Human Rights and Development

Human Rights and Development

Towards Mutual Reinforcement

Edited by

PHILIP ALSTON
and
MARY ROBINSON

This volume was prepared in collaboration with the
Center for Human Rights and Global Justice
New York University School of Law

OXFORD
UNIVERSITY PRESS

*This book has been printed digitally and produced in a standard specification
in order to ensure its continuing availability*

OXFORD
UNIVERSITY PRESS

Great Clarendon Street, Oxford OX2 6DP

Oxford University Press is a department of the University of Oxford.
It furthers the University's objective of excellence in research, scholarship,
and education by publishing worldwide in

Oxford New York

Auckland   Cape Town Dar es Salaam   Hong Kong   Karachi
Kuala Lumpur Madrid Melbourne Mexico City   Nairobi
New Delhi Shanghai   Taipei Toronto
With offices in
Argentina Austria Brazil Chile Czech Republic France Greece
Guatemala Hungary Italy Japan South Korea Poland Portugal
Singapore Switzerland Thailand Turkey Ukraine Vietnam

Oxford is a registered trade mark of Oxford University Press
in the UK and in certain other countries

Published in the United States
by Oxford University Press Inc., New York

© The Various Contributors 2005

The moral rights of the author have been asserted

Crown copyright material is reproduced under Class Licence
Number C01P0000148 with the permission of OPSI
and the Queen's Printer for Scotland

Database right Oxford University Press (maker)

Reprinted 2009

ISBN 978-0-19-928462-7

Preface

This book results from a conference held at New York University Law School in 2004, at which drafts of most of the chapters were first presented. The conference was the result of a joint initiative by two co-sponsors. The first was Realizing Rights: The Ethical Globalization Initiative (EGI), founded by Mary Robinson, and devoted to promoting a more ethical and equitable globalization process through dialogue, research, and concerted action. The second co-sponsor was the Center for Human Rights and Global Justice at New York University Law School, one of the principal aims of which is to generate high quality research into the relationship between human rights and the global economic system.

In preparation for the conference Mary Robinson consulted with James Wolfensohn, President of the World Bank group, who was extremely supportive and agreed that it would be helpful if a significant number of senior Bank officials could contribute papers, and participate in the discussions. One of the Bank's Managing Directors, Mamphela Ramphele, and her adviser, Alfredo Sfeir-Younis, then joined Mary Robinson and Philip Alston in identifying the topics and the speakers who were invited to present papers to the conference. Speakers included a range of leading scholars, as well as representatives from key international organizations including UNICEF, the International Monetary Fund, the Office of the High Commissioner for Human Rights, and the Inter-American Development Bank. NGO participants included speakers from Human Rights Watch, Amnesty International, and World Vision International. Participants from the World Bank, in addition to James Wolfensohn and Mamphela Ramphele, included Peter Woicke, Executive Vice-President of the International Finance Corporation, Jean-Luis Sarbib and Roberto Dañino, both senior Vice-Presidents, and Gobind Nankani, Ian Goldin, and Meg Taylor, all of whom are Vice-Presidents of the Bank. The Chairperson of the Bank's independent Inspection Panel, Edith Brown Weiss, and the Compliance Advisor/Ombudsman from the International Finance Corporation, Meg Taylor, also participated.

We are grateful to NYU Law School, and especially its Dean, Richard Revesz, for financial and other support for the conference. In addition the World Bank facilitated the participation of a number of participants from developing countries. In the design of the conference, Scott Jerbi and Françoise Torchiana, both from EGI, and Tish Armstrong from NYU all provided very helpful advice, as did Alan Whaites of World Vision International.

The organization of the conference was undertaken almost entirely by Tish Armstrong, of the Center for Human Rights and Global Justice, who did a superb job. Smita Narula, Executive Director of the Center, and

Meg Satterthwaite, its Research Director, also contributed a great deal to the successful outcome of the conference.

Finally, we owe a debt of gratitude to Nehal Bhuta for his first-rate work in preparing the papers for publication.

Philip Alston and Mary Robinson
New York, January 2005

Contents

D. Reform of Legal and Judicial Systems

E. The Role of the Private Sector in Promoting Human Rights

F. Building Human Rights into Development Planning Processes: The PRSP Exercise

G. The World Bank and Human Rights

Notes on Contributors

Philip Alston is Professor of Law at New York University Law School and Faculty Director of its Center for Human Rights and Global Justice. Since 2002 he has been Special Adviser to the UN High Commissioner for Human Rights on the Millennium Development Goals.

Gordon Betcherman is a Senior Economist in the Social Protection Team at the World Bank working on areas including industrial relations, core labor standards, labor law, active labor market policies, and support for unemployed workers.

Nehal Bhuta was educated at the University of Melbourne and holds graduate degrees from NYU School of Law and the New School for Social Research, New York. He is currently working for Human Rights Watch in New York.

Christina Biebesheimer is Principal Specialist in the State, Governance and Civil Society Division of the Sustainable Development Department of the Inter-American Development Bank.

Helene M. Carlsson is a Gender Specialist in the World Bank's Gender & Development Group where she is involved in an array of issues associated with mainstreaming gender into the World Bank.

Roberto Dañino, a former Prime Minister of Peru, has been senior Vice-President and General Counsel of the World Bank and Secretary-General of the International Centre for Settlement of Investment Disputes since 2003.

Jean Drèze is Professor at the Centre for Development Economics, at the Delhi School of Economics.

Jean Fares is an economist in the Labor Markets group of the World Bank's Social Protection Team. He previously taught at the American University of Beirut.

Varun Gauri is an Economist in the Development Research Group (Public Services Team) at the World Bank.

Elizabeth D. Gibbons is Chief of Global Policy at UNICEF, working on human rights approaches to poverty reduction, and analytical tools and advocacy strategies for placing children at the centre of social, economic, and juridical policies.

Stephen Golub teaches International Development and Law at Boalt Hall Law School of the University of California at Berkeley; serves as External Advisor to the UK Department for International Development on the portion of its governance website concerning Safety, Security and Accessible Justice; and consults for foundations, bilateral donors, multilateral agencies, and NGOs.

Friedrich Huebler works for the Strategic Information Section of UNICEF's Division of Policy and Planning. He specializes in the areas of education and child labor, with an emphasis on the analysis of data from household surveys.

Lindsay Judge is Consultant on PRSPs, Poverty Reduction Group, Poverty Reduction and Economic Management (PREM), at the World Bank.

Daniel Kaufmann is the Director of Global Governance at the World Bank Institute (WBI).

Edilberto Loaiza is a programme officer in the Strategic Information Section of the Division of Policy and Planning at UNICEF, New York. His work is mainly focused on education, child protection, and child mortality.

Amy Luinstra is a member of the Social Protection Team at the World Bank and specializes in labour issues.

Karen O. Mason is Director of Gender and Development of Poverty Reduction and Economic Management (PREM) at the World Bank and is the Bank's senior spokesperson on gender and development issues.

Gobind Nankani is Vice-President for Poverty Reduction and Economic Management (PREM), at the World Bank.

John Page is Director of the Poverty Reduction Group, Poverty Reduction and Economic Management (PREM), at the World Bank.

Mark W. Plant is Assistant Director, Policy Development and Review Department, at the International Monetary Fund.

Robert Prouty is a member of the Social Protection Team at the World Bank and specializes in education issues.

Kerry Rittich is Associate Professor at the Faculty of Law and the Institute for Women's Studies and Gender Studies at the University of Toronto.

Mary Robinson founded Realizing Rights: The Ethical Globalization Initiative in 2002. Previously she was President of Ireland (1990–1997), and UN High Commissioner for Human Rights (1997–2002).

Olivier de Schutter is Director of the Research Unit on Fundamental Rights (CRIDHO) at the Centre for Philosophy of Law, and Professor at the Law Faculty, at the Catholic University of Louvain.

Frances Stewart is Professor of Development Economics and Director, Centre for Research on Inequality, Human Security and Ethnicity at the International Development Centre, Queen Elizabeth House, Oxford University.

Janet Walsh is deputy director of the Women's Rights Division of Human Rights Watch. Previously she practised law at several international law firms and in the Legal Office of the United Nations in New York.

Michael Wang teaches in the Department of Economics at Oxford University.

Peter Woicke is the Executive Vice-President of the International Finance Corporation and a Managing Director of the World Bank Group.

James D. Wolfensohn was President of the World Bank for ten years until June 2005.

List of Tables

List of Figures

Abbreviations

ACIT	Academic Consortium on International Trade
ADB	Asian Development Bank
ADR	alternative dispute resolution
ALGs	Alternative Law Groups
APL	above poverty line
BITs	bilateral investment treaties
BMI	body mass index
BP	British Petroleum
BPL	below poverty line
BTC	Baku-Tbilisi-Ceyhan
CAO	Compliance Advisor/Ombudsman
CBO	community-based organization
CDC	Center for Disease Control and Prevention
CEDAW	Convention on the Elimination of All Forms of Discrimination Against Women
CEE	Central and Eastern Europe
CEO	Chief Executive Officer
CESCR	Committee on Economic, Social and Cultural Rights
CFOs	Cheif Finance Officers
CLE	clinical legal education
CRC	Convention on the Rights of the Child
CRS	Catholic Relief Services
CRWHUM	Cingranelli, Richards, and Webster Human Rights Codification
CSOs	Civil Society Organizations
CSR	Corporate Social Responsibility
DFID	Department for International Development
DFIDB	DFID Bangladesh
DG	democracy and governance
DHS	Demographic and Health Surveys
EBRD	European Bank for Reconstruction and Development
EFA	Education For All
EGI	Ethical Globalization Initiative
EMP	environmental management plan
EOS	Executive Opinion Survey
EPZs	export processing zones
EU	European Union
FDI	foreign direct investment
FGM	female genital mutilation

FSU	former Soviet Union
FTI	Fast Track Initiative
GAC	governance and anti-corruption diagnostics
GDP	gross domestic product
GER	gross enrollment rates
GPI	gender parity index
GRESEA	Groupe de recherche sur les stratégies économiques alternatives
HAART	highly active anti-retroviral therapy
HGAs	Host Government Agreements
HIPC	Heavily Indebted Poor Countries
IBRD	International Bank for Reconstruction and Development
ICCPR	International Covenant on Civil and Political Rights
ICDS	Integrated Child Development Services
ICESCR	International Covenant on Economic, Social and Cultural Rights
ICFTV	International Confederation of Free Trade Unions
ICSID	International Center for the Settlement of Investment Disputes
IDA	International Development Association
IDB	Inter-American Development Bank
IELRC	International Environmental Law Research Centre
IFC	International Finance Corporation
IFES	International Foundation for Election Systems
IFIs	international financial institutions
IGA	Inter-Governmental Agreement
ILO	International Labour Organization
IMF	International Monetary Fund
INGOs	international NGOs
IPEC	International Program on the Elimination of Child Labor
I-PRSP	Interim Poverty Reduction Strategy Paper
LDCs	least developed countries
LRC	Legal Resources Centre
LTCs	Land Tenure Certificates
MAI	multilateral agreement on investment
MDGs	Millennium Development Goals
MICS	Multiple Indicator Cluster Survey (UNICEF)
MIGA	Multilateral Investment Guarantee Agency
MLIs	multilateral lending organizations
NACC	National AIDS Control Council (Kenya)
NAFRE	National Alliance for the Fundamental Right to Education
NAFTA	North American Free Trade Agreement
NAR	net attendance ratio

NGO	non-governmental organization
NNMB	National Nutrition Monitoring Bureau
NYU	New York University
OAS	Organization of American States
ODI	Overseas Development Institute
OECD	Organization for Economic Co-operation and Development
OHCHR	Office of the High Commissioner for Human Rights
PCR	primary completion rates
PDS	public distribution system
PIL	Public Interest Litigation
PISA	Program for International Student Assessment
PPAs	Participatory Poverty Assessments
PREM	Poverty Reduction and Economic Management
PRGF	Poverty Reduction Growth Facility
PROBE	Public Report on Basic Education in India
PRSs	Poverty Reduction Strategies
PRSPs	Poverty Reduction Strategy Papers
PSIA	Poverty and Social Impact Analysis
RAPs	Resettlement Action Plans
RBA	rights-based approach
RDI	Rural Development Institute
ROL	rule of law
SDC	Swiss Agency for Development and Cooperation
SIDA	Swedish International Development Cooperation Agency
SSA	sub-Saharan Africa
SSAJ	Safety, Security, and Access to Justice
SUBIR	Sustainable Use of Biological Resources Project
TB	tuberculosis
TBP	Time-bound Programme
TNCs	transnational corporations
TRC	Truth and Reconciliation Commission (South African)
TRIMs	Trade-Related Investment Measures
UDHR	Universal Declaration of Human Rights
UNAIDS	Joint United Nations Programme on HIV/AIDS
UNCTAD	United Nations Conference on Trade and Development
UNCTC	United Nations Centre on Transnational Corporations
UNDP	United Nations Development Program(me)
UNESCO	United Nations Educational Scientific and Cultural Organization
UNHCR	United Nations High Commissioner for Refugees
UNICEF	United Nations Children's Fund
UNIFEM	United Nations Development Fund for Women
USAID	United States Agency for International Development

WBES   World Business Environment Survey
WBI   World Bank Institute
WDR   World Development Report
WEF   World Economic Forum
WHO   World Health Organization
WTO   World Trade Organization

1GHR   first generation human rights
2GHR   second generation human rights

1

The Challenges of Ensuring the Mutuality of Human Rights and Development Endeavours

PHILIP ALSTON AND MARY ROBINSON

The focus of this volume is on ways in which the strengths, resources, and support of the international human rights and development communities can be mobilized in order to reinforce one another in their efforts to achieve shared goals. Endeavours to promote meaningful and productive linkages between the agendas of these two communities are hardly new. Indeed, one of the main achievements of the first World Conference on Human Rights, held in Teheran in 1968, was precisely its assertion that 'the achievement of lasting progress in the implementation of human rights is dependent upon sound and effective national and international policies of economic and social development'.[1] Almost a decade later, in 1977, the UN Commission on Human Rights gave a new impetus to these efforts by proclaiming the existence of a human right to development.[2] That in turn led to the launching of a major push by developing countries to broaden the focus of international human rights debates to include a range of economic and other issues which had previously been considered to lie squarely and exclusively within the domain of the national and international development agencies.[3]

But debates in the United Nations and in other international fora do not necessarily translate into change on the ground, let alone within the different disciplines which need to adjust their working assumptions and methods in order to embrace, or at least accommodate, change. While the human rights

---

[1] The Proclamation of Teheran, para. 13, in *Final Act of the International Conference on Human Rights*, UN doc. A/CONF.32/41 (1968).
[2] Commission on Human Rights res. 4 (XXXIII)(1977).
[3] For the next few years a debate raged around the pros and cons of the resolution—General Assembly res. 32/120 (1977). For some contemporary competing perspectives see various contributions in B. Ramcharan (ed.), *Human Rights: Thirty Years After the Universal Declaration* (Martinus Nijhoff, 1979).

community had recognized the need to engage with their development counterparts, they were not necessarily prepared to change their modus operandi. And, perhaps unsurprisingly, the latter group proved generally reluctant to engage in debates about international legal obligations and how to reflect the relevant norms in policies at the domestic and international levels. In the latter setting, the initial efforts to achieve some sort of practical integration of the issues came, in different ways and in response to different pressures, in the institutional arrangements dealing first with women and then with children. One of the most important of the policy initiatives during this period focused on gender mainstreaming, although it is important to note that this was not always pursued in terms of women's rights per se. Similarly, the impetus behind the Convention on the Rights of the Child, adopted in 1989, and the involvement of the UN children's agency UNICEF in the promotion of that Convention, led to measures designed to insinuate at least a part of the overall human right agenda into development activities as they related to children. Several of the chapters in this volume address the current state of the art in relation to these efforts.

In the mid-1990s the human rights community began to engage more directly and constructively with their counterparts working on development issues and a movement began to promote rights-based approaches to development.[4] But it was not until Kofi Annan directed all UN agencies, in 1997, to contribute to the mainstreaming of human rights that a comprehensive effort began in that regard. Mary Robinson's appointment as High Commissioner for Human Rights later in the same year ensured that this important policy initiative would be given a major practical impetus and one of the results was the initiation of in-depth discussions with many of the principal UN agencies.[5] Some of the results achieved in that context are noted below in Chapter 3.

But despite the very considerable progress made in recent years in terms of formal commitments to the mainstreaming of human rights there remains a great deal to be done. In his recent book, Peter Uvin presents a detailed and challenging evaluation of the role of rights-based approaches to development. One of the principal conclusions that he draws relates to the extent to which the embrace of a human rights approach by a development agency requires far-reaching change. In his view, the adoption of such an approach is:

a radical affair . . . demanding profound changes in choices of partners, the range of activities undertaken and the rationale for them, internal management systems and

---

[4] P. Alston, 'The Rights Framework and Development Assistance', 34 *Development Bulletin* (Australia), August 1995, p. 9.

[5] See e.g. M. Robinson, *Bridging the Gap between Human Rights and Development: From normative principles to operational relevance*, World Bank Presidential Lecture, Washington, 3 December 2001.

funding procedures, and the type of relationships established with partners in the public and non-governmental sectors.[6]

And the challenge is rendered all the more difficult by the continuing compartmentalization of responsibilities in the development domain. This point was emphasized in the 2004 report submitted to the UN Secretary-General by a 'High-level Panel on Threats, Challenges and Change' which explored the major challenges to the UN system in the years ahead. They noted that '[i]nternational institutions and States have not organized themselves to address the problems of development in a coherent, integrated way . . .'. The approaches of the former were said to 'mirror the fragmented sectoral approaches of Governments'.[7]

The challenge of mainstreaming or of ensuring a human rights-based approach to development is thus clearly on the international agenda, but it has to be acknowledged that there is a very long way to go before such approaches become the norm. And as Christina Biebesheimer observes in this volume, there is a great deal more that the human rights community can do in terms of developing more practical and applied approaches to demonstrate how human rights dimensions can best be integrated into work being done on many of the key challenges that confront those seeking to promote human development.

The aim of this volume is precisely to facilitate a dialogue between development and human rights practitioners and to contribute, both in conceptual and practical terms, to moving the debate forward. Rather than engaging in the type of abstract or polemical approaches which have so often been adopted in the literature dealing with these issues, the focus is on six very practical and quite specific sets of issues. They are (a) the economics of social rights; (b) land rights and women's empowerment; (c) child labour and access to education; (d) reform of legal and judicial systems; (e) the role of the private sector in promoting human rights; and (f) building human rights into development planning processes.

We turn now to a brief review of the different contributions to the book.

1.1 PROMOTING MUTUAL REINFORCEMENT: INTRODUCTORY ESSAYS

The nature of some of the challenges confronting efforts to ensure that the human rights and development agendas really can be mutually reinforcing are elucidated in the first part of the volume by two of the key players in the

---

[6] P. Uvin, *Human Rights and Development* (Kumarian Press, 2004).

[7] United Nations, *A More Secure World: Our Shared Responsibility*, Report of the High-level Panel on Threats, Challenges and Change (New York, United Nations, 2004), para. 55.

international debate, James Wolfensohn, as former World Bank President, and Mary Robinson, as former UN High Commissioner for Human Rights. Wolfensohn begins by acknowledging that the debate is one 'that I've never fully understood'. Nevertheless, by undertaking a systematic review of some of the key provisions of the Universal Declaration of Human Rights and the two International Covenants on Human Rights he concludes that this normative base could easily have provided 'the framework which led [the World Bank] to the poverty reduction strategy approach, or the comprehensive development framework'.[8] And he observes that a good many of the World Bank's other initiatives in relation to issues such as addressing the plight of the Roma Peoples of central and eastern Europe, or the role of culture in development, could equally well have been approached through a human rights lens.

Wolfensohn notes, however, that to some of the governments who constitute the Bank's shareholders 'the very mention of the words human rights is inflammatory language'. And so in order to avoid controversy the Bank has opted in the past to 'talk the language of economics and social development'.[9] He notes, encouragingly, that the Bank had been unable or unwilling to talk about the issue of corruption when he first became President and that this has since changed dramatically. In the same spirit, he suggests that 'maybe we now need to mention the "R" word which is "rights". And, maybe . . . we will talk much more about rights as we move forward.' At the end of his remarks he states that the Bank is 'deeply committed to trying to clarify the role of rights in development'. Finally he concludes by emphasizing that both the human rights and development communities share a common enemy of indifference to the plight of poverty in the world, to the neglect of the Millennium Development Goals, and to the spiralling levels of military expenditure in the world. The two communities need to join together to tackle those issues.

Mary Robinson begins her chapter by surveying the situation of global poverty and some of the factors that have exacerbated it. She then considers some of the positive developments in recent years which have seen greater attention paid to human rights issues in development discussions. They include efforts by various UN agencies to consider how they might incorporate a stronger human rights dimension in their work, leading to the adoption of a Common Understanding on the application of a rights-based approach. In addition, various bilateral development assistance programmes have adopted a human rights approach, human rights NGOs are now more engaged with these issues, and the World Bank has made a major effort to engage with human rights on a variety of fronts. Taken together, these add

---

[8] J. D. Wolfensohn, 'Some Reflections on Human Rights and Development', Chapter 2 below, p. 19.   [9] Ibid., p. 21.

up to a sea change in the relationship between the two communities, although while mutual curiosity has increased 'confidence is far from being safely established'.[10]

Robinson's chapter then turns to examine some of the major criticisms directed at human rights by development specialists. They include the claim that human rights are political, that they are unrealistic, that they are abstract and incapable of practical application, that they cannot cope with notions of change over time, and that an emphasis on law does little to help the poor. She concedes that there are elements of truth in some of these criticisms but contends that the human rights community is well able to respond to each of them. She concludes by outlining the ways in which a human rights framework can add value to development challenges and, like Wolfensohn, emphasizes the importance of promoting an effective and empowering approach to realizing the Millennium Development Goals.

(a) The Economics of Social Rights

Human rights proponents are often accused of ignoring the economic implications of the normative positions which they advocate. While this shortcoming tends to be overlooked when it affects civil and political rights, such as freedom of speech, the right to vote, or the rights to be free from torture and slavery, it is considered to be especially problematic when it arises in relation to economic and social rights. This first section of the book thus sees two economists casting a critical eye over the rights to food, health, and education, and evaluating the extent to which sound economic policy is compatible with commitments to promote respect for these rights.

In Chapter 4, Jean Drèze argues that the persistence of a serious nutrition crisis in India reflects the fact that Indian democracy is trapped in a 'vicious circle of exclusion and elitism'.[11] Despite constitutional protections of certain economic and social rights, including the right to food, and relatively stable democratic institutions, the underprivileged are excluded from actively participating in democratic politics, with the result that their aspirations and priorities are not reflected in public policy.. The elitism of public policy further disempowers the poor by perpetuating their deprivations. Drèze notes that the renowned Indian political leader Dr. Ambedkar predicted an intensification of the contradiction between political equality and economic and social inequality, in speeches given a few years after India achieved independence. Ambedkar had insisted on the inclusion of social and economic rights in the Directive Principles of the Indian Constitution in order

---

[10] M. Robinson, 'What Rights Can Add to Good Development Practice', Chapter 3 below, p. 31.

[11] J. Drèze, 'Democracy and the Right to Food', Chapter 4 below, p. 45.

to try to ensure that a concern with economic and social democracy would not be allowed to disappear from the political agenda in India. Relying on these Directive Principles, Drèze calls for a revival of concern with Constitution-based economic and social rights, in order to fully realize the democratic vision of Ambedkar and of the Indian Constitution itself. He notes that greater consciousness of elementary education as a *constitutional right* (brought about by two decades of social activism and a landmark Supreme Court decision) has helped expand the reach of the school system, and protect it—to some extent—from the fiscal cutbacks arising from structural adjustment.

In the case of the right to food, Drèze accepts that it may be harder to define and operationalize than the right to education. Defined as 'freedom from hunger', the right to food may be seen as a right to 'nutrition'. But nutrition is achieved not just through food but through clean water, basic health care, and good hygiene, among other inputs. Similarly, although the state can be regarded as bearing primary responsibility for the right to food, there is also a responsibility on local communities and families to ensure basic nutrition is equally available to all their members. Drèze accepts that this complicates the question of how the right to food can be enforced. The courts are not powerless, but may not be the best venue through which to realize the right to food. Instead of relying on an unwieldy and ad hoc judicial enforcement process, he insists that the right to food must be the basis for mobilization in the democratic public sphere, and made the object of political demands for protective legislation. Drèze sees asserting the right to food *as a fundamental right* as one way of creating a focus for public action in response to India's nutrition emergency, and for increasing the poor and underprivileged's sense of entitlement to state action on nutrition. Moreover, the more politicized the deprived are about their right to food, the more vigilant they will be in policing the various state nutrition schemes that already exist, and in combating the endemic corruption that diminishes the effectiveness of existing measures. That campaigning, combined with selective litigation over the right to food, can achieve concrete successes, is illustrated by the introduction of cooked mid-day meals in primary schools in many states, after a public campaign and a Supreme Court case in 2001.

Drèze concludes that the right to food cannot be realized in isolation from other social and economic rights, such as the right to health. The rights to health care and education are taken up by another economist, Varun Gauri, in the second contribution to this section of the volume. Gauri's carefully argued essay is a nuanced analysis of the philosophical foundations of social and economic rights, which demonstrates that disagreements between a 'rights-based' and a development economics approach to social welfare are not as significant as they might appear. He first reviews the different normative bases upon which social and economic rights are claimed to be 'rights', and the major philosophical and practical objections. He suggests that economic and social rights, such as the right to health care and education, are best understood not as legal instruments for individuals, but as 'duties for governments, international agencies, and other actors to take concrete measures on behalf of individuals, or to restructure institutions so that the rights can be fulfilled more effectively...Calling health care and education rights means, on this understanding, that everyone bears some responsibility for their fulfillment.'[12]

Gauri then reviews some of the economic literature on education and health care, observing that economists seem to accept that the realization of high standards of health and education are conducive to economic growth. Moreover, economists' concerns about how health care is best provided are not incompatible with a human rights orientation. From a human rights perspective, participation, empowerment, transparency, and accountability in relation to service delivery are important for ensuring health care and education quality and for fostering a social basis for self-esteem. From an economic perspective, the same goals are important because they help solve problems related to collective action and asymmetric information. Nevertheless, the tensions do not dissolve completely. The human rights approach regards transparency and empowerment as ends in themselves, while an economic approach sees them as instrumental to a welfare outcome. Similarly, a human rights approach typically evaluates health and education programmes in terms of distribution of outcomes, not just averages. Conversely, a human rights approach gives little or no guidance in terms of prioritizing allocative decisions or making trade-offs, and cannot easily analyse the sometimes perverse consequences of a redistributive policy, such as forms of moral hazard or free riding. Gauri concludes that there are no simple answers to some of these tensions between the human rights approach and an economic perspective, but that both approaches can learn from the limitations of the other, and should recognize their complementarities.

(b) Land Rights and Women's Empowerment

The second section of the volume explores the complementarities and possible conflicts in the relationship between human rights principles and development programmes intended to increase women's legal right to land in developing countries.

Kerry Rittich notes that programmes which promote the formal real property rights of women—in place of customary laws or other informal mechanisms—have the potential to both improve and retard women's access

[12] V. Gauri, 'Social Rights and Economics: Claims to Health Care and Education in Developing Countries', Chapter 5 below, p. 72.

to real property, depending on how such measures are implemented.[13] She argues that the programmes promoting property rights tend to go together with measures to formalize, commodify, and individualize landholdings, and that these three processes have often intensified the dispossession of women who may have had access to land under informal or customary law arrangements. Thus, the promotion of property rights from an economic perspective may well undermine the social rights and human development of women in developing countries, if specific attention is not paid to the gender-specific impact of changing property regimes. In this field, economic analysis may learn something from legal conceptions of property, which treat property not just as a resource but as a set of relations between individuals and groups. Such an approach might highlight the otherwise unforeseen distributive consequences for women of moving from an informal property regime to a formalized and individualized one. No single conception of property or set of institutional reforms in respect of land can be associated with greater gender empowerment.

Based on their extensive experience with the World Bank, Karen Mason and Helene Carlsson draw on a large amount of empirical material in their consideration of the development impact of gender equality on land rights. Their review of the literature and their own empirical investigations suggest that secure rights to land enhance human development, but that a range of factors lead to gender disparities in women's ability to benefit from reforms aimed at securing land tenure.[14] They argue that secure land rights enhance incentives to invest in the land and thus raise agricultural productivity and household incomes, and may also improve the sustainability of agricultural practices. However, despite the fact that women do the majority of agricultural labour in many developing countries, they own very little of the land they work. Mason and Carlsson note that, unless gender inequality in land holding is taken into account when implementing land tenure reforms, improved land tenure security may diminish women's land holdings. A variety of factors can lead to this result, including discriminatory inheritance laws, the application of an androcentric definition of 'head of household', and inequalities in women's capacity to participate in the market for land. However, the authors cite some examples, such as Costa Rica and Colombia, in which land reforms were undertaken in a way that improved women's ownership of land.

They argue that improving women's access to secure land holding will greatly enhance their human development, and that of the country in which they live: women who own the land they work have greater incentives to raise

---

[13] K. Rittich, 'The Properties of Gender Equality', Chapter 6 below, p. 92–3.
[14] K. O. Mason and H. M. Carlsson, 'The Development Impact of Gender Equality in Land Rights', Chapter 7 below, p. 114.

their labour productivity, and women who earn more income are more likely than men to invest in the household and in their children's education and nutrition. Overall food production may also increase. The empowerment of women that flows from having a productive economic asset may also help ameliorate the impact of the HIV/AIDS pandemic on agricultural production, and strengthen the bargaining power of women in household decisions. The reforms suggested by Mason and Carlsson at the conclusion of the chapter illustrate the importance of applying a human rights lens—specifically, the norms of non-discrimination and equal property rights—when implementing economic reforms, and suggest the indivisibility of economic and social rights from women's capacity to exercise civil and political rights.

Janet Walsh, basing herself on a lengthy report on Kenya prepared by Human Rights Watch,[15] documents the serious violations of women's human rights that arise from a discriminatory property rights regime and a lack of will on the part of courts and the government. Although the right to property can be regarded as an 'economic and social right', discriminatory laws and practices in relation to women's right to own property after the death of a husband, after a divorce, or as part of an inheritance, have immediate consequences for the civil and political rights of women in Kenya.[16] Women who lose their property due to discriminatory laws and practices face impoverishment, sexual violence, and are at increased risk of HIV/AIDS due to both homelessness and the rituals associated with the loss of their property. The inequality in gender relations that is encoded in discriminatory laws, and the indifference of state organs, jeopardizes Kenya's efforts to stem the spread of HIV/AIDS, and threatens agricultural production, indicating the concrete negative impact that human rights violations can have on the achievement of development goals.

(c) Child Labour and Access to Education

From both a development economics perspective and a human rights perspective, there are strong reasons to seek an end to child labour. Human rights advocates have long regarded child labour as implicated in the violation of many of the rights of the child. It should be eradicated in order to ensure children's human rights as ends in themselves. From the perspective of development economics, child labour amounts to an inter-generational loss of potential income, as children suffer diminished human capital (such as reductions in health and opportunities for education) that will reduce their productivity in the future. The contribution to this volume by Gordon Betcherman, Jean Fares, Amy Luinstra, and Robert Prouty notes the

---

[15] Human Rights Watch, *Women's Property Rights Violations in Kenya* (New York, 2003).
[16] J. Walsh, 'Women's Property Rights Violations in Kenya', Chapter 8 below, p. 133.

International Labour Organization's (ILO's) estimate that current levels of child labour will result in an income foregone of $5 trillion between 2000 and 2020. They review recent statistics on the extent of child labour, and estimate that a staggering 23 per cent of the world's children aged between 5 and 17 years are engaged in some form of work. They also note that there is considerable evidence to suggest that child labour adversely affects children's educational attainment.[17]

While economists and human rights activists are united in their desire to see an end to child labour, Betcherman et al. demonstrate the important insights that economic analysis can provide in understanding how best to reduce child labour. Factors contributing to child labour can be seen in terms of incentives that encourage child work, constraints that compel children to work, and decisions that may not be made in the best interests of the children. Human rights advocates often focus on the latter (whether by parents or governments), but also need to consider how the direct (books, transport) and indirect (poor quality, loss of household labour) costs of education may lead parents to regard the returns of education as not providing sufficient immediate returns to the household or the child. Understanding these factors could improve strategies for changing household decision making. Betcherman et al. consider some creative examples of government policies aimed at altering the structure of incentives and constraints affecting child labour, such as Mexico's *Progresa* programme, that indicate the important concrete contribution that a development economics perspective can bring to the question of how best to alter social and economic practices. Similarly, echoing Gauri's argument, the authors point out that standard setting legislation is of itself insufficient to alter an interacting set of incentives and constraints, and may well have the perverse effect of reducing child welfare.

Drawing on their extensive experience of working with these issues in UNICEF, Elizabeth Gibbons, Friedrich Huebler, and Edilberto Loaiza consider how, at the level of *statistical analysis*, the application of the human rights principle of non-discrimination can affect our understanding of the dimensions of child labour.[18] They note that existing methods of calculating the extent of child labour under-report the degree of child work done by girls, because the measures exclude household chores. By failing to consider 'female work' within the definition of child labour, the impact of child work on the educational and health attainment of girls is made invisible.

The authors undertake an analysis of child labour data in an attempt to make female child labour visible, revealing a one-quarter increase in the estimate of child labour among girls, and a fall in the gap between boys' and

---

[17] G. Betcherman, J. Fares, A. Luinstra, and R. Prouty, 'Child Labor, Education, and Children's Rights', Chapter 9 below, p. 175.

[18] E. D. Gibbons, F. Huebler, and E. Loaiza, 'Child Labour, Education, and the Principle of Non-Discrimination', Chapter 10 below, p. 205.

girls' child labour. Gibbons, Huebler, and Loaiza also investigate some of the factors affecting school attendance and find that, while labour and household poverty are generally constraints on attendance, a mother's educational attainment is also an important determinant that correlates positively with school attendance. This, they argue, 'shows, in dramatic and incontrovertible terms, the inter-generational payoff from an investment in girls' education'.[19] An examination of the impact of child labour on *performance* in schools (as opposed to simply attendance) leads to the conclusion that child labour does not result in a higher likelihood of grade repetition in most countries, but that household wealth and the level of education of the primary caretaker can also have a significant effect on educational attainment.[20] However, child labour does clearly increase the probability that a child will drop out of school.

On the basis of a case study of India, the chapter by Philip Alston and Nehal Bhuta considers the evidence of the qualitative impact that human rights discourse, and the constitutional entrenchment of economic and social rights, can have on the attainment of social goods such as education. They review the history of the constitutional amendment that was adopted in 2002 to make education part of the category of 'fundamental rights' in the Indian Constitution.[21] The amendment led to the inclusion of a justiciable right to education in relation to children between the ages of 6 and 14. The authors ask whether this has made any difference in terms of progress towards achieving the goal of free, universal, elementary education. The evidence is mixed, but does suggest that the public debate surrounding the constitutional amendment, and public interest litigation in state and federal courts, have provided some impetus for government authorities to address critical problems in the provision of education. Perhaps more enduringly, and in line with the analysis of the right to food undertaken by Jean Drèze in Chapter 4, the idea of education as a 'fundamental right' is becoming a focus for local political action and agitation among under-resourced and oppressed communities, who rely on the new constitutional provision as a way of pressing their demands on local and regional government decision makers.

(d) Reform of Legal and Judicial Systems

The extent to which multilateral lending agencies should use human rights criteria in assessing development projects has been subject to considerable debate over the last fifteen years. Agencies such as the World Bank and International Monetary Fund have been criticized for failing to consider

---

[19] Ibid., p. 214.   [20] Ibid., p. 230.

[21] P. Alston and N. Bhuta, 'Human Rights and Public Goods: Education as a Fundamental Right in India', Chapter 11 below, p. 244.

adequately the human rights impact of their lending.[22] At the same time, international financial institutions (IFIs) are increasingly funding 'institution-building' projects that, explicitly or implicitly, have human rights-related objectives, particularly in the form of rule of law initiatives. Christina Biebesheimer reflects on the experience of the Inter-American Development Bank (IDB), which has explicitly embraced the promotion of human rights as conducive to creating the conditions for economic development. The IDB, perhaps more than any other international financial institution, has expanded its loans to projects concerned with improving public sector institutions such as courts. It has, as a matter of policy, come to regard democratic institution-building as part of a state modernization strategy and has taken the justice sector as a particular focus. Biebesheimer reviews the kinds of projects that the IDB has supported through its 'modernization of the state' strategy, and observes that human rights principles are being used in 'interpreting the areas of justice [the IDB] can work in, in defining project content, in establishing methodologies for pre-project diagnostics, and in defining indicators for project success and impact'.[23]

In her concluding sections, Biebesheimer asks how a comprehensive human rights approach would change the way that the IDB works. Her answer is that it may lead to a greater emphasis on citizen participation in the design and implementation of justice projects, and may lead to placing greater emphasis on justice sector initiatives that combat discrimination and exclusion. She laments, however, that little practical guidance in project design and implementation can be derived presently from the materials produced by the human rights community. There is a need for human rights advocates to address their concerns to the development community in a way that demonstrates how a human rights approach will improve project effectiveness, and how improvements could be implemented in a way that is consistent with existing time and resource constraints.

In his chapter, Stephen Golub takes aim at the 'rule of law' promotion practices of the international financial institutions. He argues that these lending practices are underpinned by a 'rule of law orthodoxy' that does not adequately conceptualize the relationship between justice sector reform and human rights protection.[24] The 'rule of law orthodoxy's' focus on narrowly defined justice sector projects does not pay sufficient attention to the reality that improvements in the courts or in legal training will by no means necessarily result in the enforcement of rights or the alleviation of poverty for

---

[22] See generally M. Darrow, *Between Light and Shadow: The World Bank, the International Monetary Fund and International Human Rights Law* (Oxford, Hart, 2003).

[23] C. Biebesheimer, 'The Impact of Human Rights Principles on Justice Reform in the Inter-American Development Bank', Chapter 12 below, p. 279–80.

[24] S. Golub, 'Less Law and Reform, More Politics and Enforcement: A Civil Society Approach to Integrating Rights and Development', Chapter 13 below, p. 299.

structurally disadvantaged groups. Golub notes that project reviews of justice sector reform projects have generally found that the projects have not had a discernible impact on the poor and disadvantaged, and have not necessarily resulted in durable and sustainable changes in the functioning of legal institutions.

He argues that, instead of the 'rule of law', development agencies should promote 'legal empowerment', which he defines as 'the use of legal services and other development activities to increase disadvantaged populations' control over their lives'. He suggests that such a strategy would emphasize strengthening the capacity of NGOs and community-based organizations that defend and promote the rights of the poor, and the selection of issues flowing from the needs of the poor. It would also pay greater attention to a variety of state institutions (administrative agencies, local governments, and so forth) that can be used to advance the rights of the poor, rather than focusing on a narrowly defined justice sector. Golub marshals considerable evidence that such an approach is more sustainable and more likely to have long-term benefits for the realization of human rights and human development, than justice sector programmes. His contention is not that justice sector programmes should be abandoned, but that a better balance should be struck in 'rule of law' development funding, between legal empowerment and legal reform.

(e) The Role of the Private Sector in Promoting Human Rights

Peter Woicke reflects on the International Finance Corporation's (IFC's) efforts to incorporate human rights standards into its criteria for evaluating prospective loans to private companies. The IFC is the private sector development lending arm of the World Bank Group. In recent years it has emerged as a leader within the group in developing modalities for using human rights criteria in lending decisions. Woicke argues that this effort by the IFC should be seen as part of a broader worldwide movement for corporate social responsibility.[25] It is thus consistent with efforts by large corporations to respond to criticism of corporate behaviour and to present adherence to international human rights standards as part of their corporate and brand identity. As a financier of private companies active in developing countries, the IFC has accepted that corporate responsibility principles can and should be applied to those who fund private sector activity, as well as to those who implement them. In an informative and illuminating case study, Woicke describes in detail a project that was financed by the IFC, and how

---

[25] P. Woicke, 'Putting Human Rights Principles into Development Practice through Finance: The Experience of the International Finance Corporation', Chapter 14 below, p. 328.

the process of project assessment could have incorporated a human rights analytical framework.

Does human rights promotion and enforcement actually lead to better governance and greater human development? Are civil and political rights and economic and social rights really indivisible? While these propositions have become something of a policy and philosophical commonplace since Amartya Sen's powerfully persuasive work,[26] Daniel Kaufmann observes that the empirical basis for (or against) the claims is not easy to establish. Employing an innovative method for measuring and assessing human rights outcomes and their impact on governance, he seeks to rise to this challenge in his chapter.[27] He first reviews indicators for political and civil rights and asks whether there has been an improvement in the realization of these rights. He then explores the relationship between civil and political rights and economic and social rights, and asks how improvements in the former affect the realization of the latter. He finds that progress in the realization of civil and political rights is uneven and varies according to region, but that there is a strong correlation between income levels and respect for civil and political rights. Of course, this tells us little about the causality of the relationship between civil and political rights and economic development.

In a further series of analyses, Kaufmann makes a persuasive case for the proposition that good governance is not a 'luxury good' which every country comes to enjoy when it becomes wealthier, implying that policy makers and civil society must work hard and continuously at improving civil rights and governance. He also finds that where political and civil rights are less respected, the risks of corruption and state capture by special interests are higher, which in turn impairs socio-economic development. Conversely, better governance seems to be causally related to improved development outcomes. Kaufmann examines the case of Bolivia to contend that measures that promote participation and citizens' input into the operations of an institution were likely to reduce corruption and improve service delivery. Voice and participation are thus instrumentally related to containing corruption and realizing social and economic rights, and it may not be reasonable to expect that a purely technocratic approach to macroeconomic management will deliver such objectives.

Olivier de Schutter proposes a new way of conceiving the human rights responsibilities of transnational corporations (TNCs). He argues that the conventional approach, which focuses on the project-specific human rights consequences of a particular company in a particular locale, is inadequate to address concerns about whether the activities of TNCs promote the human

---

[26] See e.g. A. Sen, *Development as Freedom* (Oxford, Oxford University Press, 1999).

[27] D. Kaufmann, 'Human Rights and Governance: The Empirical Challenge', Chapter 15 below, p. 352.

development of the society as a whole.[28] De Schutter distinguishes between a 'micro' and a 'macro' approach to the human rights impact of TNC activity. Most current analyses take the 'micro' approach, but do not consider ways in which TNCs and foreign direct investment can be instruments in a form of growth that realizes the right to development. De Schutter contends that the 'macro' analysis must supplement the 'micro' to discern measures that can link TNC activity to national economic development. De Schutter reviews a wide range of evidence indicating that the mere presence of foreign investment will not necessarily result in balanced human development, and should be subject to a multilateral framework of development friendly rules. By contrast, the current framework for investment aims to limit as much as possible the capacity of a state to impose conditions on foreign investment and TNC activity. De Schutter argues that developed states and multilateral lending institutions should bear primary responsibility for developing a multilateral framework for 'development friendly' investment, and suggests that such a set of rules has the potential to alleviate the problem of 'regulatory competition' between national jurisdictions.

(f) Building Human Rights into Development Planning Processes: The PRSP Exercise

By far the most important single tool for development planning and for seeking to stimulate a greater and better focused flow of development assistance today is the Poverty Reduction Strategy Paper (PRSP) process. It was introduced in 1999 as a condition of eligibility for debt relief among Heavily Indebted Poor Countries (HIPC), but has since become ubiquitous in the development context. The rationale for the PRSP process was that it would promote national and local 'ownership' of macroeconomic policies and help ensure that these policies were sufficiently adapted to relieving poverty in the world's poorest countries. In principle, the process represents an embrace of the values of participation and transparency in the formulation of macroeconomic policy, and thus has the potential to shape the content of these policies in order to meet the needs of the poor. As of April 2004, thirty-nine countries had completed PRSPs on a full or interim basis.

The chapter by Frances Stewart and Michael Wang reviews the experience of participation in the preparation of these strategies over a number of countries, and assesses whether this participation has empowered the poor to alter the content of macroeconomic policy and poverty reduction strategies. They find significant variation across countries, in terms of *who* participates, *how* they participate, and *issues* in respect of which they have

---

[28] O. de Schutter, 'Transnational Corporations as Instruments of Human Development', Chapter 16 below, p. 404.

participated.[29] Troublingly, they find that a number of important actors have been consistently excluded from participation, including parliamentarians, and the representatives of trade unions, women, and marginalized groups. The amount of time allowed for consultations and participation was often inadequate, and in a number of cases civil society groups were presented with pre-prepared drafts on which to 'comment' rather than having an opportunity to participate in the design of the framework. Nevertheless, Stewart and Wang find that the PRSP process seems to have led national development plans to become more 'pro-poor' and include more ambitious social targets. At the same time, participation rarely resulted in changes to the macroeconomic policies prescribed by IFIs and there were no departures 'from the kind of advice provided under structural adjustment programmes'.[30]

Stewart and Wang conclude by asking how a more explicitly 'human rights-based' approach might alter the process and content of PRSPs. They note that even if PRSPs did use the language of rights, the change might end up being confined to language and have little consequence in reality. They recommend, instead, that PRSPs be reformed so that there is greater participation by the marginalized and the poor, and that the representation of private sector groups and external agencies be limited. Wang and Stewart note, however, that even if steps are taken to improve the PRSP process, they will not have a positive impact on the content of PRSPs unless donor countries and IFIs cede greater control to the countries concerned in defining their economic priorities.

Drawing on the experience of the World Bank, as the principal driving force behind the PRSPs, Gobind Nankani, John Page, and Lindsay Judge argue that these strategies should be seen as an important means for bringing about a convergence of human rights principles and poverty reduction policies. The PRSP process, they recall, was introduced as a way of ensuring that the voice of the poor was heard in the formulation of development strategies, and as a way of trying to avoid the failures of 'top-down' development policies.[31] The participatory process mandated by PRSPs represents a 'pact between states, their citizens, and the international community' to achieve poverty reduction. Nankani, Page, and Judge contend that the outcomes sought by a poverty reduction focused development strategy overlap considerably with the norms and values embodied in human rights instruments, although the overlap is not total. They note that, on the *supply* side, human rights advocates and development economists may be at odds over what governments need to do to ensure various possible outcomes for

---

[29] F. Stewart and M. Wang, 'Poverty Reduction Strategy Papers within the Human Rights Perspective', Chapter 17 below, p. 454. [30] Ibid., p. 466.

[31] G. Nankani, J. Page, and L. Judge, 'Human Rights and Poverty Reduction Strategies: Moving Towards Convergence?', Chapter 18 below, p. 477.

citizens (with economists focused on the question of how to ensure optimal use of finite resources), while on the *demand* side there is convergence in the emphasis on empowering marginalized people to take control of their lives and claim their entitlements.

Nankani, Page, and Judge defend the PRSP process as likely to lead to a better alignment between poverty reduction strategies and human rights principles. They argue that the process has enhanced country ownership of, and commitment to, poverty reduction policies, and has also changed donor behaviour by encouraging donors to co-ordinate more carefully their inputs with national governments. They also contend that the PRSP process has led to a more comprehensive approach to poverty reduction in countries that have undertaken it. They argue that further steps can be taken to heighten the complementarity between a human rights approach and the PRSP process, but sound a note of caution: resource and capacity constraints in developing economies mean that hard choices and some trade-offs must always be made. But there is room for thinking through these hard choices in terms of a human rights framework.

Finally, in the last chapter, the theme of hard choices and trade-offs is taken up by Mark Plant, a senior official of the International Monetary Fund. Plant revolves his comments around a set of *Draft Guidelines* for a human rights approach to Poverty Reduction Strategies which was prepared at the request of the Office of the High Commissioner for Human Rights (OHCHR).[32] He raises some challenging questions about the practical utility of incorporating human rights language into PRSPs. He notes that there is a danger that the strategy documents will become overburdened with 'wish-lists' of desired outcomes and principles, while at the same time losing their role in providing concrete guidance to the implementation of poverty reduction policies in a given national context. He asks whether the human rights community has given enough consideration to achieving the right balance between ambition and realism. He suggests that there is a real danger that the human rights approach advocated by the OHCHR will be seen by low-income countries as being unnecessarily 'grafted on to the PRS process and thus more of a burden than a help'.[33] Plant also raises an important empirical question about whether broader participation will actually result in *better* economic policy. While local level actors are well placed to identify the needs and priorities that concern them the most, these must be balanced with the maintenance of national economic stability in an international economy.

---

[32] United Nations High Commissioner for Human Rights, *Draft Guidelines: A Human Rights Approach to Poverty Reduction Strategies*, 10 September 2002 (Geneva: United Nations). It should be noted that a revised version of this document was due to be made available early in 2005.

[33] M. W. Plant, 'Human Rights, the Poverty Reduction Strategies, and the Role of the International Monetary Fund', Chapter 19 below, p. 501.

Plant contends that 'difficult macroeconomic choices cannot be avoided by adopting empty or internally contradictory policies; if this is done, the choices will be made by markets ... or postponed until later generations through indebtedness'.[34] Plant's pointed questions lead to a challenge to members of the human rights community to ask themselves whether, while demanding that development economists internalize the human rights perspective, they have failed to adequately internalize the economists' concerns. He concludes by suggesting that OHCHR should consider ways in which it can operationalize its expertise, so as to provide concrete assistance to developing countries that face difficult trade-offs in terms of how best to implement economic policies in a manner consistent with human rights principles.

(g) The World Bank and Human Rights

In the concluding chapter of the volume Roberto Dañino, who has been Senior Vice-President and General Counsel of the World Bank since 2003, offers some personal reflections on the appropriate role of human rights within the work of the Bank. His views are of particular significance in light of the influence that his predecessors, and especially Ibrahim Shihata, exerted in relation to such matters within the Bank. Dañino makes clear that while there are both legal and institutional limits that must be respected, the World Bank should in the future 'embrace the centrality of human rights to [its] work instead of being divided by the issue of whether or not to adopt a "rights-based approach" to development'. While some would suggest that such an approach would represent a significant change in Bank policy, others would argue that the Bank already has a very extensive de facto policy in relation to a wide range of human rights issues and that Dañino's approach would serve mainly to bring the theory into line with the practice and thus encourage a more systematic approach to human rights within the work of the most influential of the international community's development agencies.

[34] M. W. Plant, 'Human Rights, the Poverty Reduction Strategies, and the Role of the International Monetary Fund', Chapter 19 below, p. 503.

2

Some Reflections on Human Rights and Development[1]

JAMES D. WOLFENSOHN

Let me start by saying that my colleague Alfredo Sfeir-Younis gave me three versions of a speech. It's very lengthy, very complicated, and frankly beyond me. He knows so much about this subject that I think he assumed that I would be able to enter immediately into a discussion at the highest possible level of human rights activists, relate it to the work of development activists, and emerge with some searing insights that I could leave you with that would set the tone for the entire day.

Sadly, I'm unable to do that because I'm really not there yet. One of my hopes is that in the course of the day we may, with my colleagues, elucidate just what some of the issues are and what is the way forward in a debate that I've never fully understood. What I'd really like to do is just to give you my feelings about this issue of human rights and development, and some of the thoughts that go through my head as I think about the subject.

As I try to lead the World Bank in a way that will profit from the activities of human rights activists and, indeed, the approach I have discussed with Mary Robinson many times: the human rights-based, or a rights-based, approach to development, as compared to what it is that I imagine we're doing already. I've said to Mary a number of times that I think that there's a tremendous coalescence between human rights and what we do every day in our institution—perhaps not speaking as much about rights as we should, but in fact giving effect to the agenda of the human rights community.

I did take the trouble before coming to this conference to read the key declarations and covenants that have been agreed to by the UN. There's quite a volume of them, but I decided that if I was going to come to this

[1] This is an edited transcript of the remarks by the former President of the World Bank group presented at the opening of a Conference on Human Rights and Development. It was held at New York University Law School on 1 March 2004, and co-organized by the Ethical Globalization Initiative and the NYU Law School Center for Human Rights and Global Justice.

meeting it might be worthwhile to read them all. And, it was a profitable activity because I started circling the key elements with my pen. First, the Universal Declaration of Human Rights,[2] then the Covenant on Civil and Political Rights[3] and the Covenant on Economic, Social and Cultural Rights,[4] then the Declaration on the Right to Development;[5] and then various other human rights instruments which have been added over the years.[6]

And, when you go through it, starting with the preamble to the Universal Declaration, and looking at the various articles you start with the right to life, liberty, and security of every person. You move to issues of recognition of rights before the law and think of things that we incorporate in our work in legal, social, and judicial reform and of various aspects of what that law should be, including issues like the right to a nationality.

When I read about that right I thought about something the Bank did six months ago. We ran a conference in Europe, which we organized along with six central European governments, on the Roma Peoples.[7] We didn't call it a rights conference, but we did gather the representatives of 12 million people together, whose countries will join the European Union, but many of whom suffer from not having passports. We had what I thought was a fantastic conference, and I never mentioned the word human rights. But, this project jumped out at me as I thought of the many activities we do every day that seem to be in keeping with the focus of our present discussion on human rights and development.

I then looked at Article 17 of the Universal Declaration on property rights. I looked at the right to freedom of thought, conscience, and religion. I thought of the Bank's activities in seeking to reach out and have a dialogue on faith and development. Over the last five years, we put together three separate meetings of faith leaders from around the world. We have engaged in this dialogue despite the fact that some have expressed the view that such a dialogue pollutes our institution, by having religion as an aspect of our activities.

The Declaration also goes on to talk about culture. I had the same experience on that topic. We ran a conference in Florence on culture and

---

[2] G.A. res. 217A (III), U.N. Doc A/810 at 71 (1948).

[3] International Covenant on Civil and Political Rights (ICCPR), G.A. res. 2200A (XXI), 21 U.N. GAOR Supp. (No. 16) at 52, U.N. Doc. A/6316 (1966), 999 U.N.T.S. 171, *entered into force* 23 Mar. 1976.

[4] G.A. res. 2200A (XXI), 21 U.N. GAOR Supp. (No. 16) at 49, U.N. Doc. A/6316 (1966), 993 U.N.T.S. 3, *entered into force* 3 Jan. 1976.

[5] Declaration on the Right to Development, G.A. res. 41/128, annex, 41 U.N. GAOR Supp. (No. 53) at 186, U.N. Doc. A/41/53 (1986).

[6] See generally United Nations, *Human Rights: A Compilation of International Instruments* (New York, United Nations, 1994).

[7] See the report on the conference: *Roma in an Expanding Europe: Challenges for the Future* (Washington DC, World Bank, 2003), available at http://lnweb18.worldbank.org/eca/ecshd.nsf/links_roma/F2C41F5522F19F8EC1256E70002F295A/$FILE/Roma%20Proceedings.pdf.

development which was attended by 700 people, although we had expected only a couple of hundred. And, that, too, was resisted by many of our shareholders as being exotic, elitist, and not the sort of thing that a development institution should do.

I remind you of these criticisms because the Bank works for the same people whose governments adopted the Universal Declaration. But in actuality their application of the principles to which they have so vigorously attested sometimes differs from the notions that they had when they signed it. I raise that point because we are not an institution just composed of my colleagues and myself, able to do what we'd like to do. We're an institution which is owned and, to an extent, dominated by the very same people who wrote the Universal Declaration of Human Rights and the subsequent human rights instruments.

I've said to Mary Robinson many times: 'One of the things we have to do in our institution is to try and do something on these issues, but to some of our shareholders the very mention of the words human rights is inflammatory language. It's getting into areas of politics, and into areas about which they are very concerned. We decided just to go around it and we talk the language of economics and social development.'

As I continue to read the Universal Declaration it refers to social security, equal employment, the right to adequate standards of living, motherhood, children, education, a just international order, etc. All these are the things which I would have told you, before rereading this document, add up to the charter of our institution. It's actually what we do every day. We come in and we, basically, have a motto just inside our door which says that we should fight poverty with passion and that we should do it every day.

And, I have 10,000 colleagues, some of whom probably have never read the Universal Declaration of Human Rights, and have certainly not read the Covenants in detail as I can now claim I have. We deal with this development agenda in a way that is, we think, pretty strong. The people feel morally pretty strong. They don't actually think that they're any less strong than rights activists. They actually think, correctly or not, that they're on pretty high moral ground and that their job is to deal with the question of poverty. And, when you look at what they're dealing with, speaking candidly, it is everything that is in the rights agenda and the Declaration and Covenants.

I was really fascinated when I read this, although I have only mentioned a couple of the issues that struck me. I could see from this document that, if I had read it thoroughly before articulating the Bank's programme, this could have been the framework which led us to the poverty reduction strategy approach, or the comprehensive development framework, or the interconnectedness of rights, which is, of course, referred to here—the interconnection of rights which we have said is reflected in terms of our approach to poverty and development. You need to have all the different elements functional because, if you don't, you're going to fall because of inadequate attention to those things which will make the achievement of your objectives on poverty attainable.

So, there are an enormous number of parallels between what we have, as one might say, lucked into, or arrived at over 50 years and the integrated rights-based approach to world development which is so prominent in the human rights literature these days.

But then I thought, also in relation to the Bank, what is there to argue about? Why is there any heat in this debate when all of us face a much more difficult and significant problem? We can argue with each other and debate these issues but I think the papers presented at this conference demonstrate a considerable set of shared interests between the two communities and I hope, at the end, they will advance a methodology to enable us to move forward in a better, more complementary and mutually supportive way. When I came to the Bank we were not allowed to mention the word 'corruption'. It was called the 'C' word. I was told by the General Counsel within days of my getting to the institution, and in great secrecy, 'Don't mention the "C" word'. So I asked, 'What's the "C" word?' He replied, 'Corruption'.

Well, maybe we now need to mention the 'R' word which is 'rights'. And, maybe coming down the line we will talk much more about rights as we move forward. But, in the case of rights it's not because I think there is any difference of view. I think that, because of the history of our organization and because of the nature of how we need to progress things with our Board and with our client countries, we tend to approach such matters from an economic and from a social point of view, staking out objectives which are articulated in the Universal Declaration and in the Covenants. But rather than referring back to those documents, we reflect their contents within the context of seeking to address the question of poverty.

Let me return now to the issue of why it is that we're debating while Rome is burning. There is an issue that I think each of our communities needs to face, and that is our shareholders who set the Millennium Development Goals (MDGs).[8] And, who, as a result of the meetings in Monterey and Johannesburg set a basis on which these goals might be achieved. The fact is that these Millennium Goals have, in most cases, very little chance of being achieved because of the lack of interest and support and priority that is given to the question of achieving those goals at this time.

There is a fair chance that statistically we will achieve the poverty goal. But, if you read the statistics, they are highly biased by the inclusion of China and India. And, if you take a look at 47 countries in sub-Saharan Africa

---

[8] The MDGs derive from the Millennium Declaration, a statement adopted by the UN General Assembly in 2000 at a special meeting attended by 147 Heads of State or Government. See General Assembly Res. 55/2 (2000), available at: http://www.un.org/millennium/declaration/ares552e.htm.

you'll find that the statistics are, in fact, going in the other direction. If you look at education, the goals of primary school education—which, by the way, is mentioned many times in the Covenants and the Universal Declaration—we started with the fact that there are 130 million kids, the majority of whom are girls, not in primary school. And, so we thought, let's take that as the first target for the millennium goals because no one can disagree with it.

I probably should have said, and may well have done, 'Every child has the right to primary school education. They have a right. It's written here. And, we just want to support that right. So, the right is agreed to by all the nations of the world. Now, let's get on with it.' Well, having selected it as the first of the MDGs, we focused on 18 countries plus five more—the large countries, so that we could tackle the question of how to finance the efforts of those countries that have an effective and integrated approach to education—an interdependent approach as the human rights documents would say—and which are capable of applying such programmes but who lack only the resources.

And, we arrived at a figure of a couple of billion dollars a year for a period of seven to ten years that was needed as supplemental support for this right to education and for this MDG education objective. Well, we succeeded in the first round of trying to get money for this in reducing the number to seven countries—less than seven per cent of the kids involved. And, we succeeded, if that's the word, in putting together a total of $200,000,000 for three years. We then went back again and got a catalytic fund of a few hundred million dollars to help to get this small number of kids into school.

Now, this is the issue as we define it. It's not the issue of advocacy. It is the simple fact that today people are really not interested in pursuing these goals if it requires extra finance. You hear about numbers—such as the five billion dollars extra being put up by the United States to increase it's overall commitment from ten to fifteen billion, and there's another eight to twelve billion which will be forthcoming from the European Union.

People will tell you as a result that the last year reflected an increase of six billion dollars in available funding for development assistance. And indeed, if you look at the statistics, the total has gone from 52 to 58 billion. But, I asked my colleagues, since I used to be in the business of analysing numbers, let's take them apart.

So, we took them apart. What is the six billion increase? Three billion of it is debt relief which is a zero contribution. It is money that would not other-wise have been paid and is now written off. (In fact, of the 58 billion today, six billion is debt relief.) A further two billion is an increase in the money that goes to consultants and scholarships. So, that makes five billion. And, two billion more goes to Pakistan and Afghanistan in special transfers, and we're not yet talking about special transfers to Iraq which also will probably embellish and strengthen the numbers.

So, far from an increase, when you really dig into it, it's at best a line ball. And, then when you do the analysis of the $52 billion, which we'd done already some months ago, you dig down and you'd be lucky to find $26–28 billion in cash.

Against that, you have agricultural subsidies of $300 billion plus. And, you have military expenditures and defence. In 1999 they came to $800 billion and our estimates today are around a thousand billion.

They are the statistics. And, then we talk about achieving the objectives because the world is united in supporting them. It's nonsense. We're spending 20 times the amount of our development funding on military expenditures. And, the developing world, by the way, is itself spending $200 billion a year on military expenditures. This is very largely China and some of the other large countries, but the amounts are still much too significant in Africa and other places.

Forgive me for this diversion, but I thought it was important before we beat each other up that we understand that we have a common enemy. And, it is an enemy of indifference. It's the enemy of a lack of focus on the concerns that each of our communities, the development and rights-based communities, think about. And, it is here that I think together we could make a big addition. By joining together to try and put pressure on our leaders to make this world a more focused and a better and a more effective place in terms of development and in terms of rights.

I look forward to the results of these discussions very much. And, I can assure you that, from the point of view of the Bank, and from the International Finance Corporation, we are deeply committed to trying to clarify the role of rights in development. How we can go beyond terminology to try and make our work more effective, and how we can, from the point of view of advocacy, join together to get some effective results. When the two of us are talking about our respective disciplines, let's not forget that there are people out there who care about neither rights nor development.

3

What Rights Can Add to Good Development Practice

MARY ROBINSON

Let me begin by saying what poverty means to me, and from where I come at it.

While the focus since 9/11 in developed countries has been on state security and combating acts of terrorism, millions of other people on the planet have continued to be at daily risk from violence, disease, and abject poverty. Their insecurity stems from worry about where the next meal will come from, how to acquire medicines for a dying child, how to avoid the criminal with a gun, how to manage the household as a ten year old AIDS' orphan—theirs is the comprehensive insecurity of the powerless.

For women, gender is itself a risk factor threatening human security: the secret violence of household abuse, the private oppressions of lack of property or inheritance rights, the lifelong deprivations that go with lack of schooling, and the structural problem of political exclusion.

Freedom from want is an empty promise today for more than 800 million people who suffer from undernourishment,[1] for the 30,000 children around the world who die each day of preventable causes,[2] for the thousand million people still without access to clean water supplies or the 2.6 billion who lack access to basic sanitation.[3]

An unprecedented number of countries actually saw their human development indicators slide backwards in the 1990s. In 46 countries people are poorer today than in 1990. In 25 countries more people go hungry than

[1] World Food Progamme, 'Fighting the Global War on Hunger From the Frontline', at http://www.wfp.org/index.asp?section=1 (accessed 23 September 2004).

[2] United Nations Children's Fund, 'Facts on Children: Early Childhood', at http://www.unicef.org/media/media_9475.html (accessed 23 September 2004).

[3] World Health Organization, 'World facing "silent emergency" as billions struggle without clean water or basic sanitation, say WHO and UNICEF', at http://www.who.int/mediacentre/news/releases/2004/pr58/en/ (accessed 23 September 2004).

a decade ago.[4] The picture that emerges is increasingly one of two very different groups of countries: those that have benefited from more open markets, free movement of capital, and new technologies and those that have been left behind.

Of course, the reasons for this situation are many. For example, more and more people are conscious of the intolerable burden of debt on the poorest countries—a debt often incurred over long periods by former dictators which never benefited the general population. What is less appreciated is that poor countries are currently financing the huge deficit here in the United States. A recent World Bank report puts it this way: 'Since 2000, the developing world has been a net exporter of capital to the advanced economies'.[5] This is one of the global inequities we must bear in mind. Not only is more debt relief for the poorest countries essential but rich countries such as the United States should no longer borrow cheaply from poorer ones who need those resources for development at home.

Statistics give us the numbers we account for in addressing inequalities, but they fail to convey the humiliation, the hopelessness, the lack of dignity involved. Listening to a family living in absolute poverty it is this lack they speak of: the lack of self-respect, the indignity and humiliation of a refugee camp, the invisibility of being homeless, the helplessness in the face of violence, including violence caused by those in uniform who should protect.

This is where I begin. In the rest of this paper, I would like to describe recent progress which I think the international community has made in bringing human rights into discussion of development, and then to discuss in a little more detail some of the reasons why many development and economics specialists still remain critical of human rights as an approach. To end, I will indicate briefly where I believe fuller use of human rights principles and values adds to the best practices of those working in development.

3.1 THE CHALLENGE

In December 2001, I was invited to give the World Bank Presidential Lecture in Washington D.C. It was part of a deepening engagement with the Bank, and it was followed by a series of contacts between the staff of the World Bank and the Office of the High Commissioner for Human Rights that have

---

[4] United Nations Development Programme, *Human Development Report 2004: Cultural Liberty in Today's Diverse World* (New York, UNDP, 2004), available at http://hdr.undp.org/reports/global/2004/pdf/hdr04_complete.pdf.

[5] World Bank, *Global Development Finance: Harnessing Cyclical Gains for Development* (Washington DC, World Bank, 2004) 7.

since continued. These contacts informed my own thinking about poverty and rights. In that speech I set out what I still believe to be the key questions: 'What can human rights offer to development work? How can those who are working for universal observance of human rights impact effectively on poverty—itself a violation of human rights—powerlessness, and the conflict and human suffering which poverty underpins?'[6]

I went on to discuss a prior question: What has the activity of promoting and protecting human rights got to do with development? Are these not wholly different fields of national and international endeavour? What does it add to try to relate them?

The international human rights documents, including the Declaration on the Right to Development of 1986, are replete with references to the interdependent or mutually reinforcing relationship that exists between all categories of rights within national protection systems. But they go one step further. They assert that these rights must be effectively enjoyed, whether a country is developing or developed, and that a participatory democracy, based on the rule of law, is the only system of government that can ensure the implementation of all rights.

In this, human rights take a holistic approach which is surely not far removed from the approach taken by development NGOs since the 1970s, by OECD donor governments since the 1990s, and by the World Bank today. Yet historically, a distance has always separated those who work on development and those who work on human rights. In the words of the *Human Development Report 2000*, which discussed the relationship: 'Until the last decade human development and human rights followed parallel paths in both concept and action—the one largely dominated by economists, social scientists and policy-makers, the other by political activists lawyers and philosophers. They promoted divergent strategies of analysis and action—economic and social progress on the one hand, political pressure, law reform and ethical questioning on the other.'[7]

And yet, it is not the case that development and human rights specialists have been separated intellectually by the way they have defined the issue. In its Annual Report 2001, the World Bank talked about poverty in the following terms: 'Poor people often lack legal rights that would empower them to take advantage of opportunities and protect them from arbitrary and inequitable treatment. They, more than any other group in society, are adversely affected by laws permitting discrimination, deficient laws and institutions that fail to protect individual and property rights, and insufficient enforcement of

[6] Mary Robinson, *Bridging the Gap between Human Rights and Development: From normative principles to operational relevance*, World Bank Presidential Lecture, Washington, 3 December 2001.

[7] UNDP, *Human Development Report 2000: Human Rights and Human Development* (New York, UNDP, 2000) 2.

these laws, as well as other barriers to justice.'[8] This assessment of the effects of poverty is little different from the definition which the Office of the High Commission adopted at the very end of my term of office in 2002: 'the sustained or chronic deprivation of the resources, capabilities, choices, security and power necessary for the enjoyment of an adequate standard of living and other civil, cultural, economic, political and social rights'.[9] The Bank's emphasis on powerlessness and discrimination was even more forcefully articulated in its ground-breaking work on poverty, 'Voices of the Poor'.[10]

While convergence can clearly be seen, however, the challenge remains: How in practical terms are we to make the links useful? How can the affirmation of principles in the Universal Declaration of Human Rights, developed through treaties and legal standards, help to construct operational programmes that contribute practically to development and the elimination of poverty?

We might begin by asking where progress has already occurred. What has already been done to bring convergence closer, make mainstreaming more real, and apply human rights in ways that make some difference to development policy and to the poverty from which so many people suffer?

3.2 WHAT HAS BEEN ACHIEVED SO FAR?

When I started my term as High Commissioner in September 1997, the Cold War had ended and I felt there was at last an opportunity to take political and civil, and economic and social, rights equally seriously, as the drafters of the Universal Declaration of Human Rights intended. Several positive steps were taken at the international level in the next five years.

Under new mandates the UN Commission on Human Rights appointed special rapporteurs in areas such as education, food, and the highest attainable standard of health as well as an independent expert on the right

[8] World Bank, *The World Bank Annual Report 2001*, Vol. 1, Year in Review (World Bank, Washington DC, 2002) 58, available at http://www.worldbank.org/annualreport/2001/pdf/wbarvol1.pdf.
[9] This definition was adopted by Professors Paul Hunt, Manfred Nowak, and Siddiq Osmani when they prepared draft guidelines on a human rights approach to poverty reduction strategies. The Guidelines were published in September 2003 (United Nations Office of the High Commissioner for Human Rights, *Human Rights and Poverty Reduction: A Conceptual Framework*, Geneva, 2004) and subsequently revised in November 2004.
[10] D. Narayan et al., *Can Anyone Hear Us? Voices From 47 Countries* (Washington DC, World Bank, 1999) 26–51, available at http://www1.worldbank.org/prem/poverty/voices/reports/canany/vol1.pdf.

to development—all of whom have made substantial contributions to advancing the agenda on these issues.[11]

Important strides were made after Kofi Annan asked UN agencies and programmes in 1997 to mainstream human rights throughout the UN system. Some of the UN's key bodies, including the UN Development Program, the World Health Organization, and the UN Children's Fund (UNICEF), included human rights within their mandates and started to integrate them in their programming.[12] In 2003, they and a number of UN agencies agreed to a 'Common Understanding' of how they would apply a rights-based approach.[13] The Millennium Declaration, signed by all the world's political leaders, makes specific references to human rights.[14]

Within the Office of the High Commissioner for Human Rights we developed human rights guidelines for poverty reduction strategies,[15] and worked more closely with UN country teams on economic and social issues. In regional meetings, we reviewed national case law and shared experiences of how different national courts and regional systems were addressing international commitments concerning economic, social, and cultural rights.

Not for the first time, bilateral agencies were often ahead of international agencies in this work. The Nordic countries had already applied human rights principles in their programming for many years. The Netherlands, DFID, the Swiss Development Cooperation programme and some other countries were not far behind.[16]

---

[11] For details of the work of the Special Rapporteurs on the right to education, the right to food, and the right to housing, as well as of the independent expert of the Commission on Human Rights on the right to development see: http://www.unhchr.ch/.

[12] WHO has published a series of papers on health and human rights: *Twenty Five Questions and Answers on Health and Human Rights* (2002), *WHO's Contribution to the World Conference Against Racism, Racial Discrimination, Xenophobia and Related Intolerance: Health and Freedom from Discrimination* (2001), *The Right to Water* (2003), and *International Migration, Health and Human Rights* (2003). See http://www.who.int/hhr/activities/publications/en/. For a summary of UNICEF's rights-based approach see: http://www.unicef.org/publications/index_16271.html. For UNDP's goals in integrating rights into development see http://www.undp.org/governance/humanrights.htm.

[13] 'The Human Rights Based Approach to Development Cooperation Towards a Common Understanding Among UN Agencies', 2003, available at http://www.undp.org/governance/docshurist/030616CommonUnderstanding.doc.

[14] General Assembly Res. 55/2 (2000) at http://www.un.org/millennium/declaration/ares552e.htm.   [15] See above n. 9.

[16] On the Swedish International Development Corporation Agency's approach to human rights: http://www.sida.se//Sida/jsp/polopoly.jsp?d=514&a=9175. DFID has published several policy documents on their rights-based approach, including *Realising Human Rights for Poor People* (London, DFID, 2000) at http://62.189.42.51/DFIDstage/Pubs/files/tsp_human.pdf. The Swiss Agency for Development and Cooperation (SDC) lists respect for human rights as a vital piece of their goal 'to promote the sound management of public affairs'. http://www.sdc.admin.ch/index.php?navID=299&userhash=14402823&l=e.

Over the same period, human rights activists and NGOs in every region also turned more actively to the advancement of economic and social rights. Numerous new NGOs formed to work on these rights, and many of the established international NGOs—including both Human Rights Watch and Amnesty International—amended their mandates to permit them to give economic and social rights more attention.[17] My travels as High Commissioner brought me in contact with human rights activists and NGOs in every region who were finding innovative ways to hold their governments accountable for the commitments they had made under the International Covenant on Economic, Social and Cultural Rights, the Convention for the Elimination of Discrimination against Women, and the Convention on the Rights of the Child, each of which also include specific provisions concerning economic, social, and cultural rights.

I recall, for example, the way in which a wide cross-section of Brazilian NGOs prepared an alternative report to the UN Committee on Economic, Social and Cultural Rights in order to bring home the government of Brazil's failure to produce a required report to the Committee within the time allowed under the International Covenant on Economic, Social and Cultural Rights. This effort resulted in more constructive debate on rights throughout Brazil and caused the government to step up efforts to fulfil its international human rights commitments.

Development NGOs also moved towards using human rights. Many chose to integrate human rights within their programmes, a trend that accelerated after the shock of the Rwanda genocide in 1994. One of the first to do so was Oxfam International:[18] the choice of someone with my background to be its president—following in the illustrious footsteps of the economist Amartya Sen—is itself significant. I find it very positive that Amnesty International has launched a campaign to highlight violence against women and that, for the first time, Amnesty and Oxfam have co-operated in a joint campaign (for the control of small arms).

During Jim Wolfensohn's Presidency, the World Bank has greatly increased its attention to the relationship between human rights and development. In his

[17] In August 2003, Amnesty International amended their mandate to 'mak[e] the advancement of ESCR an integral part of the movement's human rights strategy' (http://www.amnestyusa.org/activist_toolkit/amnestyinaction/esc_rights.html). Human Rights Watch has also increasingly focused on economic, social, and cultural rights (http://hrw.org/doc/?t=esc). See K. Roth, 'Defending Economic, Social and Cultural Rights: Practical Issues Faced by an International Human Rights Organization', 26 *Human Rights Quarterly* 63 (2004). Several NGOs focus predominantly on ESC rights such as the Center for Economic and Social Rights (www.cesr.org) and ESCR-Net (http://www.escr-net.org/EngGeneral/home.asp).

[18] See Oxfam International's *Strategic Plan 2001–2004*, available at http://www.oxfam.org/eng/pdfs/strat_plan.pdf, and the address given by Oxfam International Policy Director Jeremy Hobbs at the 2004 World Social Forum in Mumbai, India: http://www.oxfam.org/eng/pdfs/doc040119_wsf_human_rights_jeremy_speech.pdf.

address to the Board of Governors of the Bank in Dubai, President Wolfensohn noted that we face an immense challenge in creating a new global balance 'Human rights lie at the heart of that global challenge . . .'. The close links forged with my Office as High Commissioner have been continued with 'Realizing Rights: the Ethical Globalization Initiative'. The participation of President Wolfensohn and his senior colleagues at the Bank in the March 2004 New York Law School conference on 'Human Rights and Development' is a recent manifestation of that relationship. In his address to the Conference, Roberto Danino, Senior Vice-President and General Counsel of the Bank, made clear his view that the economic and political restrictions reflected in the Bank's Articles do not inhibit a proactive and explicit consideration of human rights as part of the Bank's work. Following the conference, President Wolfensohn assigned Mr Danino the task of co-ordinating further thinking on the Bank's approach to human rights. More recently, President Wolfensohn invited me and my colleagues to the Ethical Globalization Initiative to comment on the draft World Bank management Response to the Extractive Industries Review, and I was the keynote speaker at the Bank's Workshop on Gender-based Violence in November 2004. I have every confidence that this very useful dialogue with former President Wolfensohn and the senior officials of the Bank will continue.

In my own view, these developments indicate that a sea change is occurring in the relationship between development and human rights. At the same time, no informed observer can avoid noting that the process of integration has not been an easy one. Whether you consider the UN's difficulties in mainstreaming, the experience of NGOs, or the frustrations felt by many government development officials, we are far from arriving at a position where those working in the human rights tradition and those working in the development tradition feel they speak the same language. If mutual curiosity has increased, confidence is far from being safely established. Let me turn therefore to the reasons why development experts and officials who implement development policies remain somewhat ill at ease with human rights, or at least unconvinced at present that they are helpful.[19]

---

[19] Interestingly, many of the points I mention were raised in an article by the Executive Director of Human Rights Watch, see Roth, n. 17 above. His aim was to explain why, in certain respects, it remains more difficult to campaign for economic and social rights than civil and political rights. The interest, not to say controversy, which his article generated signals perhaps that the human rights community is beginning to address many of the criticisms of the human rights framework that development specialists and economists have made. Here too I detect progress. See the following exchange: L. Rubenstein, 'How International Human Rights Organizations can Advance Economic, Social, and Cultural Rights: A Response to Kenneth Roth', 26 *Human Rights Quarterly* 845 (2004); Mary Robinson, 'Advancing Economic, Social, and Cultural Rights: The Way Forward', 26 *Human Rights Quarterly* 866 (2004); and K. Roth, 'Response to Leonard S. Rubenstein', 26 *Human Rights Quarterly* 873 (2004).

3.3 CRITICISMS OF HUMAN RIGHTS

Three principal criticisms of the human rights approach are made by those who work in the field of development.

3.3.1 Human Rights Are Political

Development experts often feel that human rights are 'political', by which they mean that they are overly focused on the state, and use adversarial and judgemental techniques to monitor state performance that politicize the development process unhelpfully. Connected to this is the complex issue of sovereignty. They argue that, by appealing to international standards, human rights advocates diminish the notion of national sovereignty, irritating national governments and undermining efforts to make them nationally responsible. Without local ownership, critics say, development cannot be achieved.

This claim is worth a more extended discussion than can be had here. I make three remarks. The first is that the human rights framework does focus first and foremost on the responsibilities of states; and it does indeed have an adversarial critical tradition. At the same time, more human rights organizations now also work with states on issues of reform and in doing so they come closer to the methodologies and programmes of development agencies. Human rights organizations are broadening their work to address other actors too, notably business, and this trend can also be observed at every level—international, national, in civil society, and so forth.

My second remark concerns the issue of sovereignty. The human rights approach does put the state at the centre of responsibility. This means that human rights advocates consider national governments, and national societies, to be the key locus of action. It is a misunderstanding to conclude that, because the human rights system draws legitimacy from international standards, it is essentially interested only in the international dimension. The importance of international standards is that they establish an agreed objective, a minimum—rarely a maximum—standard, to ensure that all people are protected in key areas of their lives. There is a benchmark, in other words, for states to attain—but this is not the end goal. The end goal is the creation of a government and a society (and in our existing legal order that means national government) that protects rights because both governments and members of society are adequately accountable.

My third observation is to note that the issue of sovereignty presents itself just as acutely in the work of development agencies. Not surprisingly: in a world of highly unequal nation states, it is not easy to escape. Development agencies are regularly accused of promoting policies that reflect their cultural traditions or serve their national interests at the expense of smaller and poorer states. They are often accused of failing to address questions of abuse, because they are politically sensitive, even though they undermine the credibility of their development strategies. The merit of the human rights framework in this respect is that it makes judgements on performance in relation to objective standards that have been agreed by the international community as a whole—including, in most cases, the government in question. As a result, the case for arbitrariness and bias, or abuse of unequal power, is that much more difficult to make.

3.3.2 Human Rights Are Unrealistic

A second criticism is that human rights advocates want instant reform, reform by decree. Critics argue that human rights reformers overstate the importance of law and presume the state has a capacity that it often does not have. They are accused of failing to take proper account of underlying social and cultural causes of underdevelopment and failing to understand that development is necessarily a long-term process, extending over several generations. They are accused of ignoring the fact that successful reform processes must cope with numerous failures and political backsliding.

To some extent I think this used to be a fair criticism; however, the situation has been changing rapidly. Many human rights organizations now recognize the need to go beyond 'naming and shaming' alone. They are engaging with government reform processes, in capacity building through human rights technical co-operation programmes, and in working out how to co-operate with government while retaining their critical independence. Their thinking is evolving and they are gaining experience. At the international level, this is also true. I believe the Office of the High Commissioner for Human Rights, for example, is now in a much stronger position to contribute in practical and useful ways to development programmes than it was just a few years ago. We are learning how to contribute to large multi-dimensional development programmes and how to complement the work of other agencies.

The movement is not all one way, of course. Development specialists— from the World Bank outwards—are today much more conscious of the importance of governance than they used to be. The link between transparency, accountability and political inclusion—all values central to human rights—is very widely recognized, as is the frequently devastating impact on development of corrupt and oppressive rule.

With respect to 'unrealism', I would also add that development agencies are not immune from the same charge. They are frequently accused of failing to co-ordinate their programmes, failing to consider underlying social and economic conditions, preferring simple even faddish fixes to long-term strategic investment and commitment, etc. Though to a less extreme degree than human rights campaigners, they, too, are said to apply conditionality insensitively, and to withdraw aid whenever it is politically expedient to do so. The point is that these are inherently difficult policy questions: I do not have plain answers to any of them. My aim is to point out that development agencies and human rights organizations have here elements of an agenda in common. Neither the fault, nor the virtue, are all on one side.

3.3.3 Human Rights Are Abstract, Cannot Be Applied Practically

The third criticism I hear is a rather specific one. It is usually made by economists who say that human rights advocates appeal to high principle but cannot apply themselves to practical decision making. A critic of this sort claims that economists and administrators must regularly choose one 'good' outcome at the expense of another because there is not enough money to go round; accepting such 'real world' constraints, they rationalize their decisions as responsibly as they can. By contrast, it is argued, human rights advocates are not only unable to choose between two 'goods' using their principles; they refuse to do so or to acknowledge the real constraints of scarcity, but say minimum standards must be met immediately, across the board. In this respect, the critic goes on, human rights advocates are irresponsible: they claim too much, they refuse to trade, they will not address the problem of resource limits—in short, they are all norms and no teeth.

This criticism also deserves a more extended answer than I can give here. In fact I agree that human rights advocates often find it difficult to trade—to negotiate, to do deals—but believe this is not (or is not necessarily) because they are unrealistic or 'other worldly' in their thinking. The human rights framework is systemic. Its ambitious aim has been to develop a body of principles that, taken together, provide points of reference for all cases where issues of rights arise. It is the systemic nature of human rights which explains why advocates of rights often speak of their universality and indivisibility. This is not jargon—it highlights the belief that respect for any right cannot be achieved in the absence of respect for other rights.

As a result, however, rights advocates find it difficult to bargain—to set aside protection of one right in favour of protecting another. Unlike development, human rights is not a pragmatic tradition. And since human rights advocates are often unfamiliar with other traditions—just as other traditions are unfamiliar with the systemic nature of human rights thinking—difficulties of communication are almost inevitable.

For at least three reasons, however, I do not accept that the human rights approach is inherently unrealistic. First of all, the human rights standards do take account of resource constraints and were drafted in a quite practical spirit—governments would not have consented to them otherwise. I cannot give you many examples here, but to illustrate I would point to the increasingly skilful way those working for child rights are analysing national budgets to see whether the allocation for education is being progressively implemented, or whether there is new expenditure for example on unnecessary military equipment.

Secondly, I believe that a lot of good work is now being done that in time will enable decision makers to draw upon human rights standards in ways that will help to improve the transparency and accountability and *quality* of their decisions. I do not say that all decisions will be assisted by referring to human rights; but many could be. Taking account of human rights obligations will often suggest indicators that can assist decision making; and evaluating decisions against human rights criteria will often assist decision makers to identify where their policies are likely to produce, or have produced, discriminatory outcomes or outcomes that are otherwise undesirable.

My third remark concerns the claim that human rights is 'too normative'. It is true that the human rights system is based on norms, on values. In my view, so it should be. My comment is really that other systems are also. Let me again be a little provocative and suggest that classical economics is open to a very similar charge. Its notion of economic man, or economic woman, postulates a norm of human behaviour that is highly unrealistic, though useful. I do not believe for one moment (and nor do most economists) that most human beings act in practice in ways that maximize their economic advantage. Altruistic behaviour is commonplace, as indeed are financial incompetence and simple lack of interest in economic matters. In this respect, human rights is not a uniquely normative approach and its strengths and weaknesses should not be judged as if it was.

3.3.4 Human Rights Cannot Cope with Time

A related criticism is that the human rights methodology proceeds in a single tense, the present, and is unable to cope with time. The notion of 'progressive realization', for example, seems unilinear: it assumes that progress must be continuous, and that it is never acceptable for policy makers to 'go backwards' at one point in order to go forwards later on. This is important for development economists, who take it for granted that most development programmes cause damage en route, either for a minority or for the majority of long-term beneficiaries. Further, they argue that human rights analysts are often unwilling to deal with differential advantage: when a minority suffer from the impact of progress, they tend to condemn this, irrespective of the scale of benefits for the majority or the benefits that those who suffer immediately may eventually receive.

My own view is that these are interesting questions; I tend to agree that human rights analysts have not thought enough about them. Their significance can easily be exaggerated, nevertheless. The great merit of the human rights approach is that it draws attention to discrimination and exclusion. It permits policy makers and observers to identify those who do not benefit from development, and refuses to marginalize their interests by reference to benefits that are received by others, or may be received in the future. This is extremely important in this context, precisely because so many development programmes have caused misery and impoverishment inadvertently or out of sight, because planners only looked for macro-scale outcomes and did not consider the consequences for particular communities or groups of people. The ability of human rights to force attention towards those who lose out is a specific contribution they can make to development planning.

3.3.5 Law and Poor Don't Mix

A final criticism of human rights organizations is less often made explicitly, at least by development professionals, but is of great relevance for the next phase of work that human rights organizations should prepare for.

In general, protection of human rights is most easily, most successfully, achieved when governments are well resourced, responsible, and respectful of the rule of law. Equally, individual protection is more easily achieved where those whose rights are threatened are well educated, well-connected, and well off. Except in the case of industrialized totalitarian regimes, the worst violations tend to occur where governments are unskilled and lack resources and where those at risk are in the same position. But everywhere, however competent they are, and even if they are committed to protecting rights, governments find it difficult to adequately fulfil their obligations towards the very poor, and those who are most alienated and marginalized.

This is a problem for development activists but much more so for human rights organizations, precisely because human rights law does place explicit emphasis on the responsibility of states, while it is characteristic of many marginalized communities that they don't look towards the state to meet their needs—on the contrary many positively flee in the other direction. Where a relatively small number of people are affected, as in most industrialized societies, the problem should be manageable (though it remains an intellectual challenge that must be worked through). In large areas of the world, however, great numbers of people are poor and their governments clearly lack resources as well. The people in question not only look primarily to their own communities for support and assistance; in addition they are not aggregated in large organized social units that can be easily reached and, being extremely vulnerable, they cannot afford to confide in, or easily trust, outsiders who claim to want to help them. To create conditions in which the human rights of very poor or marginalized communities can be protected, governments will need to find new ways of reaching into and serving such communities, and human rights organizations will need to find new ways of winning their trust. In my view, these things can probably only be done by building alliances with organizations that have a long-term presence in such communities—religious organizations, community groups, representatives of social movements, development NGOs, etc.[20]

This is a challenge which human rights organizations have only recently understood. It is also a challenge governments need to face. It is another argument in favour of convergence. If we share an interest in ending poverty and creating more inclusive, prosperous, and fairer societies, we all have an interest in working more closely together.

3.4 WHERE HUMAN RIGHTS ADDS VALUE

Overall, I suggest there is gathering evidence of *mutual* need. Development agencies have adopted and integrated within their policies some key values and operational terms. Some are explicitly promoted in PRSPs, though they are rooted in an older tradition which first emerged among development NGOs in the 1970s and were subsequently adopted by the OECD in the early 90s. Key terms include:

- inclusion and non-discrimination
- national and local ownership
- accountability and transparency
- participation and empowerment.

These are also values that underpin the fundamental principles of human rights law—as Jim Wolfensohn has pointed out. In his chapter in this volume he notes that he had read through the principal human rights documents beforehand and 'could see that [human rights] could have been the framework which led us to the poverty reduction strategy approach, or the comprehensive development framework'. He went on to emphasize the interconnectedness of rights, observing that 'you need to have all the different elements functional because if you don't, you're going to fail because of inadequate attention to those things which will make the achievement of

---

[20] International Council on Human Rights Policy, *Enhancing Access to Human Rights* (Geneva, ICHRP, 2004) at http://www.ichrp.org.

your objectives on poverty attainable'. 'So,' he went on, 'there are an enormous number of parallels between what we have [in the development community] arrived at over 50 years and the integrated rights-based approach to world development which is so prominent in the human rights literature these days.'[21]

This observation needs to be given attention. As I have suggested, we need to see the system of human rights clearly for what it is in order to understand what it can offer. It is essentially an ordered body of principles, incorporated in international law, which therefore reflects the character of international law (based on states and state sovereignty), that elevates the importance of individual rights (and also responsibilities) in relation to the state, and the state's responsibilities (and by implication rights) vis-à-vis the individual. As I noted in the Presidential Address I gave to the World Bank in 2001:

A rights-based approach is a conceptual framework for the process of human development that is normatively based on international human rights standards and operationally directed to promoting and protecting human rights. The rights-based approach integrates the norms, standards and principles of the international human rights system into the plans, policies and processes of development. The norms and standards are those contained in the wealth of international treaties and declarations that I have mentioned. The principles in question are: participation, empowerment, accountability, non-discrimination, and express linkages to international human rights norms and standards. But it should be emphasized that at the heart of a human rights approach must be the legal character of the international treaties that creates rights and duties.[22]

Drawing from existing research and development experience, we might say that a human rights approach provides:

- enhanced accountability;
- higher levels of citizens' empowerment, ownership, and free, meaningful, and active participation;
- greater normative clarity and detail;
- easier consensus and increased transparency in national development processes;
- a more complete and rational development framework;
- integrated safeguards against unintentional harm by development projects;
- more effective and complete analysis; and
- a more authoritative basis for advocacy.

Rights lend moral legitimacy and reinforce principles of social justice that already underpin much development thinking. They help shift the focus of analysis to the most deprived and excluded, especially to deprivations caused

---

[21] J. D. Wolfensohn, Chapter 2 in this volume.   [22] Note 6 above.

by discrimination. They require those involved in development processes to provide information and a political voice for all people. They affirm that civil and political rights need to be exercised in practice as well as theory in the course of successful and legitimate development, and that economic, social, and cultural rights need to be recognized and implemented as human rights, rather than aggregated in a general way or idealized.

There is an answer, I believe, to the important question posed by Jim Wolfensohn.[23] What does recognition of a 'right' to health or education add to the high priority already placed on improvements in health and education as a matter of the Bank's existing development strategy? The recognition of a 'right' to health or education, arising out of treaties and other international commitments, implies corresponding legal obligations of national governments as well as of the international community. As a consequence of that recognition, those who are poor and marginalized are empowered, and their participation rendered effective. Thus, as only one example, the participation of civil society in the PRSP is necessarily enhanced where it can be framed in terms of enforcement of legal obligations.

In my view, the most defining attribute of human rights in development is its focus on accountability. I have in the past called for a more critical approach to the integration of human rights into the work of development— one that asks hard questions about obligations, duties, and action. Adoption of human rights principles and methods will require all partners in the development process—local, national, regional, and international—to accept higher levels of accountability. Establishing ways to operationalize and evaluate institutions and mechanisms for accountability in development programming is therefore a defining challenge in the years ahead. I recognize the important conceptual work produced by the Bank in this area.

Let me recall again why human rights values are considered indivisible and universal. This is not a matter of jargon: advocates emphasize them precisely because they believe that respect for any right cannot be achieved in the absence of respect for other rights. A hungry child cannot successfully educate herself. A sick man cannot exercise his right to work.[24]

Enthusiastic advocates of human rights have perhaps too often thought of themselves as bringing 'good news' to development professionals, however— a 'new and better way' of doing things that, by implication at least, should cause such professionals to sweep aside some of the practices that they have painfully fashioned from long experience. This is significant when we consider the areas of unease that I have described. For, if human rights values really are universal, we should be astonished to discover that good development

---

[23] Chapter 2 in this volume.

[24] International Council on Human Rights Policy, *Duties sans Frontières: Human Rights and Global Social Justice* (Geneva, ICHRP, 2003) 17–22, available at http://www.ichrp.org.

practice did not fairly accurately reflect them. In this sense, I think it is inappropriate to speak of 'the human rights approach' as if it is wholly new or has revolutionary implications. I believe this is a misunderstanding of the situation we are in. Convergence is the better term because essentially it is more accurate. Truly good practice—in government, in development, in other domains—tends everywhere to be consistent with human rights principles and values and, to the extent that this is so, the question we need to ask is: What *additional* benefits can fuller use of human rights principles and methods bring? The question is less one of replacement than enhancement and improvement. One distinct benefit is a 'buy-in' by civil society groups through having tools which empower them.

The Commission on Human Security describes the concept of empowerment, as:

People's ability to act on their own behalf—and on behalf of others . . . People empowered can demand respect for their dignity when it is violated. They can create new opportunities for work and address many problems locally. And they can mobilize for the security of others.[25]

I saw this for myself in every country I visited as High Commissioner. Human rights groups, women's groups, environmental movements, child advocates, minority groups, those tackling poverty were all increasingly seeing the value of applying their governments' human rights obligations to budget analysis, legislation, and social policies to expose failures to implement progressively rights to the highest standards of health, to education, and adequate housing among others. They were also challenging money spent on unnecessary military equipment or projects benefiting only a small elite. Invariably, the work was under-resourced, undervalued, and often resented by those in power. But change was possible.

Now these groups have additional tools available in the commitments both developed and developing countries have made to achieve the Millennium Development Goals by 2015, which will be reviewed and debated at the General Assembly in 2005.

An opportunity presents itself to reinforce the empowerment of grass-roots organizations in every region by linking two processes that provide them with tools of accountability. We should help them to link their country's undertaking to achieve the Millennium Development Goals, and the country's legal commitments to progressively implement economic and social rights under the relevant international treaties, together with developed countries' commitment to substantial new resources for financing this development.

To date, large parts of civil society have not been actively engaged in promoting the MDGs and mobilizing to pressure their governments to take

---

[25] Commission on Human Security, *Human Security Now* (New York, United Nations, 2003) 11, available at http://www.humansecurity-chs.org/finalreport/index.html.

effective action. Indeed, my experience of speaking to audiences in the United States, including political scientists, sociologists, and economists, is that a substantial majority has never heard of the MDGs! Some human rights groups have expressed concern that the Millennium Goals sideline more pressing issues or ignore previous commitments such as the women's rights platform of the 1990s including violence against women and reproductive rights. Another criticism is that the MDG process is top-down. Civil society was not involved in formulating the MDGs which are seen by some as an attempt at a one-size-fits-all approach.

While I recognize that these are legitimate concerns, we should not forget that the MDGs were placed within the context of commitments that governments reaffirmed in September 2000 in the Millennium Declaration, to promote human rights, democracy, and good governance. These commitments include:

- to respect and fully uphold the Universal Declaration of Human Rights;
- to strengthen the capacity of all countries to implement the practices of democracy and human rights;
- to implement the Convention on the Elimination of All Forms of Discrimination against Women (CEDAW);
- to ensure respect and protection for the rights of migrant workers and their families;
- to work collectively for a more inclusive political process, allowing genuine participation by all citizens in all countries; and
- to ensure the freedom of the media and public access to information, which are vitally important to achieving the development goals and should be given greater prominence.

The assessment of progress on the MDGs to be carried out in 2005, and the debate in the General Assembly in September 2005, provide an ideal context for the further convergence of those working in the fields of human rights and development.

Part A

The Economics of Social Rights

4

Democracy and the Right to Food

JEAN DRÈZE*

4.1 INTRODUCTION

The right to food can be seen from at least three different perspectives. One is the perspective of the Indian Constitution, including the Directive Principles of State Policy. Secondly, we can refer to international declarations and conventions on this matter, starting with the Universal Declaration of Human Rights. Thirdly, it is possible to argue for the right to food as a moral and social right, independently of all these documents. Indeed, it is a basic premise of the human rights movement that all human beings have some fundamental rights, whether or not these rights are already incorporated in national or international law. To illustrate, one can argue that a child has a right to protection from physical punishment at school, whether or not physical punishment is legally permissible.

These three perspectives, of course, are not mutually exclusive. In fact, they complement each other. In this paper, however, I shall concentrate on the first approach, and particularly on the right to food as one of the economic and social rights affirmed in the Directive Principles.[1] There are two reasons for this. One is that this approach appears to me to be particularly coherent and far-reaching. The other reason is that it is important to place the right to food in the larger context of the need to revive the Directive Principles, and their underlying vision of radical social change.

* Reprinted from *Economic and Political Weekly*, with kind permission of the publisher. The original article was adapted from the third C. Chandrasekaran Memorial Lecture, delivered at the International Institute for Population Sciences (Mumbai) on 7 November 2003. The author is grateful to P. Arokiasamy and T. K. Roy for inviting me to deliver this lecture, and for their overwhelming hospitality.

[1] On the international perspective, see e.g., R. Gaiha, 'Does the Right to Food Matter?' *Economic and Political Weekly*, 4 October 2003; S. Mahendra Dev, 'Right to Food in India', Working Paper 50 (Hyderabad: Centre for Economic and Social Studies, 2003). H. Mander, 'Social, Economic and Cultural Entitlements and Legal Rights' (mimeo, New Delhi: Action Aid, 2003).

The Directive Principles are chiefly due to Dr. Ambedkar, and they build on his visionary conception of democracy. This vision, in turn, was intimately related to his notion of the good society as a society based on 'liberty, equality, and fraternity'. Democracy, as he saw it, was both the end and the means of this ideal. It was the end because he ultimately considered democracy itself as synonymous with the realization of liberty, equality, and fraternity. At the same time, democracy was also the means through which this ideal was to be attained.

Indeed, in Dr. Ambedkar's perspective, democracy was intrinsically geared to social transformation and human progress. In one of the most inspiring definitions of the term, he described democracy as 'a form and method of government whereby revolutionary changes in the economic and social life of the people are brought about without bloodshed'.[2] For this to happen, it was essential to link political democracy with economic and social democracy. This was one of the main objectives of the Indian Constitution, and particularly of the Directive Principles. Dr. Ambedkar himself put it as follows:

Our object in framing the Constitution is really two-fold: (1) To lay down the form of political democracy, and (2) To lay down that our ideal is economic democracy and also to prescribe that every Government whatever is in power shall strive to bring about economic democracy. The directive principles have a great value, for they lay down that our ideal is economic democracy.[3]

This revolutionary conception of democracy, however, fell into oblivion soon after independence. Indian democracy essentially went the same way as parliamentary democracy in Europe, which Dr. Ambedkar considered as 'a name and a farce'.[4] Fifty-five years down the road, economic democracy has been quietly buried as a principle of public policy, and even political democracy is not exactly in the pink of health.

---

[2] Quoted in B. Das, ed., *Thus Spoke Ambedkar: Volume I* (Jalandhar: Buddhist Publishing House, 1963) 61. Strictly speaking, this was not so much a definition of democracy as a 'test' of it. Dr. Ambedkar added: 'It is perhaps the severest test. But when you are judging the quality of a material you must put it to the severest test.' Note also that in other contexts he insisted that democracy was not just a method of government but also a 'form of social organization' and a 'way of life'.

[3] Proceedings of the Constituent Assembly of India, Friday 19 November 1948; available at http://www.parliamentofindia.nic.in/debates/vol17p9.htm.

[4] 'The second wrong ideology that has vitiated parliamentary democracy [in western Europe] is the failure to realize that political democracy cannot succeed where there is no social or economic democracy...Democracy is another name for equality. Parliamentary democracy developed a passion for liberty. It never made a nodding acquaintance with equality. It failed to realize the significance of equality and did not even endeavour to strike a balance between liberty and equality, with the result that liberty swallowed equality and has made democracy a name and a farce.' Quoted in V. Rodriguez, ed., *The Essential Writings of B. R. Ambedkar* (New Delhi: Oxford University Press, 2002) 62.

4.2 THE NUTRITION EMERGENCY IN INDIA

With this background, let me turn to the question of food. On this, the first point to note is the catastrophic nature of the nutritional situation in India. The second National Family Health Survey (1998–1999) provides ample evidence of the problem. To illustrate, according to this survey, 47 per cent of all Indian children are undernourished, 52 per cent of all adult women are anaemic, and 36 per cent have a body mass index (BMI) below the cut-off of 18.5 commonly associated with chronic energy deficiency.[5] These nutritional deficiencies have devastating consequences for the well-being and future of the Indian people. To start with, hunger and undernutrition are intrinsic deprivations and severely diminish the quality of life. Further, under-nutrition is associated with reduced learning abilities, greater exposure to disease, and other impairments of individual and social opportunities.

In international perspective, India is one of the most undernourished countries in the world. According to the latest *Human Development Report*, only two countries (Bangladesh and Nepal) have a higher proportion of undernourished children than India, and only two countries (Bangladesh and Ethiopia) have a higher proportion of infants with low birthweight.[6] Even after taking into account various gaps and inaccuracies in the international data, there is another indication here that undernutrition levels in India are extremely high.

The second National Family Health Survey contains a wealth of further evidence on different aspects of the nutrition situation in India. Consumption data, for instance, bring out the frugal nature of food intakes for a majority of the population. Only 55 per cent of adult women in India consume milk or curd at least once a week, only 33 per cent eat fruits at least once a week, and 28 per cent get an egg. The evidence on child morbidity is no less sobering. Among children under the age of three, 30 per cent had fever during the two weeks preceding the survey, 19 per cent had diarrhoea, and another 19 per cent had symptoms of acute respiratory infection.[7] Even after allowing for some overlap between these different groups, this suggests that at least half of all Indian children below the age of three suffer from one of these conditions within any given interval of two weeks.

All the figures cited so far are national averages. It goes without saying that the situation gets worse—far worse—as we consider the poorer states

[5] International Institute for Population Sciences, *National Family Health Survey (NFHS-2) 1998–99: India* (Mumbai: IIPS, 2000) 246, 250, and 270. The 'child undernutrition' figures are based on weight-for-age data for children under the age of three.

[6] United Nations Development Programme, *Human Development Report 2003* (New York: UNDP, 2003) 258–261.

[7] International Institute for Population Sciences, above n. 5, 219 and 244.

(e.g., Jharkhand, Chhattisgarh, Orissa), and the more deprived regions within these poorer states (e.g., Palamau in Jharkhand, Sarguja in Chhattisgarh, Kalahandi in Orissa), not to speak of the poorer communities within these deprived regions. Among the Sahariyas, Musahars, Kols, Bhuiyas and other marginalized communities, the nutritional situation can only be described as a permanent emergency. To illustrate, in a recent survey of 21 randomly-selected households in a Bhuiya hamlet of Palamau district in Jharkhand, 20 reported that they had to 'skip meals regularly'.[8] At the time of the survey, most of the households in this hamlet survived on *chakora* (a local spinach) and *gheti* (a wild root), supplemented with some broken rice on lucky days. Some had nothing to eat but plain *chakora*.

Another disturbing aspect of the nutrition situation in India is that it shows little sign of major *improvement* over time. There is evidence of a steady decline of extreme hunger and severe undernutrition.[9] But the general progress of anthropometric indicators (e.g., the heights and weights of Indian children) is very slow. The point is illustrated in Figure 4.1, which shows the average weight of Indian children at different ages in 1992–1993 and 1998–1999, based on the first and second rounds of the National Family Health Survey. There is some improvement, but it is not exactly dramatic. Based on the weight-for-age criterion, the proportion of undernourished children declined from 53 per cent in 1992–1993 to 47 per cent in 1998–1999.[10] If

---

[8] B. Bhatia and J. Drèze, 'Still Starving in Jharkhand', *Frontline*, 16 August 2002.

[9] To illustrate: (1) according to the National Sample Survey (unpublished data), the proportion of households that are not getting 'two square meals a day throughout the year' declined from 19 per cent in 1983 to 3.3 per cent in 1999–2000; (2) according to the National Nutrition Monitoring Bureau (NNMB), the proportion of 'severely undernourished' children (weight-for-age criterion) in eight sample states declined steadily from 17.2 per cent in 1975–1980 to 6.4 per cent in 1999–2000, and clinical signs of acute undernutrition such as marasmus and kwashiorkor have virtually disappeared. See National Institute of Nutrition, *25 Years of National Nutrition Monitoring Bureau* (Hyderabad: National Institute of Nutrition, 1997) 69–70 and 104, and National Nutrition Monitoring Bureau, 'Diet and Nutritional Status of Rural Population', Technical Report 21 (Hyderabad: National Nutrition Monitoring Bureau, 2002) 74. On related matters, see also National Institute of Nutrition, *Report of Repeat Surveys (1988–1990)* (Hyderabad: National Institute of Nutrition, 1991). H. P. S. Sachdev, 'Nutritional Status of Children and Women in India: Recent Trends' (2003), available at www.nutritionfoundationofindia.org/archives/apr2003c.htm/archives/ auth-s2v.htm; H. P. S. Sachdev, 'Recent Transitions in Anthropometric Profile of Indian Children: Clinical and Public Health Implications', paper presented at IX Asian Congress of Nutrition, New Delhi, 23–27 February 2003, available at www.nutritionfoundationofindia. org/archives/apr2003c.htm; C. Gopalan, 'Changing Nutrition Scene in South Asia', paper presented at IX Asian Congress of Nutrition, New Delhi, 23–27 February 2003, available at www.nutritionfoundationofindia.org/archives/apr2003c.htm.

[10] International Institute for Population Sciences, *National Family Health Survey 1992–93: India* (Mumbai: IIPS, 1995) 283, and International Institute for Population Sciences, above n. 5, 266. A similar picture of sluggish nutritional improvement emerges from independent surveys carried out by the National Institute of Nutrition, Hyderabad; see e.g., National

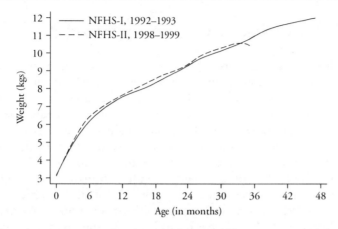

Figure 4.1. Average weight of Indian children at different ages

Source: Alessandro Tarozzi, unpublished analysis of National Family Health Survey (NFHS) data. The graph relates to boys and girls combined, in rural and urban areas combined.

the child undernourishment figures continue to decline at this sluggish rate of one percentage point per year, it will take another *forty* years before India achieves nutrition levels similar to those of China today.

The comparison between the two surveys also points to the growth of nutritional *inequality* in the nineties: anthropometric indicators improved more for urban areas than for rural areas, and more for boys than for girls. For instance, the proportion of undernourished children (based on weight-for-age criteria) declined by 7 percentage points for urban boys between 1992–1993 and 1998–1999, but only 3 percentage points for rural girls. In other words, the time required for rural Indian girls to 'catch up' with their Chinese counterparts if present rates of improvement continue is not forty years, but eighty years or so. These patterns are consistent with independent evidence of a sharp increase in economic inequality in the nineties.[11]

Institute of Nutrition, *Annual Report 2001–2* (Hyderabad: NIN, 2002) and *Annual Report 1999–2000* (Hyderabad: NIN, 2000).

[11] See e.g., A. Deaton and J. Drèze, 'Poverty and Inequality in India: A Reexamination' *Economic and Political Weekly*, 7 September 2002; also M. S. Ahluwalia, 'Economic Performance of States in Post-reforms Period' *Economic and Political Weekly*, 6 May 2000; N. J. Kurian, 'Widening Regional Disparities in India: Some Indicators' *Economic and Political Weekly*, 12 February 2000; R. Nagaraj, 'Indian Economy since 1980: Virtuous Growth or Polarisation?' *Economic and Political Weekly*, 5 August 2000; A. Banerjee and T. Piketty, 'Top Indian Incomes, 1922–2000' (mimeo, Department of Economics, Cambridge MA: Massachussetts Institute of Technology, 2003).

4.3 DEMOCRACY AND SOCIAL RIGHTS

Perhaps the most startling aspect of the nutrition situation in India is that there is virtually no discussion of it, outside specialized circles. Chronic hunger rarely figures in public debates and electoral politics. To illustrate, consider the coverage of nutrition issues in the mainstream media. *The Hindu*, one of the finest English-medium dailies, publishes two opinion articles every day on its editorial page. In a recent count of these opinion articles over a period of six months (January to June 2000), it was found that health, nutrition, education, poverty, gender, human rights, and related social issues *combined* accounted for barely 30 out of 300 articles. Among these 300 articles, not *one* dealt with health or nutrition.[12] As this simple exercise illustrates, the basic needs of the Indian people count for very little in public debates and democratic politics, and nutrition issues are particularly out of focus.

This neglect of social issues in general, and of chronic hunger in particular, is often attributed to 'lack of political will'. This diagnosis is plausible enough, but it does not take us very far since it begs the question as to why there is no political will in the first place. In a democracy, political will is an outcome of democratic politics. Seen in this light, the deafening silence surrounding hunger and nutrition issues in India is an invitation to reflect on the nature and limitations of Indian democracy.

As far as democratic institutions are concerned, India is doing reasonably well in historical and international perspective. To illustrate, in comparison with the United States (the self-proclaimed torch-bearer of democracy in the contemporary world), India fares much better in many respects. For instance, India has much higher voter turnout rates (the United States are near the rock bottom of the international scale in that respect); it has more extensive provisions for the political representation of socially disadvantaged groups; and it is less vulnerable to the influence of 'big money' in electoral politics. There is also far greater pluralism in Indian than in US politics. Dozens of political parties, from extreme left to extreme right, are represented in India's lower house, in contrast with two parties (with virtually identical political programmes) in the United States. Even the quality of the Indian press is much higher, in many respects, than that of its counterpart in the United States. The comparison is not entirely to India's advantage (for instance, the US fare better in terms of the freedom of information), and there is of course plenty of scope for improving democratic institutions in

---

[12] J. Drèze and A. Sen, *India: Development and Participation* (New Delhi and Oxford: Oxford University Press, 2002) 302. When I repeated the exercise for the period of January–June 2003, I did find an article dealing with health—it was about the SARS crisis in China!

India.[13] Nevertheless, by contemporary world standards, Indian democracy appears in a reasonably good light as far as its institutional foundations are concerned.

Having said this, Indian democracy has one minor flaw, namely that most people are unable to participate in it due to economic insecurity, lack of education, social discrimination, and other forms of disempowerment. Voter turnout rates may be reasonably high (about 60 per cent for parliamentary elections), but informed participation in democratic institutions on a sustained basis is confined to a tiny minority. And even voting is a very limited form of democratic participation when most people are unable to distinguish clearly between the different political parties and their respective programmes.[14]

In short, Indian democracy is trapped in a vicious circle of exclusion and elitism. Because underprivileged sections of the population are excluded from active participation in democratic politics, their aspirations and priorities are not reflected in public policy. The elitist orientation of public policy, in turn, perpetuates the deprivations (poverty, hunger, illiteracy, discrimination, etc.) that disempower people and prevent them from participating in democratic politics.

The root of the problem was identified quite clearly by Dr. Ambedkar in the context of his argument for linking political democracy with economic and social democracy. 'On the 26th January 1950,' he said, 'we are going to enter into a life of contradictions. In politics we will have equality and in social and economic life we will have inequality.'[15] The contradiction is still with us today and, in some respects at least, the problem is even intensifying at this time of growing inequality and elitism. India is in some danger of becoming a 'business-driven society', to use Noam Chomsky's telling characterization of US democracy.[16] It is in this context that there is an urgent

---

[13] The reform of democratic institutions is a subject of lively debate and action in India at this time, involving issues such as the right to information, the eradication of corruption, the decriminalization of politics, the representation of women, the devolution of powers, the need for greater democracy within political parties, and electoral reforms (e.g. the possibility of a move towards proportional representation). For a useful introduction, see e.g., J. Narayan, 'We, the Losers', *Humanscape*, December 2003.

[14] See e.g., B. Bhatia, 'The Naxalite Movement in Central Bihar', Ph.D. thesis, University of Cambridge, 2003. The author describes the predicament of Dalit women during the 1995 Assembly elections in central Bihar as follows: 'Most of the women I interviewed had never voted before, nor did they understand the meaning or significance of *chunav* (elections), vote or parties. While some of them were able to recognize some party symbols, they were often unable to relate the symbol to the party, and none of them could relate it to a particular candidate or programme.'

[15] Government of Maharashtra, *Dr. Babasaheb Ambedkar: Writings and Speeches. Vol. 13: Dr. Ambedkar: The Principal Architect of the Constitution of India* (V. Moon, ed., Mumbai: Department of Education, 1994) 1216.

[16] See e.g., Noam Chomsky, *World Orders, Old and New* (Delhi: Oxford University Press, 1998). There are many interesting similarities between Ambedkar and Chomsky's views on

need to revive the concern with economic and social rights expressed in the Directive Principles of the Constitution, including the right to food. Indeed, as mentioned earlier, the main object of the Directive Principles was precisely to lay the foundations of 'economic and social democracy'.[17]

4.4 TWO ILLUSTRATIONS

An example or two may help to convey the potential empowerment value of economic and social rights. One interesting example is the right to education. Until quite recently, the right to education was out of focus in education policy. For instance, the issue is not mentioned in the National Education Policy of 1986. The basic assumption in those days was that large proportions of children were beyond the pale of the schooling system, and that this situation would continue to prevail for many years. Since then, however, there has been a healthy revival of public concern for the right to education. Today, the notion that every child has a fundamental right to elementary education has gained wide acceptance. For instance, if a village does not have a school, the case for providing one immediately does not need to be made— it is taken for granted. And even children belonging to highly disadvantaged families or communities, such as migrant labourers or (so-called) primitive tribes, are widely considered to have an inalienable right to elementary education. This broad recognition of elementary education as a fundamental right of every child (recently incorporated in the Constitution) has contributed to the relatively rapid expansion of schooling facilities and school participation in the nineties.[18]

This does not mean that spectacular progress has been made in realizing the right to education. Indeed, there are also tendencies on the other side (i.e. tendencies inimical to the right to education), such as the crisis of state

democracy, even though Ambedkar was rather less critical of state power. It is perhaps not an accident that both were strongly influenced by John Dewey, an outspoken critic of the concentration of power who viewed politics as 'the shadow cast on society by big business' (quoted in Chomsky, 87).

[17] Whether the Directive Principles went far enough in that respect is another matter. Ambedkar's own blueprint for a 'socialist constitution', sketched in an early memorandum submitted to the Constituent Assembly (B. R. Ambedkar, 'States and Minorities', memorandum submitted to the Constituent Assembly; reprinted in Government of Maharashtra, *Dr. Babasaheb Ambedkar: Writings and Speeches* (V. Moon, ed., Mumbai: Department of Education, 1979–1998), Volume 1), included more sweeping changes in economic institutions, especially property rights.

[18] On the accelerated progress of literacy and school participation in the nineties, see Drèze and Sen, above n. 12, 151–152, 327–329. On the right to education in India, see R. Srivastava, 'The Right to Education in India' (mimeo, New Delhi: Centre for Development and Human Rights, 2003) and the literature cited there.

finances and intense hostility to the 'welfare state' in the corridors of power. Some recent developments, such as the growing reliance on low-quality, 'second-track' schooling facilities to raise enrolment figures, can even be seen as an attack on the fundamental right to education.[19] Nevertheless, it is interesting that the reach of the schooling system has expanded so fast in a period of structural adjustment and general disengagement of the state. The growing recognition of elementary education as a fundamental right of every child has played a part in this achievement. Also, this consensus has given education activists a powerful foothold to resist any attempt to dilute the constitutional commitment to free and compulsory education until the age of fourteen.

There is an instructive contrast here with the corresponding situation in the field of health care. Unlike elementary education, health care is yet to be widely accepted as a basic right of all Indian citizens.[20] This ambiguity has facilitated the continuation if not intensification of state abdication in this field in the nineties. Public expenditure on health has declined as a proportion of GDP, from an abysmally low base (about 1 per cent).[21] And the lack of any major initiative in the field of health care during the last ten years contrasts with wide-ranging innovations in the field of elementary education. Correspondingly, the pattern of accelerated progress in educational achievements in the nineties does not apply to health indicators. In fact, there have been some major setbacks, such as the slowdown of infant mortality decline,[22] and, more recently, the reduction of child vaccination rates in some states.

Another enlightening example is the right to information. Anyone who has worked in rural India is bound to be familiar with the tremendous disempowerment experienced by ordinary citizens due to lack of information and the inaccessibility of public records. Many examples can be given: some people have ration cards, but do not know what they are entitled to buy from the ration shop and at what price; others take bank loans without understanding the conditions of borrowing; TB patients are sent away from public health centres with cough syrups; labourers are unaware of the legal

[19] See e.g., A. Sadgopal, 'Education for Too Few', *Frontline*, 5 December 2003.

[20] There is, however, rapid change in this respect; see e.g., R. Duggal, 'Health and Development in India: Moving Towards Right to Healthcare' (mimeo, Mumbai: Centre for Enquiry into Health and Allied Themes, 2003) and A. Shukla, 'The Right to Health Care: Moving from Idea to Reality' (mimeo, Mumbai: Centre for Enquiry into Health and Allied Themes, 2003).

[21] The ratio picked up again towards the end of the nineties, but mainly because of rapid increases in salaries (based on the recommendations of the Fifth Pay Commission), with little increase—if any—in real inputs.

[22] P. N. Mari Bhat, 'Has the Decline in Infant Mortality Rate Slowed Down? A Review of SRS Evidence', paper presented at a national workshop on Infant Mortality, New Delhi, 11–12 April 2002.

minimum wage; and so on.[23] Another manifestation of the problem is corruption in public life, which thrives on secrecy and the dissimulation of information.

In response to this situation, one could try a 'case by case' approach, in the form of addressing the problem in the specific domain where it occurs. The visionary insight of the 'right to information movement', however, is that the problem can also be tackled across the board, in a lasting manner, by demanding a blanket right of access to *all* public records at *all* times for *all* citizens.[24] This led to a campaign for 'right to information laws', combined with efforts to enable people to use these laws. Going beyond this, the right to information movement can be seen as a step in the larger journey towards public accountability and participatory democracy.

The right to information movement has already led to some concrete results. In Rajasthan, for instance, it has played a crucial role in eradicating the earlier practice of endemic 'fudging' of muster rolls on relief works.[25] This may look like a small victory, but it is actually a significant breakthrough, which paves the way for further action in this field. Ten years ago, the suggestion that corruption in public life can be eradicated, or even substantially reduced, would have seemed very naïve. Today, there is a new sense of possibility in this respect.

4.5 THE RIGHT TO FOOD

The right to food is, in some ways, a more complex right than the right to education or the right to information. To start with, the entitlements and responsibilities associated with the right to food are far from obvious. In the

---

[23] I recently observed an extreme example of such situations in Allahabad district, where some Dalit labourers had land titles (received under some 'land distribution' scheme) but did not know where their land was. The *gram sevak* would not show it to them without a hefty bribe, and they were unable to pay. Some of them even suspected that they were working as casual labourers on their own land, encroached by powerful landlords.

[24] The right to information movement has been particularly active in Rajasthan during the last 15 years or so, but it has deep roots, going back at least to Jayaprakash Narayan. Another interesting precursor is Jotirao Phule, who was apparently checking muster rolls more than a century before Mazdoor Kisan Shakti Sangathan: '[Phule] enjoyed the company of the labourers and organised them . . . [He] studied for two or three years how corruption was practised by high officials and engineers. He knew well how they made up accounts by showing false attendance of labourers and how they divided the profits among themselves': D. Keer, *Mahatma Jotirao Phooley: Father of Our Social Revolution* (Bombay: Popular Prakashan, 1964) 90.

[25] See Drèze and Sen, above n. 12, 367–368, and S. Vivek, 'A Message of Hope', *Humanscape*, December 2003. For further discussion of the right to information movement, see particularly N. Mishra, 'People's Right to Information Movement: Lessons from Rajasthan', Discussion Paper 4, Human Development Resource Centre (New Delhi: UNDP, 2003).

case of, say, the right to information, some basic entitlements and responsibilities are easy to identify: every citizen has a right of access to public records (subject to specific exceptions, pertaining for instance to 'national security'), and conversely every civil servant has a duty to part with the relevant records under pre-specified terms. If he or she refuses to do so, action can be taken. To a large extent, the right to information can therefore be translated into legal entitlements and enforced in a court of law. In other words, it is justiciable.

In the case of the right to food, however, matters are more complicated. Broadly speaking, the right to food can be interpreted as a claim of individuals on society (starting but not ending with the state). It is an entitlement to be free from hunger, which derives from the assertion that the society has enough resources, both economic and institutional, to ensure that everyone is adequately nourished. However, difficulties arise as soon as we try to flesh out this broad definition and translate it into specific entitlements and responsibilities.

The term 'freedom from hunger', for instance, lends itself to several interpretations: getting two square meals a day, meeting specific calorie norms, avoiding nutrition-related ailments, and so on. Ideally, the right to food should be seen as a right to 'nutrition', and this is indeed the term used in Article 47 of the Constitution.[26] However, good nutrition itself depends in complex ways on a wide range of inputs: not just adequate food intake but also clean water, basic health care, good hygiene, and so on. Even if we confine our attention to food intake, the constituents of good nutrition are a matter of debate among nutritionists. For instance, there is some controversy about the importance of various 'micronutrients' for good nutrition. For all these reasons, it is hard to translate the right to food into a specific list of entitlements.

Similar difficulties arise in clarifying the responsibilities associated with the right to food. The primary responsibility is surely with the state, because the state alone commands the resources (economic and institutional) required to protect everyone from hunger, and because the state is generally responsible for safeguarding constitutional rights. However, the right to food is not the responsibility of the state alone. To illustrate, suppose that I come across someone who is dying of starvation on the street. If I am able to do something about it, and if I recognize that every citizen has a right to be free from hunger, it would clearly not be right for me to wash my hands of the situation

---

[26] More precisely, one could say that a person's right to food is realized if her life is not impaired or limited by nutritional deficiencies of any kind, or (in a similar vein) that a person's right to food is violated if nutritional deficiencies of any kind prevent her from leading a dignified life. The last definition would make it possible to link the right to food with recent judicial interpretations of the fundamental right to life (Article 21) as a right to 'live with dignity'. I leave it to others to unravel the full implications of this approach, e.g., whether a professional weightlifter has a right to 'more food' than an unemployed clerk.

and say that it is the responsibility of the state. The fact that the state bears the primary responsibility for letting this happen does not absolve me from the duty of intervening, if I am in a position to do so. In other words, in some circumstances at least, the responsibility for protecting the right to food is a shared responsibility, involving not only the state but also other institutions or individuals.

To take another example, suppose that a girl is undernourished because she does not get a fair share of food within the family. Clearly, her right to food would be violated. But who is responsible? At some level, state responsibility would be involved, since the state has an overarching duty to eradicate social discrimination. But surely, the girls' parents (or whoever controls the distribution of food within the family) would also bear a substantial part of the responsibility for this situation. Here again, there is a difficulty in apportioning responsibilities for protecting the right to food.

The last example also brings out a related problem, namely that the right to food is not always 'justiciable', in the sense of being enforceable in a court of law. If a girl is undernourished because of discrimination within the family, I doubt that the best response would be to take her parents (or for that matter the government) to court.[27] Other means of intervention would be required. Similar problems arise with other economic and social rights, and for this reason, among others, legal enforcement of the Directive Principles was explicitly ruled out in the Constitution. This applies in particular to the directives relevant to the right to food, such as Article 47 (which stresses that 'the State shall regard the raising of the level of nutrition . . . and the improvement of public health as among its primary duties') and Article 39A (which directs the state to ensure that 'the citizens, men and women equally, have the right to an adequate means of livelihood').

At this point, the reader may wonder whether the right to food has any 'teeth' at all, if it is so difficult to define and so hard to enforce. I would argue that it does have a cutting edge, for at least three reasons.

First, even if the right to food is not always justiciable, some *aspects* of the right to food (at the very least) are amenable to legal enforcement. This is one crucial lesson of the public interest litigation initiated by the People's Union for Civil Liberties (Rajasthan) in April 2001 with a writ petition to the Supreme Court.[28] The litigation is far from over, but some useful orders have already been passed, such as the interim order of 28 November 2001, directing all state governments to introduce cooked mid-day meals in primary schools. We can plausibly envisage that entitlements of this kind might

---

[27] This does not mean that it is pointless to make intra-family discrimination *illegal*. Most of the time, laws are enforced by institutions other than the courts. Legal provisions can also have important effects on public perceptions of what is right and wrong.

[28] Writ Petition (Civil) 196 of 2001, *PUCL v. Union of India and others*; for further details, see www.righttofood.com.

become part of the law of the land, just as the right of access to public records has found expression in 'right to information laws'.

Indeed, this approach would be highly consistent with the scheme of things initially envisaged by the Constitution. It is often forgotten that while Article 37 explicitly states that the Directive Principles 'shall not be enforced by any court', it goes on to stress (1) that these principles are nevertheless 'fundamental to the governance of the country', and (2) that 'it shall be the duty of the State to apply these principles in making laws'. The application of these prescriptions to the right to food is potentially far-reaching. Some good work has been done, for instance, on the possibility of introducing a 'framework law' that would translate a wide range of aspects of the right to food into legal provisions.[29]

I submit that this approach would be more productive than the common proposal that the Directive Principles should somehow be declared 'justiciable'.[30] For one thing, there are serious difficulties in making the right to food fully justiciable. Much of it ultimately belongs to the domain of democratic politics rather than of legal enforcement. For another, even if the right to food is deemed fully justiciable, it will remain necessary to spell out the constructive interventions through which this right is to be protected. Leaving it to the courts to settle this issue as and when it arises would be both risky and inappropriate. The need would therefore remain for additional legislation, framed through democratic processes, clarifying how the right to food is to be realized. And this is precisely what I am advocating in the first place.

The approach proposed here does not detract from the possibility of claiming the right to food in court as a corollary of the fundamental 'right to life' under Article 21. Indeed, this claim is one aspect of the public interest litigation initiated in April 2001 by the People's Union for Civil Liberties. And the Supreme Court itself has already clarified on various occasions that the right to life implies the right to food.[31] In some circumstances, this

---

[29] See e.g., M. Vidar, 'Implementing the Right to Food: Advantages of a Framework Law', paper presented at a seminar convened by FIAN International, held at the Indian Social Institute, New Delhi, 24–26 February 2003 and G. Moore, 'Note on National Framework Legislation', available at http://www.nutrition.uio.no/iprdf/Encounterdocuments/DocO18. html.

[30] Variants of this proposal include: (1) converting some Directive Principles into Fundamental Rights (as happened with the right to education), (2) elastic interpretations of the Fundamental Rights to encompass these Directive Principles (as with the argument that the right to food is implicit in the fundamental 'right to life'), and (3) a constitutional amendment making all Directive Principles justiciable (see e.g., Duggal, above n. 20, in the context of the right to health). On related issues, see M. Singh, 'The Statics and the Dynamics of the Fundamental Rights and the Directive Principles: A Human Rights Perspective' (mimeo, Delhi: University of Delhi, 2003) and the literature cited there.

[31] For instance, in *Shantistar Builders v. Narayan Khimalal Totame* (1990) 1 SCC 520, the Supreme Court stated: 'The right to life is guaranteed in any civilized society. That would take

recognition can be invoked with good effect. Yet, the persistence of mass hunger in India more than twenty years after the Supreme Court effectively accepted the right to food as a fundamental right clearly indicates that more specific legal provisions are required.

The second reason why the right to food does have a cutting edge, even when it is not enforceable in a court of law, was clearly spelt out by Dr. Ambedkar in his defence of the Directive Principles. Essentially, he argued that in a democracy, legal action is not the only means of holding the state accountable to its responsibilities. In cases where rights cannot be enforced through the courts, they can be asserted through other democratic means, based for instance on parliamentary interventions, the electoral process, the media, international solidarity, street action, or even civil disobedience.[32]

This process has worked relatively well with respect to one specific aspect of the right to food—the prevention of famines. As Amartya Sen has noted, in a democratic political system, allowing a famine to develop would be political suicide for the party in office. This is the main reason why every threat of famine in independent India has been boldly dealt with (at least in terms of avoiding excess mortality). The latest example is the drought of 2002–2003 in Rajasthan. In the absence of public intervention, drought-affected people would have perished in large numbers. With Assembly elections round the corner, however, the government did not take any chances. In late June 2003, close to 4 million labourers were employed on relief works and related programmes in rural Rajasthan.[33] This was one of the largest public employment programmes ever, in terms of the proportion of the population employed. Famine was averted, not because there is a law against it but because of other democratic safeguards.[34]

Outside the specific context of famine prevention (and other extreme circumstances, such as 'starvation deaths'), democratic practice has delivered rather little, so far, in terms of holding the state accountable to its responsibility for protecting the right to food. However, this situation is not

within its sweep the right to food . . .'. On this and other legal foundations of the claim that the right to life implies the right to food, see Human Rights Law Network, 'The Right to Food and the Right to Work for Food: Case Law' (mimeo, New Delhi: Human Rights Law Network, 2002); also National Human Rights Commission, 'Proceedings', Case No. 37/3/97-LD (starvation in KBK districts) (mimeo, New Delhi: NHRC, 17 January 2003).

[32] Dr. Ambedkar himself focused mainly on electoral politics as the means of holding the state accountable to the Directive Principles: '[The party in power] may not have to answer for their breach in a Court of Law. But [it] will certainly have to answer for them before the electorate at election time . . .' (in Rodriguez, above n. 4, 490). The point, however, can be extended to other tools of democratic practice.

[33] See http://www.rajasthan.gov.in/relief2002/relief2report/2.pdf.

[34] As it turns out, the Congress Party lost the 2003 elections in Rajasthan. But this does not invalidate the argument. It simply shows that preventing famines is not a *sufficient* condition for winning elections.

immutable. In fact, I would argue that there are vast possibilities of radical change in this field. These possibilities arise mainly from the growing participation of underprivileged groups in democratic politics, and the fact that food security is one of their main concerns. Another positive development in this context is that the tools of democratic participation are becoming more diverse over time. In his defence of the Directive Principles, Dr. Ambedkar focused on the electoral process as the principal means of holding the state accountable outside the courts. Since then, we have learnt not to expect too much from electoral competition in this respect, for reasons discussed earlier. But at the same time, we have good grounds for enhanced confidence about the possibilities of public action outside the traditional arena of electoral politics. These possibilities have already been creatively harnessed for various causes, ranging from gender equality and Dalit liberation to war resistance and the defence of civil liberties. There is no reason why these initiatives should not be extended to the assertion of economic and social rights, as is already happening to some extent.

The third argument for asserting the right to food is that, even when they are not enforceable in court, economic and social rights can have a profound influence on public *perceptions* of who is entitled to what. These perceptions, in turn, can make a concrete difference in diverse ways. For instance, in situations where the effectiveness of food security programmes depends on the vigilance of the public, perceptions of rights can matter a great deal.

To illustrate, consider the public distribution system (PDS). One reason (among others) why the PDS is not in very good shape today is endemic corruption. Now, recent analyses indicate that the extent of corruption in the PDS is much higher in north India than in south India. In north India, about half of the grain meant for distribution to poor households through the PDS seems to end up in the black market, rising to 80 per cent in Bihar and Jharkhand. In south India, the 'leakages' are much smaller, to the extent that they do not show up in secondary data.[35] One reason for this contrast is that people's perceptions of their entitlements under the PDS differ radically between the two regions. In large parts of north India, poor people have very little awareness of their entitlements and how they can be enforced.[36] They

[35] See J. Drèze, 'Food Security Programmes in Uttar Pradesh: An Autopsy', paper presented at a seminar on Labour and Poverty in Uttar Pradesh, G. B. Pant Social Science Institute, Allahabad, 22–23 November 2002 (to be published in the proceedings of the seminar); also Government of India, *Report of the High Level Committee on Long-Term Grain Policy* (New Delhi: Department of Food and Public Distribution, 2002) 158. These estimates are obtained by 'matching' food grain off-take from Food Corporation of India godowns with National Sample Survey data on household purchases from the public distribution system.

[36] To illustrate, a recent study of the PDS in Allahabad district found that only one per cent of the 1,400 sample households had correct knowledge of their entitlements: B. Mazumder, 'Public Distribution System in India: A Study of the District of Allahabad, Uttar Pradesh' (mimeo, Allahabad: G. B. Pant Social Science Institute, 2003) 21.

are sitting ducks for corrupt PDS dealers, and consider themselves lucky if they get anything at all.[37] In this respect, the situation is very different in the southern region. In Tamil Nadu, for instance, even illiterate Dalit women seem to have a sharp awareness of their entitlements, and of the redressal mechanisms that are available in the event where they are cheated.[38] The two factors (awareness of rights and accountability mechanisms) reinforce each other and preserve the integrity of the system. If India's public distribution system is to be revitalized, close attention needs to be paid to the circumstances that shape people's perceptions of their rights as well as their ability to enforce them.

It is in this respect, among others, that the recent division of the rural population between 'BPL' and 'APL' households (below poverty line and above poverty line, respectively), with PDS entitlements being effectively restricted to BPL households, is so pernicious. This division undermines the notion that PDS entitlements are a matter of right, since no one has a 'right' to a BPL card. It also weakens the ability of BPL households to enforce their rights, by destroying the solidarity between APL and BPL households, and sometimes even pitching one group against the other. The fact that 'vigilance committees', the local watchdogs of the public distribution system, often turn out to consist mainly of APL members, who have no stake in the integrity of the system, does not help either. The need of the hour is to empower disadvantaged households vis-à-vis PDS dealers, but the present targeting system goes in the opposite direction.

4.6 MID-DAY MEALS AND THEIR WIDER SIGNIFICANCE

These diverse roles of the right to food can be further illustrated with reference to the issue of mid-day meals in primary schools. This is one aspect (perhaps the only aspect) of the right to food that has been significantly

[37] See e.g., J. Drèze, 'Food Security and the Right to Food', in S. Mahendra Dev, K. P. Kannan, and N. Ramachandran, eds., *Toward a Food Secure India* (New Delhi: Institute for Human Development, 2003). In one village of Sendhwa (Madhya Pradesh), the PDS dealer has apparently struck a deal with the local residents, whereby he keeps all their cards, gives them twenty rupees in cash each month, and takes care of the rest. The most interesting part of the story is that the villagers are apparently satisfied: 'twenty rupees is better than nothing', they say. This contentment reflects their low expectations of the PDS in ordinary circumstances (Sachin Jain, personal communication).

[38] Personal observations based on field work in Dharmapuri district, one of Tamil Nadu's most deprived districts (see also J. Drèze, 'Where Welfare Works: Plus Points of the TN Model', *Times of India*, 21 May 2003). In one village, Dalit women were intrigued by the suggestion that the local dealer might be cheating them. 'Where would he go after doing this?', they said. 'He lives here, and we will catch him if he cheats us.' Their confidence was refreshing, especially in comparison with the disempowerment and helplessness commonly observed among poor households in north India.

consolidated in India in recent years. I believe that this experience is of some significance not only from the point of view of child nutrition but also as a pointer to the scope for further action in this field.

The case for providing cooked mid-day meals in primary schools is very strong. At least three arguments can be invoked in this connection. First, mid-day meals boost school attendance, especially among girls. Secondly, they protect children from classroom hunger and also enhance child nutrition, if the meal is nutritious. Thirdly, mid-day meals contribute to social equity, in several ways: they teach children to share a common meal irrespective of caste and class, act as a form of income support for poor households, and provide employment opportunities to poor women. The wide-ranging personal and social benefits of mid-day meals have been well demonstrated in states that made an early start down this road, notably Tamil Nadu and Gujarat. More recent experiences in Karnataka, Rajasthan, and elsewhere suggest that similar achievements are possible all over the country. In Rajasthan, for instance, girl enrolment in Class 1 jumped by nearly 20 per cent in a single year after mid-day meals were introduced.[39]

On 28 November 2001, the Supreme Court directed all state governments to introduce cooked mid-day meals in primary schools within six months. This interim order came up in the context of the public interest litigation mentioned earlier. Several states (notably Bihar, Jharkhand, Uttar Pradesh, and West Bengal) are yet to implement this order. Nevertheless, the coverage of mid-day meal programmes is steadily expanding. Fifty million children are already covered, making this the largest nutrition programme in the world by a long margin. With adequate public pressure, another 50 million children are likely to get on board within a year or so, and the quality of mid-day meal programmes could also be radically enhanced. This would be no small achievement at a time of growing abdication of state responsibility for the well-being of Indian citizens.

With this background, let me clarify how recent experience with mid-day meals illustrates the three possible roles of the right to food discussed earlier. To start with, this experience shows the possibility of bringing some aspects of the right to food within the ambit of legal enforcement. Some commentators are quite unhappy about the Supreme Court 'meddling' with policy issues such as the provision of mid-day meals in primary schools. Having witnessed the court's deliberations at close quarters, I share some of these apprehensions.[40] Yet, the interim order on mid-day meals seems quite

---

[39] For further discussion, see J. Drèze and A. Goyal, 'Future of Mid-day Meals' *Economic and Political Weekly*, 1 November 2003, and earlier studies cited there.

[40] The proceedings often reminded me of Kropotkin's indictment of the lawyers of his time: '. . . a race of law-makers legislating without knowing what their laws are about; today voting a law on the sanitation of towns, without the faintest notion of hygiene, tomorrow making regulations for the armament of troops, without so much as understanding a

reasonable, considering that we are dealing here with very basic rights of Indian children (not only the right to food but also the fundamental right to education), and that the effectiveness of mid-day meals in furthering these rights is well established. As things stand, the directive on mid-day meals is only an 'interim order', but there is no reason why mid-day meals should not be given permanent legal status, just as the right to work has found expression in Maharashtra's 'employment guarantee act'.

Secondly, the mid-day meal story also highlights the importance of campaigning for economic and social rights outside the courts, using all democratic means available. Indeed, had the Supreme Court order on mid-day meals been allowed to take its own course, it is doubtful that it would have been implemented. In this connection, it is worth noting that on the same day (28 November 2001), the Supreme Court also issued a similar order relating to the Integrated Child Development Services (ICDS), calling inter alia for the provision of functional *anganwadis* (child care centres) in 'every habitation'. This order, however, has made no impact so far, and one reason for this is the failure to supplement the court order with active public pressure. Mid-day meals, by contrast, have been the focus of lively campaigns in many states during the last two years. The steady progress of mid-day meals reflects this effective combination of legal action and social action.

Thirdly, mid-day meals provide another useful illustration of the role of economic and social rights in shaping people's perceptions of their entitlements and enhancing their determination to get their due. Here again, the point can be appreciated by looking at contrasts between different states. In Tamil Nadu, where mid-day meals go back to 1925, and were universalized in 1982, the whole arrangement is widely accepted as a basic entitlement of all children and has been internalized by all parties concerned—parents, teachers, cooks, administrators, and children themselves. Mid-day meals are provided on every day of the year, including holidays, and any lapse in this regard would be considered a serious matter. In (say) Chhattisgarh or Madhya Pradesh, by contrast, mid-day meals are still far from being perceived as a basic entitlement of all children. This is one reason why the implementation of mid-day meals remains quite casual in these states, to the extent that the meal often fails to materialize on a particular day, without anyone making a fuss.[41]

gun; . . . legislating at random in all directions, but never forgetting the penalties to be meted out to ragamuffins, the prison and the galleys, which are to be the portion of men a thousand times less immoral than these legislators themselves'. (Kropotkin, 'Law and Authority', quoted in A. Bose, *A History of Anarchism* (Calcutta: World Press, 1967) 266.)

[41] Personal observations in Tamil Nadu, Chhattisgarh, and Madhya Pradesh. In both Chhattisgarh and Madhya Pradesh, it is not uncommon to find that the mid-day meal has failed to materialize for trivial reasons such as alleged lack of firewood. In one such school, visited at four o'clock in the afternoon, the teachers were not the least concerned about the fact

Beyond these specific lessons, there is a larger message here about the possibility of bringing democratic politics to bear on issues of hunger and nutrition. The point emerges most sharply in Tamil Nadu, where mid-day meals have been a lively political issue ever since M. G. Ramachandran (alias 'MGR') threw his weight behind this idea in the early 1980s. In fact, many observers consider this initiative as one of the pillars of MGR's lasting popularity.[42] The prominence of social development issues in Tamil Nadu politics (at least in comparison with other states) is also a major reason for the relatively good quality of nutrition and health services in general, from *anganwadis* to primary health centres.[43] Elsewhere in India, social issues are nowhere near getting the same attention in state politics, but, as argued earlier, this situation is not immutable. There are growing possibilities of public mobilization on these issues, and the future course of the right to food depends a great deal on the extent to which these opportunities are seized.

4.7 CONCLUDING REMARKS

The basic argument of this paper is something like this. First, the Indian Constitution and its underlying ideas (chiefly due to Dr. Ambedkar) provide a sound framework for thinking about the right to food. In this framework, the right to food is one of the basic economic and social rights that are essential to achieve 'economic democracy', without which political democracy is at best incomplete. Indeed, there is an obvious sense in which mass hunger is fundamentally incompatible with democracy in any meaningful sense of the term.

Secondly, the right to food is nowhere near being realized in India. In fact, undernutrition levels in India are among the highest in the world. Further, the improvement of nutrition indicators over time is very slow. There is also some evidence of increasing disparities in nutritional achievements (between rural and urban areas as well as between boys and girls) in the nineties. The recent accumulation of nearly 70 million tonnes of grain against a background of widespread hunger is a particularly startling violation of the right to food.

Thirdly, the nutrition situation in India is a sort of 'silent emergency': little attention is paid to it in public debates and democratic politics. This

that the children had not eaten anything since early morning, and even since the previous evening in a few cases. In response to a pointed question about the Supreme Court order, one of them promptly argued that the order required mid-day meals to be served on '200 days in the year only'.

[42] See e.g., A. Pratap, 'Strike Against Hunger', *Outlook*, 18 August 2003.

[43] For further discussion, see Drèze and Sen, above n. 12, 213–218; see also Drèze, 'Where Welfare Works: Plus Points of the TN Model', above n. 38.

illustrates a more general feature of Indian democracy—its tremendous lack of responsiveness to the needs and aspirations of the underprivileged. Against this background, economic and social rights have a crucial role to play as built-in safeguards against the elitist biases of public policy.

Fourthly, the right to food is a somewhat complex right that does not readily translate into well-defined entitlements and responsibilities. The scope for enforcing it through the courts can be significantly enlarged (e.g., by consolidating legal provisions for the right to food), but serious difficulties are involved in making it fully justiciable. Nevertheless, the right to food can bring new interventions within the realm of possibility in at least three different ways: through legal action, through democratic practice, and through public perceptions.

Fifthly, I have illustrated these different roles of the right to food with reference to the provision of mid-day meals in primary schools. It goes without saying that I am not proposing mid-day meals as an answer to India's massive nutrition problem. Yet, this experience is a helpful illustration of the possibility of effective action in this field. Similar things can be done with respect to many other means of intervention: employment guarantee acts, the public distribution system, social security arrangements, *anganwadi* facilities, and land rights, among others.

I end by reiterating that, if the right to food is to be achieved, it needs to be linked with other economic and social rights, such as the right to education, the right to work, the right to information, and the right to health. These economic and social rights complement and reinforce each other. Taken in isolation, each of them has its limitations, and may not even be realizable within the present structure of property rights. Taken together, however, they hold the promise of radical change in public priorities and democratic politics. This is why it is so important to revive the Directive Principles of the Constitution as well as the visionary conception of democracy that informs them.

5

Social Rights and Economics: Claims to Health Care and Education in Developing Countries[1]

VARUN GAURI

5.1 INTRODUCTION

Human rights are increasingly important in international development discourse, particularly in the areas of health and education. The legal foundations for those rights are the Universal Declaration of Human Rights 1948,[2] and the International Covenant on Economic, Social and Cultural Rights 1966.[3] In addition, references to the right to education and health care are found in the European Social Charter 1961,[4] the African Charter on Human and Peoples' Rights 1981,[5] and the Convention of the Rights of the Child 1989.[6] A number of international and bilateral development agencies have endorsed a human rights orientation in the provision of health care and education in developing countries.[7] Social rights are also important at the

[1] The author would like to thank Claudio Montenegro for able research assistance, Imran Hafiz and Hedy Sladovich for help in preparing the manuscript, and Paul Clements, Deon Filmer, Mead Over, Thomas Pogge, Jamie Radner, and two anonymous referees for insightful comments. The findings, conclusions, and interpretations expressed in this paper are those of the author and do not necessarily express those of the World Bank or its Executive Directors. This chapter has been reprinted from 32 *World Development* 465 (2004), with kind permission of the publisher.   [2] G.A. res. 217A (III), U.N. Doc A/810 at 71 (1948).
[3] G.A. res. 2200A (XXI), 21 U.N. GAOR Supp. (No. 16) at 49, U.N. Doc. A/6316 (1966), 993 U.N.T.S. 3, *entered into force* 3 January 1976.

[4] European Social Charter, 529 U.N.T.S. 89, *entered into force* 26 February 1965.

[5] African [Banjul] Charter on Human and Peoples' Rights, adopted 27 June 1981, OAU Doc. CAB/LEG/67/3 rev. 5, 21 I.L.M. 58 (1982), *entered into force* 21 October 1986.

[6] G.A. res. 44/25, annex, 44 U.N. GAOR Supp. (No. 49) at 167, U.N. Doc. A/44/49 (1989), *entered into force* 2 September 1990.

[7] See, for example, UK Department for International Development (DFID), *Realising Human Rights for Poor People*, DFID Target Strategy Paper (London: DFID, 1997). Human

national level. One analyst found that 110 national constitutions make reference to a right to health care.[8] A review conducted for this paper assessed constitutional rights to education and health care in 187 countries. Of the 165 countries with available written constitutions, 116 made reference to a right to education and 73 to a right to health care. Ninety-five, moreover, stipulated free education and 29 free health care for at least some population sub-groups and services.[9]

Brazil offers a compelling example of the force of human rights language. The Brazilian Constitution of 1988 guarantees each citizen the right to free health care. Although the constitutional guarantee has not eliminated shortages and inequalities in the sector, that provision had real 'bite' in 1996, when a national law initiated a program of universal access to highly active anti-retroviral therapy (HAART) for AIDS patients, free of charge. Partly as a result, in major Brazilian cities AIDS deaths have dropped sharply, falling over 40 per cent during 1997–2002. The program is costly: even after prices declined 48 per cent from 1997–2001 as a result of generic production and government pressure, drugs alone still cost the government $2,530 per patient for 113,000 patients on HAART in 2001.[10] Meanwhile,

Rights Council of Australia, *The Rights Way to Development: A Human Rights Approach to Development Assistance* (Sydney: HRCA, 1995). United Nations Development Program (UNDP), *Human Development Report* (New York: Oxford University Press, 2000). United Nations Educational Scientific and Cultural Organization (UNESCO), *World Education Report 2000: The right to education: Towards Education for All throughout Life* (Paris: UNESCO, 2000); World Health Organization (WHO), 25 *Questions & Answers on Health & Human Rights* (Geneva: WHO, 2002). Summary reviews are B. I. Hamm, 'A Human Rights Approach to Development' 23 *Human Rights Quarterly* 1005 (2001); S. P. Marks, *The Human Rights Framework for Development: Five approaches*, Working Paper Series, No. 6. (Cambridge MA: Francois-Xavier Bagnoud Center for Health and Human Rights, Harvard School of Public Health, 2001).

[8] E. D. Kinney, 'The International Human right to Health: What does this mean for Our Nation and World?' 34 *Indiana Law Review* 1457 (2001).

[9] The coding system identified a right to education or health care if a constitution used the word 'right', stated that the service was 'guaranteed', stated that government was to provide the service to 'all', or stated that everyone was 'entitled' to the service. Weaker formulations (e.g. the 'state shall endeavor to provide education') were not considered constitutional rights. The analysis identified a provision for free health care if any population sub-group was to receive free services (usually the poor or indigent) and a provision for free education if any level of education was free (usually primary and/or secondary education). The analysis of the right to health care focused on the right of access to medical services, not population-based preventive measures. The later a constitution was written, the more likely it incorporated a right to education (correlation ¼0.22) and a right to health care (correlation ¼0.21). The constitutions were found at: http://www.psr.keele.ac.uk/const.htm, http://confinder.richmond.edu/, http://doc-iep.univ-lyon2.fr/Ressources/Liens/constitution-etr.html, http://www.cia.gov/cia/publications/factbook/. The review was conducted in November 2002.

[10] Ministry of Health of Brazil, *National AIDS drugs policy* (Brasilia: Ministry of Health, 2002).

many basic antibiotics remained too expensive for or inaccessible to millions of citizens.

Reactions to Brazil's AIDS drugs program are divided, so much so that an account of it is an almost perfect screening instrument for distinguishing people inclined to a rights-based approach to health care from those who gravitate to an economic analysis. On the one hand, rights advocates contend that the Brazilian program is based on a constitutional guarantee and an explicit human rights orientation, prevents at least some Brazilians from dying prematurely while the country possesses the resources to save them, and more generally illustrates why health care is not a mere 'commodity'. On the other, economists argue that to the degree that providing those drugs displaces private expenditures, it is merely an income transfer; that AIDS treatment might be a lower priority than other health initiatives that could save more lives at lower social cost, such as disease prevention and the provision of clean water; and that, more generally, without the information that prices convey health care providers would slack off, innovation and scientific progress in those fields would slow, and consumers would have a harder time distinguishing good from bad providers.

This chapter will argue that the disagreements between the approaches are not as large as they appear, and that, with regard to practical policy consequences for health care and education, rights advocates and economists are not far apart. Both approaches recommend wider access to information, more local organizations for clients, stronger advocacy, and changes in sectoral governance. The goal of both approaches is to strengthen the position of service recipients. Still, there remain differences. Whether procedures for service delivery are ends in themselves, the degree of disaggregation at which outcomes should be assessed, and the consequences of long-term deprivation are all areas where the approaches diverge. This chapter argues, however, that even in these areas the differences are not irreconcilable. More difficult to reconcile are issues that emerge from two pointed questions from the economic critique: given scarce resources, why allocate according to a principle other than social welfare; and why ignore the behavioral distortions that follow from subsidies? Although other moral entitlements and immunities, such as subsistence rights and the right to physical security, have obvious relevance for health and education outcomes, this chapter focuses on the direct rights to health care and education services. Moreover, it addresses only some of the most common approaches: it is impossible to do justice to the vast literature on these topics in a short space. Section 2 assesses the foundations and uses of social rights in development. Section 3 outlines an economic approach to improving health and education service provision. Section 4 highlights differences and similarities. And Section 5 draws inferences for policy work in these sectors in developing countries.

5.2 SOCIAL RIGHTS: FOUNDATIONS, USES, AND CRITICISMS

Genealogically, the concept of human rights is related to Locke's notion of the natural right to one's labor, Rousseau's and Kant's ideas of innate liberty, and before that to Stoic and Christian conceptions of natural law, or the divinely inspired respect that is owed to human beings.[11] There is a lively debate about whether this historical relationship necessarily makes the existing human rights regime parochial; but one can argue that the regime can in fact be built on a variety of philosophical foundations.[12] There are 'plural foundations'[13] because human rights, while conceptually vague for reasons described below, are the product of a powerful intuition, common across many if not most cultures and religions, that human beings are especially important in the cosmos and deserve special treatment. Ideas inspired by that intuition have caught on in a variety of forms and circumstances, sometimes in conjunction with conquest, in the cases of Islam in the Middle East and liberalism in the colonial world, but frequently independent of it, such as Buddhism in India, Christianity in the Mediterranean world, and Islam in Indonesia.[14] The foundations of human rights can be secular or religious, and religious in a variety of forms, because the notion that human beings are worthy of respect recurs throughout history. It is arguable, moreover, that human rights do not have, and do not need, any particular philosophical foundation: they might be a 'freestanding moral idea'[15] or a 'common agreement' that constrains institutions, describes goals, and furnishes the grounds of political criticism.[16]

[11] For a history of these transitions, see R. Tuck, _Natural Rights Theories: Their Origin and Development_ (New York: Cambridge University Press, 1987). Primary sources for the concept of human rights include I. Kant, _Groundwork for the Metaphysics of Morals_ (A. Wood and J. B. Schneewind, eds, New Haven, CT: Yale University Press, 2003); J. Locke, _The Second Treatise of Government, and; A Letter Concerning Toleration_ (New York, Dover: Newton Abbot, 2002). J-J. Rousseau, _Discourse on the Origin of Inequality_ (P. Coleman, ed., New York: Oxford University Press, 1994).

[12] For discussions of the parochialism of human rights from the East Asian perspective, see J. R. Bauer and D. Bell, _The East Asian Challenge for Human Rights_ (Cambridge, UK: Cambridge University Press, 1999).

[13] A. Guttman, 'Introduction' in A. Guttman ed., _Human Rights as Politics and Idolatry_ (Princeton, NJ: Princeton University Press, 2001).

[14] C. Taylor, 'Explanation and Practical Reason' in M. Nussbaum and A. Sen, eds, _The Quality of life: Studies in Development Economics_ (Oxford, UK: Oxford University Press, 1993).

[15] M. C. Nussbaum, 'Aristotle, Politics, and Human Capabilities: A Response to Antony, Arneson, Charlesworth, and Mulgan' 111 _Ethics_ 102 (2000); M. C. Nussbaum, _Women and Human Development: The Capabilities Approach_ (Cambridge, UK: Cambridge University Press, 2000).

[16] C. R. Beitz, 'Human Rights as a Common Concern' 95 _The American Political Science Review_ 269 (2001).

As the preceding paragraph indicates, the theoretical issues surrounding human rights are complex, and this chapter can only illustrate a few of the principal concerns. One key issue is what counts as a right. The list of possibilities is long but can be distilled into five types: personal rights (life, liberty, security, property, conscience); legal rights (due process, equal protection under the law); political rights (participation, suffrage, assembly); social and economic rights (standard of living, employment, health care, education, nutrition); and collective rights (ethnic self-determination, minority rights).[17]

Secular justifications for social rights, such as health care and education, which are the concern of this chapter, usually depend on the selection and defense of a set of basic needs, primary goods, or essential human capabilities. (The key difference between an approach based on human needs or primary goods and one based on capabilities is that the latter recognizes that different people need different levels of resources: a disabled person, for instance, needs more resources to function in society than someone who is not disabled.[18]) There are at least two general approaches to establishing social rights. In the first, which emphasizes human agency, it is argued that in a fully human life a person makes important decisions, such as where to live, what to work on, how to worship, whom to marry, on her own, in accordance with her own understanding of the elements of a good or worthy life, and that abject poverty, disease and disability, and illiteracy and ignorance can so impair a person's ability to imagine and realize plans that her own human life fails, in an important way, to be realized.[19] Disease and

---

[17] This list borrows from Beitz, above n. 16. Philosophical treatments of human rights include J. Baker, *Group Rights* (Toronto: University of Toronto Press, 1994), R. M. Dworkin, *Taking Rights Seriously* (Cambridge, MA: Harvard University Press, 1977), A. Gewirth, *The Community of Rights* (Chicago: University of Chicago Press, 1996), W. Kymlicka, *Multicultural Citizenship: A Liberal Theory of Minority Rights* (Oxford, UK: Oxford University Press, 1995), M. J. Perry, *The Idea of Human Rights: Four Inquiries* (New York: Oxford University Press, 2000), T. Pogge, *World Poverty and Human Rights: Cosmopolitan Responsibilities and Reforms* (Cambridge, UK: Polity Press, 2002) J. Rawls, *The Theory of Justice* (Cambridge, MA: Belknap Press, 1971) and J. Rawls, *The Law of Peoples* (Cambridge, MA: Harvard University Press, 1999), R. Rorty, 'Human Rights, Rationality, and Sentimentality' in S. Shute and S. Hurley, eds, *On Human Rights: The Oxford Amnesty Lectures 1993* (New York: Basic Books, 1993).

[18] Primary goods is the term used in Rawls, above n. 17, basic needs is in H. Shue, *Basic Rights: Subsistence, Affluence, and US Foreign Policy* (Princeton, NJ: Princeton University Press, 1996), and the capabilities approach is developed in M. C. Nussbaum, 'Capabilities and Human Rights' 66 *Fordham Law Review* 273 and A. Sen, 'Equality of What?' in S. McMurrin, ed., *Tanner Lectures on Human Values* (Cambridge, UK: Cambridge University Press, 1980) and *Choice, Welfare, and Measurement* (Oxford, UK: Blackwell Publishing, 1982). Pogge, above n. 17, describes criteria for basic goods. On the differences between Rawls and Sen, see G. A. Cohen, 'Equality of What? On Welfare, Goods, and Capabilities' in M. C. Nussbaum and A. K. Sen, eds, *The Quality of Life* (Oxford, UK: Oxford University Press, 1993).

[19] An argument of this kind is found in Nussbaum, above n. 15. Somewhat similar is Shue, above n. 18, who argues that basic subsistence is essential to the exercise of human capacities;

ignorance are akin to enslavement in the sense that those afflicted cannot experience themselves as beings whose lives are significant.

The second approach, which emphasizes human dignity, emphasizes not falling victim to fate but being left in that condition by one's fellow citizens. It points out that enjoying a healthy, vigorous life and being well educated are desirable in contemporary societies worldwide, which, at least in their urbanized centers, generally admire health and material well-being.[20] Being denied education and health care, then, is tantamount to being excluded from modern society, with its attendant social and psychological consequences. The rights to health care and education become elements in the 'social bases of self-respect', which Rawls[21] defines as perhaps the most important of his 'primary goods'. Closely related are Sen's notion (drawing on Adam Smith) of 'the ability to appear in public without shame'[22] and Feinberg's idea that 'having rights enables us to stand up like men, to look others in the eye, and to feel in some fundamental way the equal of anyone'.[23] There can also be, of course, religious foundations for broad access to health care and education, such as commandments to love one's neighbor or engage in charity, as well as communitarian approaches.[24]

Some critics of social rights fear that an expansive list causes 'rights inflation' and cheapens 'genuine' human rights, particularly the rights of the person.[25] Others contend that guaranteeing minimal income, health care, and education necessarily entails large government, or even socialism.[26]

---

see also O. O'Neill, *Faces of Hunger: An Essay on Poverty, Justice and Development* (London: Allen & Unwin Hyman, 1986) and *Bounds of Justice* (Cambridge, UK: Cambridge University Press, 2000).

[20] As Walzer points out, centuries ago in Europe access to a spiritual advisor was considered indispensable for every soul, whether a noble or a serf, whereas access to health care and education was not a prerequisite for meaningful participation in society: M. Walzer, *Spheres of Justice: A Defense of Pluralism and Equality* (New York: Basic Books, 1993). Now close to the reverse is true.

[21] Rawls, *A Theory of Justice*, above n. 17, and J. Rawls, *Justice as Fairness: A Restatement* (Cambridge, MA: Harvard University Press, 2001).

[22] A. K. Sen, *Development as Freedom* (New York, NY: Knopf, 1999).

[23] J. Feinberg, *Rights, Justice, and the Bounds of Liberty: Essays in Social Philosophy* (Princeton, NJ: Princeton University Press, 1997).

[24] W. T. De Bary, *Asian Values and Human Rights: A Confucian Communitarian Perspective* (Cambridge, MA: Harvard University Press, 2000), L. S. Rouner, *Human Rights and the World's Religions* (Notre Dame, IN: University of Notre Dame Press, 1988).

[25] M. Ignatieff, *Human Rights as Politics and Idolatry* (Princeton, NJ: Princeton University Press, 2001).

[26] This disagreement was acute during the Cold War, leading to the bifurcation of the international instruments meant to codify the Universal Declaration of Human Rights into one on economic, social, and cultural rights, and another on civil and political rights: See P. G. Lauren, *The Evolution of International Human Rights: Visions Seen* (Philadelphia, PA: University of Pennsylvania Press, 1998). Libertarian critics contend that only restraints are

Political and philosophical concerns such as these have partly motivated the theoretical effort to distinguish 'negative rights', which set constraints on other actors (e.g., the right to personal liberty enjoins unjustified detention and is the principle behind the common law doctrine of habeas corpus), from 'positive rights', which entail intervention or resource support from others (e.g., the right to health care). Again, the arguments are complex; but one can show that for their fulfillment all rights require restraint, protection, and aid from the entity from whom rights are claimed, and that a reasonably effective and well funded state is a sine qua non for all rights.[27]

In addition to these theoretical difficulties with social rights, a practical objection concerns judicial enforcement. Because education and health care services involve considerable discretion at the point of delivery on the part of numerous independent providers, and because they entail a large number of transactions,[28] it is difficult for courts, the entities to which claims of rights violation are typically taken, to determine whether a given student or patient is being denied his right to education or health care. The example of desegregation in the United States is illustrative. When courts intervened on the grounds that separate schooling for black and white students was inherently in conflict with the equal protection clause of the national constitution, the courts discovered that school management, financing, and politics were so intertwined that remedies, such as court ordered bussing, affected the entire educational system in ways that could not be determined in advance. As a result, in some cases courts had to operate school systems themselves, which in turn created a backlash that weakened the educational rights of black students.[29] Judicial remedies for social inequalities would be even more difficult in developing countries, where legal systems are often weak and less than impartial.

Do these criticisms mean that a human rights approach to health care and education in developing countries is vague, impractical, or self-defeating? If rights are understood as binding constraints on government action, it is hard to avoid those conclusions. Governments in developing countries cannot provide or assure adequate levels of health care and education. Given that

justified because taxation for the purposes of economic redistribution or social support amounts to unjustified taking: see R. A. Epstein, 'Imitations of Libertarian Thought' 15 *Social Philosophy & Policy* 412 (1998) and R. Nozick, *Anarchy, State, and Utopia* (New York: Basic Books, 1974).

[27] S. Holmes and C. Sunstein, *The Cost of Rights: Why Liberty Depends on Taxes* (New York: W. W. Norton, 1998); Shue, above n. 18.

[28] L. Pritchett and M. Woolcock, *Solutions when the Solution is the Problem: Arraying the Disarray in Development*, Center for Global Development Working Paper #10 (Washington D.C.: Center for Global Development, 2002).

[29] J. L. Hochschild, *The New American Dilemma* (New Haven, CT: Yale University Press, 1984).

legal systems in most developing countries are inequitable and under-developed and that enforcement mechanisms are weak, allowing citizens to make legal claims of inadequate service provision will further politicize courts, weaken their capacity to adjudicate existing rights, and possibly increase government spending even where it is inequitable or inefficient.

If understood not as binding constraints but high priority goals, rights to health care and education can be meaningful and useful.[30] In this view, rights are not legal instruments for individuals (though they can be, if governments codify them in domestic law), but duties for governments, international agencies, and other actors to take concrete measures on behalf of individuals, or to restructure institutions so that the rights can be fulfilled more effec-tively.[31] Failure to develop plans, achieve benchmarks, or establish and fin-ance implementing agencies constitute violations of the duties associated with the rights, and invite legitimate criticism, moral pressure, and, in egregious cases, justifiable external intervention.[32] Failure to pursue actions in pursuit of the goals might also raise serious issues concerning the legitimacy and long-term stability of governments and international institutions because social rights have become critical elements of the modern social compact and the modern personality. With rights so conceived, the problem of whether people can hold a right without a designated person or entity bearing a duty to fulfill or protect it becomes less important. Calling health care and edu-cation rights means, on this understanding, that everyone bears some responsibility for their fulfillment. If individuals in developing (or for that matter, developed) countries receive miserably inadequate health care and education, their rights impose duties on their local governments, national governments, foundations, neighbors, international agencies, and citizens of the rich countries—on all people who might be in a position to help. The fact that no one actor bears responsibility for them means that co-ordinating a response might be difficult, but, as Sen notes, they remain rights nevertheless: 'But it is surely possible for us to distinguish between a right that a person has which has not been fulfilled and a right that the person does not have.'[33]

On this view, the problems of adjudicating what exactly the rights to health care and education entail and how to ensure their attainment are affected, and appropriately so, by political processes within countries. This might mean that standards of health care and education, as well as the means of delivery, vary from place to place. It is possible, however, to distinguish between governments and other actors that recognize the fundamental importance of those goods but depart from international norms of provision, and those that

---

[30] J. Feinberg, *Social Philosophy* (Englewood Cliffs, NJ: Prentice-Hall, 1973); J. Nickel, *Making Sense of Human Rights* (Berkeley, CA: University of California Press, 1987) and J. Nickel, *Human rights as goals* (mimeo, 2002).   [31] Pogge, above n. 17.   [32] Beitz, above n. 16.   [33] Sen, *Development as Freedom*, above n. 22, 230–231.

fail to recognize their importance altogether.[34] Similarly, on this understanding of rights, the problem of judicial enforcement is re-framed and made
far less damaging for the rights approach. If rights are not binding constraints,
then every perceived shortcoming is not actionable in courts, though certain
categories, such as those premised on equal protection claims, might be.

The notion of rights as high-priority goals is implicit in some of the legal
documents underlying the rights approach to development. The WHO
Constitution 1946, and the Declaration of Alma Ata 1978, for instance,
make reference to the 'highest attainable standard of health', which implicitly
acknowledges that many developing countries cannot provide comprehensive
health care for all of their citizens. The WHO interprets the principle to
mean that governments should put into place 'policies and action plans
which will lead to available and accessible health care for all in the shortest
possible time'.[35] The UN also describes the right to education as a mandate
that is being progressively realized.[36]

Understanding social rights as goals brings out their self-reinforcing
quality and helps clarify the somewhat opaque assertion that rights are
'indivisible'.[37] From the perspective of human agency, certain social goods,
such as health care and education, are indispensable for the exercise of one or
more critical human faculties, such as self-understanding or reason, because
they provide essential physical and cognitive infrastructure; but reason and
self-understanding in turn facilitate the articulation, assertion, and defense of
social and political rights. Where a society supports education, for example, a
woman is more likely to understand a clinical diagnosis, demand appropriate
treatment, and complain if her health needs are not met; but reasoning
ability and rhetorical skills also help position her to organize and participate
in community oversight of clinics and schools. There is a parallel argument
from the perspective of dignity: individuals for whom social rights are fulfilled are more likely to consider themselves fully equal participants in
decision making, both within the household and outside it, and are therefore
emboldened to speak and organize in defense of their social rights. This

---

[34] It might even be necessary for standards to vary. Local understandings of agency and
social inclusion, arrived at through rich democratic self-government, have to be incorporated
into norms of service provision because it is in principle impossible for an outsider to predict
in advance what services a person will say are essential for her ability to live a good or worthy
life. As a result of these varying standards, there will remain sharp disagreements across regions
regarding some aspects of social policy, notably in gender roles and reproductive health,
though these too can be the subject of persuasion and reasonable argument (Nussbaum, above
n. 15). Despite this, it is still possible to determine whether a government or an agency is
making a good faith effort to provide adequate health care and education services according to
its own understanding.   [35] WHO, above n. 7.

[36] UNESCO, above n. 7.

[37] Declaration on the Right to Development, G.A. res. 41/128, annex, 41 U.N. GAOR
Supp. (No. 53) at 186, U.N. Doc. A/41/53 (1986).

structure of arguments for rights brings out that they are both ends of and instruments for development. To the extent that they are instruments, the policy consequences of a rights approach overlap considerably with a modern economic approach to health care and education.

5.3 AN ECONOMIC APPROACH TO HEALTH CARE AND EDUCATION

The consumption of education and health care services is positively related to household productivity and economic growth. Although empirical work has identified a significant relationship between health and nutrition in childhood and lifetime cognitive and motor skills,[38] it has been more difficult to establish that health mitigates poverty and enhances labor productivity. The reasons for this difficulty include measurement problems related to the fact that health is multidimensional, changes over time, and is unreliably reported. In addition, there are conceptual problems related to the dynamic relationship between health and income, including the facts that labor can be substituted for within households, that health falls in importance as the physical intensity of labor declines, and that health is in general both a cause and effect of labor productivity.[39] Recent studies have demonstrated some success in identifying an effect. For instance, at the individual level there is a correlation between adult height, a measure of long-term nutrition, and income even among uneducated Brazilian men and women.[40] At the macrolevel writers have argued that nutritional gains account for a large part of economic growth in Europe over the past two centuries,[41] that malaria and endemic diseases depress economic growth in Africa,[42] and that declining mortality and fertility rates were associated with the unprecedented economic growth in East and Southeast Asia from the 1960s to the 1990s.[43] Of course, factors such as income, access to clean water, and education might be as or more important in promoting health than access to health care. While just

[38] R. Martorell, 'Promoting Healthy Growth: Rationale and Benefits' in P. Pinstrup-Andersen, D. Pelletier, and H. Alderman, eds, *Child Growth and Nutrition in Developing Countries* (Ithaca, NY: Cornell University Press).

[39] J. Strauss and D. Thomas, 'Health, Nutrition, and Economic Development' 36 *Journal of Economic Literature* 766 (1998).

[40] D. Thomas and J. Strauss, 'Health and Wages: Evidence on Men and Women in urban Brazil' 77 *Journal of Econometrics* 159 (1997).

[41] R. Fogel, 'Economic Growth, Population Theory, and Physiology: The Bearing of Long-term Processes on the Making of Economic Policy' 84 *American Economic Review* 369 (1994).

[42] J. L. Gallup and J. Sachs, *The Economic Burden of Malaria*, CID Working Paper No. 52 (Cambridge, MA: Harvard Center for International Development, 2000).

[43] Asian Development Bank, *Emerging Asia: Changes and Challenges* (Manila: ADB, 1997).

how important health care is for health status remains controversial,[44] there is enormous evidence at the micro-level that some health care interventions (skilled birth attendance, for example) have enhanced health outcomes,[45] and compelling arguments that publicly provided and financed health care services were important in mortality declines in some countries.[46] In addition, partly because purchasers of health insurance can hide their actions and health status from insurers, health insurance is expensive and unavailable for many. Governments have a role in subsidizing or regulating insurance for catastrophic health events, which in developing countries can take the form of the direct financing of hospital care.[47]

The evidence for the impact of education on private wages is more strongly established. Calculations of the annual private returns to educational investments average about 6 per cent in industrialized countries and 11 per cent in developing countries.[48] These remain rough estimates because they do not control for school quality, and there remain problems in controlling for the endogeneity of the schooling enrollment decision. But a review of studies that used compulsory schooling laws and other variables as instruments for completed education found that estimates for the returns to education were as big as or bigger than standard ordinary least squares estimates.[49] At the national level, the relationship between educational attainment and growth in output per worker at the national level is weaker.[50] But a study that measures labor force quality, based on international mathematics and science test scores, finds that is strongly related to national growth rates.[51]

[44] D. Filmer, J. Hammer, and L. Pritchett, 'Weak Links in the Chain: A Diagnosis of Health Policy in Developing Countries' 15 *The World Bank Research Observer* 199 (2000).

[45] V. De Brouwere, R. Tonglet, and W. V. Lerberghe, 'Strategies for Reducing Maternal Mortality in Developing Countries: What Can We Learn From the History of the Industrialized West?' 3 (10) *Tropical Medicine and International Health* 771 (1998).

[46] S. R. Johansson and C. Mosk, 'Exposure, Resistance and Life Expectancy: Disease and Death during the Economic Development of Japan, 1900–1960' 41 *Population Studies* 207 (1987).

[47] D. Filmer, J. Hammer, and L. Pritchett, 'Weak Links in the Chain II: A Prescription for Health Policy in Poor Countries' 17 *The World Bank Research Observer* 47 (2002).

[48] G. Psacharopoulos, 'Returns to Investment in Education: A Global Update' 22 *World Development* 1325 (1994).

[49] D. Card, *Estimating the Return to Schooling: Progress on some Persistent Econometric Problems*, NBER Working Paper #7769 (Cambridge, MA: NBER, 2000).

[50] J. Benhabib and M. Spiegel, 'Role of Human Capital in Economic Development: Evidence from Aggregate Cross-Country Data' 34 *Journal of Monetary Economics* 143 (1994); M. Bils and P. Klenow, 'Does Schooling Cause Growth?' 90 *American Economic Review* 1160 (2000); L. Pritchett, *Where Has All the Education Gone?* Policy Research Working Paper #1581 (Washington D.C.: World Bank, 1996).

[51] E. A. Hanushek and D. Kimko, 'Schooling, Laborforce Quality, and the Growth of Nations' 90 *American Economic Review* 1184 (2000).

Given that education and health care services are desirable, how should they be provided? An economic approach to service provision begins with an analysis of private markets. If individuals were left to finance and purchase education and health care services, particularly basic education and disease control, on their own, spending would be less than optimal because individuals would not take account of benefits to others when making consumption decisions. Pure private provision does not spontaneously lead to professional associations and provider networks, which are important for the efficient provision of some aspects of health care, such as clinical referrals. Private provision would also make it difficult for patients and students to monitor the diligence of health care workers, who necessarily have large discretion in decision making, and therefore make it hard for consumers to assess quality.

For reasons such as these, governments have involved themselves in the financing and provision of health care and education. But government provision is bedeviled by the same problems that affect private provision. It is hard for clients and citizens to monitor the work of civil servants and bureaucrats; and, indeed, in government service delivery the one power clients have over service providers, the power to seek services elsewhere, by design usually has no effect on the behavior of government providers. Governments, at least democratic ones, are in theory accountable to citizens through elections rather than through market power. But because elections in modern states are relatively infrequent, are votes for candidates and parties and not single issues, and occur in relatively large districts without much voter deliberation, the existence of elections is weakly related to service quality, especially in developing countries. In other words, although elections can confer legitimacy, they do not assure accountability.[52] These problems are compounded by the fact that several different principals, the various ministries and institutions of government, share responsibility for health and education services, and thereby dilute accountability to their agents, the citizenry.[53] In addition, the interests of civil servants are often not aligned with those of service recipients, and civil servants mobilize in pursuit of their own interests more easily than the public at large.

There exists no optimal solution to the accountability problem for the provision of health and education services. Instead, there are a variety of mechanisms through which health and education service delivery can be made more accountable to clients. These include (a) strengthening citizens' power with respect to providers, either by granting them authority over or

[52] M. Lane, 'Accountability, Transparency, Legitimacy: The New Staples of Democratic Discourse and their Implications for Non-elected Institutions', Paper presented at the Annual Meeting of the American Political Science Association, 2002.

[53] A. Dixit, 'Power of Incentives in Private versus Public Organizations' *AEA Papers and Proceedings*, May 1997.

participation in health and education facilities or by allowing them more market choices; (b) making contracts between government and frontline providers explicit, so that provider performance is linked to rewards and sanctions; and (c) amplifying citizens' voice in health and education by changing electoral rules, creating advocacy groups, and releasing information. Examples include service 'report cards' in Bangalore, India, community control over the river blindness reduction campaign in West Africa, participatory budget formulation in Porto Alegre, Brazil, the publication of budget allocations targeted to each school in Uganda, explicit contracting for all city services in Johannesburg, South Africa, and direct cash transfers to households that send their children to school and obtain immunizations in Brazil and Mexico.[54]

5.4 SIMILARITIES, DIFFERENCES, AND THE HARD QUESTIONS

The preceding sections make clear that a rights orientation and an economic approach prescribe similar methods for service delivery in heath care and education. From the perspective of social rights, participation, empowerment, transparency, and accountability in service delivery are important for ensuring health care and education quality; and in some forms, such as informed consent so that patients can make fully informed treatment decisions and parental participation so that local understandings of respect for elders and holidays are included in classroom practices, they are also constitutive of the kind of social respect that is critical for self-esteem. From the economic perspective, participation, empowerment, transparency, and accountability are important because problems related to collective action and asymmetric information lead to inefficiencies in publicly provided services. Both private and public provision are also suboptimal because the quality and cost of education and health care (particularly health insurance) are related to who else is in one's school or health care program, which leads people of similar backgrounds to sort themselves into the same schools or programs.

It is not surprising that a rights orientation shares certain principles with an economic approach because both are genealogically related to the renewed emphasis on reason and individualism that emerged in the Enlightenment. Both recognize individuals, not societies, tribes, or other entities, as the principal locus of moral value and meaning in the world. One way to see this is to view both political systems, including electoral democracies, skeptically.

---

[54] World Bank, *World Development Report (2004): Making Services Work for Poor People* (New York: Oxford University Press, 2003).

Both are compatible with democracy, of course, and a commitment to human rights probably requires universal suffrage and contested elections. But, in both cases, empowerment, participation, and information become critical because regular elections do not as a matter of routine lead to universal access to minimally decent health care and education.

From the human rights perspective, the reason for this is that explicit legal discrimination, prolonged social exclusion, patterns of prejudice, and/or the internalization of low expectations lead to inadequate service utilization for some groups and individuals. Problems such as these are acute in developing countries, where former colonial powers bequeathed varying group-based civil law for different ethnicities and religions, and where liberal constitutions are contemporaneous with feudal, clientelist, and patriarchal practices.[55] The remedy requires correcting legal defects, as well as empowering citizens and the civil society organizations that act on their behalf to campaign against the informal cultural, social, and economic practices that sustain unfairness in access and utilization.

The economic approach is skeptical that electoral democracy by itself creates accountability in the health and education sectors for two reasons. Drawing on public choice theory, some economic analysts argue that interest groups, such as teachers unions, 'capture' the institutions of service delivery for their own purposes.[56] Using the principal findings of social choice theory, others contend that the preferences of service recipients are so heterogeneous that efforts to aggregate them, whether through democratic procedures or through market provision of jointly provided services like health care and education, are invariably bedeviled by impossibility, arbitrariness, and instability.[57] Economic solutions to interest group capture entail strengthening the market and political position of recipients by giving consumers choices, exposing providers to competitive pressures, and, where services remain publicly provided, allowing service recipients more direct participation in decision making and monitoring. One solution to the aggregation problem involves group deliberation and the development of trust.[58]

In spite of these similarities, the economic and the human rights approaches result in at least three important, though not irreconcilable, differences in policy. First, the mechanisms and processes for the delivery of health and education services are, in the rights approach, themselves morally

[55] M. Mamdani, *Citizen and Subject* (Princeton, NJ: Princeton University Press, 1996).

[56] N. Birdsall and E. James, 'Efficiency and Equity in Social Spending: How and Why Governments Misbehave', Policy, Research, and External Affairs Working Paper No. WPS 274 (Washington D.C.: World Bank, 1990).

[57] K. J. Arrow, *Social Choice and Individual Values* (New Haven, CT: Yale University Press, 1970).

[58] J. Dryzek and C. List, 'Social Choice Theory and Deliberative Democracy: A Reconciliation' 33 *British Journal of Political Science* 1 (2003).

compelling. This follows from understanding the rights to health care and education as critical elements of social inclusion. If protecting and fostering the social basis of self-esteem partly motivates the provision of health care and education services, either because the denial of those services is a marker of low status or is related to a pervasive sense of personal ineffectiveness, then service delivery should be structured to support self-esteem. That means that consent to treatment, norms for due process in delivery and allocation, participation and consultation, and transparency regarding professional and bureaucratic decision making not only facilitate good service delivery but are constitutive of it. On the other hand, the economic approach views those processes instrumentally: they could in principle be reconciled with authoritarian styles in medicine and school governance if those lowered mortality and raised literacy. But the entire thrust of normative micro-economic theory is to expand choices available to consumers, both because choices raise utility directly and because competition among providers increases social welfare. In addition, benchmark theories of competitive equilibrium require full information on prices, quantities, quality, and pre-ferences; and contemporary accounts of service delivery endorse reducing information asymmetries among principals and agents. In other words, the processes of service delivery are critical in the economic approach, even if they do not have intrinsic value.

Second, in the rights approach, evaluations of health and education pro-grams emphasize distributions in outcomes, not only averages. The entire distribution is of concern because rights theories take seriously the idea that every human being is worthy of respect. If systematic discrepancies appear among large populations, rights advocates take this as evidence that services are unavailable or inadequate for some groups. Typically, the rights approach views these discrepancies as direct evidence of inequity, whereas the eco-nomic approach would first examine whether they are the result of household choices. Rights advocates pay particular attention to disaggregated data among ethnic and religious minorities, women, and the poor because they are particularly liable to practices and prejudices that weaken their agency and the social basis of their self-esteem. Economists, of course, are also concerned with the distribution of outcomes. But usually, economists dis-aggregate data by income level because standard assumptions regarding the poor and the rich, such as the degree of risk aversion and the marginal utility of consumption, are available to build positive accounts of individual and household behavior. But there is nothing inherent in economic theory that conflicts with a normative concern for excluded groups, or with the devel-opment of new behavioral assumptions regarding women or ethnic groups.

Third, rights approaches accommodate adaptive preferences. Some constraints to the fulfillment of rights are external. For example, many cannot afford the direct or opportunity costs of schooling, do not receive information about how to receive medical care, or live in communities where collective action is costly or impossible. Economic analyses highlight the important role of these factors—resources, information, and co-ordination—in the quality of service delivery. Especially in the guise of the capabilities framework, rights approaches emphasize, in addition to these, constraints internal to individuals, such as adaptive preferences—the habit of individuals subject to deprivation to lower their standards regarding what they need, want, and deserve. Rights advocates call for consciousness raising, political education, and other measures to expand the imagination and demands of excluded groups. The discipline of economics does not easily accommodate individuals who do not maximize their welfare. But many of the mechanisms through which economists propose second best solutions involve changes in available information, participation, and incentives that, in practice, also change people's awareness of what they have and what they deserve. In practice, then, the policy consequences that follow from this aspect of rights approaches overlap, at least in part, with the economic solutions.

There are two additional and less easily reconciled challenges that economic analysis poses for rights approaches. First, rights-based approaches have no distributional metric. The question arises: in the rights framework, just how high is the high priority status of educational and health care goods and services, and how should governments and other actors make allocative decisions, both within and across sectors? Economics offers alternative approaches. Allocations can be based on consumer preferences and existing endowments, or on an objective social welfare function, such as cost per life saved or real social returns to human capital investments. Both of these approaches are problematic. The former simply assumes that market allocations are just and offers no ground for moral criticism, and the latter places no value on deliberative procedures and on actual preferences, which might or might not prioritize welfare and material well-being. Still, the approaches have the virtue of being clear and calculable.

Rights-based approaches do not offer an explicit metric for making trade-offs, and are in fact premised on the incommensurabilty of human dignity. It is true that some aspects of health care and education, such as skilled attendance at birth and literacy, can be identified as more fundamental to agency, social inclusion, and life chances than others, say contact lenses and earth science. But there are also countless close calls, both within and across sectors. As a result, from a rights perspective, there are always ambiguous trade-offs, and recommended allocations are not robust to small changes in circumstances.[59] Sorting out the various claims and counter-claims in a large

[59] Allocations are also ambiguous because they not only favor some services over others but some people over others. The claims of any person to health or education services are always

population is, from the rights perspective, inevitably an activity without a formula, and one that relies on judgment guided by principle. Because ambiguities in trade-offs stem from disagreement about priorities, and not only from lack of information about the priorities that people already have, fair procedures that adjudicate claims according to principles of representative self-government are critical. Those procedures might in turn entail a collective decision to employ disability adjusted life years (DALYs), net present value of human capital investments, or some other welfare function; but the justification for the use of any welfare function would not be independent of the adequacy of the political procedures and principles of the society. As a result of complexities like these, when making policy proposals, some rights advocates tend for the sake of simplicity to fall back on modest versions of social rights, such as the right to subsistence, basic education, and minimal health, note that even these are not available in developing countries, and argue that, globally, resources are available to fulfill at least some basic rights without having to confront the most vexing trade-offs.

The second tough problem that economic analysis poses for rights involves the behavioral distortions associated with subsidies. If a rights approach leads to subsidies or otherwise more accessible services for at least some individuals or groups, those who receive the (implicit or explicit) subsidies will spend less of their own money on the services, or will engage in more costly activities (moral hazard), with the result that the government or the entity supporting the services will buy them at a higher social cost than anticipated. In health care, providing HAART for HIV patients might, to some extent, encourage risky behavior and reduce the effectiveness of prevention efforts. To take a different example, the more strictly a state regulates the adoption process, on the understanding that it is protecting the well-being of potential adoptees, the greater the number of prospective parents who will be deterred by the regulatory costs, leading to larger numbers of children who are not adopted. The general problem is that subsidies change relative prices, which in turn changes the decisions that individuals make.

Economists charge that rights advocates ignore these reactive behaviors, which might in some cases be large enough to undermine the right that the policies are designed to promote. It is a fair criticism. On the other hand, rights advocates note that unanticipated behavioral changes that lower social costs can also follow from subsidies. For example, after Brazil, India, other countries, nongovernmental organizations (NGOs), and other actors started

---

broader than her membership in any group, including the poor, the socially excluded, or those afflicted with a particular disease or condition. His or her moral claims might also involve how the person came to have the need. For instance, deprivation as the direct result of negligence or malfeasance, as a result of military or other national service, or as a consequence of oppressive family or political circumstances, all affect the claims independently of being poor or socially excluded.

to argue for the right to HAART, surprising pressure to lower prices worldwide resulted. When Uganda abolished user charges in schools, enrollments increased far beyond expectations because the move established a new norm that everyone deserves to go to school.[60]

Responses associated with subsidies can have perverse effects, but in other instances making something a right can affect norms and customs, resulting in large and desirable changes in household behavior.

5.5 CONCLUSION

Rights are an increasingly important component of international development discourse. At the same time, they are also subject to a number of criticisms. In reality, the criticisms both over- and underestimate the contentions of rights advocates. They overestimate the contentions because most accounts of social rights interpret them as goals and grounds for moral criticism, not as legally binding constraints on the policies and programs of governments and international agencies. Most accounts also hold that rights cannot be realized at once, and that the provision of services can take several forms. The criticisms underestimate the contentions of rights advocates because they fail to recognize the enormous rhetorical importance of rights, both at the international level and within developing countries, and their historical role in the mobilization of social movements, professionals, and others in the expansion of education and health care services. Although there remain significant differences between a rights-based approach and an economic approach to health care and education, particularly regarding the issues of long-term deprivation, trade-offs, and the behavioral effect of subsidies, their policy consequences overlap considerably. Both are skeptical that electoral politics and de facto market rules by themselves provide sufficient accountability for the effective and equitable provision of health and education services, and believe that further intra-sectoral reforms in governance, particularly those that strengthen the hand of service recipients, are essential.

Three implications for development policy follow. First, the analysis shows that not only are sectoral reforms that strengthen the bargaining positions of students, families, and patients useful for enhancing service delivery, but that, because they are constitutive of the social basis of self-respect, they are intrinsically valuable. Seen this way, existing efforts to restructure sectoral governance in health and education become even more

---

[60] K. Deininger, 'Does Cost of Schooling affect Enrollment by the Poor? Universal primary education in Uganda' 22 *Economics of Education Review* 291 (2003); 'Brazil and AIDS drugs—A cure for high prices', *The Economist*, 21 June 2001, 64.

important. Second, the analysis highlights the problem of internal constraints, and particularly the tendency for people accustomed to deprivation to lower their expectations, for the achievement of health and education outcomes. Initiatives to augment information and participation in health care and education could also, as Appadurai puts it, incorporate efforts to enhance the 'capacity to aspire'.[61] Third, the analysis shows that, in typical formulations, both the economic and right-based approaches ignore behavioral changes that might follow interventions: the right-based approach can miss the effects of subsidies, and the economic approach can fail to anticipate discontinuous changes following the emergence of new norms. The identification of the potential, unforeseen consequences of policy change remains critical both for development research and practice.

[61] A. Appadurai, 'The Capacity to Aspire: Culture and the Terms of Recognition' in V. Rao and M. Walton, eds, *Culture and Public Action* (Stanford, CA: Stanford University Press, 2004).

Part B

Land Rights and Women's Empowerment

6

The Properties of Gender Equality

KERRY RITTICH

6.1 INTRODUCTION

It has long been observed that there is a gross disparity between men and women in the control of property.[1] Because women's lack of property is a fact about the world, and in many places women lack rights to property as a matter of cultural or juridical norms as well, equality in land rights holds a central place in the narrative of gender empowerment.[2] Indeed, important exceptions aside,[3] the idea that rights to land are critical to gender equality at this point seems obvious, even banal, rather than seriously contested.

The importance of gender equality in land is accepted not only from the standpoint of human rights; it is also becoming conventional wisdom within mainstream development debates. Because of a confluence of events in the field of development in the last few years—the move to 'socialize' the development agenda,[4] an important, if tentative, merger of the goals of development and human rights,[5] the recognition that gender equality is

---

[1] 'While women represent half the global population and one-third of the labor force, they receive only one-tenth of world income and own less than one percent of world property...': Report to the UN Commission on the Status of Women, cited in Robin Morgan, 'Introduction: Planetary Feminism: The Politics of the 21st Century', Robin Morgan, ed., *Sisterhood is Global: The International Women's Movement Anthology* (Garden City, NY: Anchor Books, 1984) 1.

[2] Convention on the Elimination of All Forms of Discrimination against Women (CEDAW), G.A. res. 34/180, 34 U.N. GAOR Supp. (No. 46) at 193, U.N. Doc. A/34/46, *entered into force* 3 September 1981, Article 16 (h); United Nations Fourth World Conference on Women, Declaration and Platform for Action (Beijing Platform), 15 September 1995, 35 I.L.M. 401 (1996), c. IV, a; U.N.G.A., Report of the Ad Hoc Committee of the Whole of the Twenty-third Special Session of the General Assembly (Beijing + 5), A/S-23/10/Rev.1 (Suppl. No. 3), 10 June 2000, para. 8.

[3] See for example the reservations to the Beijing Platform, above n. 2, in respect of women's inheritance rights.

[4] James D. Wolfensohn, *A Proposal for a Comprehensive Development Framework (A Discussion Draft)* (Washington D.C.: World Bank, 1999).

[5] Amartya Sen, *Development as Freedom* (New York: Anchor, 1999).

'good for development',[6] and the increasing references to gender equality in development agendas as a result[7]—it is no longer a struggle, at least at the normative level, to make the case for gender equality in rights to property in general and rights to land in particular.

To date, concerns have centered primarily around norms which limit or exclude women from access to land. In both development and human rights literature, customary and religious law, social norms, and/or inadequate or discriminatory formal laws are typically characterized as 'the problem' for women; transforming such norms and ensuring the formal equality of women to hold property is 'the answer'.[8]

There are clearly ongoing concerns around entitlements to land for women.[9] The pursuit of gender empowerment without attention to the distribution of land is an enterprise that is fatally hobbled from the outset as, for a large percentage of the world's population, real assets come primarily in the form of entitlements to land. However, it would be a mistake either to assume that formal equality exhausts the issues of interest around property rights and gender empowerment or to conclude that ensuring gender equality in respect of land rights is simply a matter of transforming social norms, enforcing the law, or compelling outlier states to bring their legal regimes into conformity with current human rights and development norms.

Instead we need to consider the nature of property regimes as well. The growing attention given to gender equality, human rights, and the social dimension of development and globalization has been accompanied by an increasing preoccupation with good governance, the rule of law, and legal and institutional reforms that promote economic growth. A central part of this legal-institutional reform project is the commitment to a particular type of property regime. This regime is one in which property entitlements are: secured through formalization of title; entitlements are consolidated and individualized; ownership is largely privatized; and regulation is minimized or eliminated. The aim of these reforms is to enhance the value of land as an asset and, by creating markets in land and facilitating the transfer of both

---

[6] World Bank, *Engendering Development: Through Gender Equality in Rights, Resources and Voice* (Washington D.C.: World Bank, 2001).

[7] World Bank, *World Development Report 2002: Building Institutions for Markets* (New York: Oxford, 2001); World Bank, *World Development Report 2003: Sustainable Development in a Dynamic World* (Washington D.C.: World Bank, 2002).

[8] See generally, World Bank, *Engendering Development*, above n. 6. The World Bank's policy research report on gender and development identifies equality in land rights as one of the four areas in which legal reforms are required to ensure gender equality.

[9] See for example Florence Butegwa, 'Mediating Culture and Human Rights in Favour of Land Rights for Women in Africa: A Framework for Community-level Action', in Abdullahi A. An-Na'im, ed., *Cultural Transformation and Human Rights in Africa* (London and New York: Zed Books, 2002) 108.

land titles and interests in land, increase the overall levels of productivity and commercial use of land, thereby spurring greater economic growth.[10]

It is now recognized that the wider constellation of institutional and regulatory reforms of which these property regimes are a part is profoundly important for gender equality and human rights. Indeed, it lies at the center of a host of distributive justice concerns in the global economy.[11] This chapter seeks to link these observations to the agenda for land reform, and to suggest that the commitment to transforming property regimes so that they better conform to the ideals of formalization, individualization, and commercial exploitation poses a distinct set of risks and challenges for women. The effects are certain to vary from context to context. However, because of the far-reaching effects of these regimes, it is unsafe to assume that gender equality is achievable simply by ensuring the formal legal equality of men and women.

There are two sets of problems, one focused on the effects of property regimes themselves, and the other on the larger vision of development in which such property regimes are embedded. Paradoxically, efforts to promote security of tenure through the formalization of title may both improve the status of women and go hand in glove with dispossessing women of property. Among other things, it depends on who gets title and what interests get recognized in the process of formalization.

Happily, there may be efficiency benefits to a better allocation of entitlements: a more equal distribution of land may contribute to future growth[12] and a more equal allocation of land and other resources between men and women may be especially good for growth.[13] However, the distributive concerns do not stop at this point. The consolidation of interests and the individualization of title may also function to limit or exclude the claims of those other than the title holder, many of whom, as a consequence of gender norms, we should expect to be women. In addition, women face a particular set of risks and disadvantages in market transactions and labor markets, a result of which may be that more intense commercialization of land exacerbates gender inequality. Ultimately, all of these effects may be

---

[10] References to the benefits of such regimes are legion in development literature. For a recent effort to re-articulate the theoretical bases of such regimes, see World Bank, *Land Policies for Growth and Poverty Reduction* (New York: Oxford University Press, 2003).

[11] Gerry Helleiner, 'Markets, Politics and Globalization: Can the Global Economy be Civilized', United Nations Conference on Trade and Development (UNCTAD) 10th Raul Prebisch Lecture, Palais des Nations, Geneva, 11 December 2000; J. Gatthi, 'Good Governance as a Counter-Insurgency Agenda to Oppositional and Transformative Social Projects in International Law', 5 *Buffalo Human Rights Law Review* 107 (1999). Balakrishnan Rajagopal, *International Law from Below: Development, Social Movements and Third World Resistance* (Cambridge, UK: Cambridge University Press, 2003).

[12] World Bank, *Land Policies for Growth and Poverty Reduction*, above n. 10, 18–20.

[13] World Bank, *Engendering Development*, above n. 6, 11.

equally, or even more, important to the question of gender equality than whether men and women have equal formal legal rights to land. Thus, the status of women is a function not only of formally equal entitlements to land, but of the 'gendered properties' of different property regimes, the ways that they affect participation in the market, and the vision of development in which they play such a central role.

6.2 PROPERTY AND HUMAN RIGHTS UNDER GLOBALIZATION

It can no longer simply be assumed that what is good for growth is good for human rights in general or for particular constituencies such as women or indigenous groups. Indeed, an important part of the critique of the first generation development agenda was predicated upon the conflict between the canonical set of 'Washington consensus' principles, rules, and policies and aspirations for greater social justice.[14]

As human rights have emerged as the universal language of social justice,[15] so they have become the main counter-discourse to globalization. Concerns about disempowerment, disenfranchisement, and dispossession in the context of market reforms and global economic integration are typically expressed in terms of human rights. The social deficit of globalization is almost invariably described as a lack of attention to human rights, and human rights principles are advanced as at least part of the solution to demands for greater empowerment and distributive justice in the global economy.[16]

The actual and potential risks to human rights, gender equality, and economic, social, and cultural rights in particular, under conditions of what

[14] G. Cornia, R. Jolly, and F. Stewart, *Adjustment with a Human Face* (New York: UNICEF/Clarendon, 1987); 'Washington consensus' stabilization policies have also been heavily criticized by economists for their impact on domestic capital formation, domestic financial intermediation, and industrial structure in developing economies. These critiques are not principally concerned with the distributional consequences of the stabilization policies but with macroeconomic and microeconomic effects. See, e.g., Lance Taylor and Ute Pieper, 'The Revival of the Liberal Creed: The IMF, The World Bank and Inequality in a Globalized Economy' in D. Baker, G. Epstein, and R. Pollin, eds, *Globalization and Progressive Economic Policy* (Cambridge, U.K.: Cambridge University Press, 1998) 37–64.

[15] Margaret E. Keck and Kathryn Sikkink, *Activists Beyond Borders: Advocacy Networks in International Politics* (Ithaca and London: Cornell, 1998) Introduction.

[16] United Nations, Committee on Economic, Social and Cultural Rights (CESCR), 'Substantive Issues Arising in the Implementation of the International Covenant on Economic, Social, and Cultural Rights: Poverty and the International Covenant on Economic, Social, and Cultural Rights', statement adopted by the CESCR on 4 May 2001, E/C.12/2001/10. Available at: http://www.unhchr.ch/tbs/doc.nsf/0ac7e03e4fe8f2bdc125698a0053bf66/ 518e88bfb89822c9c1256a4e004df048?OpenDocument.

Stiglitz has termed 'market fundamentalism',[17] have now been well documented. A range of policies and strategies associated with contemporary 'good governance' norms—structural adjustment programs, privatization, 'deregulation', and the emphasis placed on efficiency and fiscal austerity— have all been identified as potential threats to human rights or as actual violations of human rights.[18]

Yet despite their centrality to the 'good governance' project, contemporary property reforms have not appeared on the radar of the human rights community. Disputes over the reach of intellectual property rights[19] and conflicts with indigenous rights aside, securing property rights is more commonly accepted as simply part and parcel of respect for human rights. Linkages between human rights and property rights are proliferating everywhere. For example, the reformed development agenda of the World Bank puts property rights on par with human rights.[20] Following de Soto,[21] a recent International Labour Organization (ILO) report on the social dimensions of globalization identifies the formalization of property rights as a critical component of poverty reduction and social progress in developing states.[22] The right to property is itself now identified as basic to the idea of development as freedom.[23]

The powerful arguments about the relationship between property rights and economic growth,[24] and the associated assumption that growth is the precondition to social progress and the realization of social and economic rights, make it easy to conclude that the protection of property rights is something to which social justice activists and the human rights community should be uncritically committed. This conclusion should give us pause.

[17] Joseph E. Stiglitz, *Globalization and its Discontents* (New York: Norton, 2002) Ch 1.

[18] United Nations Office of the High Commissioner for Human Rights, Committee on Economic, Social and Cultural Rights, 'Statement on Globalization and Economic, Social and Cultural Rights', Geneva, 11 May 1998, available at: http://www.unhchr.ch/tbs/doc.nsf/MasterFrameView/adc44375895aa10d8025668f003.

[19] World Trade Organization, *Doha WTO Ministerial 2001: Ministerial Declaration*, 20 November 2001, available at: http://www.wto.org/english/thewto_e/minist_e/min01_e/mindecl_e.htm.

[20] Wolfensohn, *A Proposal for a Comprehensive Development Framework (A Discussion Draft)*, above n. 4.

[21] Hernando de Soto, *The Mystery of Capital: Why Capitalism Triumphs in the West and Fails Everywhere Else* (New York: Basic Books, 2000).

[22] ILO, *A Fair Globalization: Creating Opportunities for All*, Final Report, World Commission on the Social Dimensions of Globalization, 24 February 2004, available at: http://www.ilo.org/public/english/wcsdg/index.htm, para. 256.

[23] Sen, *Development as Freedom*, above n. 5.

[24] Ibrahim Shihata, 'Law, Development and the Role of the World Bank', *Complementary Reform: Essays on Legal, Judicial and Other Institutional Reforms* (The Hague: Kluwer, 1997); World Bank, *Doing Business in 2004: Understanding Regulation* (Washington D.C.: World Bank, 2004).

The heightened emphasis on the protection of property is institutionally and politically related to the current character of development thinking and to the shifting perceptions about appropriate roles and functions of different social institutions. It is a marker of the influence of financial markets and the international financial institutions on the development of policy and regulatory priorities at the national and international levels. It is also a reflection of the important role assigned to private actors in the advancement of social, economic, and political goals and the effort to contain the reach of the state. For example, a recent World Bank report on the links between legal regimes and economic growth contends that, while governments generally do 'too much', the one area in which they fail to do enough is the protection of property rights.[25] In other words, the prominence of property reflects much more than simply a set of empirical observations about the connection between property rights and growth. Rather, it is linked to a host of deeply contested debates about the organization of economic, social, and political life, and the role envisaged for property rights in development should be thought of as part of a broader effort to promote more entrepreneurial societies.

The enhanced importance of both the distribution of property and property regimes is also a structural outcome of reforms in another sense. The 'deregulation' of markets, whether they are markets in land, labor, or anything else, does not leave a legal vacuum but rather a regime in which transactions are structured largely by property, contract, and other private rights. The privatization of assets changes not only the locus of title but typically the distribution of assets and the class of beneficiaries within societies as well. Reducing the redistributive and risk-spreading activities of the state leaves individuals and households more dependent on their own assets, making access to property of greater importance.

There is no necessary conflict between the protection of property rights and greater social justice; property reform may indeed be an essential ingredient of social justice. However, despite claims to the contrary, the protection of private property does not necessarily enhance either the general level of social welfare or the extent of social justice. It is worth recalling that fierce social and political struggles are often played out in and around property rights. For example, property norms are well-known instruments of conquest,[26] and demands for land reform are often central to social protest and revolutions. Property reforms have strengthened the power of the commercial class and at the expense of the agrarian;[27] they have been invoked to defeat legislative efforts to enhance worker rights;[28] and they are currently

---

[25] World Bank, *Doing Business in 2004: Understanding Regulation*, above n. 24.

[26] *Johnson v. M'Intosh* 21 US 543, 5 L.Ed. 681, 8 Wheat. 543 (1823).

[27] E. P. Thompson, *Whigs and Hunters: the Origin of the Black Act* (London: Allen Lane, 1975).					[28] *Lochner v. New York*, 198 U.S. 45 (1905).

the locus of struggle over control of biological resources between indigenous communities in the developing world and pharmaceutical companies.[29] The disposition of property and the status of property rights have been critical in transitions from colonial to post-colonial rule and apartheid to post-apartheid states. This is reflected in the Declaration on the Right to Development, which asserts the sovereignty of peoples over their natural resources and the right of states to formulate development policies to the benefit of all, and emphasizes the importance of distributive justice.[30] As these scenarios disclose, the critical questions are not simply whether property rights should be protected, but rather what those rights should be, who should possess them, to what extent, and to what effect in any given context.

To date, property rights have attracted the attention of women's rights and human rights scholars largely because of concerns about discrimination in entitlements to land. The argument is that, here as in other contexts, it is important to both widen the inquiry and flip the lens. Given the centrality of property reforms and the claims that formalization of title is not only good for growth but now good for the poor as well, it is critical to scrutinize the gendered effects—the effects on women's human rights—of the drive to formalize property rights in land, consolidate title in a single owner who possesses the power to conclusively dispose of the interests at stake, promote the creation of markets in land in order to link local with global markets, and encourage the use of land as security and collateral for other economic ventures.

6.3 PROPERTY IN DEVELOPMENT

Reforms to property rights now center around three types of transformation: formalization, individualization, and commodification.

6.3.1 Formalization

The importance of formalization lies in the key role that certainty of entitlement and security of tenure play in promoting the most efficient use of land.[31] The basic argument is that property holders will under-invest in their property to the extent that they cannot be certain of reaping the rewards, and

---

[29] World Trade Organization, *Doha WTO Ministerial 2001: Ministerial Declaration*, 20 November 2001, available at: http://www.wto.org/english/thewto_e/minist_e/min01_e/mindecl_e.htm.

[30] G.A. res. 41/128, annex, 41 U.N. GAOR Supp. (No. 53) at 186, U.N. Doc. A/41/53 (1986).

[31] World Bank, *Land Policies for Growth and Poverty Reduction*, above n. 10, 8.

growth will suffer as a result.[32] In addition, there are considerable benefits to formalization because of savings on transaction costs. Finally, formalization is necessary to 'modernize' the economy and to enable producers to branch out beyond local markets and participate in the global economy.[33]

According to its proponents, formalization of title can be especially beneficial to the poor, for the reason that the poor generally lack access to capital other than land. Formalization thus serves to transform land into an active resource that can be used for economic development.[34] Formalization may also have collateral benefits, such as increasing the available resources of central and local governments by increasing property tax revenues.[35]

6.3.2 Individualization

Individualizing property rights is advocated on the basis of the 'tragedy of the commons'. The argument is that optimal property use will invariably suffer when it is under common control, while '[i]ndividual assignment of property rights is the arrangement that provides the greatest incentives for efficient resource use'.[36] For similar reasons, the privatization of land is assumed to be beneficial, while the nationalization of land is presumptively bad.[37]

The basic efficiency argument is accompanied by a dynamic analysis which holds that property rights tend to become more precise as land values rise while control becomes both more important and more contested. Individual title, too, becomes more functional in the course of development: while there are instances in which collective rights are the best way to deal with externalities, these tend to decline with modernization.[38] The merits of individualization also provide a set of arguments against the regulation of land. Like multiple interests, regulation can function as a 'clog' on title, slowing transactions, impeding transferability, and generally reducing the efficient use of property.

However important, the arguments for individual title and unimpeded control are not exhausted by economic concerns: there are political and

---

[32] See Karen O. Mason and Helene M. Carlsson, 'The Development Impact of Gender Equality in Land Rights', in this volume, Chapter 7.

[33] World Bank, *Land Policies for Growth and Poverty Reduction*, above n. 10, 24.

[34] de Soto, above n. 21.

[35] Inter-American Development Bank (IDB), Loan Agreement with the Government of Belize, Land Management Program, (BL–0017), executive summary on file with the author.

[36] World Bank, *Land Policies for Growth and Poverty Reduction*, above n. 10, 24 citing Robert Ellickson, 'Property in Land', 102 *Yale Law Journal* 1315 (1993). For a consideration of this argument in the context of transition, see Michael Heller, 'The Tragedy of the Anti-Commons: Property in the Transition from Marx to Markets', 111 *Harvard Law Review* 621 (1998).   [37] Id. at 4–5.

[38] World Bank, *Land Policies for Growth and Poverty Reduction*, above n. 10. These ideas have a fairly established pedigree in development economics.

institutional concerns as well. At the heart of this claim is a particular image about the inherent nature of property rights: property rights confer a Blackstonian sphere of unfettered control and dominion upon the right holder.[39] While encroachments may be justified for compelling economic reasons, the baseline assumption is that property rights confer total, rather than fractional, ownership and control. Except with respect to the property rights of shareholders to a corporation, the burden of proof lies upon those who wish to argue for restraints on this control. This burden is intensified in the context of development for at least two reasons. One is the association of regulation with government failure and corruption.[40] The other is the argument, especially salient in the context of post-communist economies, that property rights function to insulate the individual from the predations of the state.

6.3.3 Commodification

An important reason for both the formalization and individualization of title is to enhance the commercial value of land. Once formal title is secure and the number of interest holders reduced, ideally to one, land can be used more effectively to promote growth in a variety of ways. It can be alienated outright or rented to those who may use it more productively. It also becomes transformed from a 'dead asset' into something that can be used as collateral for loans, whether to access equipment or enable investments to enhance the value of the land itself or as security for other economic enterprises.[41] These processes, in turn, can be expected to reduce the demand for agricultural labor and increase the available labor supply for other ventures. Thus, the particular *purposes* for which property rights are introduced—hooking local markets up to global markets and facilitating transactions—come to determine the nature of the rights themselves.

6.4 PROPERTY AND GENDER EQUALITY

Gender theorists and activists have enumerated a number of ways that standard approaches to property in development thinking might pose problems for women, undermining rather than enhancing their status and empowerment. The perils of property reforms are well documented in the

---

[39] William Blackstone, *Commentaries on the Laws of England* (Chicago and London: University of Chicago Press, 2002); Joe Singer, 'The Reliance Interest in Property', 40 *Stanford Law Review* 611 (1988).

[40] World Bank, *Land Policies for Growth and Poverty Reduction*, above n. 10.

[41] de Soto, above n. 21.

post-communist economies too: dramatic concentrations of wealth[42] and the impoverishment of large sectors of society resulted from privatization efforts gone awry. It would be a mistake to assume that these problems lie in the past, now remedied by greater attention to institutions and gender equality. Rather, institutionalization itself can be the problem. For this reason, attention to who holds title to property is crucial. Land reforms that fail to require either joint titling or special rights for women may undermine the status of women. Similarly, reliance upon market mechanisms may deprive women of access to land that they would otherwise have under customary law.[43]

These types of property regimes may generate systematic disadvantages for women and actually increase the degree of inequality between men and women, for a number of reasons, such as gendered differences in the ownership and control of property, the presence of plural legal systems, the gendered distribution of paid and unpaid work, and the differences in men and women's capacity to both participate in markets and derive economic benefit from that participation. However, whether disadvantages are generated may depend on the presence or absence of a host of other legal and social entitlements and institutions, and on the wide variety of ways in which property claims are adjudicated or otherwise disposed of. In other words, calculating the effects of transformations in property regimes for women requires much more than simply projecting a set of economic effects of property rights in the abstract; it requires an assessment of the wider institutional matrix in which they operate.

This is no easy task. Because the relationship between property regimes and social and economic outcomes is contingent, there is no single property regime that can be safely associated with gender empowerment or the protection or advancement of human rights across context and time. Yet while it is impossible to specify *ex ante* a set of property entitlements that is unequivocally associated with the promotion of gender equality, it may be possible to say quite a lot about what structure of entitlements might exacerbate or mitigate gender inequality in a given context, and why. And it is possible to say still more about why the property regime now promoted as the precondition of economic integration and growth, without more, might systematically work against the interests of women, or some groups of women, even if it appeared to be efficient in the aggregate in the sense of generating greater measurable market returns. However, the reasons for which it fails to improve the status of women also say a great deal about why it might not actually be efficient either, certainly in the medium to long term. The short answer is that, while there has been intense interest in the potential

[42] Adrian Levy and Cathy Scott-Clark, 'He won, Russia lost', *The Guardian* (Manchester, UK), 9 May 2004.
[43] World Bank, *Engendering Development*, above n. 6, 120–122.

benefits of such regimes, there has been a distinct failure to tally, and sometimes even to recognize, the total costs that are typically involved in moving from one regime to another. What follows is an effort to say more about what might actually be at stake in the processes of formalization, individualization, and commodification.

Whatever the motivation, efficiency-enhancing measures like titling systematically generate distributive outcomes and effects that tend to be persistently underplayed, if not ignored outright.[44] The basic argument is that the benefits of reforms, whether to property rights or other rules, cannot be untethered from these distributive effects. Women may experience both benefit and harm from reforms to property. However, we are well past the point in experiments with legal and institutional reform at which it is possible to simply assert, as either a theoretical or empirical claim, that the institution of property rights amounts to progress per se, or that 'in the long run' we will be better off. This is particularly true if egalitarian and distributive concerns rank highly in the social welfare calculus. There are repeated instances, both contemporary and historical, in which the transformation of property rights has been associated with income polarization, significant declines in welfare, and/or outright dispossession.[45] At minimum, we need to investigate how and why this might occur in the course of development and market reform. By now, we should also *expect* the process of redistribution to occur. In investigating these issues, the real question in any event is not 'property, good or bad', but rather the structure of property rights and the manner in which they are allocated.

6.5 RETHINKING THE PROPERTY NARRATIVE

However persuasive from within the discipline of economics,[46] from the standpoint of law the conventional arguments for the formalization, individualization, and commodification of property seem incomplete at best, and seriously misleading at worst. Although a comprehensive analysis is not possible here, because it is so central both to the logic of development *and* to understanding the potential for ongoing, even increased, gender equality, it seems important to at least briefly sketch an alternative account of the operation and effects of property regimes. A number of general observations about the account of property given in development thinking can be made.

[44] For a more sustained exploration of this argument, see Kerry Rittich, *Recharacterizing Restructuring: Law, Gender and Distribution in Market Reform* (The Hague: Kluwer, 2002).

[45] Katherine Verdery, *The Vanishing Hectare: Property and Value in Postsocialist Transylvania* (Ithaca, NY: Cornell University Press, 2003); Rittich, *Recharacterizing Restructuring: Law, Gender and Distribution in Market Reform*, above n. 44.

[46] I am leaving aside here any internal economic critiques of such property regimes.

One is the functionalist, evolutionary view that is taken of the transformation of property rights; another is the orientation towards efficiency to the exclusion of other concerns and effects; yet a third is the belief in the efficacy of formal rights.

Reading mainstream economic accounts, one would think that the transformation of property can be accounted for by efficiency concerns and that property rights induce both a defined set of responses from economic actors and a defined set of legal conclusions from adjudicators. However, even passing familiarity with property laws in market societies confirms that property rights vary significantly both among societies and within societies over time, and that even formally similar regimes seem to be associated with very different economic outcomes. Definitions of property rights are affected as much by social and political conflict as by economic progress. Efficiency criteria often seem marginal to judges in the disposition of property claims; sometimes they are totally eclipsed. In short, from the inside of law, property rights seem both conceptually and mechanically quite different.

6.5.1 Realist and Post-Realist Ideas about Property

Property is conventionally described in post-realist legal analysis[47] as a bundle of infinitely divisible rights that can be combined, recombined, and allocated in a number of ways.[48] Whatever the merits of secure property rights, the *structure* of property rights is not something that can be simply assumed. Nor can it be determined by invoking the importance of property alone: it is the very question to be answered.[49] And however appealing the prospect of unfettered control from an efficiency standpoint, the property rights of owners cannot be absolute without defeating a host of other interests and values.[50]

One reason is that property is in essence a set of relations among people in respect of things tangible and intangible: to put it another way, property has a social, rather than a merely economic, function.[51] Although property

---

[47] For a survey of the literature of the realist tradition in American legal thought, see William W. Fisher III, Morton J. Horwitz, and Thomas A. Reed, *American Legal Realism* (New York: Oxford, 1993).

[48] Thomas C. Grey, 'The Disintegration of Property', in J. Roland Pennock and John W. Chapman, *Property: Nomos XXII* (New York: New York University Press, 1980) 69.

[49] Felix S. Cohen, 'Transcendental Nonsense and the Functional Approach', 35 *Columbia Law Review* 809 (1935); Singer, 'The Reliance Interest in Property', above n. 39, 637–641.

[50] Joe Singer, *Entitlements: The Paradoxes of Property* (New Haven and London: Yale University Press, 2000).

[51] Greg Alexander, *Commodity and Propriety: Competing Visions of Property in American Legal Thought, 1776–1970* (Chicago and London: University of Chicago Press, 1997).

rights are often figured as a counterweight to state or local power in development literature,[52] the scope of property rights is a public, not private, matter: where rights are formalized, property amounts to a delegation of sovereignty from the state and a decision about the extent and nature of control to which owners are entitled vis-à-vis non-owners.[53] Because property rights often confer a significant amount of control over the lives of others,[54] determinations about their character and reach are inherently political, in the sense that they concern the allocation of resources and power among different social groups. Property rights do not merely protect wealth or reduce the costs of transactions; they also *produce* wealth. The assertion, that as property becomes more valuable it attracts more legal protection, does not capture either the process or the interests at stake. Legal regimes both enhance and impair the value of property; property may not even *exist* except as an effect of law. For example, it is the law which produces almost all of the value of new pharmaceutical products. By securing their exclusive entitlement to produce the product, the law confers enormous leverage on patent holders in setting price levels and capturing future profits. Moreover, property rights produce a particular *distribution* of wealth: they not only create value, but determine who can draw on the value that is created and by how much. Where access to property is crucial for survival, well-being, or even simply status, this means that property rights impose costs and burdens on others.[55] This is why the manner in which property rights are structured powerfully influences the distribution of gains in the market.

There are multiple possible ways of configuring property regimes in market societies. Property rights can be divided up in many ways, and they are routinely rather than exceptionally regulated in a variety of ways. Entitlements may be allocated to multiple interest holders internally through property law doctrine notwithstanding that title is vested in a single owner. The common law, for example, can effect a separation between legal and beneficial ownership though trust instruments and allocate entitlements across time through the creation of life and other estates. The scope and

---

[52] See for example World Bank, *Land Policies for Growth and Poverty Reduction*, above n. 10.

[53] Morris Cohen, 'Property and Sovereignty', 13 *Cornell Law Quarterly* 8 (1927).

[54] C. B. Macpherson, *Property: Mainstream and Critical Positions: a Reader* (Toronto: University of Toronto Press, 1978) Introduction; Robert Hale, 'Coercion and Distribution in a Supposedly Non-Coercive State' (1923) 38 *Political Science Quarterly* 470; Max Weber, 'Freedom and Coercion', in M. Rheinstein, ed., *Max Weber on Law in Economy and Society*, trans. E. Shils and M. Rheinstein (Cambridge, MA: Harvard University Press, 1954) 188–189.

[55] W. Hohfeld, 'Some Fundamental Legal Conceptions as Applied in Judicial Reasoning', 23 *Yale Law Journal* 28 (1913).

operation of property entitlements are also inevitably affected by the nature of other legal entitlements. While the resulting structure of property rights may be complex, there is nothing mysterious about the reason for the complexity: there are simply myriad individual and social interests at stake which are expressed and ratified through the medium of property law. The point of rehearsing these facts is simply to emphasize that development discourse and policy tends to deploy a radically compressed range of property regimes that operate, or that might potentially operate, within market-based societies.

Developing and transitional states are frequently advised to simplify ownership structures and reduce the degree of regulation, whether because of the absence of developed legal systems, the presence of corruption, or the possibility of regulatory capture. However, these arguments seem less persuasive once it is recognized that customary property rights, too, can be very complex,[56] and that developing states are typically under simultaneous pressure to adopt other economic laws that are relatively complicated and expensive to administer. But the more important point is simply that the trade-offs and losses involved in simplifying and deregulating property regimes may be very high. Whatever the concerns about the capacity of the state or the local administration, it is not possible, without damage, to simply dismiss the functions that such institutions perform. For example, land regulation may be efficiency-enhancing even in conventional terms, because of some imperfection in land markets themselves; in the alternative, it may preclude uses that, while efficient from the standpoint of the owner, impair either future use or other valuable ends. This is well recognized in theory, even if it tends not to be reflected in legal reform prescriptions. Property regimes are incredibly complex social institutions that are ultimately inseparable from the welfare, power, and resources of particular groups. Decisions about property rights amount to fundamental decisions about social ordering; they both make and reflect those decisions. Disruptions to entrenched property rights can thus amount to disruptions to the social order. While this does not in and of itself tell us whether changes to particular property regimes are likely to be beneficial, it does put us on notice that the transformation of property regimes entails something much broader than the mere promotion of efficiency and growth. At minimum, it suggests that potential dislocations to potentially wide networks of people who depend in some way on access to land must be taken seriously. This in turn suggests that the rejection of the 'one-size-fits-all' approach, now standard in other areas of development thinking, should apply to property rules and regimes too.

---

[56] See for example Sally Falk Moore, *Law as Process: An Anthropological Approach* (London; Boston: Routledge & K. Paul, 1978).

6.6 PROPERTY IN DEVELOPMENT REVISITED

This brief review of the mechanics of property rights in action suggests a number of insights, all of which may be relevant to the question of property reforms and to the matter of gender empowerment.

- We are always *in medias res*: there is never any system of 'non-allocation' of property rights, even if those rights are incompletely specified under formal or customary law.
- Formalization is unlikely to merely record pre-existing interests. Rather, providing greater security, certainty, and predictability, whatever the underlying motivation, will necessarily alter the existing distribution of property rights.
- Because property rights operate in a relational fashion and because they normally empower the owner to exclude, to say that property provides security is to say both too little and too much: they are simultaneously a source of security and insecurity. Thus, advocating the security of property rights does not answer the critical question: security for whom?
- The different elements of property reforms—formalization, individualization, and commodification—are not in any way entailed by each other. Rather, they are distinct and separable. Nor do the benefits of formalization necessarily justify the individualization of title or intensified efforts to commodify land. The costs and benefits of each element need to be considered independently and in context.
- It is unsafe to simply equate formalization with the creation of legal certainty. Because property rights function as a conclusion rather than a premise,[57] property disputes can be decided in a variety of ways. Judges face a range of choices in the process of adjudicating claims. The decisions they reach may both affect the power and position of the claimants and modify, strengthen, or subvert the property right itself.
- Property rights will inevitably operate differently and generate different effects in different contexts. Formal property rights inevitably function in tandem with other normative orders, ranging from customary law to informal social and cultural norms, including gender norms.[58] This fundamental insight about legal pluralism is curiously absent, or at least under-explored, in much mainstream development literature. However, it, too, complicates the claim that property rights engender certainty and security in fundamental ways. The presence of social or cultural norms about the proper uses of property, for example, may affect the way that

[57] Cohen, 'Transcendental Nonsense and the Functional Approach', above n. 49, 809.
[58] Moore, *Law as Process: An Anthropological Approach*, above n. 56.

property disputes are decided, notwithstanding the structure of formal entitlements.[59] This suggests that where there are multiple interests at stake, decisions about the disposition of property are unlikely to be completely governed by efficiency even where property rights are formalized.

- Because property rights in action include the total complex of norms and decisions in operation, it is unrealistic to simply transplant legal regimes from one context to another with the expectation that they will produce roughly similar results. Even if the idea is to generate a set of economic effects and outcomes, there is unlikely to be any single, 'right' regime that will do so in a predictable way.
- The relationship between property rights and growth is complicated rather than straightforward; generating economic growth almost certainly involves much more than instituting the right set of legal incentives.[60] How should we account for the fact that growth may be robust, notwithstanding relatively uncertain property rights?[61] Or that, as a historical matter, growth has been associated with instability and disruption to established property rights, as well as certainty and stability of entitlements?[62]
- The protection of property rights is in no way incompatible with regulation; notwithstanding the arguments in favour of unfettered control, property is typically regulated in myriad ways in market societies. The regulation of property (and contract) may actually preserve the viability of markets and preserve the physical, social, and human capital that enables them to function in the long term.[63]
- It is also unsafe to assume that intensified market activity in land is always welfare enhancing. Countries experiencing the transition from communism and planned economies are good examples. Processes such as

---

[59] Celestine I. Nyamu, 'Gender, Culture and Property Relations in a Pluralistic Social Setting', SJD dissertation, on file at the Harvard Law School library, 2001; Celestine I. Nyamu, 'How Should Human Rights and Development Respond to Cultural Legitimization of Gender Hierarchy in Developing Countries?' 41 *Harvard International Law Journal* 381 (2000); Leslye Amede Obiora, 'Remapping the Domain of Property in Africa', 12 *University of Florida Journal of Law and Public Policy* 57 (2000).

[60] Verdery, *The Vanishing Hectare: Property and Value in Postsocialist Transylvania*, above n. 45.

[61] Matthew C. Stephenson, 'A Trojan Horse Behind Chinese Walls? Problems and Prospects of US-Sponsored "Rule of Law" Reform Projects in the Peoples' Republic of China', CID Working Paper no. 47, Center for International Development, Harvard University, 2000.

[62] Frank Upham, 'Mythmaking in the Rule of Law Orthodoxy', Working Paper no. 30, Rule of Law Series, Democracy and Rule of Law Project, Carnegie Endowment for International Peace, September 2002.

[63] This is an old insight about market economics. See Karl Polanyi, *The Great Transformation* (Boston: Beacon, 1957).

privatization and commercialization may be 'captured' by local or external elites, leading to the dispossession and impoverishment of substantial numbers of local people.[64]

- It has long been recognized that property holding can be a form of risk management or insurance against economic misfortune.[65] This is especially true in the absence of markets for particular goods or services or in states or regions without extensive, or any, social insurance or income protection. Where access to land is a crucial social resource, preserving life and livelihood, it is unsafe to assume that particular property arrangements are 'inefficient' in the sense of failing to serve any overriding or rational economic interest, even where they impede the easy transferability of land interests on the market. As paradoxical as it may seem, facilitating markets in land may require the concurrent implementation of new legal institutions to provide insurance, protection, and resources that would otherwise be unavailable.

- It has long been observed that the degree of bargaining power that parties have in the course of market transactions is intimately connected to the distribution of property; to put it another way, actual freedom of contract is subject to the distribution of property.[66] Thus, any claims about the benefits of greater market participation for groups such as women are inseparable from the manner in which property is distributed. However, it also means that the general claims about the benefits of commercializing and commodifying land are inseparable from how land and land entitlements are distributed.

6.6.1 Property and Gender Equality

With these insights in mind, we can see that mere formal equality of property rights under the law is unlikely to ensure gender equality. Paradoxically, the wholesale effort to commodify or commercialize land may be just as likely to contribute to inequality between men and women. Without more, women face a number of inherent risks in any shift to a regime of property rights configured along the lines described above.

---

[64] Verdery, *The Vanishing Hectare: Property and Value in Postsocialist Transylvania*, above n. 45.

[65] Donald McCloskey, 'The Persistence of English Common Fields', in William N. Parker and Eric L. Jones, eds, *European Peasants and their Markets: Essays in Agrarian Economic History* (Princeton, N.J.: Princeton University Press, 1975) 73.

[66] Robert Hale, 'Coercion and Distribution in a Supposedly Neutral State', above n. 54; C. B. Macpherson, *Property: Mainstream and Critical Positions*, above n. 54, 'Introduction', 'Weber', and 'Marx'.

6.6.1.1 Formalization and Individualization

Where women gain formal title to land, one obvious possibility is an improvement in their social and economic position. Apart from the benefits that accrue from ownership alone, title to land may also improve women's labor market position; as gender scholars have observed, land ownership may affect the reserve price of labor.[67] Asset ownership and income in the market also appears to improve women's bargaining position within the household. Analyses of the household as a locus of co-operation and conflict,[68] one affected deeply by the gendered balance of power, make the idea that household members are simply happily engaged in welfare-maximizing activities the benefits of which will be altruistically shared among them decidedly unpersuasive. However, even if women have equal rights to land, gender equality is by no means assured simply by the move to formalize title. One reason is that the merits of formalization and individualization of title are typically promoted independently of the question of land distribution; to put it starkly, it would be a mistake to equate the protection of property rights with the 'right to property' for any particular group. Because land distribution is inherently political (and often seen as 'cultural' too, especially where women are concerned), it is often avoided in the context of reforms, no matter how pressing it might be to development objectives. But where questions of distribution are put to one side and title goes to men rather than women, the detriments are obvious: women may end up worse off. The more general point is that formalization may simply further empower those who are already powerful.

It is also important to recognize that cultural norms and other normative orders continue to operate, notwithstanding the formalization of title. Nor does formalization necessarily push such norms in a more 'progressive' direction. Rather formalization, especially when accompanied by the ideology of individualization, may function to enhance the position of men, permitting them to claim more than they would otherwise receive under customary law.[69] Another reason for caution is the distinction between ownership and control. Even where women have title to land or other assets, it may be unsafe to equate ownership with effective control, especially if there are cross-cutting norms and obligations that impede the exercise of control. Conversely, women may have obligations (obligations of labor, for example) in respect of land that they do not own. This phenomenon raises important

---

[67] Bina Agarwal, *A Field of One's Own: Gender and land rights in South Asia* (Cambridge, UK: Cambridge University Press, 1994).

[68] Sen, *Development as Freedom*, above n. 5; Agarwal, *A Field of One's Own: Gender and land rights in South Asia*, above n. 67.

[69] Nyamu, 'Gender, Culture and Property Relations in a Pluralistic Social Setting', above n. 59.

questions: might the superior productivity of family-run farms,[70] for example, reflect men's capacity to command the unpaid work of women?[71]

Moreover, even where women benefit from the formalization of title they may be disadvantaged by the individualization of property interests or the efforts to commodify land. Formalization need not entail the elimination of customary entitlements; there is no reason, at least in theory, that myriad different interests might not be formalized in the titling process or recognized in the course of adjudication. For example, common law judges can and do use devices such as constructive trusts to recognize both customary norms and the economic contribution of women to property held in the name of their husbands or partners.[72] However, in practice formalization often serves to wipe out customary entitlements, many of which are held by women. Indeed, by relying upon and recirculating absolutist claims about the nature of property rights, the current ideology about property reform may encourage such outcomes.

It is well known that women are much less likely to be recognized as the formal heads of households; it is also recognized that presumptions of male headship have often operated in tandem with formalization to facilitate the elimination of women's entitlements.[73] Particularly where title is vested in husbands or fathers alone, titling provides increased opportunities to alienate land and to deprive others of access and resources. Thus, a basic risk is simple dispossession in the process of titling.

What is important is that this is not merely accidental nor even undesirable, in current development logic. Part of the *point* of individualizing title is to reduce or eliminate the number of recognized interests so as to facilitate the transfer of title and interests. However, given the gendered division of labor, women are very likely to lose not simply property rights in the abstract: they are likely to have material investments, in time and labor if not money, that may be eliminated in the eyes of the law in the process of formalization/individualization.

6.6.1.2 Commodification

For a variety of reasons, men appear to be much more likely than women to benefit from markets in land: they have also often been the main beneficiaries

[70] Klaus Deininger and Gershon Feder, 'Land Institutions and Land Markets', Policy Research Working Paper 2014, World Bank, Development Research Group, Rural Development, November 1998.

[71] Ambreena Manji, 'Remortgaging Women's Lives: the World Bank's Land Agenda in Africa', 11 *Feminist Legal Studies* 139 (2003).

[72] This has been an important device in common law in jurisdictions such as Australia and Canada; see for example *Pettkus v. Becker* [1980] 2 S.C.R. 834. It has also been used in Kenya; for a discussion see Nyamu, 'Gender, Culture and Property Relations in a Pluralistic Social Setting', above n. 59.

[73] Nyamu, 'Gender, Culture and Property Relations in a Pluralistic Social Setting', above n. 59.

of the transformations of land use, such as cash cropping, associated with integration into global markets. Thus, in the absence of countervailing and compensatory reforms, there is reason to think that the commodification of land may exacerbate rather than ameliorate gender inequality. Among the adverse effects of land commodification for women that have been documented to date are: loss of traditional entitlements to land use; loss of access to communal lands; increased labor contributions to crops whose proceeds are controlled by men; greater difficulty in discharging traditional (and persisting) obligations to provide for the subsistence and other needs of dependents; and increased engagement in and reliance upon marginal self-employment or wage labor on terrible terms.[74] Even apart from these concerns, the benefits of commodification may also be overstated in ways that matter to women in particular. Where produce is marketed rather than consumed, for example, an increase in economic activity is registered, even though it may not reflect any actual increase in output and may even coincide with a decrease in welfare for some parts of the population.[75]

Yet the implications of commodification extend beyond these concerns. The move to transform the uses of property is linked to a particular path of economic progress and transformation, one in which both men and women spend less time in agricultural and other subsistence activities and are ever more intensively and productively employed in an expanding range of market activities. Here it becomes important to recognize that women are situated differently than men in their ability to take advantage of market opportunities. Although social norms may play a role, this is a structural as well as cultural matter. Since market participation is the projected future, the route to both development and gender equality,[76] it is crucial to try to understand the factors and processes that might affect women's capacity to participate in markets. Once property reforms are seen as part of a larger process to create a more mobile, productive labor force, it becomes particularly important to take account of the gendered operation of labor markets.

One thing to take into consideration is that, in virtually every society, non-market obligations fall much more heavily on women than on men. This has the effect of limiting women's work options, typically by constraining women's mobility and reducing the time that can be devoted to the pursuit of market opportunities. To make this observation is not to say that women are not active participants in markets or are not important economic producers; the opposite is true. But it may not be the case that women are the ones capturing the cutting edge opportunities to participate in global market activities, particularly where information and trust circulate within gendered

---

[74] Agarwal, *A Field of One's Own: Gender and land rights in South Asia*, above n. 67.

[75] The *locus classicus* on this is M. Waring, *If Women Counted: A New Feminist Economics* (San Francisco: Harper and Row, 1988).

[76] World Bank, *Engendering Development*, above n. 6.

sub-communities. Will women remain in small-scale, traditional sectors, while men capture the gains in the new?[77]

Another reason is that bargaining power, both in households and in labor markets, is linked to alternatives and exit options.[78] If either formalization or individualization of title has the effect of reducing both women's entitlements and property holdings, we should expect women to fare less well in the market too. The ability to use land as security is, in theory, beneficial to both women and to men. At first glance, it may seem *more* important to women than men, as lack of access to credit may limit women's capacity to engage in productive activity in the market. But women may also be more at risk from the use of land as security. Imagine, for example, that, once title is formalized, land is now used as collateral for some new economic venture. Who will labor to pay the debt? Will women necessarily benefit from the economic venture supported by the loan? Past experience with microcredit finance[79] and export production encouraging cash cropping suggests perhaps not. What if the venture fails? Foreclosure on the land is the likely outcome, with the loss of probably the only real source of economic security. The risk of loss may be relatively high, particularly where ventures are to any degree speculative. There are similar, if not greater, risks with efforts to promote the alienation of land outright.

Earlier privatization experiments resemble the land reform agenda in that they subscribed to similar hopes about the welfare-enhancing properties of new markets, and made similar assumptions about the desire and capacity of individuals to participate in markets and maximize their economic returns. However, 'taking advantage' of the market needs to be understood in both its positive and negative senses; there are both dangers and opportunities, and we now know that the capacity of individuals to benefit from both legal transformations and markets varies enormously. More sophisticated, well-positioned, or unscrupulous parties can be expected to move quickly to seize the opportunities presented by legal transformations such as titling. A tremendous redistribution of entitlements in a short time frame can accompany property reforms, some of which can have very long-term consequences. For example, assets may be captured by outsiders or domestic elites, while others are dispossessed.[80] These are serious concerns; in the wake of accumulating experience with reforms, it is unsafe to assume that these are collateral

---

[77] World Bank, *Engendering Development*, above n. 6, 187, 223.

[78] A. Sen, 'Gender and Co-operative Conflict' in I. Tinker, ed., *Persistent Inequalities: Women and World Development* (New York: Oxford University Press, 1990); Bina Agarwal, ' "Bargaining" and Gender Relations: Within and Beyond the Household', 3(1) *Feminist Economics* 1 (1997).

[79] Toni Williams, 'Requiem for Microcredit? The Demise of a Romantic Ideal', 19 *Banking and Finance Law Review* 145 (2003).

[80] Research indicates that the creation of markets in land through titling in Honduras led to the dispossession of indigenous people from 70% of their traditional lands in the space of 10 years. Liza Grandia, 'Fronteras de Progreso o Desarrollo de Pobreza? Dinámicas

problems that are outweighed by the potential benefits of regime change as a whole. Rather, given the potential losses to individuals, households, and local economies, it seems important to ask what contingency plans are in place. What would constitute adequate protection? And are there reasons that the loss of land might bite deeper for women than men? For example, ongoing obligations of care for others make the consequences both more serious for women and the wider community, while more limited options in the labor market mean that the loss of land is more likely to lead to poverty for women than for men.

While the answers will vary from context to context, it seems clear that the effort to push people from subsistence labor into wage labor or simply into more productive market opportunities needs more attention if gender inequality is not to be exacerbated. The emergence of new labor markets almost invariably produces a range of gender-specific problems, and occupational segregation is endemic everywhere. It will almost certainly induce the continued dislocation of people from rural to urban areas. Apart from the capacity of urban markets to absorb this labor, something that cannot be assumed, rural-urban migration often implies the dissolution of households, the disruption to household income, and a greater workload for women. Once these costs are accounted for, how does the cost/benefit calculation come out? What might be needed to redress these concerns?

What about the regulation of land use once land is commercialized? Environmental degradation is a pressing concern, especially when transformation of land use is at issue, as land may be rendered effectively unusable for its original purposes. In light of these well-documented problems, is it responsible, even from a purely economic standpoint, to promote more intensified commercial use of land without adequate regulation in place? Can the presumption against the regulation of land be simply reduced to the question of government capacity or failure?[81] Where capacity to adequately regulate land use really is a problem, might it change the assessment of whether more intense commercialization is a good thing in the first place?

6.7 CONTESTING PROPERTY REGIMES

The foregoing questions do not mean that property rights in land should not be formalized or transformed, or that new, more productive commercial uses of land should not be pursued. However, they do indicate why the efforts to

Fronterizas de la Migración Q'eqchi' a las Tierras Bajas de Petén, Izabal, y Belice en el Contexto de Globalización Corporativa', Centro Universitario de el Petén, CUDEP, Universidad de San Carlos, Guatemala, 6 March 2004, paper on file with the author.

[81] World Bank, *Land Policies for Growth and Poverty Reduction*, above n. 10.

strengthen property rights, without more and in the context of weakened state regulation, may well generate greater gender inequality as well as a host of other social problems.

If the aim is to promote the transferability of interests in land, a range of rules and policies beyond simple propertization need to be implemented simultaneously if the furtherance of gender equality and other social objectives is to be taken seriously. Unless the only metric is their functionality in the context of global markets, the merits of property regimes cannot be determined at the abstract level. The question is not merely land rights, but their place in the larger regulatory scheme, their connection to different development trajectories, and their interaction with other normative orders, including human rights. In order to assess their relation to gender empowerment, we need to ask who is likely to benefit under these schemes and why. If the egalitarian and distributive concerns seem compelling, we should be prepared to either reconsider the regimes themselves or institute compensatory rules and mechanisms to address these concerns.

There are numerous human rights principles that might be invoked to counter property reforms that have an adverse effect on the empowerment of women.[82] Arguably, the right to equality and non-discrimination contained in the international covenants and conventions provides a basis upon which to contest any regulatory strategy which has the effect, if not the purpose, of impairing the relative status of women.[83] Depending on the circumstances, such rights might also be invoked to advance property regimes that differ from the current regulatory ideal. Because access to economic resources influences so many things—from social and family status to educational opportunities, political participation, and market opportunities—the structure of property reforms is likely to intersect with the full range of women's human rights concerns at numerous points. And since women are critical to the well-being of so many communities, the de facto linchpin in the achievement of social and economic rights, the possible lines of interest and connection between property regimes and human rights are virtually limitless.

What should be stressed is that no single conception of property or set of institutional reforms in respect of land can be associated with gender empowerment, either negatively or positively; rather, their relationship may be more contingent than we normally suppose. Figuring out the relationship between property regimes and gender empowerment is not a simple task: as

---

[82] Robert Wai, 'Countering, Branding, Dealing: Using Social Rights in and around the International Trade Regime', 14 *European Journal of International Law* 35 (2003).

[83] International Covenant on Civil and Political Rights (ICCPR), G.A. res. 2200A (XXI), 21 U.N. GAOR Supp. (No. 16) at 52, U.N. Doc. A/6316 (1966), 999 U.N.T.S. 171, *entered into force* 23 March 1976, Articles 2, 26; International Covenant on Economic, Social and Cultural Rights (ICESCR), G.A. res. 2200A (XXI), 21 U.N. GAOR Supp. (No. 16) at 49, U.N. Doc. A/6316 (1966), 993 U.N.T.S. 3, *entered into force* 3 January 1976, Articles 2, 3.

the discussion has indicated, there are a wide variety of factors that can complicate the calculus. However, the complexities of land reform suggest that some of the conventional assumptions in the field of human rights need to be revisited. For example, although cultural norms that discriminate against equal land rights for women are typically the object of concern from the standpoint of human rights,[84] such assumptions may be part of the problem rather than the solution in the context of current property reforms. Customary property rights may be fluid and/or disputed, cultural and formal norms may be overlapping rather than distinct,[85] and the formalization of title, even when accompanied by gender equality norms, may leave women worse off. When the vagaries of adjudication are taken into consideration too, it becomes progressively more problematic to assume that culture rather than formal law is the problem.

Moreover, there will be unavoidable conflicts, both within the framework of human rights and when other legal rights are at stake. In courts of human rights, indigenous groups have successfully invoked property rights against outsiders seeking to exploit the commercial potential of traditional lands.[86] However, both in courts of general jurisdiction and specialized trade and investment dispute tribunals, there are far more instances in which investors have invoked property rights to limit competing claims or exclude other concerns, many of which, such as labor or environmental rights, are germane to the concerns of the human rights community. Hence, human rights advocates arguing that taking 'all appropriate means' to progressively realize human rights requires a reconsideration of property rights should expect powerful and well-articulated response from those who argue that a straight line runs from property rights through economic growth to enhanced human welfare and human rights. Similarly, those arguing for an idea of non-discrimination and equality focused on effects rather than intent or form will run up against the opportunity models of equality[87] and other 'market-friendly' notions of human rights now so popular among the international financial and economic institutions.[88]

Although they are foundational to liberal conceptions of freedom and rights,[89] and hence the origins of human rights, property rights have received much less direct consideration in the field of human rights than they have in

[84] See for example, CEDAW, Article 2 (f).

[85] Nyamu, 'How Should Human Rights and Development Respond to Cultural Legitimization for Gender Hierarchy in Developing Countries?', above n. 59.

[86] *Mayagna (Sumo) Awas Tingni Community v. Nicaragua*, Inter-American Court of Human Rights, Series C, Case No. 79, Judgment of 31 August 2001.

[87] See, for example, World Bank, *Engendering Development*, above n. 6.

[88] Philip Alston, 'The Myopia of the Handmaidens: International Lawyers and Globalization', 3 *European Journal of International Law* 435 (1997); Upendra Baxi, 'Voices of Suffering and the Future of Human Rights', 8 *Transnational Law and Contemporary Problems* 125, (1998).

[89] John Locke, *Second Treatise of Government* (Indianapolis, Ind.: Hackett Pub. Co., 1980).

the field of development. While justifications for current property reforms can be found in countless pieces of development literature, there is no analysis of property that is of equivalent depth, breadth, or prominence within human rights doctrine and literature. One reason is that the status and degree of protection that should be afforded to property rights have been highly contentious in the international order. Prior to 1989, no international agreement on such issues would have been possible, given that the geo-strategic divisions among states of the post-World War Two era also tracked deep differences in their internal economic organization. Much of the controversy over the New International Economic Order, too, concerned property, revolving around issues such as the status of natural resources and the degree of compensation to be paid in the course of nationalization and expropriation.[90] Although the protection of private property was a key issue in the social and political transformation of post-communist states,[91] the nature and extent of property rights, especially those granted to investors, continue to generate conflict and resistance.[92]

Property rights are protean. Rather than merely accept the argument that particular property regimes are essential to the protection of civil liberties, democratic freedom, and the promotion of social and economic rights, those in the human rights community need to approach these claims with a skeptical eye and develop a nuanced appreciation of the larger issues to which they are often connected. We might ask, for example, who is calling for such rights, in what context, and why? When do calls for the protection of property further the project of greater social or distributive justice, and when do they advance other interests? When are they signposts of governance regimes that have already been identified as problematic from the standpoint of human rights because, for example, they function as arguments against other forms of legal regulation or protection that might otherwise appear both desirable and available?

In addition, human rights scholars need to continue to draw attention to the actual distribution of assets. Although the promotion of property reforms is conventionally separated from this question, it is critical to insist upon the

---

[90] Mohammed Bedjaoui, *Towards a New International Economic Order* (New York: Holmes and Meier, 1979); Thomas W. Walde, 'A Requiem for the "New International Economic Order"—The Rise and Fall of Paradigms in International Economic Law', in N. Al-Nauimi and R. Meese, eds, *International Legal Issues Arising under the United Nations Decade of International Law* (Kluwer Law International, 1995) 1301.

[91] G. Alexander and G. Skapska, 'Introduction', in G. Alexander and G. Skapska, eds, *A Fourth Way? Privatization, Property and the Emergence of the New Market Economies* (London: Routledge, 1994).

[92] For a discussion of the concerns around investor protections granted under NAFTA and the general trend towards the 'constitutionalization' of investment protections, see David Schneiderman, 'Investment Rules and the New Constitutionalism', 25 *Law and Social Inquiry* 757 (2000).

connection between them in order to assess whether, and how much, the protection of property rights is likely to advance the human rights claim at stake.

If there is useful analytic territory that could be staked out in respect of property, an important part of it lies in resisting the advance of neo-formalist ideas about property rights. Against this tide, human rights scholars and others need to elucidate the range of available choices about property rights and to try to make as clear as possible what is at stake for particular groups and issues in the decisions that are made. In addition to demonstrating their impact on human rights concerns, it is also crucial for human rights advocates to contest the functionalist explanations that circulate in the realm of development policy about the nature of property rights. Whatever their role in enhancing efficiency, the idea that particular legal regimes can be reduced to, or explained by, efficiency considerations has long been challenged and discredited in legal thought.[93] This is particularly important as such instrumentalist ideas are powerfully entrenched, both discursively and institutionally, in the development agenda. The point is not merely of theoretical interest. What fall from view when functionalist explanations dominate the discussion of property rights are precisely the concerns most of interest through the lens of human rights: questions of power, conflict, equality, and disadvantage.

To reiterate, property rights are the question, not the answer. For the purposes of human rights, it is important to insist that neither the structure nor the content of property regimes can be assured in advance, and they cannot be divorced from the larger regulatory matrix of which they are a part. The status of property rights cannot be untethered from their distributive consequences, consequences which are in turn contingent upon myriad other norms and facts specific to each context.

No single conception of the right to property will suffice to either advance or protect all the interests that might be at stake in a human rights claim. Because property regimes are inseparable from the basic structure and character of societies that they regulate and help constitute, it is hard to imagine that any single conception would be desirable.

Because of the impact that property rights can have on a wide range of egalitarian and distributive objectives, human rights scholars need to become much better versed in the structure, history, and operation of property law in particular contexts, and the counter-arguments to current claims that might be available. While they may not be able to hope to match the resources that are currently devoted to establishing the centrality of property rights to development, there is much analysis in the common law tradition that human rights scholars could usefully recuperate to ensure that efforts to

[93] Robert Gordon, 'Critical Legal Histories', 36 *Stanford Law Journal* 57 (1984).

address complex problems of social ordering and social justice are not defeated by simplistic conceptions of property.

One such source is the realist and post-realist literature referred to earlier.[94] Another is the important emerging literature on the colonial antecedents of contemporary economic norms, practices, and institutions,[95] much of which is indispensable to understanding the context and reception of contemporary development and legal reform projects. As this analysis reveals, there are more and less useful approaches to unpacking property rights, especially where the issue is the relationship between property rights and wider questions of economic and social justice. Property rights need to be approached as relational constructs that both empower and disempower at the same time. The domains of sovereignty they create may provide protection or create risk; they can create both wealth and impoverishment simultaneously.

At the end of the day, many debates over property rights can be understood as proxies for struggles over the character and shape of social life. Sometimes property reforms will be congruent with human rights goals, sometimes they will be neutral with respect to those goals, and sometimes they will conflict with those goals. If there is an overemphasis on property rights in development, perhaps the problem in the field of human rights is the reverse. But whatever the position that advocates might stake out on any particular issue, the human rights community should take their rising significance in the field of development as a sign of their increasing relevance to the field of human rights as well.

[94] See Greg Alexander, *Commodity and Propriety: Competing Visions of Property in American Legal Thought, 1776–1970* (1997); Singer, *Entitlements: The Paradoxes of Property*, above n. 50.
[95] Antony Anghie, 'Time Present and Time Past: Globalization, International Financial Institutions, and the Third World', 32 *New York University Journal of International Law and Politics* 243 (2000); Antony Anghie, 'Colonialism and the Birth of International Institutions: Sovereignty, Economy, and the Mandate System of the League of Nations', 34 *New York University Journal of International Law and Politics* 513 (2002).

7

The Development Impact of Gender Equality in Land Rights

KAREN O. MASON AND
HELENE M. CARLSSON

7.1 INTRODUCTION

One of the most common forms of gender inequality in the developing world is men's disproportionate control of land and real property. Even in regions where women farm independently of men and produce a majority of the food crops, women's claim to land is typically indirect or insecure. In these regions, when husbands die or disappear, wives often lose their access to land or are forced to engage in costly and often unsuccessful legal struggles to retain their rights to it. Because women collectively represent an enormous productive potential and often invest their resources in ways that result in better economic and social outcomes than men do, women's lack of secure claim to land has undesirable consequences for development and human well-being as well as for women's own empowerment. Strengthening women's land rights can set in motion a wide range of social and economic benefits that are likely to improve the quality of life for all citizens.

The advent of industrialization and other forms of high-value production have made wealth less dependent on land ownership than it once was, but land remains one of the most valuable resources in both urban and rural economies. In rural areas, land is the primary vehicle for generating a livelihood and is a key element of household wealth. Indeed, in some areas of the world, whether rural households have title to land is a fundamental determinant of whether they are poor. In urban areas, land ownership also helps to determine the economic status of households. Because land remains an important economic resource, disparities in land rights affect equality, growth, and well-being. Unequal title to land is thus an important issue in economic development.

This chapter focuses specifically on gender disparities in land rights. In the chapter, we identify the reasons why secure rights to land generally enhance sustainable development and human well-being; document gender disparities in the control of land and discuss some of the factors that underlie these disparities; and describe the specific benefits to be gained by ensuring gender equality in rights to land. The chapter also makes policy recommendations to enhance women's title to land and the benefits that this secure titling can bring. Because we are interested in the broad development implications of gender inequality in land ownership and control, not in the legal or philosophical specifics of women's human rights to land, we use such terms as land rights and land ownership interchangeably.

Although the chapter focuses on the welfare rationale for ensuring women's land rights, existing human rights conventions make clear that rights to land are one of women's human rights. The Convention on the Elimination of All Forms of Discrimination Against Women (CEDAW), which was adopted by the General Assembly in 1979,[1] is regarded as the most important international bill of rights of women, both because it spells out women's rights in detail and because it is binding on governments that ratify it. As of March 2004, over 90 per cent of the members of the United Nations (177 countries) were party to the Convention.[2] CEDAW requires states to eliminate discrimination against women in the enjoyment of all civil, political, economic, and cultural rights. In article 14, it explicitly calls on states to 'take all appropriate measures to eliminate discrimination against women in rural areas' by ensuring to these women 'the right to . . . equal treatment in land and agrarian reform as well as in land resettlement schemes'. Thus, although CEDAW does not explicitly state that *all* rights to land should be equal between women and men, it makes clear through its general requirements and its specific statements about rural women's rights that women have equal rights to land with men. CEDAW's full potential is still to be realized, but in several cases it has been used successfully to persuade domestic courts to uphold women's rights to land. One such case was in Tanzania:

In *Ephrohim v. Pastory*, a Tanzanian woman named Holaria Pastory challenged Haya customary law, which prevented her from selling clan land. Pastory had inherited clan land from her father, but when she tried to sell the land, her nephew applied to have the sale voided. Tanzania's Declaration of Customary Law stated that 'women can inherit, except for clan land, which they may receive in usufruct but may not sell', thereby prohibiting Pastory's sale of the land. In making its decision, the court relied on the Government of Tanzania's ratification

---

[1] G.A. res. 34/180, 34 U.N. GAOR Supp. (No. 46) at 193, U.N. Doc. A/34/46, *entered into force* 3 September 1981.

[2] United Nations, CEDAW website, Division for the Advancement of Women. http://www.un.org/womenwatch/daw/cedaw/.

of CEDAW, as well as the African Charter on Human and Peoples' Rights, and found that women were constitutionally protected from discrimination. The court eventually overruled customary law.

Source: UNIFEM, *Bringing Equality Home: Implementing the Convention on All Forms of Discrimination Against Women, CEDAW* (New York: UNIFEM, 1998).

7.2 WHY LAND RIGHTS ARE IMPORTANT FOR SUSTAINABLE DEVELOPMENT

Throughout history, land has been a primary source of wealth, social status, and power. For both rural and urban populations, land continues to be a key asset, providing the foundation for economic activity and household survival, especially in poorer households. In Uganda, for example, land constitutes between 50 and 60 per cent of the asset endowment of the poorest households.[3] And in India, landlessness, poverty, and status as a *dalit* (untouchable) are often strongly correlated, making landless *dalits* the poorest of the poor in many communities.

There are several reasons why strengthening the land rights of the rural poor can increase their wealth and welfare, and contribute to economic growth and development. One reason is that secure land rights are often a necessary condition for the rural poor to invest in their land to increase its productivity and economic value. If claims to land are uncertain, households living at the margin are unlikely to see the value of—or feel they can afford—investing precious resources in soil quality, irrigation systems, or higher value crops that require expensive inputs or offer delayed economic returns (e.g., tree crops). With insecure tenure, it may well be the landlord who benefits from these investments rather than the poor household itself.

In addition, insecure tenure may also increase the probability of becoming embroiled in land conflicts. Such conflicts increase the need to spend scarce resources on defending land rights (for example, by investing in guards, fences, or other demarcation devices), rather than using these resources for productive investments.[4]

The under-investment induced by insecure tenure not only results in lower incomes for the landed poor, it also lowers total aggregate output. Secure land tenure for the rural poor thus can improve their economic status and produce higher per capita rates of economic output in the community.

Studies in many different parts of the developing world have found that secure title to land is positively correlated with agricultural investments and

---

[3] K. Deininger, *Land Policies, Growth and Poverty Reduction* (Washington D.C.: Oxford University Press for the World Bank, 2003) 17.　　　　　[4] Ibid. 23.

outputs. For example, Jacoby, Li, and Rozelle[5] compared plots planted with the same crop by the same household under different tenure systems in China, Pakistan, and Vietnam, and found that farmers tend to apply more labor and manure and obtain significantly higher yields on plots that are privately owned and are therefore more secure. Similarly, in Ghana, one study found that plots with greater transferability (interpreted as more secure tenure) increased the probability that individuals would plant trees and undertake a wide range of other investments such as drainage, irrigation, and mulching.[6] In Thailand, a study found that gaining title to land induced higher investment in farming capital. As a result, output was 14–25 per cent higher on titled land than on untitled land of equal quality.[7]

A second, closely related reason that secure land rights promote development is the enhanced ability to access credit when rights to land are secure and fully transferable. Poor households that lack secure and easily transferable ownership rights to land are unlikely to have the collateral to secure the substantial loans needed to install irrigation systems or invest in expensive, high-value crops. Evidence from Thailand and Honduras, for example, shows that holders of land titles have three-to-four times the access to credit as those without title to their land.[8] To be sure, where financial markets are underdeveloped or non-existent, tenure security is less likely to have an impact on access to credit, but, for the majority of the world's rural poor, secure land title increases access to credit and hence facilitates increased agricultural productivity.[9]

Secure land rights also encourage conservation and environmental sustainability, as people tend to be more inclined to adopt environmentally friendly practices where they can be confident that the land will remain in their hands for the long haul. In India, for example, investments in conservation are much lower on leased plots and on plots that are subject to sales restrictions than on plots to which owners have full, secure title.[10] In Brazil,

---

[5] H. G. Jacoby, G. Li, and S. Rozelle, 'Hazards of Expropriation: Tenure Insecurity and Investment in Rural Chile' 92 *American Economics Review* 1420 (2002).

[6] T. Besley, 'Property Rights and Investment Incentives: Theory and Evidence from Ghana' 103 *Journal of Political Economy* 903 (1995).

[7] G. Feder, *Land Policies and Farm Productivity in Thailand* (Baltimore and London: The Johns Hopkins University Press, 1988).

[8] G. Feder, 'The Intricacies of Land Markets: Why the World Bank Succeeds in Economic Reform through Land Registration and Tenure Security', paper presented at the Conference of the International Federation of Surveyors, 19–26 April 2002, Washington D.C.

[9] A recent presentation at the World Bank by Renee Giovarelli, a land rights expert, noted that banks are often unwilling to lend to women who hold title to land, but who do not have other obvious sources of income, because of the high costs of amortizing collateral in cases of loan default. Giovarelli agreed, however, that land ownership is often a necessary, even if not sufficient, condition for accessing credit.

[10] J. Pender and J. Kerr, 'Determinants of Farmers' Indigenous Soil and Water Conservation in Semi-Arid India' 19 *Agricultural Economist* 113 (1998).

tenure insecurity has been identified as a key factor in deforestation.[11] Where households hold full title to their land, they are less likely to strip it of trees than where tenure is insecure.

Secure tenure may also contribute to the welfare of poor households by providing a form of insurance that can be used in the event of shocks or economic distress. Illness, the death of a breadwinner, or an economic crisis can leave landless households with few resources to fall back on; in these circumstances, landowning households may be able to sell or lease out land in order to tide them through the crisis. Such income smoothing can benefit households and, if the shock is widely shared, may help to maintain the health of the local economy (although this depends on the availability of buyers for distress land sales).

Measures to increase households' and individuals' ability to control land can also empower them, give them greater voice in the community and create the basis for more participatory, democratic local development. Where households have reason to believe that raising their voice will undermine their access to land and other resources, they are much less likely to do so.[12] Although secure tenure does not guarantee voice or power in local affairs, it helps reduce a fundamental form of insecurity faced by many poor households.[13]

The value of secure tenure cuts across both rural and urban sectors of the economy. The United Nations Centre for Human Settlements, for example, has identified secure tenure as one of the most important catalysts for stabilizing urban communities.[14] Squatter settlements in urban or peri-urban areas whose occupants are under threat of eviction are, like their rural counterparts, less likely to invest in improved infrastructure, permanent housing, and community amenities than are the urban poor living on land to which they have clear rights. Thus, in both urban and rural areas, secure rights to land, especially for poor families, offers benefits not only to these families, but to the economy and society as a whole.

7.3 THE PREVALENCE AND CAUSES OF GENDER INEQUALITY IN LAND RIGHTS

In all regions of the world, evidence of large gender disparities in land ownership exists. For example, data for five Latin American countries (Brazil,

---

[11] A. Cattaneo, 'Deforestation in the Brazilian Amazon: Comparing the Impacts of Macroeconomic Shocks, Land Tenure, and Technological Change' 77 *Land Economics* 219 (2001).   [12] Deininger, above n. 3, 3.

[13] D. Narayan, with R. Patel, K. Schafft, A. Rademacher, and S. Koch-Shulte, *Voices of the Poor: Can Anyone Hear Us?* (Oxford: Oxford University Press for the World Bank, 2000).

[14] United Nations Centre for Human Settlements, *The Global Campaign for Secure Tenure* (Geneva: UNCHS, 1999).

Table 7.1 *Distribution of landowners by gender, various countries, and years*

Country & year	Women	Men	Couple	Total	N
Brazil, 2000[a]	11.0	89.0	—	100.0	39,904
Mexico, 2003[b]	22.4	77.6	—	100.0	2.9 m
Nicaragua, 1995[c]	15.5	80.9	3.6	100.0	839
Paraguay, 2001[d]	27.0	69.6	3.2	100.0	1,694
Peru, 2000[e]	12.7	74.4	12.8	100.0	1,923

N—The number of units in each category.
a—For farms larger than 50 ha., derived from Censo Comunitario Rural 2000, Confedracao Nacional Agraria, Brasilia.
b—Ejido sector only, includes ejidatarios, posesionarios, and arecindados.
c—Excludes members of production co-operatives, FIDEG rural household survey.
d—Based on households with land titles, derived from LSMS, MECOVI survey, 2000–2001.
e—Based on distribution of ownership of titled land parcels: excludes non-household members. Derived from LSMS, ENNVI survey 2000.

Source: C. D. Deere and M. Leon, 'The Gender Asset Gap: Land in Latin America' 31 *World Development* 925 (2003).

Mexico, Nicaragua, Paraguay, and Peru) show that women constitute one-third or less of all landowners (Table 7.1).[15] In Brazil, women are only 11 per cent of the landowners, while in Paraguay—which has the highest percentage of female landowners among the five countries—women make up 30 per cent of all owners. In a region where gender disparities on most human development indicators are relatively small, and inheritance laws relatively egalitarian, gender differences in land ownership nonetheless stand out.

Similar differences in land ownership by gender exist in other regions of the world. In Cameroon, where women make up more than 51 per cent of the population and do more than 75 per cent of the agricultural work, only 3.2 per cent of all land titles in the Northwest Province and 7.2 per cent in the Southwest Province are held by women. For the country as whole, women are estimated to hold under 10 per cent of all land certificates.[16]

Household surveys in Kenya and Nigeria show that women have substantially less control over land disposition than men do. For example, only about 30 per cent of female household heads in Kenya and Nigeria have the right to sell the land they are using, compared to about 60 per cent of male heads.[17] A 1960s study of the ownership of 960 plots of land in three villages

[15] C. D. Deere and M. Leon, 'The Gender Asset Gap: Land in Latin America' 31 *World Development* 925 (2003).
[16] World Bank, *Towards Gender Equality: The Role of Public Policy* (Washington D.C.: World Bank, 1995).
[17] K. Saito, with H. Mekonnen and D. Spurling, *Raising the Productivity of Women Farmers in Sub-Saharan Africa*, World Bank Discussion Papers 230, Africa Technical Department Series (Washington D.C.: World Bank, 1994).

in a district of Tanzania found that men owned 61 per cent of the plots.[18] A 1994 survey in rural Punjab, Pakistan found that only 36 women owned land in their own name across the 1,000 households that were surveyed.[19] A 2001 household survey in Pakistan showed that women own only 2.8 per cent of the plots, even though 67 per cent of the sampled villages reported that women have a right to inherit land.[20]

There are many reasons for the existence of gender inequality in rights to land. Ultimately, inequality in land rights reflects traditional norms about the appropriate roles and rights of the sexes, the way that family relationships are structured, and the resulting economic and power inequalities between males and females. Where men are defined as the breadwinners and heads of household while women are defined as men's dependents, responsible for child care and other household consumption work, inheritance of land almost invariably favors male heirs. Even when women are recognized as important breadwinners—as is the case in much of sub-Saharan Africa—the conditions under which women gain access to land often leaves them with less secure land rights than men enjoy.

What are some of the specific determinants of gender inequality in land rights that are potentially amenable to policy intervention? Although factors influencing the gender-based distribution of land rights tend to be highly context specific, general determinants that are important across a variety of settings include (i) inheritance laws, either customary or statutory, (ii) the manner in which land reforms are effected, (iii) the concept of the 'head of household' and its application in land titling, and (iv) the economic inequality of males and females in land markets. We discuss each of these in turn.

7.3.1 Inheritance Laws

In most family systems found in the developing world, inheritance laws favor male heirs. A majority of the world's family systems are implicitly or explicitly organized on patrilineal principles, meaning that it is male heirs who represent the continuity of the family across the generations and who are therefore seen as the right and fitting ones to inherit land, particularly if it is an important basis on which the family gains its livelihood. For example, in much of South Asia and East Asia, the ideal family was traditionally a multigenerational extended unit in which one or more adult sons continued

---

[18] E. Boserup, *Woman's Role in Economic Development*, (New York: St. Martin's Press, 1970) 59.

[19] S. Kazi, 'Gender Inequalities and Development in Pakistan' in S. R. Khan, ed., *Fifty Years of Pakistan's Economy* (Oxford: Oxford University Press, 1999).

[20] World Bank, *Gender Assessment for Pakistan* (Washington D.C.: World Bank, 2003).

to live with their parents along with their wives and children. In these systems, the land that was the basis for the economic support of the multi-generational family naturally devolved to sons after the death of the parents. Daughters had no status as heirs, either in relation to their own parents or to their husband's parents. Although many Asian societies have seen considerable change in family relations in recent decades,[21] the tendency to favor sons in inheritance remains strong, especially in rural agrarian families.

Although patrilineal family systems are far more common than are matrilineal systems, the latter are found in parts of Southeast Asia, in the state of Kerala in India, in areas of Sri Lanka, and in some sub-Saharan groups (e.g., the Akan groups in Ghana). Land is inherited through the female line in these systems, meaning that children inherit land via their mothers rather than their fathers. It is important to recognize, however, that this method of determining inheritance does not necessarily give women ownership or control of land. Indeed, in some matrilineal family systems, it is males who control the family's land—land they have inherited from their mother's brother rather than from their father, and which their sisters' sons will in turn inherit from them. Matrilineal inheritance *can* give women stronger rights to land than men enjoy. For example, among the Lemba of Zaïre, women inherit land from their parents, and it is they, not men, who continue to live in their natal villages after marriage and who allow their husbands to use their land for farming.[22] But it does not necessarily give women control of land.

Islamic law provides more explicit rights and protections for women in inheritance than do many traditional systems of inheritance. Shar'ia law specifies that daughters should inherit one-half of what sons inherit. Although this division is more even-handed than in many customary systems, it does not always result in the ownership of land by females. Many families choose to pass real property to sons while providing daughters with movable property (sometimes in the form of a dowry—movable property that the bride's parents contribute for the support of their daughter and son-in-law in return for the land that the son-in-law brings to the marriage). In other settings, daughters typically cede their claims to land in favor of their brothers on the understanding that, if they are widowed or abandoned by their husbands, the brother will take them in. Thus, among most Muslim

---

[21] L.-J. Cho and M. Yada, *Tradition and Change in the Asian Family* (Honolulu, HI: University of Hawaii Press for the East-West Center, 1994); K. O. Mason, N. O. Tsuya, and M. K. Choe, *The Changing Family in Comparative Perspective: Asia and the United States* (Honolulu, HI: University of Hawaii Press for the East-West Center, 1998); A. Thornton and H.-S. Lin, *Social Change & the Family in Taiwan* (Chicago, IL and London: University of Chicago Press, 1994).

[22] Similar practices exist in parts of South East Asia, for example, in Thailand. There, the youngest daughter traditionally remained with her parents, her husband moved in with her, and, after the death of the parents, the daughter inherited the house and land.

groups, despite the formal protections to women's interests offered by the shar'ia, gender disparities on land ownership favoring males are the norm.

7.3.2 Land Reforms

The manner in which land reforms are conducted can influence gender equality in land ownership. In many instances, these reforms have either reinforced or exacerbated gender inequality in rights to land. More than thirty years ago, Ester Boserup[23] noted that efforts by the colonial powers in sub-Saharan Africa to formalize land ownership during the nineteenthth and early twentieth centuries deprived women of title to land, thereby undermining their traditional use rights. Because the colonial powers had Western ideas about gender roles—man the breadwinner, woman the caregiver—they gave title to men on the erroneous assumption that only men were farmers. In several instances, female farmers were so enraged that they rioted—but to little avail.

Even recent land reforms have often favored men. For example, in Kenya, the introduction of statutory inheritance laws endangered widows' entitlement to the use of land owned by their husbands. Sons who inherit land now can legally sell it without their mother's permission, often leaving widows without a livelihood.[24]

Fortunately, in some instances, land reforms have been conducted in a way that has resulted in women's increased ownership of land. Costa Rica, for example, undertook a land reform in the early 1990s that resulted in the proportion of female title holders rising from 12 to 45 per cent. Similarly, in Colombia the percentage of land under adjudication that was jointly titled rose from 18 to 60 per cent in just one year after a 1995 ruling on joint titling.[25] The success of these programs suggests that land reforms that are designed to reduce gender disparities in land ownership can, indeed, accomplish this goal.

7.3.3 The Concept of the Household Head

One reason that land reforms and the introduction of formal land titling has resulted in gender disparities in land ownership is a heavy reliance on

---

[23] Boserup, above n. 18, ch. 3.

[24] J. Davidson, ed., *Agriculture, Women and Land: The African Experience* (Boulder, CO: Westview Press, 1988).

[25] Although Latin America has relatively egalitarian traditions compared to many other world regions, not all land reforms in Latin American countries have improved gender equality in land rights. In Bolivia and Ecuador, for example, there was no movement toward joint titling or special rights for women during the negotiations in the 1990s that led to new agrarian codes.

the concept of the family or household head—and the designation of this head as the 'natural' or fitting holder of the title. In many countries, the registration of property is only allowed in the name of one person, with the result that the male household head is chosen as the one person. This practice has been as common in countries with official policies of gender equality—for example, the transition countries in Eastern Europe and Vietnam—as in countries without such policies. Even where there is no formal prohibition to joint titling, government officials and householders themselves often conceive of the household head as the individual to whom land should be titled. Because most formal or customary systems define the husband the household head if the household contains both a husband and wife—even when the husband is absent due to labor migration or the wife is the primary agriculturalist—men end up owning a disproportionate share of the land.

One example of how the concept of the household head and land registration initiatives together can deprive women of title to land is found in the Lao People's Democratic Republic. The Laos Forest Law of 1996 and the Land Law of 1997 provide a comprehensive legal framework for land use and ownership rights. Both laws are intended to be gender neutral: women are neither explicitly excluded from nor included in land allocation and titling processes. In practice, however, land titling and other registration procedures use official forms that ask for the head of household. So although custom allows Laotian women to inherit land from their parents, the legal documents that are gradually supplanting customary property rights exclude women from land ownership. As a result, men are acquiring greater control of land at the expense of women.[26]

Examples of land titling that give both women and men rights to use land are emerging, however. The following describes a pilot project in Vietnam that gave wives and husbands equal claims to land:

A pilot project in north central Vietnam sponsored by the World Bank has instituted an approach to land titling that gives both women and men rights to land. Before the pilot, Land Tenure Certificates (LTCs) had space for only one name per family, and since registrants were usually the male head of the household or the husband, the policy resulted in male control of land, despite the gender neutrality of the national policy. To recognize the interests of both women and men, the pilot project re-issued LTCs, with space for more than one name per family, for households in two rural communes in Nghe An Province. In partnership with the local government, leaflets about laws on gender equality in

[26] M. Viravong, 'Reinforcing Property Rights in Laos' in I. Tinker and G. Summerfield, eds., *Women's Rights to House and Land (China, Laos, Vietnam)* (Boulder, CO: Lynn Reinner Publishers, 1999).

land use rights were printed and distributed. Village meetings and loudspeakers were also instrumental in spreading the word about the new LTCs. The Land Tenure Certificates now bear the names of both the husband and wife. As joint holders of LTCs, women and men can both take advantage of the opportunities that such property rights entail for the well-being of the rural economy.

Source: World Bank, *Promising Approaches to Engendering Development: Land Use Rights and Gender Equality in Vietnam* (Washington D.C.: World Bank, 2002).

7.3.4 Inequality in Land Markets

The final cause of gender disparities in land ownership found across a range of countries is inequality between women and men in their ability to participate successfully as buyers in land markets. Women tend to have less bargaining power in markets than men do for several reasons: (a) because they earn less money than men due to labor market discrimination or because of the time poverty that arises from their responsibility for most household chores; (b) because they typically have less control over the use of the household's economic resources than male household members do; (c) because they are excluded from informal networks through which sales may be arranged or bargains struck to lower the price to buyers; and (d) because both women and men tend to regard the man as the head of the household who rightfully should represent the household in the market place.

The result of these inequalities is that women find it more difficult to compete successfully as buyers in land markets than men do. Even in settings where women are legally able to purchase and own title to land, and where they enjoy relatively equal rights with men, the underlying economic and social inequalities between the sexes may result in male dominance in land markets. For example, evidence from *hacienda* land sales in Peru in the 1950s and 1960s found that women tended to buy smaller parcels and paid higher prices than men for land of similar size and quality.[27]

In summary, many factors that reflect normative traditions about the roles of women and men and the structure of family relations result in women having fewer rights to land and less land ownership than men. In the next section, we trace some of the consequences of this inequality in land titling—for women themselves and for the economic well-being of the society at large.

[27] C. D. Deere, 'Institutional Reform of Agriculture under Neoliberalism: The Impacts of the Women's Indigenous Movements', keynote address prepared for the Centre for Latin American Research and Documentations, Research School for Resources Studies for Development, and Wageningen Agricultural University conference on 'Land in Latin America: New Context, New Claims, New Concepts', Amsterdam, 26–27 May 1999.

7.4 THE IMPACTS OF GENDER INEQUALITY IN LAND RIGHTS

This section examines the impact of women's and men's unequal control of land on women's empowerment, economic growth, and the well-being of men, women, and children. The general conclusion suggested by the available evidence is that greater gender equality in land rights helps to empower women and enhances economic growth and human well-being.

7.4.1 Women's Empowerment

Although there are no simple formulas for empowering women, most observers agree that control of assets or productive resources is likely to contribute to women's empowerment. Because land remains a valuable asset in both rural and urban settings, greater equality in ownership of land would presumably help to empower women vis-à-vis men. This idea is consistent with recent microeconomic analyses of intra-household bargaining, which suggest that command over economic resources such as assets, unearned income, and transfer payments increase an individual's bargaining power within the household.[28] Women's ownership of land is thus likely to empower them vis-à-vis other household members, particularly husbands or other adult men.

One issue on which the literature provides little guidance is the consequences for women's empowerment of joint husband–wife land titling versus sole titling of a portion of their land in the name of the wife. Although one might speculate that sole titling would be more empowering than joint titling, at least in settings where the state is able to enforce title to land, such effects are likely to be highly contingent on women's access to the state's legal and judicial machinery, the extent to which they have other economic opportunities, their attitudes about their roles and rights, and their voice in community decision making, among other factors. Research that compares joint versus single titling of land across comparable settings would be very helpful for understanding the land policies most likely to empower women.

7.4.2 Economic Growth and Human Well-Being

Gender equality in rights to land tends to enhance economic growth and improve human well-being for two principal reasons. The first is that,

---

[28] S. Lundberg and R. A. Pollak, 'Bargaining and Distribution in Marriage' 10 *Journal of Economic Perspectives* 139 (1996).

contrary to the widespread stereotype of men as the breadwinners, rural women often are major producers of food. Conditions that enable them to increase their productivity therefore increase agricultural outputs, including those used to feed family members. The second reason is the universal tendency for women to invest more heavily than men in the well-being of their children and other family members. Resources that enable women to generate income therefore tend to improve the 'quality' of the next generation and enhance the potential for economic growth by improving the stock of human capital. Although estimates of the magnitude of these effects are not available, in sub-Saharan Africa, the effects appear to be large and particularly critical in light of the AIDS pandemic.

7.4.2.1 Women as Food Producers

Rural women are estimated to be responsible for half the world's food production, and in developing countries produce 60–80 per cent of the food. In Asia, between 50 and 90 per cent of the work in rice fields is done by women, and in sub-Saharan Africa and the Caribbean women produce up to 80 per cent of basic foodstuffs.[29]

Because of women's importance as food producers, improving the security of their title to land is likely to improve productivity, thereby generating greater outputs and higher incomes. For the reasons noted earlier, secure tenure enables investment in the productivity of the land. Particularly where women are farming independently of their husbands, their outputs are likely to increase when they have secure land tenure.

The effect of secure title on productivity is especially germane to rural sub-Saharan Africa, where women not only produce an unusually high proportion of foodstuffs, but typically do so as independent farmers. Because of the historical emphasis in this region on the lineage (as opposed to the household), and the frequent practice of polygamy, married women have long been responsible for feeding their children and husband, regardless of the husband's level of income or wealth. Thus, even when husbands farm, their wives typically farm independently from them.

Most women farmers in rural sub-Saharan Africa also gain access to agricultural land through their husbands. One consequence of this, reported by Goldstein and Udry in a study of a district in eastern Ghana,[30] is that wives may avoid fallowing their land for optimal periods of time out of fear that this will lead to the loss of their use rights. This restriction on fallowing

---

[29] Food and Agriculture Organization, *Gender and Access to Land*, Land Tenure Studies 4, Rome, 2002.

[30] M. Goldstein and C. Udry, 'Gender, Power and Agricultural Investment in Ghana', unpublished manuscript, 2004.

appears to be the main reason why women's land in this area typically yields smaller crops and profits than men's land does.

Another consequence of insecure tenure for women in sub-Saharan Africa is that, in the event of a divorce or the husband's death, women are likely to lose the use of his land, either because the land is returned to his lineage or becomes the property of his male heirs. If this happens while dependent children are still in the mother's care, the consequences for their welfare are often disastrous. Moreover, even when women fight to retain their rights to land, their productivity and incomes are likely to suffer. A study of land conflicts in Uganda, for example, found that female-headed households and widows were significantly more likely to be involved in land-related conflicts than were other groups. Not surprisingly, the study also found that land conflicts have a significant negative impact on productivity: controlling for other factors, output on a plot affected by conflict is more than 30 per cent lower than on plots free from conflict.[31]

The combination of independent farming and access to land only through the husband produces particular problems for food productivity in sub-Saharan Africa. Even before the advent of the AIDS pandemic, studies of agricultural productivity in African countries suggested that the unequal allocation of household resources between male and female farmers was reducing total agricultural output. Studies estimated that, were household resources reallocated so that wives shared them equally with husbands, total agricultural output would likely increase by 5–20 per cent.[32] Although secure land tenure was not the specific focus of these studies, their findings nonetheless are consistent with the hypothesis that women's dependency on their husbands for access to arable land reduces their agricultural productivity.

The problems associated with African women's insecure land tenure have been exacerbated by the AIDS pandemic. Because husbands are increasingly likely to die while the wife is young and has dependent children in her care, the loss of agricultural land associated with the husband's death has more far-reaching negative consequences for the family than was the case in the past. Not only is the widow likely to suffer a disastrous loss of income, her children are, too. To be sure, secure title to land might not guarantee women's continued productivity in the face of the AIDS pandemic if women are forced to give up farming in order to care for sick family members. Nonetheless, one wonders if their uncertain hold on the land they farm is contributing to their decision to stop farming in order to care for their sick or dying husband. If women know they are likely to lose their claim to his land

---

[31] K. Deininger and R. Castagnini, *Incidence and Impact of Land Conflict in Uganda*, World Bank Policy Research Paper No. 3248 (Washington D.C.: World Bank, 2004).

[32] C. M. Blacken and C. Bhanu, *Gender, Growth, and Poverty Reduction: Special Program of Assistance for Africa, 1998 Status Report on Poverty in Sub-Saharan Africa*, World Bank Technical Paper No. 428 (Washington D.C.: World Bank, 1999).

after he dies, they may be more inclined to give up farming while he is alive than were they certain they would retain title to the land on their own. In any case, the rapid increase in deaths among men in the prime adult ages has meant a further loss of agricultural productivity—specifically of foodstuffs—in sub-Saharan Africa.[33]

In summary, there is much evidence to support the hypothesis that rural women would generate higher incomes were their title to the land they farm secure and their share of land greater. Equality in land rights would thus improve productivity. Let us now turn to the issue of how women versus men spend their incomes, a factor that helps to determine the welfare of family members and the well-being of future generations.

7.4.2.2 *Women's Investments in Children*

Many empirical studies from around the world suggest that women are more likely than men to spend their incomes on children. In countries as diverse as Bangladesh, Brazil, Canada, Cote d'Ivoire, Ethiopia, Indonesia, South Africa, Taiwan, and the United Kingdom, studies have found that patterns of household consumption vary according to the amount of income contributed by husbands versus wives.[34] Although the precise effects differ from study to study, all find that increases in the relative resources controlled by women translate into a larger share of household resources going to family welfare, especially expenditures on children. These effects have been observed for a variety of child inputs and outcomes, including investments in children's schooling, in the time children spend studying outside of school, in children's nutrition, and for child survival.

For example, with regard to nutrition and child survival, almost all studies show that an increase in *total* household income is associated with improvements in these outcomes, regardless who controls this income. Marginal improvements are substantially larger, however, if the mother controls the income rather than the father. For child survival, the marginal effect of female income is almost twenty times as large as the effect of male income. For weight-for-height and height-for-age—two measures of child nutrition—the marginal effects of female income are about four-to-eight times as large as the effects of male income.[35] In Cote d'Ivoire, increasing women's share of cash income in the household significantly increases the share of the household budget allocated to food, controlling for income,

---

[33] World Bank, *Intensifying Action Against HIV/AIDS in Africa: Responding to a Development Crisis* (Washington D.C.: World Bank, 1999); Food and Agriculture Organization, *HIV/AIDS and Food Security*, 2004, available at http://www.fao.org/hivaids.

[34] World Bank, *Engendering Development: Through Gender Equality in Rights, Resources, and Voice* (Washington D.C.: Oxford University Press for the World Bank, 2001).

[35] Ibid. 81.

Table 7.2. *Percentage change in selected household outcomes associated with a 10 per cent increase in borrowing: Bangladesh microcredit programs*[a]

Outcome	Grameen Bank		BRAC[c]		RD-12[d]	
	Male borrowing	Female borrowing	Male borrowing	Female borrowing	Male borrowing	Female borrowing
Boys in school	0.07	0.61	−0.08	−0.03	0.29	0.79
Girls in school	0.30	0.47	0.24	0.12	0.07	0.23
Boys' nutrition[b]	−2.98	14.19	−2.98	14.19	−2.98	14.19
Girls' nutrition[b]	−4.92	11.63	−4.92	11.63	−4.92	11.63

a—Equations also include outcomes for per capita spending, net worth, contraceptive use, and recent fertility.
b—Percentage changes here represent average impacts across all three micro-finance programs.
c—Bangladesh Rural Advancement Committee, an NGO.
d—Rural Development Project 12 of the Government of Bangladesh's Rural Development Board.
Source: S. Khandker, *Fighting Poverty with Microcredit: Experience in Bangladesh* (Washington D.C.: Oxford University Press for the World Bank, 1998) 161.

household size, and demographic characteristics.[36] Similarly, in Brazil, additional income in the hands of women results in a greater share of household budgets devoted to education, health, and nutrition-related expenditures.[37]

Further evidence that income in the hands of women tends to have greater benefits for the welfare of children comes from studies of microcredit programs in Bangladesh. These studies find that borrowing by women from the Grameen Bank and other micro-finance institutions has greater positive impacts on child welfare than does borrowing by men (Table 7.2). Mothers' borrowing increases the enrollment of both girls and boys more than fathers' borrowing does, and has an even more substantial positive effect on children's nutritional status.[38] Because women's access to commercial credit is

[36] J. Hoddinott and L. Haddad, 'Does Female Income Share Influence Household Expenditures? Evidence from Cote d'Ivoire', 57 *Oxford Bulletin of Economics and Statistics* 77 (1995).
[37] D. Thomas, 'Income, Expenditure, and Health Outcomes: Evidence on Intrahousehold Resource Allocation' in L. Haddad, J. Hoddinott, and H. Alderman, eds., *Intrahousehold Resource Allocation in Developing Countries: Models, Methods, and Policy* (Baltimore, MD: The Johns Hopkins University Press, 1997).
[38] S. Khandker, *Fighting Poverty with Microcredit: Experience in Bangladesh* (Washington D.C.: Oxford University Press for the World Bank, 1998).

often limited by their lack of title to land, investments in children and the potential for long-term economic growth could be increased with more gender equality in land tenure.

In this section we have reviewed evidence that gender equality in land rights is likely to empower women, enhance economic growth and improve the welfare of men, women, and children. Control of valuable assets tends to increase the bargaining power of individuals within households, suggesting that, if women held title to land on an equal footing with men, they would have a greater say in household decisions. Because rural women are major producers of foodstuffs, their land rights can affect agricultural productivity and determine rates of economic growth. Finally, because women are more inclined to invest their incomes in the well-being of children than men are, the more that women control productive resources, including land, the higher the likely quality and productivity of the next generation. In short, ensuring women's ownership of land is an important development investment, especially in rural areas.

7.5 POLICY RECOMMENDATIONS

Women's relative lack of control over land is a reflection of unequal rights and opportunities between males and females generally. Does this mean that gender equality in land rights can only be achieved once the entire system of unequal relations between the sexes is transformed?

We think not. Indeed, ensuring women's land rights may be a relatively straightforward and potentially powerful entry point for promoting gender equality and the empowerment of women, and thus for achieving the third Millennium Development Goal. In this section, we suggest some specific steps that governments might take to enhance women's land rights and the development benefits likely to flow from them.

7.5.1 Introduce Legal Reforms to Increase Women's Rights to Land

Many societies have enacted laws that embody the principle of equal rights to land ownership between women and men. Although these laws have not always succeeded in increasing gender equality in land ownership, they are often a necessary precondition for achieving such equality. Governments would therefore be wise to ensure that legislation is in place that explicitly gives women and men equal rights to land. Laws making joint titling mandatory in monogamous, landowning households may also provide a strong foundation for ensuring women's land rights. Affirmative action that gives women beneficiaries priority in government land reform programs might also be considered.

7.5.2 Undertake Advocacy to Draw Attention to the Importance of Gender Issues in Land Policy

One reason that laws specifying equality of rights to land between women and men fail to translate into equal ownership is a lack of awareness of these laws among both women and men as well as among policy makers and land registration workers. Governments should therefore consider legal literacy education for women and men, policy makers, and registration workers regarding women's rights to land and the benefits to families that follow from these rights. Specific attention to CEDAW as a basis for equal claims to land should be featured in legal literacy programs.

7.5.3 Integrate Land Reforms into a Broader Approach to Development

In particular, provide effective institutional structures that can protect and strengthen equitable access to land within the framework of a society's particular land policy goals. Another reason that laws nominally giving women equal rights to land with men fail to result in equality on the ground is the absence of effective institutions to implement these laws. Building such institutions is important. Ensuring that grass-roots women are consulted about land reforms may help to increase their voice in determining laws and implementation, thereby making those responsible for implementation more accountable. Providing assistance to grass-roots groups in the form of capacity building or resources for pressing legal cases may also help to establish more accountable and effective institutions that deal with claims to land.

7.5.4 Consider Dropping the Concept of the Household Head

During the 1970s and 1980s, feminists in the United States successfully sought to have the U.S. Bureau of the Census drop the concept of the household head on the grounds that the concept is male biased and results in a disproportionate share of resources and voice going to male household members (the U.S. Census now asks about 'householders' and their relationship to each other, rather than asking about the 'head' of the household and the relationship of other household members to this head). Governments in developing countries should consider eliminating the legal status of household head, at least for purposes of land titling and registration. Even if the concept is retained, joint titling to heads and their spouses should be the norm.

7.5.5 Strengthen International Agreements on Women's Rights to Land

Although CEDAW makes clear that land rights are part of women's human rights, the references to these rights are not as explicit as they might be. Strengthening the language in international agreements to make women's rights to land explicit would help to guarantee women all their rights by ensuring their entitlement to one of the fundamental bases for livelihoods and economic opportunities—land.

7.6 CONCLUSION

This chapter has argued that women's land rights and land ownership contribute to women's empowerment, economic growth, and improved welfare, both in current and future generations. Because land remains a valuable asset in both rural and urban areas, women's control of land provides a resource that they can leverage economically, socially, and polit- ically. Secure land tenure among rural women is also likely to facilitate improvements in land productivity and women's income, and protect the environment. And improved incomes are in turn likely to benefit family members—especially children—because of the widely observed tendency for women to invest their incomes in family welfare more than men do.

To be sure, because land is a valuable asset, political resistance to increasing women's land rights may be strong. It is therefore important for governments to recognize that, in the long run, men, women, and children all suffer a loss of welfare from the unequal rights to land between women and men that typically prevail today. Wise governments will therefore engage in the struggle needed to bring greater equality to this important area of human rights and development.

8

Women's Property Rights Violations in Kenya

JANET WALSH[1]

8.1 INTRODUCTION

Women's rights to property are unequal to those of men in Kenya. Their rights to own, inherit, manage, and dispose of property are under constant attack from customs, laws, and individuals—including some government officials—who believe that women cannot be trusted with or do not deserve property. The devastating effects of property rights violations—including poverty, disease, violence, and homelessness—harm women, their children, and Kenya's overall development. For decades, the government ignored this problem. After a change of government in January 2003, some preliminary steps were taken to eliminate this insidious form of discrimination, yet much remains to be done. Unless Kenya acts to protect women's property rights, it will see its fight against HIV/AIDS, its economic and social reforms, and its development agenda stagger and fail.

Many women are excluded from inheriting, evicted from their lands and homes by in-laws, stripped of their possessions, and forced to engage in risky sexual practices in order to keep their property. When they divorce or separate from their husbands, they are often expelled from their homes with only their clothing. A woman's access to property usually hinges on her relationship to a man. When the relationship ends, the woman stands a good chance of losing her home, land, livestock, household goods, money, vehicles, and other property. These violations have the intent and effect of perpetuating women's dependence on men and undercutting their social and economic status.

[1] This chapter is based upon a report by Human Rights Watch, *Kenya: Double Standards—Women's Property Rights Violations in Kenya* (New York: Human Rights Watch, 2003). Reproduced with permission of Human Rights Watch.

Women's property rights violations are not only discriminatory, they may prove fatal. The deadly HIV/AIDS epidemic magnifies the devastation of women's property violations in Kenya, where approximately 7 per cent of the population between the ages of fifteen and forty-nine is infected with HIV. Widows who are coerced into the customary practices of 'wife inheritance' or ritual 'cleansing' (which usually involve unprotected sex) run a clear risk of contracting and spreading HIV. AIDS deaths expected in the coming years will result in millions more women becoming widows at younger ages than would otherwise be the case. These women and their children (who may end up AIDS orphans) are likely to face not only social stigma against people affected by HIV/AIDS but also deprivations caused by property rights violations.

A complex mix of cultural, legal, and social factors underlies women's property rights violations. Kenya's customary laws—largely unwritten but influential local norms that coexist with formal laws—are based on patriarchal traditions in which men inherited and largely controlled land and other property, and women were 'protected' but had lesser property rights. Kenya's constitution prohibits discrimination on the basis of sex, but undermines this protection by condoning discrimination under personal and customary laws. The few statutes that could advance women's property rights defer to religious and customary property laws that privilege men over women. Sexist attitudes are infused in Kenyan society: men that Human Rights Watch interviewed said that women are untrustworthy, incapable of handling property, and in need of male protection. The guise of male 'protection' does not obscure the fact that stripping women of their property is a way of asserting control over women's autonomy, bodies, and labor— and enriches their 'protectors'.

Currently, women find it almost hopeless to pursue remedies for property rights violations. Traditional leaders and governmental authorities often ignore women's property claims and sometimes make the problems worse. Courts often overlook and misinterpret family property and succession laws, although the establishment of a family court in Nairobi provides one ray of hope. Women often have little awareness of their rights and seldom have means to enforce them. Women who try to fight back are often beaten, raped, or ostracized. Yet bills that could improve women's property rights have languished in parliament and government ministries have only recently begun considering ways to promote equal property rights. Although some government officials are now speaking out about the injustice of women's property rights violations, many still shrug this off as a cultural issue with which they will not interfere. Fortunately, many women's organizations in Kenya and some donor agencies recognize the seriousness of this issue and are working on many fronts to combat this form of discrimination.

As important as cultural diversity and respecting customs may be, if customs are a source of discrimination against women, they—like any other norm—must evolve. This is crucial not only for the sake of women's equality, but because there are real social consequences to depriving half the population of their property rights. International organizations have identified women's insecure property rights as contributing to low agricultural production, food shortages, underemployment, and rural poverty. In Kenya, more than half of the population lives in poverty, the economy is faltering, and HIV/AIDS rates are high. If Kenya is to meet its development aims, it must address the property inequalities that hold women back.

8.2 BACKGROUND

Women's limited ability to own, acquire, and control property in Kenya is the product of historical, political, legal, and social developments in a society that has only haltingly addressed its extreme gender inequalities.[2] After decades of authoritarian rule under President Daniel arap Moi, Kenya has recently emerged with a new government, an initiative for a new constitution, and a citizenry electrified by the possibility of real social change. In this context, it is critical for women's property rights to be high on Kenya's legislative and policy agendas.

Women's property rights abuses are not exclusive to one social class, ethnic group, religion, or region. This is not to say that no women inherit, own, or

---

[2] This background section is intended as a basic introduction to the history of women's property rights in Kenya, and does not attempt to capture the many variations of the different ethnic groups' histories and customs. It is based on a variety of sources, including: Eugene Cotran, *Casebook on Kenya Customary Law* (Nairobi: Professional Books Limited, 1987); Smokin C. Wanjala, *Essays on Land Law: The Reform Debate in Kenya* (Nairobi: Faculty of Law, University of Nairobi, 2000); Abdullahi A. An-Na'im, *Cultural Transformation and Human Rights in Africa* (New York: Zed Books Ltd., 2002); Kivutha Kibwana and Lawrence Mute, *Law and the Quest for Gender Equality in Kenya* (Nairobi: Clairpress Limited, 2000); Marjolein Benschop, *Rights and Reality: Are Women's Equal Rights to Land, Housing and Property Implemented in East Africa?* (Nairobi: United Nations Human Settlements Programme, 2002); Patricia Kameri-Mbote, 'Gender Dimensions of Law, Colonialism and Inheritance in East Africa: Kenyan Women's Experiences', International Environmental Law Research Centre (IELRC) Working Paper No. 2001–1 (2002); Task Force for the Review of Laws Relating to Women, *Women's Status and Rights in Kenya: Report of the Task Force for the Review of Laws Relating to Women* (Nairobi, 1998); Kenya Human Rights Commission, *Women and Land Rights in Kenya* (Nairobi: Kenya Human Rights Commission, 2000); Human Rights Watch interview with Odenda Lumumba, co-ordinator, Kenya Land Alliance, Nairobi, 18 October 2002; Human Rights Watch interview with Jennifer Miano, senior program officer (advocacy), Kenya Human Rights Commission, Nairobi, 16 October 2002; and Human Rights Watch interview with Mbugua Mureithi, co-ordinator, Kituo Cha Sheria, Nairobi, 26 October 2002.

control property. Some certainly do. Rather, it is important to understand that the problems cut across populations. Human Rights Watch interviewed illiterate women and those with advanced degrees, and found their property experiences remarkably similar. Urban women lost their possessions just like rural women, with a slightly greater chance of staying in their (looted) homes. Though western Kenya is notorious for its discriminatory customary practices related to property, women from all over the country told Human Rights Watch of abuses. Rich and poor, in monogamous and polygamous unions, women struggled not just with losing their property, but also with being ostracized by their families and communities if they attempted to assert their rights. While the details varied, women described the same end result: men or in-laws got the property, and women lost out. 'Even in middle-class, educated households, women are not able to exercise their property rights', said the head of the government Women's Bureau. 'Men are too adamant. It's a tug of war, and women let go.'[3] The one notable difference was that more educated and wealthier women, especially those with monetary income, were more likely to hire legal counsel to assert their rights.

Prior to the colonial era, property in Kenya was primarily controlled and allocated at the clan level. Land in particular could not be transferred without approval of clan elders, who were almost always men. Women's access to most property was through male relatives (usually husbands, fathers, brothers, or sons). In most of Kenya's ethnic groups, which number over forty, a husband's clan essentially 'absorbed' a woman upon marriage. Marriage resulted from a process involving family negotiations (including dowry payment by the man to the bride's family) and ongoing social practices, as opposed to a single wedding event. Married women left their parents' homestead to live and work on their husbands' clan's land. Men typically controlled land allocation, yet women were responsible for most aspects of crop production. Although women's property rights were limited, social structures protected both women and men against exclusion from land, Kenya's most important asset.

In most ethnic groups, inheritance was patrilineal. A married woman did not inherit from her parents since her husband's family was expected to provide for her. Unmarried daughters could expect to inherit something, but not on an equal basis with their brothers. Women did not inherit from their husbands, but if they had sons they could continue to live and work on the husband's land, holding it in trust for the sons. Sometimes, women were 'inherited' by male relatives of the deceased husbands.

Customary divorce rules varied among the ethnic groups, but women generally got either nothing, the items their own families gave them, or

[3] Human Rights Watch interview with Mary Wambua, head, Women's Bureau, Nairobi, 6 November 2002.

personal effects and a small portion of the family property (if they contributed to its acquisition). Divorced women normally returned to their parents, who were to provide for and allocate land to the women. Divorce in many clans was contingent on repayment of the dowry.

After the British colonized Kenya in the late 1800s, communal, clan-based property systems eroded as colonial authorities expropriated land, uprooted many indigenous Kenyans from their ancestral lands, crowded them onto 'native reserves', and later introduced an individual titling system. The land titling system recognized men's right to allocate land for agricultural use as more akin to ownership, and men gained title deeds. Women's right to use land received no legal recognition. Their secure land tenure evaporated as land became a commodity that men could sell without clan approval. As the cash economy developed and land grew scarce, men could sell land whether their families agreed or not. Moreover, men as title holders had sole rights to agricultural surplus although women provided most of the labor. Colonial authorities also introduced piecemeal legislation on marriage, divorce, and inheritance, applying different rules to different populations.

Kenya gained independence from the British in 1963 after a struggle inspired in part by inequalities in the colonial land regime. In the decades following independence, some colonial-era laws lingered and many new laws were introduced, none of which adequately protected women's property rights. Women continue to suffer property discrimination sanctioned by Kenya's constitution, laws, and practices. Legislative reforms have faltered, but the constitutional reform process holds some promise.

8.3 WOMEN'S STATUS IN KENYA

By just about any measure, women in Kenya are worse off than men. Their average earnings are less than half those of men.[4] Only 29 per cent of those engaged in formal wage employment are women, leaving most to work in the informal sector with no social security and little income.[5] The numbers of women in formal employment are decreasing.[6] Women head 37 per cent of all households in Kenya, a number likely to grow as AIDS claims more victims.[7] Eighty per cent of female-headed households are officially classified

---

[4] Republic of Kenya, *National Development Plan 1997–2001* (Nairobi: Government Printer, 1997) 146. In 1999, the per capita annual income in Kenya was estimated at U.S.$306. United Nations Development Program, *Kenya Human Development Report 2001* (Nairobi: UNDP, 2002) 30.

[5] Republic of Kenya, *Poverty Reduction Strategy Paper for the Period 2001–2004* (Nairobi: Ministry of Finance and Planning, 2001) 36.

[6] Republic of Kenya, *Economic Survey 2002* (Nairobi: Government Printer, 2002) 2.

[7] Ibid. 8.

as poor or very poor, in part due to their limited ownership of and access to land.[8] Girls receive less education than boys at every level, and women's literacy rate (76 per cent) is lower than men's (89 per cent).[9] Violence against women is commonplace: 60 per cent of married women reported in a 2002 study that they are victims of domestic abuse.[10] In another study published in 2002, 83 per cent of women reported physical abuse in childhood and nearly 61 per cent reported physical abuse as adults.[11]

Women's land ownership is minuscule despite their enormous contribution to agricultural production. Women are said to account for only 5 per cent of registered landholders nationally.[12] Women constitute over 80 per cent of the agricultural labor force, often working on an unpaid basis, and 64 per cent of subsistence farmers are women.[13] Women provide approximately 60 per cent of farm-derived income,[14] yet female-headed households on average own less than half the amount of farm equipment owned by male-headed households.[15] Rural women work an average of nearly three hours longer per day than rural men.[16] With so many women working in the agricultural sector and so few in formal employment, it is all the more devastating when women lose their land.

Kenya's high HIV/AIDS prevalence also reflects women's subordinate status.[17] According to the United Nations, an estimated 1.2 million individuals had HIV/AIDS in Kenya at the end of 2003, including 6.7 per cent of those between ages fifteen and forty-nine.[18] Of those infected, 720,000

---

[8] Gita Gopal and Maryam Salim, *Gender and Law: Eastern Africa Speaks* (Washington D.C.: The World Bank, 1998) 20.

[9] United Nations Development Program (UNDP), *Human Development Report 2002* (New York: UNDP, 2002) 224.

[10] Tony Johnston, *Domestic Abuse in Kenya* (Nairobi: Population Communication Africa, 2002) 10.

[11] Tony Johnston, *Violence and Abuse of Women and Girls in Kenya* (Nairobi: Population Communication Africa, 2002) 12.

[12] Celestine Nyamu-Musembi, 'Are Local Norms and Practices Fences or Pathways? The Example of Women's Property Rights' in Abdullahi A. An-Na'im, *Cultural Transformation and Human Rights in Africa* (New York: Zed Books Ltd., 2002) 136.

[13] Republic of Kenya, *A Gender Analysis of Agriculture in Kenya* (Nairobi: Ministry of Home Affairs, Heritage and Sports, 2000) 1 and Gopal and Salim, *Gender and Law: Eastern Africa Speaks*, above n. 8, 22.

[14] Task Force for the Review of Laws Relating to Women, *Women's Status and Rights in Kenya*, above n. 2, 294.

[15] World Bank, *Engendering Development* (New York: Oxford University Press, 2001) 52.

[16] Ibid. 66.

[17] For more detailed information on AIDS in Kenya, see Human Rights Watch, 'In the Shadow of Death: HIV/AIDS and Children's Rights in Kenya', *A Human Rights Watch Report*, vol. 13, no. 4(A), June 2001.

[18] Joint United Nations Programme on HIV/AIDS (UNAIDS), *Epidemiological Fact Sheets on HIV/AIDS and Sexually Transmitted Infections: 2004 Update* (Geneva: UNAIDS, 2004) 1.

were women and girls between ages fifteen and forty-nine.[19] As is the case in many African countries, HIV prevalence in Kenya is higher among women (8.7 per cent) than among men (4.5 per cent).[20] The HIV infection rate in girls and young women fifteen to nineteen years old is about six times higher than that of their male counterparts in the heavily affected Kisumu area,[21] and about three times higher than males of that age in the country overall.[22] The large number of AIDS deaths has reduced life expectancy by thirteen years to fifty-one years.[23]

Kenya's failure to eliminate discriminatory property inheritance practices exacerbates the already unimaginable havoc caused by HIV/AIDS. Women with AIDS in Kenya, virtually all of whom were infected by husbands or regular male partners, are essentially condemned to an early death when the women's homes, lands, and other property are taken. They not only lose assets they could use for medical care, but also the shelter they need to endure this debilitating disease. Moreover, the failure to ensure equal property rights upon separation or divorce discourages women from leaving violent marriages. Those women risk exposure to HIV infection due to the correlation between HIV/AIDS and domestic violence, which often involves coercive sex, diminishes women's ability to negotiate safe sex and condom use, and impedes women from seeking health information and treatment. The Kenyan government only belatedly outlined how it intends to mainstream gender concerns in its HIV/AIDS strategic plan.[24]

8.4 CUSTOMARY LAWS TODAY

Since customary laws to this day have a profound impact on women's property rights, it is important to understand their nature, their place in Kenya's legal system, and basic principles. Customary laws are mostly

---

[19] Ibid.   [20] Ibid.

[21] UNAIDS, *Report on the Global HIV/AIDS Epidemic* (Geneva: UNAIDS, 2003) 26–27.

[22] Dorah Nesoba, 'Women Hardest Hit by HIV/AIDS, Says Health PS', *East African Standard*, 28 November 2002 [online], http://allafrica.com/stories/200211280190.html (retrieved 20 January 2003).

[23] UNAIDS, *Epidemiological Fact Sheets on HIV/AIDS and Sexually Transmitted Infections: 2004 Update*, above n. 18, 2.

[24] See Gender and HIV/AIDS Technical Sub-Committee of the National AIDS Control Council, *Mainstreaming Gender into the Kenya National HIV/AIDS Strategic Plan 2000–2005* (Nairobi: Office of the President, 2002) 19. This document sets out objectives, including establishing an institutional policy framework for integrating gender into all HIV/AIDS policies and programs; creating a gender responsive legal framework for HIV/AIDS prevention, treatment, and care; and ensuring that adequate human and financial resources are available for gender responsive HIV/AIDS programming. It acknowledges that explicit strategies focused specifically on gender were not included in the development of HIV/AIDS policies and programs in Kenya.

unwritten and constantly evolving norms that exist in parallel with statutory law but derive legitimacy from tradition and custom rather than a government act. There are as many customary laws as there are ethnic groups, and each has its own nuances. Kenya's legal system formally recognizes customary laws. The Judicature Act provides that courts' jurisdiction must be exercised in conformity with the constitution, statutes, and other sources of formal law, adding that courts should be guided by customary law so far as it is 'applicable and is not repugnant to justice and morality or inconsistent with any written law'.[25] Traditional leaders (such as elders) and local authorities (such as government-appointed chiefs) are the primary enforcers of customary laws. Judges and magistrates also apply customary laws in some court proceedings. In terms of their content, customary laws largely follow pre-colonial patterns with regard to women and property rights. Customary law is fluid and prone to subjective interpretation. This malleability can have advantages for those trying to effect social change through local norms, but one cannot assume that the local norms support women's equality. One legal expert explained, '[Most] customary law is unwritten. Those interpreting it bring their own biases and women-unfriendly notions.'[26]

8.4.1 Wife Inheritance and Ritual Cleansing

The customary practices of wife inheritance and ritual cleansing continue in parts of Kenya with some permutations. The original practice of wife inheritance was a communal way of providing widows economic and social protection. Since widows were not entitled to inherit property in their own right, being inherited was a way to access land. An inheritor was supposed to support the widow and her children. Although the terms 'wife inheritance' and 'cleansing' are sometimes used interchangeably, wife inheritance generally refers to the long-term union of a widow and a male relative of the deceased, and cleansing typically refers to a short-term or one-time sexual encounter with a man paid to have sex with the widow. These practices reflect the common belief that women cannot be trusted to own property and the belief that widows are contaminated with evil spirits when their husbands die.

Wife inheritance and cleansing practices take a number of different forms depending on the clan. First, there is non-sexual wife inheritance, whereby the coat of an inheritor is placed in a widow's house overnight to symbolically cleanse her. This generally applies to widows beyond childbearing age. Second, there is inheritance involving long-term sexual relations, typically with a brother of the deceased, in what amounts to a marriage. Third, there is a

---

[25] Judicature Act, chapter 8, article 3.
[26] Human Rights Watch interview with Dr. Patricia Kameri-Mbote, director (policy research and outreach), African Center for Technology Studies, Nairobi, 17 October 2002.

combination of cleansing and inheritance, whereby a widow first has sex with a social outcast (known as a *jater* in western Kenya) who is paid to have sex with her to cleanse her of her dead husband's spirits, and is then inherited by a male relative of the dead husband. Fourth, there is cleansing alone, where a widow has sex with a *jater* to cleanse her but is not inherited permanently.

Women's property rights closely relate to wife inheritance and cleansing rituals in that many women cannot stay in their homes or on their land unless they are inherited or cleansed. According to one women's rights advocate, 'Women have to be inherited to keep any property after their husbands die. They have access to property because of their husband and lose that right when the husband dies.'[27] Women who experienced these practices told Human Rights Watch they had mixed feelings about them. Most said the cleansing and inheritance were not voluntary, but they succumbed so that they could keep their property and stay in their communities.

Men clearly benefit not just from their inherited wife's labor and child-bearing potential, but also from the property the deceased husband leaves behind. A law professor observed, 'Wife inheritance is a very common way to access property. If women resist, they are sent out of the household.'[28] A paralegal who works with widows added: 'Men feel that if they stay with a woman, they will get the dead man's clothes and property. Younger brothers of a husband feel that since the husband died, now he can take the brother's belongings. They don't consider the wife of any consequence.'[29] Thus, even if wife inheritance was originally protective and if cleansing is supposed to be a benevolent way to 'purify' widows, these practices are now in many ways predatory and exploitive.

Wife inheritance and cleansing practices also pose frightening health risks. These practices are common in western Kenya, among the poorest and most heavily AIDS-affected areas in the country. According to one news report, one in three widows in western Kenya is forced to undergo the cleansing ritual.[30] Condom use has lagged, in part because cleansing is not considered complete unless semen enters the widow and because women's inequality makes it difficult to demand condom use.

Human Rights Watch learned of the cleansing practices in one village from Guy Udoyi, a *jater* who has cleansed at least seventy-five widows in the two years he has worked as a *jater*. He has not been tested for HIV. Udoyi,

---

[27] Human Rights Watch interview with Wambui Kanyi, Collaborative Centre for Gender and Development, Nairobi, 27 October 2002.

[28] Human Rights Watch interview with Dr. Patricia Kameri-Mbote, director (policy research and outreach), African Center for Technology Studies, Nairobi, 17 October 2002.

[29] Human Rights Watch interview with Eunice Awino, paralegal, Education Centre for Women in Democracy, Siaya, 2 November 2002.

[30] Beatrix Nyakisumo, 'A vile custom that must go', *Africanews*, May 1997 [online], http://www.peacelink.it/afrinews/14_issue/p6.html (retrieved 14 January 2002).

who is paid in cash (approximately KSh5,000 or U.S.$63)[31] or livestock (cows, goats, and hens) by widows' in-laws, told Human Rights Watch:

I don't use condoms with the women. It must be body to body. I must put sperm in her. . . . If no sperm comes out, she is not inherited. . . . I don't do anything to stop pregnancy. Two widows have had my children. I don't act as the father or give assistance, but I'm considered the father.

I've heard about how you get AIDS. I'm getting scared. You get it by having sex, and you must use a condom to prevent it. But the widows don't want to hear about condoms. They want skin to skin. There are inheritors who are infected with HIV. They don't use condoms.[32]

Udoyi explained that superstitions, which he shares, motivate this custom. He explained that if a widow is not cleansed, she and her children will have bad luck and be ostracized. 'Women are forced to do this', he acknowledged. He said there is no comparable cleansing for widowers.

8.5 WOMEN'S PROPERTY RIGHTS VIOLATIONS AND THEIR CONSEQUENCES

Human Rights Watch documented women's property rights violations in Kenya across a range of ethnic groups, social classes, religions, and geographic regions. These violations can occur at any point in a woman's life, but are most frequent and extreme when it comes to inheritance and division or control of matrimonial property. The personal accounts below illustrate property rights abuses suffered by widows from rural and urban areas, women whose parents have died, divorced or separated women, and married women who lack control over their matrimonial property.

8.5.1 Widows from Rural Areas

Rural widows told Human Rights Watch that their in-laws took their property, including their land, homes, vehicles, livestock, furniture, and household items, when their husbands died. Many were subsistence farmers who lost their basis of survival when they lost their land. Rural widows, even more than urban widows, are often expected to undergo wife inheritance or cleansing rituals. Most of those who did the rituals said they could keep their property. Those who refused not only lost their property but were also ostracized. They often returned to their parents' homes or moved to urban centers, including Nairobi's notorious slums.

---

[31] Throughout this report the exchange rate used is 79 Kenya shillings to the U.S. dollar, the rate on 6 January 2003.
[32] Human Rights Watch interview with Guy Udoyi, Siaya district, 3 November 2002.

Emily Owino, a fifty-four-year-old widow from the Luo ethnic group, lived and farmed on her husband's land from the time she married at age fifteen until her husband died several years ago. With four children, she depended on that land, her simple home, and her meager possessions to subsist. When her husband died, her in-laws took everything. 'Things started disappearing from the time of the burial ceremony', she said. 'They took farm equipment, livestock, cooking pans, bank records, pension documents, house utensils, blankets, and clothes. . . . This happened in the three months after my husband died. I was desperate.'

Owino's in-laws also pressured her to be cleansed by a *jater*. They hired a herdsman to cleanse Owino, paying him KSh500 (U.S.$6). She had sex with this man—against her will and without a condom. 'They said I had to be cleansed in order to stay in my home', she recalled. 'I tried to refuse, but my in-laws said I must be cleansed or they'd beat me and chase me out of my home. They said they had bought me [with the dowry], and therefore I had no voice in that home.' Succumbing to the cleansing ritual did not, however, save Owino from losing her home and land. The situation became unbearable:

I was suffering so much that I went home to my parents for assistance. I had young children who were sick, and no one would assist us. I couldn't buy clothes, we couldn't eat, and I had no cooking pots. When I came back from my mother's home, I saw that my land and last few possessions were taken. I was destitute.[33]

While she was gone, Owino's in-laws rented out her land, which the renter was cultivating, and took the title deed. 'The land was supposed to be mine. My husband had verbally willed it to me', Owino said. 'There were witnesses. My in-laws knew it was my land, but they didn't care.' When Owino complained, her in-laws threatened to assault her. Owino reported the incursion on her land to a village elder. 'I told the elder "I've come from my parents' home and found that someone planted cassava on my land." The elder asked for a bribe before he would take action. He said, "If a lady wants assistance, she must pay." I didn't have the money.' She then took her case to the local chief. According to Owino, the chief considered this an inconsequential 'family case' and referred Owino back to the elder, who again refused to handle her case. She did not go to the police: 'I had no money to go to the police. I was told that unless I have money, I couldn't go to the police.' She could not afford a lawyer for a court claim.

Since the local authorities were unhelpful, Owino again asked her mother-in-law if she could cultivate part of the land. 'My mother-in-law refused, and told me to go back to my parents', Owino said. 'I had to leave my home. I couldn't stay because I had nothing to eat, no land to till.' Owino moved

[33] Human Rights Watch interview with Emily Owino, Siaya, 2 November 2002.

with her children from place to place until someone offered her a small, leaky hut made of poor-quality grass. None of her children are educated beyond pre-school. Though still young, they work as herders and maids. 'If I could have stayed on my property, my children could have gone to school', Owino said.[34]

Monica Wamuyo, a forty-year-old widow from the Kikuyu ethnic group, said her in-laws evicted her when her husband died in 1996. She and her husband had lived in a spacious house in Nyeri on land where she grew vegetables. Soon after Wamuyo's husband died, her in-laws pressured her to leave. 'My father-in-law would kick my door at night and tell me I should leave because it was his land. He said if I wanted land, I should go to my mother and ask for land.' When Wamuyo protested, her father-in-law demanded that she be his second wife. 'I told him I had never heard of such a thing in our tradition', she said. 'I went to the elders because I wanted to continue living there. . . . The elders said I had to move out.' Wamuyo moved to Nairobi's Kangemi slum, where she earns money washing clothes. She said she was crushed by losing her land and now struggles to make ends meet: 'Sometimes I'm unable to buy food for my children. They haven't been in school since 1997. . . . I told my daughters to look for housework.'[35]

Having no sons is a serious liability for rural widows: women with no children or only daughters are often considered worthless and undeserving of property. 'I was thrown out of my home when my husband died because I had only given birth to girls', said Theresa Murunga, a widow from rural Bungoma. Until her husband's death in 1994, Murunga lived in a hut on her husband's homestead, where she grew potatoes and maize. She recalled:

When my husband died, his relatives came and took everything. They told me to take my clothes in a paper bag and leave. I left, because if I had resisted they would have beat me up. The relatives identified someone to inherit me. It was a cousin of my husband. They told me, 'Now you are of less value, so we'll give you to anyone available to inherit you.' I didn't say anything. I just left and went to my parents' home. . . . This is customary. If I had married the cousin, I could have lived where I was. I decided not to because he was polygamous—he had five other wives. . . . I know if a woman is inherited, she is normally mistreated by the one who inherits her.

If I had sons instead of daughters, they would have apportioned land to me. . . . When they told me to leave, they said there was no way they could recognize my daughters since they'll marry and leave the homestead. They said I shouldn't have given birth at all. . . . My in-laws took everything—mattresses, blankets, utensils. They chased me away like a dog. I was voiceless.[36]

Murunga's in-laws expected her to undergo a traditional ritual involving sexual intercourse with her dead husband's body, but she avoided this

---

[34] Human Rights Watch interview with Emily Owino, Siaya, 2 November 2002.
[35] Human Rights Watch interview with Monica Wamuyo, Nairobi, 28 October 2002.
[36] Human Rights Watch interview with Theresa Murunga, Nairobi, 20 October 2002.

because her brothers were there with machetes to protect her. Her in-laws were angry, and they and other villagers harassed her. One night, a group of five men came to her hut shouting threats. She believes that the village elder sent them to punish her for rejecting tribal traditions.

Frightened, Murunga left her home and went to her parents, where she stayed for four years without getting land to cultivate. 'I felt like a foreigner in that homestead', she remarked. In 2001, Murunga was having so much trouble paying her children's school fees that she went back to her in-laws to ask permission to cultivate her late husband's land. 'My brother-in-law sent me away. He said I am no longer his relative and he doesn't know who I am.' Murunga now lives in Nairobi in a dilapidated one-room shack without electricity. 'Even feeding my children is hard now', she said. She did not seek help from authorities. 'Whom could I tell?' she asked. 'I felt that if I went to the elders, they wouldn't attend to me because I only have daughters.'[37]

Having sons does not always help women keep their property, at least not all of it. Rimas Kintalel, a Maasai widow with four sons and three daughters, lost all of her cattle and sheep to her brother-in-law. One month after her husband died, her brother-in-law 'took twelve cattle and twenty sheep. He said, "I want you to go from here because I want my brother's property." ' Kintalel managed to stay on her land because she and her husband, who worked for her father, lived on her father's land. Kintalel told her village elders that her brother-in-law had taken her livestock, but they did nothing. Her troubles did not stop there. In 2001, her brother-in-law abducted six of her children. She said he felt entitled to them because she married into his family even though some were fathered by a man other than her late husband. 'For Maasais, this doesn't matter', she said. 'Once you're married, they consider any children part of the husband's family.' Kintalel reported the abduction and the earlier property grabbing to the police. 'The police asked if it was possible for me to go live with my brother-in-law, and I said no.' She got her children back, and the brother-in-law was fined two sheep and one cow. She did not get the other livestock.[38]

8.5.2 Widows from Urban Areas

Widows living in urban centers when their husbands died described to Human Rights Watch how their in-laws invaded their homes to take household goods and furniture, whether or not the woman had bought them, and transported them along with the deceased husband's body to his ancestral home (generally in a rural area). In-laws also interfered with urban widows' access to pensions, death benefits, and bank accounts. Property

---

[37] Ibid.
[38] Human Rights Watch interview with Rimas Kintalel, Ngong, 24 October 2002.

located in rural areas, such as land, livestock, homes, and household items, was often taken without compensating the widow. Some urban widows were pressured into remaining in their deceased husband's home village and becoming a junior wife of an in-law. Women told Human Rights Watch that when they protested being inherited they were attacked and forced to leave. Others acquiesced, citing cultural expectations that prevent women from challenging in-laws.

While many widows Human Rights Watch interviewed were not forced to leave their urban homes, they were impoverished after losing their property. They toiled to feed, clothe, and educate their children after losing virtually everything they owned. Monica Olola, a fifty-year-old Luo widow, said that she and her husband lived on and cultivated land in rural Siaya for fifteen years. They had moved to Nairobi, but kept their land and a small house in Siaya. When Olola's husband died, her in-laws took the rural land, home, and household goods. 'My brothers-in-law immediately took everything', she said. 'They took land in Siaya, household goods, a radio, bicycle, and cupboards. . . . One brother moved into the house and started to till the land.' Olola told him she wanted the property back. 'My brother-in-law told me to go back to Nairobi. . . . He felt that whatever property my husband had was his.' Olola returned to Nairobi and now lives in a slum. She hawks fish in a market to earn a meager living. Her daughters dropped out of school because Olola could not afford school fees.[39]

Adhiambo Nyakumabor, whose husband died of AIDS in 1998 and left her HIV-positive with five children, went from being relatively affluent to destitute after her husband's family took her property. Her in-laws grabbed household items from her Nairobi home and took over her house and land on the island of Rusinga even though Nyakumabor helped pay to construct the house. Soon after her husband's death, Nyakumabor's father-in-law called a family meeting, told her to choose an inheritor, and ordered her to be cleansed by having sex with a fisherman. Nyakumabor refused, causing an uproar. She felt ostracized and quickly returned to Nairobi. A brother-in-law took over her land and livestock on Rusinga without compensating Nyakumabor. She now struggles to meet her family's needs, and her landlord in Nairobi's Kibera slum has threatened to evict her because she cannot always pay rent on time.[40]

Dowry can exacerbate property rights violations: if it is paid, some people consider the woman herself as property, and she has less bargaining power to defend her rights or resist wife inheritance. Patricia Wairium, a thirty-six-year-old widow from the Maragoli ethnic group, lived in Nairobi when her

[39] Human Rights Watch interview with Monica Olola, Nairobi, 18 October 2002.
[40] Human Rights Watch interview with Adhiambo Nyakumabor, Nairobi, 19 October 2002.

husband died in 1995. Shortly after he died, Wairium's in-laws raided her Nairobi home and stripped it bare. They wanted her to be inherited because they had paid dowry. With her Nairobi home empty and her in-laws pressuring her to be inherited, Wairium decided to move back to her parents' home, where she stayed for two years. 'I went back to my parents with just the few things that I had locked up', she said. 'I had to start over to buy things. My in-laws refused to give me my things.'[41]

Many women, particularly in urban areas, cohabit with men but do not complete all steps for a customary, civil, or religious marriage to be definitively recognized. Many of these women consider themselves married and in fact may have enforceable rights under the common-law doctrine of presumption of marriage. Women in this status are prime candidates for disinheritance. In-laws use this hazy marital status along with other excuses, such as having no sons, to disinherit these women.

Although urban widows are somewhat less connected to traditions than rural widows, this does not stop their in-laws from threatening violence if the widows refuse to be inherited. It also does not stop women from abandoning their property to flee the danger, nor from silencing themselves so as not to transgress cultural norms. Pamela Adhiambo, a thirty-two-year-old Luo woman, said that, after her husband's burial in 2001, she heard rumors that her in-laws wanted her to be inherited. She quickly left her husband's homestead without the livestock and household goods she and her husband kept there. 'I heard that if I refused to be inherited, they'd come in a group and rape me. . . . The elders would look for people to do it. I had heard of this in the vicinity where I was married.' Adhiambo was not aware that she might have some right to that property: 'I really had no right. As much as they were my husband's belongings, I had no right.'[42]

8.5.3 Women Whose Parents Have Died

Although statutory law provides that daughters and sons should inherit equally from parents when there is no will, it is uncommon for women in Kenya to inherit property from their parents on an equal basis with brothers. Daughters typically inherit less, and in some cases nothing, since they are expected to get married and be supported by their husbands.

Married women are even less likely than unmarried women to inherit from their parents because they are deemed to belong to the husband's clan. It is so uncommon for married women to inherit that none of the women Human Rights Watch interviewed tried to get a portion, much less an equal share, of their parents' estate. Susan Wagitangu, a fifty-three-year-old Kikuyu

---

[41] Human Rights Watch interview with Patricia Wairium, Nairobi, 22 October 2002.
[42] Human Rights Watch interview with Pamela Adhiambo, Kisumu, 4 November 2002.

woman, said that when her parents died, her three brothers inherited the
family land. 'My sister and I didn't inherit', she said. 'Traditionally, in my
culture, once a woman gets married, she does not inherit from her father.
The assumption is that once a woman gets married she will be given land
where she got married.' This was not the case for Wagitangu: when her
husband died, her brothers-in-law forced her off that homestead and took
her cows. She said she 'never dared to ask' about inheriting her parents'
property. 'I would like to claim a part of the land left by my father, but I feel
so overwhelmed', she said. Wagitangu now lives in a Nairobi slum. 'Nairobi
has advantages', she said. 'If I don't have food, I can scavenge in the garbage
dump.'[43]

Custom not only interferes with women's statutory inheritance rights, but
also with Muslim women's already unequal inheritance rights under Islamic
law. The chief Kadhi, Kenya's top authority on Islamic law, said, 'Disinheritance of daughters is one of the biggest problems I have. I try to show this
is not correct. You must allow women to have a share. It becomes acrimo-
nious, and there is violence.'[44] Farida Mohammed, a thirty-four-year-old
Muslim woman whose father died in 2000, said, 'I didn't inherit. There was
land that my big brother inherited. . . . None of the sisters inherited. My
brother inherited because he's a man.' Two of her sisters are unmarried and
live on her late father's land, but still did not inherit.[45] Mona Hassan, a
thirty-seven-year-old Muslim woman of Asian descent, said that she and her
sisters did not inherit anything when her father died. 'My father had land,
money, and houses. My brothers got it all. The sisters got nothing.' She
attributes this to custom:

My problem was custom. In my custom, the estate goes from the father to the son
with the understanding that the son should take care of his sisters. My brothers do
not take this responsibility seriously. We're a Muslim family but still the tribal
customs are so strong. Our negative traditions drag us back. We tend to abide by
those systems more than religion.[46]

8.5.4 Divorced or Separated Women

Divorced and separated women told Human Rights Watch of leaving their
homes with nothing but clothing and never getting a share of the family
property. Despite case law establishing that women can be awarded half of

---

[43] Human Rights Watch interview with Susan Wagitangu, Nairobi, 29 October 2002.

[44] Human Rights Watch interview with Sheikh Hammad Mohamed Kassim, chief Kadhi,
Nairobi, 7 November 2002.

[45] Human Rights Watch interview with Farida Mohammed, Nairobi, 8 November 2002.

[46] Human Rights Watch telephone interview with Mona Hassan, Nairobi, 16 November
2002.

the family property, men typically keep the house and almost everything in it, and women leave with practically nothing. Women are expected to go 'home' and live with their parents, which is not always an option. Domestic violence victims are hardest hit, often staying in abusive relationships for years because they think it is hopeless to have their husbands leave, and the women have nowhere else to go. 'In most cases it's the women who leave the matrimonial home upon separation. . . . Lots of abused women are held back by that', said a lawyer who handles domestic violence and property cases.[47]

Human Rights Watch interviewed women whose husbands had significant property during the marriage, but the women got none of it upon separation or divorce. Many said they had no idea they could claim a share of the family property. Tipira Kamuye, a thirty-five-year-old Maasai woman, was abused by her husband for years before they divorced in 1999. 'My husband cut me on the head', she said. 'He was going to kill me. . . . He told me, "I'll cut your neck", and tortured me.' Kamuye and her three children fled to her parents' home, and her father returned the dowry to her husband. At the time, her husband owned at least two hundred sheep and cattle, but she got none of them. Kamuye did not try to get a share of the matrimonial property: she believed elders would never allow a woman to keep family property and her husband would attack her if she tried to claim it. When asked whether she considered hiring a lawyer, she laughed. 'There's nothing like that here', she said. 'Maasais don't have that.'[48]

Some women who suffered domestic violence knew they were entitled to family property, but were so frightened of further attacks they did not attempt to claim a share. Mary Atieno, a Luhya woman living in Nairobi, separated from her husband in 1998 after his beatings and rapes became life threatening. She had briefly left her husband and reported the violence to police in 1996, but they took no action. Having nowhere else to stay, Atieno went back to her husband. When Atieno left the marriage for good, she did not take property. 'I didn't try to get the property because I was trying to save my life. I don't even want to dream about getting the property. I want nothing to do with my husband. I won't bother.' The family property at the time consisted of a commercial plot, money in a bank, a pension fund, household goods, and furniture. Atieno purchased most of the household goods and furniture. The house she shared with her husband had a tile roof, brick walls, cement floor, electricity, and running water. She and her children now live in Nairobi's Kibera slum in a one-room mud and iron shelter, where they initially slept on cardboard boxes. Her slum shelter has no electricity, water, or sanitation, and there are no public schools nearby. Atieno's parents

---

[47] Human Rights Watch interview with Ann Gathumbi, co-ordinator, Coalition on Violence Against Women, Nairobi, 17 October 2002.
[48] Human Rights Watch interview with Tipira Kamuye, Ngong, 24 October 2002.

would not let her live with them: 'To them it was not good that I left my husband and was spoiling tradition. Leaving a husband is like being a prostitute.'[49]

Even women who pay for property and have title solely in their name are not immune from property rights violations. Ndunge Ritah, a thirty-four-year-old Kamba woman, was separated from her husband on and off for several years. During one period of separation, she borrowed money, purchased land, and constructed a house, all in her name alone. When she reconciled with her husband in 2001, they moved into the house together. He became violent again, and accused her of sleeping with everyone who helped her construct the house. He threatened to kill her, slashed her face with a knife, and beat her so severely she could not get out of bed for three days. Ritah fled to her mother's house. She obtained legal services from a women's organization and filed for legal separation. Ritah's lawyer sent her husband a letter demanding that he move out of the house, which he ignored. At a preliminary hearing, a judge refused to order Ritah's husband to vacate the house even though the judge knew that Ritah paid for it herself and had title to the house. Ritah still pays the mortgage while she stays with friends and family, and her husband pays nothing.[50]

Dowry also impedes women from getting a share of family property upon divorce. For the Maasai, payment of dowry even means that the woman and any children she has or property she acquires for the rest of her life belong to her husband. Unless the dowry is returned to the husband, he can even take children the woman has with other men. Divorced women in such communities do not get family property because the dowry is supposed to suffice, even if the woman does not benefit from the dowry. Naiyeso Samperu, a forty-five-year-old Maasai woman who was forced to marry at age ten, separated from her husband because of his savage beatings. 'I was tortured all over my body', she said, and pointed out scars on her head, legs, and arms. Samperu's husband had more than one hundred cattle and sheep, but when she ran away from him she took only the clothes she was wearing. Her husband asked her father to return the dowry, but her father refused. Later, her husband took a child Samperu had had with another man. She reported this to the chief and elders in her village. The elders told her to 'let the child stay with him to represent the dowry that was not repaid. . . . I just cried and left.' The child was two years old at the time, and Samperu has not seen him for the last seventeen years.[51]

Of the sixteen divorced and separated women Human Rights Watch interviewed, only two were able to stay in their home from the time of

---

[49] Human Rights Watch interview with Mary Atieno, Nairobi, 28 October 2002.
[50] Human Rights Watch interview with Ndunge Ritah, Nairobi, 10 November 2002.
[51] Human Rights Watch interview with Naiyeso Samperu, Ngong, 24 October 2002.

separation. In one case, the woman was wealthy and thus had resources to afford an expensive court battle to keep her there. In the other, the woman was able to stay because her husband moved out of their dilapidated Nairobi shelter and into a modern Mombasa house.

Some Kenyans say that divorced women should not get property because they can go back to their parents. With the transformation that community and family structures have undergone since pre-colonial days, this is not always an option or the desire of the woman. Women who do turn to their families are often ordered to go back to their husbands, even when they are abusive. Women who have lost their property have a hard time contributing to costs in their families' homes and are considered an unwelcome economic burden. Mary Abudo, a fifty-four-year-old Luo woman with eight children, said that, when she and her husband separated, he kept all of the property, including vehicles, the land she cultivated, household goods, furniture, and bicycles, and she received nothing. Her violent husband forced her out of their home, and she went to her parents. They wanted her to return to her husband, but he would not take her back. Abudo stayed in her mother's hut, but was forced out when her mother died. Abudo did not try to claim any matrimonial property: 'I didn't dare to go back. My husband had issued threats.' He told Abudo's sister that if he saw Abudo he would 'kill her, and he was certain the government wouldn't do anything to him'. Abudo, who now has HIV, lives in a Nairobi slum and cannot afford medical treatment.[52]

Divorced and separated women from all social classes and ethnic groups experience property rights violations. In several cases, educated, formally-employed women who married men with high salaries and ample property told Human Rights Watch that they were evicted and left empty-handed just like poorer women. These women had enough knowledge of their rights to pursue legal claims, but had only limited success.

8.6 CONSEQUENCES OF WOMEN'S PROPERTY RIGHTS VIOLATIONS

As the accounts above illustrate, when a woman's property rights are violated, the consequence is not just that she loses assets. The repercussions reverberate throughout women's lives, often resulting in poverty, inhuman living conditions, and vulnerability to violence and disease for women and their dependents. Each of these consequences is amplified by Kenya's high HIV/AIDS rate: with increasing AIDS deaths, there are more widows who face potential property grabbing and its consequences. HIV infected and affected

---

[52] Human Rights Watch interview with Mary Abudo, Nairobi, 29 October 2002.

women and their dependents experience the hardships of losing property all the more intensely.

Living in squalor is one common consequence of women's property rights violations. The housing women resort to when evicted by their relatives is often decayed, cramped, and unsafe. In the case of women with HIV/AIDS, these conditions can lead to earlier death. As reflected in many of the testimonies above, women whom Human Rights Watch interviewed consistently described being forced to live in sub-standard housing: the physical structures are dilapidated; services (including running water, energy, and sanitation) are unavailable; and the locations (in terms of schools, health-care facilities, and safety) are bad. For example, Mary Adhiambo was forced to leave her rural home and land in 1998 after her husband beat her and demolished her home. 'Where I live now is a bad place in the Kibera slums', she said. 'It's a very small room. When it rains, water comes through the roof. I have no money for a better house. I have no electricity. I buy water from a stand pipe, but when I have no money, I have no water.'[53]

Women who lose their property lose their economic base and often descend into abject poverty. Many of the women Human Rights Watch interviewed said the property rights violations left them poor and struggling to pay school fees, buy food and water, obtain medical treatment, and meet other subsistence needs. Some were poor before the property rights violations but became infinitely poorer when their possessions, and especially their land, were taken from them. The traditional solutions to this dilemma—being inherited by a male in-law, remaining with an abusive husband, or returning to a father's homestead—keep women economically dependent on men and preserve their inequality. The poverty resulting from women's property rights abuses affects children, too. A teacher said: 'It's very common for children to drop out of school when their mothers are disinherited. . . . Some drop out because of general poverty, but when it comes to widows, it's even more serious. . . . I know a lady whose husband had built a house, but her mother-in-law came after the husband died and grabbed it. The child dropped out of school last week because the mother couldn't pay the school fees.'[54]

Violence is another by-product. Some women said they stayed in violent relationships for years because they believed no court or other authority would give them a share of the family property or remove the abusive partner

---

[53] Human Rights Watch interview with Mary Adhiambo, Nairobi, 28 October 2002.
[54] Human Rights Watch interview with Doris Adem, teacher, Siaya, 3 November 2002. President Kibaki declared in January 2003 that his government would comply with the legal requirement under the Children's Act of 2001 that primary schools not charge fees. 'If consistently enforced, this will help many dispossessed women.' Andrew Teyie and Ben Agina, 'Primary Education is Free from Monday, Says Kibaki', *East African Standard*, 4 January 2003 [online], http://www.eastandard.net/headlines/news0401200304.htm (retrieved 4 January 2003).

from the home. Some women were beaten, threatened, and harassed by husbands or relatives when they protested property rights violations. Women are also abused for trying to learn about their property rights. A paralegal who offers trainings on property rights said, 'Husbands have threatened, "don't ever go [to a training] again or I'll kick you out. . . . " One woman was beaten senseless for coming to our meeting.'[55]

Property rights violations also threaten women's health. Women who succumb to customary practices like wife inheritance and cleansing are vulnerable to all types of sexually transmitted diseases. An expert on HIV/AIDS and the law said women's property rights violations increase their vulnerability to HIV/AIDS: 'Because women do not own property as such, men have more say over them. They can't negotiate safer sex, and this increases infection.'[56] Many women with HIV/AIDS are likely to die sooner because of their unequal property rights, depriving them of the resources and shelter they need to survive. Women who have lost their property often cannot afford medical treatment.

8.7 CONTRIBUTING FACTORS

Women's property rights violations in Kenya are caused and aggravated by a blend of discriminatory laws, customs, and attitudes combined with ineffective institutions, official disregard, widespread ignorance of rights, and other obstacles to their enforcement.

8.7.1 Discriminatory Laws

Kenya's constitution outlaws discrimination on the basis of sex, but exemptions largely eviscerate the non-discrimination provisions. Article 70 of the constitution provides that all Kenyans are entitled to fundamental rights and freedoms, whatever their sex. Article 82(1) prohibits any law that is 'discriminatory either of itself or in its effect' and article 82(3) defines discrimination to include discrimination on the basis of sex. However, article 82(4) exempts certain laws from the discrimination prohibition. It permits discrimination 'with respect to adoption, marriage, divorce, burial, devolution of property on death or other matters of personal law' and with respect to 'the application in the case of members of a particular race or tribe of customary law with respect to any matter to the exclusion of any law with

---

[55] Human Rights Watch interview with Samson Michura, paralegal, Education Centre for Women in Democracy, Nairobi, 25 October 2002.
[56] Human Rights Watch interview with A. D. O. Rachier, advocate, Nairobi, 11 November 2002.

respect to that matter which is applicable in the case of other persons'.[57] In other words, in areas vital to women's property rights, such as marriage, inheritance, and the application of customary law, discrimination is sanctioned. As one lawyer observed, the current constitution 'gives with one hand and takes away with the other'.[58]

The Law of Succession Act of 1981, which attempted to bring some uniformity to succession in Kenya, should have improved women's inheritance rights. However, it contains several discriminatory provisions. This law governs both testamentary and intestate succession (succession with or without a will). Where there is no will, female and male children should inherit from their parents equally. If there is one surviving spouse and a child or children, the surviving spouse is entitled to (i) an absolute interest in the deceased's personal and household effects and (ii) a life interest in the rest of the estate. This means the surviving spouse becomes the absolute owner of personal and household items and can use other property (such as land and houses) during the spouse's lifetime. The spouse cannot dispose of the second category of property without court permission. If the surviving spouse is a woman, her interest in the property terminates if she remarries. A surviving husband's interest does not terminate upon remarriage. When the surviving spouse dies (or, in a woman's case, remarries), the estate goes to the children. The intestate succession rules also provide that, if one dies without a spouse or children, the estate goes first to the father, and if the father is dead to the mother. Thus, even though women have inheritance rights under this Act, men have greater rights.

Exceptions and misinterpretations also undermine the Law of Succession Act. The Act was amended in 1990 to exempt Muslims, who protested the equality provisions.[59] In addition, section 32 of the act exempts agricultural land, crops, and livestock in certain 'gazetted' districts (districts designated in a legal notice in the official gazette) from the intestacy rules. In those districts, customary law applies. Although the Law of Succession Act is clear about the exceptions, some judges and magistrates assert that all rural land, not just land in gazetted districts, is exempt from the Act. A justice on Kenya's highest court told Human Rights Watch, 'The Law of Succession Act can't apply [to rural land] because women are supposed to be married and go away.'[60]

Statutory law on division of family property remains so undeveloped that lawyers must resort to England's 1882 Married Women's Property Act[61] and

---

[57] Constitution of Kenya, article 82(4). The constitution was last amended in 1998.

[58] Human Rights Watch interview with Ann Njogu, executive director, Centre for Rehabilitation and Education of Abused Women, Nairobi, 16 October 2002.

[59] Act No. 21 of 1990. Muslims are subject only to Islamic laws on succession.

[60] Human Rights Watch interview with Justice Richard Otieno Kwach, Court of Appeal, Nairobi, 7 November 2002.

[61] The MWPA applies in Kenya as a statute of general application pursuant to a 1971 High Court decision.

Kenyan case law interpreting that Act. Case law establishes that women are entitled to half of the family property if they can prove contribution. This principle applies even to customary and Muslim marriages. However, the absence of a statute regulating division of property makes the application of this case law uneven. 'The gap in the law is glaring', said one women's rights lawyer. 'Why are we using an 1882 Act forty years after independence?'[62] Moreover, when Human Rights Watch discussed family property division with local officials, many had no idea that women could be entitled to anything, much less half of the family property, upon separation or divorce.

Land laws in Kenya, while not discriminatory on their face, have exacerbated women's inequality by recognizing men's traditional allocation rights as worthy of registration while ignoring women's user rights to clan land. Moreover, although a non-binding administrative decree instructs land control boards—bodies with authority to approve certain land transactions—to take families' interests into account, this guideline is not always effective. Men have reportedly bribed land control boards, fraudulently brought imposter 'wives' to the boards to consent to land transfers, and threatened their wives with violence or eviction if they withhold consent.[63]

Finally, customary property laws, as described above, overtly discriminate on the basis of sex by giving men greater rights than women to own, inherit, acquire, manage, and dispose of property. With the drastic changes in family and social structures since pre-colonial times as well as the health risks of HIV/AIDS and other diseases that thrive on women's subordination, this gender differentiation and the profound inequalities it produces are no longer justifiable.

8.7.2 Biased Attitudes

Many men—and some women—in Kenya believe that women should not be entitled to property rights, at least not on an equal basis with men. These attitudes influence the interpretation of customary laws, and vice versa. This cycle legitimizes women's subordination and inequality.

Traditional leaders and local government officials, whose views are influential in their communities and form the basis of customary laws, were candid with Human Rights Watch about their attitudes toward women and their property rights. A government-appointed senior chief in Kajiado district spelled out women's status as chattel: 'A woman and the cows are a

---

[62] Human Rights Watch interview with Martha Koome, Martha Koome & Co. Advocates, Nairobi, 6 November 2002.

[63] Human Rights Watch interview with Akinyi Nzioki, gender program officer, Royal Netherlands Embassy, Nairobi, 7 November 2002 and Human Rights Watch interview with Mary Wambua, head, Women's Bureau, Nairobi, 6 November 2002.

man's property', he said. 'The Maasai believe that the property within their
homestead is theirs—the children, the wife, the cows, the land—is all a man's
property. There are no disputes.'

An elder in rural Siaya district said he has never heard of a divorced
woman taking property, and only a man's name can go on a land title deed.
He said he knows the Law of Succession Act applies in his village, but in
practice, only sons inherit. He said, 'In the case of land, you can't let girls and
boys inherit equally because girls may marry. Even fifty years from now it
should be that way.' When asked whether these customs should change, he
replied, 'While making changes, women shouldn't be given freedom because
they will misuse property.'[64]

Individual men revealed similar attitudes. Kotet ole Supeyo, a Maasai
farmer, said 'In Maasai land, a woman can't have property on her own.' He
has given his sisters livestock during hard times, but their husbands, not his
sisters, actually own the livestock. 'The husband has to own the property
because the wife belongs to the husband', he explained. 'The husband owns
the wife.' He elaborated: 'Most women are not literate. They can't do anything by themselves. So in Maasai land, women have to rely totally on
men. . . . A woman can't sell property without consulting her husband. But
he can sell without consulting his wife.' In terms of land, he said, 'We don't
trust women. Women could go and sell the land.' He said some people give
land to unmarried daughters, but he has not done so.

Steven Oketch, a farmer in Siaya district, chuckled when asked if women
take property upon divorce. 'If there is a divorce, the woman returns to
her parents', he said. 'When she goes, she leaves everything. It would be
funny to hear of a woman leaving with property.' When asked if a divorced
man would ever leave the family home, he replied, 'Here it is the woman
who leaves. It is the man who brought the woman to the ancestral
land. . . . Even if they don't live on ancestral land, it is the woman who
leaves.' He thinks this would happen even if a woman bought the land, but
added, 'Actually, a woman has never bought land. It never happens that
a woman buys land.' In terms of women independently owning property,
he said this was impossible because 'they would automatically commit
adultery.'[65]

Some women are resigned to having inferior property rights, and others
even oppose the idea of women having equal property rights. Anna
Adhiambo, a Luo woman from Kisumu, said, 'I didn't inherit from my
parents because when parents die, daughters do not get anything. Boys
inherit, but girls do not. . . . This started much earlier. No one bothers to

[64] Human Rights Watch interview with Thomas Ojuang, elder, Siaya district, 3 November
2002.
[65] Human Rights Watch interview with Steven Oketch, Siaya district, 3 November 2002.

question it. We're born into it.' This is true even for her children: 'As much as I want to see change, it will be difficult. If I die, I know my son won't share with my daughters.'[66] A women's rights lawyer said an elderly woman recently told her, 'If we give land to a woman . . . she will be arrogant and won't serve her man.'[67] An NGO representative attributes this attitude to socialization:

Very few women have property registered in their name. Why? Patriarchy. The message is always reinforced that women can't own property. Even some women believe this. Women are socialized in many ways to think that this is the domain of men. . . . Even well-educated women fall in the same trap.[68]

Many supporters of women's equal property rights have a hard time realizing such rights in their own families. A fair number of individuals and officials expressed concern about the property rights violations perpetrated against women, yet few had co-registered property with their wives or written wills to ensure that wives and daughters would inherit. A district officer in the Rift Valley Province said that cultural limitations on women's property ownership stunt their development, but then said, 'All my property is in my name. I don't see any reason to put it in my wife's name. It's cultural.'[69] One former minister, who said 'a lot needs to be done to change attitudes and values in society' and supports women's equal property rights, acknowledged that he has not co-registered his property with his wife and has no written will to protect her from disinheritance.[70] An official in the Women's Bureau clearly supports women's equal property rights, but she and her husband have not co-registered their property: 'We bought land, and it's not in my name. We put up a small house, and my husband called it "his" house. My contribution is not considered.'[71]

Fear of community scorn also stops some families from respecting women's property rights. 'Even if a father is enlightened and wants his daughter to inherit,' said one property lawyer, 'he won't do this because he will be looked down on by his community. Society dictates this.'[72] According

[66] Human Rights Watch interview with Anna Adhiambo, Kisumu, 1 November 2002.

[67] Human Rights Watch interview with Judy Thongori, then deputy head of litigation, International Federation of Women Lawyers (FIDA-Kenya), Nairobi, 16 October 2002.

[68] Human Rights Watch interview with Ann Gathumbi, co-ordinator, Coalition on Violence against Women, Nairobi, 17 October 2002.

[69] Human Rights Watch interview with [name withheld], district officer, Rift Valley Province, 25 October 2002.

[70] Human Rights Watch interview with [name withheld], [title withheld], Nairobi, 7 November 2002.

[71] Human Rights Watch interview with [name withheld], Women's Bureau, Nairobi, 6 November 2002.

[72] Human Rights Watch interview with Jane Michuki, partner, Kimani & Michuki Advocates, Nairobi, 6 November 2002.

to one women's organization representative, 'Neighbors would laugh at a man if he left property to his daughter.'[73]

8.7.3 Unresponsive Authorities and Ineffective Courts

Since many women in Kenya never make it to court to claim property, they often turn to local authorities, both governmental and traditional, to resolve disputes. Although informal dispute resolution can help limit the financial and social costs of claiming property rights, local officials are more apt to apply customary law than statutory law, which can disadvantage women. Women told Human Rights Watch that local authorities were occasionally helpful but more often unresponsive or ineffective. 'We have poor local leadership', one NGO representative remarked. 'They're not responsive to the community.'[74] Moreover, police and central government officials acknowledged that women do not have equal property rights in Kenya, but officials do not consider this a pressing issue. Many local officials are loath to get involved in women's property cases, which they justify as a desire 'not to interfere with culture'.[75]

Women seldom go to police about property problems—unless their children are endangered—because they believe the police will turn them away, dismissing them as family or clan disputes. 'The problem with the police is that they don't like these cases of disinheritance of widows', said a paralegal in western Kenya. 'They say it's normal.'[76] A police official acknowledged: 'Women can't come here [for property cases]. We can't go into family cases on inheritance. Each tribe has its custom. Unless the law is changed to come to the criminal point, [we can't get involved]. For now, the elders sit together and decide.... When it comes to physical harm, we step in.... Evictions [by families] are handled under customary law.'[77]

Overall, the Kenyan government has not made women's property rights a priority. In 2002, Human Rights Watch interviewed officials in ministries and other government departments who could have played a role in preventing or redressing property rights violations, or at least in alleviating the hardships victims endure. These officials could not identify any program

[73] Human Rights Watch interview with Rose Mary Moraa, program manager, Maendoleo Ya Wanawake Organization Nairobi, 7 November 2002.
[74] Human Rights Watch interview with Elijah Agevi, regional director, Intermediate Technology Development Group, Nairobi, 20 October 2002.
[75] Human Rights Watch interview with Wilson Tulito Molill, senior chief, Ngong, 25 October 2002.
[76] Human Rights Watch interview with Eunice Awino, paralegal, Education Centre for Women in Democracy, Siaya, 2 November 2002.
[77] Human Rights Watch interview with P. O. Etyang, officer in charge, Police Division, Siaya, 4 November 2002.

aimed specifically at alleviating women's property rights violations. Since then, there have fortunately been some improvements in the official response to women's property rights violations, but on a relatively small scale. For example, Kenya's new National Commission on Human Rights initiated a human rights education program which includes women's property rights as a topic, but the pilot program is reaching only a small number of districts. The family court is said to be improving in how it handles inheritance cases, but it serves only litigants in Nairobi. The lands ministry has reconstituted land boards (which approve sales of family land) to include one-third representation of women, which may improve the treatment of women appearing before these boards. There are other examples of minor progress, but taken together, considering the massive scale of abuses, all these improvements probably make only a minuscule difference to the women of Kenya.

Even with the Kenyan government's increasing attention to the AIDS pandemic, official efforts to curb customary practices like wife inheritance and ritual cleansing, both of which can cause HIV transmission, have been inadequate. A UNAIDS official said that Kenya has not done enough to address women's property rights and their vulnerability to HIV/AIDS. 'Women's disinheritance in Kenya is terrible, a tragedy', he remarked. He said the government should discourage traditional rituals, which are 'shrouded in secrecy, and [require] that if a man dies, the woman has to sleep with a scum of society'.[78] An NGO representative said government officials put tradition over health concerns: 'I've not seen many government efforts to educate people about the HIV risks of widow inheritance and cleansing practices. I was at a meeting of government and religious leaders where they said a cure should be found first because these traditions should continue.'[79] Even the government-sponsored National AIDS Control Council acknowledges that Kenya's serious policy and strategic gaps relating to women's rights have contributed to the spread of HIV/AIDS.[80]

[78] Human Rights Watch interview with Dr. Warren Naamara, country programme adviser, UNAIDS, Nairobi, 31 October 2002.

[79] Human Rights Watch interview with Alie Eleveld, co-ordinator, Society of Women against AIDS in Kenya, Nairobi, 28 October 2002.

[80] A National AIDS Control Council (NACC) publication identifies the following gaps: a lack of strategies to implement inheritance rights; lack of specific interventions to address property ownership and inheritance by women in female-headed households; lack of interventions to address women's land ownership; lack of appropriate guidelines for marriage, separation, divorce, and ownership of property; and failure to outline measures to eliminate harmful cultural practices such as wife inheritance. Gender and HIV/AIDS Technical Sub-Committee of the National AIDS Control Council, *Mainstreaming Gender into the Kenya National HIV/AIDS Strategic Plan 2000–2005* (Nairobi: Office of the President, 2002) 4–5. NACC also confirmed in this publication that losing family property when a husband or father dies and practices such as wife inheritance increase widows' vulnerability to HIV infection. Ibid. 8–9.

Problems with Kenya's courts also contribute to the lack of redress for women's property rights violations. Lawyers and individual women complain that Kenya's courts are biased against women, slow, corrupt, and often staffed with ill-trained or incompetent judges and magistrates. These perceptions discourage women from using courts to assert property claims. 'There are biases on the bench', observed a lawyer at one women's NGO. 'Access to justice is lacking, but actually biases against women in the court are worse than anything else.... We see bias in both succession and marriage cases.'[81] Some say judges embody the attitude that women are inferior to men. 'Judges are men who were brought up to believe less in the rights of women', said one property rights lawyer. 'Judges say, "Why should women get property?" '[82] Even a government official who handles succession matters admits: 'Men judges do not apply the law. Our men are men whether they are judges or not. [Men judges] may believe a wife should not inherit.'[83]

Sometimes, courts simply do not enforce laws that could protect women's property rights. 'Most law is in writing, not in practice. The courts are far behind.... I don't think the courts enforce the law per se', said one government official.[84] This can happen if they think they have no jurisdiction, as exemplified by the remarks of a magistrate who, when asked if a court could order a man to leave the family home upon divorce, said: 'A woman can't come to court if she wants her husband to leave rather than her.... We don't interfere with the community set-up.'[85] It may also be due to ignorance of the law, although the head of the Family Division said she trained all judges and magistrates on family law.

Secular courts are not the only ones with problems. Kadhis' courts— religious courts that determine questions of Islamic law relating to personal status, marriage, divorce, and inheritance where all parties are Muslims—are also accused of being inept, slow, and costly. One lawyer who handles property cases for Muslim women said she prefers the secular High Court for divorce cases. 'A Kadhis' court is like a kangaroo court. It's frustrating to litigants and lawyers', she said. 'Kadhis are insensitive to women's issues.... More often than not, Muslim lawyers go to civil courts to advocate for rights of women.'[86] In some areas, the pull of custom is so strong that the

---

[81] Human Rights Watch interview with Judy Thongori, then deputy head of litigation, FIDA-Kenya, Nairobi, 16 October 2002.

[82] Human Rights Watch interview with Martha Koome, Martha Koome & Co. Advocates, Nairobi, 6 November 2002.

[83] Human Rights Watch interview with Mary Njoki Njuya, principal state counsel, Office of the Attorney General, Nairobi, 11 November 2002.

[84] Human Rights Watch interview with Mary Njoki Njuya, principal state counsel, Office of the Attorney General, Nairobi, 11 November 2002.

[85] Human Rights Watch interview with Francis Makori Omanta, senior resident magistrate, Siaya, 4 November 2002.

[86] Human Rights Watch interview with Abida Ali-Aroni, lawyer, Nairobi, 23 October 2002.

Kadhis have difficulty applying Islamic law. Kenya's Chief Kadhi said, 'Where custom is strong, it may be hard for a Kadhi because people will be hostile to him if he judges according to Islamic law, so they encourage some sort of settlement. Sometimes this may not be beneficial for women.'[87]

8.7.4 Other Obstacles to Women Claiming Property

Obstacles to women asserting their property rights in Kenya abound. The most serious are women's lack of awareness about their legal rights, the time and expense of pursuing property claims, violence, social stigma, poverty, and harassment of NGOs working on women's property rights.

Kenya's pluralistic legal system is complex and confusing even for those with high levels of education and access to information. For women not in that privileged position, it is unusual for them to know their legal rights. Many women interviewed by Human Rights Watch had not heard of laws relating to property at all or knew little of their content. The time it takes to pursue property claims, especially in court, is also an obstacle for many women. 'Many women give up going to court because it takes so long', said the head of a women's organization.[88]

The cost of claiming property rights is another deterrent. If a woman initiates a legal case, lawyers are her biggest expense. Of the women Human Rights Watch interviewed, two whose cases went the furthest had to pay legal fees of approximately KSh5 million (U.S.$62,893) and KSh8 million (U.S.$100,645), respectively. 'To go to court you just pay', said Patrice Nayoke, a widow from western Kenya. 'You're wasting money.'[89] Local dispute resolution, such as arbitration by elders or chiefs, can also be unaffordable. Susan Wagitangu, a widow from central Kenya, said, 'If you want to be assisted, you have to produce money. Even to go to the chief or the land department, they will always ask for money.'[90] A women's rights educator who trains local officials said, '[Informal] village courts are harsh to women. In most cases, widows spend a lot of money trying to pay a bribe to the elders to handle their [property] cases.'[91]

Threats of violence also inhibit women from pursuing property claims. Many divorced and separated women told Human Rights Watch that they feared their husbands would attack or kill them if they pursued their property

[87] Human Rights Watch interview with Sheikh Hammad Mohamed Kassim, chief Kadhi, Nairobi, 7 November 2002.

[88] Human Rights Watch interview with Tabitha Seii, executive director, Education Centre for Women in Democracy, Nairobi, 22 October 2002.

[89] Human Rights Watch interview with Patrice Nayoke, Kisumu, 1 November 2002.

[90] Human Rights Watch interview with Susan Wagitangu, Nairobi, 29 October 2002.

[91] Human Rights Watch interview with Zedekia Ouma, paralegal, Education Centre for Women in Democracy, Siaya, 4 November 2002.

rights. These women were also willing to tolerate abuse because their housing alternatives were limited. Some widows also said they feared violence from their in-laws if they tried to regain their property. Social stigma discourages women from claiming their property rights. Women who pursue property claims are often considered greedy traitors of custom. The near certain alienation they face from their families and communities stops many women from asserting property claims.

Poverty not only contributes to women's property rights violations, it also discourages women from claiming their rights. Some women simply cannot afford to pay what it takes to pursue property claims. Poverty can also increase the strain on families, leading to perceptions that a woman pursuing her rights is competing against her male relatives.

Finally, activists' and NGOs' ability to help women claim their property rights is jeopardized by harassment they face for doing their work. A paralegal who conducts civic education on women's property rights was once threatened after holding a training in a village: 'I received a call on my cell phone with a man's voice saying "If you ever set your foot in this place again, then you will not leave here alive. You will know there are men in charge here, not women."...I felt threatened. I thought I was going to lose my life.'[92] Another paralegal who works on inheritance cases said, 'The villagers get angry. Brothers who want to take widows' property say "I'm going to kill you" or that they'll do a witchcraft curse.'[93]

8.8 INTERNATIONAL LEGAL STANDARDS

When women in Kenya are forced out of their homes, stripped of their belongings, and coerced into risky sexual behaviors in order to keep their property simply because they are women, and when the government does little to prevent and redress this, they are experiencing human rights violations.

International human rights law proscribes discrimination, including on the basis of sex. It sets out certain civil, political, economic, social, and cultural rights and requires governments to respect and fulfill those rights in a non-discriminatory way. Human rights law also contains the principle that states have a duty to affirmatively protect human rights even from abuses committed by private actors. Kenya has ratified or acceded to international human rights treaties and has legal obligations under them, including with

---

[92] Human Rights Watch interview with Samson Michura, paralegal, Education Centre for Women in Democracy, Nairobi, 25 October 2002.

[93] Human Rights Watch interview with Zedekia Ouma, paralegal, Education Centre for Women in Democracy, Siaya, 4 November 2002.

respect to women's property rights.[94] A number of treaties and rights are implicated when women's property rights are violated.[95]

The principles of non-discrimination and equality are central to human rights. The core international treaty on women's rights, the Convention on the Elimination of All Forms of Discrimination against Women (CEDAW), defines discrimination against women as:

any distinction, exclusion or restriction made on the basis of sex which has the effect or purpose of impairing or nullifying the recognition, enjoyment or exercise by women, irrespective of their marital status, on the basis of equality of men and women, of human rights and fundamental freedoms in the political, economic, social, cultural, civil or any other field.[96]

CEDAW obliges states to 'refrain from engaging in any act or practice of discrimination against women and to ensure that public authorities and institutions shall act in conformity with this obligation' and to 'take all appropriate measures to eliminate discrimination against women by any person, organization or enterprise'.[97] It also requires that states 'take all appropriate measures, including legislation, to modify or abolish existing laws, regulations, customs and practices which constitute discrimination against women'.[98] The fact that men in Kenya have greater rights than women when it comes to owning, accessing, and inheriting property under the constitution, the Law of Succession Act, and customary laws violates the principle of non-discrimination.

CEDAW also recognizes that many women's rights abuses emanate from society and culture, and compels governments to take appropriate measures to correct these abuses. CEDAW requires governments to 'modify the social and cultural patterns of conduct of men and women, with a view to achieving the elimination of prejudices and customary and all other practices which are based on the idea of the inferiority or the superiority of either of the sexes or

---

[94] For example, Kenya has ratified or acceded to the following treaties: Convention on the Elimination of All Forms of Discrimination against Women (CEDAW), G.A. Res. 34/180, U.N. Doc. A/34/46, entered into force 3 September 1981 and acceded to by Kenya on 9 March 1984; the International Covenant on Civil and Political Rights (ICCPR), 999 U.N.T.S. 171, entered into force 23 March 1976 and acceded to by Kenya on 1 May 1972; the International Covenant on Economic, Social and Cultural Rights (ICESCR), G.A. Res. 2200 (XXI), 21 U.N. GAOR Supp. (No. 16), U.N. Doc. A/6316, entered into force 3 January 1976 and acceded to by Kenya on 1 May 1972; Universal Declaration of Human Rights (UDHR), G.A. Res. 217A(III), U.N. GAOR, 3d. Sess., pt. 1, at 71, U.N. Doc. A/810 (1948); and the African (Banjul) Charter on Human and Peoples' Rights (African Charter), adopted 26 June 1981, OAU Doc. CAB/LEG/67/3 rev. 5, 21 I.L.M. 58 (1982), entered into force 21 October 1986 and acceded to by Kenya on 23 January 1992.

[95] For an extensive overview of the international human rights instruments relating to women's equal rights to land, housing, and property, see Benschop, *Rights and Reality*, above n. 2.   [96] CEDAW, above n. 94, article 1.

[97] Ibid., article 2.   [98] Ibid.

on stereotyped roles for men and women'.[99] The Kenyan government has done little or nothing to comply with this requirement with respect to women's property rights. The constitution and statutes expressly permit the application of customary laws based on women's inferiority and stereotyped roles for women. Officials condone customary laws and practices even when they realize that they discriminate against women. The government's acquiescence to social and cultural patterns of conduct that harm women's property rights violates CEDAW.

Human rights law also requires that governments address the legal and social subordination women face in their families and marriages. Under CEDAW, states must:

take all appropriate measures to eliminate discrimination against women in all matters relating to marriage and family relations and in particular to ensure, on a basis of equality of men and women:

. . .

(b) The same right freely to choose a spouse and to enter into marriage only with their free and full consent;

(c) The same rights and responsibilities during marriage and at its dissolution; [and]

. . .

(h) The same rights for both spouses in respect of the *ownership, acquisition, management, administration, enjoyment and disposition of property*, whether free of charge or for a valuable consideration. [Emphasis added.][100]

Interpreting these provisions, the Committee on the Elimination of Discrimination against Women (CEDAW Committee) noted that violations of women's marriage and family rights are not only discriminatory, but stifle women's development. The CEDAW Committee observed:

[A]ny law or custom that grants men a right to a greater share of property at the end of a marriage or de facto relationship, or on the death of a relative, is discriminatory and will have a serious impact on a woman's practical ability to divorce her husband, to support herself or her family, and to live in dignity as an independent person.[101]

Kenya's laws and customs violate women's marriage and family rights under CEDAW. The coercive nature of wife inheritance arrangements, where widows do not have a reasonable alternative and cannot choose the union freely, violates the right to choose a spouse and enter into marriage with free

[99] CEDAW, above n. 94, article 5(a).

[100] Ibid., article 16. The ICCPR also provides that governments must guarantee the equal rights of spouses as to marriage, during marriage, and at its dissolution. ICCPR, above n. 94, article 23(4).

[101] CEDAW Committee, General Recommendation 21, Equality in marriage and family relations (Thirteenth session, 1992), Compilation of General Comments and General Recommendations Adopted by Human Rights Treaty Bodies, U.N. Doc. HRI/GEN/1/Rev.1 at 90 (1994), para. 28.

and full consent. Women and men have vastly different property rights, especially under customary law, during marriage and at its dissolution. Since women are unable to inherit and retain family property upon separation or divorce on an equal basis with men, their rights are unequal to men's in respect of owning, acquiring, enjoying, and disposing of property. Women are less able than men to manage, administer, and dispose of property during marriage: customarily and in practice, men have far greater rights than women to determine how family property will be used or transferred. All of this violates CEDAW and other sources of international law.

International human rights law increasingly recognizes women's right to sexual autonomy, including the right to be free from non-consensual sexual relations. The right to sexual autonomy is reflected in a number of international declarations and conference documents.[102] Sexual autonomy is closely linked to the rights to physical security and bodily integrity,[103] the right to consent to and freely enter into a marriage, as well as equal rights within the marriage.[104] When women are subjected to sexual coercion with no realistic possibility for redress, a woman's right to make free decisions regarding her sexual relations is violated. Lack of sexual autonomy may also expose women to serious risks to their reproductive and sexual health. In Kenya, women's rights to sexual autonomy, physical integrity, and security of person are violated when women are forced to undergo traditional rituals like cleansing and wife inheritance involving non-consensual sex and when they are physically abused in connection with property rights violations.

Protections against abuses associated with HIV/AIDS are, at least by inference, included in international treaties. In 1998, the Office of the

---

[102] At the U.N. International Conference on Population and Development held in October 1994 in Cairo, Egypt, and the U.N. Fourth World Conference on Women held in September 1995 in Beijing, China, governments explicitly endorsed women's sexual autonomy. In the 1994 Cairo Programme of Action on Population and Development, delegates from governments around the world pledged to eliminate all practices that discriminate against women and to assist women to 'establish and realize their rights, including those that relate to reproductive and sexual health'. In the 1995 Beijing Declaration and Platform for Action, delegates from governments around the world recognized that women's human rights include their right to have control over and decide freely and responsibly on matters related to their sexuality free of coercion, discrimination, and violence. See United Nations, *Programme of Action of the United Nations International Conference on Population and Development* (New York: United Nations Publications, 1994), A/CONF.171/13, 18 October 1994, para. 4.4(c) and United Nations, *Beijing Declaration and Platform for Action* (New York: United Nations Publications, 1995), A/CONF.177/20, 17 October 1995, para. 223.

[103] ICCPR, above n. 94, article 9. Article 9 of the ICCPR guarantees to everyone 'liberty and security of person'. This right, although traditionally applied to conditions of arrest or detention, has been expanded over time to cover non-custodial situations.

[104] ICCPR, above n. 94, article 23 and CEDAW, above n. 94, article 16. See also article 16 of the UDHR.

U.N. High Commissioner for Human Rights and UNAIDS issued 'HIV/ AIDS and Human Rights: International Guidelines', which provide a framework for governments seeking to incorporate human rights protections related to HIV/AIDS into national law. The guidelines cover a range of issues, such as the need for protection against discrimination and eliminating violence against women, including harmful traditional practices, sexual abuse, and exploitation.[105] According to the Committee on Economic, Social and Cultural Rights (CESCR), the right to the enjoyment of the highest attainable standard of health under article 12 of the International Covenant on Economic, Social and Cultural Rights (ICESCR) includes the right to information and education concerning prevailing health problems, their prevention, and control.[106] Similarly, under the African Charter, states must 'promote and ensure through teaching, education and publication' respect for and understanding of human rights.[107] The Kenyan government's failure to combat women's property rights violations as a means of halting the spread of AIDS and its failure to ensure that people in Kenya understand the HIV/AIDS and other health risks associated with women's property rights violations and harmful customary practices violate these rights and obligations.

Women also have a human right to equal legal capacity. CEDAW calls on governments to accord women a legal capacity identical to that of men and the same opportunities to exercise that capacity. It provides that governments must 'give women equal rights to conclude contracts and to administer property and shall treat them equally in all stages of procedure in courts and tribunals'.[108] Similarly, the International Covenant on Civil and Political Rights (ICCPR) provides that everyone has a right to be recognized everywhere as a person before the law.[109] Unlike men in Kenya, women face significant obstacles to realizing their right to administer property, an aspect of the right to equal legal capacity. Moreover, the Human Rights Committee says that this right means that 'women may not be treated as objects to be given together with the property of the deceased husband to his family'.[110] Wife inheritance in Kenya violates this human right.

The 'right to property' is guaranteed under the African Charter on Human and Peoples' Rights (African Charter), which also requires that all rights be

---

[105] Office of the United Nations High Commissioner for Human Rights and the Joint United Nations Programme on HIV/AIDS, 'HIVAIDS and Human Rights: International Guidelines' (from the second international consultation on HIV/AIDS and human rights, 23–25 September 1996, Geneva), U.N. Doc. HR/PUB/98/1, Geneva, 1998.
[106] Committee on Economic, Social and Cultural Rights (CESCR), General Comment 14, The right to the highest attainable standard of health, U.N. Doc. E/C.12.2000.4, paras. 12(b), 16 and note 8.   [107] African Charter, above n. 94, article 25.
[108] CEDAW, above n. 94, article 15.   [109] ICCPR, above n. 94, article 16.
[110] Human Rights Committee, General Comment 28, Equality of rights between men and women (article 3), U.N. Doc. CCPR/C/21/Rev.1/Add.10 (2000), para. 19. The Human Rights Committee is the U.N. body charged with monitoring implementation of the ICCPR.

implemented in a non-discriminatory way.[111] The Universal Declaration of Human Rights, which is widely regarded as customary international law, provides, 'Everyone has the right to own property alone as well as in association with others.'[112] At a minimum, this right means that men and women must have equal property rights. That is not the case in Kenya, where women have lesser rights than men to inheritance and, in practice, division and control of matrimonial property.

Women's equal right to inherit, while not explicit in international treaties, can be inferred from rights to equality and non-discrimination. It is also supported by a protocol on women's rights in the African human rights system, although this protocol is not yet in force. Moreover, several international treaty bodies have recognized women's equal inheritance rights. The Human Rights Committee noted in a general comment, 'Women should also have equal inheritance rights to those of men when the dissolution of marriage is caused by the death of one of the spouses.'[113] The CEDAW Committee, in interpreting women's right to equality in marriage and family relations, elaborated:

There are many countries where the law and practice concerning inheritance and property result in serious discrimination against women. As a result of this uneven treatment, women may receive a smaller share of the husband's or father's property at his death than would widowers and sons. In some instances, women are granted limited and controlled rights and receive income only from the deceased's property. Often inheritance rights for widows do not reflect the principles of equal ownership of property acquired during marriage. Such provisions contravene the Convention and should be abolished.[114]

International law also guarantees housing rights, which include equal rights to security of tenure and access to housing and land. The ICESCR recognizes 'the right of everyone to an adequate standard of living for himself and his family, including adequate...housing'.[115] CEDAW also requires states to ensure rural women's right to enjoy adequate living conditions, particularly in relation to housing.[116] The ICCPR prohibits arbitrary or unlawful interference with one's home[117] and guarantees the right to choose

---

[111] African Charter, above n. 94, article 14.   [112] UDHR, above n. 94, article 17.
[113] Human Rights Committee, General Comment 28, para. 26.
[114] CEDAW Committee, General Recommendation No. 21, para. 35.
[115] ICESCR, above n. 94, article 11(1). The CESCR interpreted this right in its General Comment 4, which set forth the following factors for analyzing adequacy of housing: (a) legal security of tenure; (b) availability of services, materials, facilities, and infrastructure; (c) affordability; (d) habitability; (e) accessibility; (f) location; and (g) cultural adequacy. CESCR, General Comment 4, The right to adequate housing (art. 11(1) of the Covenant) (Sixth session, 1991), Compilation of General Comments and General Recommendations Adopted by Human Rights Treaty Bodies, UN Doc. HRI/GEN/1/Rev.1 (1994), p. 53.
[116] CEDAW, above n. 94, article 14(2)(h).   [117] ICCPR, above n. 94, article 17.

one's residence.[118] Other international treaties, such as those relating to children, race, and refugees, also include housing as a human right.[119] States must progressively realize the right to adequate housing and immediately end discrimination that creates a barrier to the enjoyment of this right.[120] Women's insecure tenure in their homes and on their land, as well as the dismal housing conditions they typically experience after their property is grabbed, are evidence of housing rights violations. The government's failure to remedy discrimination against women with respect to property leads to and exacerbates housing rights violations.

Finally, states must not only facilitate women's exercise of their human rights by ensuring that the conditions for such exercise are free of coercion, discrimination, and violence,[121] but they must also provide an effective remedy if human rights are violated and enforce such remedies.[122] The Kenyan government has done far too little to create conditions conducive to women's exercise of their property rights, as evidenced by the coercive wife inheritance and cleansing practices, discriminatory laws and customs, and the violence women face if they try to assert their rights. Moreover, the fact that some judges, magistrates, police officials, and local authorities outright admit that they do not apply legislation and case law on inheritance and division of property demonstrates that Kenya is violating its obligation to provide an effective remedy to women's property rights violations.

8.9 CONCLUSION

Property rights abuses inflicted on women in Kenya should be recognized for what they are: gross violations of women's human rights. Discriminatory property laws and practices impoverish women and their dependents, put their lives at risk by increasing their vulnerability to HIV/AIDS and other diseases, drive them into abhorrent living conditions, subject them to violence, and relegate them to dependence on men and social inequality. Despite the slow recognition that property rights violations harm not just women and their dependents but Kenya's development as a whole, little has been done to prevent and redress these violations. Averting these abuses in a country where

---

[118] ICCPR, above n. 94, article 12.

[119] Convention on the Rights of the Child, U.N. Doc. A/44/25, entered into force on 2 September 1990 and ratified by Kenya on 30 July 1990, article 27(3); International Convention on the Elimination of All Forms of Racial Discrimination, 660 U.N.T.S. 195, entered into force on 4 January 1969 and acceded to by Kenya on 13 September 2001, article 5(e)(iii); Convention relating to the Status of Refugees, 189 U.N.T.S. 150, entered into force 22 April 1954 and acceded to by Kenya on 16 May 1966, article 21.

[120] ICESCR, above n. 94, article 2(1).

[121] United Nations, Programme of Action of the United Nations International Conference on Population & Development, para. 7.3. [122] ICCPR, above n. 94, article 2(3).

dispossessing women is considered normal will be difficult. A concerted effort is needed not just to improve legal protections, but to modify customary laws and practices and ultimately to change people's minds. With extreme poverty, a weak economy, rampant violence, and catastrophic HIV/AIDS rates, Kenya can no longer afford to ignore women's property rights violations. Eliminating discrimination against women with respect to property rights is not only a human rights obligation; for many women, it is a matter of life and death.

Part C

Child Labour and Access to Education

9

Child Labor, Education, and Children's Rights

GORDON BETCHERMAN, JEAN FARES,
AMY LUINSTRA, AND ROBERT PROUTY[1]

Nonetheless, if the fundamental rights behind our cause are not sufficient to move people to act, then let it be the economic and social
rationale behind it. Either way, we are going to challenge people to act.

> Nelson Mandela and Graca Machel, in calling for
> a global partnership for children in May 2000.

9.1 INTRODUCTION

Over 200 million children between 5 and 14 years of age are working
worldwide. This figure represents one-fifth of the total population of girls
and boys in this age group. About 111 million children are in what has
been termed as 'hazardous work' which refers to forms of labor which are
likely to have adverse effects on the child's safety, health, and moral development. Nearly 10 million of these children are engaged in some form of
slave labor, armed conflict, prostitution or pornography, or other illicit
activities. Some observers believe that these figures understate the real
magnitude of child labor.

The implications of this situation are significant, complex, and multidimensional. The hazardous and worst forms of child labor are of universal
concern, given the obvious harm that they inflict on the lives of these
children and their possibilities for a hopeful future. Child labor also has

[1] The authors are in the Human Development Network of the World Bank. This chapter
has been prepared under the direction of Jean-Louis Sarbib, Senior Vice President, Human
Development at the World Bank. All opinions expressed in this paper are those of the authors
and do not represent the views of the World Bank, its member countries, or its Board of
Executive Directors.

important economic implications. Most notable are the substantial future income losses that working children will incur because of the negative consequences working will have on their human capital, including their health and education. Since children are more likely to work and not go to school if their parents worked as children, the economic losses associated with child labor and their implications for poverty are often transmitted across generations.

Studies have concluded that eliminating child labor and putting these children into education would have huge aggregate developmental benefits. Gains would primarily be through the added productive capacity of future generations that had the benefit of education, as opposed to having worked as children. Very recently, the International Labour Organization (ILO)[2] has published estimates that the discounted present value of this economic gain would be in the order of US$5 trillion over the 2000–2020 period. While such a calculation is inherently imprecise, any plausible set of assumptions would yield a very large benefit, far in excess of the costs that would be incurred. Of course, in addition to the economic argument, there are compelling, if difficult-to-quantify, moral concerns with the worst forms of child labor, as noted above.

As the international community rallies around the Millennium Development Goals (MDGs) as a comprehensive vision for development, child labor, in fact, stands as a serious obstacle to achieving a number of the goals including poverty reduction. Most directly, child labor has obvious implications for meeting the goal of universal primary education. In April 2000, the international community committed to Education For All (EFA), a partnership to achieve education for every citizen in every society. This initiative will not meet its objectives by focusing only on the education system itself. Because of its implications for schooling, child labor must be addressed if the rights to education at the heart of EFA are implemented meaningfully.

Child labor, of course, has already received considerable attention. Most countries have long had prescriptive legislation as well as compulsory education laws. At the international level, child labor has been the focus of various conventions and recommendations. Most significant have been the UN Convention on the Rights of the Child (1989)[3] and two ILO conventions, the Minimum Age Convention (No. 138, 1973)[4] and the Worst Forms of Child Labor Convention (No. 182, 1999).[5] In promoting children's

---

[2] ILO, *Investing in Every Child, An Economic Study of the Costs and Benefits of Eliminating Child Labour* (Geneva: ILO, 2004).

[3] G.A. res. 44/25, annex, 44 U.N. GAOR Supp. (No. 49) at 167, U.N. Doc. A/44/49 (1989), *entered into force* 2 September 1990.

[4] 26 June 1973, 1015 U.N.T.S. 297, *entered into force* 19 June 1976 (Convention 138).

[5] 38 I.L.M. 1207 (1999), *entered into force* 19 November 2000 (Convention 182).

rights, each of these instruments—in very different ways—has been motivated by an interest in protecting children from exploitation through their labor and providing for education as a preferable alternative.

As Myers has argued,[6] the content of these conventions reflects an evolution within the international community in thinking about how children's rights should be applied to child labor and education. Starting from a Euro/American-centric view of the meaning of childhood which dominated the international debate for much of the twentieth century, the Convention on the Rights of the Child and, even more so, the Worst Forms of Child Labor Convention reflect a recognition that child labor is a complex phenomenon, with various forms, diverse underlying causes, and different meanings in different cultural contexts. Understanding these realities sharpens the discussion on child labor and builds consensus on appropriate responses. It would be difficult for any concerned individual or organization to not support the goal of Convention 182 to eliminate children working in the unconditional worst forms (slavery, prostitution, armed conflict, drug trafficking, etc.) or in work that is unsafe, unhealthy, or hazardous to mental, emotional, and physical development.

However, while consensus may have been established against the very visible forms of child labor targeted by Convention 182, these do not describe the work life of tens of millions of working children. The reality is quite complicated. The vast majority of child workers are involved in agricultural work, typically in family-run farms. In Africa, where the incidence of child labor is highest, rural children are at least twice as likely to be working as urban children. A significant proportion of working children are enrolled in school as well, although there is a lot of evidence confirming the adverse impact of child labor on educational achievement.

Reflecting this complex reality, addressing child labor and, thus, achieving universal education goals requires complex approaches. Effective policy responses depend 'upon recognizing that most children work with or for their parents in economies where markets are underdeveloped and the legal and political infrastructure is thin'.[7] Understanding household decision-making and the incentives and constraints facing families is essential, then, to comprehend why child labor exists and to consider interventions that can effectively address the underlying causes.

It is true that the incidence of child labor is associated with poverty, so policies that alleviate poverty are likely to have beneficial outcomes. However, empirical research in recent years has shown that the relationship between poverty and child labor is weaker than is often believed. Other forces clearly

[6] W. Myers, 'The Right Rights? Child Labor in a Globalizing World', *The Annals of the American Academy of Political and Social Science*, May 2001, 38–55.

[7] S. Bhalotra and Z. Tzannatos, 'Child Labor: What have we learnt?', Social Protection Discussion Paper No. 0317 (Washington D.C.: World Bank, 2003) 54.

come into play. For example, children may work because the economic returns to working may be greater than returns they would be able to accrue in low-quality, inaccessible schools. Or families in vulnerable situations may put children to work because they need the immediate benefits of their labor due to lack of access to credit instruments or social safety nets. These situations require multi-sectoral approaches that can involve, at a minimum, education, social protection, and health interventions, as well as enforcing compulsory education and child labor regulations. This comprehensive approach reinforces children's rights and solidifies the efforts to achieve a broad range of goals set by the Convention on the Rights of the Child.

In the next section, we review the international legal framework relating to child labor and access to education. In Section 9.3, we present a statistical portrait of child labor and educational participation. Section 9.4 looks at why children work from the perspective of household decision making. In Section 9.5, we consider policy options, discussing how interventions can improve the incentives to education relative to labor, remove constraints to schooling, and increase education participation through legislation. Conclusions are drawn in the final section.

9.2 HUMAN RIGHTS INSTRUMENTS

As noted above, the principal international legal instruments for addressing child labor include the Convention on the Rights of the Child which covers both child labor and the right to education and two ILO conventions, Convention 138 and Convention 182, 1999. The UN Universal Declaration on Human Rights[8] and the International Covenant on Economic, Social and Cultural Rights[9] also address the right to education but the above-listed instruments provide more detail and are commonly seen as the key international instruments for addressing children's rights. These instruments are summarized in Table 9.1.

The Convention on the Rights of the Child and the ILO child labor conventions have received widespread international support, the former being ratified by 192 countries—all U.N. members, in fact, save the United States and Somalia. Convention 182, prioritizing action against the worst forms of child labor, was the first convention adopted unanimously and has been the most rapidly ratified convention in the organization's 85-year history.

While widely supported, international human rights laws related to children do have limitations. Negotiated by governments (and, in the case of the

---

[8] G.A. res. 217A (III), U.N. Doc A/810 at 71 (1948).
[9] G.A. res. 2200A (XXI), 21 U.N. GAOR Supp. (No. 16) at 49, U.N. Doc. A/6316 (1966), 993 U.N.T.S. 3, *entered into force* 3 January 1976.

Table 9.1. *International human rights instruments related to education and child labor*

Title	Date	Ratified*	Provisions (Articles)
Universal Declaration on Human Rights	1948	N/A	Right to Education (26)
International Covenant on Economic, Social and Cultural Rights (CESCR)	1966	148	Compulsory and free primary education (13)
ILO Convention 138: Minimum Age	1973	131	Minimum Age of 15; exceptions for LDCs and 'light work'. Consolidated and replaced earlier Child Labor conventions
Convention on the Rights of the Child (CRC)	1989	192	Freedom of association (15); primary education (28); rest and leisure (31); no hazardous child labor (32); protection from sexual exploitation (34) and trafficking (35)
ILO Convention 182: Worst Forms of Child Labor	1999	147	Ban slavery, use in armed conflict, prostitution, drug trade; Work harmful to health safety, morals

*As of February, 2004.

Source: United Nations High Commissioner for Human Rights (http://www.un.org/rights/) and International Labour Organization (www.ilo.org).

ILO, social partners), they are the result of political consensus. They reflect what governments and interest groups could agree on, not necessarily what experts believe should be done. Once adopted by the international bodies, individual countries voluntarily decide to ratify and apply the convention in their national laws. While the international system provides mechanisms for oversight and monitoring, there are no international enforcement provisions; ratifying countries are responsible for enforcing their own laws. Some bilateral trade agreements, however, do refer to ILO conventions and provide options for sanctions. Despite these limitations, international conventions provide important standards or points of reference for developing national policy as well as benchmarks against which national policies and interventions can be monitored and assessed.

Standards for child labor and education policy are established with varying degrees of specificity in the three key instruments under discussion.

Convention 138 is the most specific international instrument pertaining to child labor. When adopted in 1973, it replaced ten previous ILO conventions referring to minimum working age in various industries. Unlike the Convention on the Rights of the Child, this convention does not refer to children as having rights; the purpose is simply to establish a minimum age at which they ought to be allowed to work. That age is set to 15 or not less than the end of compulsory schooling, with an exception for developing countries of 14. There are also exceptions for light work, defined as work which is not harmful to a child's health and development and which does not prejudice school attendance or participation in vocational training nor the capacity to benefit from the instruction received. Light work is allowed for ages 13–15, or 12–14 in developing countries. Hazardous work is to be generally banned for children under 18 but conditionally allowed at 16 if adequate protection and training is provided.

Convention 138 has been criticized for promoting a Euro-American view of children and childhood.[10] Critics note that it promotes a concept of an 'ideal childhood' as one free of responsibilities, including work, and dominated by education and leisure within the family context. Ethnographers in various contexts point to different models and realities of childhood.[11] A developed-country bias is also evident in the assumptions made about the institutional framework for implementation: a well-functioning labor inspectorate operating in primarily industrial settings; an adequate legal system; and compulsory, accessible, and high-quality education.

The Convention on the Rights of the Child was an ambitious attempt to safeguard the rights of children. In contrast to Convention 138, the Convention on the Rights of the Child articulates principles and objectives, giving broad scope to states to choose policy interventions that best fit their situation.[12] The Convention on the Rights of the Child establishes a right to education, acknowledging that fulfilling this right must be achieved progressively. It calls on states to make primary education compulsory and free and encourages the development of secondary education, including vocational training. Under the Convention on the Rights of the Child, governments must take measures to ensure regular attendance and the reduction of drop-outs. International co-operation to support developing countries in meeting these obligations is encouraged.

The Convention on the Rights of the Child also includes provisions related to child labor, including much of the language later adopted in Convention 182. The Convention on the Rights of the Child focuses on

---

[10] Myers, above n. 6.

[11] R. Baker and R. Hinton, 'Approaches to Children's Work and Rights in Nepal', *The Annals of the American Academy of Political and Social Science*, May 2001, 176–193.

[12] Myers, above n. 6.

protecting children from work that may harm them or 'their physical, mental, spiritual, moral, or social development' (Article 27). There is no blanket provision against children working, thereby acknowledging the reality of families in poor countries who may rely on their children's work, particularly in agriculture. The Convention on the Rights of the Child also breaks new ground in establishing the principle of acting in the best interests of the child (Article 3) and, importantly, giving the child who is capable of forming views the right to express them in all matters affecting the child (Article 12).

In 1999, the ILO adopted Convention 182, calling on all governments to take 'immediate and effective measures to secure the prohibition and elim-ination of the worst forms of child labour as a matter of urgency'. The worst forms identified by Convention 182 include slavery, trafficking, prostitution, and work likely to harm the health, safety, or morals of the children. An accompanying Recommendation (190) offers guidelines on what types of work may be considered hazardous, although the responsibility for defining such work rests with national governments. The Convention also calls for special attention to the situation of girls.

Convention 182 has received acclaim for achieving consensus between developed and developing countries, as well as among practitioners, advo-cates, and academics. It is largely viewed as having avoided Euro-American bias, incorporating relativist principles even as it established monitorable responsibilities for signatories. A strong consensus on Convention 182 has fueled mobilization of significant resources aimed at eliminating the worst forms of child labor.

The promotion of children's participation and empowerment in the Convention on the Rights of the Child and Convention 182 reflects a key contribution of the rights-based approach to development more broadly. This approach, which has been adopted by a number of bilateral and mul-tilateral development organizations, emphasizes the participation of poor people in development; social inclusion and equal access for all; and sup-porting governments in meeting their obligations under international law.[13] Rights-based approaches expand development objectives beyond physical assets and income growth, thereby promoting a wider range of possible policy interventions. By placing the interests of the child first and seeking ways to involve children and families in solutions, the Convention on the Rights of the Child and Convention 182 allow for complexity in under-standing the phenomenon of child labor as it varies by location, cultural context, and sector.

---

[13] Department for International Development, *Strategies for Achieving the International Development Targets: Human Rights for Poor People*, Consultation Document (London: DFID, 2000).

9.3 BASIC STATISTICS AND STYLIZED FACTS

In reviewing the incidence and severity of child labor, this section addresses three important questions: What is child labor? How prominent is it around the world? And what is the current state of knowledge regarding its key determinants?

While it seems straightforward, the definition of child labor is not simple and can be controversial. At the basis of this debate is the fact that child labor (unlike adult labor) is not only defined by the activity but also by its consequences. The age definition, subject to a lesser controversy, is guided by the Convention on the Rights of the Child and covers all children less than 18 years old. However, this definition does not reflect culture-specific experiences relating to when children start to make their own decisions and/or when they are no longer part of their parents' household.

The definition of 'labor' is subject to considerable debate. The broadest definition includes all children involved in any form of economic activity (for at least one hour during the reference week), encompassing most productive activities by children.[14] Because some of these activities fall within acceptable social and cultural norms, a distinction is made among various types of work. Convention 138 (Article 7), for example, stipulates that 'light work' should (a) not be harmful to a child's health and development and (b) should not prejudice attendance at school and participation in vocational training, nor the capacity to benefit from the instruction received. As we have already seen, the ILO also identifies activities that are hazardous, and which are unambiguously the worst forms of child labor. In several instances, disagreement about these definitions has postponed the ratification of ILO conventions.

According to the child labor statistics published by ILO's International Program on the Elimination of Child Labor (IPEC), in 2000 an estimated 211 million children aged 5–14 years, and 140 million children aged 15–17 years old were engaged in some form of economic activity (Table 9.2). Of this total number of children involved in economic activity, there are around 245 million in child labor, according to the ILO definition, including 170.5 million children engaged in hazardous work.[15] In addition to the number of

---

[14] As defined by the UN System of National Accounts (1993 Rev. 3), this includes unpaid and illegal work, work in the informal sector, and production of goods for own use. This definition does not include household chores, which are considered non-economic activities and therefore outside the 'production boundary', according to the System of National Accounts.

[15] The ILO estimates of child labor refer to all economically active children less than 12 years old; children between 12 and 14 who are performing non-light work; children between 15 and 17 working in hazardous occupations (e.g., mines, sporting goods and garments, glass bangles, matches and fireworks, carpet looms, tanning leather, breaking stones in quarries,

Table 9.2. *Children in economic activities, 2000*

	Levels (millions)	% of Total	% in total child population
5–14 Years Old	**211**		**17.6**
Industrialized economies	2.5	1	2
Transition economies	2.4	1	4
Asia and the Pacific	127.3	60	19
Latin America & Caribbean	17.4	8	16
Sub-Saharan Africa	48	23	29
Middle East/North Africa	13.4	6	15
15–17 Years Old	**140**		**42.4**
Industrialized economies	11.5	8.1	31.3
Transition economies	6.0	4.2	29.1
Asia and the Pacific	86.9	61.7	48.4
Latin America & Caribbean	10.3	7.3	25.0
Sub-Saharan Africa	18.1	12.8	44.8
Middle East/North Africa	7.5	5.3	31.8
Total	**351**		**23.0**

Source: ILO, *Every Child Counts: New Global Estimates on Child Labour* (Geneva: ILO, 2002).

children in hazardous work, it is estimated that about 8.4 million children are involved in the worst forms of child labor as defined by Convention 182. These children, including the sexually exploited and child soldiers (referred to immediately below), are the most vulnerable and need special and urgent attention.

The distribution of working children aged 5–14 years old varies significantly across regions. As shown in Table 9.2, Asia-Pacific has the largest number (127 million), while Sub-Saharan Africa has the highest incidence (29% of children are in child labor). For children aged 15 to 17 years old, Asia and the Pacific has the largest number of working children and the highest incidence of child labor.

Child Soldiers

More than 300,000 children under 18 are fighting in armed conflicts in over 30 countries worldwide. Of that total, approximately 120,000 are in sub-Saharan Africa. While the majority of child soldiers are between the ages of 15 and 18, children as young as 7 or 8 years old are known to participate in armed conflicts.

---

street vendors and porters, polishing surgical instruments, making bricks, working on garbage dumps); and the worst forms of child labor (e.g., trafficking, sexual exploitation, child soldiers, all such activities with direct harm to health, safety, and morals of children).

The 'forced or compulsory recruitment of children for use in armed conflict' is recognized as one of the worst forms of child labor under ILO Convention 182. The UN Optional Protocol on the Use of Children in Armed Conflict raises the minimum compulsory recruitment age to 18 for service in State Party armed forces. It also calls on ratifying governments to work to ensure that members of their armed forces who are under 18 do not take direct part in hostilities, and it promotes international co-operation in the rehabilitation and social integration of victims of acts contrary to the protocol. The immediate challenges to address this problem are:

- *PREVENTION:* Any action to prevent the recruitment and use of children in armed groups must be based on a sound understanding of the children's situation in the specific context in which recruitment is taking place;
- *DEMOBILIZATION:* Prior to demobilization, child soldiers must be disarmed, which entails assembling combatants and collecting the weapons used within the conflict zone. Demobilization refers to the process by which parties in a conflict begin to disband their military structure, and combatants begin their reintegration into civilian life;
- *REINTEGRATION:* Children are inevitably returning to an environment profoundly affected by war. Families may have changed; communities may be hostile to the former combatants; schools may be closed or destroyed; and families may have limited access to income-generating opportunities.

Sources: U.S. Department of Labor, Bureau of International Labor Affairs, International Child Labor Program.

In general, child labor takes two forms: unpaid work in the household or in the family farm/enterprise, and paid work in the labor market. The vast majority of working children are in agriculture work, typically on family-run farms. For example, in Africa, the incidence of child labor is at least twice as high in rural areas (see Table 9.4 below).

In recent years, there has been a growing literature describing the patterns of child labor and its causes and consequences. To illustrate some key dimensions of child labor, we briefly summarize the empirical findings on gender, income, and education.

- *Boys are more likely to be engaged in economic activity than girls, with the gender gap frequently substantial. However, this varies across regions and depending on the definition used.* Table 9.3 shows how boys' involvement in child labor as well as hazardous work exceeds that of girls.

These global estimates are supported by regional evidence. For example, in 11 of 15 countries included in a Latin American study, boys' economic activity rate was at least double that of girls, and in five, boys' economic activity rate was three times as great. These estimates, however, do not, consider household chores, which are technically non-economic activities

Table 9.3. *Gender distribution of child labor, children aged 5–14 years old, 2000*

	Levels (millions)	% of Total	% in total child population
Child Labor	**186.3**		**15.5**
Boys	97.8	52.5	15.9
Girls	88.5	47.5	15.2
Hazardous Work	**111.3**		**9.3**
Boys	61.3	55	9.9
Girls	50.0	45	8.5
Total	**211**	**100**	**17.6**

Source: ILO, *Every Child Counts: New Global Estimates on Child Labour* (Geneva: ILO, 2002).

and therefore outside the 'production boundary', according the UN System of National Accounts (1993 Rev. 3).

Indeed, since responsibility for household chores typically falls disproportionately on girls in most countries, estimates of involvement in work based solely on economic activity are likely to understate girls' participation in work relative to that of boys. Table 9.4 shows that, in Africa, the incidence of girls involved in household chores is 50 per cent higher than boys. In fact, once we include household chores in the child work definition, the gender gap in children's work disappears.

- *Cross-country evidence displays a negative relationship between the incidence of child labor and income; on the other hand, evidence from household data shows a weak correlation between child labor and household income.* Figure 9.1 displays a clear drop in the incidence of child labor as GDP per capita increases for low-income countries. However, the evidence also indicates a non-linear relationship, with child labor incidence elasticity decreasing as the level of per capita income rises.

This pattern is evident in Africa, where Table 9.4 shows the incidence of child labor significantly higher among the poorest households. However, more recently, micro data on the household level have been used to disentangle the income effect from other associated factors, including the development of legal and political infrastructure. The evidence shows a surprisingly weak correlation between child labor and household income once these other factors are taken into account.[16]

---

[16] E. Edmonds, 'Does Child Labor Decline with Improving Economic Status?' *NBER Working Paper No. 10134* (Washington D.C.: National Bureau of Economic Research, 2003); S. Bhalotra and C. Heady, 'Child Farm Labor: Theory and Evidence', Development Economics Working Paper #24 (London: Suntory and Toyota International Centre for Economic

Table 9.4. *Distribution of children in Africa, by category of activity*

	Work only (%)	Work and school (%)	School, no work (%)	Only HH chores (%)	Idle (%)
Age					
5–9 years	13.7	8.9	28.1	18.1	31.2
10–14 years	20.5	32.8	33.7	9.3	3.7
Gender					
Male	16.1	21.0	31.0	11.5	20.4
Female	17.6	19.3	30.5	16.6	16.0
Sector					
Urban	9.5	14.7	46.5	12.2	17.0
Rural	19.8	21.8	24.9	14.6	19.0
Income quintile					
Poorest	23.2	19.3	21.0	16.3	20.3
Richest	7.4	16.1	50.6	10.8	15.1
Mother's Education					
Formal	11.3	20.5	36.0	13.4	18.7
No Formal	20.9	19.7	23.8	15.9	19.8
Total	**16.9**	**20.1**	**30.7**	**14.1**	**18.2**

Notes: (a) The UNICEF definition of child work applies (economic activity or 4 or more hours of household chores per day); (b) The category 'only HH chores' is for children spending less than 4 hours on household chores per day.

Sources: UNICEF, MICS, DHS. Sample includes 18 countries.

- *There is a lot of evidence confirming the adverse impact of child labor on educational attainment.* A significant proportion of children are simultaneously working and enrolled in school. While the evidence on the effect of child labor on school enrollment is not very strong, there is evidence of a strong negative effect on school attendance, test scores, and grade completion.[17] This has important ramifications for achieving Education for All (see The Challenge of Education for All, below). On the other hand, as we will go on to emphasize, household decisions regarding children's activities are also affected by the relative returns to education, compared to returns from child labor activities.[18] A closely related issue is mothers'

and Related Disciplines, 2000); C. Rogers and K. Swinnerton, 'Inequality, Productivity, and Child Labor: Theory and Evidence' unpublished manuscript, 2001.

[17] P. Orazem and V. Gunnarsson, 'Child Labour, School Attendance and Performance: A Review' *ILO/IPEC Working Paper*, October 2003.

[18] M. Ravaillon and Q. Wodon, 'Does Child Labor Displace Schooling? Evidence on Behavioural Responses to an Enrolment Subsidy' 110 *The Economic Journal* C158 (2000); N. Ilahi, 'Children's Work and Schooling: Does Gender Matter? Evidence from Peru LSMS

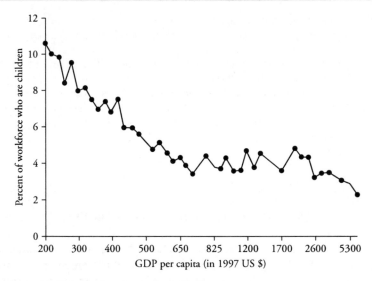

Figure 9.1. Child labor incidence and GDP per capita

education as an important determinant of children's activities (see Table 9.4 on Africa).

The Challenge of Education for All

An estimated 104 million children are currently without any access to primary schooling, of whom 56% are girls. South Asia and East Asia account for almost half of these children though, if current trends prevail, by 2015 more than half of out-of-school children will be African. An estimated 130 million children worldwide do not attend school regularly. Many of these children do not attend school because they are working.

Worldwide access to primary schooling has increased modestly in recent years. Both gross and net primary enrollment rates increased by 2 percentage points worldwide between 1990 and 2000, and by the same amount in developing countries. In sub-Saharan Africa, gross enrollment rates increased by 7 percentage points while net enrollment increased by 3 percentage points. Some countries achieved dramatic progress in expanding enrollments, improving schooling retention and completion rates, and reducing gender disparities. Enrollments in Uganda, Malawi, and Mauritania doubled between 1995 and 2000. These are positive trends, but unevenly distributed, and the scale of the EFA challenge remains huge. One child in four drops out without completing 5 years of basic education. Some 600 million women and 300 million men remain illiterate, and their children, as a group, are far less likely to be schooled than others.

Panel Data' Background Paper for the World Bank Research Report on Gender (Washington D.C.: World Bank, 1999).

Enrollment rates in many countries are stagnant. At present trends, as many as 86 countries will fail to meet the Millennium Development Goal of universal primary education completion by 2015.

Girls' enrollment trends have generally been positive. The annual EFA Global Monitoring Report for 2003–2004 shows a consistent narrowing of the gender gap. The gender parity index (GPI) worldwide in 1991, for instance, was 0.89. By 2000, it had increased to 0.93. Most of this gain was in developing countries, where the GPI increased from 0.87 in 1991 to 0.92 in 2000. Nevertheless, the gains are slow, and about 14 million more girls than boys were out of primary school in 2000.

9.4 UNDERSTANDING CHILD LABOR

While recognizing that child labor is influenced by various social and cultural factors, in this brief section we present an *economic* framework for understanding child labor. This allows us to shed light on important aspects of child labor, and offers a useful guide to policy in this arena. We use household decision making as the unit of analysis. Following Bhalotra[19] and Bhalotra and Tzannatos,[20] we describe a framework where children work instead of going to school because of some combination of the following: (i) *incentives* favor work, (ii) *constraints* compel children to work, and/or (iii) decisions are not made in the child's best interest (*agency* problem).

The incentives problem arises when the economic benefits of a child working will be greater than expected benefits of schooling. In these cases, then, parents can be making economically rational decisions in sending their children to work. This situation—in effect, where the ratio of the net returns to education relative to work is negative—will typically arise where education is too costly or offers little benefit. High costs can refer to either direct or opportunity costs of education. Direct costs may be high because of access issues: for example, fees may be expensive or transportation may be costly because schools are far away. Opportunity costs may be high when children are needed for non-school activities that are critical for household welfare (e.g., helping with the harvest, fetching water). On the other side of the cost-benefit equation, the returns to education may be low because of quality issues such as a lack of teaching materials, poor curricula, or inadequately trained teachers.

Even when expected returns to education are favorable, and parents have an economic incentive to send their children to school, they might not be able to afford the current costs of schooling (including opportunity costs stemming

[19] S. Bhalotra, 'Is Child Work Necessary?', Discussion Paper No. 26, (London: Suntory and Toyota International Centre for Economic and Related Disciplines, 2000).

[20] Bhalotra and Tzannatos, above n. 7.

from the income losses for children not working). Parents may be constrained from sending their children to school because of poverty or insurmountable short-term economic concerns. The direct costs of schooling may simply be unaffordable for chronically poor families or for families that are in a situation of transitory poverty because of a shock (e.g., job loss of a parent, drought, etc.). In a world of perfect markets, parents could borrow against the future income gains from the higher human capital of their children to finance current education expenditures. However, such instruments are normally not available, especially for poor or otherwise vulnerable families lacking collateral. In fact, for some households, child labor constitutes the only mechanism for intertemporal allocation of resources (i.e., using child labor to borrow from the future for present consumption). Imperfect labor markets may also pose constraints for households. Monitoring costs (and incomplete contracts) can make the employment of non-family members costly and lead households to use the labor of their own children as an alternative.[21]

The agency problem arises when children go to work instead of school because parents or others making decisions for them do not act in their interests. In some cases, the problem may be informational—i.e., parents are unaware of the economic benefits of education. In other cases, parents may simply not act altruistically relative to their children. Finally, a growing number of children have been orphaned or separated from their families because of HIV/AIDS and/or conflict. As a result, these children do not have parents or anyone else to act on their behalf.

9.5 POLICY OPTIONS

Understanding why children work is essential for designing appropriate interventions that reduce child labor and increase educational attendance. As discussed in the preceding section, parents face a variety of incentives and constraints in making choices on behalf of their children. In some cases, children do not have parents or other altruistic agents to make appropriate decisions for them nor are they given the right to participate in any decisions. Child labor may also result from market failures that can be addressed through public policy. Each of these problems has different policy implications so it is important to understand the relevance of each in any real situation in considering policy responses.

An additional aspect of public policy in the area of child labor concerns providing protection and services to children who are working. This is a controversial issue, since this line of discussion might be interpreted as

---

[21] In fact, one of the puzzles of the literature has been the finding that child labor *increases* with land ownership. This 'wealth effect' is not what one would expect when child labor is seen as driven primarily by poverty.

explicitly accepting child labor. However, as we have seen, child labor remains essential for some families and, at any rate, will not be eliminated immediately. Thus, policy makers need to be concerned with enforcing workplace health and safety and other labor standards, making educational and health services accessible to child workers, and offering vocational training and rehabilitation services. In addition to these interventions, all efforts should be made to remove children from hazardous and other worst forms of child labor.

Table 9.5 summarizes the policy options associated with the incentive, constraint, and agency issues. In the following subsections, we consider these in greater detail.

Table 9.5. *Examples of policy approaches to address child labor and school attendance*

Improving **incentives** for children to go to school	Removing **constraints** stopping children from going to school	Using **legislation** to encourage schooling and discourage labor
—Make school attendance more accessible (more schools, flexible scheduling) —Reduce or eliminate school fees —Eliminate discrimination against girls in school —Improve education quality (teaching, materials, etc.) —Improve basic services (e.g., access to clean water) —Eliminate wage discrimination against children (thereby reducing demand for child labor)	—Poverty-reduction strategies —Social safety nets —Conditional cash or food transfers (linked to participation in education or health services) —Financial instruments that allow access to credit, collateralize assets —Better labor market functioning	—Enforce compulsory education laws —Introduce and enforce appropriate child labor laws —Enforce labor laws to eliminate wage discrimination, etc.
Providing protection and rehabilitation **services for working children**		
—Remove children from hazardous and worst forms of child labor —Enforce health and safety and other employment standards —Provide access to education and health services —Offer vocational training and other rehabilitation services		

9.5.1 Improving Incentives for Schooling

In developing countries, one in five children aged 6–11 is not in school—more than 100 million children in total. In many areas, rural primary school enrollments are below half of enrollment rates in urban areas. The out-of-school rates for children with disabilities are up to ten times higher than for the population as a whole. For every four children who are in school, one will drop out before completing primary education. The children who do drop out of school, in part because of poor teaching and learning conditions, are predominantly poor, generally rural, and disproportionately female. Figure 9.2 shows a wide range across countries in terms of persistence in schooling and overall primary completion. Educational policies that reduce the costs of education or increase the expected returns will shift household incentives away from sending children to work and towards sending them to school. Making schools accessible, improving their quality, and reducing direct schooling costs can all serve to improve incentives.

Education may be costly because of inaccessibility. Some children are living in remote, under-served areas and do not have reasonable access to school. Only 32 per cent of children in rural Senegal, for example, live within walking distance of a school offering the full six-grade cycle. Available education services may be inaccessible for children with learning or other disabilities. A range of cultural and safety issues may also limit children's ability to seek out schooling opportunities. Lehman and Buys,[22] working in Chad, found that, contrary to initial hypotheses, enrollment drops off precipitously for children in satellite villages located less than 1 km from a school (Figure 9.3). This suggests that it is not just physical distance that is the problem, but also cultural distance can affect enrollment. The idea of sending one's child to a 'foreign' village may be one of the primary constraints.

Costs of education can also be high because of fees that are unaffordable for poor families. One option is that school be free. Another possibility is that schools serve food supplements which, in effect, can create a situation of 'negative fees' for the most disadvantaged children. As we will see in the next subsection, various social protection interventions can reduce the opportunity costs families can face in sending their children to school.

Poor quality can be a major issue that reduces the expected benefits of education and, thus, can be a disincentive to schooling. Schools in many developing regions suffer from problems such as overcrowding, inadequate sanitation, and under-skilled or apathetic teachers. As a result, parents may see little use in sending their children to school when they could be home

---

[22] Douglas Lehman and Piet Buys, 'Bringing the School to the Children: Shortening the Path to EFA' *Education Notes* (Washington D.C.: World Bank, 2002).

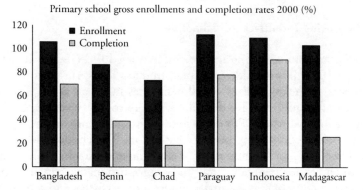

Figure 9.2. High enrollments may not produce high completion rates

Note: In many countries, school enrollment rate provides a very different picture from one given by the completion rate. In Madagascar, for example, 80 per cent of the students do not manage to complete the primary school education despite the country's high enrollment rate.

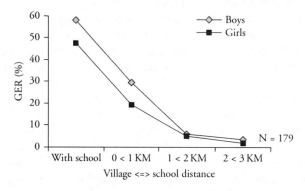

Figure 9.3. Distance and school attendance

learning a skill (for example, agriculture) and supplementing family income. Enhancing quality through better teachers, curricula and materials, or other reforms can increase the expected returns to education and thus increase the incentives for sending children to school. Because of the control parents have over the decision making process, their perception of the value of school is a main determinant of child attendance. Parents who are educated understand the importance of schooling from personal experience.

In 2002, the Fast Track Initiative (FTI) was launched in an effort to accelerate progress toward universal primary education. The FTI built on specific commitments expressed by the international community at the Monterrey conference in 2002. This involved committing to a boost in development aid in support of the MDGs within a framework of mutual responsibility and accountability in which donors would provide additional support to countries implementing sound policies and willing to be held accountable for results. This includes a set of key education policy and financing parameters which constitute an indicative framework against which countries' plans may be evaluated and monitored. These parameters are explicitly designed to ensure that children are able to complete a full program of primary schooling, and the benchmarks are outlined below:

Policy Benchmarks for Universal Primary Education by 2015*

Service Delivery

Avg. annual teacher salary	3.5 × per capita GNP
Pupil-teacher ratio	40:1
Non salary spending	33% of recurrent education spending
Average repetition rate	10% or lower
Annual hours of instruction	850 or more

System Expansion

Unit construction cost	$10,000 or less

System Financing

Government revenues	% of GDP 14–18 per cent (depending on p/c GDP)
Education spending	20% (as share of Government revenues)
Primary education spending	50% (as share of total education recurrent spending)

* *Benchmarks to be applied flexibly on the basis of country circumstances*

The FTI countries, as a group, have been moving in a more positive direction over the past decade than the developing countries as a whole (Figure 9.4). For the first ten FTI countries, gross enrollment rates (GER) averaged an increase of 33 percentage points, while primary completion rates (PCR) averaged 14 percentage point gains.

These positive outcomes suggest that, with sufficient political support both in a country and from the donor community, the goal of universal primary completion is attainable for most countries within the time frames suggested. This will also represent an important step in moving towards eradication of child labor.

9.5.2 Removing Constraints through Better Social Protection

As we have noted, children sometimes go to work, not because there is no incentive to send them to school but because of constraints families face in doing so. These constraints can stem from chronic poverty or from shocks of a more transitory nature—in either case, families sometimes are compelled to

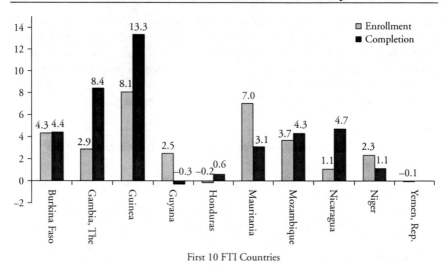

First 10 FTI Countries

Figure 9.4. GER and PCR annual growth: 1990–2002 (or most recent year)

Notes: For Gambia and Honduras, PCR start year is 1991; for Nicaragua, 1988; for Honduras, 1991; for Yemen, 1993. For purposes of comparability, Mauritania figures reflect Gr.5 completion (primary cycle changed from 5 to 7 years in 2000).

For Guyana, PCR MRY is 1999; for Mauritania, Honduras, and Guinea, 2001; for the Gambia and Yemen, 2000. For Burkina Faso, GER MRY is 2003; for Gambia, Guinea, Honduras, Mauritania, Mozambique, Nicaragua, Niger and Yemen, 2000; and for Guyana, 1999.

Source: World Bank, 'Education For All—Fast Track Initiative Progress Report,' 26 March 2004, prepared for Development Committee at the Spring Meetings of the World Bank and IMF based on statistics collected by the World Bank Education Statistics Unit and the UNESCO Institute for Statistics.

make decisions that may be necessary for the short run but are suboptimal in terms of their long-run welfare. Instruments that can effectively support families in managing risks related to poverty and other forms of vulnerability can reduce or eliminate these obstacles and give families choices beyond resorting to sending their children to work. This management of social risk is the task for social protection.

Social risk management includes market-based and informal arrangements (such as access to financial assets and insurance, and extended families), as well as public measures.[23] Table 9.6 identifies some examples in each of these categories that can help families manage risks that might otherwise lead to child labor. These can involve *ex-ante* (risk reduction or risk mitigation) strategies or *ex-post* (coping) strategies. Faced with a shock—for example, job

---

[23] Human Development Network of the World Bank, *From Safety Net to Springboard: Social Protection Strategy* (Washington D.C.: World Bank, 2001).

Table 9.6. *Examples of managing risks that can lead to child labor*

	Informal, household	Market	Public
Risk reduction			• Good economic policies • Good labor market policies (including labor standards)
Risk mitigation	• Multiple (adult) earners • Crop diversification	• Asset/social/ other types of insurance	• Social insurance plans
Risk coping	• Personal savings • Assistance from extended families • Selling assets	• Borrowing instruments	• Social safety nets • Good financial market policies

loss or disability of a breadwinner or a bad harvest—families may have to consider putting a child to work. However, there may be other household strategies, such as having the insurance of other adult earners or relying on savings or transfers from extended family to make up for the lost income. Studies from countries as different as Russia, the Philippines, and Kyrgyzstan have found that private transfers and savings are very important for families to cope with shocks. Some forms of social protection can be provided by financial markets in the form of private insurance (e.g., crop insurance, disability insurance) or in the form of credit instruments that allow families to cope with temporary income loss.

While such informal and market-based arrangements can provide social protection to families, they are, by themselves, insufficient. So public measures are a critical source of social protection in terms of helping families to deal with obstacles that might prevent them from sending their children to school. These include good economic and labor market policies that encourage growth, reduce poverty, and thus reduce the likelihood that families will be vulnerable to risks that might force them to put their children to work. In addition to a role in reducing risk, public policies and interventions can provide families with instruments that help them insure themselves against shocks such as job loss, disability, or crop failure. This can happen either through providing an effective and efficient framework for regulating privately-provided insurance or through directly providing the insurance, as in the case of unemployment insurance. In some cases, for example, pensions and disability insurance, governments may play both roles.

In situations where risks that may lead to child labor cannot be prevented or insured against, families wind up coping through various means (including child labor). Public safety nets are important here and, when effective, can offer families alternatives beyond sending children to work. Virtually all countries have some safety net programs in place, although their extent, sophistication, and effectiveness vary considerably. In many countries, these programs are in need of reform if they are going to offer the necessary support.[24]

However, there are many successful programs around the world, and different options for useful interventions. Public works, or workfare, programs have probably been the most widely used type of safety-net intervention in low-income countries. When designed well, these programs offer needed income (or food, in some cases) to poor households and can help them smooth consumption, without having to rely on strategies such as child labor.[25] Public works can also build badly-needed infrastructure in underdeveloped areas, such as roads, schools, and health clinics, that will directly increase access to education. Social funds in many countries have played a similar role.

Conditional transfers represent a type of safety net program with particular relevance to reducing child labor and increasing school attendance. These programs tie cash or, in some cases, food transfers to poor families that meet specific conditions such as sending children to school. They have been used most widely in Latin America.[26] One of that region's best known conditional cash transfer programs is Mexico's Progresa, which links cash grants and nutritional supplements to school and clinic attendance:

Mexico's *Progresa* Program

Progresa is a major program in Mexico aimed at developing the human capital of poor households. The program provides monetary transfers to families that are contingent upon their children's regular attendance at school. The benefit levels are intended to offset the opportunity costs of not sending children to school and

---

[24] Problems vary. In some cases, spending is too low to make much of a difference. In others, timing is the main problem—i.e., where countries cannot or do not increase spending in periods when need increases (e.g., crisis, recession). Sometimes implementation is the problem. For example, programs are poorly targeted, efforts are too fragmented among many programs, and interventions are not sufficiently evaluated in terms of their effectiveness.

[25] For a review of the experience with public works, see K. Subbarao, 'Systemic Shocks and Social Protection: Role and Effectiveness of Public Works Programs', Social Protection Discussion Paper No. 0302 (Washington D.C.: World Bank, 2003).

[26] There may be other conditions—e.g., attendance at health clinics. For a review of conditional cash/food transfers in Latin America, see L. Rawlings and G. Rubio, 'Evaluating the Impact of Conditional Cash Transfer Programs: Lessons from Latin America', unpublished manuscript, World Bank, 2003.

increase with the grade level in school—recognizing that the opportunity cost of children's time increases as they grow older. In order to ensure the gender lags in secondary enrollment are reversed, it offers higher transfers for girls than for boys attending secondary school. Evaluation of the program indicates that it has significantly increased the enrollment of boys and girls, particularly of girls, and above all, at the secondary level. The results imply that the children will have an average of 0.7 years of extra schooling because of *Progresa,* although this effect may increase if children are more likely to go on to senior high school as a result of the program.

Evaluations have shown that this program has reduced child labor and increased education levels among the poor. Bangladesh has had an innovative Food for Education program, which provided a free monthly ration of rice or wheat to poor families if their children attend primary school. Turkey has recently introduced a conditional cash transfer as part of a comprehensive initiative to increase school attendance and to improve health care utilization of children.

In many developing countries, especially low-income ones, resources available for conditional transfer programs and other types of safety nets are limited. As a result, targeting is very important if public policy is going to be successful. Effective safety nets targeted on the poor and most vulnerable are absolutely essential if these families are going to have choices to invest in their children.[27]

9.5.3 Addressing Agency Problems and Market Failure

Thus far, we have argued that the supply of child labor is a decision made at the household level based on incentives and constraints. Here, the government can only indirectly influence the decision-making process through provision of better, more accessible schools or social protection interventions such as conditional cash transfers. In this section we discuss the use of legal instruments, namely, setting a minimum age for employment, banning child labor or certain forms of child labor, and/or establishing mandatory education.

There is considerable debate about the effectiveness of legislative interventions in the fight against child labor. In the worst case, sudden dismissal of children from work in relatively safe, well-remunerated jobs can lead poor children into considerably more dangerous and hidden worst forms of child labor. In the best case, legal bans on child labor can reduce the supply of and

[27] Disability provides a good example. With about 10% of the world's people disabled and only 5% of disabled children receiving formal education worldwide, the education for all goal is out of reach unless special support to this vulnerable group is given.

demand for child labor, raising wages for adults and increasing household income, making child labor unnecessary. There are no guarantees, however, that bans on child labor will have significant impact on reducing the incidence of child labor. Before exploring the conditions in which legal mechanisms are likely to have the most effect, it is important to emphasize that the worst forms of child labor should be banned in every circumstance. State authorities ought to do all in their power to enforce laws protecting children from the exploitative circumstances identified in Convention 182.

The first child labor law was passed in Britain in 1802. The 200-year history of attempts to eliminate child labor by legislative fiat since then shows mixed results. Srivastava and Raj[28] cite Basu's review of the literature that finds examples where bans on child labor played an important role in its elimination, such as in the cotton mills of Manchester. In other cases, however, dramatic reductions in child labor were achieved with no legislative intervention (e.g., Belgium in the nineteenth century). The decline in the incidence of child labor between 1880 and 1920 in industrialized countries is thought to be due to both economic and legal reasons, with the former predominating.

Governments almost universally have laws establishing a minimum age for employment, banning certain types of child labor, and requiring attendance at school. The international human rights instruments discussed in Section 9.2 offer important guidance for these laws. Nonetheless, a recent comparative review of child labor legislation by the OECD found many examples of child labor laws that were unclear, fragmented, or inconsistent with compulsory education laws.[29]

Furthermore, given the incentives and constraints influencing household behavior discussed in previous sections, we know that such laws are not always sufficient for preventing child labor. There are various scenarios, however, in which legal interventions can be expected to play a critical role in reducing child labor. Three such cases are discussed below.

The first concerns the problem of children's agency. Much of the economic analysis on child labor assumes that (a) parents are making the decision about whether to send a child to work and (b) that parents act altruistically, that is, in the best interest of the child. There are circumstances in which neither may be the case. When adults are exploiting children, legal bans on child labor or mandatory schooling policies can raise child welfare. This also applies in situations where the parents may not have full information about the long-term returns to education versus work. Laws related to child labor are also particularly important in areas affected by conflict or HIV/AIDS, when

---

[28] R. Srivastava and N. Raj, 'Education and Child Labour: Some Insights from the Carpet Belt', 6 *Labour and Development* 1 (2000).

[29] OECD, *Combating Child Labour: A Review of Policies* (Paris: OECD, 2003).

children find themselves as heads of households or in the care of non-parent adults or institutions who may not act in their best interest.

In the other two scenarios, banning child labor and requiring school attendance are important interventions to correct for market failure.[30] In the first case, individual households decide to send their children to work instead of school in order to earn a certain subsistence level of household income. Assuming that children and adults are perfectly substitutable in the labor market, the aggregate effect—on wages as well as human capital development—of individual households sending children to work instead of school is socially suboptimal. Government intervention in the form of child labor laws can correct for this externality. A ban on child labor which effectively reduces the demand for and supply of child labor could raise adult wages sufficiently to increase household income above subsistence levels. In this case, the 'bad equilibrium' characterized by low wages and high incidence of child labor is replaced by a 'good equilibrium' characterized by high wages and low incidence of child labor.[31]

Likewise, a ban on child labor can correct the market failure that arises when employers prefer to hire children instead of adults because they can do so at a lower price. The gap in wages between children and adults due to differences in productivity will not provide enough motivation for employers to hire children instead of adults. However, in some cases, employment of children is driven by employer desire to exploit, that is, pay wages lower than the marginal productivity of child workers, who have less power to negotiate wages, individually or collectively. Here, laws against child labor can be an important policy tool.

Even in these cases where legal intervention can be expected to reduce the incidence of child labor, implementation may be problematic. Child labor laws are very difficult to enforce for a number of reasons: labor inspectorates are under-resourced; most child laborers work in rural areas far from inspectors; many children are in inaccessible workplaces such as domestic homes and unregistered establishments. Compulsory education is often seen as a more effective legislative avenue for addressing child labor as it is easier to ensure the presence of children in schools than to enforce their absence from work.[32]

---

[30] Basu identifies an additional justification for banning child labor on the basis of fundamental preferences. He defines a household choice as 'fundamental' if it can be agreed that no one should have to pay a price for having such a preference. He then notes that households that choose not to send children to work may pay a price vis-à-vis those who do in the form of reduced adult wages due to the additional supply of (child) labor in the market. Because households ought not to pay a price for having a fundamental preference, a legal ban on child labor may be justified. K. Basu, 'Child Labor: Cause, Consequence and Cure, With Remarks on International Labor Standards', 37 *Journal of Economic Literature* 1083 (1999).

[31] See generally Basu, ibid.   [32] Srivastava and Raj, above n. 28.

In some circumstances, legal efforts to ban child labor, potentially even those derived from Convention 138 which establishes minimum ages for employment, may actually reduce child welfare. When concerns about child labor in developing countries began to attract attention in North America and Europe, many consumer advocates and activists called for banning imports of products made with child labor or boycotting companies using child labor in their supply chains. Fearing sanctions from key trading partners, the Bangladesh garment industry conducted a sweep of factories and threw 50,000 children out of work. According to UNICEF, the children, mostly girls under age 14, ended up in more dangerous jobs with less pay.[33]

While media, consumer, and activist attention has focused on child labor in export industries, well-meaning efforts at removing children from work in the domestic market can have unintended consequences as well. The Child Labor Deterrence Act in India established fines for employers, making the employment of children more costly. The wages of working children thus dropped causing either more children in the household to work or those already working to work more hours.[34]

Convention 182 recognizes that efforts to end child labor work best when linked to comprehensive measures to combat poverty and promote education. Countries ratifying this convention are required to take immediate and effective measures to secure the prohibition and elimination of the worst forms of child labor as a matter of urgency. The Time-Bound Programme (TBP) approach constitutes one of the means put in place by the ILO to assist countries in fulfilling their obligations under the convention. TBPs are designed as a comprehensive framework that governments can use to chart a course of action with well-defined targets. They comprise a set of integrated and co-ordinated policies and interventions with clear goals, specific targets, and a defined time frame, aimed at preventing and eliminating a country's worst forms of child labor. They emphasize the need to address the root causes of child labor, linking action for the latter's elimination to national development policy, macroeconomic trends and strategies, and demographic and labor market processes and outcomes, with particular emphasis on economic and social policies to combat poverty and to promote universal basic education and social mobilization. El Salvador, Nepal, and Tanzania are the first three countries to implement TBPs. Three other countries, the Dominican Republic, Costa Rica, and the Philippines, started implementation during 2002–2003.

---

[33] UNICEF, 'Poverty and Children: Lessons of the 90s for Least Developed Countries', Policy Review Document, Division of Evaluation, Policy, and Planning (New York: UNICEF, 2001) 20.

[34] K. Basu and Z. Tzannatos, 'The Global Child Labor Problem: What Do We Know and What Can We Do?', 17 *The World Bank Economic Review* 147 (2003).

9.6 CONCLUSION

Child labor is a significant phenomenon, large in scope, and with very important social and economic implications. It takes a variety of forms, from children working on family farms or in family businesses to children engaged in sweatshop labor, prostitution, armed conflict, or other illicit activity. It also has serious implications on human capital accumulation and in perpetuating poverty and therefore is closely linked to progress against the MDGs, especially the goal of achieving universal primary education. Given the connections between child labor and schooling, the efforts of the Education For All partnership will not be fully successful without addressing child labor.

An economic framework, such as the one presented in this chapter, based on household decision making—specifically regarding the school/work choice for children—is an effective tool for understanding the phenomenon of child labor and targeting policies that can address it. Children work for different reasons. In some cases, families have a greater incentive to put children to work than to send them to school because the expected returns to education are less than the returns to work. In other cases, economic returns may favor school but families are unable to educate their children because of various obstacles or constraints. These most often apply to poor or vulnerable families that cannot afford the direct costs of education or the opportunity costs of losing the labor of their children. Still other cases of child labor stem from the fact that children do not have parents or some other agent acting in their interest.

These different circumstances point to the need for multi-sectoral approaches to child labor and increasing school participation. Where incentives are the problem because expected returns are greater for work than school, educational reforms are the most important policy instrument. The goals of these reforms should focus on reducing the costs of education, increasing the quality and hence the returns to education, or both. Where the problem is that poor or vulnerable families face constraints in sending their children to school, social protection interventions that provide a safety net or overcome failures in financial or labor markets are the key. There is also room for child labor and compulsory school attendance legislation to play an important role. This approach is especially relevant where children face an 'agency' problem or when labor market imperfections result in wage discrimination or a socially unfavorable substitution of child labor for adult labor.

The international human rights instruments we described relating to child labor and the right to education have effectively raised awareness about child labor and have helped mobilize significant resources and political will to address the issue. Convention 182, in particular, reflects the lessons learned over the last three decades about the causes and effects of child labor. In appreciating the reality of low income countries and severe constraints faced by poor households, Convention 182 prioritizes urgent action against the worst forms of child labor and promotes a pragmatic and multi-sectoral approach, with flexibility for developing countries to adapt policy interventions in line with country-level circumstances and priorities. Such an approach is fully consistent with the economic analysis presented in this chapter.

Finally, the Oslo Agenda for Action, unanimously adopted at the 1997 International Conference on Child Labour, lays out the priorities for the international community to address child labor. The Agenda specifically identified the crucial need for better information on the child labor phenomenon, its extent and nature, its causes and consequences, and the effectiveness of policies and programs to address it. The Oslo Conference also articulated the need to strengthen co-operation and co-ordination among the international development agencies in the child labor field. There was a general recognition in Oslo that, despite a common policy framework (in the form of ILO Conventions 138 and 182, the Convention on the Rights of the Child, and the MDGs), action on child labor was poorly co-ordinated across agencies. As a result, the many potential synergies in the agencies' work in the child labor field were unexploited. The World Bank has responded to these calls by forging partnerships with the ILO and UNICEF to address the challenge of child labor.

10

Child Labour, Education, and the Principle of Non-Discrimination

ELIZABETH D. GIBBONS, FRIEDRICH
HUEBLER, AND EDILBERTO LOAIZA[1]

10.1 THE HUMAN RIGHTS FRAMEWORK FOR ANALYSING CHILD LABOUR AND EDUCATION

10.1.1 International Conventions against Child Labour: Standards and Reality

As early as 1921, when the International Labour Organization (ILO) passed the first Minimum Age Convention, the world has attempted to protect children's right to an education and to prevent any child labour which would prejudice their school attendance.[2] The ILO's Minimum Age Convention 138 of 1973[3] set the standard for the minimum age for admission to employment as 15 years, or in special cases where economic and educational facilities are insufficiently developed, 14 years; light work not harmful to the child or prejudicial to his or her attendance at school is permissible after age 12. Since 1990, with the entry into force of the Convention on the Rights of the Child,[4] the child's right to be protected from 'any work that is likely to be

[1] Invaluable inputs to this paper were received from Anna-Karin Irvine, Meredith Slopen, and Radhika Gore of the Global Policy Section, Division of Policy and Planning, UNICEF. The views expressed in this paper are those of the authors and do not necessarily represent the views of UNICEF.

[2] 'Children under the age of fourteen years may not be employed or work in any public or private agricultural undertaking, or in any branch thereof, save outside the hours fixed for school attendance. If they are employed outside the hours of school attendance, the employment shall not be such as to prejudice their attendance at school.' Article 1 in: ILO. 1921. *C10: Minimum age (agriculture) convention.* http://www.ilo.org/ilolex/cgi-lex/convde. pl?C010 (accessed 17 May 2004).

[3] 26 June 1973, 1015 U.N.T.S. 297, *entered into force* 19 June 1976 (Convention 138).

[4] G.A. res. 44/25, annex, 44 U.N. GAOR Supp. (No. 49) at 167, U.N. Doc. A/44/49 (1989), *entered into force* 2 September 1990.

hazardous or to interfere with the child's education' (Article 32) and his or her right, on an equal, non-discriminatory basis to 'primary education compulsory and available free to all' (Article 28) have gained the status of internationally recognized norms, while imposing an obligation on the 192 states parties to the Convention to realize these rights for the children under their jurisdiction.[5] In 2000, children were provided further protection through the entry into force of ILO Convention 182,[6] which was ratified by 150 countries as of May 2004.[7] Convention 182 prohibits the worst forms of child labour, defined as all forms of slavery and similar practices; child prostitution and pornography; illicit activities (in particular the production and trafficking of drugs); and work that is likely to harm the health, safety, or morals of children.

However, as is well known, many governments have thus far failed to realize these rights for their children. For 2002, the United Nations' Children's Fund (UNICEF) estimated that 121 million children were out of school, 65 million of them girls.[8] In 2002, the ILO estimated that, worldwide, 211 million children aged 5 to 14 years were economically active, 111 million of them in hazardous work.[9] In fact, since this figure only counts children working in economic activities and excludes those working on household chores (which, if excessive, can also affect school attendance), the number of working children in the world is likely to greatly exceed this estimate. For these millions of children, their rights to education, to a childhood protected from work detrimental to their development, and to human dignity, are all being violated. This is a scandal for the twenty-first century, a harvest of ignorance and lost potential which mortgages the future of these children and their countries.

10.1.2 Implications of a Human Rights Approach to Development

Since 1996, when UNICEF adopted a Mission Statement whereby the Organization in all its work is 'guided by the Convention on the Rights of the Child and strives to establish children's rights as enduring ethical principles',[10] it has struggled to understand and apply a human rights approach to development in its programmes of co-operation. Learning is continuous,

---

[5] UNICEF, *First call for children: World declaration and plan of action from the World Summit for Children, Convention on the rights of the child* (New York: UNICEF, 2000).

[6] 38 I.L.M. 1207 (1999), *entered into force* 19 November 2000 (Convention 182).

[7] Database of International Labour Standards. http://www.ilo.org/ilolex/cgi-lex/ratifce.pl?C182 (accessed 17 May 2004).

[8] UNICEF, *The State of the World's Children 2004* (New York: UNICEF, 2004) 7.

[9] ILO, *Every Child Counts: New Global Estimates on Child Labour* (Geneva: ILO, 2002) 20.

[10] UNICEF, *The Mission of UNICEF*, UN Doc.E/ICEF/1996/AB/L.2.

but to date we have seen, among other effects of the rights approach, that UNICEF is driven, beyond the utilitarian principle of the greatest good for the greatest number of children, to give attention to those children and vulnerable members of society living at the margins of the mainstream, and to push for services to reach the 'last 10 per cent' of the unreached. As a corollary, applying the principles of universality and non-discrimination pushes UNICEF to direct the state's attention and resources to marginalized children and their families. This includes children engaged in child labour. Likewise, application of human rights principles has led UNICEF into actions which identify, advocate for, and support communities of ethnic and racial groups suffering from discrimination, and to seek gender equity in all its actions. This means that the gender dimension of child labour has to be visible, as a prelude to being understood and acted upon.

Applying the principle of indivisibility of human rights has led to programmes which incorporate the interrelatedness of causes and are increasingly inter-sectoral in content, addressing the rights of the whole child. This has particular relevance for programmes simultaneously seeking to increase school attendance and decrease child labour, acting through a complex nexus of interacting factors. Thus, the rights approach to child labour calls for a profound analysis of the causes contributing to child labour, and a multi-sectoral response to the problem: provision of accessible, affordable, and quality education; interventions aimed at increasing household income of poor families; reform and implementation of laws on minimum age of employment, truancy, teachers' minimum qualification, and mandatory teaching hours; birth registration (without which it is impossible to establish whether a child is old enough to attend school or to work); and civic education aimed at all levels of society to promote and respect the fulfilment of child rights, and ensure that law enforcement effectively suppresses the demand for child labour.

Overall, applying human rights principles derived from the Convention on the Rights of the Child has resulted in a shift in the mix of strategies undergirding UNICEF's development work:

a) Increased support to *capacity building* of the state, its policies, and its institutions, so as to enable it to better meet its obligations to the citizenry.
b) Considerable *widening of partnerships*, well beyond the state, into civil society organizations at all levels, and greater clarity on the importance of community capacity building and citizen empowerment.
c) A deeper causal analysis for non-realization of rights, leading to a better understanding of the interrelationship of causes impeding children's growth and development, and to *programmes which address structural causes of inequity*. Prior to adoption of the human rights approach,

structural causes of children's problems—including poverty, which is often at the root of child labour—were taken as a given and not subject to change through programme action.

d) A much higher investment by UNICEF programmes in *advocacy* with (for example) parliaments to change discriminatory laws and to increase budgets for social development, with international financial institutions, and with power brokers in general.

e) A considerable *decrease in direct support to service delivery* (except in situations of humanitarian emergency), as this is the state's duty, to which UNICEF contributes indirectly through capacity building of its institutions, through empowering communities to demand the quality services to which they have a right, and to know how they can hold state agents accountable for poor services.

10.1.3 Education as a Preventive Strategy against Child Labour

Stimulated by the Oslo International Conference on Child Labour in 1997, UNICEF, with support of seven partners,[11] developed the Global Child Labour Programme, whose most important sub-programme was 'Education as a Preventive Strategy against Child Labour'. Implemented in 30 countries between 1999 and 2002, the programme used a multi-sectoral, child rights approach to implementing four components: provision of quality, relevant, and affordable education; improvement in family economies; raising of awareness in and respect for children's rights; and the enforcement of child labour laws. All four components were to be implemented at policy, institutional, school, and community level.

In 2003, the programme was evaluated.[12] The experience showed that it *is* relevant to use education as a main entry point for the targeted children (i.e., those engaged in child labour), but there was only partial effectiveness in interventions. The evaluation concluded that education can only be an adequate alternative to child labour if it is accessible, affordable, of good quality, non-discriminatory, safe, and linked with other programmes in an integrated way. This finding reinforces the multi-sectoral approach to development problems, as derived from the human rights principle of indivisibility. However, the complexity of the determinants and the inter-relationship between child labour and education were such that predictive

[11] These funding partners were Finland, Luxembourg, the Netherlands, Norway, Sweden, the ILO, and the World Bank.
[12] UNICEF, *Education as a preventive strategy against child labour: Evaluation of the cornerstone programme of UNICEF's global child labour programme*, Evaluation Working Paper (New York: UNICEF, 2003).

factors, favouring the abandonment of child labour and enrolment in school, were difficult to identify. The present study attempts to fill this gap by analysing the constraining effect of child labour on school attendance and achievement.

Overall, the programme failed to systematically collect and synthesize quantitative data which could have helped to further explain the inconclusive results. However, the programme confirmed that there is not invariably an inverse relationship between school attendance and child labour, as many other factors determine whether a child will or will not attend school. Furthermore, the programme 'focused on working children, children who have never been to school, and children at risk of dropping out of school to join the workforce. . . . Except for an intended link to girls' education, there was no particular attention to girls at work.'[13] To that degree the programme failed to address the gender dimensions of child labour, perhaps because the tools for assessing the extent of household chores did not exist, and because there are, to date, no internationally accepted definitions of child labour that include the tasks disproportionately carried out by girls, as well as the corresponding indicators to measure and report the existing empirical evidence.

10.2 OVERCOMING THE DISCRIMINATION AGAINST GIRLS IN ANALYSES OF CHILD LABOUR

10.2.1 Existing Data Sources for Assessing Child Labour

The vast majority of studies on child labour limit themselves to analysing time spent in economic activity (whether inside or outside the home); they do not take into account time spent on household chores. Since girls are almost always more likely to be occupied in household chores than are boys, this way of analysing the extent of child labour, and its impact on schooling, is significantly biased against girls. Non-discrimination is a key human rights principle; it is important to develop an 'equalizing' indicator of child labour, so that its impact on girls' access to education, and school attainment, is made visible in similar terms as the effect of child labour on boys.

UNICEF has been able to collect data on the time children spend in household chores through its Multiple Indicator Cluster Survey (MICS). The MICS is a household survey developed by UNICEF to fill data gaps in areas critical to the survival of children. The methodology was developed in collaboration with the World Health Organization (WHO), UNESCO, the

---

[13] Ibid. 49.

United Nations Statistics Division, MEASURE (USAID), the London School of Hygiene and Tropical Medicine, and the United States Center for Disease Control and Prevention (CDC). Specifically, MICS was developed to obtain data on key indicators for assessing progress towards the goals of the World Summit for Children for the year 2000. The end-decade MICS (MICS2) collected data for 63 of the 75 *Indicators for Monitoring Progress at End-Decade*.[14] MICS2 drew heavily on experiences with the mid-decade MICS, which was conducted around 1995, and the subsequent mid-decade MICS evaluation.

By 2001, 65 developing countries had carried out MICS2 studies. The studies were conducted between 1999 and 2001 by government agencies (mostly Statistical Offices and Ministries of Health) with the technical and financial support of UNICEF. The MICS2 model questionnaire includes 19 core modules and 4 optional modules to obtain information for households, household members, women 15 to 49 years of age, and children under five years of age. Since the main objective of MICS2 was to help countries fill data gaps, not all modules were necessarily included in a country's questionnaire. With the data from the surveys, the respective governments completed country reports that documented the progress toward the end-decade goals defined at the World Summit for Children. The results are presently being used by national governments to define priorities regarding women and children for the period 2000–2005.[15] UNICEF used the results to prepare the report *We the Children* that the UN Secretary-General presented at the Special Session for Children in May 2002,[16] the accompanying statistical review,[17] and the outcome document, *A World Fit for Children*.[18] The survey data also helped define UNICEF's medium-term strategic plan for the period 2000–2005.[19]

The MICS surveys collected information on the number of hours children aged 5 to 14 years spent working for others (paid or unpaid); working for the family, whether on a farm or in a business (paid or unpaid); and on the time

[14] The World Summit for Children adopted 27 goals with 75 related indicators. The goals and indicators are listed in Appendix 1 to: UNICEF, *End-decade assessment: Indicators for assessing progress globally*, UNICEF Executive Directive CF/EXD/1999–03, New York, 23 April 1999.

[15] MICS documentation and results can be obtained at a dedicated UNICEF website, www.childinfo.org.

[16] UNICEF, *We the Children: Meeting the promises of the World Summit for Children* (New York: UNICEF, 2002).

[17] UNICEF, *Progress since the World Summit for Children: A statistical review* (New York: UNICEF, 2001).

[18] United Nations, *A world fit for children*, UN Doc. A/S-27/19/Rev. 1. (New York: UN, 2002).

[19] UNICEF, *Medium-term strategic plan for the period 2002–2005*, UN Doc. E/ICEF/2001/13, 7 November (New York: UNICEF, 2001).

spent in household chores such as cleaning, fetching water, laundry, or child care. However, due to limitations of the methodology, it was not possible to collect data on the kind of work children engaged in. Thus, MICS data cannot be used to analyse the worst forms of child labour (bonded labour, prostitution, drug trafficking, etc.).

A further source of data is the Demographic and Health Surveys (DHS) that are conducted by Macro International with funding from the U.S. Agency for International Development (USAID). As a result of co-ordination between USAID and UNICEF, some countries implementing DHS surveys decided to include the child labour module from the MICS.[20]

10.2.2 Creating an Equalizing Indicator between Girls and Boys: The Role of Household Chores in the Measurement of Child Labour

Because MICS and DHS provide data on household chores it is possible to apply the principle of non-discrimination by making the extent of girls' engagement in child labour visible. A study by Friedrich Huebler and Edilberto Loaiza of UNICEF's Strategic Information Section compared the rates of child labour with and without household chores in 25 countries from sub-Saharan Africa.[21] To ensure that the extent of girls' labour is not underestimated, UNICEF includes household chores in excess of four hours per day in calculations of child labour. Household chores of less than four hours per day are, for the sake of argument, not considered harmful to the child's development, and hence are not counted as child labour. Of course, depending on the chore, one could question this assertion; four hours a day carrying heavy buckets of water could certainly be both physically detrimental to the child, and prevent him or her from attending school.[22] Even though with a minimum measure of four hours' household chores per day, the extent of child labour may be underestimated, without some arbitrary cut-off, almost all children could be considered to be engaged in child labour.

The inclusion of at least 28 hours per week of household chores in UNICEF's definition of child labour creates, however imperfectly, an

---

[20] Documentation and survey data can be obtained at the DHS Web site, www. measuredhs.com.

[21] Friedrich Huebler and Edilberto Loaiza, *Child Labour and school attendance in Sub-Saharan Africa: Empirical evidence from UNICEF's Multiple Indicator Cluster Surveys*, Working Paper (New York: UNICEF, 2002).

[22] Researchers at the joint ILO-UNICEF-World Bank project 'Understanding Children's Work', based at UNICEF's Innocenti Research Centre in Florence, are currently engaged in studies to determine at what threshold the number of hours of household chores becomes detrimental to school attendance and achievement.

'equalizing indicator' between boys and girls, and expands the usual ILO definition of child labour as shown in Table 10.1.

The study of 25 African countries by Huebler and Loaiza indeed shows that once household chores are included, the disparity in child labour rates for boys and girls narrows by more than half, as illustrated by Table 10.2.

When household chores are taken into account, the estimate of child labour among girls is increased by more than one-quarter, from 23.6 per cent to 30.2 per cent. In contrast, the estimate of child labour among boys is increased by one sixth, from 27.0 per cent to 31.5 per cent. The gap between boys' and girls' child labour falls from 3.4 per cent, to 1.5 per cent. Thus, despite its imperfections, the UNICEF indicator of child labour, which includes household chores, contributes to a better visibility and understanding of gender disparities in child labour. As such, its use allows policy makers to better apply the human rights principle of non-discrimination.

Table 10.1. *Adjusting child labour definitions for household chores*

Indicator	Definition
1. Child labour (with household chores)	Ages 5–11: at least (a) one hour of economic activity or (b) 28 hours of household chores per week. Ages 12–14: at least (a) 14 hours of economic activity or (b) 28 hours of household chores per week.
2. Child labour (without household chores)	Ages 5–11: at least one hour of economic activity per week. Ages 12–14: at least 14 hours of economic activity per week.

Table 10.2. *Child labour in sub-Saharan Africa, 25 countries, children 5–14 years*

	Without Household Chores	With Household Chores
Total Child Labour	25.3%	30.8%
Girls	23.6%	30.2%
Boys	27.0%	31.5%
Difference boys-girls	3.4%	1.5%

Source: Friedrich Huebler and Edilberto Loaiza, *Child labour and school attendance in Sub-Saharan Africa: Empirical evidence from UNICEF's Multiple Indicator Cluster Surveys*, Working Paper (New York: UNICEF, 2002).

10.3 DOES PARTICIPATION IN CHILD LABOUR SIGNIFICANTLY CONSTRAIN SCHOOL ATTENDANCE AND ACHIEVEMENT?

10.3.1 Data Coverage and Analytical Model

The present study, stimulated by the ambiguous results of the UNICEF programme 'Education as a Preventive Strategy against Child Labour', seeks, through analysis of household survey data, to understand quantitatively (a) the extent to which child labour is, in and of itself (i.e., independent of other factors), preventing school attendance and contributing to repetition and drop-out rates, and (b) the extent to which other factors may influence the realization of children's right to education. The present study covers the 18 countries listed in Table 10.3, which is a reduced sample from that in the study by Huebler and Loaiza.[23] For 14 countries, data from MICS surveys was used and, for the remaining four countries, DHS data was used.

We use the same definition of child labour as the earlier study, whereby household chores of 28 hours or more per week are included, in order to introduce an equalizing indicator and make girls' work as visible as boys' work. Our working hypothesis is that being engaged in child labour invariably constrains school attendance. To test this, we want to investigate the extent to which child labour, together with other socio-economic factors such as gender and wealth, is a significant factor constraining school attendance and educational attainment among children 7 to 14 years of age.[24]

For the purpose of this study we define a child to be in school if he or she was attending either primary or secondary education at the moment of the survey. Children in pre-school or in non-standard schools are counted as not attending school. A child is considered to have dropped out from school if he or she was attending school the year before the survey and is not currently attending. Similarly, a child is considered to be a repeater if, at the moment of the survey, the grade of school attended is the same as during the year before the survey. Repetition and drop-out rates are taken as proxies for educational achievement, although it is recognized that such measures cannot fully reflect school performance. Since the surveys represent a point in time,

---

[23] In some of the 25 sub-Saharan African countries in the earlier study, surveys were conducted during a period of school vacation, which means that no concurrent data on child work and school attendance was available. In these countries it is thus not possible to evaluate the trade-off between school attendance and child labour.

[24] Although child labour data for children aged 5 to 14 years is available, we limit the analysis to children 7 years and older because 7 years is the minimum age by which children in all countries are supposed to attend primary school, according to national legislation.

Table 10.3. *Data sources and country population*

Country	Survey	Year	Population in 2000 (1,000)
Burundi	MICS	2000	6,267
Central African Rep.	MICS	2000	3,715
Comoros	MICS	2000	705
Congo (DRC)	MICS	2000	48,571
Côte d'Ivoire	MICS	2000	15,827
Gambia	MICS	2000	1,312
Guinea-Bissau	MICS	2000	1,367
Kenya	MICS	2000	30,549
Lesotho	MICS	2000	1,785
Malawi	DHS	2000	11,370
Mali	DHS	2001	11,904
Niger	MICS	2000	10,742
Senegal	MICS	2000	9,393
Sierra Leone	MICS	2000	4,415
Somalia	MICS	1999	8,720
Swaziland	MICS	2000	1,044
Tanzania	DHS	1999	34,837
Uganda	DHS EdData	2001	23,487

Population figures complied from: United Nations Population Division, *World Population Prospects: The 2002 revision* (New York: United Nations, 2003).

they cannot account for the cumulative effect of child labour on attainment over time.

A regression analysis of the data seeks to show the relative weight of six factors in influencing school attendance, grade repetition, and dropping out. These factors are: age (7–10 or 11–14 years), gender, area of residence (rural or urban), household wealth (indicated by wealth quintile), mother's or caretaker's education (for more than 9 out of 10 children the caretaker is the mother), and child labour. This is a very simple model that cannot take into account any variable related to access to school (in terms of the non-existence of a school as a reason for non-attendance), to the quality of education (availability of books, materials, or trained teachers, which is known to have a strong influence on parents' preference for work over school), or to the intensity of child labour (beyond the hourly threshold established by the definition above). As previously noted, due to data collection limitations, the extent of the worst forms of child labour cannot be analysed. However, the model does have the merit of producing quantitative data, comparable over a large number of countries. By showing the relative weight of each of these factors, analysis of the data should present some considerations for policies aimed at increasing school attendance and eliminating child labour.

10.3.2 School Attendance and Child Labour: Descriptive Statistics

Table 10.4 and Figure 10.1 summarize the school attendance and child labour rates from the 18 countries in this study.

In the sample overall, 60 per cent of children 7 to 14 years of age are attending school. It is also evident that, for many children, labour is part of their daily lives: 38 per cent of all children are labourers. Among these children, slightly more than half (or 20 per cent) also attend school while another 18 per cent are only engaged in labour and have their right to education denied. On the other hand, among the non-labouring children, two-thirds attend school. In spite of significant overlap between school

Table 10.4. *School attendance and child labour in sub-Saharan Africa (%), children 7–14 years*

Category	Attending school	Child labour	School only	School and CL	CL, no school	No school, no CL
Burundi	47.3	28.2	36.0	11.3	17.0	35.7
CAR	49.8	60.8	21.6	28.2	32.6	17.6
Comoros	35.9	29.0	25.7	10.2	18.8	45.3
Congo (DRC)	61.7	31.8	48.2	19.3	12.4	20.1
Côte d'Ivoire	61.7	39.0	41.9	19.7	19.3	19.1
Gambia	52.7	21.6	43.5	9.2	12.5	34.8
Guinea-Bissau	43.3	54.7	25.8	17.5	37.1	19.5
Kenya	81.3	28.8	59.6	21.7	7.1	11.6
Lesotho	75.3	20.0	61.4	14.0	6.0	18.7
Malawi	83.4	20.9	66.1	17.3	3.5	13.1
Mali	38.7	40.8	27.7	11.0	29.7	31.6
Niger	30.2	71.8	12.2	17.9	53.8	16.0
Senegal	47.0	39.5	33.2	13.8	25.7	27.3
Sierra Leone	43.2	58.5	19.3	23.8	34.6	22.2
Somalia	13.4	41.9	8.9	4.5	37.4	49.2
Swaziland	77.8	10.1	70.1	7.8	2.3	19.9
Tanzania	51.1	42.4	31.6	19.5	22.9	26.0
Uganda	87.8	43.4	49.2	38.6	4.8	7.4
Male	62.4	37.9	42.8	21.1	16.8	19.3
Female	58.3	38.2	40.1	19.2	19.0	21.7
Total	60.3	38.0	41.4	20.1	17.9	20.5

Notes: Averages are weighted by country population.—School attendance rate for Congo (DRC) is for children 7–14 years, remaining columns for Congo show estimates for children 10–14 years because no child labour data was available for ages below 10 years.

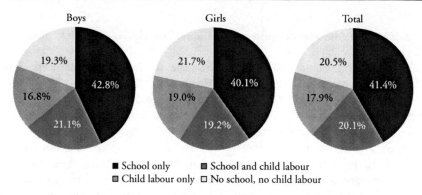

Figure 10.1. Activity status, children 7–14 years

attendance and child labour, 41 per cent of the children attend school only and the remaining 21 per cent are neither in school nor working.[25]

Girls attend school less than boys (58 per cent compared to 62 per cent) but, thanks to the inclusion of household chores in the analysis, we are able to see that the share of child labourers among girls is the same as among boys—about 38 per cent. Because of their lower attendance rate, girls are more likely to be engaged in child labour only (19 per cent compared to 17 per cent for boys), or to neither attend school nor do child labour (22 per cent compared to 19 per cent for boys).

Figure 10.2 plots the child labour and school attendance rates against each other. We observe that in countries with a high proportion of child labourers, school attendance tends to be low. At the extreme ends of the distribution are Swaziland, with a school attendance rate of 78 per cent and a child labour rate of 10 per cent, and Niger, with a school attendance rate of 30 per cent and a child labour rate of 72 per cent. Uganda and Somalia appear to be two outliers. In Uganda, 43 per cent of all children are labourers and yet 88 per cent of all children are in school. Somalia has the lowest school attendance rate of all countries, with 13 per cent, but with a share of 42 per cent there are almost as many child labourers as in Uganda.

The evidence from Table 10.4 and Figures 10.1 and 10.2 indicates that child labour is a constraint for school attendance but many other factors can have an effect on the schooling decision for a child. A multivariate analysis is necessary to examine the relative weight of some of the other determinants of school attendance. As a first step, Table 10.5 disaggregates the estimates for the activities of children in the 18 countries in our sample by various background characteristics.

---

[25] The 21% not in school and not in child labour includes 2% doing light work (1 to 13 hours of economic activities per week among children 11–14), 13% doing 1 to 27 hours of household chores per week, and 6% that are idle (no school and no work at all).

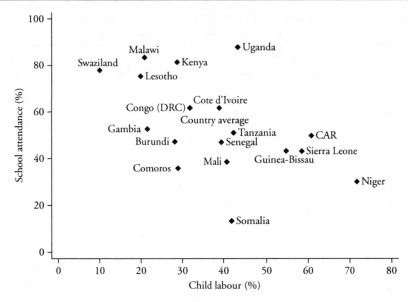

Figure 10.2. Child labour and school attendance in sub-Saharan Africa, children 7–14 years

A number of important observations can be made from Table 10.5. The school attendance rate of girls is 4 percentage points below that of boys. School attendance increases with age, reaching a peak at 11 years and falls again. If the child lives in an urban area, his or her chance of attending school is three in four, compared to roughly one in two if he or she lives in a rural area.

As one might expect, a child in the richest 20 per cent of the population is much more likely to be in school and not working than one in the poorest 20 per cent; children from the richest households are approximately twice as likely to be in school only, and the gap between the two groups of children is 31 percentage points. Further, a child from the richest quintile is almost half as likely to be working as a child from the poorest quintile. Children from the poorest quintile have a fifty-fifty chance of not being in school at all, but at the same time it is important to emphasize that even among the richest 20 per cent of the population one fifth of all children do not attend school. This could be due to lack of access to schools, even for the richest, poor quality of education (leaving parents to believe school is a waste of time for their children), or simply that in poor countries only the top 5 per cent of families have the wherewithal to fulfil their children's right to an education.

The other very striking observation is the role of mothers' education as a determinant of school attendance, with 73 per cent of children of educated

Table 10.5. *School attendance and child labour by background characteristics (%), 18 countries in sub-Saharan Africa, children 7–14 years*

Category	Attending school	Child labour	School only	School and CL	CL, no school	No school, no CL
7 years	41.8	29.6	30.0	11.0	18.6	40.4
8 years	53.9	36.6	36.4	17.3	19.3	27.0
9 years	60.4	43.2	36.9	23.7	19.5	19.8
10 years	63.8	47.6	36.3	27.5	20.1	16.1
11 years	68.2	50.2	36.6	31.6	18.5	13.2
12 years	67.4	32.2	50.9	16.4	15.8	16.8
13 years	66.5	34.1	49.4	17.0	17.1	16.5
14 years	65.2	35.8	48.0	17.2	18.7	16.1
7–10 years	54.7	39.9	35.6	21.2	18.7	24.5
11–14 years	66.7	37.7	46.5	20.3	17.5	15.8
Female	58.3	38.2	40.1	19.2	19.0	21.7
Male	62.4	37.9	42.8	21.1	16.8	19.3
Rural	55.5	42.7	35.6	21.4	21.3	21.7
Urban	73.3	24.6	58.6	15.3	9.3	16.7
Poorest quintile	48.8	44.7	31.2	19.4	25.3	24.1
Second quintile	52.1	43.9	33.0	20.3	23.7	23.0
Third quintile	57.1	39.5	38.0	20.6	19.0	22.4
Fourth quintile	65.8	36.4	44.9	22.3	14.2	18.7
Richest quintile	78.4	23.8	61.9	16.7	7.1	14.2
Caretaker no ed.	51.4	40.6	34.4	18.4	22.1	25.1
Caretaker ed.	72.7	33.1	51.4	22.6	10.5	15.5
Total	60.3	38.0	41.4	20.1	17.9	20.5

Note: Averages are weighted by country population.

mothers attending, compared with only 51 per cent of children of uneducated mothers.[26] This shows, in dramatic and incontrovertible terms, the inter-generational pay-off from an investment in girls' education. The potential development gain from that inter-generational pay-off also reinforces the need to understand and address the obstacles preventing girls from attending school today, and hence for non-discriminatory indicators capable of revealing those obstacles.

[26] A mother or caretaker is considered to be educated if she or he has attended any formal education at primary level or higher. Those who attended only pre-school or non-standard schools are considered to have no formal education.

10.3.3 Regression Analysis: Determinants of School Attendance

To assess the statistical significance of the findings in the preceding section, a multivariate analysis was implemented for all 18 countries. In the model, the probability of school attendance is assumed to be a function of six factors: the child's age and gender, the place of residence (urban or rural), the wealth of the household, the mother's or caretaker's education, and the child labour status. For each country, the set of binary variables set out in Table 10.6 is created.

For households in the poorest wealth quintile, all four household wealth variables are equal to 0. We use a probit regression to test the model, with school attendance as the dependent variable.

The results of the regression are presented in Table 10.A1 in the appendix. For each country, the table shows the net attendance ratio (NAR), that is the share of all children aged 7–14 years who are in school, as well as the number of observations in the sample.[27] For example, the Burundi sample consisted of 5,166 children between 7 and 14 years, with a net school attendance ratio of 47.3 per cent.

Instead of regression coefficients, the marginal effects are listed. The marginal effect is the change in the dependent variable for a one-unit change in the independent variable—from girl to boy (0 to 1) or rural to urban (again 0 to 1), for example. In Burundi, the marginal effect of the variable 'Male' on school attendance is 0.092; this means that compared to girls, boys have a probability of attending school that is 9.2 percentage points higher. The marginal effect of the variable 'Child labour' is −0.104 in Burundi, meaning that the probability of attending school is 10.4 percentage points lower for child labourers compared to non-labourers.

Statistical significance is indicated with asterisks; if a marginal effect has no asterisk the effect of the respective variable on school attendance is statistically insignificant. In the case of Burundi, belonging to a household in the second wealth quintile has no statistically significant effect on school attendance; this means that there is no difference in school attendance between these children and those from the poorest quintile (the reference category for the household wealth variables).

To ease interpretation, the regression results are summarized in Table 10.7. The table counts the countries where each of the independent variables has (a) a positive and statistically significant effect on school attendance, (b) a negative and statistically significant effect, or (c) no statistically significant

---

[27] In a few cases (Congo, Somalia, Swaziland) the school attendance rates differ from those in Table 10.4. This is because the regressions were run with a reduced number of observations, due to missing values in some of the variables.

Table 10.6. *Variables in assessing school attendance*

Variable	Description
Dependent variable:	
School attendance	1 if the child is attending school, 0 if not
Independent variables:	
Age 11–14 years	1 if the child is 11–14 years old, 0 if 7–10 years old
Male	1 if the child is male, 0 if female
Urban	1 if the household is located in an urban area, 0 if in a rural area
Second quintile	1 if the household is in the second poorest wealth quintile, 0 if not
Third quintile	1 if the household is in the third wealth quintile, 0 if not
Fourth quintile	1 if the household is in the second richest wealth quintile, 0 if not
Richest quintile	1 if the household is in the richest wealth quintile, 0 if not
Caretaker educated	1 if the mother or caretaker has a formal education, 0 if not
Child labour	1 if the child is a labourer, 0 if not

Table 10.7. *Summary of multivariate analysis in Table 10.A1: determinants of school attendance, children 7–14 years (18 countries, average attendance rate 60.3%)*

Variable	Positive and significant*	Negative and significant*	Insignificant	Average marginal effect	
				Positive and significant*	Negative and significant*
Age 11–14 years	12	2	4	0.185	−0.030
Male	10	2	6	0.120	−0.026
Urban	11	3	4	0.079	−0.064
Second quintile	8	1	9	0.058	−0.053
Third quintile	16	—	2	0.075	—
Fourth quintile	17	—	1	0.131	—
Richest quintile	18	—	—	0.210	—
Caretaker educated	18	—	—	0.170	—
Child labour	1	10	7	0.017	−0.092

* Minimum 5% level of significance.—Averages are weighted by country population.

effect. The last two columns list the mean values of the positive and negative marginal effects, weighted by country population.

The most striking finding of this analysis is that belonging to the richest household quintile and having a formally educated mother or caretaker have a positive and statistically significant effect on school attendance in all 18 countries. These effects are statistically significant regardless of other variables in the model (age, sex, place of residence, and child labour). Moreover, their marginal effect is substantial. A wealthy child's chances of attending school are increased on average by 21 percentage points (compared to a child from the poorest 20 per cent of the population) and the chances of a child with an educated mother by 17 points. Compared to the bottom 20 per cent of the population in terms of household wealth, children from the third and fourth wealth quintiles also have a significantly increased probability of attending school.

Almost as striking is that child labour, as a constraining determinant of school attendance, is significant in more than half of all countries (10 of 18). Among these countries, the strongest negative effect of child labour can be observed in Mali and Senegal, where the likelihood of attending school is reduced by 14 percentage points for child labourers. The average among the countries in which child labour has a negative and significant effect on school attendance is − 9 points, ranging from −14 points to −4 points in Lesotho. In other words, in and of itself, being a labourer would on average decrease a child's likelihood of attending school by 9 percentage points, compared to a child who is not working.

In one country, Uganda, the opposite is observed; here child labour has a positive effect on school attendance (+2 points). In the remaining 7 countries, no relationship between child labour and school attendance can be observed. Although child labour should be eliminated because of its violation of children's basic rights, the findings for these 7 countries indicate that doing so, even if possible, would not significantly increase school attendance nationwide.[28] Thus other strategies are required for children to realize their right to education. In the Central African Republic, for example, where child labour is not significantly associated with school attendance, the findings point to the importance of poverty (being in the richest quintile of the population produces a 30 point difference in the levels of school attendance, compared to the poorest quintile), mother's education (20 points difference), gender and place of residence (13 points difference in both cases).

For 11 of the 18 countries we also found that children living in urban areas tend to have greater levels of school attendance. However, in 3 other countries (Côte d'Ivoire, Kenya, and Uganda) this relationship works in the opposite direction, meaning that residents of rural areas tend to have greater levels of school attendance. In the remaining 4 countries the relationship between area of residence and school attendance is statistically insignificant.

---

[28] This conclusion does not preclude that child labour may have an effect on school attendance at a sub-national level. Interventions targeted at certain provinces or parts of the population may help increase school attendance.

The average marginal effect for the 11 countries in our sample in which living in an urban area has a positive and significant effect on school attendance, compared with rural residents, is 8 percentage points. Conversely, for the 3 countries in which the opposite is true, there is an average marginal effect of 6 percentage points in favour of rural children. Policy interventions that target urban or rural populations need to be informed by the findings presented here, and tailored to the specific situation.

10.3.4 The Role of Gender in Determining School Attendance

It is frequently argued that, in general, girls tend to attend school less than boys. For the 18 countries in our sample, boys have an attendance rate that is 4 percentage points above that of girls, as shown in Table 10.8. The gender disparity is greatest in the Central African Republic, Côte d'Ivoire, Mali, and Niger, with about 12 percentage points difference between boys' and girls' school attendance ratios.[29] In a few countries, girls are more likely to be in school than boys, including Lesotho (9 points difference) and Tanzania (3 points difference).

The regression analysis confirms that, controlling for all other factors, girls are less likely to attend school than boys in 10 of the 18 countries. In 2 of the other 8 countries (Lesotho and Malawi), boys are at a disadvantage compared to girls, and in the remaining 6 countries being a boy or a girl does not have a significant effect on the likelihood of school attendance (Comoros, Kenya, Somalia, Swaziland, Tanzania, and Uganda).

However, when we examine the regressions to select only countries where there were significant gender disparities in school attendance, we find a much stronger correlation between child labour and school attendance than in the sample as a whole. While, overall, in 10 out of 18 countries child labour has a strong negative effect on school attendance, 7 of these 10 countries (Burundi, Congo, Côte d'Ivoire, Gambia, Mali, Niger, and Senegal) are among the 10 countries that also have school attendance rates favouring boys (in the Central African Republic and Guinea-Bissau the impact of child labour on school attendance is not significant, and in Lesotho girls are more likely to be in school). Without further analysis at the country level it is not possible to say with certainty why child labour tends to affect school attendance more in countries with significant gender disparities. We can say, however, that child labour and gender are important determinants of school attendance, as shown in Table 10.7, although their net effects may be in the opposite direction of the conventional wisdom.

---

[29] These countries continue a widespread practice of early marriage, which may contribute to girls' lower school attendance.

Table 10.8 *School attendance in sub-Saharan Africa by gender (%), children 7–14 years*

Country	Total	Male	Female	Male-Female
Burundi	47.3	51.2	43.8	7.4
CAR	49.8	55.7	44.0	11.7
Comoros	35.9	35.5	36.3	−0.8
Congo (DRC)	61.7	66.0	57.6	8.4
Côte d'Ivoire	61.7	67.6	55.3	12.3
Gambia	52.7	56.5	49.2	7.3
Guinea-Bissau	43.3	46.7	39.9	6.8
Kenya	81.3	80.7	81.8	−1.1
Lesotho	75.3	71.0	79.6	−8.6
Malawi	83.4	82.6	84.2	−1.6
Mali	38.7	45.0	32.7	12.3
Niger	30.2	36.2	24.2	12.0
Senegal	47.0	51.1	42.9	8.2
Sierra Leone	43.2	45.9	40.4	5.5
Somalia	13.4	14.2	12.7	1.5
Swaziland	77.8	77.7	78.0	−0.3
Tanzania	51.1	49.6	52.6	−3.0
Uganda	87.8	87.8	87.7	0.1
Total	60.3	62.4	58.3	4.1

Note: Averages are weighted by country population.

Delving further into the question of gender, we divided the samples for the 18 countries and ran separate regressions for boys and girls. The results for the individual countries are shown in Tables 10.A2 and 10.A3 in the appendix, and summaries are presented in Tables 10.9 and 10.10. In the 9 countries in which child labour has a negative and statistically significant effect on school attendance, a girl engaged in child labour is on average 11 percentage points less likely to attend school (Table 10.9), while a boy in the same circumstances would be close to 8 percentage points less likely to attend school (Table 10.10), compared to their non-working peers. Moreover, while in three countries (Central African Republic, Comoros, and Uganda) being a boy child labourer has a positive and significant impact on his school attendance (possibly because it gives him both needed financial resources and time-management skills), this is never the case for girls. In other words, the impact of child labour on girls' school attendance, when statistically significant, is always negative and on average more severe than for boys. This gender-differentiated effect is an important finding, one that may have been impossible to observe without the inclusion of household chores in our definition of child labour. The separate regressions also confirm a result from

Table 10.9. *Summary of multivariate analysis in Table 10.A2: determinants of school attendance, girls 7–14 years (18 countries, average attendance rate 58.3%)*

Variable	Positive and significant*	Negative and significant*	Insignificant	Average marginal effect	
				Positive and significant*	Negative and significant*
Age 11–14 years	10	4	4	0.175	−0.053
Urban	9	4	5	0.148	−0.089
Second quintile	7	1	10	0.068	−0.071
Third quintile	15	—	3	0.078	—
Fourth quintile	17	—	1	0.141	—
Richest quintile	18	—	—	0.220	—
Caretaker educated	18	—	—	0.178	—
Child labour	—	9	9	—	−0.108

* Minimum 5% level of significance.—Averages are weighted by country population.

Table 10.10. *Summary of multivariate analysis in Table 10.A3: determinants of school attendance, boys 7–14 years (18 countries, average attendance rate 62.4%)*

Variable	Positive and significant*	Negative and significant*	Insignificant	Average marginal effect	
				Positive and significant*	Negative and significant*
Age 11–14 years	12	—	6	0.203	−0.055
Urban	9	1	8	0.113	—
Second quintile	6	—	12	0.069	—
Third quintile	14	—	4	0.089	—
Fourth quintile	17	—	1	0.120	—
Richest quintile	18	—	—	0.199	—
Caretaker educated	18	—	—	0.161	—
Child labour	3	9	6	0.026	−0.076

* Minimum 5% level of significance.—Averages are weighted by country population.

the summary regression shown in Table 10.7: for both boys and girls, having an educated mother or being in the richest 20 per cent of the population is not only positively associated with school attendance, it also has the greatest net effects on attendance, compared to other factors like area of residence.

10.3.5 Child Labour, Repetition, and Drop-Out

The analysis in the previous section showed that in our sample of 18 countries in sub-Saharan Africa child labour had no effect on school attendance in 7 countries, in one country the effect was positive, and in the remaining

Table 10.11. *Levels of school attendance, repetition, and drop-out in sub-Saharan Africa (%), children 7–14 years*

Category	Attending school	Attended school last year	Repeaters	Drop-outs
Burundi	47.3	40.0	23.8	4.3
CAR	49.8	48.2	33.9	5.6
Comoros	35.9	41.4	36.4	27.5
Congo (DRC)	61.7	57.1	20.9	10.2
Côte d'Ivoire	61.7	56.8	13.3	1.9
Gambia	52.7	45.1	3.6	1.6
Guinea-Bissau	43.3	34.5	16.5	4.9
Kenya	81.3	70.9	9.4	2.1
Lesotho	75.3	62.3	10.0	3.7
Malawi	83.4	75.6	29.9	2.2
Mali	38.7	34.6	10.4	1.3
Niger	30.2	25.5	8.8	3.5
Senegal	47.0	46.7	14.5	14.1
Sierra Leone	43.2	30.1	11.1	8.4
Somalia	13.4	10.4	3.3	13.1
Swaziland	77.8	68.1	13.2	6.4
Tanzania	51.1	39.8	0.9	1.9
Uganda	87.8	75.8	10.9	1.7
Total	60.3	52.9	13.0	5.1

Note: Averages are weighted by country population.

10 countries the effect on attendance was negative. In addition, we found that the effect of child labour on girls' school attendance was substantially greater than the effect on boys' attendance. In this section we examine the effect of child labour on academic performance. Could it be that child labourers who manage to attend school are too tired to learn? If this is so, then one would expect that children repeating a grade or dropping out of school would be disproportionately those engaged in child labour. As a recent study from Ghana and a review of similar studies by the ILO have shown, work has a detrimental effect on learning achievements in the key areas of language and mathematics.[30]

To test the hypothesis that children engaged in labour would have higher repetition and drop-out rates, the survey data was further analysed. Table 10.11 lists the attendance rates among children aged 7 to 14 years in the current

[30] C. Heady, *What is the effect of child labour on learning achievement? Evidence from Ghana*, Innocenti Working Paper No. 79 (Florence, Italy: UNICEF, 2000). P. Orazem and V. Gunnarsson, *Child labour, school attendance and academic performance: A review*, ILO/IPEC working paper (Geneva: ILO, 2003).

and previous year, the share of repeaters, and the drop-out rate. On average, 13 per cent of the children in school are repeaters, with a range of 1 per cent in Tanzania to 36 per cent in Comoros. Of the children who were in school during the year preceding the survey, 5 per cent had dropped out by the time the surveys were conducted. The drop-out rate ranges from 1 per cent in Mali to 28 per cent in Comoros.

In Table 10.12 the data is disaggregated by various background characteristics. Young children, boys, and rural children are more likely to repeat a grade. The drop-out rate falls from age 7 to age 11 and then rises again. Girls and rural children are in greater danger of dropping out than boys and urban children. However, with the average drop-out rate at 5 per cent, there is on average less than one point difference between girls and boys, between urban and rural children, and between children aged 7 to 10 and 11 to 14 years. Both the repetition and drop-out rate fall with increasing household wealth. Children with a formally educated mother or caretaker are less likely to repeat a grade or drop out of school. Finally, child labour is associated with higher repetition and drop-out rates.

To test whether these findings are statistically significant, we ran probit regressions with repetition and drop-out as the dependent variables. The set of explanatory variables is the same as in the regressions for school attendance.

Complete regression results for each country are shown in Tables 10.A4 and 10.A5 in the appendix. Table 10.14 summarizes the results for grade repetition from Table 10.A4.[31] The most important determinant of repetition seems to be age: in 11 of 17 countries children 11 to 14 years old are less likely to repeat a grade than children 7 to 10 years old; the average marginal effect is -7 percentage points. This is not surprising, given that young children (most of whom will not have benefited from pre-school education) have to adapt to the rhythm and demands of school. The data may also show the existence of a selective process which tends to promote students with higher abilities. However, in 3 countries the net effect of age is reversed: in Mali, Niger, and Senegal older children are more likely to repeat a grade.

The other explanatory variables are insignificant in the majority of countries. Increasing household wealth reduces the likelihood of repetition, but this effect is mostly limited to children from the richest quintile, and here only in 8 countries. Having an educated caretaker reduces the repetition rate in 6 countries, on average by 3 percentage points. Children from urban areas are less likely to repeat a grade in 5 countries and the average marginal effect is relatively strong with -6 percentage points.

The evidence for child labour is mixed. As Table 10.14 shows, child labour has a significant net effect on grade repetition in 7 of 17 countries.

---

[31] The summary table for grade repetition excludes Somalia because of unreliable regression results for this country.

Table 10.12. *School attendance, repetition, and drop-out for 18 countries in sub-Saharan Africa (%), children 7–14 years*

Category	Attending school	Attended school last year	Repeater	Drop-out
7 years	41.8	21.7	23.4	6.8
8 years	53.9	38.5	16.7	4.8
9 years	60.4	50.3	14.8	4.5
10 years	63.8	57.9	12.9	4.5
11 years	68.2	63.7	11.9	4.2
12 years	67.4	65.8	10.2	4.8
13 years	66.5	67.0	11.0	5.7
14 years	65.2	66.8	11.6	6.3
7–10 years	54.7	41.6	15.7	4.7
11–14 years	66.7	65.8	11.1	5.3
Female	58.3	51.2	12.8	5.3
Male	62.4	54.6	13.2	4.8
Rural	55.5	47.8	14.5	5.4
Urban	73.3	67.0	9.3	4.5
Poorest quintile	48.8	41.0	15.6	6.4
Second quintile	52.1	44.5	15.0	6.4
Third quintile	57.1	49.9	14.1	5.8
Fourth quintile	65.8	58.6	12.9	4.8
Richest quintile	78.4	71.4	9.3	3.2
Caretaker has no formal ed.	51.4	44.7	14.1	6.6
Caretaker has formal ed.	72.7	64.1	12.5	3.8
No child labour	65.3	58.3	11.8	4.3
Child labour	55.9	50.7	13.2	6.7
Total	60.3	52.9	13.0	5.1

Note: Averages are weighted by country population.

However, in three of these countries (Malawi, Senegal, and Uganda), children who worked were on average 2 percentage points less likely to repeat a grade than the average child. In the countries where child labourers are more likely to repeat a grade (Comoros, Guinea-Bissau, Mali, and Swaziland), the average marginal effect is 3 percentage points.

We can conclude that in most countries the likelihood of repeating a grade is not significantly associated with changes in the independent variables included in the model used in the present study. It would also seem that, contrary to our prior expectations, being a child labourer does not

Table 10.13. *Variables for repetition or drop-out*

Variable	Description
Repetition	1 if the child is repeating a grade, 0 if not
Drop-out	1 if the child dropped out of school, 0 if not

Table 10.14. *Summary of multivariate analysis in Table 10.A4: determinants of grade repetition, children 7–14 years* (17 countries, average repetition rate 13.0%)

Variable	Positive and significant*	Negative and significant*	Insignificant	Average marginal effect	
				Positive and significant*	Negative and significant*
Age 11–14 years	3	11	3	0.047	−0.072
Male	4	1	12	0.017	−0.020
Urban	1	5	11	0.075	−0.064
Second quintile	—	2	15	—	−0.046
Third quintile	1	1	15	0.100	−0.044
Fourth quintile	—	4	13	—	−0.045
Richest quintile	—	8	9	—	−0.051
Caretaker educated	1	6	10	0.053	−0.031
Child labour	4	3	10	0.028	−0.023

* Minimum 5% level of significance.—Averages are weighted by country population.

Note: Somalia is excluded from this table because of unreliable regression results; marginal effects near 1 for the third, fourth, and richest wealth quintile would strongly skew the mean values.

automatically affect school performance, or at least not so dramatically that the child cannot pass his or her end-of-year exams. At the same time, we also need to recognize that household wealth and education of the primary caretaker have significant net effects on grade repetition in more than one third of the countries in our sample; for school attendance, as will be recalled, these factors had a significant effect in all countries studied.

The regression results for school drop-out, presented in Table 10.A5 in the appendix (and as summarized in Table 10.15), are similarly mixed. In the majority of the 18 countries, the determinants included in our model have no effect on the probability of dropping out. On the other hand, we find that children with educated caretakers are less likely to drop out in 8 countries, with an average marginal effect of −3 percentage points. In 7 of 18 countries, children from the richest household quintile are less likely to drop out; compared to children from the poorest quintile their drop-out rate is 5 percentage points lower. The effect of the area of residence on the drop-out rate is ambiguous. The marginal effect is statistically significant in only

Table 10.15. *Summary of multivariate analysis in Table 10.A5: determinants of dropping out of school, children 7–14 years* (18 countries, average dropout rate 5.1%)

Variable	Positive and significant*	Negative and significant*	Insignificant	Average marginal effect	
				Positive and significant*	Negative and significant*
Age 11–14 years	5	1	12	0.013	−0.031
Male	1	1	16	0.050	−0.031
Urban	4	3	11	0.037	−0.052
Second quintile	1	2	15	0.062	−0.019
Third quintile	—	3	15	—	−0.015
Fourth quintile	1	6	11	0.042	−0.033
Richest quintile	—	7	11	—	−0.054
Caretaker educated	—	8	10	—	−0.034
Child labour	8	1	9	0.029	−0.010

* Minimum 5% level of significance.—Averages are weighted by country population.

7 countries, and among those we observe a positive effect in 4 countries and a negative effect in 3 countries. In 5 countries, younger children are more likely to drop out than older children, and in one country, they are less likely to drop out.

The results for child labour as a determinant of dropping out are clearer than they were for repeating a grade. Child labour increases the probability of dropping out of school in 8 countries, with an average marginal effect of 3 percentage points. In one country, the Central African Republic, being a child labourer lowers the probability of dropping out, but only by 1 percentage point.

In summary, it is fair to say that, in one-third to half of all countries, we observed significant net effects on dropping out of school that can be associated, though not uniformly or predictably, with age, place of residence, household wealth, mother's education, or child labour. Once again we see that any policy aimed at school drop-outs or repeaters must be designed for each country individually.

10.4 CONCLUSIONS AND POLICY RECOMMENDATIONS

10.4.1 The Human Rights Principle of Non-Discrimination Applied to Statistical Analyses

The gender-differentiated impact of child labour revealed by this study confirms the importance of applying the human rights principle of non-discrimination to analyses of the nexus between school attendance and child labour. A universally recognized and applied gender-equalizing indicator of child labour, such as that used here on an experimental basis, must take household chores into account. The human rights approach to analysis of issues in human development aims to reveal, as a prelude to appropriate policy responses, whose rights are not being fulfilled and why. This demands a more refined approach to statistical analysis, requiring investigators to:

a) Use household survey data: Survey data can provide more accurate information than administrative records. Survey data can be disaggregated and analysed at various levels, which helps reveal discrimination. Surveys are a good (perhaps the best) tool to collect information on child labour; however they are unlikely to capture hidden child labour (this includes the worst forms of child labour: prostitution, bonded labour, drug trafficking).

b) Use appropriate indicators: Indicators developed with the idea of revealing discrimination provide a more accurate picture. Deciding what indicators to use requires an understanding of prevailing cultural, ethnic, and gender patterns which may produce discrimination. A child labour indicator that considers household chores shows that girls work as much as or more than boys. This indicator also reveals that girls fall into stereotypical roles assigned to women by traditional society (cook, caretaker of children, etc.).

c) Propose new data collection methods: Current indicators based on available data may hide existing discrimination. Equality in school attendance rates, for example, does not mean that there is no discrimination: teacher attitudes may mean that girls are not given as much opportunity to participate in class as boys, reducing their learning achievement. Our analysis showed that child labourers are more likely to drop out, but we do not know if child labourers who stay in school perform worse or the same as their non-working peers. Thus, we need data on school achievement but existing data is insufficient. The Program for International Student Assessment (PISA), which was begun in 2000, provides data on reading, mathematical and scientific literacy of 15-year-olds in school but these surveys are mostly implemented in OECD countries where child labour is less widespread than in Africa and other parts of the world.[32]

However, even when all these measures to reveal discrimination are considered, we are often left with a result which will only show statistical averages within a larger population. A weak link between child labour and education

---

[32] OECD, *Literacy skills for the world of tomorrow: Further results from PISA 2000* (Paris: OECD, 2003).

at the country level may hide stronger relationships between the two variables in certain areas of the country or among minority populations, which cannot always be identified because the survey data may not be representative at a lower level. Thus, even in countries where child labour is not a statistically significant constraint to school attendance, it still may prevent large numbers of children from enjoying their right to education. More refined analysis will always be required to determine who those children at the margins actually are, and whether they are statistically invisible due to discrimination, poverty, or other factors. The human rights principle of universality means that, ultimately, all children must have their rights fulfilled. Policy makers cannot be satisfied with averages which hide disparities.

10.4.2 Limitations of Survey Data and Child Labour Indicator

In addition to inherent difficulties of applying the human rights principle of non-discrimination to statistical analyses in general, the weak results with regard to child labour for some countries in this study may at least partly be due to the way child labour is measured. The data from the MICS and DHS surveys does not tell us exactly what kind of work children do, only whether they work for a family farm or business, for someone who is not a member of the household, or whether they are engaged in domestic work. Tending cows for one's parents, perhaps accompanied by friends, and working long hours on a cacao plantation far away from home both carry the same weight in our analysis.[33] Yet, these two activities are likely to have a different impact on a child's physical and mental well-being. If we find that child labour has no statistically significant effect on school attendance and achievement in a country, then this is perhaps due to the fact that the children engage in relatively light forms of labour.[34] If such work does not interfere with children's education it would be less cause for concern from a human rights perspective, even though there could be other implications, such as the child's reduced enjoyment of the right to recreation, which is integral to his or her human development.

10.4.3 Some Reasons why Children in Sub-Saharan Africa are not Attending School

The main conclusion to be drawn from this study of 18 countries in sub-Saharan Africa is that the strongest determinants of school attendance are,

---

[33] Both activities are child labour, as long as they meet the minimum threshold of one hour per week for children aged 5 to 11 years, and 14 hours per week for children aged 12 to 14 years.

[34] The authors thank Craig Scott of York University for bringing this point to our attention.

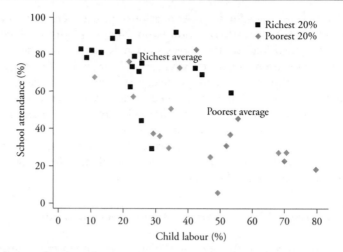

Figure 10.3. Child labour and school attendance in sub-Saharan Africa, by household wealth, children 7–14 years

Note: Each country is represented by two points, one for the richest and one for the poorest household quintile.

overwhelmingly and without exception, household wealth and mother's education. This finding clearly indicates that, in order to increase the levels of school attendance, policies should focus on poverty reduction, for example through income transfers to poor families. This would allow parents to forgo the contribution of their children to household income, were the latter attending school instead of working. The effect of household wealth is clearly seen in Figure 10.3, which plots child labour and school attendance rates for the poorest and richest 20 per cent of the population in 18 countries. Children from the poorest households are more likely to work and less likely to be in school than children from the richest households.

Similarly, the findings related to mother's education indicate that educating the mothers and caretakers of the future will lead to increased levels of school attendance. This finding should give renewed vigour to the international community's commitment to reach gender parity in primary school by 2005.[35]

The second conclusion to be drawn from the present study is that child labour is one of the major factors constraining school attendance for the majority of the countries analysed. For 10 of 18 countries, being engaged in child labour adds on average 9 percentage points to the probability that a

[35] Target 4 of the Millennium Development Goals, adopted at the UN Millennium Summit in 2000, aims to 'eliminate gender disparity in primary and secondary education, preferably by 2005 and in all levels of education no later than 2015' (UNDP, *Human Development Report 2003*, New York: Oxford University Press, 2003).

child will not attend school. It is important to mention also that the probability of not attending school is disproportionately skewed against girls. For girls, the marginal effect of child labour on school attendance (-11 percentage points) is, in relative terms, 40 per cent higher than the marginal effect of child labour on boys' school attendance (−7 percentage points). Considerably more research is required to understand why this should be. One hypothesis could be that the countries with high gender disparities are also those with the least developed economic and social infrastructure. The absence of such infrastructure, such as rural electrification, community water systems, preventive health services, and pre-schools, all increase the time which girls must spend on household chores, thus limiting time available for attending school.

However, it is also important to mention that the net effects of child labour on school attendance were not statistically significant in 7 countries. Our original hypothesis, that child labour invariably constrains school attendance, has thus been proved false. This study shows that there are other factors besides time spent working that prevent children from realizing their right to education; these factors need to be identified on a case by case basis to ensure that policy interventions are appropriate. Such factors can include the quality of education, the physical access to schools, the child's nutritional and health status as well as cultural barriers. More research is especially required to determine the causes of apparently anomalous results. For example, of particular concern is the finding that around one in five children from the richest 20 per cent of the population are not attending school, even though household wealth is the strongest determinant of school attendance.

With more than half of all child labourers also attending school, we expected that, due to less time available for studying, they would be more prone to repeat grades or drop out of school, compared to their non-working peers. With regard to repetition, this hypothesis is true for 4 countries, but the opposite is observed in 3 other countries. For the remaining 10 countries, the marginal effects are not significant, which would also appear to indicate that time spent in child labour does not affect school performance enough to keep the child from being promoted to the next grade. One must also keep in mind that with the MICS and DHS data it is not possible to show if this result would hold over time because the surveys only show the relationship between labour and repetition at one moment in time.

Finally, for 8 countries child labour increases the probability of dropping out of school by 3 percentage points on average. On the other hand, in one country, the Central African Republic, children involved in child labour tend to have drop-out rates that are on average 1 percentage point lower than among non-labouring children. In the remaining 9 countries, child labour was not significantly associated with the probability of dropping out of school. Thus, the conventional wisdom that child labour significantly increases the probability of dropping out of school has been proved true for only half of the countries in the sample. This confirms the need for much more sophisticated causal analyses when designing policy responses to the problem of retention in school. Attention must be paid, for example, to the structure of the local economy (which could be a 'pull' factor on children's participation in the labour market), the legal framework (including the age until which schooling is compulsory), the minimum age of employment, and the minimum age of marriage.[36]

10.4.4 Policy Recommendations

Based on the results presented in this study, several recommendations for policy can be made.

a) The importance of using a human rights lens when analysing the data has been confirmed. The human rights approach to statistical analysis is a useful tool for getting at the causes of violations of each child's right to education, revealing discriminations on the basis of gender and poverty. Better indicators, more refined survey methodologies, and deeper analyses are needed to identify the scope of the child labour problem and who is affected, and its relationship with school attendance and achievement. A universally accepted 'gender equalizing' indicator of child labour must be created.

b) The present study, by demonstrating that the relationship between child labour and education is not a simple or predictable one, has also confirmed that a holistic, multi-sectoral development approach, consistent with the principle of indivisibility of rights, is needed to address both issues. Only through a multi-sectoral response will all children be enabled to enjoy the rights laid down in the Convention on the Rights of the Child.

c) Poverty reduction strategies must be vigorously pursued as an integral response to poor school attendance, given that in all 18 countries in the study poverty was a constraining factor on school attendance for both boys and girls.

d) The mother's education as a determinant for assuring a child's school attendance reinforces and gives renewed impetus to the Millennium Development Goals for gender equity in schools by 2005, and universal primary education for girls and boys by 2015. Countries must invest in girls' education over the long term.

---

[36] These ages can be inconsistent. Niger, for example, the country with the lowest rate of school attendance in the study (with the exception of Somalia), has a school-leaving age of 16, a minimum employment age of 14, and no legally-established minimum age of marriage.

As with most of the research in social sciences, the analysis in the present study leaves unanswered many questions about the determinants of school access and achievement. The reality is perhaps as complex and diverse as the analysed countries. Overall, the study establishes that there is an intricate nexus of factors that influence whether a child attends school or not, and child labour is but one of them. Even though most parents want education for their children, some may perceive school as irrelevant, since they see that children end up doing the same work as their peers who have dropped out of school and are seen as getting a head start in the labour market. Other factors affecting school attendance and achievement can include teachers' and administrators' attitudes, biased and irrelevant curricula, discriminatory and abusive treatment of children such as corporal punishment and sexual abuse, or deprived conditions (poor infrastructure, no books, poorly prepared teachers). In reality, the lack of respect for children's rights within the school, along with the poor quality of education itself, can drive children out of the system and into child labour. To what extent this may be so is a topic for further research.

APPENDIX: REGRESSION RESULTS

Table 10.A1. *Multivariate analysis (probit regression): marginal effects of the determinants of school attendance in 18 sub-Saharan countries, children 7–14 years*

	Burundi NAR 47.3 Marg. effect (z stat.)	CAR NAR 49.8 Marg. effect (z stat.)	Comoros NAR 35.9 Marg. effect (z stat.)	Congo (DRC) NAR 67.5 Marg. effect (z stat.)	Côte d'Ivoire NAR 61.7 Marg. effect (z stat.)	Gambia NAR 52.7 Marg. effect (z stat.)	Guinea-Bissau NAR 43.3 Marg. effect (z stat.)	Kenya NAR 81.3 Marg. effect (z stat.)	Lesotho NAR 75.3 Marg. effect (z stat.)
Age 11–14 years	0.136** (9.56)	0.050** (7.38)	0.084** (6.50)	0.015 (1.10)	-0.034** (3.89)	0.089** (6.93)	0.148** (11.02)	0.112** (15.40)	0.139** (13.26)
Male	0.092** (6.43)	0.134** (20.04)	-0.006 (0.44)	0.114** (10.46)	0.141** (15.98)	0.091** (7.22)	0.109** (8.57)	-0.011 (1.49)	-0.092** (8.81)
Urban	0.102** (3.23)	0.134** (15.78)	0.108** (6.39)	0.034* (2.10)	-0.029* (2.53)	0.075** (4.74)	0.295** (16.58)	-0.091** (5.59)	-0.031 (1.88)
Second wealth quintile	0.022 (0.91)	0.128** (12.02)	0.019 (0.95)	-0.053* (3.14)	0.091** (6.95)	0.087** (4.93)	0.019 (0.90)	0.055** (5.76)	0.089** (6.28)
Third wealth quintile	0.057* (2.35)	0.146** (13.74)	0.073** (3.64)	0.016 (0.95)	0.106** (8.10)	0.115** (6.17)	0.051* (2.43)	0.063** (6.48)	0.141** (10.15)
Fourth wealth quintile	0.139** (6.20)	0.241** (21.10)	0.083** (4.07)	0.113** (6.73)	0.177** (12.02)	0.223** (11.35)	0.162** (7.32)	0.105** (10.24)	0.190** (13.55)
Richest wealth quintile	0.204** (8.50)	0.304** (25.44)	0.095** (4.37)	0.212** (10.47)	0.243** (15.26)	0.310** (13.50)	0.252** (9.41)	0.087** (5.75)	0.234** (15.85)
Caretaker has formal ed.	0.165** (9.86)	0.199** (28.17)	0.097** (6.18)	0.211** (17.97)	0.218** (21.52)	0.126** (6.04)	0.218** (11.28)	0.163** (18.55)	0.146** (8.21)
Child labour	-0.104** (6.55)	0.002 (0.34)	0.013 (0.92)	-0.068** (5.78)	-0.105** (10.98)	-0.053** (3.39)	-0.025 (1.77)	-0.062** (7.63)	-0.040** (3.09)
Observations	5166	24,780	5858	7671	13055	6697	7448	11206	6827

Probit regressions: * significant at 5%; ** significant at 1%

	Malawi NAR 83.4 Marg. effect (z stat.)	Mali NAR 38.7 Marg. effect (z stat.)	Niger NAR 30.2 Marg. effect (z stat.)	Senegal NAR 47.0 Marg. effect (z stat.)	Sierra Leone NAR 43.2 Marg. effect (z stat.)	Somalia NAR 13.7 Marg. effect (z stat.)	Swaziland NAR 78.1 Marg. effect (z stat.)	Tanzania NAR 51.1 Marg. effect (z stat.)	Uganda NAR 87.8 Marg. effect (z stat.)
Age 11–14 years	0.053** (8.71)	−0.002 (0.25)	−0.015 (1.13)	−0.023* (2.55)	−0.006 (0.34)	0.054** (5.59)	0.027* (2.46)	0.430** (25.83)	0.083** (12.00)
Male	−0.016** (2.70)	0.148** (17.95)	0.147** (11.63)	0.096** (10.89)	0.073** (5.02)	0.013 (1.33)	−0.001 (0.12)	−0.026 (1.56)	0.001 (0.14)
Urban	0.036** (3.10)	0.119** (9.37)	0.208** (9.27)	0.076** (5.92)	0.121** (6.31)	−0.019 (1.55)	−0.022 (1.03)	0.038 (1.45)	−0.053** (3.56)
Second wealth quintile	0.020* (2.31)	0.027* (2.06)	0.030 (1.38)	0.010 (0.72)	0.023 (0.99)	0.001 (0.05)	0.091** (6.46)	0.012 (0.47)	0.005 (0.46)
Third wealth quintile	0.033** (3.91)	0.055** (4.15)	0.030 (1.48)	0.070** (5.00)	0.105** (4.50)	0.081** (4.06)	0.109** (7.21)	0.102** (3.86)	0.043** (4.60)
Fourth wealth quintile	0.080** (9.66)	0.144** (10.67)	0.029 (1.36)	0.167** (10.22)	0.172** (7.33)	0.151** (6.40)	0.108** (6.51)	0.175** (6.76)	0.070** (7.58)
Richest wealth quintile	0.108** (11.40)	0.332** (19.60)	0.228** (9.36)	0.247** (13.28)	0.286** (10.54)	0.250** (9.44)	0.089** (4.23)	0.332** (11.02)	0.085** (8.06)
Caretaker has formal ed.	0.123** (19.47)	0.240** (16.72)	0.240** (10.25)	0.268** (21.44)	0.249** (12.68)	0.095** (8.00)	0.120** (9.48)	0.127** (7.24)	0.060** (8.71)
Child labour	−0.003 (0.37)	−0.143** (16.69)	−0.102** (7.05)	−0.135** (14.83)	0.010 (0.60)	−0.016 (1.56)	0.001 (0.05)	−0.117** (6.64)	0.017* (2.51)
Observations	13886	15567	5787	14309	5119	4599	5434	4179	8627

Probit regressions: * significant at 5%; ** significant at 1%

Note: Data for Congo (DRC) is for girls 10–14 years of age.

Table 10.A2. *Multivariate analysis (probit regression): marginal effects of the determinants of school attendance in 18 sub-Saharan countries, girls 7–14 years*

	Burundi NAR 43.8	CAR NAR 44.0	Comoros NAR 36.3	Congo (DRC) NAR 62.4	Côte d'Ivoire NAR 55.3	Gambia NAR 49.2	Guinea-Bissau NAR 39.9	Kenya NAR 81.8	Lesotho NAR 79.6
	Marg. effect (z stat.)	Marg. effect (z stat.)	Marg. effect (z stat.)	Marg. effect (z stat.)	Marg. effect (z stat.)	Marg. effect (z stat.)	Marg. effect (z stat.)	Marg. effect (z stat.)	Marg. effect (z stat.)
Age 11–14 years	0.114** (5.81)	0.003 (0.32)	0.069** (3.72)	0.004 (0.22)	−0.070** (5.25)	0.065** (3.68)	0.118** (6.30)	0.102** (10.10)	0.139** (10.12)
Urban	0.128** (2.87)	0.174** (14.55)	0.075** (3.08)	0.046 (1.94)	−0.026 (1.53)	0.078** (3.56)	0.284** (11.55)	−0.119** (5.18)	−0.077** (3.49)
Second wealth quintile	−0.019 (0.57)	0.092** (5.85)	0.021 (0.72)	−0.071** (2.80)	0.111** (5.38)	0.072** (2.85)	0.053 (1.65)	0.059** (4.55)	0.062** (3.44)
Third wealth quintile	0.037 (1.08)	0.141** (9.14)	0.086** (2.97)	−0.032 (1.28)	0.103** (5.08)	0.119** (4.57)	0.079** (2.56)	0.074** (5.54)	0.109** (6.13)
Fourth wealth quintile	0.118** (3.79)	0.235** (13.88)	0.109** (3.70)	0.126** (4.98)	0.193** (8.49)	0.225** (8.03)	0.211** (6.44)	0.102** (7.26)	0.163** (9.13)
Richest wealth quintile	0.190** (5.65)	0.311** (17.94)	0.105** (3.38)	0.239** (7.79)	0.243** (9.88)	0.302** (9.33)	0.330** (8.66)	0.104** (5.26)	0.196** (10.28)
Caretaker has formal ed.	0.166** (7.36)	0.215** (21.48)	0.092** (4.06)	0.247** (14.29)	0.235** (15.90)	0.163** (5.72)	0.217** (8.14)	0.141** (11.52)	0.130** (5.64)
Child labour	−0.132** (5.95)	−0.019 (1.86)	−0.015 (0.72)	−0.065** (3.82)	−0.140** (10.12)	−0.068** (3.14)	−0.016 (0.78)	−0.095** (8.22)	−0.007 (0.41)
Observations	2706	12378	2842	3890	6248	3526	3719	5600	3419

* significant at 5%; ** significant at 1%

	Malawi NAR 84.2	Mali NAR 32.7	Niger NAR 24.2	Senegal NAR 43.0	Sierra Leone NAR 40.4	Somalia NAR 12.9	Swaziland NAR 78.2	Tanzania NAR 52.6	Uganda NAR 87.7
	Marg. effect (z stat.)	Marg. effect (z stat.)	Marg. effect (z stat.)	Marg. effect (z stat.)	Marg. effect (z stat.)	Marg. effect (z stat.)	Marg. effect (z stat.)	Marg. effect (z stat.)	Marg. effect (z stat.)
Age 11–14 years	0.038** (4.57)	−0.025* (2.19)	−0.049** (2.96)	−0.063** (5.04)	−0.025 (1.11)	0.029* (2.15)	0.023 (1.46)	0.418** (17.56)	0.062** (6.46)
Urban	−0.010 (0.65)	0.082** (4.81)	0.291** (9.78)	0.083** (4.68)	0.108** (4.04)	−0.038* (2.18)	−0.031 (1.06)	0.024 (0.67)	−0.070** (3.33)
Second wealth quintile	0.025* (2.22)	0.019 (1.07)	0.021 (0.74)	0.021 (1.04)	0.000 (0.01)	0.003 (0.09)	0.083** (4.08)	0.049 (1.32)	0.017 (1.24)
Third wealth quintile	0.036** (3.11)	0.040* (2.23)	0.074** (2.63)	0.111** (5.50)	0.120** (3.53)	0.089** (3.14)	0.105** (4.85)	0.041 (1.11)	0.069** (5.45)
Fourth wealth quintile	0.092** (8.14)	0.138** (7.44)	0.035 (1.25)	0.208** (8.90)	0.206** (6.06)	0.183** (5.23)	0.117** (4.92)	0.180** (4.93)	0.087** (6.99)
Richest wealth quintile	0.103** (8.02)	0.346** (14.79)	0.178** (5.54)	0.285** (10.81)	0.330** (8.46)	0.243** (6.39)	0.068* (2.29)	0.334** (7.97)	0.094** (6.60)
Caretaker has formal ed.	0.128** (14.69)	0.275** (13.97)	0.228** (7.38)	0.291** (16.33)	0.222** (7.93)	0.074** (4.41)	0.090** (5.04)	0.125** (5.16)	0.067** (6.98)
Child labour	−0.007 (0.68)	−0.120** (10.47)	−0.119** (6.62)	−0.132** (10.29)	0.036 (1.60)	0.000 (0.03)	0.011 (0.42)	−0.147** (5.87)	0.008 (0.86)
Observations	7162	7938	2920	7187	2523	2211	2666	2087	4390

* significant at 5%; ** significant at 1%

Note: Data for Congo (DRC) is for girls 10–14 years of age.

Table 10.A3. *Multivariate analysis (probit regression): marginal effects of the determinants of school attendance in 18 sub-Saharan countries, boys 7–14 years*

	Burundi NAR 51.2	CAR NAR 55.7	Comoros NAR 35.5	Congo (DRC) NAR 72.8	Côte d'Ivoire NAR 67.6	Gambia NAR 56.4	Guinea-Bissau NAR 46.7	Kenya NAR 80.7	Lesotho NAR 71.0
	Marg. effect (z stat.)	Marg. effect (z stat.)	Marg. effect (z stat.)	Marg. effect (z stat.)	Marg. effect (z stat.)	Marg. effect (z stat.)	Marg. effect (z stat.)	Marg. effect (z stat.)	Marg. effect (z stat.)
Age 11–14 years	0.161**	0.099**	0.101**	0.023	−0.001	0.113**	0.172**	0.124**	0.138**
	(7.83)	(10.42)	(5.51)	(1.25)	(0.06)	(6.07)	(9.10)	(11.83)	(8.77)
Urban	0.073	0.090**	0.140**	0.020	−0.025	0.072**	0.301**	−0.055*	0.018
	(1.63)	(7.61)	(5.97)	(0.91)	(1.64)	(3.13)	(11.85)	(2.41)	(0.74)
Second wealth quintile	0.063	0.158**	0.017	−0.036	0.074**	0.100**	−0.005	0.050**	0.119**
	(1.86)	(11.24)	(0.60)	(1.66)	(4.61)	(4.08)	(0.17)	(3.64)	(5.38)
Third wealth quintile	0.075*	0.151**	0.060*	0.058**	0.107**	0.107**	0.032	0.053**	0.175**
	(2.18)	(10.55)	(2.16)	(2.72)	(6.51)	(4.07)	(1.14)	(3.76)	(8.15)
Fourth wealth quintile	0.158**	0.243**	0.059*	0.098**	0.156**	0.217**	0.124**	0.109**	0.219**
	(4.98)	(16.15)	(2.09)	(4.48)	(8.42)	(7.94)	(4.11)	(7.36)	(10.05)
Richest wealth quintile	0.216**	0.291**	0.086**	0.180**	0.238**	0.313**	0.175**	0.065**	0.275**
	(6.36)	(18.02)	(2.85)	(6.84)	(11.80)	(9.61)	(4.57)	(2.85)	(12.10)
Caretaker has formal ed.	0.164**	0.176**	0.103**	0.174**	0.198**	0.086**	0.218**	0.185**	0.164**
	(6.64)	(18.08)	(4.73)	(11.11)	(14.60)	(2.83)	(7.83)	(14.74)	(6.09)
Child labour	−0.073**	0.024*	0.042*	−0.071**	−0.066**	−0.036	−0.036	−0.028*	−0.068**
	(3.23)	(2.43)	(2.07)	(4.39)	(5.09)	(1.62)	(1.78)	(2.38)	(3.54)
Observations	2460	12402	3016	3781	6807	3171	3729	5606	3408

* significant at 5%; ** significant at 1%

	Malawi NAR 82.6	Mali NAR 45.0	Niger NAR 36.2	Senegal NAR 51.1	Sierra Leone NAR 45.9	Somalia NAR 14.4	Swaziland NAR 78.0	Tanzania NAR 49.6	Uganda NAR 87.9
	Marg. effect (z stat.)	Marg. effect (z stat.)	Marg. effect (z stat.)	Marg. effect (z stat.)	Marg. effect (z stat.)	Marg. effect (z stat.)	Marg. effect (z stat.)	Marg. effect (z stat.)	Marg. effect (z stat.)
Age 11–14 years	0.071** (8.00)	0.020 (1.61)	0.021 (1.08)	0.016 (1.30)	0.012 (0.53)	0.076** (5.58)	0.031* (1.98)	0.448** (19.04)	0.104** (10.48)
Urban	0.093** (5.57)	0.152** (8.25)	0.114** (3.42)	0.065** (3.56)	0.133** (4.90)	0.001 (0.03)	−0.011 (0.34)	0.050 (1.30)	−0.034 (1.58)
Second wealth quintile	0.013 (1.08)	0.035 (1.87)	0.043 (1.31)	0.002 (0.12)	0.047 (1.47)	−0.001 (0.03)	0.098** (5.05)	−0.024 (0.66)	−0.007 (0.48)
Third wealth quintile	0.030* (2.41)	0.068** (3.62)	−0.005 (0.16)	0.034 (1.77)	0.097** (3.02)	0.066** (2.38)	0.113** (5.38)	0.175** (4.62)	0.015 (1.11)
Fourth wealth quintile	0.067** (5.58)	0.145** (7.61)	0.023 (0.74)	0.133** (5.83)	0.141** (4.34)	0.115** (3.65)	0.100** (4.30)	0.168** (4.56)	0.051** (3.71)
Richest wealth quintile	0.115** (8.30)	0.315** (13.10)	0.271** (7.64)	0.214** (8.21)	0.245** (6.49)	0.249** (6.77)	0.114** (3.87)	0.334** (7.64)	0.076** (4.93)
Caretaker has formal ed.	0.116** (12.71)	0.199** (9.67)	0.241** (7.06)	0.243** (13.93)	0.273** (9.93)	0.115** (6.90)	0.148** (8.31)	0.129** (5.05)	0.052** (5.35)
Child labour	0.004 (0.40)	−0.159** (12.75)	−0.079** (3.51)	−0.139** (10.71)	−0.017 (0.76)	−0.028 (1.91)	−0.007 (0.27)	−0.086** (3.46)	0.026** (2.69)
Observations	6724	7629	2867	7122	2596	2388	2768	2092	4237

* significant at 5%; ** significant at 1%

Note: Data for Congo (DRC) is for boys 10–14 years of age.

Table 10.A4. Multivariate analysis (probit regression): marginal effects of the determinants of grade repetition in 18 sub-Saharan countries, children 7–14 years

	Burundi Repeaters 23.8	CAR Repeaters 33.9	Comoros Repeaters 36.4	Congo (DRC) Repeaters 17.4	Côte d'Ivoire Repeaters 13.3	Gambia Repeaters 3.6	Guinea-Bissau Repeaters 16.5	Kenya Repeaters 9.4	Lesotho Repeaters 10.0
	Marg. effect (z stat.)	Marg. effect (z stat.)	Marg. effect (z stat.)	Marg. effect (z stat.)	Marg. effect (z stat.)	Marg. effect (z stat.)	Marg. effect (z stat.)	Marg. effect (z stat.)	Marg. effect (z stat.)
Age 11–14 years	−0.093** (4.67)	0.002 (0.22)	−0.066** (2.86)	−0.064** (4.51)	0.013 (1.60)	−0.020** (2.94)	−0.072** (4.72)	−0.040** (5.84)	−0.092** (9.19)
Male	0.001 (0.07)	−0.014 (1.56)	0.007 (0.29)	0.005 (0.48)	0.003 (0.36)	0.017* (2.56)	0.005 (0.31)	0.012 (1.89)	0.025** (2.71)
Urban	−0.041 (1.18)	−0.013 (1.17)	0.022 (0.77)	−0.079** (5.28)	−0.005 (0.45)	0.002 (0.28)	−0.035 (1.54)	−0.049** (3.89)	−0.040** (3.40)
Second wealth quintile	−0.056 (1.62)	0.028 (1.60)	−0.023 (0.58)	0.001 (0.07)	−0.008 (0.54)	0.018 (1.76)	0.021 (0.56)	−0.012 (1.27)	−0.011 (0.68)
Third wealth quintile	−0.010 (0.29)	0.005 (0.32)	−0.008 (0.20)	−0.025 (1.39)	−0.013 (0.94)	−0.007 (0.72)	0.100** (2.66)	−0.003 (0.28)	−0.008 (0.49)
Fourth wealth quintile	−0.037 (1.21)	−0.022 (1.26)	0.061 (1.65)	−0.007 (0.39)	−0.013 (0.87)	−0.008 (0.78)	0.041 (1.16)	−0.006 (0.65)	0.006 (0.40)
Richest wealth quintile	−0.030 (0.92)	−0.076** (4.26)	−0.023 (0.60)	−0.037 (1.76)	−0.045** (2.92)	−0.010 (0.88)	0.072 (1.93)	−0.031* (2.00)	−0.009 (0.57)
Caretaker has formal ed.	−0.023 (1.10)	0.053** (5.71)	−0.079** (3.06)	−0.009 (0.74)	0.001 (0.15)	−0.018 (1.85)	0.009 (0.50)	−0.028** (3.46)	−0.065** (3.49)
Child labour	−0.022 (0.99)	0.011 (1.22)	0.123** (4.70)	0.021 (1.69)	0.002 (0.19)	−0.001 (0.09)	0.042* (2.47)	0.007 (0.99)	0.008 (0.67)
Observations	1976	11560	1814	4827	7013	2877	2595	7688	4082

Probit regressions: * significant at 5%; ** significant at 1%

	Malawi Repeaters 29.9	Mali Repeaters 10.4	Niger Repeaters 8.8	Senegal Repeaters 14.5	Sierra Leone Repeaters 11.1	Somalia Repeaters 3.1	Swaziland Repeaters 13.3	Tanzania Repeaters 0.9	Uganda Repeaters 10.9
	Marg. effect (z stat.)	Marg. effect (z stat.)	Marg. effect (z stat.)	Marg. effect (z stat.)	Marg. effect (z stat.)	Marg. effect (z stat.)	Marg. effect (z stat.)	Marg. effect (z stat.)	Marg. effect (z stat.)
Age 11–14 years	-0.164** (18.06)	0.036** (4.30)	0.051** (4.01)	0.055** (5.83)	-0.097** (5.81)	-0.004 (0.51)	-0.033** (2.89)	-0.005 (1.56)	-0.078** (9.97)
Male	0.005 (0.59)	-0.020* (2.36)	-0.016 (1.22)	-0.007 (0.78)	-0.022 (1.50)	0.000 (0.04)	0.027* (2.38)	0.002 (0.68)	0.016* (2.15)
Urban	-0.085** (5.76)	0.019 (1.58)	0.024 (1.32)	0.025 (1.94)	-0.033 (1.85)	0.009 (1.06)	0.075** (3.22)	-0.005 (1.73)	-0.042** (3.10)
Second wealth quintile	0.026 (1.76)	-0.006 (0.38)	-0.047* (2.30)	-0.027 (1.54)	0.055 (1.44)	0.983 (.)	-0.032* (2.04)	0.006 (0.95)	0.001 (0.07)
Third wealth quintile	-0.026 (1.83)	0.014 (0.86)	-0.025 (1.24)	-0.010 (0.62)	0.005 (0.15)	0.948** (8.22)	-0.044** (2.71)	0.003 (0.54)	-0.005 (0.43)
Fourth wealth quintile	-0.052** (3.71)	0.000 (0.01)	-0.054** (2.68)	-0.034 (1.92)	0.041 (1.36)	0.838** (8.02)	-0.047** (2.72)	-0.006 (1.12)	-0.038** (3.34)
Richest wealth quintile	-0.120** (8.12)	-0.016 (0.93)	-0.062** (2.68)	-0.050** (2.60)	-0.015 (0.49)	0.628** (7.67)	-0.065** (3.11)	0.008 (1.33)	-0.038** (3.00)
Caretaker has formal ed.	0.003 (0.37)	-0.026* (2.45)	0.023 (1.38)	-0.036** (3.38)	-0.033* (2.08)	-0.011 (1.50)	0.003 (0.19)	0.005 (1.76)	0.011 (1.52)
Child labour	-0.022* (2.07)	0.019* (1.97)	-0.000 (0.02)	-0.028** (2.73)	0.026 (1.60)	-0.010 (1.34)	0.051** (2.61)	0.001 (0.49)	-0.021** (2.77)
Observations	10505	5250	2007	5600	1488	388	3467	1809	6489

Probit regressions: * significant at 5%; ** significant at 1%

Notes: Data for Congo (DRC) is for children 10–14 years of age.—The results for Somalia are unreliable, possibly due to a small sample size. Somalia is therefore excluded from the summary in Table 10.14.

Table 10.A5. *Multivariate analysis (probit regression): marginal effects of the determinants of dropping out in 18 sub-Saharan countries, children 7–14 years*

	Burundi Drop-outs 4.3		CAR Drop-outs 5.6		Comoros Drop-outs 27.5		Congo (DRC) Drop-outs 10.0		Côte d'Ivoire Drop-outs 1.9		Gambia Drop-outs 1.6		Guinea-Bissau Drop-outs 4.9		Kenya Drop-outs 2.1		Lesotho Drop-outs 3.7	
	Marg. effect	(z stat.)	Marg. effect	(z stat.)	Marg. effect	(z stat.)	Marg. effect	(z stat.)	Marg. effect	(z stat.)	Marg. effect	(z stat.)	Marg. effect	(z stat.)	Marg. effect	(z stat.)	Marg. effect	(z stat.)
Age 11–14 years	0.002	(0.23)	0.005	(1.26)	0.000	(0.01)	0.003	(0.25)	0.003	(1.08)	0.001	(0.21)	−0.007	(0.87)	0.006*	(2.05)	0.018**	(3.22)
Male	0.000	(0.05)	0.005	(1.16)	0.050**	(2.84)	−0.031**	(3.86)	0.001	(0.46)	−0.005	(1.16)	−0.007	(0.90)	0.002	(0.54)	0.007	(1.28)
Urban	0.013	(0.69)	−0.011*	(2.19)	0.034	(1.57)	0.048**	(4.24)	−0.001	(0.21)	0.003	(0.55)	−0.045**	(3.34)	0.015*	(2.13)	−0.002	(0.22)
Second wealth quintile	−0.005	(0.35)	−0.015*	(2.25)	0.062*	(2.04)	−0.012	(0.93)	−0.003	(0.68)	0.008	(1.05)	0.039	(1.82)	0.001	(0.33)	−0.008	(1.02)
Third wealth quintile	−0.014	(1.11)	−0.009	(1.31)	0.014	(0.49)	−0.018	(1.52)	−0.003	(0.59)	−0.005	(0.81)	0.011	(0.57)	−0.014**	(3.57)	−0.016*	(2.18)
Fourth wealth quintile	−0.017	(1.50)	−0.029**	(4.32)	−0.011	(0.38)	−0.054**	(4.68)	−0.004	(0.73)	0.003	(0.45)	0.021	(1.13)	−0.010*	(2.46)	−0.020**	(2.68)
Richest wealth quintile	−0.025*	(2.05)	−0.024**	(3.30)	0.034	(1.12)	−0.095**	(7.31)	−0.010	(1.93)	−0.012	(1.76)	0.023	(1.15)	−0.009	(1.53)	−0.032**	(3.99)
Caretaker has formal ed.	−0.015	(1.66)	−0.014**	(3.16)	−0.055**	(2.74)	−0.040**	(4.33)	−0.002	(0.52)	0.014	(1.93)	−0.014	(1.47)	−0.005	(1.41)	−0.016	(1.64)
Child labour	0.053**	(5.00)	−0.010*	(2.24)	0.016	(0.78)	0.043**	(4.76)	0.005	(1.46)	0.000	(0.01)	−0.015	(1.62)	0.023**	(5.91)	0.020**	(2.72)
Observations	2065		12262		2560		5346		7186		2929		2740		7840		4250	

Probit regressions: * significant at 5%; ** significant at 1%

	Malawi Drop-outs 2.2	Mali Drop-outs 1.3	Niger Drop-outs 3.5	Senegal Drop-outs 14.1	Sierra Leone Drop-outs 8.4	Somalia Drop-outs 13.0	Swaziland Drop-outs 6.4	Tanzania Drop-outs 1.9	Uganda Drop-outs 1.7
	Marg. effect (z stat.)	Marg. effect (z stat.)	Marg. effect (z stat.)	Marg. effect (z stat.)	Marg. effect (z stat.)	Marg. effect (z stat.)	Marg. effect (z stat.)	Marg. effect (z stat.)	Marg. effect (z stat.)
Age 11–14 years	0.014** (5.75)	0.006* (2.11)	0.041** (5.33)	−0.031** (3.93)	−0.009 (0.64)	0.015 (0.51)	0.009 (1.14)	0.012 (1.94)	0.005 (1.71)
Male	0.004 (1.89)	−0.003 (1.23)	−0.002 (0.31)	0.014 (1.81)	−0.011 (0.85)	−0.005 (0.17)	−0.003 (0.33)	−0.008 (1.63)	−0.001 (0.38)
Urban	−0.007 (1.77)	−0.001 (0.19)	0.004 (0.42)	−0.069** (6.18)	−0.008 (0.50)	0.110** (2.98)	−0.004 (0.29)	0.007 (0.96)	0.015* (2.19)
Second wealth quintile	−0.004 (1.51)	−0.002 (0.40)	0.006 (0.38)	0.002 (0.13)	−0.031 (1.14)	0.186 (1.35)	−0.031** (3.10)	0.005 (0.59)	0.002 (0.42)
Third wealth quintile	−0.002 (0.52)	0.006 (1.18)	−0.003 (0.26)	−0.006 (0.45)	−0.046 (1.90)	0.191 (1.60)	−0.027* (2.57)	−0.011 (1.45)	0.003 (0.69)
Fourth wealth quintile	−0.010** (3.33)	−0.004 (0.86)	0.042* (2.35)	−0.013 (0.90)	0.020 (0.78)	0.094 (0.89)	−0.036** (3.16)	0.002 (0.21)	−0.006 (1.32)
Richest wealth quintile	−0.014** (4.13)	−0.007 (1.35)	0.010 (0.73)	−0.041* (2.50)	−0.012 (0.47)	0.015 (0.15)	0.009 (0.59)	−0.003 (0.28)	−0.010* (2.08)
Caretaker has formal ed.	−0.016** (6.64)	−0.007 (1.82)	−0.018* (2.25)	−0.100** (9.81)	−0.040** (2.82)	−0.007 (0.23)	−0.005 (0.59)	−0.008 (1.53)	−0.015** (4.72)
Child labour	0.008** (2.97)	0.001 (0.28)	0.014* (2.01)	0.041** (4.75)	−0.007 (0.47)	−0.000 (0.00)	0.006 (0.46)	0.018** (3.12)	0.005 (1.81)
Observations	10731	5320	2084	6512	1653	494	3718	1844	6610

Probit regressions: * significant at 5%; ** significant at 1%

Note: Data for Congo (DRC) is for children 10–14 years of age.

11

Human Rights and Public Goods: Education as a Fundamental Right in India

PHILIP ALSTON AND NEHAL BHUTA

This chapter explores some of the key issues that arise in the context of efforts to bring the discourses of human rights and development closer together. It does so by focusing on the right to education, and in particular on an unusually interesting and instructive case study of India. The Indian experience with the right to education illustrates both the central issues that arise in relation to resource constraints and the role played by key actors in relation to economic and social human rights, including civil society, the judiciary, and the legislature. In some respects it is a cautionary tale, while in others it provides an invaluable insight into some of the steps that need to be taken if a right to education is to gain community acceptance, take constitutional form, and have a significant impact on both policy and practical outcomes in the field of education.

11.1 LEGAL VERSUS DEVELOPMENTALIST PERSPECTIVE ON EDUCATION

It is relatively uncontentious to say that human rights and development objectives are for the most part complementary. We can even go further and suggest, as does the title of this volume of essays, that they are capable of mutually reinforcing one another. But the sticking point comes when it is suggested that it follows that a human rights lens is not only a desirable way of viewing some of the fundamental challenges facing development, but is actually a superior and perhaps even a mandatory one. Such a formulation immediately raises three questions: (a) is a human rights approach meaningful and thus useful in the context of complex issues of resource allocation affecting sectors such as education, food, and housing? (b) are there ways in which such an approach can be shown to be better than non-rights-based ways of approaching those issues? and (c) is a human rights approach mandatory, or obligatory, and if so what does that mean?

The backdrop against which such questions often arise is the disconnect that generally seems to characterize the approaches taken by human rights lawyers on the one hand and development economists on the other. One way of contrasting these two approaches is by thinking of them in terms of overdrawn depictions, almost caricatures, of the positions adopted on each side. Although caricatures are, by definition, distorted or extreme in some respects, they can nonetheless assist us to get a sense of the strengths and weaknesses of the approaches. A caricature of the international law approach (the equivalent of a drawing by Honoré Daumier of a lawyer in nineteenth-century France) posits the absoluteness and immediacy of human rights and a refusal to take account of financial constraints in relation to a fundamental value which must take priority over all else. In at least some cases, this would apply equally to a right like the right to education.

A comparable caricature of the development economist's approach posits an open-ended set of policy options, an emphasis on individual and ideally rational decision making, and a preoccupation with the financial dimensions of any social options that might be considered. As one World Bank economist has observed, many economists think that 'human rights principles, as commonly defined today, tend to violate the basic principles of traditional' welfare economics,[1] presumably because the rights approach seeks to pre-empt at least some choices and to tie the hands of decision makers in certain respects.

In reality, economists, whatever their starting point, are rarely likely to adopt the position that human rights considerations have no legitimate place in the overall equation. Similarly, international lawyers rarely entertain an absolutist approach to the right to education, even when they adopt a more dogmatic approach to civil and political rights, such as the right to free speech or the right to freedom from torture. And even in relation to those rights, there is room for a degree of relativism in any sophisticated and frank analysis.

The bigger problem for international human rights lawyers is that they are unaccustomed to having to provide justificatory analyses. For most of them, the issue of justification has long since been settled, whether through the adoption of the Universal Declaration of Human Rights of 1948, the widespread ratification of key treaties (such as the two International Human Rights Covenants) adopted in the 1960s and 1970s, the virtually universal

---

[1] Alfredo Sfeir-Younis, 'Human Rights Day Interview: How may "human rights" enhance our development mission?', available at http://web.worldbank.org/WBSITE/EXTERNAL/NEWS/0,,contentMDK:20143686 ~ menuPK:34457 ~ pagePK:34370 ~ piPK:34424 ~ the SitePK:4607,00.html#.

acceptance of the Convention on the Rights of the Child of 1989, or simply the evolution of the customary international law of human rights.

While leaving aside the broader philosophical challenge of defending either the concept of human rights or the catalogue of rights adopted by governments within the United Nations framework, the issue of justification is especially relevant in relation to the cost dimensions of rights and particularly those commonly conceived of as positive rights. In this respect, economists would point, and not without cause, to the reluctance of many human rights proponents to engage in debates over the resource implications of taking seriously a range of economic and social rights such as the right to education. They might cite, by way of example, the very lengthy General Comment on that right adopted by the UN Committee on Economic, Social and Cultural Rights[2] which addresses the resources issue only in order to emphasize that states must use their available resources to the maximum, and that, in some respects, a lack of resources can be no defence to a failure to take appropriate measures.

In recent years, however, economists have been increasingly prepared to factor into the overall equation a relatively new set of considerations under the rubric of good governance. The result is that development policy literature and relevant programmes are now replete with references to the importance of governance, defined to include not only free elections, the absence of corruption, and the presence of various market freedoms, but also accountability, transparency, and participation. These elements are not, however, generally viewed in the way that human rights proponents might present them—as matters of justice, fairness, and right which must simply be included whatever their cost. Instead they are seen in instrumental terms as factors which are empirically justified in economic terms. Similarly, education has long been considered as an important element in the economic balance sheet but the perceived returns on investments in education had not led to the conclusion that it should be supplied to every child regardless of his or her productive potential. But while this approach has now been replaced by the language of universal access, it continues to be a programme which is put forward and justified, at least in the discourse of international development organizations, essentially in terms of its economic benefits. Thus, for example, an important study on child labour by the International Labour Organization, subtitled 'An Economic Study of the Costs and Benefits of Eliminating Child Labour', was entitled 'Investing in Every Child'.[3] While

---

[2] Committee on Economic, Social and Cultural Rights, General Comment No. 13 (Twenty-first session, 1999), 'The right to education (article 13 of the Covenant)', UN doc. HRI/GEN/1/Rev.6 (2003) p. 70, see paras. 31, 43, 45, and 50.

[3] *Investing in Every Child: An Economic Study of the Costs and Benefits of Eliminating Child Labour* (Geneva, ILO, 2003). In fairness it should be noted that a companion ILO study entitled *Every Child Counts* (Geneva, ILO, 2002) adopts more of a human rights type

the study does not ignore the issue of values, the language of rights is comprehensively avoided. In order to assert that its inspiration is not solely instrumentalist the report notes that the ILO's perspective is that 'child labour is not only, nor perhaps even primarily, an economic problem. The justifications for [its Conventions on child labour] are largely ethical and social in nature, although the economic consequences of child labour are taken into account.'[4]

But rather than highlighting the rights or values dimension, the report's emphasis is very clearly on economic justifications. Thus while it acknowledges the 'personal development and social inclusion' benefits of eliminating child labour it clearly states that the 'two principal benefits' are 'the added productive capacity a future generation of workers would enjoy due to their increased education' and the 'economic gains' which would flow from healthier workers if the worst forms of child labour, such as those that are hazardous, are eliminated.[5] This then leads inexorably into what might be termed a supply-, rather than a demand-, style approach. The challenge is to 'supply' education through 'an expansion of school capacity and an upgrading of school quality'.[6]

The International Monetary Fund takes an even more determinedly 'neutral' or economistic approach to the issue, while the Fund now acknowledges, which was not the case only a few years ago, that user fees for primary education, 'whether taking the form of compulsory benefit taxation or voluntary user fees, are . . . second-best compared with free access'.[7] But rather than invoking ethical, let alone human rights, based arguments, the Fund simply observes that requiring payment 'is generally considered undesirable'.[8] The reason, it transpires, has nothing to do with the rights of children, but rather 'because of the burden placed on parents, particularly in low-income households'.[9] The thrust of the report, which includes an analysis of three countries in which user fees had recently been eliminated in relation to primary education (Uganda, Malawi, and Tanzania) is that economically rational considerations should determine how a given education budget should optimally be allocated. The report thus sums up the classic dilemma in the following terms:

[V]oluntary user fees introduce a dilemma in the choice between efficiency and equality. A decision regarding user payments may, for example, require a judgment about whether 45 children attending school and 5 children excluded is preferable to 50 children not attending school.[10]

---

approach but the separation of the two approaches nevertheless confirms the point being argued here.

[4] Ibid. 15.   [5] Ibid. 3.   [6] Ibid. 1.

[7] A. Hillman and E. Jenkner, *User Payments for Basic Education in Low-Income Countries*, IMF Working Paper WP/02/182 (2002) 1.   [8] Ibid. 3.

[9] Ibid. 24.   [10] Ibid. 25.

But this analysis takes for granted the refusal of the government involved to prioritize comprehensive access to free primary education, and assumes that an agency such as the IMF has no role whatsoever in factoring into the equation either the individual government's human rights obligations (an almost universal obligation in relation to the Convention on the Rights of the Child) or the rights of the child in the country concerned to enjoy access to primary education as of right. It is hardly surprising then that the report cautions that 'a strong preference for equality could . . . lead to a judgment rejecting financing, through user payments, even when public expenditure cannot provide reasonable schooling, so as to avoid the unequal exclusion of some children. Equality may then mean that all children are functionally illiterate.'[11]

Even studies produced by international organizations which focus specifically on the situation of primary education in India have tended to pay little or no attention to the human rights dimension of the equation. This is well illustrated by a comprehensive 300-page analysis undertaken by the World Bank which opens with the observation that '[t]he vision of education for India is contained in article 45 of its Constitution',[12] but fails to make any significant reference to this dimension of the issue in the remainder of the report. Even when responding to the question of why children are out of school, in the context of an analysis of potential demand-side interventions, the report mentions a range of factors but does not consider the possibility that characterizing education as a right rather than a possible opportunity might contribute to changing community expectations and stimulating demand for education.[13]

While it is obvious that the instrumentalist and rights approaches are not necessarily incompatible, and that one can advocate universal access to education both on the grounds that it is a right and that it is a sound investment, the point is that most of those who take one approach are at best reluctant to embrace also the other. Thus the language of investment can be an attractive formulation for those who wish to play down, or even deny, the human rights dimension of a right to education. Thus for example the Country Reports on Human Rights Practices, issued by the United States Government in February 2004, contrasts its discussion of the need to protect civil liberties and political rights (or at least to make sure that other countries do) with its references to the desirability of 'investing' in education and health.[14] This enables the State Department to both insist on the importance

---

[11] A. Hillman and E. Jenkner, *User Payments for Basic Education in Low-Income Countries*, IMF Working Paper WP/02/182 (2002) 25–26.

[12] *Primary Education in India* (Washington DC, World Bank, 1997) 14.

[13] Ibid. 72. The demand-side factors identified are 'the poor quality of much schooling, weak implementation of compulsory schooling laws, grade repetition, and high demand for child labor'.

[14] *2003 State Department Country Reports on Human Rights Practices* (Washington DC, 2004).

of education while maintaining its position that economic and social rights should be seen not as entitlements but rather in terms of opportunities.

The language of public goods provides a helpful bridge towards bringing the two approaches together. Few people would disagree that the provision of and access to education is a social good, and an indispensable component of human development, sustainable economic growth, and poverty reduction. A number of economists have argued that the provision of education is a public good which produces a variety of beneficial externalities, including health improvements, slowed population growth, the strengthening of democracy, and good governance[15]—all dimensions of any reasonable definition of 'human development' and 'human security'.[16] Drèze and Sen, adopting Sen's notion of development as the enhancement of capabilities and freedoms, enumerate five ways in which a successful programme of universal education contributes to development: education is intrinsically important inasmuch as it directly improves a person's effective freedom in basic social interactions; education facilitates the attainment of employment and other sources of income, and helps persons negotiate and cope with circumstances that may threaten their livelihood (education as self-defence); education facilitates public discussion of social needs and encourages informed collective demands, which can produce better governance and greater effectiveness in the use of public resources; education can help eradicate specific social problems, such as child labour; and educational achievement among disadvantaged groups increases their ability to resist oppression, organize politically, and alter distributive outcomes.[17] Invoking the example of Kerala, Drèze and Sen observe that basic education is a catalyst of social change:

[T]he historical analysis of Kerala's experience...brings out the dialectical relationship between education progress and social change: the spread of education helps to overcome the traditional inequalities of caste, class, and gender, just as the removal of these inequalities contributes to the spread of education.[18]

Drèze and Sen's final example points us towards the close conceptual kinship between the idea of education as a 'public good' conducive to development, and the idea of education as a human right. At the very least, the notion of human rights connotes the equal dignity and autonomy of human beings in their pursuit of their conception of a good life, a life worth living. At a foundational level, to speak of something as a human right is to not just make

[15] For a review of the arguments concerning public provision of education, see J. B. G. Tilak, 'Public Subsidies in Education in India', *Economic and Political Weekly*, 24 January 2004, 343–359, at 344–345.

[16] A. Sen, 'Basic Education and Human Security', paper delivered at workshop on 'Basic Education and Human Security' in Kolkata, India, 2–4 January 2002.

[17] J. Drèze and A. Sen, *India: Economic Development and Social Opportunity* (New Delhi, Oxford University Press, 1996), 14–15.　　　　　　　　　　　　　　　　[18] Ibid. 109.

a legal claim to resources or for protection against an abuse of power, but it is also to insist that, without those resources or that protection, one's equal dignity, autonomy, and participatory parity are fundamentally impaired. The externalities that make the public provision of education welfare-enhancing as a public good (health, greater reproductive choices, employment opportunity, slowing of diminishing marginal returns) are also effects that broadly correspond with the achievement of equal dignity and autonomy. At a certain level of abstraction, then, we might readily conclude that education qua public good and education qua human right share an essential affinity.

It is against this background that we turn in this chapter to explore the practical consequences of entrenching education as a legally enforceable right. What does the idea of education as a human right add to the way in which governments and civil society develop strategies to ensure access to education? This chapter seeks to address these questions through a case study of India, which in 2002 amended its Constitution to make education a 'fundamental right' for children between the ages of 6 and 14. Before addressing those issues it is appropriate to note briefly the status of the right to education in international law.

11.2 THE INTERNATIONAL LEGAL SETTING FOR THE RIGHT TO EDUCATION

While the right to education has been recognized in a great many international human rights treaties, the formulations used and the nature and the scope of the resulting obligations undertaken by states tend to vary significantly.[19] In view of the fact that these different provisions have been analysed in considerable detail elsewhere,[20] it will suffice for the purposes of the present chapter to note that the relevant provision in the UN Convention on the Rights of the Child is binding on 192 states which have opted to become parties to it and that the only states in the world which are not covered by its provisions are Somalia and the United States. The Convention thus provides a virtually universal basis for examining the right to education.

The key provision of the Convention is article 28 (1) which provides that:

States Parties recognize the right of the child to education, and with a view to achieving this right progressively and on the basis of equal opportunity, they shall, in particular:

(a) Make primary education compulsory and available free to all; . . .

[19] One study lists over 40 international conventions and declarations that refer to education as a human right. See A. Fernandez and S. Jenkner, eds., *International Declarations and Conventions on the Right to Education and the Freedom of Education* (Frankfurt, Info-3 Verlag, 1995).

[20] See e.g. Manfred Nowak, 'The Right to Education', in Eide, Krause & Rosas, eds., *Economic, Social and Cultural Rights: A Textbook* (The Hague, Kluwer, 2nd edn., 2001) 245–272.

It is also pertinent to note that many state constitutions within the United States recognize a right to education and that they are by no means alone in recognizing education in the context of formulations dealing with rights.[21] The UN Special Rapporteur on the Right to Education indicated that in 2001 there were explicit guarantees of the right to education in the constitutions of 142 countries, and that only 44 countries did not include such provisions within their national constitutions.[22] While the relevant provisions have been significant in the context of a state such as India, they have also had an impact within some developed countries. This is true, for example, of the United States where education is characterized in rights terms, albeit in widely varying formulations, in the constitutions of some 40 or more states of the United States. While many of these provisions seem to have lain almost dormant for a good period of time, there have been notable exceptions. Suffice it to note for present purposes that the Constitution of New York State guarantees every child the opportunity for a 'sound basic education'.[23] In 2005 this provision was relied upon by the NY State Supreme Court in Manhattan to order that $5.6 billion per year be spent on the City's schools over and above current levels. An additional $9.2 billion was ordered to be spent over the following five years to shrink class sizes, relieve overcrowding, and provide the city's 1.1 million students with adequate laboratories, libraries, and other learning places. The case had been initiated twelve years earlier by the Campaign for Fiscal Equity and had been fought strongly by the State Government. The New York Times commented that:

The decision is a major landmark in one of the nation's biggest school-finance cases, and may have ripple effects across all school districts in the state. Though virtually every state in the nation has been embroiled in lawsuits over school spending, the New York suit has been more closely watched, in part because of the number of students and the dollar figures at stake.[24]

The extent to which a right to education has thus found recognition within a wide variety of constitutional instruments and traditions serves to highlight the potential importance of the experience of any country in which

---

[21] For a cross-section of the literature see R. Levesque, 'The Right to Education in the United States: Beyond the Limits of the Lore and the Lure of the Law', 4 *Annual Survey of International and Comparative Law* (1997) 205; S. Steinke, 'The Exception to the Rule: Wisconsin's Fundamental Right to Education and Public School Financing', *Wisconsin Law Review* [1995] 1387; and M. Mills and W. Quin II, 'The Right to a "Minimally Adequate Education" as Guaranteed by the Mississippi Constitution', 61 *Albany Law Review* (1998) 1521.

[22] K. Tomaševski, Free and Compulsory Education for all Children: The Gap between Promise and Performance (Lund, 2001) 19, available at http://www.right-to-education.org/.

[23] For background to this case see H. Hershkoff and B. Kingsbury, 'Crisis, Community, and Courts in Network Governance: A Response to Liebman and Sabel's Approach to Reform of Public Education', 28 *N.Y.U. Rev. of Law & Soc. Change* (2003) 319.

[24] Greg Winter, 'Judge Orders Billions in Aid to City Schools', *New York Times*, 15 February 2005, 1.

the right has been taken seriously in terms of public advocacy, national constitutional arrangements, and international supervision of treaty undertakings. We turn therefore to examine the situation in India, which constitutes a prime example in this regard.

11.3 THE STATE OF EDUCATION IN INDIA

India is an interesting and tractable case study for the actual and potential impact of constitutionalizing the right to education, for two reasons. On the one hand, India is a developing country facing considerable resource challenges, particularly in light of its rapidly growing population and the fiscal constraints of the state and federal governments. On the other hand, India has a well-developed judicial system and a recent history of constitutional rights litigation that, in the breadth of issues that it has touched upon and the scope of remedial judgments delivered, is almost unparalleled in either the developing or the developed world.[25]

In a nutshell, almost 50 per cent of the population remains illiterate, and an estimated 58 million out of 185 million children aged between 5 and 14 years are not in school.[26] The Indian Government reported in 2003 that the enrolment rate in rural areas nationwide was only 71 per cent, with a gender disparity of 0.84, meaning a 16 per cent lower rate for girls. In some states the levels are considerably lower. In Bihar only 59 per cent are enrolled and in Rajasthan the rate is 61 per cent with a gender disparity of 46 per cent for girls.[27] This result is hardly surprising given that the provision of education (particularly elementary education) appears to have been a relatively low priority for central and state Indian governments from 1947 to 1980, with less than 2 per cent of GDP being expended annually on education until 1979.[28] Expenditures on education grew substantially after the central government was granted concurrent responsibility for education through a 1976 constitutional amendment,[29] but remained lower (as a share of total

---

[25] For a brief history of constitutional litigation, see Burt Neuborne, 'The Supreme Court of India', 1 *International Journal of Constitutional Law* (2003) 476.

[26] R. Banerji, 'Poverty and Primary Schooling: Field Studies from Mumbai and Delhi', *Economic and Political Weekly*, 4 March 2000, 795 (citing data from the 50th National Sample Survey).

[27] Report of India to the Committee on the Rights of the Child, UN doc. CRC/C/93/Add.5 (2003) para. 801.

[28] Government of India, Department of Education, *Selected Educational Statistics*, at http://www.education.nic.in/htmlweb/edustats_03.pdf, cited in V. Sripati and A. K. Thiruvengadam, 'India: Constitutional Amendment making the right to Education a Fundamental Right', *International Journal of Constitutional Law* (2003) 149, 151.

[29] A. Shariff and P. K. Ghosh, 'Indian Education Scene and the Public Gap', *Economic and Political Weekly*, 15 April 2000, 1396–1406.

government expenditure) than most low-income countries.[30] Significantly, the share of expenditure allocated to elementary education through the 1980s remained below 50 per cent, which is low relative to other countries that sought to universalize elementary education at a comparable stage of economic development. Shariff and Ghosh note that:

Japan invested 84 percent of its educational budget in six years of elementary education in 1885 and a meager 8 percent on higher education. By 1960, the share of higher education had increased to 13 percent. . . . In Sri Lanka too, the case is similar. Sri Lanka allocated 70 percent of its educational budget to the first level of education and 6 percent to higher education in 1970. By 1978, when primary education had become universal, the share of higher education had increased (marginally) to 8.7 percent.[31]

The nature of the resulting challenge is made all the greater by the fact that the overall social picture in the country has been far from rosy. Thus, over the past ten years, India's ranking in the United Nations' Human Development Index has fallen dramatically.[32] A former Supreme Court Justice and former Chairman on the National Commission on Human Rights, M. N. Venkatachaliah, put the situation of education in its broader context by observing in 2000 that:

Today we have the dismal situation of a social infrastructure where 670 million people in this country don't have basic sanitary facilities, and 260 million don't have potable water. Forty percent of the world's tuberculosis patients are in India, 25 percent of the world's blind are in India . . . Then there is the issue of the enormous corruption in public life, electoral malpractices, the tyranny of wealth, and the insolence of authority.[33]

The poor state of primary education is thus but one of several urgent developmental priorities that the Government of India must balance, and this balancing may well mitigate the value of constitutionally entrenching education as a right.

11.4 THE RESPONSE OF THE SUPREME COURT

Beginning in the early 1980s, the Supreme Court of India waived traditional doctrines of standing and pleadings to permit concerned citizens, public interest advocates, and non-government organizations to petition it on behalf of individuals or communities suffering violations of constitutionally

---

[30] World Bank, *Primary Education in India* (1997) 219.
[31] Shariff and Ghosh, above n. 29, 1399.
[32] See *Human Development Report 2004* (New York, Oxford University Press, 2004).
[33] *Frontline* (Madras), Vol. 17, No. 4, 19 February–3 March 2000, www.flonnet.com/fl1704/17040300.htm.

protected rights. As a consequence, the Court entertained applications for constitutional protection on behalf of a wide range of traditionally powerless persons, including bonded labourers, rickshaw drivers, pavement dwellers, inmates of mental infirmaries and workhouses, and victims of environmental damage. In conducting these cases, the Court created its own fact-finding commissions to investigate alleged violations, and dramatically expanded its remedial powers to include detailed supervision of government institutions and the ordering of programmes to mitigate the effects of systematic injustice. Through the development of its 'Public Interest Litigation' (PIL) jurisdiction, the Supreme Court of India came to act as a 'combination of constitutional ombudsman and inquisitorial examining magistrate, vested with responsibility to do justice to the poor litigant before it by aggressively searching out the facts and the law, and by taking responsibility for fully implementing its decisions . . . PIL provides a model for courts struggling to balance the transformative aspect of law against the law's natural tendency to favour those rich enough to invoke it.'[34]

It was in fact a Supreme Court public interest case that set in train the movement to create an enforceable constitutional right to education in India. The unamended text of the Constitution of India (adopted 1950) had included a right to education under the title of a 'Directive Principle of State Policy'.[35] In the Constitution of India, a Directive Principle was distinguishable from a Fundamental Right in so far as a Directive Principle 'shall not be enforced in any court'.[36] A Directive Principle is phrased in terms of an important duty incumbent upon the state, but one that is to be implemented by the executive and legislative arms of government without intervention or oversight by the judiciary. Thus, the 'right to education' as contained in the original text of the Constitution of India was cast in imperative terms:

The State shall endeavour to provide, within a period of ten years from the commencement of this Constitution, for free and compulsory education for all children until they complete the age of fourteen years.

The ten-year deadline for the provision of free, universal elementary education was not met, and remains unmet to this day.

In 1992 and 1993, the Supreme Court of India decided two PIL cases in which the plaintiffs claimed a judicially enforceable right to education.[37] Although both cases concerned the impact of certain state laws on private educational institutions of higher learning, the Court took the opportunity to develop a precedent that also governed the public provision of elementary

---

[34] Neuborne, above n. 25, 503.   [35] Constitution of India, Part IV, art 45.

[36] Constitution of India, Part IV, art 37.

[37] *Mohini Jain v State of Karnataka*, AIR 1992 SC 1858; *Unni Krishnan J.P. v State of Andhra Pradesh*, AIR 1993 SC 2178.

education. Expressing concern at the obvious failure of the Government of India to uphold its duty under article 45 to ensure free and compulsory elementary education, the Court in *Unni Krishnan* stated:

It is noteworthy among the several articles in Part IV [of the Constitution], only article 45 speaks of a time-limit... Does not the passage of 44 years—more than four times the period stipulated in article 45—convert the obligation created by the article into an enforceable right? In this context, we feel constrained to say that the allocation of available funds to different sectors of education in India discloses an inversion of priorities indicated by the Constitution.[38]

Based, it appears, on the view that the central and state governments of India had consistently and systematically failed to apply the Constitution in their decision making in relation to funding allocations for elementary education in India, the Court held that the right to education up to fourteen years of age contained in article 45 amounted to a 'fundamental right' that was enforceable by the courts. It also relied upon a link between the right to life recognized in article 21 of the Constitution as a fundamental right, and the right to education as a directive principle. Sripati and Thiruvengadam observe that the immediate effect of the *Unni Krishnan* decision was that any child below the age of fourteen who was denied facilities for primary education could approach a court for an order directing the authorities to initiate appropriate measures.[39]

While human rights proponents have consistently welcomed the Court's activist approach in this area, and its effective re-characterization of the right to education as a fundamental right, despite the arguably clear contrary intent of the drafters of the Constitution, it must be asked whether such a powerful judicial reinterpretation of the relevant principles could be achieved in any other constitutional system and whether it is desirable. But whatever the outcome of such an inquiry in relation to other countries, it is essential to note that within India the Court's initiative had a huge impact in terms of mobilizing civil society, legitimating demands for a right to education, and unleashing extensive pressures on the government to formally amend the Constitution so as to bring it into line with the Court's approach.

11.5 RESPONDING TO THE COURT'S AGENDA-SETTING ROLE

Community activists and non-government organizations began utilizing the decisions as a means of pushing the executive and legislature toward action on primary education. At the same time, the decisions became a catalyst for political advocacy and public sphere debate over the state of primary

---

[38] *Unni Krishnan*, at 2232.   [39] Sripati and Thiruvengadam, above n. 28, 153.

education in India, galvanizing a number of different children's rights groups into a coalition demanding government implementation of the 'fundamental right to education'. The central government responded by establishing two committees to investigate both the desirability and financial implications of amending the Constitution to establish primary education as a fundamental right. A joint committee of state government Ministers of Education (the Saikia Committee) concluded in 1997 that the Constitution should be amended to create as a 'fundamental right' the right to free and compulsory education from six to fourteen years of age, and to impose a 'fundamental duty' on parents to provide opportunities for education to their children in this age group. A second expert committee (the Majumdar Committee) concluded in 1999 that the universalization of elementary education for children aged six to fourteen years would require an additional expenditure of Rs 140,000,000,000 per year for ten years; on the assumption of annual GDP growth of 5 per cent, this amounts to an additional 0.7 per cent of GDP dedicated to education per year, raising education expenditure to approximately 5 per cent of GDP.

The Saikia Committee report resulted in a Bill to amend the Constitution to introduce a new article 21A, which provided: '[t]he State shall provide free and compulsory education to all citizens of age six to fourteen years in such manner as the State may, by law, determine'. It also introduced a new article 51A which imposed a duty on parents and guardians to provide their children with educational opportunities, in the terms recommended by the Saikia Committee. The Bill was tabled in 1997, but would not pass into law until December 2002. In the meantime, a number of important criticisms were made of the proposed new right during the hearings of the Parliamentary Standing Committee on Human Resource Development.[40] The Standing Committee noted that the 'general feeling' of submissions was that the age restriction was arbitrary and neglected the rights of children below six and above fourteen years of age. The exclusion of the application of the right to children under six years of age was noted to be contrary to the Supreme Court's ruling in *Unni Krishnan*. It was also submitted to the Standing Committee that, at the time of the drafting of the original article 45 (which encoded the fourteen year age limit), a child received a formal certification of education at 7th grade; in modern India, no formal certification was awarded until 10th grade, or when a child would be aged about sixteen years. The constitutional amendment as proposed would thus not ensure that impoverished children could continue until their formal certification had been obtained. Submissions to the Standing Committee also argued that there was a need (potentially in subsequent legislation pursuant to the amendment) to define the meaning of 'free' as referred to in article 21A, and to include some definition of the quality of education that was to be provided.

---

[40] Available at http://arunmehta.freeyellow.com/page144.html.

Two factors which warrant emphasis in the present context are the role played by civil society in mobilizing to demand the formal constitutional recognition of a right to education and the role played by commentators and scholars, both domestic and foreign, in highlighting the claim that resources were not in fact the sole or even the main barrier to a major improvement in India's educational performance. The latter case was pressed with particular force and perseverance by Myron Weiner who rejected outright the claim that the low educational rates in India were due to the lack of financial resources needed to fund universal compulsory primary school education. Focusing on the question of why widespread child labour persisted despite avowed government opposition, he suggested three alternative explanations: (a) child labour was sustained by weak and unenforced government policies on primary education; (b) the middle classes were more concerned to expand government funding for higher education than for primary education; and (c) even more controversially, that child labour was in fact 'part of the government's industrial strategy to promote the small scale sector and to expand exports'.

Weiner depicted compulsory education as a *sine qua non* for the reduction and abolition of child labour. He concluded that: '[t]he sooner India acts, the quicker will be the fall in the illiteracy rate, the more likely it is that child labour will be reduced, and the greater are the prospects for a reduction in fertility rates as children are no longer seen as financial assets to the family'. He was particularly critical of what he saw as ameliorative half-measures which involved programmes such as the promotion of adult literacy campaigns, the provision of non-formal education to working children, and the provision of free school lunches. In his view, nothing short of a compulsory and constitutionally recognized right to primary education would suffice.[41]

Civil society groups also took up the struggle to give constitutional status to the right to education. As one observer put it, the proposed amendment 'is an initiative which could have far-reaching consequences... [It] has the potential to be a major catalyst in achieving the elusive goal of universal elementary education.'[42] Much of the groundwork for this support had also been laid by a major public initiative which produced the path-breaking Public Report on Basic Education in India (PROBE Report).[43] The Report was important not only because of its sophisticated advocacy approach but because it was based upon a detailed empirical study of the situation in five states of northern India, accounting for 40 per cent of the total population but well over half of its children not attending school.[44] In contrast to the

[41] Myron Weiner, 'Child Labour in Developing Countries: The Indian Case', 2 *International Journal of Children's Rights* (1994) 121.

[42] R. Wazir, 'Profiling the Problem' in Wazir, ed., *The Gender Gap in Basic Education: NGOs as Change Agents* (New Delhi, Sage Publications, 2000) 18.

[43] PROBE Team, *Public Report on Basic Education in India* (New Delhi, Oxford University Press, 1999). [44] Ibid. 2.

economic instrumentalist approach favoured by so many developmental economists, the Report identifies eight arguments which can be invoked to justify the case for universal elementary education. They are: (1) elementary education is a fundamental right, as stated in the Constitution and determined by the Supreme Court; (2) there is massive popular demand for universal schooling; (3) it represents an important investment in human capital; (4) it should contribute to the joy of learning; (5) education helps individual well-being in diverse ways; (6) education assists the social progress of the whole community; (7) education facilitates effective political participation; and (8) universal elementary education is a requirement of social justice.[45]

The Report concluded that 'the notion of a fundamental right has great value in overcoming the objections and excuses that are consistently invoked to continue postponing the goal of universal elementary education'.[46] To some degree, the very process of drafting and debating the amendment generated popular mobilization around the need to improve basic education in India, with 40,000 citizens from distant villages and towns around India rallying in New Delhi on the day that the amendment was passed.[47] The protest was organized by a coalition of several thousand grass-roots organizations from all over India, the National Alliance for the Fundamental Right to Education (NAFRE), and demanded a common school system providing free education of equitable quality.

The role played by civil society in bringing about the constitutional amendment is instructive. Human rights demands are all too often promoted in a top-down fashion, whether pushed by the international community, or by domestic elites. Although this process is not necessarily doomed to failure, it is less likely to succeed and, more importantly, it is less likely to generate the level of societal support which will, over time, ensure that the relevant value is internalized within the community so that, at least at the level of ideas, it is no longer a matter of contention. While India's vibrant civil society, its relatively long-standing democratic traditions, and its legal heritage might all have combined to provide particularly fertile ground for such an initiative, this does not necessarily mean that a campaign based on the assertion of education as a matter of human rights will not work in other countries.

11.6 THE CONSTITUTIONAL AMENDMENT

Despite the minimum age restriction also being criticized by the government-sponsored National Commission to Review the Working of

[45] PROBE Team, *Public Report on Basic Education in India* (New Delhi, Oxford University Press, 1999) 4–5.   [46] Ibid. 141.

[47] Anil Sadgopal, 'A Convenient Consensus', *Frontline* (Madras), 22 December 2001–4 January 2002, www.frontlineonnet.com/fl1826/18261070.html.

the Constitution,[48] the amendment establishing the fundamental right to education passed in the form originally proposed.[49] While controversial in its terms, the constitutional amendment was nevertheless hailed by activists and education-focused non-government organizations as an important step towards improving the condition of basic education in India.

To understand how the constitutional amendment might (or might not) assist in realizing this demand, we need briefly to consider the state of basic education in India and some of the reasons why the goal of universal elementary education remains elusive after 58 years of independence. India's achievements in elementary education have been far less impressive than other developing countries that were similarly situated 40 years ago.[50] As already noted, close to half of the Indian population is still illiterate and almost one-third of the children to whom the Constitutional amendment will apply are not in school.[51] Enrolment rates are suspected of being inflated, and say nothing of whether children actually attend school or learn anything.[52] The PROBE Report and other studies have documented very low levels of learning among enrolled students in those states and regions with high numbers of out of school children.[53] Studies and analyses investigating the reasons behind this poor performance indicate a combination of causes: inadequate financing of education, entrenched social division and discrimination on the basis of caste, class, and gender, political apathy, and an institutional and management incentive structure that inhibits accountability, responsiveness, and quality teaching.[54]

As noted above,[55] elementary education in India has suffered from 'five decades of underinvestment',[56] a problem compounded by the fact that state governments are responsible for more than 80 per cent of education expenditure. This entails very considerable inter-state disparities in education expenditure, but has also meant that national expenditure on education has

[48] National Commission to Review the Working of the Constitution, *Final Report*, vol. 1, ch. 3 (2002) para. 3.20.2, recommending that every child have the right to free education until he completes the age of fourteen years, and that girls and members of the scheduled castes and the scheduled tribes benefit from the right until the age of eighteen years.

[49] Sadgopal, n. 47 above.   [50] Drèze and Sen, above n. 17, 114.

[51] Banerji, above n. 26, 795 (citing data from the 50th National Sample Survey).

[52] Drèze and Sen, above n. 17, 113.

[53] PROBE Report, above n. 43; World Bank, *India: Primary Education: Achievements and Challenges* (1997); Banerji, above n. 26, 799.

[54] See, *inter alia*, Wazir, above n. 42; PROBE Report, above n. 43; Drèze and Sen, above n. 17; S. Shukla and R. Kaul, eds., *Education, Development and Underdevelopment* (New Delhi, Sage Publications, 1998); A. Vaidyanathan and P. R. Gopinathan Nair, eds., *Elementary Education in Rural India* (New Delhi, Sage Publications, 2001); R. Govinda, ed., *India Education Report* (New Delhi, Oxford University Press, 2002).

[55] See notes 26–31 and text.

[56] B. J. Tilak, 'Five Decades of Underinvestment in Education', *Economic and Political Weekly*, 6–12 September 1997; see also PROBE report, above n. 43, 134.

suffered as a consequence of the fiscal crisis of state governments throughout India, over the 1990s. Shariff and Ghosh observe that, during the 1990s, the share of state budgets devoted to elementary education has declined in all but three states in India to levels below that achieved in the 1980s.[57] The growth in per pupil expenditure on elementary education also declined over this period in all but three states. While the 1980s saw a steady growth of central and state government expenditure on education generally and on elementary education in particular, the share of GDP devoted to education expenditure fell from 4.1 per cent in 1990–1991 to 3.8 per cent in 1995–1996.[58] Drèze and Sen observe that the increased education expenditure of the 1980s went almost entirely toward teachers' salaries, even as there was an absolute decline in the number of primary and upper primary teachers between 1991 and 1993.[59]

Adequate expenditure on education is by no means a sufficient condition for universal elementary education of an equitable standard, but it is undoubtedly a necessary condition. Access to lower and upper primary schools within safe walking distance of a settlement remains a problem in the states most afflicted by illiteracy and poor educational attainment, and, as the PROBE Report has documented, the mere presence of a school building does not mean that the school is adequately equipped to educate children at a suitable quality. The PROBE survey of settlements in four traditionally underdeveloped states found a widespread absence of basic facilities like roofing, toilets, water supply, teaching kits, and book resources. One third of the schools surveyed by PROBE were de facto single teacher schools, and the pupil-teacher ratio averaged 50:1.[60] The consequence of such resource shortages is that school facilities, while available, may be inadequate to enable learning.[61]

A major problem identified by numerous studies, and a strong disincentive to impoverished parents to bear the opportunity cost and the real cost of sending children to school, is the poor quality of schooling provided. Studies reveal not so much a lack of demand for education among the rural poor and so-called 'backward castes' and 'backward tribes',[62] as a disaffection with the lack of learning that occurs after very considerable sacrifices are made to send children to school.[63] As one interviewee of a field study stated:

We are poor, but not so poor that we cannot send our children to school . . . But how is it possible for them to continue? They don't learn anything here. We had to spend so much money on the books, and then the teacher is sitting so far away from the

---

[57] Shariff and Ghosh, above n. 29, 1403.   [58] Ibid. 1405.

[59] Drèze and Sen, above n. 17, 123.   [60] PROBE Report, above n. 43, ch. 4.

[61] See also Vaidyanathan and Gopinathan Nair, above n. 54, 43–44.

[62] An important exception to this result is the attitude towards the education of girl-children, which is more consistently negative.

[63] Banerji, above n. 26; G. K. Lieten, 'Children, Work and Education—I', *Economic and Political Weekly*, 10 June 2000, 2037.

children that absolutely nothing is learned there. Everybody thinks so about the teachers. The only thing they can do is beat up the children. So when Raju came home, and I kept telling him everyday to go to school, he just burned his books.[64]

The quality problem identified in so many studies is in part a reflection of inadequate resources: it is hard for teachers to teach and students to learn in class sizes of fifty or more, in schools with no roof or without teaching aids. However, numerous authors[65] have suggested that complete indifference and inactivity on the part of teachers is to blame, and that this is a result not only of the difficult environment in which teachers must work but of a systematic institutional failure to produce and ensure good teaching through the provision of training, peer review, and accountability to local communities.[66] Animating these general quality constraints in any specific case, and particularly in underdeveloped states and locales, are social hierarchies of caste, class, and gender. From curricula that are completely unsuited to the educational needs and lived experience of first generation learners in rural areas or urban slums,[67] to discrimination against scheduled caste and scheduled tribe members in the location of schools and in the attitude of higher caste teachers, caste and class remain important determinants of access to and the quality of elementary education in India.[68] Likewise, important barriers remain to the education of girl-children from impoverished families.

This cursory overview of the obstacles to the provision of universal elementary education in India leaves out many important issues, such as the tendency toward the expansion of a 'two track' education system. But it does allow us to observe that the achievement of universal elementary education is not only a matter of the availability of resources or even just their distribution: it is a product of the interaction of social, political, and institutional forces, of community mobilization and empowerment, and of challenging bureaucratic inertia and deeply embedded social hierarchies.

[64] Ibid. 2175.
[65] For an overview, see G. Kingdon and M. Muzammil, *The Political Economy of Education in India: Teacher Politics in Uttar Pradesh* (New Delhi, Oxford University Press, 2003) Ch. 1.
[66] R. Sudarshan, 'Educational Status of Girls and Women: The Emerging Scenario' in Wazir, ed., above n. 42, 64; Vaidyanathan and Gopinathan Nair, above n. 54, 44–45; Govinda, above n. 54, 11.
[67] See, e.g., M. Talib, 'Observations from a School in a Working Class Settlement in Delhi' in Shukla and Kaul, eds., above n. 54, 189–199; PROBE Report, above n. 43, 68–75; Anita Rampal, 'Texts in Context: Development of Curricula, Textbooks, and Teaching Learning Materials' in Govinda, ed., above n. 54, 154–166.
[68] G. Nambissan and M. Sedwal, 'Education for all: The Situation of Dalit Children in India' in Govinda, ed., above n. 54, 72–86; K. Sujatha, *Education of Indian Scheduled Tribes: A Study of Community Schools,* (Paris International Institute for Educational Planning, UNESCO, 1999) 87–95; Banerji, above n. 26; Vaidyanathan and Gopinathan Nair, above n. 54, 27–29.

On the one hand, the complexity and durability of the social structures militating against the universalization of elementary education appears to be a strong argument against the proposition that litigation and court orders upholding the right to education could be effective. The American experience with court-ordered desegregation demonstrates the limitations of attempting to alter deep-seated social structures, such as race segregation, through case by case court orders that are ultimately unable to retrench the social forces which reproduce inequality of opportunity between black and white Americans. The prospect of having to try to re-engineer the United States' schools and school districts, one by one, perhaps led the Supreme Court of that country to narrow its jurisprudence on desegregation.[69] While the Supreme Court of India has shown itself to be more willing to undertake Olympian tasks of investigation and supervision of government conduct, the record of government compliance with the Court's sweeping orders concerning social problems, such as bonded labour,[70] is not encouraging: 'a judge can only give directions: and in regard to many of the gravest problems these directions have to be given to the very institutions whose negligence has compounded the malady in the first place'.[71]

Indeed, in the first budget after the passage of the constitutional amendment establishing the fundamental right to education, the central government ignored the expert committee report and failed to allocate the amount deemed necessary to universalize elementary education; in fact, the amount allocated was less than 50 per cent of the estimated requirement of Rs 140,000,000,000 per annum[72] and less even than the Rs 98,000,000,000 recommended in the Financial Memorandum to the constitutional amendment bill.[73] The central government has commenced preparation of a Free and Compulsory Education Bill to provide legislative machinery for the constitutional right, but a noted expert on education in India comments that the administrative structure envisaged by the Act describes 'a mechanism of abdication of responsibilities by higher levels of authorities in favour of lower levels; and not a method of devolution of powers and resources, but a mechanism of mobilization of non-governmental resources'.[74]

[69] James Liebman and Charles Sabel, 'A Public Laboratory Dewey Barely Imagined: The Emerging Model of School Governance and Legal Reform', 28 *New York University Review of Law and Social Change* (2003) 183, 192–201.

[70] A. Shourie, *Courts and Their Judgments* (New Delhi, Rupa, 2001) Ch. 3.

[71] Ibid. 400.

[72] At 2005 exchange rates this would be equivalent to around US$3.2 billion.

[73] Azim Premji Foundation, 'Union Budget 2003–4 in the context of Elementary Education' (on file with authors); A. Sadgopal, 'Education for Too Few', *Frontline* (Madras), 5 December 2003, www.flonnet.com/fl2024/stories/20031205002809700.htm.

[74] J. B. Tilak, 'Free and Compulsory Education—Legislative Intervention', *Economic and Political Weekly*, 14 February 2004.

But to accept that courts cannot do everything does not imply acceptance of the opposite view, that they can do nothing at all. The last decade has seen a number of innovative responses to the problems of elementary education in India, and an important part of these innovations has been the embrace of education as a site of community mobilization and popular struggle.[75] The notion of education as a fundamental right has the potential to operate at a number of different levels to assist these kinds of innovations. First, the diffusion of 'rights consciousness' could provide a basis for political organization within communities against discrimination and division on the basis of caste and gender, and thus be an instrument towards the creation of a 'social consensus' on the entitlement of equal access to quality elementary education. Articulating education in terms of a constitutional and human right, with reference to the content of that term as it has evolved at the international level, may be a useful and effective argumentative strategy within 'public spheres' at the local and national level. A 2001 review of a Kenyan access to justice project supported by the United Kingdom Department for International Development concluded, 'the empowering influence of rights awareness is a catalyst for social organization and community-driven development. The activist function recognizes that legal rights . . . can [best] be achieved . . . through articulation of rights using advocacy and lobbying in an activist manner.'[76]

Second, litigation or the threat of litigation may greatly enhance the bargaining power of local communities vis-à-vis state and national bureaucracies and other centres of political power. Because the fundamental rights provisions of the Constitution apply to both state and central governments, villages and communities have the potential to build state-specific campaigns and cases that concern the specific needs of their locales, and to present these claims in the state courts. Of course, the realization of the opportunities presented by strategic litigation depends heavily upon effective, accessible, and carefully conducted community lawyering (which is far from alien to India). As examples from the South African context illustrate, constitutional rights litigation can be a powerful process for community mobilization and the assertion of a hitherto latent political subjectivity by the disenfranchised and the oppressed.[77] As Stephen Golub argues, the very process of preparing litigation through consultations with and education of the affected community

---

[75] See, e.g., R. Govinda and R. Diwan, *Community Participation and Empowerment in Primary Education* (New Delhi, Sage Publications 2003); S. Chowdhury, 'Universal Elementary Education in Rajasthan: A Study with Focus on Innovative Strategies' in Govinda, ed., above n. 54, 346; P. Clarke, 'Education Reform in the Education Guarantee Scheme in Madhya Pradesh, India and the Fundescola Program in Brazil', March 2003, World Bank.

[76] S. Golub, *Beyond the Rule of Law Orthodoxy*, Carnegie Endowment for International Peace, Rule of Law Working Paper No. 41 (October 2003).

[77] See Ashwin Desai, *We are the Poors: Community Struggles in Post-Apartheid South Africa* (New York, Monthly Review Press, 2002).

enhances rights awareness, strengthens knowledge of government processes, and gives decision makers the sense that they are under scrutiny from those affected by their actions—even if the litigation itself is unsuccessful: 'A value of legal empowerment is that it can constitute a feedback loop, through which grassroots experience feeds legal and regulatory change, which further grassroots work in turn converts from reform on paper to reform in practice.'[78]

Third, successful litigation may help to change the budgeting priorities of the state, and start a process towards a more authentic institutional commitment toward education. Thus, for example, this commitment has been a decisive factor in the success of educational achievement in the state of Himachal Pradesh.[79]

11.7 DRAWING CONCLUSIONS FROM THE INDIAN EXPERIENCE

While we have accorded considerable attention to the distinctive role played by the courts in India in the struggle to recognize and give effect to the right to education, it would be a mistake to focus only, or even primarily, on litigation as the key to promoting the realization of this right. While the Indian Supreme Court has certainly played an important catalytic role, the key ingredients of the Indian case study include the formal constitutional recognition of the right in the 1949 Constitution, the role of civil society in insisting that substance be given to that commitment, the contribution of sustained analytical critiques of the state of education, and the political salience of these demands.

The emphasis on treating education as a right brings two important dimensions which are all too often downplayed in the context of other approaches to education policy. They are empowerment and accountability. While each of these terms has been overused in the social science and development literature in recent years, their significance in this context is nonetheless considerable.

In terms of empowerment, the recognition of a right to education, and the adoption of an approach to education policy which accords some prominence to that dimension, serves to emphasize that the individual holder of the right is entitled to make certain demands, not only upon a government, but perhaps more importantly upon the right holder's immediate community. The responsibilities which attach to human rights apply not only to governments in accordance with the traditional state-centric analysis of the

---

[78] Golub, above n. 76.
[79] J. Drèze and A. Sen, above n. 17, 129; and Report of India, above n. 27, 248.

functioning of international human rights norms. They also encapsulate and help to inform community expectations. In the context of the right to education, for example, this will play out as much at the family and village levels as it will in any of the more routine bureaucratic levels. Where a child is being denied educational opportunities, whether for reasons of gender, disability, caste, race, order in the family, or whatever, a community which has come to internalize a sensibility to, and set of expectations about, every child's inherent right to education will react to the perceived deprivation. The same applies at the village or community level where a right to education based obligation of those in charge will have an impact regardless of the insistence of those responsible that there are simply no available resources.

In the longer term, the objective of rights such as the right to education is to internalize a value assumption to the point where a sense of injustice or even outrage follows automatically from any denial of access to primary education. Just as we respond instinctively against arbitrary physical violence exerted against another person, so too would a fully internalized sense of the right to education lead to an instinctive reaction against a government, a community, or parents or guardians denying a child access to that right.

Closely linked to the concept of empowerment is the sense that the demand for education, by both parents and students, will be enhanced and legitimated by the deeper inculcation of the notion that every individual has not just an opportunity or a duty to learn but a right to education. While this demand-side effect cannot be taken for granted, nor should it be viewed only in terms of rational economic decision making. As Lant Pritchett has observed, there may well be economic conditions that are sufficiently stagnant as to warrant considering a decision not to attend school as 'the *optimal* decision from a narrowly drawn economic calculation'. But, as he notes:

I would never recommend adopting this narrow view [because] the view that basic education is a human right and an essential element of well-being in the modern world is pretty compelling. But it is worth pointing out that when returns are low the economic calculation and the human rights desire may be at odds.[80]

This dimension of empowering the individual to put forward justified and internationally and constitutionally legitimated claims is a vital part of the human rights paradigm. It is also directly related to the notion of accountability which is an essential part of the human rights concept. As noted in the *Human Development Report 2000*, in asserting that there is a human right to primary education it follows that 'if some persons avoidably lack access to it,

[80] Lant Pritchett, *Towards A New Consensus for Addressing the Global Challenge of the Lack of Education*, Center for Global Development, Working Paper No. 43, June 2004, available at http://www.cgdev.org/docs/cgd_wp043.pdf, 56.

there must be some culpability somewhere in the social system'.[81] As the Report explains:

This focus on locating accountability for failures within a social system can be a powerful tool in seeking remedy. It certainly broadens the outlook beyond the minimal claims of human development, and the analysis of human development can profit from it. The effect of a broader outlook is to focus on the actions, strategies and efforts that different duty bearers undertake to contribute to the fulfilment of specified human rights and to the advancement of the corresponding human development. It also leads to an analysis of the responsibilities of different actors and institutions when rights go unfulfilled.[82]

The importance of these elements of empowerment and accountability which flow from treating education as a human right also serve to underscore the importance of distinguishing those policy approaches which are pre-mised, to a greater or lesser degree, upon the recognition of the right to education, from those that set broader development goals relating to edu-cation. Michael Clemens, for example, has been highly critical of the practice of 'a succession of international meetings' of adopting 'a litany of utopian international goals' which inevitably fail to be realized.[83] He lists eighteen occasions between 1934 and 2001 when governments explicitly approved the goal of universal primary education. They range from the 1934 International Conference on Public Education to the adoption of the Universal Declara-tion of Human Rights in 1948, and a succession of UNESCO Regional Conferences in the 1950s and 1960s, through the 1990 World Conference on Education for All and the 2000 Dakar World Education Forum to the Millennium Development Goals.

From a human rights perspective, his list is significantly incomplete since he lists only the Universal Declaration of 1948 and manifests no awareness of the more substantive commitments undertaken in a variety of specific international and regional-level treaties, such as the International Covenant on Economic, Social and Cultural Rights of 1966, and the Convention on the Rights of the Child of 1989. Of course, Clemens might well respond that the substantial lengthening of his list, which would result from the addition of all of the relevant undertakings made in the human rights context, only serves to reinforce his argument that repeated invocations of principle make little if any difference on their own. But there is a qualitative difference between treaty-based human rights commitments which give rise to binding legal obligations and undertakings given at regional conferences or in other contexts in which governments are convinced that they are making general

---

[81] *Human Rights and Human Development, Human Development Report 2000* (New York, Oxford University Press for UNDP, 2000) 21.   [82] Ibid. 22.

[83] Michael Clemens, *The Long Walk to School: International Education Goals in Historical Perspective*, Center for Global Development Working Paper No. 37, March 2004.

policy statements which will have no direct domestic consequences and no sustained or obligatory international follow-up. The human rights undertakings, by contrast, import an obligation to take a variety of specific steps at the national level, and to acknowledge various forms of accountability at the international level.

While this is not the place in which to explore in detail the ways in which these international accountability mechanisms do or should function, it is appropriate to note that in 2003 the Indian Government prepared a very detailed report to the UN Committee on the Rights of the Child, including over eighty pages of detailed statistical and other information on the strengths and weaknesses of the system designed to give effect to the child's right to education.[84] This report was the occasion for the preparation of a range of 'alternative' reports prepared by civil society groups and also submitted to the UN Committee.[85] While the 'concluding observations' adopted by the Committee were very general in nature[86] and likely to be of little specific import, the process as a whole was clearly an important one.[87] Its capacity to provoke the Government to undertake a systematic inventory, its involvement of civil society both at the domestic and international level, its garnering of extensive domestic press coverage, and its formal evaluation of India's performance in relation to its obligations, all contribute to promoting an element of accountability which is almost entirely absent in the case of other international undertakings relating to education.

---

[84] Report of India, above n. 27, 232–314.

[85] For example, 'The Alternate Report by the National Movement of Working Children, India, submitted to the Committee on the Rights of the Child, July 2003'.

[86] 'Concluding Observations: India', UN doc. CRC/C/15/Add.228 (2004).

[87] The extent to which the process is relevant, despite its shortcomings, is well illustrated by a highly critical assessment published in one of India's leading weekly magazines immediately after the Committee had reported:

The reporting process is like a diplomatic ritual . . . Even a cursory look at the concluding observations made by the same committee in 2000 on the basis of the earlier report indicates that the committee has mechanically repeated this part of the observations and identified the same set of factors responsible for the poor status of children in India as it had last time. This highly limited level of analysis indicates a lack of engagement with the ground realities on part of the official delegation as well as the committee. The committee also played friendly by not listing 'lack of political will' and 'poor allocation of resources' as reasons for the dismal record . . . Some observations are stale, and have been rendered over and over again; some are new and have been keenly awaited; and some are completely missing . . .

Archana Mehendale, 'Children's Rights: Lessons on Monitoring', *The Economic and Political Weekly*, 17 April 2004, 8.

Part D

Reform of Legal and Judicial Systems

12

The Impact of Human Rights Principles on Justice Reform in the Inter-American Development Bank

CHRISTINA BIEBESHEIMER[1]

12.1 INTRODUCTION

This chapter discusses the Inter-American Development Bank's (IDB) rule of law and justice reform program, the way in which human rights principles are currently incorporated into that program, and how the program might be different if a rights perspective were taken further.

The IDB's rule of law program began in the context of a broad and integrated approach to economic reform, poverty reduction, and social equity. The IDB funds projects that promote health, education, land ownership rights, infrastructure, micro-enterprise projects, rural development, environmental protection, the rights of indigenous peoples, women and minorities, good governance, and anti-corruption. This chapter, however, does not deal with human rights promotion as a general matter in the wide diversity of IDB lending; rather, it focuses on the IDB's work in the area of justice or rule-of-law reform, and the way in which human rights concepts and concerns influence the content and structure of that work.

Rule of law work, by its very nature, operates directly within the framework of international human rights obligations. This work obviously involves and impacts upon civil and political rights, since it is justice institutions that make it possible for citizens to have a fair trial, to be treated decently while in detention, and to petition for freedom from discrimination. Justice institutions also have a key role in making it possible for citizens to enforce their economic, social, and cultural rights. To some considerable degree, then, rule of law work *is* human rights work. Yet the IDB, even when

---

[1] The opinions expressed herein are those of the author and do not necessarily reflect the official views of the Inter-American Development Bank.

developing and implementing justice projects, does not closely resemble a human rights organization in either the content of its work or the methodologies it employs in going about that work.

12.2 THE IDB'S APPROACH TO RULE OF LAW AND HUMAN RIGHTS

It was probably not primarily concern for human rights implementation in the region that led the IDB into supporting projects that promote the rule of law; it was the conviction that rule of law is key to democratic governance as well as to human rights enforcement, and that these are fundamental to economic growth and social equity. We are, however, funding a number of projects that work directly with human rights organizations and human rights issues, and our policy and strategy make it clear that human rights protections must be a part of our work in justice reform.

The IDB's rule of law program includes everything from constitutional reform to access to justice projects to criminal justice reform to violence prevention to human rights education to court management. The justice program—which involves judges, prosecutors, police, prison administrators, legal aid lawyers, citizens organized against gang violence, public defenders, community groups assisting the reintegration of released inmates, and many others—is a broader program than that of other multilateral development banks working on justice reform. How did we get to this point?

12.2.1 The IDB's Policy Framework on Rule of Law and Human Rights

In 1994, the Governors of the IDB—the highest-level representatives of our member governments—met to discuss an eighth capital replenishment for the IDB. The reports that the Governors issue on the occasion of replenishments of capital discuss the state of development in Latin America and the Caribbean, and set out the strategic directions that the IDB is to follow. The Eighth Replenishment Report, still in effect because we have not needed a subsequent replenishment, established a mandate for the IDB to work with a comprehensive approach to development that seeks to consolidate economic reforms while also promoting poverty reduction and social equity, regional integration, environmental protection, and modernization of the state.

The Eighth Replenishment Report dealt explicitly with governance as a development issue, stating that long-term economic growth based on private sector activity requires an efficient public sector, and that the IDB can thus work to strengthen public institutions, since 'effective and efficient government will require institutional strengthening of the executive, legislative, and judicial branches, and other public entities'.[2] The report deals at some length with judicial reform, calling for simultaneous action on a variety of fronts in the justice sector, and requiring that IDB support be geared towards ensuring that judicial systems are independent and effective, guarantee the rights of citizens, and contribute to effective and rapid settlement of disputes. Most pertinently, the report also explicitly recognizes that *'democracy and respect for human rights have helped create appropriate conditions for development'*.[3]

The discussion in the Eighth Capital Replenishment Report has had an important impact on IDB projects. With the report's blessing, we intensified efforts to improve public sector institutions, began working directly with courts and other justice sector institutions, and pursued projects whose aims included those of improving human rights protections and increasing citizen participation in governance.

12.2.2 Democratic Governance and its Impact on Justice and Human Rights

Just last year the institution approved a new strategy on Modernization of the State. This strategy was highly consulted, inside and outside the organization. The strategy represents a shift in IDB governance policy in that it makes it clear that the IDB will pursue not just *good* governance, but *democratic* governance. The strategy defines governance as

the process through which authority is exercised in a given political community, including: (i) the form through which the holders of authority are elected, monitored, and replaced; (ii) the principles and norms guiding the interactions between the state, the private sector, and civil society organizations . . . and (iii) the capacity of the political authority to identify needs, collect resources, and define and implement policies.[4]

The strategy states that governance is democratic when a series of requirements are met in respect to how authority should be exercised and under what socio-economic conditions:

First, the requirement of representativeness that legitimizes public authority through free elections; second, the existence of mechanisms for the effective constraint and division of power, for ensuring the accountability of public officials to citizens and respect for citizen rights and liberties; third, controls on arbitrariness so that authority is exercised in a manner consistent with the law and the constitution, with effectiveness and efficiency in the assignment of resources to social needs and with

---

[2] IDB, *Report on the Eighth General Increase in the Resources of the Inter-American Development Bank*, AB-1704, 12 August 1994 (Washington D.C.: IDB) 27.

[3] Ibid. (emphasis added).

[4] IDB, *Modernization of the State Strategy Document*, GN-2235, July 2003 (Washington D.C.: IBD) (in English at www.iadb.org/sds/doc/SGC-GN-2235-1-e.pdf and in Spanish at www.iadb.org/sds/doc/SGC-GN-2235-1-s.pdf) 1.

transparency and integrity in the behavior of public officials; and finally, democratic governance requires conditions in which the enforcement of the principles of solidarity and subsidiarity permit a consensual and effective relation between different social actors in a context of social cohesion.[5]

This definition of democratic governance, then, clearly encompasses the effective enforcement of the rule of law, as well as the attributes of a political and administrative regime and the capacity of a society to face the challenges confronting it and to create solutions based on a solid social consensus. Democracy is necessary for *sustainable* growth. The strategy states: 'the success of efforts to reduce poverty and achieve sustainable development requires a substantial increase of institutional capacity and a favorable political environment'. And democracy is not valuable only in that it promotes sustainable growth, but because it promotes human rights: 'The recognition of the positive contributions of democracy to development is now added to the recognition of its intrinsic value in respect to the promotion of freedom and human rights.'

Poverty and inequality are some of the most serious problems countries face, and economic growth in Latin America and the Caribbean has not tended to lift all boats equally. The focus on democratic governance in the IDB thus comes about in part as an effort to bring about the sort of economic growth that will allow more people a way out of grinding poverty:

Under democratic governance conditions the poor are empowered, which tends to better ensure that growth is widely inclusive and participative. In solid democratic systems, there are more opportunities for the interests of the poor to be represented systematically in the process of formulating and implementing public policies.[6]

In sum, then, IDB policy and strategy documents make it clear that the institution considers that building the rule of law is one of the steps to building democratic governance, and democratic governance is valued in part because it promotes freedom and human rights, which have value in and of themselves and also tend to create appropriate conditions under which development—particularly equitable and sustainable development—can occur.

12.2.3 The Regional Human Rights Context for IDB Rule of Law Programs

The IDB's rule of law work takes place in the context of an established regional structure for the enforcement of human rights. The American Convention on Human Rights[7] (the Convention) was adopted by the

---

[5] IDB, *Modernization of the State Strategy Document*, GN-2235, July 2003 (Washington D.C.: IBD) (in English at www.iadb.org/sds/doc/SGC-GN-2235-1-e.pdf and in Spanish at www.iadb.org/sds/doc/SGC-GN-2235-1-s.pdf) 1.   [6] Ibid. 8.
[7] O.A.S. Treaty Series No. 36, 1144 U.N.T.S. 123, *entered into force* 18 July 1978, reprinted in Basic Documents Pertaining to Human Rights in the Inter-American System, OEA/Ser.L.V./II.82 doc.6 rev.1 at 25 (1992).

Organization of American States (OAS) in 1969 and has been ratified by 25 countries, including all but three of the IDB's regional member countries. The Inter-American Commission on Human Rights (the Commission) is an organ of the OAS that reviews complaints arising under the Convention, and both the Commission and individual governments can bring cases to the Inter-American Court of Human Rights.

The views of the governments of the region on the relation between democratic governance, rule of law, and human rights are manifest in mandates of Summits of the Americas from 1994 to the present, which make it very clear that the governments of the region consider that there are important interrelations between development, governance, rule of law, and human rights (although the precise causal connections between those concepts are left a bit murky). The Summit mandates state that democracy guarantees human rights and rule of law; and that the rule of law is necessary to consolidate democracy. Respect for rule of law and the democratic system are declared to represent goals and shared values which will be pursued and maintained for their own sake; and there is discussion to indicate that the value of democracy lies in part in its potential contribution to combating poverty and inequality. Importantly, Summit documents also reaffirm a commitment to all human rights—civil, political, economic, social, and cultural.[8]

Many civil and political rights that are relevant to justice institution functioning are already explicitly recognized in Latin American legislation, and have been for some time. Many countries of the region enshrine rights

[8] A few excerpts from these summit mandates follow:
Declaration of Miami, 1994: 'Democracy is the sole political system which guarantees respect for human rights and the rule of law; it safeguards cultural diversity, pluralism, respect for the rights of minorities, and peace within and among nations.'
Declaration of Santiago, 1998: 'Confident that an independent, efficient, and effective administration of justice plays an essential role in the process of consolidating democracy, strengthens its institutions, guarantees the equality of all its citizens, and contributes to economic development, we will enhance our policies relating to justice and encourage the reforms necessary to promote legal and judicial cooperation.'
Declaration of Quebec, 2001: 'The maintenance and strengthening of the rule of law and strict respect for the democratic system are, at the same time, a goal and a shared commitment and are an essential condition of our presence at this and future Summits.... Democracy and economic and social development are interdependent and mutually reinforcing as fundamental conditions to combat poverty and inequality. We will spare no effort to free our fellow citizens from the dehumanizing conditions of extreme poverty.'
Declaration of EU–Latin America and the Caribbean Summit, Madrid, 2002: 'We believe that democracy, the Rule of Law and economic and social development are elements of fundamental importance for peace and stability ... We reaffirm our commitment for all human rights, civil, political, economic, social and cultural rights, including the right to development, and fundamental freedoms taking into account their universal, interdependent and indivisible character in accordance with the UN Charter and the human rights instruments agreed internationally, together with the 1993 Vienna Declaration of Human Rights and the Programme of Action.'

such as the right to a fair trial and free legal assistance for those who cannot afford a lawyer in their constitutions, and enabling legislation often provides for due process protections such as a maximum time limit within which a detainee must be brought to trial. There seems to be genuine consensus around these ideals: judges, bar associations, civil society organizations, the media, and citizens all agree that the due process of law is fundamental and that independent justice institutions should guarantee this process to all.

The problem in the area of rule of law in many Latin American countries is not that the law does not adequately recognize due process rights; the problem is that justice institutions are not actually providing fair and timely justice for all in spite of constitutional mandates that they do so, and in spite of a general regional consensus around the importance of an effective justice system. And it is proving difficult to bring about the reform necessary to make the goals set out in law a reality in the lives of ordinary citizens. Some of the oft-cited reasons for the difficulty in bringing about reform to the justice sector are: the judiciary suffers from a legacy of being ignored or commandeered by the executive and legislative powers for many years (though one important result of a decade of reform efforts is that today most courts and other justice institutions are receiving more budgetary resources, and the indices of judicial independence from interference by other powers of government are considerably improved in Latin America);[9] courts have tended to operate at a great distance from citizens and justice institutions do not have sophisticated accountability mechanisms in place; the justice system cannot offer salaries comparable to those of the private sector and has not necessarily been regarded as providing work that is interesting and of high social standing (though this latter aspect has begun to change in a number of countries); justice institutions are weak in terms of organization and management; procedures for bringing and moving cases through the system are astonishingly complicated and byzantine; the justice system *status quo* provides advantages to some groups of society, such that reform movements have enemies as well as proponents; public and media understanding of the working of the justice system, and willingness to lobby for change to that system, is not high; and, perhaps most worrisome, public trust in the justice system is low and getting lower (See Figure 12.1).

12.2.4 The IDB's Approach to Making Rights Real

The question becomes, then: how best to go about implementing goals and laws that will make rights real for citizens and litigants? The IDB's

---

[9] See U.S. Agency for International Development (USAID), *Guidance for Promoting Judicial Independence and Impartiality*, Technical Publication Series, Office of Democracy and Governance (Washington D.C.: USAID, November 2001) 100–143.

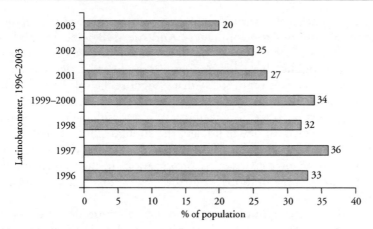

Figure 12.1. Confidence in the judiciary

Modernization of State strategy makes it evident that the IDB takes an institutional-change view of this problem. That is, the IDB asks 'What would need to happen in order for rule of law to be strong in Latin America?' and the answer is set out in the strategy: courts and other justice institutions would have to issue decisions that are fair, offer broad access, be timely in rendering service, be both independent and publicly accountable, and be free of discrimination.[10] This is not a manner of analysis that is at odds with human rights objectives, but neither is it a fully rights-based approach. That is, the IDB does not state its goals in rule of law reform by citing provisions of international human rights covenants (though judicial independence and freedom from discrimination figure in treaty provisions) or by stating that the IDB goal is to make it possible for courts and justice institutions to enforce countries' human rights obligations. Instead, the focus is on which institutions would need to be able to carry out which functions in order for justice to be administered effectively.

This seems to me to be a legitimate method of analysis and a legitimate focus, so long as it is one that brings about changes that benefit citizens, and especially poor and marginalized citizens. It is also a focus that results in a set of priorities and methodologies that are different from those that might be established under a more exclusively rights perspective. Development institutions focus on the capacity of public sector institutions because we have learned that the quality of public institutions is an essential ingredient for sustainable and equitable economic growth;[11] the IDB focuses on the

[10] IDB, *Modernization of the State Strategy Document* above n. 4, 14.
[11] See, e.g., Douglass C. North, 'Institutions Matter', Economics Working Paper Archive at Washington University in St. Louis, available at: http://ideas.repec.org/p/wpa/wuwpeh/9411004.html.

democratic capacity of institutions because we have learned that democracy matters to a country's development.[12] And the IDB tends to think about state institutions because most of our funds move through loans to governments; that is, public sector institutions are the beneficiaries and targets of much of our work. This is not to say that we ignore the role of civil society or the private sector: the strategy on modernization of the state insists that IDB work recognize that there is a reciprocal and complementary relationship between state reform on one hand, and the strengthening of civil society on the other.[13] We have some grant funds available to civil society organizations, and we work to involve civil society organizations in the implementation of our loans; but the organizations we are best set up to affect are public sector institutions.

One of the gratifying things about working on reform of justice systems in the IDB is that we have not needed to limit our work to courts alone, or to civil (as opposed to criminal) law. Our projects work with courts, prosecutors, ministries of justice, legal aid lawyers, law schools and students, justices of the peace, ombudsmen's offices, public defenders, police, prison administrators, parole departments, human rights organizations, community groups organized to prevent violence, primary and secondary schools with programs on mediation and peaceable dispute resolution, representatives of indigenous communities who administer community dispute resolution mechanisms, victims' rights organizations, church groups assisting with re-entry of former inmates into society, businesses willing to participate in work-release programs and in delinquency-prevention programs, think tanks and criminology institutes, chambers of commerce, and domestic violence shelters.

It was not always this way: the first project or two stuck to civil court administration and case management. By the second or third project, we were discussing judicial reform in a country emerging from civil war and dealing with the very serious impact of juvenile crime on the justice system— and we wound up funding violence prevention and youth rehabilitation programs, refurbishing infrastructure so that young offenders were not confined with adults (and so that they had running water and electricity), and supporting inter-institutional, sector-wide co-ordination of justice policy. Project by project, we built a tradition of sector-wide analysis, and now it is official that we are to examine the whole justice sector in the assessments and diagnostics that precede project preparation, to be sure that project activities make sense in the framework of an integrated, sector-wide approach to justice reform.

We can work so broadly in part because of the mandate the Eighth Replenishment Report gave us, encouraging projects that 'ensure that judicial

---

[12] M. Payne, D. Zovatto, and F. Carrillo, *Democracies in Development: Politics and Reform in Latin America* (Washington D.C.: IDB, 2002).   [13] Ibid. ii.

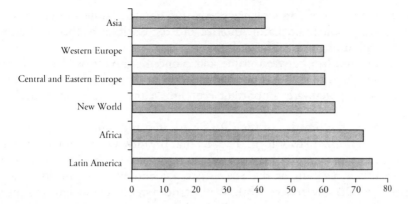

Figure 12.2. Percentage of the public victimized by any crime in urban areas, by region, 1989–1996

Source: United Nations, *Global Report on Crime and Justice* (New York: Oxford University Press (for the United Nations Office for Drug Control and Crime Prevention), 1999).

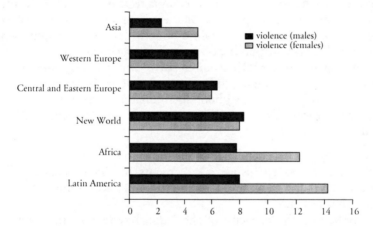

Figure 12.3. Percentage of men and women victimized by violent crimes over five years in urban areas, 1991–1996

Source: United Nations, *Global Report on Crime and Justice* (New York: Oxford University Press (for the United Nations Office for Drug Control and Crime Prevention), 1999).[14]

systems are independent and effective, guarantee the rights of citizens, and contribute to effective and rapid settlement of disputes' (that does not exclude much), and permitting a focus on human rights protection. In part the IDB has been willing (though initially cautious) to address issues of

[14] 'New World' in this figure, and also figure 12.2 refers to the U.S., Canada, Australia, and New Zealand.

criminal law reform and violence prevention because crime and violence are such grave problems in Latin America and the Caribbean, the most crime-ridden region of the world.

The relationship between crime and economic growth is clear and negative, such that the IDB has not had to strain to show that work in criminal justice has a potentially important economic consequence, particularly on the poor.[15]

I mention the breadth of the IDB's work in justice, and in particular our reach into criminal law reform, because that breadth and reach have resulted in an important interplay between human rights and our justice reform work.

The Modernization of the State strategy identifies four priority areas of action for IDB governance work: democratic system; rule of law and justice reform; state, market, and society; and public management. *Democratic system* includes strengthening the legislative branch, modernizing electoral and party systems, ensuring the neutrality and objectivity of public administration and the civil service, and supporting decentralization and democratization of sub-national governments. *State, market, and society* includes supporting economic management institutions, social and economic regulatory agencies, institutions that design development policies, and environmental governance. *Public management* includes the whole gamut of activities aimed at improving the quality and efficiency of public policies and management.

The strategy states that IDB action in *rule of law and justice reform* ought to be directed toward developing justice systems that are independent, efficient, reliable, agile, and accessible, without discrimination based on race, gender, or any similar category. The strategy sets out seven areas toward which justice programs can be oriented:

a) Supporting the independence of the judiciary;
b) Widening access to justice for segments of the population that are marginalized for geographic, socio-economic, ethno-linguistic, gender, and other reasons;
c) Strengthening the capacity of the judicial system in the fight against corruption;
d) Developing modern systems for management and administration of justice institutions and procedures;
e) Promoting alternative conflict resolution methods. (It is worth mentioning a couple of sub-categories under this item, as they have

---

[15] J-L. Londoño, A. Gaviria, and R. Guerro, *Asalto al Desarrollo: Violencia en América Latina* (Washington D.C.: IDB, 2000); A. Morrison and M. Beatriz Orlando, 'Social and Economic Costs of Domestic Violence: Chile and Nicaragua', in A. Morrison and M. L. Biehl, eds, *Too Close to Home: Domestic Violence in the Americas* (Washington D.C.: IDB and Johns Hopkins University Press, 1999); C. Moser and J. Holland, *Urban Poverty and Violence in Jamaica* (Washington D.C.: World Bank, 1997).

been important in designing projects aimed at strengthening recognition of human rights in the region. Activities in this category include 'the promotion of basic civic and legal education regarding judicial institutions, court proceedings, and basic citizen rights'; and 'improving the capacity of special indigenous jurisdictions recognized in the legislation of some countries of the region'.)

f) Updating substantive and procedural legislation;

g) And finally—and very significantly for the impact of human rights issues on rule of law projects—Protecting citizen security, and ensuring the legal control of the use of force.[16]

The paragraph on citizen security and the legal control of the use of force states:

In this area, Bank projects will seek to make human rights protection and procedural guarantees compatible with the need to combat violence, criminality and impunity that undermine the investment climate and impose a cost on citizens, especially the poorest . . . Bank activities in this area can include: (i) strengthening the offices of the public prosecutor, ombudsman, and attorney general and formulating crime prevention policies; (ii) the establishment of rehabilitation and alternative sentencing programs to reduce recidivism; (iii) training, equipping and providing infrastructure to support forensic medicine and professional investigative practices; (iv) computerizing criminal statistics and establishing criminal information and record systems; and (v) strengthening executive branch institutions in charge of ensuring the legal monopoly of the use of force, as well as civilian control of the armed forces and the police.[17]

This is not a perfect list: for example, support to prosecutors is mentioned, but public defenders are left out (in spite of that oversight, most IDB criminal justice projects incorporate support for public defenders, and operational guidelines under preparation emphasize the need to balance prosecution with defense). Still, it is a courageous list, and it is astonishing and impressive that we have come so far in the ten years since we made our first cautious entries into violence prevention and criminal justice reform.

12.3 HOW HUMAN RIGHTS CONCEPTS ARE INFLUENCING THE IDB'S RULE OF LAW AND JUSTICE PROGRAM

As the citations from the Modernization of State strategy above make clear, human rights and justice reform are directly and irreversibly linked in IDB policy. This section explores some of the ways in which human rights principles are being used in interpreting the areas of justice we can work in,

[16] IDB, *Modernization of the State Strategy Document*, above n. 4, 14–15.
[17] Ibid. 15–16.

in defining project content, in establishing methodologies for pre-project diagnostics, and in defining indicators for project success and impact.

12.3.1 Human Rights Concepts in the Interpretation of Litmus Tests

In order for the IDB to provide funding for any project (justice projects included), the IDB's Charter (the Charter) states that it must: 'contribute to the acceleration of the process of economic and social development of the regional developing member countries, individually and collectively';[18] be justified solely on the basis of economic factors; and the project must not interfere or potentially interfere in internal political matters of member countries.[19]

IDB policy posits a direct link between justice reform and economic development. The Eighth Replenishment Report explicitly recommends judicial, executive, and legislative branch strengthening to contribute to creating an efficient public sector which is necessary if private sector growth is to flourish. Similarly, the Modernization of the State strategy states that '[i]t is not possible to advance sustainable and equitable growth without progress in legal predictability and equality before the law for all citizens'.[20] These conclusions by the Board of Governors in the Eighth Replenishment and by the Board of Directors in the Modernization of State strategy are supported by academic literature on the effect of public sector effectiveness and efficiency on economic and social development.[21] There is also significant recent scholarship on the correlation between justice system reform and economic development.

When one comes to the level of individual projects, however, it can be more difficult to pinpoint the impact on economic and social development. The general way in which criminal justice reform affects *social* development may be clear, for example: the fabric of social life and peaceable coexistence is ripped apart if people live at the mercy of crime and violence, and the most basic social contract with the state is discredited if that state either cannot provide for the physical safety of its citizens on the one hand, or can detain

---

[18] Agreement Establishing the Inter-American Development Bank, Article I, Section I.

[19] Agreement Establishing the Inter-American Development Bank, Article VIII, Section 5(f); and Memorandum for the Legal Department entitled 'Limits on the Activities which may be Funded with IDB Resources' (9 April 1998).

[20] *Modernization of the State Strategy Document*, above n. 4, 14.

[21] See, e.g., A. Chong and C. Calderón, *Empirical Tests on Causality and Feedback between Institutional Measures and Economic Growth* (Washington D.C.: World Bank, 1999); D. Kaufmann, A. Kray, and P. Zoido-Lobatón, *Aggregating Governance Indicators*, unpublished manuscript, World Bank, 1999; R. La Porta, F. Lopes da Silanes, A. Shleifer, and R. Vishny, *The Quality of Government*, mimeo, Harvard University and the University of Chicago, 1998; North, above n. 11.

and imprison citizens without fair trial and presentation of credible evidence, on the other hand. But measuring precisely how IDB contributions to criminal justice projects impact social or economic development may be harder. This is because, though it is clear that lowering levels of crime and violence has a positive impact on economic development,[22] an exact measure of the extent to which an IDB project diminishes levels of crime is likely to be next to impossible to achieve, since crime levels are affected by many factors and the precise role of any IDB contribution is likely to be hard to isolate. In addition, truly comparative data rarely exists: it is rarely possible to compare a jurisdiction undergoing reform to an otherwise identical jurisdiction without reform.

We are grappling with this issue in preparing operational guidelines which will guide project teams preparing criminal justice projects. And we are leaning toward concluding that it is hard to refute that the state's ability to figure out who has committed a crime and to hand down appropriate punishment is one key element in the effort to combat crime: deterrence has to be part of the picture. Thus, IDB criminal justice projects should measure the extent to which they contribute to creating a more credible and effective process of criminal prosecution that respects due process rights.[23] Not surprisingly, then, projects are using human-rights-based indicators to measure success in project implementation. Because IDB policy holds that human rights and the rule of law contribute to growth and equity, evidence of improved respect for due process rights is thus evidence of impact on economic and social development. Examples of some of these human-rights-based indicators are: the numbers of cases thrown out by the courts for improper prosecution; the percentage of convictions of white collar crime and of the non-poor; and percentage of inmates imprisoned without sentence.

The third Charter test cited above requires that a project must not interfere or potentially interfere in the internal political matters of member countries. If this provision were very narrowly interpreted, it might be understood to prevent work in any form with the justice sector, since such work may influence the balance of power among judicial, executive, and legislative branches of government. I think it is very largely due to the common consensus around human rights in the sphere of the administration of justice—that is, common agreement as to the importance of a fair trial, of non-discrimination, and of an independent judiciary—that means that IDB work on reforming justice institutions is regarded not as interference in political matters but rather as a means of helping countries realize goals they

---

[22] See above n. 15 and references.

[23] Creating a disincentive for crime is not the only economic impact that criminal justice projects can have: some criminal justice projects will also seek to prevent crime by means of preventative police work or rehabilitation to lower recidivism rates, and crime and violence prevention has clear economic consequences.

have already voluntarily undertaken in international and regional conventions and that are often reflected in country constitutions.

But what if a government is acting in clear and intentional violation of human rights principles in the way it structures balance of power among branches of government? This issue arises, for example, in countries in which there is overt political interference that seriously impinges on judicial or prosecutorial independence. The IDB does not yet have a written position on what to do in the case of serious and intentional interference with judicial independence, though a number of policy documents, as noted, state that judicial independence is one of the priority areas of IDB justice work. We have wrestled with whether we ought to make loans for improving justice in countries in which there is little judicial independence or in which judicial independence is under threat. This is essentially a question as to whether we ought to condition our loans on a country's meeting some sort of minimum standard of independence. The Modernization of the State strategy defines judicial independence as meaning that 'the availability of budgetary resources, appointments, recruitment and career development of judges and magistrates and cooperation with other judicial institutions are not exposed to interference by political or economic interests that can compromise the objectivity and independence of judicial decision-making'. The strategy suggests several ways to work toward judicial independence, such as improving systems for selection, career development, training, disciplinary action, and remuneration of judicial officials based on principles of equality and merit, and strengthening systems that promote accountability of the judiciary to citizens.

Part of the reason that the IDB can emphasize the importance of judicial independence—in spite of the Charter provision against projects that potentially interfere with internal political matters of member countries—is that judicial independence is clearly required under most human rights conventions to which almost all of our member countries are signatories, and is thus simply a recognition of a principle already embraced by IDB member countries.[24] Reference to judicial independence as a human right is not the end of the matter, of course—it does not answer the question of whether we ought to insist on a minimum standard of independence before we

---

[24] Article 14 of the International Covenant on Civil and Political Rights (ICCPR, G.A. res. 2200A (XXI), 21 U.N. GAOR Supp. (No. 16) at 52, U.N. Doc. A/6316 (1966), 999 U.N.T.S. 171, *entered into force* 23 March 1976) and Article 8 of the Inter-American Convention on Human Rights (above n. 7) mandate 'an independent, impartial and competent judiciary'. The UN Basic Principles on the Independence of the Judiciary (Seventh United Nations Congress on the Prevention of Crime and the Treatment of Offenders, Milan, 26 August to 6 September 1985, U.N. Doc. A/CONF.121/22/Rev.1 at 59 (1985)) highlight the standards for the independence of the judiciary, including the separation of powers, technical competence, and security of tenure.

provide financing to a country for justice reform. But it facilitates raising the issue in the first place, and means that neither the IDB nor member governments consider the issue to be inconsequential or suggest that it should not constitute a priority for the Bank and the region.

The IDB has opted not to establish such a minimum standard as a condition for work in the justice sector, and it is possible we may be taken to task for that by human rights organizations. We have so opted on the basis of the conviction that it is important to work with countries in which independence is at risk or under siege to help build a consensus around its importance and definition in that society. Courts and prosecutors' offices must work continually to maintain independence, and a perfect state of independence coupled with accountability is difficult to find in any country of the world. The IDB is now considering whether we ought to recommend that, when judicial independence is weak or under siege in a given country, any IDB justice project that goes forward should address that problem head-on and work to build independence, transparency, and accountability (rather than take the tack of, for example, working in an area of grass-roots justice reform so far removed from the formal court system that the existence or not of judicial independence may seem a peripheral issue).

Criminal justice issues are linked to inherently political questions such as how a society defines and values norm and norm-deviance, life and liberty, power and violence, prevention and deterrence.[25] Here again, it is partly because of the regional consensus about the need for due process that the IDB is able to work in this area. It is noteworthy that IDB criminal justice projects have not ventured into areas that are very closely related to national security and sovereignty, such as anti-terrorism and treasonous (political) crimes against the state. These are areas that are probably more appropriate for bilateral, political aid that might take the form of military-to-military assistance or intelligence sharing, and might very possibly be determined to be ineligible for IDB funding on the basis of the 'no political interference' test.

It is in the areas of police and prison reform that the IDB has felt a need for guidelines that define which activities under what conditions are appropriate for IDB assistance and which are not. The concern with these areas is not only around the non-interference test: it is evident to us that police and prison reform projects present significant risks and require that the IDB work systematically to ensure that all reasonable precautions are taken to avoid human rights violations and to minimize opportunities for violence. However, some of these concerns make themselves manifest around the issue of the non-interference test. The draft guidelines on criminal justice reform

---

[25] It is important to point out that criminal justice projects certainly are not alone in triggering debates over essentially political issues: privatization, decentralization, and commercial law reform projects, for example, are all also political in nature in that they must reflect a balancing of a variety of political and economic interests within society.

that are in an initial stage of discussion in the institution suggest that the IDB should not work in police or prison reform at all when, for example, there is impunity for human rights abuses committed by state agents and no apparent political will to address that situation; during periods of suspension of the constitution; in countries with prisoners detained solely on political grounds; and in other similar situations. The thinking is that, because police and prisons can become a tool of political repression in situations of political instability, IDB support for them under these conditions could constitute political interference. What this amounts to, in large part, is using certain human rights considerations to help define situations in which a project might interfere or potentially interfere in internal political matters of member states.

12.3.2 Using Human Rights Principles to Define Project Content

12.3.2.1 *Access to Justice by Marginalized Groups and Enforcement of Non-Discrimination*

IDB projects in areas other than criminal law have run the gamut of substantive areas of law: constitutional law, civil procedure, contracts, administrative, labor, land, family, and property law, indigenous law, agrarian law, commercial law. It is interesting that a significant number of projects emphasize increasing access to justice, and almost no project does not include measures intended to reduce discrimination by justice institutions against women, minorities, and the disenfranchised. This is partly a reflection of the IDB's focus on poverty reduction, and it is a product of an institutional mechanism to ensure that each and every IDB project is scrutinized for its potential impact on women, minorities, and the environment.[26] This level of institutional review has done a great deal to ensure that projects include components that work for non-discrimination and equity in the way that justice is administered.

12.3.2.2 *Recognition of the Jurisdiction of Indigenous Law*

Another example of the way in which reference to human rights conventions can define project content is the area of indigenous rights and indigenous law. Many countries in Latin America are wrestling with the degree to which a national, formal justice system ought to recognize indigenous law and dispute resolution systems. This can be a delicate topic for a number of reasons—it can seem threatening to jurists in the formal system, and it can risk diminishing human rights protections to litigants proceeding under indigenous law if that law does not guarantee the same rights that the formal

---

[26] Every project is examined by the Committee on Environmental and Social Impact.

system provides for all litigants. This might not be a topic that the IDB would be working in, were it not for international conventions that define states' obligations in this regard, provisions of which are reflected in the constitutions of a number of our member countries. The IDB has established a database that analyzes the extent to which these treaty provisions are reflected in the local laws of each of our member countries in Latin America and the Caribbean (see www.iadb.org/sds/ind). We are also funding projects that assist indigenous communities, human rights ombudsmen, and other justice institutions in deciding how best to define the borders and the interplay between formal and customary law systems.[27]

12.3.2.3 Criminal Justice Reform Projects and Human Rights

In criminal justice reform projects human rights considerations have a direct role in defining project content, and may play an important role in defining diagnostic methodologies. The Modernization of the State strategy makes it clear that every criminal justice project will balance investigation and prosecution of crime with protection for due process and other human rights:

In this area, Bank projects will seek to make human rights protection and procedural guarantees compatible with the need to combat violence, criminality and impunity that undermine the investment climate and impose a cost on citizens, especially the poorest.

The IDB is able to work in criminal justice reform because its borrowing member countries are sufficiently concerned about improving public safety and respect for human rights as to be willing to allow the light of international assistance to shine on areas such as criminal trial processes, criminal investigation procedures, and penitentiary systems. Interest on the part of borrower countries to address both sides of this balance—due process protections and prosecution of crime—opens an opportunity for the IDB to work with member countries to make criminal justice systems both fairer and more effective.

The developmental needs in the area of criminal justice in Latin America and the Caribbean are many and dire. Criminal prosecutions are slow and hampered by serious debilities in investigative capacity. In much of the region, the prison population is mostly under 30, and many prisoners are of school age. Empirical studies show that most juvenile offenders do not return to school after release from prison, even in countries where schooling rates are high.[28] Those in prison are predominantly poor, without any recourse

---

[27] See, e.g., IDB, *Aceso a la Justicia de las Personas y Pueblos Indígenas*, ATN/SF-8668-RG (Washington D.C.: IDB); and IDB, *Apoyo a la Coordinación entre la Jurisdicióon Especial Indígena y el Sistema Judicial Nacional*, TC-0011050-CO (Washington D.C.: IDB).

[28] World Bank, *Trinidad and Tobago, Youth and Social Development: An Integrated Approach for Social Inclusion* (Washington D.C.: World Bank, June 2000) 21.

save what the law guarantees and with no resources save what the state provides. Many victims of crime are also poor. Too many detainees in Latin America languish in prisons waiting for trial, and those who are arrested and jailed do not know if or when they will receive a trial or how long they will be imprisoned.[29] In many countries of the region, life inside prisons—for inmates as well as prison officials—is dangerous, disease-ridden, and miserable, and there are often no programs that might help with rehabilitation. First-time offenders who have committed minor offenses are often imprisoned right along with violent, seasoned offenders, and juveniles are often incarcerated together with adults. A lack of systemic support for alternative sentencing and rehabilitation means that, even when prosecutors and judges want to sentence minor offenders to community service rather than prison time, there is no supervised community service option available.

Many of the countries in Latin America are now engaged in a historic effort to fundamentally reform their criminal procedure systems. This is an unprecedented and major reform effort in the region—nearly every country in Latin America is changing from written to oral proceedings, changing the roles of judges, prosecutors, expert witnesses, public defenders, and citizens—in an effort to improve human rights records and to move criminal cases through the system more rapidly. Some of the countries of the English-speaking Caribbean, which has a long tradition of operating with oral trials under a common-law system, are also modifying criminal procedure codes to incorporate restorative justice in order to lower recidivism rates and prevent violence.

The IDB is supporting countries in the region that seek to change their criminal procedure codes to a more transparent and oral system, and all of these projects seek to strengthen the due process rights of defendants. These projects provide training in trial advocacy to judges, prosecutors, and defense attorneys, and support to forensic sciences and to the professional collection, maintenance, and presentation at trial of evidence by police and prosecutors. They have also included support to public outreach programs meant to increase citizen input into the processes of investigating and preventing crime, as well as to increase citizen awareness of their rights and obligations vis-à-vis the criminal justice system.[30]

It makes sense that the IDB would include criminal justice reform as a priority area of work in a strategy that emphasizes democratic governance. After all, fairness in criminal justice is the bedrock of a democratic system: a key characteristic of a democratic state is that it does not deprive citizens of

---

[29] Human Rights Watch, *Global Report on Prisons 1993* (New York: Human Rights Watch, 1994).

[30] See, e.g., IDB, *Modernización del Sistema de Justicia, Etapa II*, HO-0201 (Washington D.C.: IDB, 2002); IDB, *Apoyo a la Reforma del Sistema de Justicia Penal*, VE-0057 (Washington D.C.: IDB, 2001).

life or liberty without providing a fair trial and an opportunity for the accused to defend himself or herself. Though criminal justice reform is an area in which the IDB can potentially have an important impact, it is also an area that presents serious challenges and concerns for the IDB. It is in very large part due to international and regional human rights conventions and guidelines that the IDB can work in this area, and it is those conventions— defining, for example, fair trial guidelines, principles applicable to actors in the criminal justice sector, principles applicable to persons deprived of their liberty, principles applicable to juvenile delinquents—that define project content.

Member countries have also asked the IDB to provide assistance for the construction of prisons. To date, the IDB has been cautious in financing infrastructure: it has funded improvements in infrastructure for centers for juvenile detention and rehabilitation centers (to make it possible for juvenile offenders to be housed separately from adult prisoners);[31] and it has approved funding for improvements to infrastructure necessary for improving provision of health services and job training programs to adult inmates.[32] IDB funds have also provided assistance for planning for the penitentiary system, information systems, training for prison personnel, and development of rehabilitation and work-release programs to encourage productive re-entry of inmates, both youth and adults, into society and decrease recidivism rates.[33] In including these components in loan and technical assistance projects, the IDB has recognized that planning for and managing prisons and rehabilitation programs is part of the role of the justice system, and that prison and rehabilitative systems are important to promote public safety and prevent violence.

In grappling with whether the IDB can work with police and prisons, institutions through which the state can deprive people of their liberty, the IDB must confront the reality that, if it does so in a sustained way across a number of countries, there is almost bound to be a human rights violation in one of the prisons or police forces with which we work. Should a high risk of human rights violations stop the IDB from funding programs designed to reduce human rights violations? It appears that the IDB is leaning toward a position that posits that the difficulties should not deter the IDB from lending and providing assistance to borrowing countries that evidence a high level of political will and support for reform and show a genuine commitment to key rule of law principles, including democracy, respect for

---

[31] See, e.g., IDB, *Programa de Reforma del Sistema de Justicia*, ES-0090 (Washington D.C.: IDB, 1996).

[32] See, e.g., IDB, *Apoyo a la Reforma del Sistema de Justicia Penal*, VE-0057 (Washington D.C.: IDB, 2001).

[33] See IDB, *Administration of Justice*, BA-0055 (Washington D.C.: IDB, 2001); IDB, *Citizen Security and Justice*, JA-0105 (Washington D.C., 2001).

human rights, anti-corruption, and judicial independence. The risks and difficulties should, however, cause the IDB to work systematically and carefully to make every reasonable effort to ensure that protection of the human rights of all of those in the criminal justice system is enhanced by the Bank's participation in the project and that opportunities for violence are minimized. It is worth noting that human rights organizations, specialized United Nations agencies dedicated to prison reform, and member country governments have all encouraged the IDB to be involved in criminal justice reform in general, and in work with investigatory police and prisons in particular.

We are also formulating recommendations for lines of analysis that would be appropriate to undertake as part of the pre-project diagnostic for criminal justice projects, based on best practices here in the IDB. These diagnostics could include analysis of prison population trends, pre-trial detention ratios, sentencing practices (including a review of whether there are significant regional, ethnic, or gender disparities), restorative justice measures, oversight and control of detention conditions and facilities, and public perception of crime.

12.3.2.4 *Violence Prevention and Citizen Security Projects*

We tend to distinguish between that group of projects that works with the criminal justice system to prosecute crime once it has been carried out, and projects aimed at preventing violence before it occurs—though, in practice, there is substantial overlap between these two categories of projects. The IDB has carried out numerous projects to prevent domestic violence and to increase awareness of and intervention mechanisms to deal with domestic violence. In addition, many IDB citizen safety and violence prevention projects include police education components to foster respect for human rights.

Guidelines for IDB work in violence prevention recommend that the IDB projects support: (i) the collection of reliable information on violence and crime in the region, as well as policy-oriented and best-practice research; (ii) health projects aimed at detection and treatment of violence victims, and violence prevention; (iii) education projects to improve early childhood development programs, primary and secondary education, conflict mediation and other violence prevention curricula, and programs for at-risk children and youth; (iv) justice projects designed to improve the criminal justice system and in particular rehabilitative and restorative justice programs; (v) the media to combat violence; and (vi) police forces to improve public security.[34]

---

[34] IDB Violence Prevention Guidelines, available at http://sdsnet/divisions/soc/violence/guidelines.

These guidelines state that IDB project teams should avoid financing support for police activities in which human rights abuses are a clear and present danger, including support for military police forces, counter-intelligence or state security, undercover operations, acquisition of lethal equipment, specialized units such as Special Weapons and tactics (SWAT) teams and drug eradication brigades, and training in weapons use. IDB violence prevention projects that involve police are to focus on accountability of the police to multiple constituencies—internal and external (that is, external to the police department, but internal to the government), and societal. IDB projects are also required to emphasize preventive policing.

12.3.2.5 Human Rights Projects that Work through Justice Institutions

There is also a category of projects the IDB has funded whose *raison d'être* is the promotion of human rights and which work toward that end through justice institutions. The IDB has funded a number of grants aimed at increasing knowledge about human rights and the capacity to apply international human rights in the national context in Latin America and the Caribbean. These grants include funding for a workshop on strengthening the Inter-American system for the protection of human rights, carried out by the Inter-American Court of Human Rights, which aimed to build a consensus on reforming the regional system for protection of human rights and to design specific measures for reforming that system.

The IDB has also funded a Fundamental Rights Education and Training Workshop to train judicial officials from Latin America in the international instruments and legal obligations of the Inter-American system of fundamental rights. The bilingual legal teaching materials prepared with this funding deal with the structure, function, and standards for state responsibility in key areas of fundamental rights, and domestic implementation of international fundamental rights. Law professors and lawyers report to us that human rights teaching is becoming more solid and rigorous in the region, and that judges are handling human rights concepts more knowledgeably in the context of their decisions—though this is only anecdotal evidence of progress, it is encouraging.

An operation entitled Judicial Education: Towards a Jurisprudence of Equality funds a program of workshops and seminars to provide judges and law faculties with the knowledge and skills needed to apply international standards of human rights for women in domestic court cases and jurisprudence.[35]

[35] Publications on human rights financed by the IDB include: R. K. Goldman, C. Grossman, C. Martin, and D. Rodrígues-Pinzón, *The International Dimension of Human Rights: A Guide for Application in Domestic Law* (Washington D.C., 2001); and J. Thompson, *Acceso a la Justicia y Equidad: Estudio en Siete Países de América Latina* (Washington D.C.: IDB and IIDH (Instituto *Intesmelicano de Dejectos* Humanos), 2000).

12.4 HOW MIGHT THE IDB'S RULE OF LAW PROGRAM CHANGE IF WE EMPLOYED RIGHTS-BASED METHODOLOGIES

Would a rights focus change IDB priorities in its justice work? What would an explicit human rights approach suggest is the best way to ensure that rule of law programs have greatest impact and sustainability? I will not suggest, in this discussion, that the IDB seek to adopt traditional tactics of human rights organizations such as setting human rights standards, monitoring enforcement of those standards, and pressuring governments into meeting those standards. That is, I am not exploring ways in which the IDB might act more like a human rights organization; instead, I am interested in human rights principles that might make it possible for us to better achieve our objectives regarding strengthening rule of law in Latin America and the Caribbean.

There does not seem to be a great deal written on the specific question of how a rights-based approach might redefine development work in the justice arena,[36] but a review of the literature on human rights and development generally causes me to conclude that adopting a rights-based perspective might impact the IDB's justice program in at least two ways: it might shift our focus and our requirements in terms of how we go about achieving citizen participation in justice project design and implementation; and it might cause us to place greater emphasis on the role of the legal system in maintaining or fighting systems of discrimination and exclusion.

12.4.1 Participation

Citizen participation is encouraged in the formulation of IDB-supported development plans and policies, in sector and country strategy development, and in project preparation and implementation. Projects likely to benefit from public input are required to have a consultation or participation plan, which should include some combination of three core instruments for citizen participation: information, consultation, and participation in project implementation.[37] The recently-approved strategy on participation states that

citizen participation should be treated as a core element of policy, program and project development, encouraging the creation of social organizations, networks and fabrics to build capacity in individuals and social groups, equipping them to manage their own affairs and make their voice heard in negotiations with the public sector.[38]

---

[36] Though the Lawyers Committee for Human Rights has written several documents providing an analysis and a critique of the justice work of the World Bank and the IDB.

[37] IDB, *Strategy for Promoting Citizen Participation in Bank Activities*, GN-2232-5 (Washington D.C.: IDB, May 2004) 11–15. [38] Ibid. 6.

It further requires that public participation in IDB activities observe the principles of inclusiveness, pluralism, opportunity for timely input, transparency, efficiency, and cultural sensitivity.[39] It also provides that IDB management and governance bodies must be apprised of all the comments received in consultation practices, even though the strategy recognizes that it may not be possible to incorporate all of the inevitably diverse views into any given decision. The IDB is also required to strive to inform consultation-process stakeholders of the process's outcome.

The human rights approach to development also emphasizes participation, and in particular looks to empower people to make their own decisions rather than being the passive objects of choices made on their behalf.[40] United Nations High Commissioner for Human Rights recommendations regarding key aspects of human rights principles that should be adopted in the Poverty Reduction Strategy process state that the participation of poor people in decisions affecting their lives is as important as the end result.[41] The chapter by Stewart and Wang in this volume states that participation spans a spectrum of levels of engagement of the individuals and groups involved in a decision-making process:

At one end, 'information sharing' involves very limited decision making powers but potentially important knowledge transfers. At the other lies 'initiation and control', which implies a high degree of citizen control over decision making. In between, 'consultation' exists when participants are able to express opinions but their perspectives are not necessarily incorporated into the final product; 'joint decision making', on the other hand, gives participants the shared right to negotiate the content of strategy.[42]

Stewart and Wang also note that it is important to consider who has been consulted, and whether their opinions were incorporated. They stress participation because they consider that long-term success in realization of rights 'requires that they be embedded both in legal/constitutional process and in the norms of society'.[43] And they conclude that realizing negative human rights may require comprehensive empowerment, with a particular focus on the poor.

What is the level of participation in IDB rule of law projects, and who is involved in decisions? During the stage of project preparation, information sharing and consultation are used extensively. Information is readily available

[39] Ibid. 6–8.
[40] See United Kingdom Department for International Development, *Realising Human Rights for Poor People: Strategies for Achieving the International Development Targets* (London, U.K.: DFID, October 2000) 7.
[41] Office of the High Commissioner for Human Rights, *Draft Guidelines: Human Rights Approach to Poverty Reduction Strategies* (United Nations: 2002).
[42] F. Stewart and M. Wang, 'PRSPs within the Human Rights Perspective', this volume, Chapter 17, Section 173.　　　　　[43] Ibid. at Section 17.1.

about the ongoing process of decision making regarding what are the major challenges confronting the sector, which of those challenges the IDB might be suited to assist with, and what sort of program content (objectives, activities, budget, impact indicators) it would make sense to undertake. This information is available on our website as project documents begin to be prepared and approved, and these decisions are taken jointly with those who will be implementing the project. For the set of stakeholders who will be involved in project implementation—and this usually means a government entity such as, for example, a public defenders' office—both joint decision making and initiation and control are involved. That is, we design projects shoulder to shoulder with the people who will carry them out, including many of their initiatives in the final design. We seek out civil society groups working in the legal field, and organizations representing populations who will be affected by a project such as, for example, leaders of indigenous groups, and invite them to consultations. These consultations often result in changes in our assessments of the sector and in our recommendations regarding project design.

What is hard for us, in justice projects, is figuring out ways to involve many or at least some reasonable number of the citizens who might be affected by a project. Partly, this is hard because the target beneficiary population may include everyone in the country—this would be the case if we are supporting, for instance, a project to bring about criminal procedure reform. We are likely to survey some portion of the affected population to find out about their needs and interests. We are likely to include project components on social communication and outreach, on media training, and on civic education. We are likely to allot some project money to a fund to be used to extend grants to civil society organizations or individuals who come up with good ideas for improving justice delivery in their communities. But the rights approach demands that we acknowledge that this is not the same thing as enabling citizens, and especially poor citizens, to engage with us in making decisions about what should be done to improve the justice sector.

Stephen Golub suggests a civil society approach he terms 'legal empowerment' as a way to ensure that disadvantaged populations have greater say in the legal reforms carried out to benefit them.[44] The IDB funds a number of small grant projects, often centered around rural development or development of poor inner city areas, that act much like the legal empowerment programs Golub recommends, in which citizens identify the needs most pressing for them and determine how best to pursue their goals. Some of our justice projects, too, work exclusively with civil society groups, in which case those groups are joint decision makers with the Bank and the government.

---

[44] S. Golub, 'Less Law and Reform, More Politics and Enforcement: A Civil Society Approach to Integrating Rights and Development', this volume, Chapter 13.

When justice loans to governments include grant funds set aside for civil society organizations seeking to undertake projects in the justice sector, those organizations can propose the projects that they deem most useful for their communities, which amounts to initiation and control. But the IDB was established to make it possible for governments to receive loans for public development purposes at rates lower than they would otherwise be able to obtain in the market, our shareholders and principal clients are the governments of our member countries, and most of our projects work with and through government entities. This is not necessarily bad: some much-needed justice reforms, such as the overhaul of the legal aid and public defense systems, or prison or police reform, call for approaches that bring about serious reform inside state institutions rather than inside civil society organizations. Nonetheless, serious thinking about how to make IDB justice projects more bottom-up would undoubtedly be useful. How to more effectively involve citizen participation in these projects strikes me as an issue that the rights approach brings to the front and center of conversations about how to make IDB justice projects more effective and sustainable.

12.4.2 Targeting Systems of Discrimination and Exclusion

A rights perspective encourages an emphasis on projects that seek to end patterns of discrimination and exclusion. This is clearly a major focus of the IDB, as well, in its efforts to reduce poverty. Our four Social Programs divisions, the Poverty and Inequality Unit, Women in Development Program Unit, and Indigenous Peoples and Community Development Units, focus heavily or exclusively on projects that aim to end discrimination and exclusion. As mentioned earlier, all of the IDB's projects, justice projects included, are scrutinized for their impact on women, minorities, disadvantaged groups, and the environment, and most if not all of our justice projects concern themselves with broadening access to justice in some measure.

Still, it is fair to say that IDB justice programs tend to consider that negative rights are for *all*, discriminating against neither rich nor poor, and that improvements in the quality of decisions and the quality of operations in courts or prosecutors' offices or legal aid offices will automatically advantage the poor. The rights focus may ask us to keep in mind, in each justice project, that courts and other justice system institutions are involved in the struggle to 'balance the transformative aspect of law against the law's natural tendency to favour those rich enough to invoke it'.[45] What might it mean for the IDB to pay constant attention to this balance?—perhaps that we work to a greater

---

[45] Burt Neuborne, 'The Supreme Court of India' 1 *International Journal of Constitutional Law* 476 (2003) 503.

degree on enabling public interest litigation, more projects with Offices of Human Rights Ombudsmen, or a continued focus on standards of ethics and public accountability for justice sector officials in every one of our justice projects. How to better focus on the legal system's role in creating or dismantling patterns of discrimination and exclusion may be a line of analysis that could be fleshed out in conversations with the human rights community.

12.5 CONCLUSION: SUCCESSES AND LIMITATIONS OF THE IDB'S INCORPORATION OF HUMAN RIGHTS PRINCIPLES INTO ITS LENDING ACTIVITIES IN THE JUSTICE ARENA

Our policies and projects show that human rights concepts influence the content of our justice projects in many ways. It is largely due to international and regional human rights conventions and guidelines, which provide consensus around core issues, that the IDB can work in the justice arena. Human rights conventions establish the basic definitions of concepts such as fair trials and judicial independence, which in turn become outcomes for IDB-funded projects. International treaties set standards for the ways in which countries are to recognize indigenous law and conflict-resolution methods, standards for treatment of litigants and prisoners, standards for eliminating discrimination against women and minorities, and those standards inform the content of IDB justice projects. Human rights standards also help define areas in which the IDB should not work, which is especially helpful in sensitive areas such as police and prison reform.

The existence of a regional system of human rights institutions in Latin America influences the structure of IDB justice projects, which often work through organizations such as the Inter-American Court of Human Rights or the Inter-American Institute of Human Rights. Human rights organizations are implementing IDB projects, and they are also acting as watchdog institutions to help assure that human rights violations do not occur in IDB-funded projects to improve criminal justice systems in countries in the region.

Section 12.3, above, explores the ways in which the IDB is using human rights principles to interpret our Charter provisions regarding what areas of justice we can work in, to define project content, to establish methodologies for pre-project diagnostics, and to define indicators for project success and impact. The section points out that human rights principles are significantly influencing content and methodologies of IDB justice projects.

It strikes me that those of us working on rule of law in the IDB should know more about human rights in terms of content and practices. Many of the people working on justice projects in the IDB are not human rights experts, many of them are not lawyers (the fact that we are not all lawyers is probably a good thing: diverse perspectives from anthropologists and other social scientists, experts in environmental governance, etc. bring a great deal to justice projects). But we should probably all be familiar with the international human rights framework—that should be part of the standard training for those working on rule of law reform.

I have to admit, in this regard, that I do not think the human rights community is helping us much. When I look around to understand what a rights-based approach to rule of law reform would look like, I do not find many materials. Although the IDB will always be a development and not a human rights institution, I think the human rights community would get a hearing if it were to develop some solid ideas as to how a rights-based approach might make rule of law programs more likely to get rights enforced in a sustainable manner. Project teams working on IDB programs all share one characteristic: we are pressed for time in every single project we work on, having been asked to design reform programs effectively and efficiently. That means that IDB staff have two interests: how to make projects more effective; and how to do that in a way that does not take so much time as to be unrealistic within institutional constraints. Staff will be interested in rights approaches (and anything else) that look to suggest ways to make projects more effective, and they will be paying attention to whether those approaches can be applied within reasonable time frames.

The hard fact in rule of law in Latin America is that the articulation of rights in international agreements and in country constitutions has not meant that those rights have become real on the ground for most citizens in the region. It is not a problem of legislation or even, in many areas, of consensus: most government leaders would opt for a fair, efficient, accountable, professional, non-corrupt, non-discriminating judiciary and prosecutors office and police force and prison administration if they could get it; so would most civil society organizations and most citizens and think tanks and universities and maybe even most bar associations. A process of change for the better is certainly occurring in the justice sector in Latin America, but it is a slow and difficult one. The IDB has not defined its role as holding countries' feet to the fire if they are not living up to their international human rights obligations; it sees its role as assisting those countries who have the political will but lack the resources to improve their justice systems. But even as we behave like a development institution and not a human rights organization, human rights principles play a large role in our work. It seems to me that greater understanding of the rights perspective and greater application of rights methodologies and goals could improve the ability of IDB rule of law projects to help bring justice on a sustainable basis to ordinary citizens. Certainly that is something worth experimenting with.

The important interplay between human rights and our justice reform work seems to me to indicate that IDB policy makers got it right when they decided to define the relationship between democratic governance, rule of law, human rights, and development, and to ask that that relationship be recognized in IDB projects. It takes a certain amount of institutional courage to state that the IDB will work on promoting independence of the judiciary, criminal justice reform, citizen security, and ensuring the legal control of the use of force, with police forces, prisons, and restorative justice organizations. We run the risk of funding projects and supporting agencies that may be involved in human rights abuses, even as our projects seek to strengthen human rights protections. This is a new and delicate equation for the IDB, and time will tell whether we can establish and maintain the proper balance. We have begun by trying to define clearly in policy and strategy what we are after, and by working broadly in the justice arena in countries of the region, to gain experience that will inform future policies and projects.

13

Less Law and Reform, More Politics and Enforcement: A Civil Society Approach to Integrating Rights and Development[1]

STEPHEN GOLUB

13.1 INTRODUCTION AND OVERVIEW

Foreign aid for law-oriented programs in developing countries tends to ignore the poor, whom it ultimately is supposed to benefit. The problems with many such aid programs include an expensive, excessive, and often fruitless focus on judiciaries and other state legal organizations.[2] An alternative strategy for law-oriented work, one with an arguably better track record, features support for civil society, for capacity building and other legal services for the poor, and frequently for incorporating activities and sectors beyond the legal sphere. This 'legal empowerment' approach better integrates rights[3] and development than does the dominant 'rule of law orthodoxy' reflected in state-centered programs.

I do not intend a blanket condemnation of those orthodox programs. I instead argue that legal empowerment represents a preferable alternative to rule of law (ROL) orthodoxy in some contexts, a valuable complement in others, and an effective strategy for blending rights-oriented work into many other development fields. Both within and beyond the legal sphere, then,

---

[1] This chapter partly summarizes and builds on the author's previous research and writing, most notably a lengthier paper prepared for the Carnegie Endowment for International Peace. See Stephen Golub, *Beyond Rule of Law Orthodoxy: The Legal Empowerment Alternative*, Carnegie Endowment Working Paper No. 41, Rule of Law Series, Democracy and Rule of Law Project (Washington D.C.: Carnegie Endowment for International Peace, October 2003), available at http://www.ceip.org/files/pdf/wp41.pdf.

[2] I employ the term 'organizations' rather than the more commonly used 'institutions' for reasons I explain later in this chapter.

[3] I generally use the term 'rights' rather than 'human rights' in this chapter because the former more comprehensively embraces the range of international, national, and local laws, regulations, and standards addressed by the chapter and the activities it describes.

many development initiatives would benefit from legal empowerment that features support for international and local civil society.

There are three main thrusts to this chapter: *first*, many law-oriented development programs focus too much on law and not enough on politics. For over a decade (and for nearly 20 years in some contexts) judicial and legal systems reform and its underlying assumptions—embracing a narrowly defined justice sector comprising judges, lawyers, prosecutors, prisons, laws, and the state organizations in which and through which they operate—have constituted the predominant paradigm for attempting to integrate rights and development, by building the rule of law. While not entirely without merit, this 'rule of law orthodoxy' has been too technical, narrow, and, ironically, law-oriented in nature. It pays insufficient heed to the reality that the legal problems and solutions of the poor typically reside outside the conventional 'justice sector', pertaining instead to administrative law, non-judicial dispute resolution, civil society efforts, and a host of other forums and processes.

ROL orthodoxy also tends to downplay the inherently political nature of those problems and solutions. (I mean 'political' not in the sense of competition through elections or for control over government, but rather in terms of struggles for resources and, to employ Sen's characterization, for 'development as freedom'.)[4] It accordingly minimizes the panoply of 'non-legal' strategies and actions—community organizing, group formation, political mobilization, advocacy, use of media, literacy training, and livelihood development, to name a few—useful and even necessary to effect solutions.

Second, the development community's infatuation with legal reform and with the much-misunderstood concept of institutional reform (discussed below) can blind us to the reality that such changes do not necessarily lead to the enforcement of rights or the alleviation of poverty. Reform is of course important, but development programs often treat it as an end in and of itself, rather than as a means toward the implementation of human rights and poverty alleviation. In most transitional and developing societies, laws are not self-implementing: even the best laws and state organizations do not protect the rights of disadvantaged populations if those groups lack the appropriate assistance and capacities to bring about implementation.

Third, in many contexts, civil society offers the best and sometimes the only option for providing that assistance and building those capacities. It accordingly is a crucial element in getting pro-poor laws implemented, for turning rights into reality, and for simultaneously employing the law to help alleviate poverty. In addition, funding for civil society arguably has a better track record of concretely effecting rights and development than the state-oriented efforts constituting ROL orthodoxy. Where there is a legal element involved, however explicitly or implicitly, such civil society work translates

---

[4] See Amartya Sen, *Development as Freedom* (New York: Alfred A. Knopf, 2000).

into legal empowerment—the use of legal services and other development activities to increase disadvantaged populations' control over their lives. (In fact, depending on the goals and nature of the activities, legal empowerment equals political, women's, or economic empowerment. What makes it 'legal' in nature is its attention to rights and law.)

The multifaceted nature of legal empowerment varies from context to context, but typically features assisting and building the capacities of the disadvantaged, with lawyers playing a supportive rather than lead role and the courts often not a part of the equation. It also can enable home-grown, bottom-up reform initiatives preferable to the adoption of development agencies' imported advice and models. In many contexts such support for legal empowerment best takes the form of core funding for non-governmental organizations (NGOs), together with or instead of NGO capacity building. Regrettably, in most countries funding for civil society to undertake legal empowerment work is limited or non-existent. The point is not to abandon aid to state organizations (at least not in some contexts). Rather, it is important to redress the imbalance through which such organizations receive far more development funding than civil society efforts that often address the rights and needs of the poor far more effectively.

While there is value in legal empowerment becoming a significant part of ROL programs, the even greater potential is to incorporate it into 'mainstream' socio-economic development sectors (for example, natural resources management, public health, and rural development), thereby advancing both sectoral and broader goals. Such incorporation can fuel an effective integration of rights and development. It would remove law-oriented work from the programmatic ghetto which ROL orthodoxy often inhabits, operating apart from other development fields and insights.

13.2 ROL ORTHODOXY: THE DOMINANT PARADIGM

13.2.1 The Nature of ROL Orthodoxy

The ROL orthodoxy embraced by much of the international donor community should not be confused with the rule of law itself, which incorporates such qualities as government subservience to the law, predictability of legal outcomes, and widespread access to justice. In contrast, ROL orthodoxy is a set of ideas, activities, and strategies geared toward bringing about the rule of law in a top-down, state-centered manner, often as a means toward ends such as economic growth, good governance, or poverty alleviation.

The word 'orthodoxy' is used because this approach to integrating rights and development is the dominant paradigm and, until relatively recently, has been largely unquestioned in many development organizations and other circles. My aim at this point in the chapter is to briefly question its dominance without suggesting that ROL orthodoxy is always inappropriate. I do so in order to set the stage for the core of the chapter, which argues for the civil society approach embodied by legal empowerment as an alternative paradigm in some contexts and as a complement to the orthodox approach in others.

Key features of ROL orthodoxy include:

- A focus on state organizations, particularly judiciaries.
- This focus is largely determined by the legal profession, as represented by a nation's jurists, top legal officials, and attorneys, and by foreign consultants and donor personnel.
- As a result, there is a tendency to define the legal system's problems and cures narrowly, in terms of courts, prosecutors, contracts, law reform, and other organizations and processes in which lawyers play central roles.
- Where civil society engagement occurs, it usually is as a means toward the end of the development of state organizations: consulting (NGOs) on how to reform the (narrowly defined) legal system, and funding them as vehicles for advocating reform.
- There tends to be a reliance on foreign expertise, initiative, and models, particularly those originating in industrialized societies.

These features translate into funding a distinct array of activities, including:

- drafting new laws and regulations;
- training judges, lawyers, and other legal personnel;
- establishing management and administration systems for judiciaries;
- support for judicial and other training/management institutes;
- building up bar associations;
- courthouse construction and repair;
- purchase of furniture, computers, and other equipment and materials; and
- international exchanges for judges, court administrators, and lawyers.

This orthodox paradigm is most salient in the economic sphere and among the multilateral banks that today are major sources of funds for ROL programs. The rule of law is considered essential for long-term development because it provides security for foreign and domestic investment, property and contract rights, international trade, and other vehicles for advancing economic growth. Thus, Martinez asserts that 'the liberalization of market economies . . . requires a legal order that is fair, efficient, easily accessible, and predictable'.[5] ROL orthodoxy has an even wider reach, however, as a set of

---

[5] Nestor Humberto Martinez, 'Rule of Law and Economic Efficiency' in E. Jarquin and F. Carrillo, eds., *Justice Delayed: Judicial Reform in Latin America* (Washington D.C.: Inter-American Development Bank, 1998) 3.

programs that emphasize top-down, state-centered approaches for pursuing a diversity of goals, beyond building better business environments. It infuses many law programs supported by the U.S. Agency for International Development (USAID), for example, which seeks to advance the rule of law as part of its democracy and governance (DG) program.[6] Much of the law-oriented work of the United Kingdom's Department for International Development (DFID) emphasizes state agencies as vehicles for promoting the poor's personal safety, security of property, and access to justice (SSAJ).[7]

I should emphasize though, that such funding agencies do not pursue orthodox approaches exclusively or everywhere (nor do other aid agencies that focus law-oriented aid on the state). In a number of countries, both USAID and DFID support legal services for the disadvantaged. DFID's SSAJ program explicitly aims to address the poor's urgent legal problems such as lack of security for their persons and property—though generally in a top-down, state-centered manner—rather than promoting a better business climate that may indirectly benefit them.

Even the multilateral banks are starting to support non-orthodox legal activities such as legal services. But this is being undertaken in a cautious and very limited way, with non-legal divisions often taking the lead.

International aid agencies also increasingly consult with the disadvantaged and civil society in setting priorities, and a few are broadening their perspectives on legal systems. DFID's policy papers, for example, emphasize how crucial it is to ascertain the legal needs of the poor and the multifaceted ways in which dysfunctional legal systems perpetuate their poverty.[8] But a fundamental distinction must be drawn: civil society consultation is far different than actually supporting civil society to serve the disadvantaged and build their legal capacities.

13.2.2 The Limitations of ROL Orthodoxy

The problems with the dominant paradigm reach far beyond the limitations of consultation, however. This suggests the need for alternative and complementary approaches for integrating rights and development. There is considerable doubt in some quarters of even the multilateral banks about

[6] See http://www.usaid.gov/democracy/index.html. DG programs' link to ROL is reflected in the fact that the name of the USAID unit that originally promoted the rule of law in the 1980s was the Office of Administration of Justice and Democratic Development. However, although USAID's DG goals are not inherently business-oriented, one assumption is that good governance creates the proper environment for business to flourish.

[7] See, for example, DFID, *DFID Policy Statement on Safety, Security and Accessible Justice* (London: DFID, 2003).

[8] See, for example, DFID, *Justice and Poverty Reduction* (London: DFID, 2000).

ROL orthodoxy in both principle and practice. In recent years, the criticism that I have heard within the banks' legal units addresses:

- The need to concentrate on administrative law and practices, since 'these affect far more people than judiciaries and the justice sector'.
- The weak potential of most judicial reform programs, 'but if they want the funds I guess we'll provide them'.
- The related problem of making a commitment to aid a country's judiciary without seeing much potential to productively do so, leading to a request to 'please come up with something to do with it if you can think of anything'.
- The frustrations of working with state judicial and legal organizations, with the preference to 'just work with civil society if we could'.

Commentaries that challenge the assumptions or activities of ROL orthodoxy—in whole or in part, explicitly or implicitly—reach far beyond the merely anecdotal. Several question the notion that the rule of law is necessary for (as opposed to the possibility that it correlates with) development.[9] Perhaps even more telling, many others emphasize the problematic track record, prospects, or assumptions pervading international assistance that takes the form of ROL orthodoxy.[10] Other sources challenge the

[9] See, for example, Patrick McAuslan, 'Law, Governance and the Development of the Market: Practical Problems and Possible Solutions' in Julio Fernandez, ed., *Good Government and the Law: Legal and Institutional Reform in Developing Countries* (London: Macmillan, 1997) 25–45; Richard Posner, 'Creating a Legal Framework for Economic Development' 13 *World Bank Research Observer* 1 (1998); Thomas Carothers, *Promoting the Rule of Law Abroad: The Problem of Knowledge*, Carnegie Endowment Working Paper No. 34, Rule of Law Series, Democracy and Rule of Law Project (Washington D.C.: Carnegie Endowment for International Peace, January 2003); Richard E. Messick, 'Judicial Reform and Economic Development: A Survey of the Issues' 14 *World Bank Research Observer* 117 (1999); Amanda Perry, 'International Economic Organizations and the Modern Law and Development Movement' in A. Seidman, R. B. Seidman, and T. Walde, eds, *Making Development Work: Legislative Reform for Institutional Transformation and Good Governance* (New York: Kluwer Law International, 1999) 19–32; Amanda Perry, 'An Ideal Legal System for Attracting Foreign Direct Investment? Some Theory and Reality' 15 *American University International Law Review* 1627 (2000); Katarina Pistor and Philip A. Wellons, *The Role of Law and Legal Institutions in Asian Economic Development: 1960–1995* (New York: Oxford University Press, 1999); John Hewko, *Foreign Direct Investment: Does the Rule of Law Matter?* Carnegie Endowment Working Paper No. 26, Rule of Law Series, Democracy and Rule of Law Project (Washington D.C.: Carnegie Endowment for International Peace, April 2002); Frank Upham, *Mythmaking in the Rule of Law Orthodoxy*, Carnegie Endowment Working Paper No. 30, Rule of Law Series, Democracy and Rule of Law Project (Washington D.C.: Carnegie Endowment for International Peace, September 2002); and Daniel Kauffman, *Misrule of Law: Does the Evidence Challenge Conventions in Judiciary and Legal Reforms?* draft manuscript, July 2001, available at http://www.worldbank.org/wbi/governance/pdf/misruleoflaw.pdf.

[10] See, for example, U.S. General Accounting Office (GAO), *Foreign Assistance: Promoting Judicial Reform to Strengthen Democracies*, Report GAO/NSAID-93-140 (Washington

assumption, articulated by the World Bank's Legal Vice-Presidency, that the 'the rule of law is built on the cornerstone of an efficient and effective judicial system'.[11] They detail the greater utilization by the poor of other processes and forms of dispute resolution and the greater relevance of those alternatives to directly impacting poverty.[12]

One final set of assumptions underlying the dominant paradigm merits particular scrutiny. The rationale for ROL orthodoxy also has intellectual roots in a general emphasis on the roles of institutions in development. The notion is that institutions are so fundamental that they must be addressed by international actors for development to unfold.[13]

But what do we mean by 'institutions'? There is a difference between how the concept is considered in development literature and how it is applied in development practice, at least in the legal field. North defines institutions as 'the rules of the game in a society, or . . . the humanly devised constraints that shape human interaction . . . both formal constraints—such as rules that human beings devise—and informal constraints—such as conventions and codes of behavior'.[14] He further distinguishes between institutions as 'the

D.C.: GAO, 1993); Harry Blair and Gary Hansen, *Weighing In on the Scales of Justice: Strategic Approaches for Donor-Supported Rule of Law Programs*, USAID Development Program Operations and Assessment Report No. 7 (Washington D.C.: USAID Center for Development Information and Evaluation, February 1994); Martin Bohmer, 'Access to Justice and Judicial Reform in Argentina', in Columbia University Budapest Law Center/Public Interest Law Initiative, Open Society Justice Initiative, and Fundacja Uniwersyteckich Poradni Prawnych, *Fifth Annual Colloquium on Clinical Legal Education, 15–16 November 2002* (Warsaw, Poland: 2002); William C. Prillaman, *The Judiciary and Democratic Decay in Latin America: Declining Confidence in the Rule of Law* (Westport, CT: Praeger, 2000); Thomas Carothers, *Aiding Democracy Abroad: The Learning Curve* (Washington D.C.: Carnegie Endowment for International Peace, 1999); Robert S. Moog, *Whose Interests are Supreme? Organizational Politics in the Civil Courts in India* (Ann Arbor, MI: Association of Asian Studies, 1997); John Blackton, 'Egypt Country Report', background paper prepared in 2000 for USAID and International Foundation for Election Systems (IFES), *Guidance for Promoting Judicial Independence and Impartiality*, Revised Edition (Washington D.C.: USAID Office of Democracy and Governance, January 2002); Hector Soliman, 'Philippines Country Report', background paper prepared for USAID and IFES, *Guidance for Promoting Judicial Independence*; and U.N. Development Programme, *The Status of Governance in Indonesia: A Baseline Assessment*, draft report produced on behalf of the Partnership of Governance Reform in Indonesia, October 2000.

[11] World Bank Legal Vice Presidency, *Legal and Judicial Reform: Observations, Experiences and Approach of the Legal Vice Presidency* (Washington D.C.: World Bank, 2002) 5.

[12] See, for example, Danish Ministry of Foreign Affairs, Danida, *Evaluation: Danish Support to Promotion of Human Rights and Democratisation, Volume 2: Justice, Constitution and Legislation* (Copenhagen: Evaluation Secretariat, Ministry of Foreign Affairs, 2000); and DFID, *Safety, Security and Accessible Justice*, above n. 7.

[13] Although there is some movement by DFID and other donors toward a sector-wide approach in the legal field, this promising development often translates into a focus on specific state institutions.

[14] Douglass C. North, *Institutions, Institutional Change and Economic Performance* (Cambridge, UK: Cambridge University Press, 1990) 3–4.

underlying rules of the game' and organizations (legislatures, regulatory bodies, firms, universities, unions, etc.) that both influence and are influenced by institutions.[15] In ROL orthodoxy, however, the emphasis on institutions typically reflects how the term commonly is used: institutions *as* organizations, with a particular focus on state institutions/organizations such as judiciaries.

This is not to suggest that a divergence between development theory and practice in ROL orthodoxy hinges on a semantic distinction. But the way in which this matter plays out in the legal sphere merits attention. The programmatic focus of the dominant paradigm is on the judiciary and other state organizations, as well as laws as institutions. The result is that the paradigm places great faith in a narrow view of the integration of rights and development.

In contrast, a full-fledged scrutiny of how 'the rules of the game' affect the poor would consider the diverse factors that shape both the formal and informal manifestations of how the poor interact with the law and would take both formal and informal types of law into account. That analysis might in turn learn from and apply strategies that enable the poor to affect the rules of the game and put reforms into practice. Formal laws and state organizations of course would play important parts in this analysis. But the view of how they operate—and whether and how they can be reformed—would only be part of the picture. Underlying factors that shape their operations and alternative strategies that do not wholly or mainly rely on state organizations would be taken into account. In sum, there would be less emphasis on formal laws and reforms, and more attention to politics and enforcement. There also would be, as I now discuss, more attention to civil society in many contexts.

13.3 LEGAL EMPOWERMENT: A CIVIL SOCIETY APPROACH TO INTEGRATING RIGHTS AND DEVELOPMENT

13.3.1 The Nature of Legal Empowerment

Legal empowerment is the use of legal services and other development activities to increase disadvantaged populations' control over their lives. Its distinguishing feature is that it involves the use of any of a diverse array of legal services for the poor to help advance those freedoms. At the same time, this legal work is often only a part (and not necessarily the most important part) of an integrated strategy that features other development activities—group formation, literacy training, or livelihood development, for instance. In fact, depending

---

[15] Douglass C. North, *Institutions, Institutional Change and Economic Performance* (Cambridge, UK: Cambridge University Press, 1990) 5.

on the goals and nature of the activities, legal empowerment equals political, women's, or economic empowerment. What makes it 'legal' in nature is its attention, whether central or supplemental, to rights and law.

Legal empowerment clearly is not the only mechanism, and not even the only civil society-oriented mechanism, through which rights and development can be integrated. But it is a uniquely concrete approach, in that its activities help the disadvantaged understand, act on, and enforce their rights, generally in concert with NGO or community-based organization (CBO) allies.

In contrast with ROL orthodoxy, a strategy of fostering legal empowerment typically involves:

- An emphasis on strengthening the roles, capacities, and power of the disadvantaged and civil society.
- The selection of issues and strategies flowing from the evolving needs and preferences of the poor, rather than starting with a predetermined, top-down focus on judiciaries or other state institutions.
- Attention to administrative agencies, local governments, informal justice systems, media, community organizing, group formation, or other processes and institutions that can be used to advance the poor's rights and well-being, rather than a focus on a narrowly defined justice sector.
- Civil society partnership with the state where there is genuine openness to reform on the part of governments, agencies, or state personnel, and pressure on the state where that presents an effective alternative for the disadvantaged.
- Great attention to domestic ideas and initiatives, or experience from other developing countries, rather than Western imports.

Legal empowerment involves two terms that merit explication: 'legal services' and 'other development activities'. As defined here, admittedly in a very broad way, legal services for the poor include:

- counseling, mediation, negotiation, and other forms of non-judicial representation;
- litigation, both on an individual basis and through public interest lawsuits designed to affect policies, establish precedents, or otherwise benefit large numbers of people;
- enhancing people's legal knowledge and skills through training, media, public education, advice, and other mechanisms;
- development of and services by paralegals (laypersons, often drawn from the groups they serve, who receive specialized legal training and who provide various forms of legal education, advice, and assistance to the disadvantaged); and
- advocating, advising on, and building the poor's capacities regarding legal, regulatory, and policy reform.

The 'other development activities' in legal empowerment's definition are any that complement legal services, but which themselves are not inherently law-oriented in nature. They include community organizing, group formation, political mobilization, and use of media. They may also involve other development fields, such as livelihood development, microcredit provision, literacy training, reproductive health services, and natural resources management.

Legal services can, in and of themselves, constitute and produce legal empowerment. But experience indicates that greater impact frequently flows when they are integrated with other development activities. Some links may be indirect, implicit, or initially unplanned, as in the case of a group formed for another purpose (such as microcredit) that later makes use of legal services.

Legal empowerment ultimately is about poverty alleviation, both in the narrow and broader meanings of the term. It contributes to poverty alleviation, narrowly defined, by improving material standards of living and accordingly addressing what is often called 'income poverty'. Thus, women may be less poor and have more control over their lives if they gain the right to work (and resulting employment) or a fair share of inheritances. The same applies to farmers and urban populations who respectively obtain land ownership and secure housing.

Most of the development community also views poverty alleviation more broadly, however, often using such terms as *human poverty* and reflecting the fact that the poor 'often define their own lot not so much in terms of "lack of money" as an absence of empowerment'.[16] Poverty alleviation accordingly includes increasing the capacities (such as legal knowledge and skills), participation, opportunities, and, most fundamentally, power of the poor concerning actions and decisions that affect their lives. This power dimension is inherently political in nature, transcending technical and legal perspectives. Women are less poor and have more control to the extent that they affect government or family decisions, whether effecting gender equity or halting domestic violence. Minority groups similarly may benefit where their cultures are respected and/or they influence majority perspectives and policies. Legal empowerment helps achieve those goals.

Legal empowerment should also be viewed in the context of evolving thinking that illuminates how empowerment, human rights, freedom, development, and poverty alleviation blend in practice: Reaching one such goal often equals achieving another. In *Development as Freedom*, Sen addresses the processes through which people assume increasing control over their lives.[17] The UN Development Programme has similarly linked human development, human rights, and seven essential freedoms.[18] The World

---

[16] Stephen Browne, 'Governance and Human Poverty', *Choices* (September 2002), at http://www.undp.org/dpa/choices/2001/september/essay.pdf.   [17] See Sen, above n. 4.
[18] See UNDP, *Human Development Report 2000* (New York: Oxford University Press, 2000).

Bank advocates 'facilitating empowerment' as a key means of attacking poverty.[19] Thus the notion of control contained in the definition of legal empowerment is equivalent to both freedom and power for the poor.

A number of donors have in effect endorsed the kind of cross-sectoral integration represented by legal empowerment, though carrying it out in practice has been more problematic. A USAID study found that the linkages of its democracy and governance sector (which includes law programs) 'with other sectors are an emerging development success story'.[20] DFID policy guidance highlights how its justice sector work can pursue entry points through public health, rural livelihood, or urban development projects.[21]

The potential benefits of legal empowerment work are implied in various academic studies that point to the importance of citizen engagement and civil society capacity building, organization, or political influence in improving the lives of the disadvantaged.[22] It is important to emphasize, however, that legal empowerment is not about participation for participation's sake: it aims for concrete improvements in the lives of the disadvantaged.

By building the poor's legal capacities, organization, and NGO links, legal empowerment may be particularly promising in connection with views of community-driven development articulated by Gupta et al.[23] For instance, it can help forge useful links with higher level government officials in situations where their local subordinates serve local vested interests—again, the political dimension. This can enhance project monitoring, accountability, and performance and of course serve broader development goals.

13.3.2 Legal Empowerment and Civil Society

Legal empowerment is typically a *civil society* approach to integrating rights and development for a diversity of reasons. Research commissioned by the Asian Development Bank, the World Bank, and the Ford Foundation

[19] See World Bank, *World Development Report 2000/2001* (New York: Oxford University Press, 2000) 7.
[20] USAID Center for Development Information and Evaluation, *Linking Democracy and Development: An Idea for the Times*, USAID Evaluation Highlights No. 75 (Washington D.C.: USAID, December 2001) 1.
[21] DFID, *Safety, Security and Accessible Justice*, above n. 7, 15.
[22] See, for example, J. Gaventa, A. Shankland, and J. Howard, eds, *Making Rights Real: Exploring Citizenship, Participation and Accountability, IDS Bulletin*, Vol. 33, No. 2 (April 2002); M. Edwards, 'NGO Performance—What Breeds Success? New Evidence from South Asia' 27 *World Development* 371 (1999); P. Evans, 'Development Strategies Across the Public-Private Divide' 24 *World Development* 1033 (1996); J. Fox, 'How Does Civil Society Thicken? The Political Construction of Social Capital in Rural Mexico' 24 *World Development* 1089 (1996).
[23] Monica Das Gupta, Helene Grandvoinnet, and Mattia Romani, *Fostering Community-Driven Development: What Role for the State?* World Bank Policy Research Working Paper 2969 (Washington D.C.: World Bank, January 2003).

indicates that the most successful and creative legal services for the poor across the globe generally are carried out by NGOs, often in partnership with CBOs, or occasionally by law school programs that effectively function as NGOs.[24] This does not absolutely preclude a key role for the state: sufficiently motivated government units also can carry out legal empowerment programs. However, civil society groups typically demonstrate more dedication, flexibility, and creativity than state institutions and personnel.

My aim here is not to replace ROL orthodoxy with a similarly rigid civil society paradigm that naively glorifies NGOs as a panacea for poverty or presents them as universally altruistic and honest. It is crucial for donors to separate the wheat from the chaff in supporting civil society. Where civil society is weak, it is important to put in place long-term programs that help build it. Furthermore, legal empowerment is often about good governance; state institutions are extremely relevant.

In fact, legal empowerment can and sometimes does involve NGOs in building the capacities of state institutions and their personnel, through training, informal interaction, and other devices. Thus, this approach may be civil society-focused, but it can crucially affect and benefit governments and governance. Legal empowerment is not necessarily about avoiding the state. It often functions as an alternative route for improving state entities' operations and enforcement of citizens' rights.

What NGOs and their partner populations can do far more effectively than donors, simply by virtue of civil society efforts to extract co-operation from state organizations, is identify government agencies and personnel who manifest dedication, working with them and around their reform-resistant colleagues. In this way, civil society acts as a supportive force for co-operative elements in the state and as a countervailing force against anti-reform elements. Legal empowerment catalyzes this progress in the many contexts where legal knowledge and action are important parts of reformist strategies.

Again, this certainly is not to suggest that all development NGOs are effective, competent, and dedicated. Some are far more interested in developing their own resources than in helping the populations they purportedly serve. Others are so small as to limit their effectiveness—though we should not underestimate the ability of modestly staffed legal services NGOs to generate ripple effects of impact through paralegal development, working in

---

[24] See Stephen Golub and Kim McQuay, 'Legal Empowerment: Advancing Good Governance and Poverty Reduction' in *Law and Policy Reform at the Asian Development Bank* (Manila: Asian Development Bank, 2001), available at http://www.adb.org/Documents/ Others/Law_ADB/lpr_2001.asp?p = lawdevt; Daniel Manning, *The Role of Legal Services Organizations in Attacking Poverty* (Washington D.C.: World Bank, September 1999); and Mary McClymont and Stephen Golub, eds., *Many Roads to Justice: The Law-Related Work of Ford Foundation Grantees Around the World* (New York: Ford Foundation, 2000), available at http://www.fordfound.org/publications/recent_articles/manyroads.cfm.

partnership with other civil society elements, and contributing to policy and law reform advocacy coalitions. But where these constraints apply, they constitute arguments for such steps as involving responsible international NGOs, expanding the pool of persons who could sincerely engage in legal empowerment work (through law school programs, for example), and gradually building up civil society reach and capacities.

In some war-torn, politically oppressed, or particularly impoverished societies, the presence, power, and capacities of NGOs that could engage in legal empowerment are limited. One would not expect assertive advocacy of women's rights, for instance, in areas controlled by many Afghan warlords. How development agencies might cautiously support legal empowerment under such circumstances is a matter to which I will return. For now, suffice to say that the same obstacles constricting the legal services work of legal NGOs in problematic contexts similarly limit the prospects for building effective judiciaries and other state legal organizations. Precluding support for the former while pushing ahead with the latter is a lopsided approach to rights and development.

13.3.3 Activities and Impact

An expanding array of studies documents, in both qualitative and quantitative ways, the impact of this civil society approach to rights and development. Most of that impact falls under the broad rubric of poverty alleviation. But as noted above, in many instances it also can be framed in other general terms (such as justice, human rights, freedom, and, of course, empowerment) or more specific goals (such as improved governance, gender equity, or environmental protection).

In recent years, international studies have illuminated manifold ways in which civil society mobilization, in the form of legal empowerment, reinforces both rights and development. These vehicles are inherently political in nature and that makes enforcement of reforms at least a limited reality. A seven-nation, year-long examination of legal empowerment, conducted by the Asia Foundation for the Asian Development Bank (ADB), concludes that this work 'helps to advance good governance and to reduce poverty in both substantial and subtle ways'.[25] The documented benefits range from Thai constitutional and consumer protection reforms to implementation of Pakistani women's voting rights and access to credit.

A multi-country review for the World Bank describes the poverty-alleviating impact of legal services NGOs and, by implication, of legal empowerment.[26] It highlights, *inter alia*, how such NGOs help enforce social and economic

[25] Golub and McQuay, 'Legal Empowerment' above n. 24, 12.
[26] Manning, above n. 24.

rights, facilitate the poor's engagement with local governance, assist women to reform laws that bar them from participating in development, and promote recovery in post-conflict countries.

Finally, the Ford Foundation's eighteen-month review of legal services and related work by its grantees across the globe finds considerable positive impact on equitable and sustainable development, as well as on human rights, civic participation, and government accountability.[27] The resulting book describes the impact of university-based legal aid clinics, paralegals, public interest litigation, and law-related research, even in China, Eastern Europe, and other areas where civil society is relatively weak.

The picture I so far have sketched of these civil society initiatives mainly depicts community-oriented work, but it can build on that work to have national impact (as well as impact on local levels, which in some countries are where important policy and legal decisions are made). The Ford Foundation, World Bank, and Asia Foundation/ADB reports, as well as other sources, document that impact to various degrees, describing numerous instances in which legal empowerment has helped generate such macro-level reform.

For example, the approximately two dozen Philippine legal services NGOs collectively known as Alternative Law Groups (ALGs) have contributed to scores of national regulations and laws concerning agrarian reform, violence against women, indigenous peoples' rights, environmental protection, and a host of other issues.[28] Arguably, they have played roles in the bulk of such pro-poor reforms over the past decade, providing legal expertise and other assistance for coalitions of NGOs, national federations of poor people's organizations, and (sometimes) religious groups. It must be emphasized, however, that the ALGs derive their expertise and credibility from working on a grass-roots level, where they make the most of existing laws while learning what reforms the disadvantaged want.

Legal empowerment strategies also can effectively use public interest litigation (PIL) in those circumstances where there are prospects of winning and implementing favorable decisions, where it does not exclude the disadvantaged from decision making, and where its use does not preclude complementary approaches. This approach can be found in South Africa, for instance, where PIL has built on a base of community and political activism. This has yielded a string of landmark court victories stretching over more than two decades, both under apartheid and since the transition to democracy. These victories have vindicated South Africans' rights and increased their control over their lives.

---

[27] Stephen Golub and Mary McClymont, 'Introduction: A Guide to This Volume' in McClymont and Golub, *Many Roads to Justice*, above n. 24, 5.

[28] The 'alternative' in their name reflects their development-oriented perspectives and how their operations differ from private legal practice and traditional legal aid in the Philippines.

It is important to emphasize, however, the degree to which public interest litigation draws on political mobilization and works with community concerns, not least in the identification of clients and cases. For example, as explained by the head of Legal Resources Center's Constitutional Litigation Unit:

We represent organisations which are themselves the focus for a social movement—for example the Treatment Action Campaign, which is mobilising and leading the campaign for the provision of anti-retroviral drugs to prevent transmission of HIV, and to treat HIV/AIDS.[29]

Though activist, sophisticated civil society certainly facilitates both grass-roots and national legal empowerment initiatives—witness South Africa and the Philippines—legal empowerment can have national impact even in less conducive settings. The Sustainable Use of Biological Resources Project (SUBIR) in Ecuador, undertaken by the international NGO CARE in collaboration with local Afro-Ecuadorian groups in the remote north-west part of the country, has generated national reforms and local benefits. For example, the government banned division of communal land into individual lots in response to these groups' identifying such changes as threatening their identity and way of life. The communities also successfully lobbied for Afro-Ecuadorian recognition in the national constitution, including protection for their collective rights as indigenous peoples.[30] As with the Philippines and South Africa, the national impact of this legal empowerment initiative in Ecuador has built on a base of localized work and impact, often political in nature.

In a far different context, Senegal, UNICEF provided financial and communications support that helped local NGOs and village women mobilize against female genital mutilation (FGM). The efforts facilitated the women learning about both their rights and the health implications of FGM. The result was the parliament's adoption of legislation banning the practice.[31] Once again, the national reform was linked to local mobilization, in this case:

...teaching women first about their human rights, followed by other modules related to problem solving, health, and hygiene...Although the project had originally targeted 30 villages...project organizers, facilitators and participants succeeded in expanding its reach. In November 1999 approximately 80,000 people from 105 villages participated in a ceremony during which they issued a public declaration ending the practice...[32]

---

[29] E-mail correspondence from Geoff Budlender to author, 7 January 2003.
[30] CARE, 'CARE Ecuador's Subir Project', unpublished summary produced by CARE International's Ecuador office, October 2000.
[31] Available at http://www.unicef.org/newsline/99pr1.htm.
[32] International Center for Research on Women and the Center for Development and Population Activities, 'Report-in-Brief', Promoting Women in Development Program (Washington D.C.: 1999) 1–2.

Even where foreign initiative has been involved in these developments, it tends to respond to local needs and priorities. In contrast, whatever the justifications for most ROL orthodoxy endeavors, it would not seem that the poor would see better courthouses or judicial administration as issues to rally around.

The Ecuador and Senegal experiences indicate that, where local civil society requires assistance, international organizations can play important facilitating roles regarding legal empowerment. In the end, this work must respond to community priorities, perhaps even more so when the implications are national rather than local. And preferably, the only foreign support that is needed is financial. But as with other development initiatives, there is room for other assistance (such as capacity building) where necessary.

At the same time, it is important not to become too enthralled with national impact, for changes in laws and policies mean little to the poor if they are not enforced, and enforcement is the exception rather than the rule in most developing countries. A value of civil society engagement is that it can constitute a feedback loop, through which grass-roots experience feeds legal and regulatory change, which further grass-roots work in turn converts from reform on paper to reform in practice.

With the caveat about national impact in mind, it is useful to turn to survey research, sometimes complemented by focus groups and other mechanisms, that documents the positive rights and development impact of civil society initiatives employing legal services. A World Bank assessment of an NGO legal services program it supported for poor women in Ecuador found, *inter alia*, that, as compared to demographically similar non-client populations, clients experienced significantly less domestic violence, higher rates of child support payments, and enhanced self-esteem.[33] These results have powerful, positive implications for poor women and children. For instance, above and beyond its immediate damage, the poverty-exacerbating impact of violence against women has been well documented by the World Bank and other sources.[34] Reducing the violence yields numerous benefits.

The Asia Foundation/ADB study similarly used quantitative inquiries in two of the seven countries it covered, with similarly favorable results. Survey research, focus groups, and interviews with government officials in the Philippines all indicated that farmers who received NGO capacity building

---

[33] World Bank, *Impact of Legal Aid: Ecuador* (Washington D.C.: World Bank, February 2003) 11–12.

[34] See, for example, Lori L. Heise with Jacqueline Pitanguy and Adrienne Germain, *Violence Against Women: The Hidden Health Burden*, World Bank Discussion Paper No. 255 (Washington D.C.: World Bank, 1994); and Andrew Morrison and María Beatriz Orlando, 'Social and Economic Costs of Domestic Violence: Chile and Nicaragua' in Andrew Morrison and María Loreto Biehl, eds., *Too Close to Home: Domestic Violence in the Americas* (Washington D.C.: Inter-American Development Bank, 1999).

and related legal services brought about more successful implementation of a government agrarian reform program than did farmers who did not receive such services. The research also suggested follow-on impact, in terms of greater productivity, income, farm investment, and housing quality among those recipients of legal services.[35]

In Bangladesh, the Asia Foundation/ADB study determined that two broad-based NGOs that integrate legal services with mainstream develop-ment work achieved manifold poverty-alleviating impacts. Based on com-parisons between their member populations and demographically similar control groups, these results included: restraining the widespread but illegal practice of dowry;[36] successful citizen participation in joint actions and in influencing local government decisions; fostering positive community atti-tudes toward women's rights and participation in governance; use by the poor of government-managed lands that local elites otherwise seize; and dramatically less reliance on those elites for dispute resolution. The same research found that a third NGO, a legal services group that specializes in community-level mediation, achieved modest impact in some of these regards and an even greater impact on reducing elite dominance of dispute resolution.[37]

Finally, quantitative research on a USAID-funded Women's Empower-ment Program in Nepal similarly suggests the value of integrating rights and development work. The program combined literacy classes, arithmetic education, microenterprise development and training, microcredit access, non-formal legal education, and advocacy-oriented group strengthening for 100,000 women. An impact study found that women involved with this project benefited in several ways when compared to control populations. They initiated eight times as many actions for 'social change' (such as community development and health projects, and campaigns against domestic violence, alcohol, and gambling by men), participated 30 per cent more in family and independent income allocation decisions, and better understood the importance of keeping their daughters in school.[38] A subsequent

[35] See 'Appendix 1: The Impact of Legal Empowerment Activities on Agrarian Reform Implementation in the Philippines', in Golub and McQuay, 'Legal Empowerment', above n. 24, 135–149.

[36] Dowry is the payment of money, livestock, or other material goods by the bride's family to the family of the groom, in order to secure a marriage. After the agreed payments are made and marriage occurs, the dowry demands by the groom's family frequently escalate and are accompanied by violence or other abuse against the wife.

[37] See 'Appendix 2: The Impact of Legal Empowerment on Selected Aspects of Know-ledge, Poverty, and Governance in Bangladesh: A Study of Three NGOs', in Golub and McQuay, 'Legal Empowerment', above n. 24, 135–149.

[38] Rajju Malla Dhakal and Misbah M. Sheikh, *Breaking Barriers—Building Bridges— A Case Study of USAID/Nepal's SO3 Women's Empowerment Program* (Washington D.C.: Asia Foundation, 1997).

review concluded that literacy was a key element in the women's empowerment but reaffirmed the value of integrating legal and quasi-legal (advocacy-oriented) components with the literacy training and other mainstream development activities.[39]

The findings of these various studies should be approached with some caution; the methodologies may well benefit from refinement in the future. These inquiries, therefore, should be seen as modest initial forays into issues that merit far more scrutiny. Still, the results suggest the possibility of powerful impact that affects poverty more directly and cost-effectively than does the dominant ROL paradigm. Those results also indicate that incorporation of legal services holds great potential for mainstream socio-economic development efforts.

13.3.4 Paralegal Development

Though this chapter cannot detail all of the activities carried out under the rubric of legal empowerment, paralegal development merits special mention because it transcends many societies and sectors. As noted above, paralegals are laypersons, often drawn from the groups they serve, who receive specialized training from NGOs and who provide various forms of legal education, advice, and assistance to the disadvantaged.

Depending on their level of sophistication and the needs of the populations they help, paralegal activities may range from providing basic information about people's rights on the one hand to representation in government administrative processes on the other. Paralegals can constitute key (and cost-effective) intermediaries in improving governance and getting laws enforced regarding such diverse arenas as agrarian reform, violence against women, natural resources, and a host of other issues.[40]

A recent review of Kenyan access to justice projects supported by DFID summarizes a key respect in which this aspect of civil society work is political even more than it is legal in nature:

The empowering influence of rights awareness is a catalyst for social organization and community-driven development. The activist function recognizes that legal rights ... can often [best] be achieved working outside of the [formal, narrowly defined legal system] and particularly through articulation of rights using advocacy and lobbying in an activist manner. The point is that the legal system itself can sometimes work against the best resolution of a particular problem.[41]

[39] Gwen Thomas and Ava Shrestha, *Breaking New Ground: A Case Study of Women's Empowerment in Nepal, Women's Empowerment Program* (Kathmandu: USAID/Nepal, 1998).
[40] See, for example, Stephen Golub, 'Nonlawyers as Legal Resources for Their Communities' in McClymont and Golub, *Many Roads to Justice*, above n. 24.
[41] South Consulting, 'Kenya Civil Society Programme: Review of Access to Justice Projects', Final Draft (Nairobi: South Consulting, 2001) 29.

One could quibble with that final point, by positing a broad definition of the legal system, embracing the impact of advocacy and lobbying on rights and government decision making. Regardless, the substance of the insight remains the same: paralegal efforts (and other civil society activism) often achieve the most when they transcend conventional confines of legal systems and legal work.

13.3.5 Engaging Law Students and Young Lawyers

A growing array of funding organizations, NGOs, and law schools are paving the way for future legal empowerment work and other progressive activism by providing opportunities for law students and young lawyers to work with disadvantaged populations, sometimes in ways (such as training paralegals or NGO employment) that transcend traditional legal practice. Nevertheless, the development and human rights communities as a whole pay insufficient heed to such work and the impact it generates.[42] Expanding attention and support would benefit legal communities, legal systems, and, above all, impoverished populations.

A number of options are open to concerned organizations. These options are exemplified by selected current and recent initiatives:

- a region-wide strategy, such as that undertaken by the Soros foundations network and its Open Society Justice Initiative in collaboration with a partner NGO, the Public Interest Law Initiative, in approximately 70 law schools across the former Soviet Union (FSU), Central and Eastern Europe (CEE), and Mongolia;
- building a national clinical legal education (CLE) network, as the China's Clinical Legal Education Association is doing,[43] and a national network that accesses government funds and affects the overall delivery of legal services in a country, as South Africa's Association of University Legal Aid Institutions has done, in both cases assisted by the Ford Foundation;
- adopting a sector-specific approach, as the United Nations High Commissioner for Refugees (UNHCR) and its partner NGO, Legal Assistance through Refugee Clinics, have done in helping to launch numerous law school clinics focusing on political asylum in several FSU and CEE nations;

[42] For a more detailed description of this work and impact, see Stephen Golub, *Forging the Future: Engaging Law Students and Young Lawyers in Public Service, Human Rights, and Poverty Alleviation*, an Open Society Justice Initiative Issues Paper, January 2004, at http://www.justiceinitiative.org/publications/papers/golub.

[43] See *Summary Report of Work in 2003*, Clinical Legal Education Association Committee, which can be obtained from Committee Secretary Liu Donghua at secretary@cliniclaw.cn or director@cliniclaw.cn.

- interaction with legal services and human rights NGOs, as exemplified by the roles that law school experience played in young attorneys launching the NGOs constituting the Philippines' Alternative Law Groups, a network engaged in human rights and development, and that these NGOs in turn play in employing law school graduates and shaping their careers; and
- facilitation by international NGOs, such as the Center for International Environmental Law's work with human rights and environmental NGOs, young lawyers, and law students from across the globe.

CLE-related efforts to engage law students and young lawyers in legal empowerment and other public service of course should be seen in terms of public interest law, human rights, and justice. But in many contexts they should be equally viewed as advancing poverty alleviation, good governance, and other development goals. Thus, they merit financial and technical assistance from various branches of the development and human rights communities. Just as UNHCR has helped launch refugee law clinics at numerous law schools, other sector-specific institutions should consider supporting sector-specific CLE and related work—concerning gender, children's rights, or the environment, for instance.

13.3.6 A Rights-Based Approach

Among its other applications, legal empowerment should be seen as a strategy for implementing the still-evolving concept of a rights-based approach (RBA) to development. As the Office of the High Commissioner for Human Rights (OHCHR) has noted, 'there is no single, universally agreed rights-based approach, although there may be an emerging consensus on the basic constituent elements'.[44] The OHCHR expands on this to suggest that 'while a State is primarily responsible for realizing the human rights of the people living within its jurisdiction, other States and non-State actors are also obliged to contribute to, or at the very least not to violate, human rights'.[45] It also highlights empowerment, participation, international human rights' universality, and numerous other concepts and activities as key elements of the approach.

This is not to say that legal empowerment *always* equals a rights-based approach. The important issue of whether RBA is universally appropriate is a complex matter that merits more attention than the parameters of this paper

---

[44] Office of the High Commissioner for Human Rights (OHCHR), 'Rights-Based Approaches: Is There Only One Rights-Based Approach?' at http://www.unhchr.ch/development/approaches-05.html.

[45] OHCHR, *Draft Guidelines: A Human Rights Approach to Poverty Reduction Strategies*, para.13, at http://www.unhchr.ch/development/povertyfinal.html#*.

permit. Regarding gender-oriented work, for instance, the issue may entail: consideration of what should be done where local leaders might welcome a women's development initiative that could pave the way for rights-based work down the line, but would bar it if the NGO involved emphasizes rights from the outset; or, as in rural Bangladesh (as discussed below, concerning the NGO Banchte Shekha) or Nepal, where reforming mediation practices and treatment of women can involve altering community dynamics even more than it features citation of rights; or respect for how impoverished women themselves see their needs and rights, since legal empowerment places a premium on the perspectives and priorities of the poor themselves. There are ways, then, in which legal empowerment certainly is rights-oriented, but might not always be rights-based—at least as the latter term is sometimes understood.

Nevertheless, in a crucial way legal empowerment *is* a rights-based approach: it uses legal services to help the poor learn, act on, and enforce their rights. And as indicated above, the realization of empowerment, freedom, and poverty alleviation typically equals enforcement of various human rights.

13.3.7 Integration and Mainstreaming

In a related vein, a salient feature of legal empowerment is the way in which it literally integrates rights and development by blending legal services with group formation, community organizing, or other activities pursued under the rubric of 'mainstream' socio-economic development fields—for example, rural development, public health, reproductive health, housing, natural resources—and by addressing the goals and concerns of those fields. Most of the above illustrations involve such mainstreaming. The work of the Philippines ALGs, for example, is sometimes called 'development lawyering' or 'developmental legal services' for this reason.

But it is not only legal services NGOs that take the lead in this work. Other NGOs conduct legal empowerment work, sometimes in combination with legal services groups but also on their own. Banchte Shekha, a women's movement based in rural Bangladesh, has improved its members' capacities and well-being through a combination of literacy training, rights education, livelihood development, consciousness raising, organizing, and alternative dispute resolution (ADR). By building on all of these other activities, the Banchte Shekha ADR—a reformed version of a traditional dispute resolution process called *shalish*—both addresses mistreatment of women and ameliorates the power imbalances that often tilt ADR against them. The Asia Foundation/ADB survey research cited above documents the NGO's positive impact on dowry, women's status, and other issues.

A regrettably short-lived, USAID-supported initiative in Bangladesh in the 1990s further illustrated the value of integrating law and mainstream development, in this instance legal and family planning services. Communities whose members were already familiar with reproductive health NGOs readily accepted the integrated programs. In introducing legal services, those NGOs drew on the goodwill established through many years of contact with the communities. An evaluation of the project confirmed the mutually beneficial relationship of the two kinds of work.[46]

One of the more significant forms of mainstreaming takes place where legal services facilitate agrarian reform and other land tenure improvements for the disadvantaged (for example, helping women with land claims stemming from divorce or inheritance). As the aforementioned Asia Foundation/ADB study demonstrates, NGO lawyers and paralegals can contribute to the success of agrarian reform programs.

The Rural Development Institute (RDI) similarly documents the positive contribution of legal services to such programs.[47] It also highlights the roles civil society can play more generally, urging aid donors to 'provide technical assistance and financial support to indigenous non-governmental organizations, labor organizations, and other broad-based groups that are able to conduct essential grassroots education and organizing on the land reform issue.'[48] The manifold benefits of agrarian reform include poverty-alleviating increases in crop production, nutritional welfare, and incomes; ripple effects on economic growth; and contributions to democratic development and stability.[49]

There are promising attempts at mainstreaming taking place within that most mainstream of development organizations, the World Bank. For instance, the Vice-Presidency's Legal and Judicial Reform Practice Group has started to support legal services for the poor. Nevertheless, the effort is constrained by the relative paucity of funds devoted to such services: less than $400,000 of a $10.6 million judicial reform project in Ecuador, for instance, and even this project was an exception to the rule and a very minor aspect of its overall, state-centered efforts.[50] In the past, such initiatives have been hampered by reluctance on the part of the Legal Vice Presidency's leadership to provide more than token support to legal services for the poor or to endorse

---

[46] Karen L. Casper and Sultana Kamal, 'Evaluation Report: Community Legal Services Conducted by Family Planning NGOs', a report prepared for The Asia Foundation's Bangladesh office, Dhaka, 1995.

[47] See, for example, Leonard Rolfes Jr. and Gregory Mohrman, *Legal Aid Centers in Rural Russia: Helping People Improve their Lives*, RDI Reports on Foreign Aid and Development No. 102 (Seattle: Rural Development Institute, February 2000).

[48] See, for example, Roy L. Prosterman and Tim Hanstad, *Land Reform in the 21st Century: New Challenges, New Responses*, RDI Reports on Foreign Aid and Development No. 117 (Seattle: Rural Development Institute, March 2003) 24.

[49] Prosterman and Hanstad, ibid., 4–7.

[50] See World Bank, *Impact of Legal Aid: Ecuador* (Washington D.C.: World Bank, February 2003).

law-oriented projects not operating under its rubric—a situation that many hope will change with the recent appointment of a new General Counsel.

In the meantime, other branches of the bank pursue efforts to better integrate rights and development, sometimes with legal empowerment dimensions. Its Africa Region Gender and Law Program provides matching grants for state and civil society organizations to implement legal services for women—though its funds are very limited and insecure in comparison with what the bank spends on judicial reform. The Indonesia office has launched a Justice for the Poor project that includes integration of legal services into certain mainstream development programs supported by the bank. The Poverty Reduction and Economic Management Network has provided intellectual leadership in researching and reporting on issues confronting legal systems and how they related to poverty alleviation. Whether these initiatives constitute a trend or just isolated efforts remains to be seen.

13.3.8 Questionable Assumptions about Sustainability

One final consideration regarding civil society support pertains to the question of sustainability. An important argument for investing in state legal organizations is that only such a course can offer sustainable development. The assumption is that, once reformed, the institutions will deliver improved services without continued donor input. A converse assumption is that NGOs and other civil society groups do not merit ongoing development funding, especially to cover core costs such as salaries and office rental, because they are inherently unsustainable organizations. Another is that they must generate funding themselves after a few years of donor financing. A variation on this theme is that NGOs should receive only project or capacity building support.

The DFID Bangladesh (DFIDB) office accordingly illuminates a tension and assumption that many development agencies struggle with in many countries:

... a striking conclusion is that there are few DFIDB projects with government that are making a higher-level impact for poor people . . . Thus, DFIDB faces a dilemma; it can achieve a more direct impact on poor people in the short term (possibly up to 2015) by working outside government, but for the long term only sustained improvement in delivery of public services will reach the majority of the population. A balance needs to be struck between the short and long-term goals.[51]

At least as applied to the legal field, three development myths account for this understandable but questionable assumption about the nature of sustainable change. The first is that support for state legal organizations

---

[51] DFID Bangladesh (DFIDB), *Country Strategy Review: 1998–2002 Bangladesh* (Dhaka: DFIDB, August 2002) 22.

will yield self-sustaining reforms and enduring improvements in services. As already suggested, however, the undertow of societal forces may undo promising changes: If legal systems' operations are in fact more the effect than the cause of social conditions, many systems that experience temporary improvements may revert to form. In addition, the chief justices, ministers of justice, and other officials who lead or agree to reforms often come and go rather rapidly—ironically, more rapidly than the leaders of supposedly unsustainable NGOs. The dedication to reform sometimes resides in those officials, not their institutions.

Often, however, even that personal dedication is not present. Commenting on a USAID project's short-term cuts in delay in pilot courts in Egypt, a former USAID official asks:

Will that hold up when we leave? Will our changes move from our court clusters to the nation as a whole? Have we brought about a genuine change in judicial culture—one in which reducing case delay is valued? I fear that the answer will, three years after we are gone, be 'no' to most if not all of my questions. The expat and Egyptian professionals organized within the construct of 'the project' are the ersatz substitute for political will and a new judicial culture. We [the project team] are in fact, variables in the experiment. Our presence strongly impacts the results. Donors don't like to admit how much this is true, but in justice projects in settings like Egypt, I believe it is significantly so.[52]

This problem often manifests itself from the very outset of projects, with funding organizations and personnel, rather than those of recipient countries, initiating and driving ROL programming. The result is a lack of intellectual and political ownership among recipients. Under such circumstances, the sustainability of state-centered initiatives must be questioned.

Proponents of ROL orthodoxy sometimes acknowledge that short-term reforms may hinge on persons rather than institutions and that intellectual ownership is an issue, but legitimately argue that legal systems development must be seen as a long-term process. It accordingly will take many years or even decades before it becomes clear whether and to what extent sustained impact transpires.

Fair enough, but this argument exposes a second sustainability myth: the notion that government initiatives should always be seen as potentially sustainable and that civil society efforts should not. If state institutions merit such ongoing support, especially with highly uncertain outcomes, then why exclude civil society from the long-term mix? A colleague involved with Chinese legal reform once explained to me that her time frame for lasting change is not years or decades, but centuries. While I would not argue for a 100-year development program, the core of her insight is crucial: whether on the state side or the civil society side of development, we are talking about an

---

[52] Written interview with author, 8 May 2001.

extremely long-term endeavor in many societies. Seen in that context, a long-term investment in the civil society soil in which government organizations grow is necessary.

In addition, legal services NGOs and other civil society groups can outlast the appointments of the personnel heading and staffing many government agencies and acquire a greater knowledge of their fields. Over the course of many years, such NGOs often develop track records that enable them to obtain funding from a range of donors. It is even conceivable that long-term societal changes could generate in-country resources for them in some countries, whether from their governments or private sources. With support from the Ford Foundation and other sources, over the past several years the Asia Foundation has pursued an initiative to encourage the growth of indigenous philanthropy in many Asian nations.

The third sustainability myth is that, such philanthropy-promoting efforts aside, legal services and related NGOs in many developing nations must have the potential to become wholly self-supporting if medium-term (not to mention long-term) outside support is to be justified. In fact, NGOs engaged in challenging the status quo may always depend on foreign sources for funding in many parts of the developing world, just as equivalent groups depend on foundations and other outside sources in many far more affluent industrialized societies. It is questionable whether developing country NGOs should even seek government or private money in many contexts, in view of the political strings and uncertainty that could come attached.

We also need to rethink what we mean by sustainability. Rather than *organizational sustainability*, which biases funding toward often ineffective state organizations, a key consideration should be *sustainability of impact*. If a given legal services NGO serves enough people, or builds enough capacities for the poor to effectively assert their own rights, or affects enough laws—such impact is sufficient to justify past and future donor investment. It would be unfortunate for such an organization to cease operating down the line, but its existence would still be validated by the poverty it has helped alleviate and the justice it has helped secure. This patient, realistic approach has implicitly guided some of the better donor support for NGO legal services. It has, ironically, helped sustain those services and enabled recipient NGOs to build expertise and experience that translate into impact over time.

13.4 CONCLUSIONS

13.4.1 Striking a Balance in ROL Aid

Despite this chapter's critical tone toward ROL orthodoxy, it does not aim to dismiss all assistance to state legal organizations. The objective, instead, is to press for a better balance in ROL aid. The best intentions of some donor and government officials notwithstanding, state organizations often are burdened by counter-productive incentives and constraints that outweigh or outlast efforts to ameliorate them. These include entrenched bureaucratic structures, inefficient use of resources, corruption, patronage, gender bias, general aversion to change, and other factors that work against, rather than for, the disadvantaged.

Of course, the very point of working with these organizations is to correct those problems. But this chapter has argued that, at best, this is a very difficult process. At the very least, a long-term perspective—that is, a developmental perspective—inevitably involves taking a balanced approach that incorporates support for civil society. And given the powerful and deep-seated resistance to change in many state legal organizations, there are certainly contexts in which the better investment is civil society-focused. The point is not that civil society support brings about quick, dramatic change, but that few development initiatives ever do so.

In addition, many aid agencies' law programs either do not address the legal priorities of the poor or do so ineffectively because of excessive reliance on state organizations and top-down approaches. A civil society approach to integrating rights and development is not a perfect alternative or comple-ment to such programs, but it is far preferable to the current imbalance characterizing so much of ROL aid.

The bottom line, then, is not that government is always the problem and civil society the solution. Rather, it is necessary to view the justice sector more broadly, which results in greater support for civil society efforts that address a broader assortment of legal issues and that help or pressure government to do its job better. This can yield not only greater agrarian, gender, and environmental justice, but a greater likelihood of effecting safety, security, and access for the poor even within narrow notions of the sector.

13.4.2 Mainstreaming

Blending legal services into mainstream socio-economic development pro-jects (for example, natural resources management, irrigation, rural develop-ment, public health, gender) holds considerable potential to productively integrate rights and development. Educating and enabling the disadvantaged to deal with legal matters immediately affecting them would positively impact human rights, good governance, and project performance. It could also open doors to their positive involvement with other issues important to them. For instance, Filipino farmers and Bangladeshi women respectively organized around agrarian reform and gender concerns have been better able to participate in local governance.

One potentially powerful approach to mainstreaming is to build on the group formation that occurs in many socio-economic development fields. Pulling together disadvantaged persons for purposes of microcredit, livelihood, reproductive health, public health, forest use, irrigation, or literacy training addresses their immediate priorities. It also may be tolerated or even welcomed by local leaders who might resist an initial focus on women's or farmers' rights. Once the group achieves some cohesion and acceptance in the community, members can start discussing legal issues that affect them, with paralegal development and legal activism following further down the line.

What of the many situations, however, in which civil society, legal services, and the basic capacities of the poor are torn by war, crushed by repression, stunted by severe poverty itself, or in the early stages of recovering from any of these situations? Admittedly, legal empowerment works best in the presence of a vibrant civil society. Is it beyond the reach of the poorest of the poor? Legal empowerment (or, for that matter, judiciaries and other state legal organizations) should not automatically be included in the initial mix of development efforts. Sometimes basic socio-economic recovery initiatives should be the priority.

But despite these constraints, the building blocks of legal empowerment can be put in place. As previously discussed, group formation around basic socio-economic needs can provide an entry point for mainstreaming subsequent law-oriented work. A long-term strategy of building up a rights-oriented civil society can benefit both development and human rights. Local conditions permitting, the long road toward the poorest of the poor achieving control over their lives can include introducing them to the very notion that they have rights and the ways in which those rights can benefit their daily existence.

International NGOs may play leading roles in these efforts where local conditions or insufficient capacities bar domestic NGOs and community-based groups from doing so. A goal, of course, is to build those domestic capacities over time.

13.4.3 Working with Civil Society

The effectiveness of any civil society program will hinge not just on *what* work is supported, but *how* it is supported. NGOs that show sufficient progress and potential merit ongoing core funding that enables them to pursue their own agendas in accordance with evolving circumstances and partner populations' priorities, rather than in response to sometimes rigid donor requirements. Similarly, it is best for funding agencies to take a flexible, foundation-like approach. This approach involves gradually identifying grantees, making grants, and building programs as situations evolve. It is in contrast to the project approach that tends to lock in activities at the outset.

This is not to say that the World Bank (or organizations like it) should become the Ford Foundation. But multilateral and bilateral development agencies can set up foundation-like assistance windows for supporting legal empowerment. True, there are political and structural problems in doing so. But there were political and structural problems in the World Bank addressing human rights and corruption, yet it is now doing so.

In view of multilateral banks' (and some bilateral funding agencies') possible difficulties in flexibly working with civil society, one alternative is to channel bilateral aid funds to local and international NGOs familiar with grant-making, legal empowerment, civil society, and/or grass-roots development. Although it would be a great step forward for multilateral banks to mainstream legal empowerment work into their socio-economic development projects, the funds for that work should be grants rather than loans under most circumstances and should flow through organizations that can best take a foundation-like approach.

This does not mean that a given funder should automatically commit itself to many years of support to a given NGO. But it should be open to the possibility of such ongoing assistance if the recipient shows sufficient promise and impact. It *does* mean that donors and other development agencies should move beyond repeatedly uttering the 'NGOs must make themselves sustainable' mantra and take more responsibility for assisting worthwhile partner organizations to move towards sustainability. This can include providing support that expands the fund-raising and financial management capacities of civil society groups, connecting such groups with industrialized society donors that otherwise would be logistically unable to support overseas development, and, as the Ford Foundation and USAID have done, funding self-sustaining endowments for civil society organizations.

Civil society in general and legal empowerment in particular are not panaceas for development challenges having legal dimensions. But they are under-appreciated parts of potential, albeit partial, solutions.

Part E

The Role of the Private Sector in Promoting Human Rights

14

Putting Human Rights Principles into Development Practice through Finance: The Experience of the International Finance Corporation

PETER WOICKE*

14.1 INTRODUCTION

There are three *lingua franca* of globalization: the languages of finance, environmental sustainability, and human rights. Each represents a powerful constituency and is a force for social change that continues gathering momentum. Unfortunately, until recently, there were few experts, and even fewer institutions, conversant in all three languages or in the challenges and potential their underlying activities represent. It is widely recognized today that commercial enterprises—especially large, internationally active enterprises—have an immense and rapidly expanding ability to affect positively the well-being of local communities, regions, and nations. Corporations can similarly help create or improve global public goods such as health care, education, clean air, clean water, and biodiversity. Commensurate with that power, in the mind of the public, comes a measure of responsibility. This shift in global public opinion is driving enterprises to master the three lingua franca, and the International Finance Corporation (IFC) is playing an active role in moving the debate forward.

The IFC, the private sector development lending arm of the World Bank Group, has in recent years become one of the few global financial institutions that has developed experience in the promotion of environmental sustainability. Operating only in the emerging financial markets of developing countries, IFC provides loans, equity, risk management, and technical advice

* The author wishes to thank Margaret Wachenfeld, David Cowan, and Joseph O'Keefe for their assistance in preparing this paper.

to private sector clients who meet minimum environmental and social standards, investing in projects across the full spectrum of an economy, from banks and infrastructure projects to hospitals, schools, and microcredit operations. The question that IFC is now weighing, along with an increasing number of global corporations, is whether and how human rights can be incorporated into its operations.

The question, of course, is more than a matter of rhetorical fluency. The question is whether there is a practical 'business case' for adopting human rights as a means of evaluating risks and opportunities, addressing them, and achieving results that combine profitability and a positive developmental impact. Human rights are not just a way of articulating preferred notional outcomes. They are a way of defining claims by individuals and groups against others, assigning accountability, determining preferences, and measuring outcomes. Human rights claims can be just as explicit, actionable, and complex as financial and legal claims. The question that IFC confronts is, can a global financial corporation such as IFC implement a human rights program that is internally manageable and cost-effective while being credible and accountable to external stakeholders?

14.2 CORPORATE SOCIAL RESPONSIBILITY AND HUMAN RIGHTS

Human rights can be regarded as behavioral and institutional norms expressed as injunctions and aspirations, as well as international legal requirements. Modern businesses, as capitalism has evolved, have slowly assimilated an ever-wider set of these norms, most often those directly related to their operations, such as limits on working hours, worker safety measures, sick leave, non-discrimination requirements, and so on. In some cases, these norms have been imposed by legislation. In other cases, norms have been adopted voluntarily because of idiosyncratic aspirations, societal pressures, or changing political contexts. Sometimes businesses find that they can gain an economic advantage by adopting a new norm that redefines the prevailing rules in their market. Such was the case with the auto manufacturers who began installing seat belts in their cars before laws required it.[1]

IFC, as a development institution, has witnessed these phenomena directly. In 1998, IFC adopted a comprehensive set of environmental and social safeguards for its project finance lending operations, primarily in response to external criticism.[2] However, by late 2000, management of the

---

[1] See http://www.driverstechnologyassociation.co.uk/seatbelts.htm for a short history of the seat belt and safety measures.

[2] See http://www.ifc.org/policyreview for documentation in respect of the policy review, including the Compliance Advisor/Ombudsman (CAO) review released April 2003.

corporation had come to the determination that the safeguards could provide an opportunity for market advantage and perhaps the preferred norm for project finance among major commercial banks. By June 2003, ten major international banks adopted the Equator Principles,[3] a voluntary set of guidelines based on the environmental and social guidelines and safeguard policies of IFC.

Under the principles, subscribing institutions agree, among other obligations, to require for their project finance lending investments the completion of an environmental and social assessment in accordance with the criteria and processes laid out in the relevant IFC safeguard policies. The extent of analysis and intervention is determined by a classification process. For example, projects which are classified as 'likely to have significant adverse environmental impacts that are sensitive, diverse or unprecedented' require that the borrower prepare an environmental management plan (EMP) encompassing mitigation measures, action plans, regular monitoring, management of risks, and implementation schedules. These principles will be applied to project finance activities of these banks, globally and in all industry sectors. Thus far, a total of 24 financial institutions (23 banks and one export credit agency) have adopted the Equator Principles. Collectively, these banks are estimated to account for more than 80 per cent of the worldwide project finance market.[4] In effect, IFC and the Equator Banks created a new set of global business norms for project finance, which represents more than $50 billion in investment annually.[5]

This, of course, is part of a broader trend in recent decades in which high-profile global corporations have committed themselves to corporate social responsibility and included human rights as part of that commitment.[6] Various courts have long held that private actors—although not always companies per se—can be held responsible for human rights violations.

---

[3] http://www.equator-principles.com/principles.html.

[4] The original equator banks accounted for 30% of the market, as stated in the original announcement, and this has risen to the 80% mark as other banks have joined. Figures are derived from Dealogic Projectware and are updated in reports featured on the website www.equator-principles.com.

[5] Although IFC developed the environmental and social standards embodied in the Equator Principles, it does not monitor or enforce implementation of the standards in projects unless it is a project investor.

[6] The UN Global Compact currently has almost 1,700 participants, most of which are companies around the world. The participants commit themselves to making the principles of the Global Compact, including those concerning human rights and labor rights, part of their strategy, culture, and day-to-day operations: see, www.unglobalcompact.org. See also the Business & Human Rights website for a list of 69 companies that currently have human rights policies: www.businesshumanrights.org. A number of corporate views and case studies are included in Rory Sullivan, ed., *Business and Human Rights: Dilemmas and Solutions* (Sheffield, U.K.: Greenleaf Publishing, 2003).

Throughout the 1980s and early 1990s, most companies regarded human rights as irrelevant, with the exception of a few multinationals that faced specific human rights criticisms and campaigns in relation to their operations in South Africa during the apartheid era or trade with the former Soviet bloc. However, faced with increasingly vocal critics of globalization, round-the-clock media coverage, the pressure of increased litigation from non-governmental organizations (NGOs), and the rapidly expanding power of consumer groups, a growing number of the larger global companies have come to regard human rights as relevant not only to their risks—such as their legal and financial liabilities—but to their brands. Here again, the evolutionary pattern is similar: companies first embrace norms reactively, then use the norms to manage prospective risks, and finally come to regard the norms as part of a valuable part of their market strategy.

There is a certain coincidence in the timing of all this. At the very time that businesses at the global and local level are looking to assimilate broader norms of social responsibility that foster the creation of public goods, the public sector is looking to the private sector to take a broader developmental role. This latter trend has been driven by several factors: a growing body of research that indicates far-reaching positive spillover effects from private sector growth (poverty reduction, education, training, technology transfer);[7] an emerging consensus that developmental goals for the poorer nations, such as the Millennium Development Goals, will not be met without a substantial role by the private sector; and the fact that the private sector is simply a much larger piece of the global economic equation than ever before. At the national level, domestic private sector investment averaged 10–12 per cent of gross domestic product (GDP) among the developing nations during the 1990s, compared with 7 per cent for domestic public sector investment and 2–5 per cent for foreign direct investment. Globally, in the early 1990s, there was roughly a one-to-one ratio between private-to-private cross-border capital flows and public-to-public flows. Now, for every one dollar in public sector flows, such as official development assistance, there are three to four dollars in private sector cross-border flows. During 2003, net capital flows to developing nations reached a five-year high of $200 billion, and they continue to gain strength. All of which is to say that, in the rapidly integrating global economy, there is a greater intersection of private self-interest and public goods than ever before.[8]

To demonstrate the changing role of the private sector, the intersection of private investment and the HIV-AIDS tragedy in Africa provides a

[7] This argument is advanced in B. Hadjimichael and M. Klein, *The Private Sector in Development: Entrepreneurship, Regulations, and Competitive Disciplines* (Washington D.C.: World Bank, June 2003).

[8] See World Bank, *Global Development Finance 2004* (Washington D.C.: World Bank, 2004).

convincing example. Despite substantial amounts of funding, implementation of prevention and treatment measures continues to be a huge challenge for the public sector in African nations. The disease also represents a long-term barrier to investment and economic growth. Researchers from the Center for International Health at Boston University have developed a costing model that estimates the present value of new HIV infections in the formal business sector in southern Africa. The study found that new infections can impose additional costs of between 3.4 per cent and 10.7 per cent of a company's payroll, depending on the skill level of workers affected, their level of associated benefits, and the prevalence of the disease in the area.[9] Thus private companies, recognizing both the financial risks and the opportunity to build stronger community support through public health programs, have stepped in to play a constructive role.

An IFC investment in Mozambique further illustrates the possibilities. After years of civil war, Mozambique's economy was in desperate need of jobs. With a major investment from IFC, the construction of the Mozal Aluminum Smelter in 1997 (Mozal I) and subsequent expansion in 2001 (Mozal II) represented the first major foreign investment project in the country. The project single-handedly accounted for 55 per cent of exports or 8 per cent of GDP in 2001, with Mozal I creating 745 jobs where employees were paid 6 times the legal minimum wage. Mozal contracts with many local companies for services, transport, catering, cleaning, and security, so a small and medium-enterprise empowerment and linkages program was developed by IFC's local project development facility to assist small companies in winning and delivering contracts to Mozal II. To date 12 companies have won 21 contacts valued at over $3 million. In 2000, an agreement was made between the Mozal Community Development Trust and IFC to support an additional two years' worth of an HIV/AIDS awareness program already in place. The program consists of intensive, repetitive, face-to-face encounters between trained field workers and community members.

14.3 CHALLENGES IN ADOPTING AND APPLYING HUMAN RIGHTS STANDARDS

The extent of a company's responsibility for the creation of public goods often is defined by law. However, the Mozal case illustrates that social impact and scope of responsibility can be broadened and made explicit in other

---

[9] S. Rosen, J. L. Simon, D. M. Thea, and J. R. Vincent, 'Care and Treatment to Extend the Working Lives of HIV-positive Employees: Calculating the benefits to Business' 96 *South African Journal of Science* 300 (2000). The article outlines a model for calculating the impact on business.

ways, by a combination of social norms, shared interests, and shared values within a company or a community. This is the human rights terrain where most global businesses find themselves today: the gray area between laws and other formal requirements, and new norms, proposed by a variety of sta-keholders who suggest a broader social role. The combined impact of legal and stakeholder pressure has been pronounced, and more companies in the private sector—primarily large companies with strong brands to protect—are now adopting some form of voluntary human rights code or policy. These policies range from general references to the United Nations (UN) Declaration of Human Rights incorporated in mission statements to detailed standards regarding specific types of activities, such as worker rights for employees within supply-chain operations.[10]

As for case law, there has been a slow but advancing body of judicial decisions, especially though not exclusively in U.S. courts, which have accepted the proposition that businesses can be held responsible for human rights violations.[11] In the U.S., most cases have been brought under the Alien Tort Claims Act for human rights violations that are so egregious that they have become a part of customary international law and thus fall within the wording of the statute. These claims usually involve a context where companies have been working with the government and there have been violations of human rights by the state.

IFC, as one of the handful of development finance organizations that has become a global standard-bearer for environmental and social issues, has both an opportunity and arguably a special responsibility to help companies navigate human rights concerns. Over the past year, IFC has researched and reviewed the main international human rights and labor rights conventions and other important multi-stakeholder principles on human rights in the business context and invited a diverse group of human rights experts to discussions with the senior management team. Already, IFC has identified a few of the international texts and instruments, such as additional Interna-tional Labour Organization (ILO) core labor standards[12] and the United

---

[10] See the Business & Human Rights website for a list of 69 companies that currently have human rights policies: www.businesshumanrights.org.

[11] In the United States, there are a series of cases against corporate defendants under the Alien Tort Claims Act in various federal courts in the U.S. Several have been dismissed at the trial level and a number have been appealed. None of the cases against corporate defendants has yet reached the U.S. Supreme Court. Linda Greenhouse, 'Human Rights Abuses Worldwide Are Held to Fall Under U.S. Courts', *New York Times*, 30 June 2004. In an important June 2004 case on the application of the Alien Tort Claims Act to an individual, the U.S. Supreme Court did not conclusively resolve whether corporations could be sued under the act for human rights abuses, leaving the door open to further appeals on this point. See *Sosa v. Alvarez-Machain et al.*, Case No. 03-339, 29 June 2004, US S. Ct.

[12] IFC is looking in particular at the ILO 'core labor standards' set out in the ILO Declaration on Fundamental Principles and Rights at Work (86th Session, June 1998): (a) freedom of

States–United Kingdom Principles on Security Forces and Human Rights[13] as potential supplements to its current standards.

Corporations looking to embrace human rights face several challenges. The first challenge identified by IFC is to begin the process of articulating— for itself and for stakeholders—the many different ways in which the corporation's operations are already contributing to the achievement of human rights. Businesses are full-fledged moral participants in the communities where they operate. They may influence the achievement of human rights in a number of ways. Yet, so much of what they bring to a community—both positive and negative—is rarely quantified, rarely reported, and rarely mentioned. One does not often read in a newspaper about a corporation bringing higher standards on ethnic, gender, or age discrimination into a country that may have a history of such abuses. It is only very recently that one could read about a foreign company providing fairer treatment or better health care for HIV/AIDS victims than its host country. The same type of questions could be posed on the level of media coverage of so many other issues: economic empowerment, education, and the environment. Too often the role of business with respect to human rights is viewed as either neutral or negative when, in fact, it is often quite positive. However, businesses have little incentive to step forward and show leadership on human rights issues if there is not a fair accounting in the public domain of their activities. The balance sheet has to include both the positives and the negatives. IFC has

association and the effective recognition of the right to collective bargaining (Convention concerning Freedom of Association and Protection of the Right to Organise (Convention 87, 9 July 1948, Geneva, Switzerland, *entered into force* 4 July 1950) and Convention concerning the Application of the Principles of the Right to Organise and to Bargain Collectively (Convention 98, 7 July 1949, Geneva, Switzerland, *entered into force* 18 July 1951)); (b) the elimination of all forms of forced or compulsory labour (Convention concerning Forced or Compulsory Labour (Convention 29, 28 June, 1930, Geneva, Switzerland, *entered into force* 1 May 1932) and Convention concerning the Abolition of Forced Labour (Convention 105, 320 U.N.T.S. 291, *entered into force* 17 January 1959)); (c) the effective abolition of child labour (Convention concerning Minimum Age for Admission to Employment (Convention 139, 26 June 1973, Geneva, Switzerland, *entered into force* 19 June 1976) and Convention concerning the Prohibition and Immediate Action for the Elimination of the Worst Forms of Child Labour (Convention 182, 38 I.L.M. 1207 (1999), *entered into force* 19 November 2000)); and (d) the elimination of discrimination in respect of employment and occupation (Convention concerning Equal Remuneration for Men and Women Workers for Work of Equal Value (Convention 100, 29 June 1951, Geneva, Switzerland, *entered into force* 23 May 1953) and Convention concerning Discrimination in Respect of Employment and Occupation (Convention 111, 362 U.N.T.S. 31, *entered into force* 15 June 1960)). IFC already has a safeguard policy covering two of these four core labor standards: see the IFC Policy Statement on Forced Labor and Harmful Child Labor, http://www.ifc.org/ifcext/enviro.nsf/AttachmentsByTitle/pol_ChildLabor/$FILE/ChildForcedLabor.pdf.

[13] Voluntary Principles on Security and Human Rights, http://www.state.gov/www/global/human_rights/001220_fsdrl_principles.html.

started this process by creating a Sustainability Framework, which it is using to identify and track specific developmental contributions that its investments make to a community. IFC is currently reviewing ways to refine the framework to make human rights aspects more explicit and to begin tracking the performance of these factors over time.

The second challenge IFC has identified is defining consistent principles to determine the extent of its practical engagement in human rights. Treaties, covenants, declarations, and national laws often make clear the roles and responsibilities of a state with respect to human rights. However, in many cases, the roles and responsibilities of a corporation in this realm are less clear. Corporations have a much more limited realm of activity and obligations than states, and that realm varies widely depending on the sector and type of commercial activity. Scale also matters. There is a common-sense understanding, for example, that a Chief Executive Officer (CEO) of a multinational corporation may have a different set of obligations than, say, the owner of a fruit stand. There is also presumably a recognition that owners, managers, and investors, by virtue of their proximity to operations and level of control over day-to-day decisions, have somewhat greater responsibilities than those who merely provide a portion of financing. However, there is a huge gulf between a corporate acknowledgement of legitimate, universally recognized rights, on the one hand, and the circumscribed ability of a corporation to address issues beyond its gates in a practical sense, on the other. Capacity to act on that acknowledgement, ability to influence outcomes, accessibility of appropriate venues for redress, the availability of alternative courses of action, the extent to which the causes of abuses are ad hoc, formal, communal, ethnic, or national—all these factors are likely to result in differing levels of imputed or assumed responsibility.

Part of IFC's task, as it proceeds in adopting human rights, will be to help project finance ventures, financial institutions, and the private sector companies it finances to sort through those differences in responsibility in a reasoned way. The boundaries around business responsibility for addressing human rights within its 'sphere of influence' are still in the process of being worked in light of two guideposts: key human rights documents, ranging from general principles to the brief requirements on human rights in the Global Compact to the more detailed guidance in the recent draft UN norms on business and human rights,[14] and practical experience, i.e., the specific human rights guidance that companies are developing for their staff as they confront these issues in their operations, including their supply chains. IFC's role is to take the general principles and the hands-on experience of private sector companies and provide guidance, across a wide spectrum of economic

---

[14] Norms on the Responsibilities of Transnational Corporations and Other Business Enterprises with Regard to Human Rights, U.N. Doc. E/CN.4/Sub.2/2003/12/Rev.2 (2003).

sectors and types of activity in order to inform client CEOs and Chief Financial Officers (CFOs) about circumstances in which IFC might expect them to play a constructive role. That type of guidance will need to be consistent and supported by a credible rationale.

National and international legal systems have already made progress toward defining which human rights are so essential that they are globally applicable and non-negotiable. For example, the injunctions against activities that support genocide and other crimes against humanity are quite clear and strong. However, many other rights are aspirational in nature and subject to a process of local definition, distributional trade-offs, or a pluralistic expression, such as the right to education, the right to housing, or the right to a fair and decent wage. In those cases, finding a way to support the progressive realization of a particular right in a local context within a credible, consistent framework—and within the scope of IFC's mandate—will be difficult. IFC, in effect, will have to determine, across a wide spectrum of economic sectors and types of activity, the specific and tangible responsibilities that it might assume, or that its clients might assume, to intervene and provide solutions.

14.4 HOW COULD THE IFC FACILITATE THE INCORPORATION OF HUMAN RIGHTS PRINCIPLES INTO DEVELOPMENT PRACTICE: A CASE STUDY

In order to see how these issues work out in reality, we can turn to a case study and assess the potential impact on human rights of an IFC project, based on a real project. The name of the company involved and identifying details have been excised to allow for a robust examination of the potential legal issues. The case study was one of three prepared by IFC's Compliance Advisor/ Ombudsman (CAO),[15] who was asked to identify the main human rights issues *that would have been* flagged on appraisal *if* an IFC project team had been asked to address human rights issues. That is, the case studies were conducted as a counterfactual analysis of how human rights principles could have been incorporated into IFC's analysis. The case study extracted here examines projects from a purely private sector perspective—taking issues such as country risk and the country human rights situation as a given, and then analyzing what impact the situation could have on the project, and how they could be addressed within the private sector context. The case study is not a

---

[15] The Office of the Compliance Advisor/Ombudsman was designed to enhance the development impact and sustainability of International Finance Corporation (IFC) and Multilateral Investment Guarantee Agency (MIGA) projects by responding quickly and effectively to complaints from affected communities and by supporting IFC and MIGA in improving the social and environmental outcomes of their work, thereby fostering a higher level of accountability. See http://www.cao-ombudsman.org/.

detailed analysis of the compatibility of IFC's current policies and procedures with human rights requirements, and is based on a desk review of a limited number of project documents, information from outside sources on human rights issues in the countries, and brief interviews with IFC project team members. No site visits were conducted, nor were client staff interviewed, or local NGOs who may have had information about human rights concerns about the projects. The case studies do not prescribe responses for IFC. The cases were designed to stimulate discussion as IFC grapples with how it might incorporate a more explicit recognition of rights into its projects.

The case study was assessed against the International Covenant on Civil and Political Rights (ICCPR)[16] and the International Covenant on Economic, Social and Cultural Rights (ICESCR)[17] to determine which human rights were implicated in the project. Each of the rights was examined in light of: (i) the country, its political characteristics, and the rights that may be at particular risk in the country; (ii) the project sponsor and company and any concerns on human rights issues about the sponsor and the sector of operation; and (iii) the characteristics of the project, considering what rights would and could be affected by the project preparations and operations. Only the main issues were highlighted. This and the other case studies conducted by the CAO take a positive approach to human rights, to remind the private sector of the general duties of all members of society to, as the Universal Declaration of Human Rights says, 'strive by ... progressive measures ... to secure [human rights] universal and effective recognition and observance'.[18]

14.4.1 Summary of Human Rights Issues in the Project

The project was screened against the nine main human rights issues listed below which were identified based on the country, sector, and characteristics of the project. While human rights are first and foremost a government obligation,[19] the private sector has a role to play in respecting and supporting those rights as identified in the discussion below. The analysis in this case

---

[16] G.A. res. 2200A (XXI), 21 U.N. GAOR Supp. (No. 16) at 52, U.N. Doc. A/6316 (1966), 999 U.N.T.S. 171, *entered into force* 23 March 1976.

[17] G.A. res. 2200A (XXI), 21 U.N. GAOR Supp. (No. 16) at 49, U.N. Doc. A/6316 (1966), 993 U.N.T.S. 3, *entered into force* 3 January 1976.

[18] G.A. res. 217A (III), U.N. Doc A/810 at 71 (1948).

[19] This obligation flows from the UN Charter and is reinforced in both the International Covenant on Civil and Political Rights and the International Covenant on Economic, Social and Cultural Rights which recall in their preambles 'the obligation of States under the Charter of the United Nations to promote universal respect for, and observance of, human rights and freedoms'. Article 2 of each Covenant places the obligation on State Parties to respect and implement the human rights set out in each Covenant.

study works through each relevant human right and addresses it from a private sector perspective, bearing in mind the company's relationship with those it affects, limits of the private sector's typical sphere of influence, and the factual situation. The rights are discussed in the order in which they might have arisen in the project itself. Several rights are relevant to the analysis because of the situation in the host country (security concerns, discrimination), other rights are relevant to every private sector project (participation, labor issues, accountability) and yet other rights were screened because they are often implicated in mining projects (indigenous people, right to housing, right to health, right to religion, revenue management). Not all of the rights listed were necessarily of concern in the project, as this would have depended on how the situation unfolded, the company's policies and implementation of its policies, developments in the country, etc. The following discussion is a snapshot of human rights issues that would have been highlighted during appraisal for further discussion with the client about how the issues could be investigated, addressed, and monitored within the project context.

14.4.2 Description of the Project

This 1997 project (no longer in IFC's portfolio) involved a mine in a remote region of a developing country. The project company was a joint venture among a newly formed mining company, IFC, and the national government. The objective of the project was to rehabilitate and expand the existing mining operations and to conduct further exploration in the region. As this was a 'brownfield' mining project (that is, based at an existing mine site), it required only minimal new land purchases and limited construction. The mine had been abandoned in the early 1990s. The rehabilitation involved the modification of the existing open pit mine and processing facility.

IFC acquired a 5 per cent interest in the project company and options to acquire several million shares of the project sponsor. IFC concluded that the project would have the following development impacts: revitalizing the disused mine, thereby generating much needed government revenues and foreign exchange, contributing significantly to the local economy through improved living standards and significantly higher wages for its workforce; providing the national government with first-hand knowledge of commercial transactions; and attracting further foreign investment. IFC considered political stability and security issues, risks related to the sponsor, and management and technical risks. Environmental issues included tailings treatment and disposal, waste-water treatment, a cyanide detoxification plant, potential modification to land use, and the handling of toxic and hazardous materials.

14.4.3 Project Planning Phase: Knowing the Sector and the Company and the Relevant Human Rights Issues

Compared to industrial sectors where it is possible to factor a whole range of issues into account in choosing a project location, extractive industries often have a go/no go decision dictated by the location of the deposit of interest. This lack of flexibility combined with the often considerable term of an investment means that a close look at the country and investment climate are especially crucial in the early stages of project planning. While the stability of a country has always been an important concern to extractive industries, it is only recently that companies and others have begun to explore and understand the role that a country's human rights situation plays in contributing to or jeopardizing that stability. There is not room in this brief case study to address the complex interplay that is an emerging area of study in itself. It is sufficient to say here that respect for human rights by both governments and the private sector is increasingly recognized as playing an important role in improving the stability necessary for a vibrant private sector.

The extractive industries sector has been the most common source of allegations of human rights abuses, issues ranging from land disputes and forcible relocations, violations of indigenous peoples' rights, use of bonded and child labor, denials of freedom of speech, association, and assembly, torture, disappearances, extrajudicial killings and arrests, labor rights violations, and denials of women's rights. Thus, if the project were to be appraised from a human rights point of view, the record of problems in the sector would justify close scrutiny of the relevant human rights issues. Similarly, it would have been prudent to check with national and local NGOs in the country to determine if there had been local concerns expressed about the performance or the operation of the mine before closing. While past concerns might not have been the legal obligation of the new project company, identification of those issues might have provided valuable insights into concerns and problems at the site that might nonetheless still have to be addressed within the project context going forward. Information on the past record of the previous company might also be available from the national regulatory authorities although perhaps of little value.

At the time of IFC's investment, the project sponsor was a newly created Western-based junior mining company, comprised of several experienced mining executives formerly from large multinational mining companies. As such, the project sponsor had no track record in the mining sector. A review of the international human rights media through various online services and NGO sites did not turn up any results for the project sponsor or project company. This is not surprising, given that the project sponsor and project company were both new and relatively minor players in mining.

14.4.4 Knowing the Country Context

Some states have such poor human rights records that they have become known as pariah states (such as Sudan, Myanmar, North Korea). Doing business is so difficult in these states, if not prohibited by international sanction, that there is very little foreign direct investment. Similarly, countries with a clear record of severe human rights violations such as Rwanda in 1994 or Cambodia under the Khmer Rouge would also not be hospitable to investment not just for human rights reasons, but business reasons as well. The long-running debate about engagement versus disengagement in countries that are not pariahs, but nonetheless have poor human rights records, is shifting. Many human rights organizations, including the UN Office of the High Commissioner for Human Rights and mainstream NGOs, now advocate responsible engagement in developing countries with poor human rights records as a positive support to improving human rights.[20]

In the case at hand, the host country's economy collapsed as a result of its civil war and is only slowly recovering. It is the poorest country in the region with approximately 80 per cent of the population below the poverty line. Hidden unemployment is very high, at 40 per cent. Most of the workforce is engaged in agriculture. The country has a rural, mixed ethnicity population, with people inhabiting only 7 per cent of the country's territory. A civil war soon followed after independence. Although the most active phase of the war lasted only months, hostilities continued for years afterwards. The civil war resulted from clan-based tensions, and an ensuing power struggle. With the signature of a UN-brokered peace accord and power-sharing agreement, though still not fully implemented, the UN mission of observers eventually withdrew, but small-scale fighting prevails and high levels of criminal and political violence, including hostage taking, continue.

The current regime is authoritarian and, despite the periodic but flawed elections, the government has remained in power. The government's human rights record is poor, though there have been some small improvements recently. In particular, citizens' rights to change their government remain restricted. The government uses arbitrary arrest and detention, and arrests people for political reasons. While in detention, detainees are often subject to torture that is then used in trials. The government restricts freedom of assembly and association through strict control over political organizations. There was some easing of restrictions on freedom of speech and the media in the last year. The government denied requests by the International

---

[20] Office of the High Commissioner for Human Rights, *Human Rights in Development: What, Why & How* (Geneva: United Nations, 2000) 9.

Committee of the Red Cross to make prison visits in a manner consistent with its standard modalities.

Women experience domestic violence, discrimination, and trafficking. They have diminishing educational opportunities and are subject to increasing poverty. Discrimination against religious and ethnic minorities is also prevalent. Child labor is a problem and there is some bonded labor.

With respect to labor rights, domestic law recognizes the right to freedom of association, the right to strike, and the right to collective bargaining. However, the law also appears to give the government a free hand to restrict those rights. There is a high degree of trade union membership in the country. In practice, collective bargaining does not take place, nor do strikes, driven in part by the dire status of the economy and the wish not to open conflict after the civil war that has taken place in the country.

The strained and complex ethnic relationship with the neighboring state is only now improving. Past difficulties resulted in closing of the border or restricting the flow of goods, and a good deal of the border between the countries remains seeded with land mines.

The host country is not in the group of pariah states, but it nonetheless has a well-recognized poor human rights record. IFC would not be expected to forgo investments there on the basis of the country's human rights record alone, as doing so would deprive the local population of much needed investment and development.

14.4.5 A Human Rights Approach to Business Dealings with an Authoritarian Government

While blanket prohibitions to exclude investments in countries on the basis of the country's human rights record alone (unless that record is egregious as noted above) are regarded as counter-productive, extra caution is necessary where the investment involves a contractual connection with an oppressive government. Contractual connections can be seen as an endorsement of the government's human rights record or as financially enabling the government to use resources to repress the population, or involving a joint venture partner in any human rights abuses the government might be perpetrating in connection with the project and thus exposing it to charges of complicity or benefiting from human rights abuses.

The CAO concluded that there were a number of issues concerning the joint venture with the host country government that could have been considered from a human rights perspective at the time of appraisal. First, IFC and the project sponsor would have wanted to try to limit the government's role in the project. Ideally, the government would not be involved at all in the joint venture, in order to clearly demarcate the separation of the project company (and its investors) from the government. If this could not be achieved, IFC and the project sponsor would have wanted to structure the project so as to limit the government's operational control or active involvement in operations. This objective often coincides with a number of other investment objectives and thus would not always need to be undertaken just to ensure control over operational matters for human rights reasons.

Secondly, if the government maintained a stake in the project company, IFC and the project sponsor would have wanted to examine whether there were any actions the government might take with respect to the project that could result in human rights violations. Such actions taken in the context of the project could make the project company and its investors complicit in the human rights abuses if they were reasonably foreseeable. At a minimum, the project company and its investors could be considered to have benefited from any human rights abuses perpetrated by the government that were reasonably foreseeable. If IFC and the project sponsor considered that such abuses within the project context were possible, they would have wanted to take what action they could within the project structure to ensure that those rights were not violated. For example, if land were needed for the project, the project company would not ask the government to provide the land if it knew the government would forcibly evict people from the property without compensation and without following procedural safeguards. (As it turns out the project needed only a small amount of land and the company negotiated a mutually agreeable settlement with the landowner.) IFC and the project sponsor would also have wanted to consider some ongoing 'rules of engagement' with the government with respect to actions the government might take that could affect human rights in connection with the project (see the discussion on conflict and security issues below). This could also include a forum for raising human rights concerns connected with governmental actions.

If there were concerns about serious violations in connection with the project, and absent success in addressing them, IFC and the project sponsor would have wanted to reconsider the project if a joint venture with the government were the only way forward. Recognizing that there are many unacceptable human rights situations in countries that the private sector has little or no influence to change, the choice for the private sector may ultimately come down to such a go/no go decision. In fact, the government was a passive investor in the project and played no role in the operations of the company.

Thirdly, IFC and the project company would have wanted to ensure that the project was structured in such a way as to provide the maximum beneficial return to the people and not just to the government for a number of reasons, including to justify a contractual relation with the government. Given the poverty of the country, the potential for corruption, and the potentially large payments to the government to be generated through dividends, royalties, taxes, and duties, IFC, perhaps together with the World Bank, would have considered whether revenue management arrangements could be put in place in accordance with developing best practice. These arrangements would seek to ensure that payments were not diverted into private pockets, and were instead used to address legitimate social needs and excluded uses for political repression (recognizing that ultimately money is fungible). IFC could have also encouraged the project company and government to disclose all revenue payments to the government. In addition to revenue management issues, there are other ways the project could have maximized benefit to the local population. The project company had set up a local foundation to help local businessmen start up businesses and provided funding for local schools and hospital, road works, and sewage infrastructure. Given the date of the project, unsurprisingly it had no organized or systematic community development program based on a review of community needs and input from the community. IFC would have requested such a program if the project were appraised today.

Finally, IFC and the project sponsor would also have wanted to be prepared to address concerns NGOs raised about doing business in the host country and with the government in an open and transparent manner. IFC and the project sponsor would also want to consider occasions and opportunities to raise with the government concerns about human rights abuses in the country in the context of the project.

14.4.6 Human Rights Implications of Operating in a State where Armed Conflict is a Possibility

Conflicts and human rights violations have a symbiotic relationship. The worst human rights abuses occur in conflicts. As such, it is important to understand and take what measures the private sector can within its limited sphere of influence to analyze, address, and help prevent conflicts that often arise in countries with strategic resources and oppressive governments, before they result in human rights violations connected to a project.

As noted above, the host country recently experienced a civil war. Though the war concluded with a peace accord, parts of the peace plan were not implemented. The country is still plagued by sporadic outbreaks of violence, kidnappings, and political tension. And while the main fighting during the civil war occurred in the south, away from the project area, political tensions between the central government and the regional government in the north of the country, where the project is located, have been rising. In addition, there is a large ethnic minority in the project area that have been a source of concern to the government given the strained relationship with the neighboring state.

The CAO's review suggested that a number of conflict-related issues could have been taken into account, given the situation in the country. First, given the amount of revenue the government was to earn from the project, IFC and the project company would have wanted to look at whether the funds were used for further repression against government opponents and to further entrench the current governance structure. In other words, whether the project would exacerbate governance conflicts in the region and in the country. Secondly, IFC and the project company would have wanted to know whether there was any history of resource-based conflicts around the mine. This includes inquiring into whether the mine was the subject of disputed claims by local people, whether the revenue distribution exacerbated the internal conflicts, whether revenue was shared with the local region (including the various ethnic minorities), and whether local populations would be denied access to natural resources necessary to meet basic needs as a result of the project. Finally, given the presence of a large ethnic minority in the mining area, IFC and the project company would want to understand the history and tensions between ethnic groups, as well as the relations with the neighboring state, to ascertain whether there were any ethnic or minority conflicts around the mine. There were security problems in the area but the project company did not report any specific security problems around the mine to IFC.

Related to the issue of minority rights and ethnic populations is that of indigenous peoples. Mining companies often have to decide how to interact with indigenous peoples who may live on or near the mining concession area. In particular, the use of and compensation for land traditionally occupied and used by indigenous peoples is a source of concern, conflict, and potential human rights violations around mining projects. Even though international law on indigenous peoples' rights is still developing, there is a growing recognition at the national level and international level, through the interpretation of human rights treaties, of the rights of indigenous peoples to control the use of their lands and resources, and to protect their ways of life. In this case study, there were no indigenous peoples in the project area, so these issues did not arise, but they frequently do in the mining sector.

14.4.7 Land and Housing Issues

Land acquisitions for mining operations have often been the source of conflict and human rights abuses in mining operations around the world. The large areas often required for mining exploration and operations can bring mines into contact with a cross-section of the regional population living in the concession area. While land acquisitions by a government for a company or by the company directly may comply with national law, this is no guarantee that the acquisition process complies with human rights requirements, basic notions of fair and equitable process and compensation, or good practice strategies to promote community relations and development. Eviction or involuntary resettlement, if not carried out in accordance with human rights procedural safeguards, results in violations of the human right to housing, and the rights to privacy and family, the right not to be arbitrarily deprived of property, and potentially numerous other human rights.

In this case, the project company required only comparatively little new land to carry out its mining operations because the mine was already in existence. The land acquired was used for grazing, not habitation. The land acquisition was negotiated directly between the company and the land owner/occupiers on a mutually agreed basis. A mutual arrangement is always the preferred solution, not only from a human rights point of view but also from a community relations perspective. However, the project company would need to be alert to the possibility of background government pressure on the inhabitants to settle the matter quickly or cheaply.

14.4.8 Rights of Free Speech, Assembly, and Association

The right to political participation is grounded in a number of human rights, including the right to freedom of association, assembly, and speech. Rights-based development places great emphasis on permitting people to participate in learning about and shaping projects that affect them. This is done in part through consultation that is meaningful, which requires that the information provided is appropriate (for example, translated into the local language and explained if necessary), accessible, informative (for example, more than just a short brochure that addresses only advantages without discussing negative impacts), and periodic (for example, does not end after construction). Participation also entails, most importantly, opportunities to participate in the project in some way if possible as well as the possibility to influence the parts of a project that affect the population. Participation implies that the community is able to assemble and speak freely about the project without interference from either the government or the company.

In this project, IFC did not require that the project sponsor carry out consultations in the project area. It appears that the project sponsor had some interaction with the local community. Given the considerable impacts mines have on surrounding communities, extensive and ongoing consultation is becoming best practice in the mining sector. It is also a method to allow communities to express their opinions about the project so that the company can receive the views and complaints of communities in a constructive manner and without interference by the government. Given the government's record of repressing political dissent, the project company would need to be alert to any suppression of local dissent about the project and be prepared to open an avenue whereby the local population could exercise their freedom of speech and voice their opinions about the project.

The project company provided certain benefits to the community, including a health clinic, improvements to the roads and municipal water supply, and donations to the schools and hospitals, all of which were no doubt positive, given the dire state of the economy. These types of community development projects can be an important outlet for community participation in the project process, if structured to permit the community to have a voice in and some control over the objectives and operations of the program. As part of taking a human rights approach to community development, the project company would want to ensure that community participation and the sharing of benefits were based on the most representative spectrum of the community, including women and minorities, and did not just rely on or reinforce any existing discriminatory practices.

14.4.9 Operational Phase—Labor Rights and Standards

The project company was a significant employer in the area. The ILO Declaration on Fundamental Rights and Conditions at Work[21] sets out four principles that are the core minimum rights of workers around the world: the abolition of child labor and forced labor, elimination of discrimination (equal opportunity) and the freedom of association, and collective bargaining. ILO member states have an obligation to respect, promote, and realize these four labor rights, regardless of whether they have signed and ratified the two ILO conventions underlying each right. The host country has ratified seven of the eight underlying conventions (it has not ratified the 1999 convention on the worst forms of child labor).[22] It has also ratified other ILO conventions that might have been relevant to the project. While the Declaration is not directly applicable to the private sector, it is ultimately the private sector that plays the pivotal role in ensuring these rights as employers and thus these four core labor rights are relevant to every private sector project.

14.4.9.1 Child Labor

Given the problems in the host country with both forced labor and child labor, the project team and project company would need to make more than a perfunctory inquiry to ensure that neither child labor nor forced labor was used by contractors or subcontractors during construction and operations.

---

[21] See above n. 12.

[22] Convention concerning the Prohibition and Immediate Action for the Elimination of the Worst Forms of Child Labour (ILO No. 182), 38 I.L.M. 1207 (1999), *entered into force* 19 November 2000.

14.4.9.2 Freedom of Association and Collective Bargaining

There is a high degree of unionization within the industrial sector so the employees at the project may already have had the option to join unions. The project company's role would then be to ensure that it was not interfering with the exercise of those rights (i.e., by preventing unionization), to play its part in respecting and enforcing those rights (i.e., by negotiating with employee organizations, and providing time and space for employee organization meetings and so forth), and, given the country situation, do what it could within its sphere of influence to deflect any governmental interference with its employees in exercising their labor rights.

14.4.9.3 Equal Opportunity and Non-Discrimination

The project company could have been asked to provide a preference to local people when hiring for the skilled and unskilled positions in the project in an effort to maximize local employment from the project. This may have happened by chance if not by policy, given the remote location of the project and the presence of the previously employed workers in the area. Given that discrimination is currently prevalent in the host country, the project company could also have been asked to make a principled commitment to ensuring that hiring and employment were carried out in a non-discriminatory fashion, making efforts to ensure that women and any minorities or indigenous people in the area were given at least equal consideration in hiring, employment, and advancement. In this connection, the project company would need to be sensitive to competition for the scarce jobs in such a poor economy and the tensions this might create within the community and between ethnic groups. It would need to be sensitive as well to new tensions and problems in the community if the operations attracted migrants to the area.

14.4.9.4 Other Labor Rights

The Universal Declaration of Human Rights and the ICESCR set out a number of basic workers' rights that go beyond the four core labor standards: the right to work (right to freely choose work, right to just and favorable conditions of work), wages (fair wages and equal remuneration for work of equal value and sufficient to provide a decent living for the worker and their family), working hours (a reasonable limitation of working hours and holiday with pay), employment security (social security, including social insurance, paid maternity leave), and disciplinary practices (no harsh, inhuman, or discriminatory disciplinary practices).[23]

---

[23] See UDHR, above n. 18, arts 22–26; ICESCR, above n. 17, arts 6–9, 11.

The project company raised wages early on in the project and regularized labour contracts, which were important steps in shoring up the employees' ability to exercise their labour rights. However, the project company would need to be sensitive to the impact of the improved wage structure and benefits on the surrounding community and the tensions it might create, issues that could perhaps be addressed through community development programs and community access to services. The project company could have been asked to make certain basic commitments around the other labor issues as well—working hours, employment security, and disciplinary practices, as part of its labor package.

The ICESCR calls on states to take steps to help people realize their right to work by providing technical and vocational training programs. While this is not an obligation strictly speaking on private sector employers, it is nonetheless a right that the private sector can help fulfill by providing appropriate training to their workers to improve their job and life skills. The project company provided health and safety training to the workers as well as training on handling cyanide to those who needed it. In addition, IFC secured funding from the United Kingdom's Department for International Development (DFID) to provide further health and safety training. The project company provided funds and training to local businessmen on starting small businesses.

14.4.10 Rights to Health, Safety, and Food

The ICESCR states that workers are entitled to safe and healthy working conditions, and provides for a right to health.[24] The right to health provisions call on governments and others to take steps so that people can attain the highest attainable standard of health. Governments are expected to take steps to provide medical services, treat diseases, reduce child mortality, and improve environmental and industrial hygiene. It is with respect to this last issue in particular that the private sector can and must play a role by minimizing the impacts of its operations on both the environment and workers. The right to food requires that no one be deprived of their right to subsistence—either through cutting off access to food sources, resettling people away from their food sources, or destroying food sources through pollution.

Environmental concerns are not a new issue for the private sector, and especially not for the mining sector. What is new is a convergence of ideas, focus, and pressure from a wide range of sources (environmental, corporate social responsibility, human rights, investors, industry associations, and

---

[24] ICESCR, above n. 17, arts 7(b) and 12.

regulators) on the similar objective of improving corporate environmental performance for both workers and the community. The human rights approach brings a new focus to the discussion—the health and nutritional impacts of poor environmental performance—and a new reason to address the issue: to avoid claims of abusing human rights. Thinking about environmental protection in terms of rights requires a new way of looking at environmental issues that some leading mining companies are beginning to undertake. These companies are recognizing that workers and the community are stakeholders or rights-holders in the project.

Health issues are a major concern in mining operations, both for the workers and the community. While health and safety concerns for miners have a long and documented history, it is only more recently that the effects of poor environmental performance on communities surrounding resource extraction projects has begun to be the focus of attention, protest, and conflict.

With respect to its employees, the project company had in place a safety management plan, a full-time health and safety officer, health and safety training for its employees, health screening for its employees, and a health clinic for both its employees and the local population, all of which are good steps towards supporting the right to safe and healthy working conditions for employees (provided they are carried out as required and in accordance with industry practice). This is especially true in the host country where the government recognized in its Poverty Reduction Strategy Paper that health and safety conditions were a major concern. IFC secured DFID trust funds to run further health and safety training at the project. What the company may not have considered is safety issues with respect to the political realities in the country—kidnappings and landmines, among others.

With respect to the local population, the project company had in place an environmental management system to assess and address its impacts on the surrounding environment. Given that this was a mining operation using hazardous chemicals and operating tailings dams, it would have been important for the company to monitor and control the impacts of those especially hazardous activities on the health of the community. While HIV/AIDS is often a problem in mining communities in Africa, the reported incidence of HIV/AIDS in the host country is very low (0.10 per cent). However, there may have been other health impacts caused by any influx of workers that the company would need to monitor, including sexually transmitted diseases.

With respect to the medical services provided, the company had already taken an important step in opening the doors of its medical clinic to the local population, thus supporting the right to health in a country with a failing health system. To support a human rights approach to the right to health, the project company would want to ensure that the clinic was in fact available to all on a non-discriminatory basis, ensuring, for example, that women, children, and minorities had equal access to services, equipment, and supplies.

14.4.11 Right to Security

The ICCPR provides for a right to life, a prohibition against being arbitrarily deprived of life, a right to security of person as well as a right to freedom from torture and other cruel and inhuman punishment.[25] It was violations of these rights that brought the role of the private sector in violating human rights into sharper focus. The issue arose from abuses perpetrated by security forces (private and public) protecting private sector extractive industry projects in particular. Where security forces under the control or payment of the private sector abused and killed people protesting the projects, attention began to focus on the role the private sector played in sanctioning and benefiting from those human rights abuses.

As noted, the host country has a recent history of civil war that has not been entirely resolved. Violent incidents continue, including kidnappings. In light of the circumstances in the country, the project company would want to have a security plan in place. Even if it has a plan in place, it may not have a plan or security services that are based on applicable human rights and law enforcement principles. Several major extractive industry companies, the U.S. and U.K. governments, various leading human rights organizations and trade unions recently published a set of mutually agreed-upon principles on the use of security forces in private sector operations.[26] The principles seek to balance the need for security, the realities of private sector control over situations, and human rights concerns and provide helpful guidance for companies that want to include human rights considerations in their security arrangements.

14.4.12 Accountability

The private sector is not responsible for positively delivering on the whole range of human rights, but it can be expected to respect the human rights of those with whom it comes in contact, and to take further steps concerning those human rights that it is in a position to protect or fulfill, such as treating its workers in accordance with the relevant labor rights in this project, or respecting the community's right to health by ensuring appropriate pollution control. For those rights, the private sector should be held accountable.

---

[25] ICCPR, above n. 16, arts 6, 7, 9, 10.
[26] Voluntary Principles on Security and Human Rights, http://www.state.gov/www/global/human_rights/001220_fsdrl_principles.html.

Accountability mechanisms often do exist under national law, at least in theory, but may not be very accessible for the local population. Thus, one very practical step the private sector can take to implement some kind of accountability is to provide staff and other stakeholders with an avenue of redress if there are concerns about labor and human rights issues. Accountability mechanisms should ideally be confidential with assurances of non-retribution for raising issues.

The project documentation does not address what if any accountability mechanisms the project company provided. The accountability mechanism could have been part of an ongoing community relations and consultation program that would want to address, in a transparent manner, a number of general human rights concerns that often arise around mining projects: security arrangements, revenues, employment, and community development as well as any other community concerns that may arise as operations proceed. Responding to concerns raised through any accountability mechanism presupposes that the project company would have the policies, management system, and monitoring system to track its performance against the human rights issues outlined above and to address new issues raised in an appropriate manner.

14.5 CONCLUSION—THE POTENTIAL IFC ROLE

The case above is illustrative of the challenges ahead. Should IFC incorporate human rights into its policies, the corporation would undoubtedly face questions about project compliance on a variety of fronts. IFC will be called upon, formally and informally, to resolve alleged human rights disputes associated with its projects. The mechanisms to resolve these complaints will have to be transparent, fair, and culturally appropriate. In addition, a number of institutional issues will clearly need to be debated and addressed. IFC's shareholding nations may well ask: Is it advisable for a global development finance institution to enlarge its mandate by creating a practical mechanism for addressing human rights? In operational terms, is it a good use of public funds to ask an organization such as IFC to develop a competence in this area? Would it be a distraction from its primary mission?

Assuming human rights can be integrated into IFC's lending operations, practical questions of implementation are substantial. Which office or department within the organization would perform the essential functions? Who would define the standards to be applied? Would there be an appeals mechanism? Who would be entrusted with ensuring compliance? What would be the basis to sort out legitimate allegations from false ones? This last question is particularly relevant as IFC has often been frustrated by the amount of staff time and resources devoted to responding to false allegations regarding its existing environmental and social safeguards and guidelines.

These, along with many other questions, will continue to be posed as IFC navigates a path through human rights as one of the burning issues of our day. By virtue of its unique position at the intersection of global finance, emerging markets, and environmental sustainability—as well as its new-found role as a standard-setting institution—IFC has an opportunity to be more than another voice in the global human rights debate. It has an opportunity to develop a way for businesses worldwide to explicitly and proactively address human rights issues. IFC as a development institution has a strong incentive to go beyond a low common denominator solution. Arguably, IFC also has an advantage: by putting its own money at risk in for-profit investments and facing the same market discipline as its clients, IFC has a perspective on 'what the market will bear' in terms of human rights. The challenge will be to help businesses globally reach a higher equilibrium point in their investments, not only in affirming and trans-mitting human rights but in realizing their fulfillment.

15

Human Rights and Governance: The Empirical Challenge

DANIEL KAUFMANN [1]

15.1 INTRODUCTION: HUMAN RIGHTS—THE EMPIRICAL AND GOVERNANCE CHALLENGE

In this chapter we offer a preliminary empirically-based exploration of evidence and links between human rights and governance. By doing so, in particular we challenge four notions: i) that an empirical (data-driven) approach is not productive in the field of human rights; ii) that corruption and rule of law (i.e. governance issues narrowly defined) ought not to be part of a more integrated human rights approach; iii) that first generation human rights issues (commonly known as 'negative liberties', such as civil rights/ freedoms) are not important determinants of economic development success and thus of attaining the mission of international financial institutions (IFIs); and iv) that at any rate, with economic development, progress in first generation human rights issues would take place naturally (i.e. the 'luxury good' argument for civil liberties and good governance).

To address these notions, we empirically assess data and trends on human rights, and pose questions about the links between first generation human rights issues (political and civil rights) and second generation human rights

[1] The responsibility for the errors and views in this chapter is the author's, yet credit for the work discussed here is due to many collaborators within and outside of the World Bank. In particular, the collaborative projects within the World Bank with J. Hellman and A. Kraay are noted. I have also benefited from discussions with L. Moreno-Ocampo and A. Sfeir-Younis. The excellent assistance of M. Mastruzzi, E. Hoffmann, and F. Sheikh is acknowledged. The views, data, and research findings aim to further debate and analysis, and do not necessarily reflect official views of the World Bank or its Board of Directors. The margins of error in any governance, institutional quality, and human rights dataset imply that interpretative caution is warranted in general, and in particular argue against inferring seemingly precise country rankings from the data. For details on the governance research and data: http://www.worldbank.org/wbi/governance/.

issues (of a socio-economic/development nature, often known as 'positive liberties'), as well as between these twin generation human rights aspects, on the one hand, and governance in a narrow sense (rule of law, corruption), on the other.

We first review the evidence on the first generation human rights issues (political and civil rights) and ask whether in recent times there appears to be a marked improvement in this set of rights. For this, we draw on a recently constructed human rights database which was codified based on an existing methodology, and is prepared as background to the worldwide aggregate governance indicators dataset. We then explore the links between first generation human rights (1GHR) and second generation (social, economic) human rights issues (2GHR), drawing on our recent research linking governance dimensions (utilizing aggregate governance indicators) and socio-economic outcomes.

In this research, we do address the thorny issue of endogeneity and reverse causality, thus attempting to disentangle the direction of causality between different (generations of) human rights variables. In particular, we explore whether some 1GHR (and governance) variables may possess 'luxury good' attributes, in the sense that as income growth takes place (consistent with 2GHR issues) that automatically can be expected to result in improvements in some 1GHR dimensions.[2] Whether such reverse causality is evident or not has implications for policy and interventions.

We then complement this 'macro-aggregate' empirical exploration of the link between 1GHR and 2GHR issues by reviewing our research findings at the 'micro' level, where we asked whether civil liberties and political participation do enhance the economic returns of (World Bank funded) investment projects in developing countries. Further, we briefly explore these links utilizing an in-depth country diagnostic assessment methodology, relying on a case study of Bolivia.

In the subsequent section, we address a gap in this field: the relevance of corruption and (mis-) rule of law (and thus of mis-governance in this narrow sense, yet including the challenges in both the public and corporate sectors), and their links to human rights. Corruption and rule of law were not explicitly covered in either one of the International Human Rights Covenants, or in the subsequent Declaration on the Right to Development.[3]

---

[2] Strictly speaking, the so-called second generation UN Covenant refers to social, economic, and cultural rights (1966), while in 1976 the UN adopted a Declaration on the Rights to Development. For purposes of our analysis, a simplified (and somewhat 'bundled') two-generational classification is presumed, where the focus of the first generation is on political and civil rights and liberties, while the second generational issues focus on socio-economic development issues.

[3] International Covenant on Civil and Political Rights (ICCPR), G.A. res. 2200A (XXI), 21 U.N. GAOR Supp. (No. 16) at 52, U.N. Doc. A/6316 (1966), 999 U.N.T.S. 171, *entered*

We review selected empirical links between such narrowly defined governance issues, on the one hand, and particular dimensions of human rights, on the other, and briefly explore potential implications of the omission of these (corporate and public sector) governance issues within a human-rights-based approach.

Finally, we provide a brief exploration on the variation across specific dimensions in the links between various human rights dimensions, pointing to the importance of 'unbundling' the specific human rights and governance dimensions of interest and thus going beyond the more general and aggregate findings suggested in earlier sections of this chapter. In particular, for those 'unbundled' 2GHR dimensions (for instance, some health dimensions, such as AIDS) that are not as tightly dependent by progress on 1GHR (and/or governance) factors, specific and often targeted interventions and action programs would be further warranted. Similarly, we point out that unbundling *within* each generation of human rights issues suggests that some links (and correlations) between certain human rights dimensions are weaker than others. We conclude by summarizing and pointing to some general implications for policy.

15.2 FIRST GENERATION HUMAN RIGHTS (1GHR): DATA, LEVELS, AND TRENDS

An important aim of this chapter is to challenge the notion that a rigorously empirical (evidence/data-based) approach to human rights is either not feasible or, worse, counter-productive.[4] A priori, we depart from the premise

---

into force 23 March 1976; International Covenant on Economic, Social and Cultural Rights (ICESCR), G.A. res. 2200A (XXI), 21 U.N. GAOR Supp. (No. 16) at 49, U.N. Doc. A/6316 (1966), 993 U.N.T.S. 3, *entered into force* 3 January 1976; and Declaration on the Right to Development, G.A. res. 41/128, annex, 41 U.N. GAOR Supp. (No. 53) at 186, U.N. Doc. A/41/53 (1986).

[4] While the literature on human rights is overwhelmingly prose-rich and data-poor, there are noteworthy exceptions (that prove the rule) in related dimensions, such as in the case of research on child labor. See for instance the recent study by ILO, cited in *The Economist* in 'Sickness or Symptom' (no author, 'Sickness or Symptom', *The Economist*, 5 February 2004) as well as volume 17, number 2 of the *World Bank Economic Review* on child labor, which *inter alia* features empirical articles on child labor by F. Bourguignon, F. H. G. Ferreira, and P. G. Leite, 'Conditional Cash Transfers, Schooling, and Child Labor: Micro-Simulating Brazil's Bolsa Escola Program' 17 *World Bank Economic Review* 229 (2003); K. Basu, and Z. Tzannatos, 'The Global Child Labor Problem: What do we know and what can we do?' 17 *World Economic Review* 147 (2003); S. Bhalotra and C. Heady, 'Child Farm Labor: The Wealth Paradox' 17 *World Bank Economic Review* 197 (2003); see also E. D. Gibbons, F. Huebler, and E. Loaiza, 'Child Labour, Education, and the Principle of Non-Discrimination', Chapter 10 in this volume.

that any measurement in this complex multi-disciplinary area will be difficult, subject to margins of error, and warranting caution in the analysis and interpretation.[5] Yet, as it has been shown by the insights already attained by the empirical approach taken in the field of governance and anti-corruption in recent times, embarking on a comprehensive data-driven approach to measure, monitor, and analyze the various dimensions and trends in human rights may have a significant pay-off as well. In this chapter we contribute modestly to an initial approach, to be expanded. We start by describing some of the datasets which we utilize for the analysis in this paper.

15.2.1 The Data

In this chapter, we utilize five different sources of information. The first two, which we draw heavily from in the earlier sections of this chapter, refer to cross-country data, on human rights and governance. The second set of three sources are of a more 'micro' nature, drawing first from investment project rates of return and other project characteristics of World Bank funded investments in developing countries in the past, and secondly from two worldwide surveys of enterprises. The latter part refers to the annual Executive Opinion Survey (EOS) of the World Economic Forum (WEF), with which we have collaborated in the governance component of the questionnaire and data analysis, and to the World Business Environment Survey (WBES) which was carried out by the World Bank (in collaboration with EBRD, IDB, and Harvard) in 1999–2000. In addition, we also draw on a country-specific dataset for the empirical diagnostic case study synthesis, based on the in-depth survey of public officials in Bolivia in 2000.

For this opening section, we focus on the first two datasets, namely, the more 'macro' cross-country information, which we describe below, in turn.

15.2.1.1 Human Rights Cross-Country Variables: The Cingranelli, Richards, and Webster Human Rights Codification (CRWHUM)

The human rights data was coded by Craig Webster as background for the Worldwide Aggregate Governance Indicators project (see below), utilizing the methodology by Cingranelli and Richards who first coded earlier years of such data,[6] with input by Webster. The codification draws from two sources,

---

[5] Such point of departure has governed, in fact, the empirical approach that has been undertaken for a number of years already in the field of governance and corruption. By the mid-nineties, in fact, as is still the case in human rights nowadays, there was considerable skepticism that an empirical approach could be taken in the study of governance. Yet significant strides have been made since then in the empirics of governance, rule of law, and corruption. See later sections in this chapter.

[6] D. L. Cingranelli and D. L. Richards, 'Coding Government Respect For Human Rights, Manual Version One' (State University of New York: Binghamton University, 2001).

the U.S. Department of State's Country Reports on Human Rights Practices, and from Amnesty International's Amnesty International Report. Both of these reports offer descriptions of human rights practices and conditions. Each variable is coded in an ordinal (not cardinal) scale, whose range varies between 0–2 to 0–4 (zero always reflecting the worse possible rating in the human rights dimension being measured), depending on the variable in question. For our presentational purposes, we have standardized all variables to be between zero (bad) and one (good).

In this chapter we utilize and present selected variables from such a dataset, and also construct two composites in order to illustrate aggregate trends. The first composite refers to the extent of Physical/Life Protection by the state, which is the simple average of the codified index of the following four variables: i) Absence of Killings; ii) Absence of Disappearances; iii) Absence of Torture; and iv) Absence of Imprisonments. The second composite refers to the rights of women, and is the composite of the following three variables: women's political rights; women's economic rights; and social equality of women. The full set of variables covered in the CRWHUM codification are the following: political killings; disappearances; tortures; imprisonments; independence of judiciary; government censorship; political participation; freedom to travel; workers rights; women's political rights; women's economic rights; social equality of women; coups; states of emergency; freedom of religion. In the remainder of the paper we refer to this data as the CRWHUM dataset.

15.2.1.2 Worldwide Aggregate Governance Indicators

We have defined *governance* as the set of traditions and formal and informal institutions that determine how authority is exercised in a particular country for the common good, thus encompassing: (1) the process of selecting, monitoring, and replacing governments; (2) the capacity to formulate and implement sound policies and deliver public services; and (3) the respect of citizens and the state for the institutions that govern economic and social interactions among them. For measurement and analysis, the three dimensions in this definition are unbundled to comprise two measurable concepts per each of the dimensions above, for a total of six governance components:

1) *voice and external accountability* (that is, the government's preparedness to be externally accountable through their own country's citizen feedback and democratic institutions, and a competitive press, thus including elements of restraint on the sovereign);
2) *political stability and lack of violence, crime, and terrorism*;
3) *government effectiveness* (including quality of policy making, bureaucracy, and public service delivery);

4) *lack of regulatory burden*;

5) *rule of law* (protection of property rights, judiciary independence, and so on, thus including elements of law and order); and

6) *control of corruption.*

Applying the above definition of governance and gathering data from many different sources, we have analyzed hundreds of cross-country indicators as proxies for various aspects of governance.[7] These individual variables, which serve as the inputs to our aggregate governance indicators, are produced by a range of organizations. They include the perspectives of diverse observers and cover a wide range of topics.

Imposing structure on these many available variables from diverse sources, we mapped the data to the six sub-components of governance listed above, expressed them in common units, measured the margins of error, and, thanks to a statistical methodology, aggregated into the six governance indicators—thereby improving the reliability of the resulting composite indicator and the analysis. These indicators for 1996 through 2002, for almost 200 countries, are available online. They can assist in providing global empirical perspective on governance performance today and assess the historical and other determinants and manifestations of governance.[8]

15.2.2 First Generation Human Rights (1GHR): Initial Empirics, Levels, and Recent Trends

The Economist, in their August 2001 coverage on human rights, suggested that there was a view among some NGOs and experts that significant progress in first generation human rights (1GHR) issues was a key factor in the increased focus and interest on second generation human rights (2GHR)

---

[7] For methodological details on the worldwide governance indicators presented here in brief, see D. Kaufmann, A. Kraay, and M. Mastruzzi, *Governance Matters III: Governance Indicators 1996–2002*, World Bank Policy Research Working Paper No. 3106 (Washington D.C.: World Bank), available at http://www.worldbank.org/wbi/governance/pubs/govmatters3.html. The individual indicators used for the composites came from a variety of organizations, including commercial risk-rating agencies, multilateral organizations, think tanks, and other non-governmental organizations. They are based on surveys of experts, firms, and citizens and cover a wide range of topics: perceptions of political stability and the business climate, views on the efficacy of public service provision, opinions on respect for the rule of law, and perceptions of the incidence of corruption. For a detailed explanation of sources and access to the full governance indicators databank see http://www.worldbank.org/wbi/governance/govdata2002. See also the appendix on methodological issues related to margins of error and interpretation for these indicators.

[8] The full governance dataset for 1996–2002 is available at http://www.worldbank.org/wbi/governance/govdata2002.

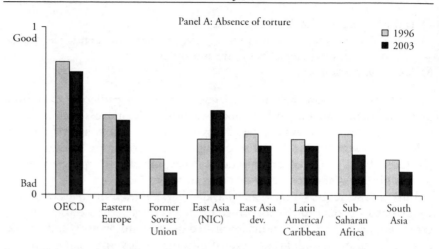

Source: Webster background compilation for Governance Indicators (GM IV, forthcoming). A high value reflects respect for human rights.

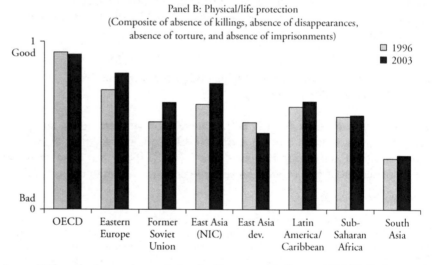

Source: Webster background compilation for Governance Indicators (GM IV, forthcoming). A high value reflects respect for human rights.

Figure 15.1. Human rights, first generation data trends

issues. Data analysis is of help to scrutinize such a view, as well as monitor trends more generally.[9] Figure 15.1 contains 6 panels covering various dimensions of 1GHR. The first 5 panels in Figure 15.1 draw from the CRWHUM dataset, while the last panel, on voice and participatory

[9] 'Special Report on Human Rights', *The Economist*, 18 August 2001.

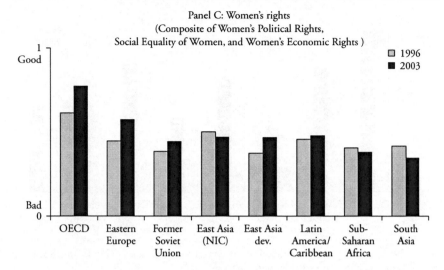

Panel C: Women's rights
(Composite of Women's Political Rights,
Social Equality of Women, and Women's Economic Rights)

Source: Webster background compilation for Governance Indicators (GM IV, forthcoming).
A high value reflects respect for human rights.

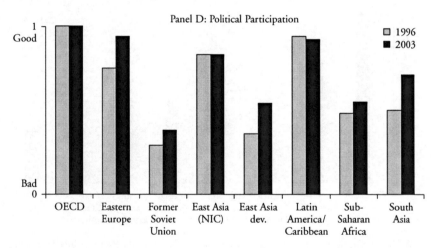

Panel D: Political Participation

Source: Webster background compilation for Governance Indicators (GM IV, forthcoming).
A high value reflects respect for human rights.

Figure 15.1. (*Continued*)

accountability (including civil liberties), is drawn from the aggregate governance database.

The data in the many panels in Figure 15.1 is suggestive in a number of respects. First, the level of first generation human right indicators, in various dimensions, is nowadays far from optimal across regions, and, second, the

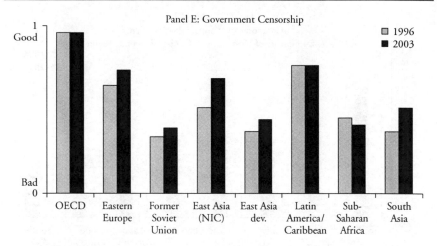

Panel E: Government Censorship

Source: Webster background compilation for Governance Indicators (GM IV, forthcoming). A high value reflects respect for human rights.

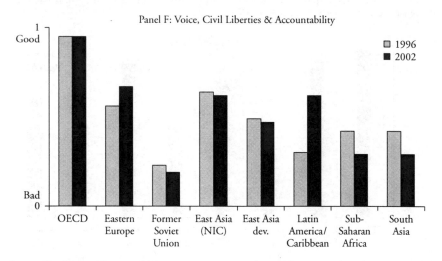

Panel F: Voice, Civil Liberties & Accountability

Source: Kaufmann, Kraay and Mastruzzi, see note 7, above. Please note the values are rescaled from the original to 0–1. However, they are not strictly comparable with the other indicators in panels A–E because they are from a different source.

Figure 15.1. (*Continued*)

trend in recent times has been uneven. While in a number of dimensions there has been some improvement (as for some of the more life-threatening human rights violations, such progress does not appear to have been dramatic overall. Further it is uneven across regions as well as across dimensions of this 'composite'. For instance, no worldwide upward trend on average is apparent in the elimination of torture (panel A), the resulting combination of some better ratings over the seven-year period for some regions and the deterioration in others. Some improvement is seen in the government censorship variable, while the trend on the rights of women is uneven. Voice and civil liberties continue to exhibit very high variation across regions (and across countries—not shown in this figure).

15.3 FIRST GENERATION HUMAN RIGHTS ISSUES AS A DETERMINANT OF SECOND GENERATION ISSUES—ARE CIVIL LIBERTIES AND GOVERNANCE 'LUXURY GOODS' THAT ACCRUE AS A RESULT OF ECONOMIC DEVELOPMENT?

Having codified the extent to which the 1GHR issues still remain a major challenge in many settings nowadays, we explore next the relevance of selected such 1GHR issues for attaining 2GHR objectives. We do so first by reporting on the cross-country research carried out with worldwide governance indicators (the 'aggregate' or 'macro' dimension), then by utilizing a 'micro' unit of observation (projects in developing countries) instead, and finally by taking an in-depth country diagnostic (case study) approach. Given the broader scope of this chapter, in each case we synthesize the main approach and the results, referencing to the available longer research available.

15.3.1 The 'Macro-Aggregate', Dimension, and Disentangling Causality Direction

The database at hand permits an initial exploration into this question of the links between first and second generation human rights issues, which we address first with the aggregate cross-country data. The first two panels of Figure 15.2 depict the very close link between voice/civil liberties, on the one hand, and socio-economic developmental variables on the other—specifically child mortality and income per capita. The voice and civil liberties indicator is drawn from the aggregate governance indicator dataset (being also one of the six governance indicators). In addition to the construction of these indicators, we posed the question of whether one can disentangle causality direction from this very high correlation between these civil liberties and governance indicators, on the one hand, and socio-economic development, on the other.

Indeed, at the most basic level, the data at first reveal a very high correlation between civil liberties/good governance and key development outcomes across countries, as depicted in the three panels in Figure 15.2. Yet these very robust correlations in themselves represent a 'weak' finding in terms of policy

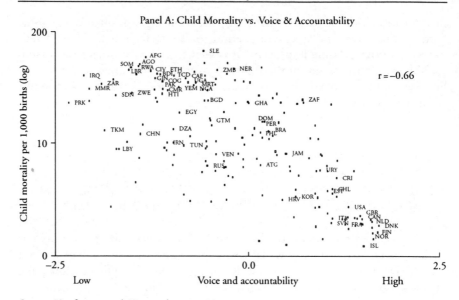

Source: Kaufmann and Kraay, above n. 10.

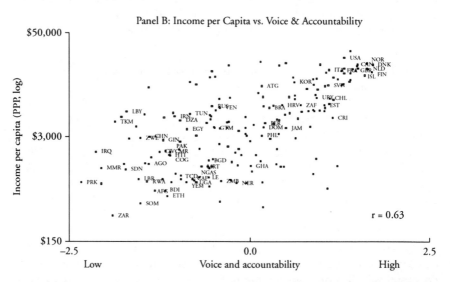

Sources: Kaufmann and Kraay, above n. 10. A. R. Heston, R. Summers, and B. Alen, *Penn World Table Version 6.1.* (Philadephia: Center for International Comparisons at the University of Pennsylvania (CICIJP), 2002) at http://pwt.econ.upenn.edu/, & CIA World Factbook.

Figure 15.2. 1GHR and 2GHR are highly correlated

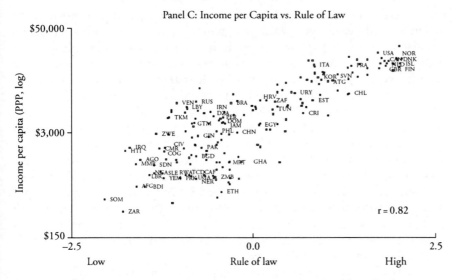

Panel C: Income per Capita vs. Rule of Law

Sources: Kaufmann & Kraay 2002, Heston & Summers, & CIA World Factbook.

Figure 15.2. (*Continued*)

application because such correlations do not shed light on the direction of causality or on whether an omitted ('third') correlated variable is the fundamental cause accounting for the effects on developmental outcomes. Thus, we need to probe deeper, which has been done in recent research with specialized statistical techniques, unbundling each causality direction.

Logically there are three possible explanations for the strong positive correlation between incomes and governance (civil liberties, rule of law, etc): (1) better civil liberties/governance exerts a powerful effect on per capita incomes; (2) higher incomes lead to improvements in governance; and (3) there are other factors that both make countries richer and also are associated with better governance. Untangling the observed high correlation between incomes and governance is important in order to ascertain whether there is an automatic 'virtuous circle' where higher incomes are automatically translated into improved governance, or if such positive feedback mechanism is absent then a concerted and continuous policy intervention effort to improve governance is needed. Consequently, we need a good understanding of the effects of governance on incomes as well as of any feedback mechanisms from incomes to governance that might exist—simply observing a strong correlation between income growth and governance does not suffice.[10]

---

[10] Untangling the directions of causation underlying the strong correlations is explained in detail in D. Kaufmann and A. Kraay, 'Growth without Governance' 3 *Economia* 169 (2003). http://www.worldbank.org/wbi/governance/pubs/growthgov.htm.

Let us consider first the effect of governance on per capita incomes. As recently as 200 years ago, per capita incomes were not very different across countries. The wide gaps in per capita income across countries that we see today reflect the simple fact that countries that are rich today have grown rapidly over the past two centuries, while those that are poor today did not.[11]

What about causation in the opposite direction, from per capita income to the quality of governance? Conventional wisdom holds that richer countries are better able to afford the costs associated with providing a competent government bureaucracy, sound rule of law, and an environment in which corruption is not condoned. This suggests that there is positive feedback from per capita income to governance as well. Yet this conventional wisdom had not been subject to in-depth empirical scrutiny. In our research we put such conventional wisdom through an empirical test. We implemented a particular methodology that permitted us to separate out the effects of per capita income on governance, and found evidence that this effect is certainly not positive, and, if anything, negative.[12]

This finding of an absence of (or even possibly negative) feedback from per capita income to governance has a number of implications. We focus here on

[11] A recent strand of research attributes a substantial fraction of these vast differences in very long run growth performance to deep historical differences in institutional quality. By isolating the part of current differences in governance performance that can be traced back to countries' colonial origins, these studies have identified the powerful effect of initial institutional quality on growth in the very long run. See for example R. Hall and C. Jones, 'Why Do Some Countries Produce So Much More Output per Worker than Others?' 114 *Quarterly Journal of Economics* 83 (1999). D. Acemoglu, S. Johnson, and J. A. Robinson, 'The Colonial Origins of Comparative Development: An Empirical Investigation' 91 *American Economic Review* 1369 (2001). We discuss some specific historical determinants in latter sections of this chapter.

[12] This of course does not mean that the simple correlation between governance and per capita income is negative, since this is dominated by the strong positive effects of governance on income. In terms of the specifics of the particular methodology used, we implemented an empirical framework allowing us to identify causal effects running in both directions between governance and per capita income. Although there is a rapidly growing literature that identifies the causation from better governance to higher per capita income, that is not the case for identifying causation in the opposite direction, from per capita income to governance. Traditionally, identification of the first direction of causality has been done with the aid of instrumental variables, such as the main language or settler mortality patterns, which we have utilized as instruments to arrive at the very large estimates of the effects of governance on income. Yet no good instruments exist for testing the reverse causality direction, namely from per capita income to improved governance. The gathering of a major governance dataset and the construction of the aggregate indicators themselves (through the particular Unobserved Component Model) give us important additional data: the margins of error for each country estimate for the governance indicators. These additional data permit us to implement a different and rarely used strategy to estimate the effect of incomes on governance, namely the utilization of non-sample information (or the 'out-of-sample' technique). Implementing this technique, we find no evidence of positive feedback from higher per capita income to better governance outcomes. See Kaufmann and Kraay, above n. 10.

two of them. First, a strategy of waiting for improvements to come automatically as countries become richer is unlikely to succeed. Second, in the absence of positive feedback from per capita income to governance, we are unlikely to observe virtuous circles when better governance improves incomes that *in turn* will lead to further automatic improvements in governance. Together, these two implications point to the fundamental importance of positive and sustained interventions to improve governance and civil liberties in countries where it is lacking. Indeed, the fact that good governance is not a 'luxury good', to which a country automatically graduates when it becomes wealthier, means in practical terms that leaders, policy makers, and civil society need to work hard and continuously at improving these civil rights and governance within their countries.

15.3.2 The 'Micro': Civil Liberties Matter for Successful Investment Projects by International Agencies

A complementary approach to a macro-aggregate investigation of the link between 1GHR and 2GHR issues is to probe at the 'micro' level. If the unit of observation to be used as an indicator of 2GHR progress is indeed at the project level, and thus it does not have aggregate effects, then it is also less complex to draw causality inferences without resorting to reverse causality tests. We therefore utilize in this section previous research findings we obtained in a research project where we investigated the determinants of success/failure of World Bank funded investment projects in emerging economies. While our (dependent) left hand side variable to be explained was at a project level (the project's socio-economic rate of return), as right hand side variables in the econometric exploration we utilized a plethora of country-wide economic policy as well as civil liberties variables.

In this past research, we focused on measuring the impact of many economic policy and participatory and civil liberties variables on project performance. We found consistent, statistically significant, and empirically large effects of civil liberties on investment project rates of return. Depending on the measure of civil liberties used, if a country were to improve its civil liberties from the worst to the best, the economic rate of return of projects could increase on average by about 15 percentage points (and by as much as 22.5 percentage points in one set of results; see Table 15.1). This impact of civil liberties is as empirically large as the better known impact of economic distortions on project returns that we obtained during such a research project as well.

Some analysts have argued that there is a trade-off between liberties and development. We find the opposite evidence, that suppressing liberties is likely to be inimical to project performance. This has obvious implications for development assistance.

Table 15.1. *Impact of civil liberties on project socio-economic rates of return: specification on independent variables*

Civil liberties variable	With exogenous control variables only	With regional dummies	With policy variables	With regional dummies and policy variables	Effect on economic rate of return of one standard deviation increase in civil liberties
Freedom House Civil liberties					
(1978–87)	1.81	1.16	1.71	1.07	
(N = 649)	(0.0005)	(0.079)	(0.002)	(0.114)	1.57
Humana					
(1982–85)	0.290	0.299	0.296	0.289	
(N = 236)	(0.003)	(0.007)	(0.002)	(0.013)	5.19
Media pluralism					
(1983–87)	4.61	4.45	3.66	3.43	
(N = 448)	(0.0001)	(0.002)	(0.001)	(0.026)	3.12
Freedom to organize					
(1983–87)	3.17	1.81	2.41	−0.26	
(N = 448)	(0.0001)	(0.184)	(0.006)	(0.854)	2.70

N = number of observations.

Note: Standard error is in parentheses. Average economic rate of return on projects is in the range of 12–19 per cent.

Source: J. Isham, D. Kaufmann, and L. Pritchett, 'Civil Liberties, Democracy, and the Performance of Government Projects' 11 *World Bank Economic Review* 219 (1997).

15.3.3 The In-Depth Country Diagnostic Perspective: The Case Study of Bolivia

Following half a century of acute political instability and numerous auto-cratic governments and economic mismanagement (including the worst hyperinflation episode for any country not at war), Bolivia embarked on a radical macroeconomic reform program in the mid-eighties—at a time of restoration of electoral democracy. A semblance of democratic political stability has basically been in place since then, and Bolivia has also stayed the course in the implementation of economic reforms, implementing trade liberalization and an ambitious privatization program, while maintaining macroeconomic stability. Yet economic growth has been disappointing, poverty alleviation has been scant, and social indicators have not improved significantly. Consequently, Bolivia, at an estimated per capita income of about US$ 1,000, continues to be one of the poorest countries in the hemi-sphere. Thus, taking the case study of Bolivia, and utilizing in-depth country diagnostic tools[13] (instead of aggregate cross-country econometric methods),

[13] Since the late nineties we have carried out detailed governance country diagnostics in scores of countries, which elicit specific information on institutional performance and its determinant factors (including voice, accountability, transparency, etc.). For a synthesis of

in a recent research project we undertook to address the question of the factors accounting for the fact that Bolivia had shown such tepid socio-economic performance—in spite of having been regarded as a stellar implementer of the so-called 'Washington Consensus' of the 1990s in terms of economic reforms and macroeconomic management.[14]

In a recent research paper we presented a framework and evidence suggesting that 'voice' and governance factors (including corruption in particular) have been the weak link in Bolivia's development. We emphasized the prevalence of patronage, 'clientelism', corruption, and political capture in the interplay between the enterprise and public sectors. These have played an important role in shaping the institutional framework under which many public institutions operate—and the resulting behavior of the enterprise sector given the incentives it faces. In this research, we presented empirical analysis based from two recent micro-level surveys: a worldwide survey of 10,000 enterprises in 80 countries carried out by the World Bank in 1999/2000 (the World Business Environment Survey),[15] which included Bolivia, as well as an in-country survey diagnostic of public officials in scores of public institutions in Bolivia, based on an interview survey (with closed quantitative questions) of over a thousand public officials.

The results from both these micro-surveys (firms and public officials) suggest the importance of specific governance factors in explaining private and public sector performance, and in particular: performance of courts, protection of property rights, corruption, transparency, and 'voice' (including feedback mechanisms by service delivery users). Figure 15.3, panels A and B, drawn from these research results based on enterprise and public official surveys, respectively, suggest the importance of these 'voice', corruption, and governance factors in affecting performance at the enterprise and for public institutions. Conversely, the empirical micro-evidence is much weaker on the potential relevance of some traditional public sector management variables, such as public sector wages (Figure 15.3, panel C), or the existence of internal rules/laws within institutions.

By contrast to aggregate cross-country studies of growth, the approach taken here of probing into some of the micro-institutional aspects—undertaken

these in-depth country diagnostic tools, see Annex 4, and visit http://www.worldbank.org/wbi/governance/capacitybuild/diagnostics.html.

[14] See D. Kaufmann, M. Mastruzzi, and D. Zavaleta, 'Sustained Macroeconomic Reforms, Tepid Growth: A Governance Puzzle in Bolivia?' in D. Rodrik, ed., *In Search of Prosperity* (Princeton, NJ: Princeton University Press, 2001) and D. Kaufmann, G. Mehrez, and T. Gurgur, 'Voice or Public Sector Management? An Empirical Investigation of Determinants of Public Sector Performance Based on a Survey of Public Officials', manuscript (Washington D.C.: World Bank Institute, 2001).

[15] World Bank, *World Business Environment Survey* (2000) available at http://www.worldbank.org/privatesector/ic/ic_ica_resources.htm.

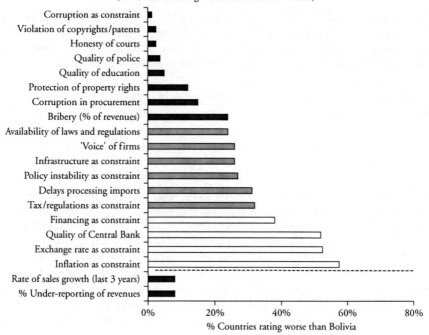

Panel A: Institutional and Governance Assessment by Firms
(% Countries Rating Worse than Bolivia—WBES)

Source: World Bank, *World Business Environment Survey* (2000) available at http://www.
worldbank.org/privatesector/ic/ic_ica_recources.htm. Based on survey of enterprises in
80 countries.

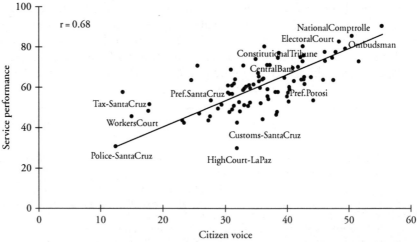

Panel B: Service Performance and Citizen Voice in Bolivia's Public Institutions

Source: Kaufmann, Mehrez, Gurgur, above n.14. Based on survey of public officials in Bolivia.

Figure 15.3. Bolivia in-depth assessment—the perspective of the firm and of the
public officials

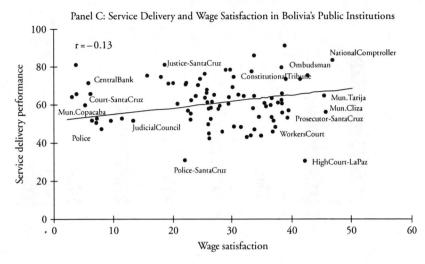

Panel C: Service Delivery and Wage Satisfaction in Bolivia's Public Institutions

Source: Kaufmann, Mehrez, Gurgur, above n. 14. Based on survey of public officials in Bolivia.

Figure 15.3. (*Continued*)

from the dual perspectives of the firm and the public agency—may prove of particular use for concrete policy advice at the country level, possibly assisting in a concrete fashion to put forth priorities for action for sustained growth, as well as pointing to the means by which such priorities ought to be detailed and carried out. These priority factors tend to be country-specific, back-stopping the need to undertake in-depth country level diagnostics, exploiting micro-level data.

15.4 GOVERNANCE, CORRUPTION, AND HUMAN RIGHTS: THE NEGLECTED LINK

In section 15.2, describing the datasets we utilize in this chapter, we discussed in some detail the aggregated governance indicators. As with the evidence on the levels and trends on human rights showcased in section 15.2, we have similarly analyzed the levels and trends of the six governance dimensions worldwide and also found rather uneven results across countries and regions. These are depicted in Figure 15.4, which contains six panels exhibiting all the governance indicators. The ordering of the panels in Figure 15.4 has been deliberately organized to go from highest congruence with 1GHR variables to the lowest. Hence voice and democratic accountability (which was also shown in 1GHR Figure 15.1, last panel), political stability and absence of violence, and rule of law and corruption do feature above government/ bureaucratic effectiveness and regulatory quality, which are farther removed

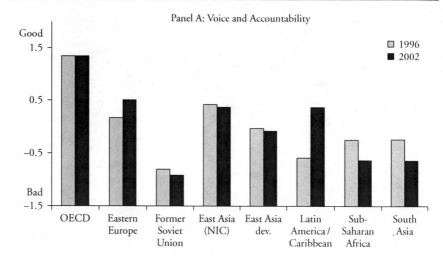

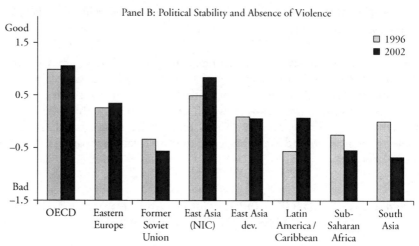

Figure 15.4. Linking governance, corruption, and human rights

from core human rights considerations. Yet it is telling that at least the lion's share of governance dimensions is highly congruent with human rights concepts (see Annex 1 depicting in detail each individual variable that was utilized in constructing each governance indicator).

And as we explore below, the linkages between governance, corruption, and human rights are multifaceted, yet there is little formal interface in the international convention or advocacy world on these issues. It is telling, for instance, the absence of any mention about absence of rule of law, independence of the judiciary, and corruption from the UN Human Rights

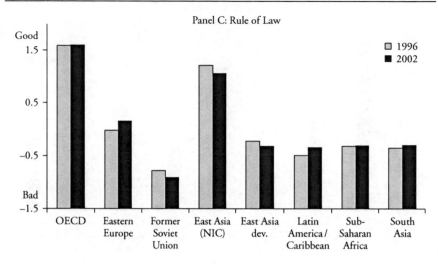

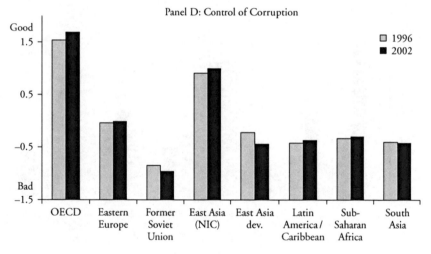

Figure 15.4. (*Continued*)

Covenants and Declaration on the Right to Development, and also the absence of any mention of human rights in the recently adopted UN anti-corruption convention (see Table C1 in Annex 3 with simple word count statistics from the various covenants and conventions).[16]

---

[16] Earlier writings have argued, however, that there is a connection between corruption and human rights. See, for instance, L. Cockroft, 'Corruption and Human Rights: A Crucial Link' Transparency International Working Paper, 1998 and E. P. Mendes, 'Corruption: The Cancer of the International Bill of Rights—Democracy and Freedom of Expression and the

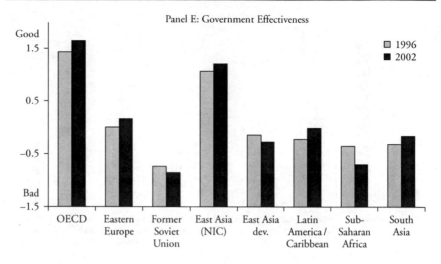

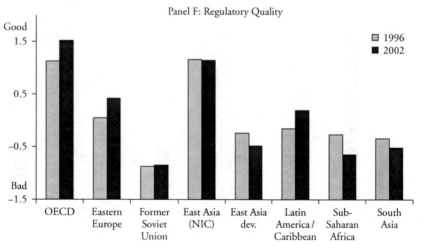

Figure 15.4. (*Continued*)

Source: Kaufmann, Kraay, and Mastruzzi, above n. 7. http://www.worldbank.org/wbi/governance/pubs/govmatters3.html.

Indeed, in the previous section we first reported on the research suggesting that 1GHR issues may be an important determinant of 2GHR issues. We also reported on the absence of automatic positive (reverse) feedback mechanism (on average) from higher incomes per capita to improved

Main Treatments?' in E. P. Mendes and A. Lalonde-Roussy, eds., *Bridging the Global Divide on Human Rights* (Aldershot, U.K.: Ashgate, 2003).

governance and civil liberties. The question we pose here refers to the mechanisms whereby 1GHR may affect 2GHR, and the factors behind the absence of reverse causality. We focus on the latter at first.

Based on empirical evidence, in that same research project we advanced an explanation for this absence of positive (or even negative) feedback mechanism: the phenomenon of *state capture*, defined as the undue and illicit influence of the elite in *shaping* the laws, policies, and regulations of the state.[17] In essence, this form of capture is a manifestation of 'grand' corruption.

When institutions of the state are 'captured' by vested interests in this way, or, more subtly, when powerful vested interests exert undue influence in shaping the rules of the game for their own benefit (discussed below), entrenched elites in a country can benefit from a worsening status quo of misgovernance and can successfully resist demands for change even as per capita income rises.

Based on in-depth governance and anti-corruption country diagnostics carried out at the World Bank in countries in various regions, as well as enterprise surveys in economies in transition, we have found significant empirical evidence on the challenge of state capture (and the related 'crony bias' or unequally distributed influence) in many countries across the world regions. Further, we find evidence that the extent of capture and crony bias is related to the degree of civil liberties in a country. In particular, in countries exhibiting quasi-authoritarian tendencies, or 'managed' democracies, the extent of state capture by the few in the elite is significantly higher than where political and civil liberties are very high. And in turn, where state capture is high, we find that socio-economic development, including income growth and private sector development, is impaired. This illustrates that important governance factors, such as grand/political corruption in the form of state capture, may be playing a key mediating role between 1GHR and 2GHR.

Thus, in countries with an environment that is 'captured' or unduly influenced by the vested interests of the powerful few, the focus of efforts to combat corruption and improve governance needs to shift from a narrow emphasis on passing laws and rules, and on procedures within the public administration, to a much broader agenda of greater political accountability, transparency, and freedom of the press.

In contrast to the absence of positive effects from income to governance, we found a *large direct causal effect* from better governance to improved

---

[17] J. Hellman, G. Jones, and D. Kaufmann, 'Seize the State, Seize the Day: State Capture, Corruption and Influence in Transition.' 31 *Journal of Comparative Economics* 751 (2003), available online at: http://www.worldbank.org/wbi/governance/pubs/seizestate.html. See also more recent evidence in some Latin American countries, emerging from the governance and anti-corruption diagnostics (GAC) of the World Bank Institute (WBI) at http://www.worldbank.org/wbi/governance/capacitybuild/.

development outcomes. Consequently, the simple relationships depicted in Figure 15.2 above (and Figure 15.5 below) in fact do approximate the causal impact of improved governance on per capita income (given the lack of positive feedback in the reverse causality direction).[18] Indeed, the effects of improved governance on income in the long run are found to be very large, with an estimated 400 per cent improvement in per capita income associated with an improvement in governance by one standard deviation, and similar improvements in reducing child mortality and illiteracy. To illustrate, an improvement in rule of law by one standard deviation from the current levels in Ukraine to those 'middling' levels prevailing in South Africa would lead to a fourfold increase in per capita income in the long run. A larger increase in the quality of rule of law (by two standard deviations) in Ukraine (or in other countries in the former Soviet Union), to the much higher level in Slovenia or Spain, would further multiply this income per capita increase. Similar results emerge from civil liberties or control of corruption improvements: a mere one standard deviation improvement in voice and accountability from the low level of Venezuela to that of South Korea, or in control of corruption from the low level of Indonesia to the middling level of Mexico, or from the level of Mexico to that of Costa Rica, would also be associated with an estimated fourfold increase in per capita incomes, as well as similar improvements in reducing child mortality by 75 per cent, as well as major gains in literacy. In Figure 15.5 below we illustrate with different data the extent to which governance factors matter for 2GHR issues.

In sum, new types of surveys and statistical methodologies permit the empirical assessment of governance and voice and civil liberties worldwide. These assessments in turn suggest that there are enormous differences in governance performance across the globe, which in turn matters significantly for growth and development outcomes. At the same time, we found that income windfalls for a country do not, however, get automatically translated into improved governance, possibly due to particular political factors related to the interface between corporate strategies of the powerful, which result in unequal distribution of influence and thus of reaping the fruits from growth.

Governance factors such as corruption and rule of law are not, however, necessarily fundamental determinants of socio-economic development, but often they are mediating factors, which in turn are related and in part determined by other factors. As suggested earlier, voice and civil liberties (and within it, components such as press freedom, rights of women, etc.) are suggested to be potential determinants of control of corruption and corporate ethics (Figure 15.6).

---

[18] In fact, due to the likelihood of a negative feedback effect from incomes per capita to governance, the actual simple correlation summarized in Figure 15.2 underestimates the extent (slope) of the causal link from governance to incomes per capita.

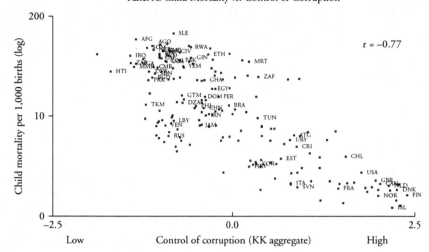

Source: Kaufmann and Kraay, above n. 10.

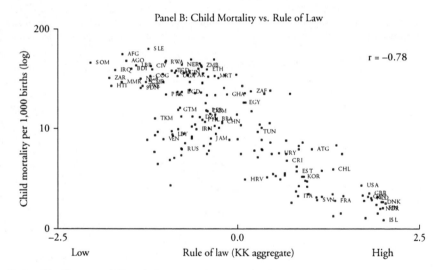

Source: Kaufmann and Kraay, above n. 10.

Figure 15.5. Governance matters for 2GHR

In sum, the evidence suggests a number of close links between human rights and governance issues. In an earlier section of this paper we showed that 1GHR and 2GHR issues are highly related in general, and possibly in a causal fashion from the former to the latter. On the basis of the evidence discussed here, we attempted to initially open the 'black box' of possible

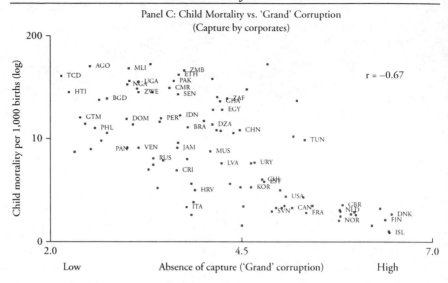

Panel C: Child Mortality vs. 'Grand' Corruption
(Capture by corporates)

Source: Kaufmann and Kraay, above n. 10. World Economic Forum and Harvard University, 'Executive Opinion Survey' (EOS) prepared for *The Global Competitiveness Report* (New York: Oxford University Press, 2003). Capture ('Grand' Corruption) variable drawn from EOS 2003 enterprise survey. Question: 'How commonly would you estimate that firms make undocumented extra payments of bribe to influence laws, policies, regulations or decrees?'

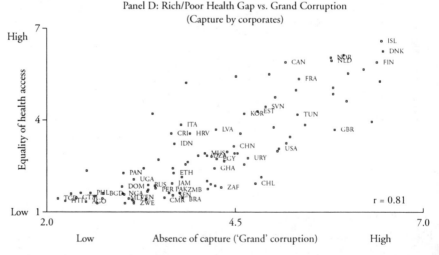

Panel D: Rich/Poor Health Gap vs. Grand Corruption
(Capture by corporates)

Source: Health gap drawn from EOS 2003. Question: 'The difference in quality of the healthcare available to rich and poor people in your country is large/small'. Capture ('Grand' Corruption) variable drawn from EOS 2003 enterprise survey. Question: 'How commonly would you estimate that firms make undocumented extra payments of bribe to influence laws, policies, regulations or decrees?'

Figure 15.5. (*Continued*)

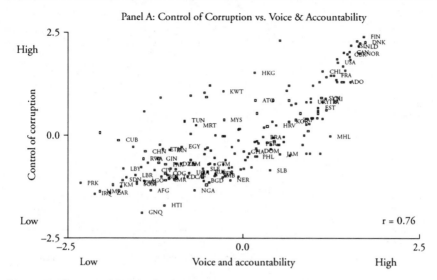

Source: Kaufmann and Kraay, above n. 10.

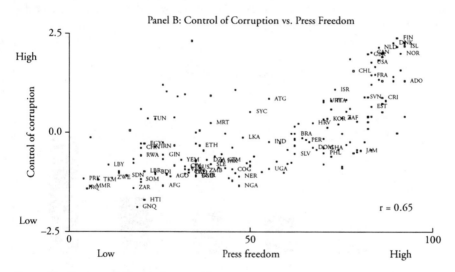

Source: Kaufmann and Kraay, above n. 10.

Figure 15.6. 1GHR matters for controlling corruption and corporate ethics—civil liberties, rights of women, and control of corruption/ethics

mechanisms linking both sets of generational issues in human rights. In particular, we posit that governance in a narrow sense, namely through corruption, rule of law, and corporate ethics, plays an important mediating role between salient 1GHR and 2GHR issues.

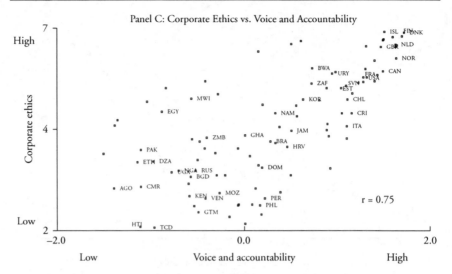

Source: Corporate ethics drawn from EOS 2003. Question: 'The corporate ethics (ethical behavior in interactions with public officials, politicians and other enterprises) of your country's firms in your industry are among the world's worst/best'. Voice and Accountability drawn from Kaufmann and Kraay, above n. 10.

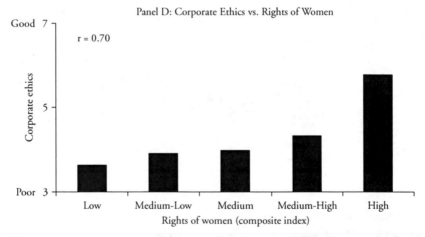

Source: Health gap drawn from EOS 2003. Question: 'The difference in quality of the healthcare available to rich and poor people in your country is large/small'. Active Capture drawn from EOS 2003. Question: How commonly would you estimate that firms make undocumented extra payments of bribe to influence laws, policies, regulations or decrees?

Figure 15.6. (*Continued*)

15.5 SIGNIFICANT EXCEPTIONS: THE CHALLENGE OF UNBUNDLING AND SPECIFICITY IN HUMAN RIGHTS

In previous sections we explored some potential causal links between 1GHR and 2GHR issues, and also between governance, rule of law, and corruption challenges, on the one hand, and 2GHR objectives, on the other. While the empirical evidence suggests that such links may indeed be present, caveats are in order. First, some of this empirical research is of a preliminary nature, and will need to be deepened and further validated by parallel research efforts.

Second, the breadth of scope encompassing human rights dimensions implies that (even if for particular components, and composites, the links suggested above substantially hold) for specific dimensions such relation between variables of interest may be weaker. It is thus important to go beyond the broad-based yet general empirical terrain we have covered so far and study in depth the extent to which the many unbundled variables of interest are highly related to each other—or not. We suggested a number of such highly correlated variables (and at times causally so) in previous sections of the chapter. Yet an important example of a weaker (although still present) link refers to AIDS, for instance. While the prevalence of AIDS is correlated with the degree of civil liberties and the extent of governance in a country (as depicted in Figure 15.7, panels A and B), such correlation is significantly lower than for other dimensions we have explored in this chapter. The fact that there are many outliers is clear from the plotgrams in Figure 15.7. Indeed, generally speaking, to attain 2GHR goals, a plethora of determinants (and thus interventions) ought to be considered, rather than taking a uni-dimensional view on what matters. And this is particularly the case for challenges such as AIDS. While focusing on 1GHR issues, and on control of corruption, is of some importance, it would be counter-productive for such focus to be exclusive, since it would obviously not suffice—or even account for the lion's share in determining the difference between successes and failures in controlling the epidemic.

AIDS is an illustration of the differential importance of various factors when unbundling human rights and governance to specific components. In this context, it is of interest to also note that for instance within 1GHR issues certain dimensions do not correlate tightly with each other. While for instance there is a high correlation (about 0.6) between various human rights components related to protection of life (for example, disappearances and torture; or killings and disappearances), the same is not the case between such 'hard-core' life protection human rights and others (such as vis-à-vis the extent of political participation, or government censorship, for instance). To illustrate further the importance of unbundling in this respect, for

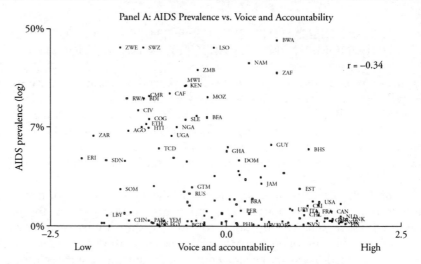

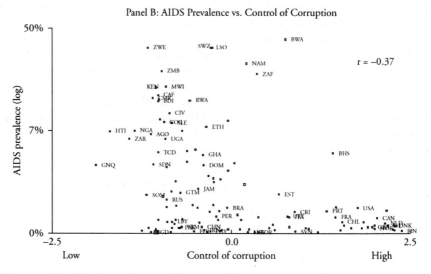

Figure 15.7. Relating AIDS to other variables

Source: Kaufmann and Kraay, above n. 10. AIDS prevalence data based on adult population only (15–49).

instance the correlation between the extent of political imprisonment and child labor is less than 0.2; similarly there is a relatively low correlation of about 0.2 between the extent of disappearances in a country and the rights of women.

15.6 CONCLUSIONS AND IMPLICATIONS

In this chapter we presented a preliminary empirically-based exploration of evidence and links between human rights and governance. We preliminarily assessed recent data and trends on human rights, and posed questions about the links between first (political and civil rights) and second (socio-economic) generation human rights issues, as well as between these twin generation human rights aspects, on the one hand, and governance, narrowly defined, on the other.

We suggested that first generation human rights issues (often called 'negative liberties') are still paramount. Both the current worldwide levels and trends in compliance with first generation human rights issues (1GHR—political and civil rights), as well as their importance as a determinant of second generation human rights outcomes, do suggest that continuing priority in addressing 1GHR is warranted. In particular, this preliminary review of worldwide evidence suggested that: i) 1GHR continue to be violated in many settings, and ii) progress towards resolution of these issues worldwide (the improving trend line) may not be apparent in some dimensions, and overall such progress may not be as pronounced as would be expected or believed in some quarters.

Progress on second generation human rights issues (2GHR—socio-economic and economic development rights, often called 'positive liberties') are (*inter alia*) found to be dependent on first generation human rights (1GHR). Consequently, there would be no empirical justification to lower the priority focus on 1GHR—even if 2GHR issues are regarded as having parity in terms of overall social welfare implications.

We also suggested that there is an important missing link—from analytical, empirical, and practical standpoints—in this realm, namely between corruption and misgovernance. Corruption and misrule of law are associated with an absence of 1GHR. Empirically, we also observe this from the standpoint of corporate ethics/governance, and not merely governance of public institutions. Some powerful elite firms engage in grand forms of corruption such as capture of the laws, regulations, and policies of the state for their benefit. Such capture is in turn related to low levels of political contestability and 'voice' in such countries. The strategies and behavior of the firm are thus linked to public sector phenomena and actions.

It was indicated that, while 1GHR issues were relevant for various forms of governance at the public and corporate levels, at the same time high corruption and capture are detrimental to the attainment of 2GHR issues. Yet in spite of the incipient evidence linking rule of law and corruption (public and corporate) issues with human rights issues, it is noteworthy that the covenants and declarations on human rights do not include freedom from corruption (and the new anti-corruption convention does not include human rights). This implies that a key mechanism linking first and second generation issues is explicitly omitted from coverage by human rights conventions, declarations, and work by activists in this area. While there may be legal (and related) justifications for such omission, it does have significant implications in terms of strategies and prospects for progress on human rights, particularly regarding 2GHR issues. Conversely, it is also paramount to further mainstream into an operational context on the ground the finding that to address corruption, misrule of law, and capture by the vested interests of powerful conglomerates, civil liberties and participatory voice and democratic accountability are of empirical significance.

Based on recent research, we presented the findings indicating that political/civil liberties and good governance are not a 'luxury good': the process of economic development does not in itself automatically ensure improved governance, civil liberties, and control of corruption. The causality direction is from improved governance to economic development, and not vice versa. This implies that specific interventions and policies on governance and 1GHR are required at every stage, rather than expecting an automatic virtuous circle whereby income growth per se will result in improved governance.

Voice and participation mechanisms are thus not only very important because of their fundamental value, but also due to their instrumental value as key to socio-economic development outcomes. And in addition to the evidence in this respect from cross-national data, this finding also applies at the ('micro') project level: investment projects funded by the World Bank in settings with better civil liberties and participatory mechanisms are found to have a much higher socio-economic impact. An in-depth case study method, utilizing diagnostic findings and research on Bolivia, was also presented in brief, further supporting the importance of 'voice' and governance mechanisms to attain 2GHR objectives—rather than expecting that a purely technocratic approach to macroeconomic management in itself will deliver such objectives.

It is also noted from the empirical work that the links between 1GHR and 2GHR and within each cluster, do vary in strength across particular issues. Some important and specific 2GHR challenges in health, for instance, such as AIDS, are not as closely correlated to 1GHR factors as others, and thus very specific focus on these (in parallel to the continuing support to 1GHR issues) is warranted. Given the breadth of scope of coverage of human rights issues, in measuring, monitoring, and drawing lessons it is paramount to unbundle the various dimensions within each generation. Some dimensions within 1GHR are not highly correlated with each other, for instance.

We suggest two concluding remarks. First, on the importance of meaningful voice (and transparency) mechanisms, and related civil and political liberties, for success in socio-economic development and thus 2GHR issues. Such 2GHR objectives, which are dependent in great measure on an environment where there is control of corruption, transparency, rule of law, and corporate ethics (and therefore absence of state capture by vested interests), thus require particular focus on these governance and integrity issues as well. These governance issues, are, however, also dependent in part on voice and civil liberties, as well as on domestic politics. Future analysis and diagnosis for successful program design will need to consider in a deeper and more integral fashion these civil liberties and political issues for enhancing aid effectiveness, even if the mandate of many IFIs preclude explicit political conditionality.

Second, on the potential for further integration between the fields of (corporate and public sector) governance, rule of law, and corruption, on the one hand, and human rights, on the other. As discussed, notwithstanding the very independent tracks that human rights, corporate governance, and corruption have taken in international fora (conventions, declarations, and covenants), in practice we find evidence of close links, which need to be further operationally exploited.

And finally, on the power of data. In this chapter we pose a challenge to data-reticence. This is akin to a development that took place almost a decade ago for the field of corruption and governance, at a time when these notions were regarded as not amenable to measurement (or, if they could be measured, it would be so unreliable to render it useless). Experience has shown that with more rigorous statistical tools, improved survey techniques, and in-depth empirical analysis, significant progress has been made. Nowadays countries and institutions are regularly monitored (and monitor themselves) on governance and corruption. Such data monitoring has become a potent tool for activism by civil society and reformists in governments worldwide. Further, the monitoring through governance indicators is likely to become an important results-oriented tool in determining aid allocations—given the impact on aid effectiveness. The investment in a major governance, rule of law, corporate ethics, and corruption databank has proven beneficial for distilling important research lessons and for challenging widely held popular notions that were not grounded on empirics.

By investing in further empirical work, collecting and analyzing data, codifying margins of error, and so forth, similar progress could take place in the human rights field in the near term. In this context, it may be pertinent to explore potential synergies between the existing in-depth country diagnostic tools for governance and corruption, and integration of relevant and measurable human rights dimensions through these surveys of enterprises, citizens, and public officials (Annex 4).

All these will require additional empirical research efforts, for which this chapter is obviously only an initial contribution. Much would need to be validated further, debated, and expanded, with additional data to be gathered and analyzed.

ANNEX 1: CODING HUMAN RIGHTS INFORMATION:
CINGRANELLI, RICHARDS, AND WEBSTER HUMAN RIGHTS
CODIFICATION AS INPUT TO WBI GOVERNANCE INDICATORS

The Human Rights data for 2002 and 2003 was coded by Craig Webster as background for the Governance Indicators project, utilizing the methodology by Cingranelli and Richards who first coded earlier years of such data, with input by Webster. The codification draws from two sources, the U.S. Department of State's *Country Reports on Human Rights Practices 2002* and Amnesty International's *Amnesty International Report 2003*. Both of these reports offer descriptions of human rights practices and conditions pertaining to the year 2002. The State Department by law must submit a human rights report to Congress and has done so for many years. Because of legal requirements of what must be covered in the report and the significant resources of the U.S. Government, it is a comprehensive source for global human rights information available. The report must be submitted to Congress by end of February each year. While Amnesty International's report is not as comprehensive in its information coverage, it does offers a valuable alternative and non-governmental source from which information can be coded for various human rights dimensions. It is available to the public usually in June of every year.

The main variables and their key characteristics are in the table annex below.

Table A1. *Cingranelli, Richards, and Webster's main variables*

Variables	Range	Description/Question
Killings	0–2 (good)	Political killings are frequent/never happen
Disappearances	0–2 (good)	Disappearances are frequent/never happen
Torture	0–2 (good)	Political killings are frequent/never happen
Imprisonments	0–2 (good)	There are many/no people imprisoned because of their political, religious, or other beliefs
Judiciary	0–2 (good)	Judiciary is a dependent/ independent institution
Censorship	0–2 (good)	Government censorship is complete/none
Political participation	0–2 (good)	Political participation is limited/free and open

Table A1. (*Continued*)

Variables	Range	Description/Question
Freedom to travel	0–1 (good)	Domestic and foreign travel is restricted/unrestricted
Workers' rights	0–2 (good)	Workers rights are not protected/protected by government
Women political rights	0–4 (good)	Women's political rights are prevented/guaranteed
Women economic rights	0–3 (good)	Women's economic rights are discriminated/equal to men
Women social equality	0–3 (good)	Social equality of women is not guaranteed by law/guaranteed
Coups	0–1 (good)	Has there been a coup?
State of emergency	0–2 (good)	Is there currently a state of emergency or martial law declared?
Freedom of religion [1]	0–1 (good)	Religions are banned by the government
Freedom of religion [2]	0–1 (good)	There are restrictions by the government on some religious practices

ANNEX 2: COMPONENTS OF AGGREGATE GOVERNANCE INDICATORS, 2002

Table B1. *Voice and accountability*

Code	Table	Concept measured
Representative Sources		
CUD	A5	To what extent does the state and/or its allied groups engage in repression of its citizens? In carrying out internal security tasks, to what extent does the state rely on tactics commonly considered illegitimate in the international community?
EIU	A8	Orderly transfers Vested interests Accountability of Public Officials Human Rights Freedom of association
FRH	A9	*Civil liberties*: Freedom of speech, of assembly and demostration, of religion, equal opportunity, of excessive governmental intervention *Political Rights*: Free and fair elections, representative legislature, free vote, political parties, no dominant group, respect for minorities Freedom of the Press
HUM	A13	*Travel*: domestic and foreign travel restrictions Freedom of political participation *Imprisonments*: Are there any imprisoned people because of their ethnicity, race, or their political, religious beliefs? Government censorship
PRS	A15	*Military in Politics*: The military are not elected by anyone, so their participation in government, either direct or indirect, reduces accountability and therefore represents a risk. The threat of military intervention might lead as well to an anticipated potentially inefficient change in policy or even in government. It also works as an indication that the government is unable to function effectively and that the country has an uneasy environment for foreign business. *Democratic Accountability*: Quantifies how responsive government is to its people, on the basis that the less response there is the more likely it is that the government will fall, peacefully or violently. It includes not only if free and fair elections are in place, but also how likely is the government to remain in power.

RSF	A16	Press Freedom Index
WMO	A18	*Institutional permanence*: An assessment of how mature and well established the political system is. It is also an assessment of how far political opposition operates within the system or attempts to undermine it from outside. A country with high institutional permanence would unquestionably survive the death or removal from power of the current leadership. A mature political system will conventionally have a clearly established relationship between the executive, legislative, and judicial branches of government.
		Representativeness: How well the population and organized interests can make their voices heard in the political system. Provided representation is handled fairly and effectively, it will ensure greater stability and better designed policies.

Non-Representative Sources

AFR	A1	Satisfaction with democracy
FHT	A9	*Political Process*: Deals with elections, referenda, party configuration, conditions for political competition, and popular participation in elections.
		Civil Society: Highlights the degree to which volunteerism, trade unionism, and professional associations exist, and whether civic organizations are influential.
		Independent Media: Press freedom, public access to a variety of information sources, and the independence of those sources from undue government or other influences.
GAL	A10	Trust in National Government
		Trust in the Parliament
GCS	A11	Firms are usually informed clearly and transparently by the Government on changes in policies affecting their industry
		Newspapers can publish stories of their choosing without fear of censorship or retaliation
		When deciding upon policies and contracts, Government officials favor well-connected firms
		Extent of direct influence of legal contributions to political parties on specific public policy outcomes
		Effectiveness of national Parliament/Congress as a law-making and oversight institution
LOB	A14	Satisfaction with democracy
WCY	A17	Transparency of Government policy

Table B2. *Political stability*

Code	Table	Concept measured

Representative Sources

Code	Table	Concept measured
CUD	A5	Assess the degree to which the decline or collapse of central political authority posed a threat to political stability in this country.
		Assess the degree to which political protest or rebellion posed a threat to political stability in the country.
		Assess the degree to which ethno-cultural and/or religious conflict posed a threat to political stability in the country.
		Assess the degree to which external military intervention posed a threat to political stability in the country.
DRI	A6	*Military Coup Risk*: A military coup d'état (or a series of such events) that reduces the GDP growth rate by 2% during any 12-month period.
		Major Insurgency/Rebellion: An increase in scope or intensity of one or more insurgencies/rebellions that reduces the GDP growth rate by 3% during any 12-month period.
		Political Terrorism: An increase in scope or intensity of terrorism that reduces the GDP growth rate by 1% during any 12-month period.
		Political Assassination: A political assassination (or a series of such events) that reduces the GDP growth rate by 1% during any 12-month period.
		Civil War: An increase in scope or intensity of one or more civil wars that reduces the GDP growth rate by 4% during any 12-month period.
		Major Urban Riot: An increase in scope, intensity, or frequency of rioting that reduces the GDP growth rate by 1% during any 12-month period.
EIU	A8	Armed conflict
		Violent demonstrations
		Social Unrest
		International tensions

HUM A13 Frequency of political killings
Frequency of disappearances
Frequency of torture

PRS A15 *Internal Conflict*: Assesses political violence and its influence on governance.
External conflict: The external conflict measure is an assessment both of the risk to the incumbent government and to inward investment.
Ethnic tensions: This component measures the degree of tension within a country attributable to racial, nationality, or language divisions.

WMO A18 *Civil unrest*: How widespread political unrest is, and how great a threat it poses to investors. Demonstrations in themselves may not be cause for concern, but they will cause major disruption if they escalate into severe violence. At the extreme, this factor would amount to civil war.
Terrorism: Whether the country suffers from a sustained terrorist threat, and from how many sources. The degree of localization of the threat is assessed, and whether the active groups are likely to target or affect businesses.

Non-Representative Sources
BRI A3 Fractionalization of political spectrum and the power of these factions.
Fractionalization by language, ethnic, and/or religious groups and the power of these factions.
Restrictive (coercive) measures required to retain power.
Organization and strength of forces for a radical government.
Societal conflict involving demonstrations, strikes, and street violence.
Instability as perceived by non-constitutional changes, assassinations, and guerrilla wars.

GCS A11 *Country terrorist threat*: Does the threat of terrorism in the country impose significant costs on firms?
LOB A14 *Country terrorist threat*: Is terrorism a serious problem in the country?
WCY A17 Risk of political instability

Table B3. *Government effectiveness*

Code	Table	Concept measured
Representative Sources		
CUD	A5	Rate the administrative and technical skills of the country's civil service (occupying middle and higher management roles).
		Rate the efficiency of the country's national bureaucracies overall.
		Rate the efficiency of the country's local-level government bureaucracies overall.
		Rate the effectiveness of co-ordination between the central government and local-level government organizations.
		Rate the state's ability to formulate and implement national policy initiatives.
		Rate the state's effectiveness at collecting taxes or other forms of government revenue.
		Does the central government produce a national budget in a timely manner?
		Do local governments produce budgets in a timely manner?
		Rate the state's ability to monitor socio-economic trends, activities, and conditions within its borders.
		Rate the state's ability to create, deliver, and maintain vital national infrastructure.
		Rate the state's ability to respond effectively to domestic economic problems.
		Rate the state's ability to respond effectively to natural disasters.
DRI	A6	*Government Instability:* An increase in government personnel turnover rate at senior levels that reduces the GDP growth rate by 2% during any 12-month period.
		Government Ineffectiveness: A decline in government personnel quality at any level that reduces the GDP growth rate by 1% during any 12-month period.
		Institutional Failure: A deterioration of government capacity to cope with national problems as a result of institutional rigidity that reduces the GDP growth rate by 1% during any 12-month period.
EIU	A8	Quality of bureaucracy
		Excessive bureaucracy/red tape
PRS	A15	*Government Stability:* Measures the government's ability to carry out its declared programs, and its ability to stay in office. This will depend on issues such as: the type of governance, the cohesion of the government and governing party or parties, the closeness of the next election, the government's command of the legislature, and popular approval of the government policies.
		Bureaucratic Quality: Measures institutional strength and quality of the civil service; assess how much strength and expertise bureaucrats have and how able they are to manage political alternations without drastic interruptions in government services, or policy changes.

| WMO | A18 | *Policy consistency and forward planning*: How confident businesses can be of the continuity of economic policy stance—whether a change of government will entail major policy disruption, and whether the current government has pursued a coherent strategy. This factor also looks at the extent to which policy-making is far-sighted, or conversely aimed at short-term economic (and electoral) advantage. |
| | | *Bureaucracy*: An assessment of the quality of the country's bureaucracy. The better the bureaucracy the quicker decisions are made and the more easily foreign investors can go about their business. |

Non-Representative Sources

AFR	A1	Trust in Police
BPS	A2	How problematic are telecommunications for the growth of your business?
		How problematic is electricity for the growth of your business?
		How problematic is transportation for the growth of your business?
BRI	A3	Bureaucratic delays
CPIA	A4	Management of external debt
		Management of development programs
		Quality public administration
FHT	A9	*Government and Administration*: Government decentralization, independence and responsibilities of local and regional governments, and legislative and executive transparency are discussed.
GCS	A11	Competence of public sector personnel
		Quality of general infrastructure
		Quality of public schools
		Time spent by senior management dealing with government officials
LBO	A14	Trust in Police
WCY	A17	Government economic policies do not adapt quickly to changes in the economy
		The public service is not independent from political interference
		Government decisions are not effectively implemented
		Bureaucracy hinders business activity
		The distribution infrastructure of goods and services is generally inefficient

Table B4. *Regulatory quality*

Code	Table	Concept measured
Representative Sources		
DRI	A6	*Regulations—Exports*: A 2% reduction in export volume as a result of a worsening in export regulations or restrictions (such as export limits) during any 12-month period, with respect to the level at the time of the assessment.
		Regulations—Imports: A 2% reduction in import volume as a result of a worsening in import regulations or restrictions (such as import quotas) during any 12-month period, with respect to the level at the time of the assessment.
		Regulations—Other Business: An increase in other regulatory burdens, with respect to the level at the time of assessment.
		Ownership of Business by Non-Residents: A 1-point increase on a scale from '0' to '10' in legal restrictions on ownership of business by non-residents during any 12-month period.
		Ownership of Equities by Non-Residents: A 1-point increase on a scale from '0' to '10' in legal restrictions on ownership of equities by non-residents during any 12-month period.
EIU	A8	Unfair competitive practices Price controls Discriminatory tariffs Excessive protections
HER	A12	Regulation Government Intervention Wage/Prices Trade Foreign investment Banking
PRS	A15	*Investment Profile.* Includes the risk to operations (scored from 0 to 4, increasing in risk); taxation (scored from 0 to 3); repatriation (scored from 0 to 3); and labor costs (scored from 0 to 2). They all look at the government's attitude towards investment.

WMO   A18   *Tax Effectiveness:* How efficient the country's tax collection system is. The rules may be clear and transparent, but whether they are enforced consistently. This factor looks at the relative effectiveness too of corporate and personal, indirect and direct taxation.

Legislation: An assessment of whether the necessary business laws are in place, and whether there are any outstanding gaps. This includes the extent to which the country's legislation is compatible with, and respected by, other countries' legal systems.

Non-Representative Sources

BPS   A2   Information on the laws and regulations is easy to obtain
                    Interpretations of the laws and regulations are consistent and predictable
                    Unpredictability of changes of regulations
                    How problematic are labor regulations for the growth of your business?
                    How problematic are tax regulations for the growth of your business?
                    How problematic are custom and trade regulations for the growth of your business?

CPIA   A4   Competitive environment
                    Factor and products markets
                    Trade policy

EBRD   A7   Price liberalisation
                    Trade & foreign exchange system
                    Competition policy
                    Commercial Law Extensiveness
                    Commercial Law Effectiveness
                    Financial Regulations: extensiveness
                    Financial Regulations: effectiveness

GCS   A11   Administrative regulations are burdensome
                    Tax system is distortionary
                    Import barriers as obstacle to growth
                    Competition in local market is limited

Table B4. (*Continued*)

Code	Table	Concept measured
		It is easy to start company
		Anti-monopoly policy is lax and ineffective
		Clusters are frequent
		Environmental regulations hurt competitiveness
		Cost of tariffs imposed on business
		Government subsidies keep uncompetitive industries alive artificially
WCY	A17	The exchange rate policy of your country hinders the competitiveness of enterprises
		Protectionism in your country negatively affects the conduct of business in your country
		Competition legislation in your country does not prevent unfair competition
		Price controls affect pricing of products in most industries
		Legal regulation of financial institutions is inadequate for financial stability
		Foreign financial institutions do not have access to the domestic market
		Access to local capital markets is restricted for foreign companies
		Access to foreign capital markets is restricted for domestic companies
		Financial institutions' transparency is not widely developed in your country
		Customs' authorities do not facilitate the efficient transit of goods
		The legal framework is detrimental to your country's competitiveness
		Foreign investors are free to acquire control in domestic companies
		Public sector contracts are sufficiently open to foreign bidders
		Real personal taxes are non-distortionary
		Real corporate taxes are non-distortionary
		Banking regulation does not hinder competitiveness

Table B5. *Rule of law*

Code	Table	Concept measured
Representative Sources		
CUD	A5	For the most part, is the state seen as legitimately representing its citizens? Rate the state's adherence to the rule of law, considering the country as a whole.
DRI	A6	*Losses and Costs of Crime*: A 1-point increase on a scale from '0' to '10' in crime during any 12-month period.
		Kidnapping of Foreigners: An increase in scope, intensity, or frequency of kidnapping of foreigners that reduces the GDP growth rate by 1% during any 12-month period.
		Enforceability of Government Contracts: A 1-point decline on a scale from '0' to '10' in the enforceability of contracts during any 12-month period.
		Enforceability of Private Contracts: A 1-point decline on a scale from '0' to '10' in the legal enforceability of contracts during any 12-month period.
EIU	A8	Violent crime
		Organized crime
		Fairness of judicial process
		Enforceability of contracts
		Speediness of judicial process
		Confiscation/expropriation
HER	A12	Black market
		Property Rights
HUM	A13	Independence of Judiciary
PRS	A15	*Law and Order*: The Law sub-component is an assessment of the strength and impartiality of the legal system, while the Order sub-component is an assessment of popular observance of the law (they are assessed separately).
QLM	A3	Direct Financial Fraud, Money Laundering, and Organized Crime

Table B5. *(Continued)*

Code	Table	Concept measured
WMO	A18	*Judicial Independence*: An assessment of how far the state and other outside actors can influence and distort the legal system. This will determine the level of legal impartiality investors can expect. *Crime*: How much of a threat businesses face from crime such as kidnapping, extortion, street violence, burglary, and so on. These problems can cause major inconvenience for foreign investors and require them to take expensive security precautions.
Non-Representative Sources		
BPS	A2	Fairness of the court system
		Affordability of the court system
		Enforceability of court decisions
		Honesty of courts
		Quickness of court decisions
		Property right protection
		How problematic is organized crime for the growth of your business?
		How problematic is the judiciary for the growth of your business?
		How problematic is street crime for the growth of your business?
BRI	A3	Enforceability of contracts
CPIA	A4	Property rights

FHT	A9	*Rule of Law:* Considers judicial and constitutional matters.
GAL	A10	Trust in the Legal System
GCS	A11	Common crime imposes costs on business
		Organized crime imposes costs on business
		Money laundering through banks is pervasive
		Money laundering through non-banks is pervasive
		Quality of Police
		Insider trading is pervasive
		The judiciary is independent from political influences of members of government, citizens, or firms
		Legal framework to challenge the legality of government actions is inefficient
		Intellectual Property protection is weak
		Protection of financial assets is weak
		Illegal donation to parties is frequent
		Percentage of firms which are unofficial or unregistered
WCY	A17	Tax evasion is a common practice in your country
		Justice is not fairly administered in society
		Personal security and private property are not adequately protected
		Parallel economy impairs economic development in your country
		Insider trading is common in the stock market
		Patent and copyright protection is not adequately enforced in your country

Table B6. *Control of corruption*

Code	Table	Concept measured
Representative Sources		
CUD	A5	Rate the severity of corruption within the state
		To what extent do the country's primary political decision makers (e.g. chief executive and cabinet members) engage in patterns of nepotism, cronyism, and patronage?
		To what extent do the country's civil service (occupying middle and higher management roles) engage in patterns of nepotism, cronyism, and patronage?
		To what extent do patterns of nepotism, cronyism, and patronage undermine the state's ability to exercise the basic functions of government effectively?
		To what extent do patterns of nepotism, cronyism, and patronage distort broad patterns of economic development?
DRI	A6	Risk Event Outcome non-price: Losses and Costs of Corruption: A 1-point increase on a scale from '0' to '10' in corruption during any 12-month period.
EIU	A8	Corruption
PRS	A15	*Corruption*: Measures corruption within the political system, which distorts the economic and financial environment, reduces the efficiency of government and business by enabling people to assume positions of power through patronage rather than ability, and introduces an inherent instability in the political system.
QLM	A3	Indirect Diversion of Funds
WMO	A18	*Corruption*: This assesses the intrusiveness of the country's bureaucracy. The amount of red tape likely to be encountered is assessed, as is the likelihood of encountering corrupt officials and other groups.
Non-Representative Sources		
AFR	A1	How common is corruption among public officials?
BPS	A2	How common is it for firms to have to pay irregular additional payments to get things done?

		On average, what per cent of total annual sales do firms pay in unofficial payments to public officials?
		How often do firms make payments to influence the content of new legislation?
		Extent to which firms' payments to public officials to affect legislation impose costs on other firms.
		How problematic is corruption for the growth of your business?
BRI	A3	*Internal Causes of Political Risk*: Mentality, including xenophobia, nationalism, corruption, nepotism, willingness to compromise, etc.
CPIA	A4	Transparency/corruption
FHT	A9	Corruption
GCS	A11	Public trust in financial honesty of politicians
		Extent to which legal contributions to political parties are misused by politicians
		Diversion of public funds due to corruption is common
		Frequent for firms to make extra payments connected to: import/export permits
		Frequent for firms to make extra payments connected to: public utilities
		Frequent for firms to make extra payments connected to: tax payments
		Frequent for firms to make extra payments connected to: loan applications
		Frequent for firms to make extra payments connected to: awarding of public contracts
		Frequent for firms to make extra payments connected to: influencing laws, regulations, decrees
		Frequent for firms to make extra payments connected to: getting favourable judicial decisions
		Extent to which firms' illegal payments to influence government policies impose costs on other firms
LBO	A14	What percentage of public employees would you say are corrupt?
WCY	A17	Bribing and corruption exist in the economy

ANNEX 3: SELECTED CONCEPTS IN KEY HUMAN RIGHTS COVENANTS AND DECLARATION

Table C1. *Simple word count of selected concepts in key human rights covenants and declarations*

	Covenant on Civil & Political Rights	Covenant on Economic, Social & Cultural Rights	Declaration on the Right to Development	Total # of Words (3 documents)	United Nations Convention Against Corruption
Total # of Words (*per document*)	7,195	3,762	1,674	12,631	18,417
Political Rights	3	1	2	6	0
Torture	1	0	0	1	0
Health	5	4	1	10	1
Food	0	5	1	6	0
Wages	0	1	0	1	0
Governance	0	0	0	0	0
Corruption	0	0	0	0	73
Rule of Law	0	0	0	0	3
Independent Judiciary	0	0	0	0	0
Data	0	0	0	0	1
Monitoring	0	0	0	0	1
Human Rights Indicators	0	0	0	0	0

ANNEX 4: SURVEY DIAGNOSTIC TOOLS FOR IN-COUNTRY GOVERNANCE ASSESSMENT

The design and implementation of agency-specific, in-depth governance diagnostic surveys for public officials, households or users, and enterprises, constitute an innovation that provides tangible inputs for countries committed to implementing capacity building and institutional change programs. New survey instruments can collect detailed information on behavior in even the most dysfunctional government agencies and on the delivery of specific services. Used with other empirical devices, such diagnostic surveys can focus the political dialogue on concrete areas for reform and rally civil society behind reform efforts.

Such country self-diagnostic data, used by a variety of in-country stakeholders and disseminated through participatory workshops, have mobilized broader support for consensus building and collective action for institutional reforms. For instance, countries such as Albania, Bolivia, Latvia, Thailand, and Slovakia, progressed from using diagnostics to taking concrete action. In other countries, similar governance improvement efforts are taking place at the municipal level, such as in a number of Ukrainian cities, as well as in the case of Campo Elias, Venezuela, where specific actions to improve the local governance were carried out following diagnostic surveys. Thus, in-depth country-specific data are powerful in mobilizing support for reforms—but the obstacles presented by the vested interests and 'state capture' of some powerful forces within the elite, resisting such reforms, are also powerful. Therefore, political leadership, civil society, private sector investors, and the donor community need to build on the insights and momentum generated by the diagnostics and utilize and disseminate statistics in conjunction with promoting civil liberties and media involvement, and resulting in higher accountability and actions against corruption.

The first set of in-depth governance diagnostic surveys of public officials, firms, and citizens was carried out in Albania, Georgia, and Latvia in 1998, and focused on diagnosing the challenge of corruption in order to identify priorities for action. More recently, implementation of refined and expanded versions of these diagnostic surveys has been carried out in dozens of other countries, focusing more broadly on the complex governance of key agencies within each country, and assessing the main institutional determinants of misgovernance and corruption. Challenging conventional wisdom, the new surveys of public officials, enterprises, and citizens find respondents willing to provide detailed information on misgovernance that they have observed and experienced (as opposed to merely indicating their vague perceptions about country-wide corruption, for instance).

Survey respondents report on embezzlement of public funds, theft of state property, bribery to shorten processing time, bribery to obtain monopoly power, and bribery in procurement. For instance, theft of state property was identified as a particular problem in Albania, where weakness in the judiciary was identified as one of the primary causes of corruption. Regulatory failures are much less important there than in Georgia and Latvia, indicating that the priorities for reform vary significantly from setting to setting, even if a priori there appear to be commonalities. In these diagnostic surveys, detailed statistics are collected on many governance and performance characteristics of the key agencies, and include important management, political, and corruption dimensions in the country such as frequency and cost of bribes paid by enterprises to regulators in different agencies as well as the shortcomings of public service delivery and other performance and effectiveness indicators. Issues such as meritocracy, discretionality, budgetary transparency, and the poverty alleviation effectiveness of various institutions are covered. The analysis of these statistics then serves as a vital input for prioritizing in the formulation of a governance improvement reform program.

When the governance diagnostic data are presented in workshops to members of the business community, major civil society, and the executive and legislative branches, the policy debate abruptly changes from vague, unsubstantiated, and often personalized accusations to one focused on empirical evidence and systemic weaknesses that need to be addressed. Action programs are often (although not always) formulated, to be followed by implementation of institutional reforms in many cases.

Indeed, the collection, analysis, and dissemination of country-specific data on governance are altering the policy dialogue on these issues, and often empowering civil society through collective action to work with reformists in the executive, judiciary, and legislative branches, as well as with the private sector.

These benefits do not always become reality, however. Important challenges remain, including the complex political dynamics that often change during the course of the diagnostics, so that the preparedness to implement an ambitious program may have waned once the diagnostic has been carried out and translated into concrete proposed actions. Another challenge refers to the evolving state of the art and methods in translating the survey evidence and its analysis into reform priorities, as well as the strategy and concrete steps in implementing the reform agenda. Once survey data and their analysis are available, countries where political will is present must begin the more difficult task of prioritizing measures according to the country reality and introducing reforms to improve governance.

16

Transnational Corporations as Instruments of Human Development

OLIVIER DE SCHUTTER

16.1 INTRODUCTION

For all the sour feelings that the acts of certain transnational corporations have aroused in developing countries where they have operated, there is one thing which, for a developing country, is even worse than to attract foreign direct investment (FDI): it is to attract none. Transnational corporations (TNCs)—corporations having business operations in countries other than their country of incorporation, either directly or through subsidiaries or affiliates[1]—have the potential to be important actors in development, not only in that they may contribute to the expansion of exchanges and therefore to economic growth, but also in that they may help fulfil a form of development oriented towards the expansion of human capabilities, of which human rights are both a main ingredient and a precondition.[2] At the same time, never have more concerns been expressed about the impunity of transnational corporations in the globalized economy: these 'leviathans'[3] or 'hydra-headed monsters'[4] occasionally commit serious human rights

---

[1] On the question raised by the definition of transnational corporations or, in his vocabulary, 'multinational enterprises', see Peter T. Muchlinski, *Multinational Enterprises and the Law* (Oxford: Blackwell, 1995) 12–15.

[2] This richer understanding of development, which cannot be reduced today to industrialization and economic growth, dates from the 1990s. The most interesting conceptualizations may be located in the *Report of the 1998 Oslo Symposium on Human Development and Human Rights* (Copenhagen: UNDP, 1998); Amartya Sen, *Development as Freedom* (New York: Anchor Books, 1999); United Nations Development Programme (UNDP), *Human Development Report 2000—Human Rights and Human Development* (New York: UNDP, 2000). In this study, it is this notion of development which is referred to under the expression 'human rights-oriented (or driven) development'.

[3] S. Joseph, 'Taming the Leviathans: Multinational Enterprises and Human Rights' 46 *Netherlands International Law Review* 171 (1999).

[4] E. A. Duruigbo, *Multinational Corporations and International Law: Accountability and Compliance Issues in the Petroleum Industry* (New York: Transnational Publishers, 2003) xviii.

violations or are complicit in such violations, and, despite their obligation under the international law of human rights to protect the human rights of populations under their jurisdiction, states hosting their investments appear too often unwilling or incapable to do so.

The complex relationship transnational corporations entertain vis-à-vis human rights in the countries in which they develop their activities is hardly surprising. Transnational corporations are simply agents of economic globalization. The very definition of economic globalization as the 'integration of national economies into the international economy through trade, direct foreign investment (by corporations and multinationals), short-term capital flows, international flows of workers and humanity generally, and flows of technology'[5] illustrates the essential function TNCs have to fulfil in this process, and this process is crucial to the economic growth and therefore also to the development of less industrialized countries. Economic globalization as such, however, is neither positive nor negative to human rights: whichever impact it has on their realization depends on the forms it takes and the kind of governance it is guided by. The argument of this chapter is based on the recognition that the forms economic globalization may take are many, and that we are not bound to any one of these forms in particular, despite the sense of fatefulness which all too often accompanies debates on globalization. The kind of globalization advocated here proposes an enriched understanding of the obligation of transnational corporations to respect human rights. The chapter moreover argues that this is, in fact, the direction in which we are moving, and that simply accentuating certain aspects of the current situation will bring us closer to this objective: transforming TNCs into instruments for a more humane kind of globalization, one which not only respects the full set of internationally recognized human rights, but which also ensures that they will be further realized, in combination with economic growth.

The general thesis is the following. Many tools have been proposed, since the mid-1990s, to ensure that companies comply with certain basic requirements in the areas of labour rights, respect for the environment, and human rights more generally, or to encourage companies to comply voluntarily with such requirements. But these tools, such as the United Nations Global Compact proposed to the business community by UN General Secretary Koffi Annan[6] or the SA8000 social accountability system proposed and managed by Social Accountability International, essentially require that, in the course of their operations, TNCs respect these internationally recognized standards. At best, they require therefore that the impact of the enjoyment of human rights be evaluated *ex ante* and *ex post*, both before the

---

[5] Jagdish Bhagwati, *In Defense of Globalization* (Oxford: Oxford University Press, 2004) 3.
[6] http://www.unglobalcompact.org.

corporation enters into a particular project and in the course of the implementation of that project. An impact-analysis approach to foreign direct investment, where it remains confined to an examination of the impact of a particular investment or project on the human rights of the population concerned (what may be called 'micro-analysis'), may however not be sufficient. The human rights perspective should and can be applied at the 'macro' level of analysis—the level at which the contribution of foreign direct investment to development may be appreciated in its fuller dimension. Mirroring Article 28 of the Universal Declaration of Human Rights,[7] the 1986 United Nations General Assembly Declaration on the Right to Development[8] defines this right as 'an inalienable human right by virtue of which every human person and all peoples are entitled to participate in, contribute to, and enjoy economic, social, cultural and political development, in which all human rights and fundamental freedoms can be fully realized'.[9] The question of which conditions are to be realized for foreign direct investment to contribute to the right to development, defined by the realization of human rights it facilitates, is quite distinct from the question whether, as foreign investors, transnational corporations respect the full panoply of internationally recognized human rights in their operations. One of the implicit proposals of this chapter is that human rights lawyers should move from the 'micro', where their presence is now well established, to the 'macro', which is still largely unchartered territory for them—that they should propose mechanisms through which not only transnational corporations should respect human rights where they act, but through which moreover their presence can contribute to a form of growth conducive of the right to development.[10]

There is no automatic relationship between the arrival of foreign investors in a country and the human rights-driven development of that country: even where the TNCs concerned respect the full range of labour rights, environmental standards, and human rights which their activity could potentially affect, there is no certainty that their presence in the country will contribute to that country moving towards the full realization of human rights of all

---

[7] G.A. res. 217A (III), U.N. Doc A/810 at 71 (1948).

[8] G.A. res. 41/128, annex, 41 U.N. GAOR Supp. (No. 53) at 186, U.N. Doc. A/41/53 (1986). [9] Ibid.

[10] In her Presidential Lecture at the World Bank in December 2001, then UN High Commissioner for Human Rights Mary Robinson noted: 'Lawyers should not be the only voice in human rights and, equally, economists should not be the only voice in development. The challenge now is to demonstrate how the assets represented by human rights principles, a form of international public goods, can be of value in pursuing the overarching development objective, the eradication of poverty.' M. Robinson, 'Bridging the Gap between Human Rights and Development', Presidential Lecture, World Bank, Washington D.C., December 2001, http://www.unhchr.ch/development/newsroom.html. I am grateful to Manfred Nowak for providing me with this reference.

its population. We could, of course, leave it to the economists to study the conditions which have to be created to ensure that foreign direct investment is conducive not only to economic growth, but also to human development. This has been, in fact, the implicit division of tasks between human rights lawyers and development economists in the discussion about the regulation of the activities of TNCs: while the former have devised tools to oblige TNCs to comply with internationally recognized human rights, the latter have demonstrated which benefits can be expected from an expansion of the private sector and the inflow of foreign capital in developing economies. This chapter, which is programmatic in that respect, seeks to identify the contours of a human rights approach as applied to—beyond the discrete activities of companies—the structural, macroeconomic, questions raised by FDI. The legal framework of FDI, in particular, must be critically examined from that perspective. Otherwise there exists a real risk that, while we devote our energies to scrutinizing the activities of TNCs in developing states, we forget about the structural dimensions of their presence in those states, such as the pressure under which developing states are to attract FDI and the concessions they make to ensure that foreign capital flows in, or the consequences of FDI on the situation of local producers and investors or on the relative wages.

Once we adopt a human rights approach to the question of foreign direct investment in its structural dimension—as distinguished, in this chapter, from the question of specific activities of companies—we are led to consider foreign direct investment also as a lever to promote human rights in the country where it is made, and identify the corresponding obligations not only of the private economic actors, but also of the states concerned and of multilateral lending institutions which finance the private sector. What is needed is to channel FDI to ensure that it serves development, understood as a process ensuring the full enjoyment of all the human rights, rather than contradicts it. This requires a 'macro-analysis' of the impact of FDI on developing countries, going beyond the examination of the impact of particular investment projects and their immediate consequences to the concerned communities, and enlarged to an analysis of the general context in which the investment is made and its consequences for a human rights-driven development of the country. This rejoins the conclusion recently presented by the 2003 Report on Trade and Investment published by the United Nations Conference on Trade and Development (UNCTAD), which states that 'the contribution of FDI to capital formation, technical progress and growth depends crucially on the policies adopted by recipient countries vis-à-vis foreign investors'.[11] It also develops the view put forward by the World Commission on the Social Dimension of Globalization set up on the

---

[11] UNCTAD, *Trade and Development Report 2003* (Geneva: UNCTAD, 2003) 76.

initiative of the ILO, the Final Report of which, released on 24 February 2004, calls for 'a development-friendly multilateral framework of rules for investment'.[12]

Sections 16.2, 16.3, and 16.4 of this chapter examine what may be labelled the failings of the micro-analysis approach to include the responsibilities of TNCs towards human rights-driven development. The general thrust of these sections is as follows. Until recently, the mechanisms which existed to ensure a better accountability of transnational corporations for human rights violations that they commit or make themselves complicit in simply sought to ensure that, in the course of their activities, these corporations would not violate, or aid and abet in violating, human rights. This understanding of the responsibility of corporations, however, fails at three levels. It appears insufficient to guard against the risk that the investments of TNCs in developing countries, although not directly the source of human rights violations, will not contribute effectively to the development of that country, because of the way they are directed or the general context in which they are made (section 16.2). It also does not ensure that the presence of the TNC in a developing country will contribute to improving the record of that country in the field of human rights, despite the fact that the investor may potentially encourage such improvements (section 16.3). Finally, at a third level, such an understanding of the responsibility of TNCs towards human rights does not prevent that, as a consequence of inter-jurisdictional competition between states, the wages of the less skilled workers in more developed countries will be lowered, out of fear of the outsourcing of certain activities to developing countries with less demanding requirements and because of a diminished leverage power of the unions, and that, in the host country of the investment, inequalities will rise between the better paid, skilled workers and the low skilled workforce (section 16.4).

Of course, the insufficiencies at each of these levels correspond to different concerns. The first insufficiency relates to the situation of a developing country which does not benefit as much as it should from the foreign direct investment, because of the conditions under which the investment is made and which the investor has been granted by exercising its bargaining power, or by relying on provisions from bilateral investment treaties or multilateral agreements on investment which favour the interests of investors. The second insufficiency relates to the situation of a developing

---

[12] World Commission on the Social Dimension of Globalization, *A Fair Globalization: Creating Opportunities for All* (Geneva: ILO, 2004) 106. The World Commission on the Social Dimension of Globalization was created by a decision of the International Labour Organization Governing Body in November 2001. Its mandate was to prepare a major authoritative report on the interaction between the globalization of economy and the world of work. The Commission has acted as an independent body and its members have been serving in their individual capacities.

country whose government commits human rights violations, which the foreign investor is or should be aware of, and could contribute to combating. The third insufficiency corresponds to the situation where the conditions which are or could be obtained by an investor in a foreign jurisdiction are used by that investor, in more or less explicit ways, to pressure the workforce in industralized countries or the public authorities in those countries to lower certain requirements which impose costs on the investor and may lead it to relocate certain segments of production elsewhere. These concerns are quite distinct from one another. They present, however, one common departure point: they have their source in a refusal to consider that the consequences of economic globalization are not automatically benevolent, for both the developing and the industrialized countries. Therefore TNCs, as vectors or channels of globalization, not only should be obliged not to violate human rights in the course of their operations. We should also identify ways in which they could be used as instruments to bring about positive changes, commensurate to the influence they already exercise de facto. In other terms, we should conceive of TNCs as a tool of international governance, which should be used to bring about the kind of globalization we believe will best contribute to the realization of the right to development.

Sections 16.5 and 16.6 of this chapter identify some mechanisms which could be used to move in the direction proposed. These sections lay the emphasis on the responsibilities of developed states and multilateral lending institutions. These are the actors which set the rules of economic globalization: these are the actors who should take action to ensure that, in the argot of the times, FDI becomes regulated by a development-friendly multilateral framework of rules. TNCs are to be incentivized to work to the good. But the current framework, in many respects, while protecting the rights of investors and strictly limiting the range of conditions which may be imposed on them by the host states, does nothing to facilitate this. TNCs are encouraged to seize upon the opportunities created for them by economic globalization: while they have to respect human rights in their activities, they are essentially to go about their business, without having to worry about the broader consequences of their presence or about whether or not their presence is conducive of the human development of the communities in which they operate. Because the imposition of further obligations directly on TNCs is fraught with difficulties—for instance, how should we define an obligation to contribute to the right to development?—the more promising path is to examine how the states where TNCs are incorporated and multilateral lending institutions could contribute to TNCs becoming, instead, the agents of a benevolent form of economic globalization, one which works in favour of human development and the eradication of poverty rather than simply contributes to economic expansion.

16.2 THE INCAPACITY OF MICRO-ANALYSIS TO TACKLE THE NOTION OF ECONOMIC RESPONSIBILITY[13]

An understanding of the responsibility of TNCs which remains confined to an examination of the impact of a particular investment or project on the human rights of the population concerned is inadequate because it does not guarantee that such an investment will contribute to the realization of the right to development, i.e., will truly benefit the populations of the country where the investment is made. Although the imposition of human rights obligations on companies through an impact analysis of each individual project may be adequate for imposing a responsibility vis-à-vis labour rights (social responsibility), the environment (environmental responsibility), or other human rights directly affected by the activities of the corporation (ethical responsibility), it fails to tackle adequately what may be styled the economic responsibility of the corporation, which we may define as its responsibility to act in order to contribute to the reduction of poverty in the country concerned. The Draft Guidelines on a Human Rights Approach to Poverty Reduction Strategies elaborated upon request of the UN High Commissioner for Human Rights mention that TNCs must 'establish accessible, transparent and effective monitoring and accountability procedures in relation to *their poverty reduction and human rights responsibilities*'.[14] But it is striking, for instance, that, where the responsibility of TNCs is evoked today, very little attention is paid to the economic context in which they operate and the impact their investment may have on the general economic situation of the country concerned, for instance the level of unemployment or the debt-repaying capacity of the state. The following paragraphs offer four examples of such potential impacts, and of how these may depend on the framework regulating FDI.

16.2.1 The Contribution of TNCs to Capital Flows

To take one first example, the form under which the FDI is made by the TNC makes a crucial difference to its impact on the local community, and

[13] The idea that an 'economic responsibility' should be imposed on private transnational actors has been suggested to me by my colleagues from the Groupe de recherche sur les stratégies économiques alternatives (GRESEA), see www.gresea.be. I would like to take this opportunity to state my admiration and solidarity for the work done in that research centre, which has been a source of inspiration for me for many years.

[14] United Nations Office of the High Commissioner for Human Rights, *Draft Guidelines: A Human Rights Approach to Poverty Reduction Strategies*, 10 September 2002 (Geneva: United Nations) para. 247 (my emphasis) (under Guideline 18: 'Monitoring and Accountaibility of Global Actors'). These guidelines were requested by Mary Robinson, then UN High

yet it is a factor rarely if ever taken into account by the current tools for improving the accountability of TNCs towards human rights. Different channels of FDI ought, indeed, to be carefully distinguished.[15] FDI can be the result of *privatizations*. These were especially important during the 1980s and the first half of the 1990s, under the influence of macroeconomic programs which sought to improve the debt-repaying capacity of the developing states *inter alia* by cutting down the public sector, especially by privatizing public enterprises for the sake of ameliorating productivity and efficiency. Often, in the absence of adequate accompanying measures, this led to more unemployment, because of the important lay-offs this led to, without alternatives being created for the employees from the public sector suddenly considered redundant.[16] FDI also can take the form of *acquisitions of local private firms*, by mergers and acquisitions. Although this form of FDI has been rising since the early 1990s,[17] its expansion has been continuing in the period 1998 to the present. Such FDI translates into the transfer of the property of local undertakings to foreign corporations, but not necessarily to new investments and growth. Finally, some FDI leads to the creation of new infrastructures, 'investment in bricks and mortar'.[18] FDI in the latter form, sometimes referred to as 'greenfield investment', is the most promising from the point of view of capital formation and economic growth, but investments under this form have been steadily declining and have been selectively distributed among countries. Moreover, when such investments are made under special economic conditions set up with the specific purpose of attracting

Commissioner for Human Rights, from three experts, Professors Paul Hunt, Manfred Nowak, and Siddiq Osmani. The initiative was taken in July 2001 by the Chair of the United Nations Committee on Economic, Social and Cultural Rights, to ask the Office of the High Commissioner for Human Rights (OHCHR) to develop such guidelines for the integration of human rights into poverty reduction strategies.

[15] For a useful overview, see Rémi Bachand and Stéphanie Rousseau, 'International Investment and Human Rights: Political and Legal Issues', background paper for the Think Tank of the Board of Directors of Rights & Democracy—International Centre for Human Rights and Democratic Development, 'Investment in Developing Countries: Meeting the Human Rights Challenge', 11 June 2003, Ottawa, Canada. On the different forms of foreign direct investment, see 4–9.

[16] See, e.g., Joseph Stiglitz, *Globalization and its Discontents* (New York: W. W. Norton & Co., 2002) ch 1, and the reference to reports either internal to the International Monetary Fund or commissioned to external experts on this detrimental impact of the so-called 'structural adjustment programs'. For a synthesis of these reports, see IMF Staff, *Distilling the Lessons from the ESAF Reviews* (Washington D.C.: IMF, July 1998).

[17] See, for example, David Kucera, 'The Effects of Core Workers' Rights on Labour Costs and Foreign Direct Investment: Evaluating the "Conventional Wisdom"', EP/130/2001, Decent Work Research Programme, ILO, 2001, at 4 (reporting that, for the least developed countries, the value of mergers and acquisitions in relation to total FDI inflows increased from about 15 to 30 per cent from 1993 to 1998).

[18] UNCTAD, *Trade and Development Report 2003*, above n. 11, 76.

foreign investors, for instance through export processing zones (EPZs) where social and environmental regulations may be lighter or underenforced or where no or only minimal levels of taxes are imposed,[19] they often represent short-term gains for the host country, in the job creations they imply. But these short-term gains may be offset by the departure of the investor to other, still more competitive jurisdictions. The International Confederation of Free Trade Unions (ICFTU) notes in this respect that the globalization of the economy 'has accentuated competition for investment between the EPZs of the various countries. In the fight to secure investments, even greater financial rewards are offered to investors (resulting in lower gains for the country itself) or measures are taken to make workers even more compliant.'[20] It adds:

The growth of the global production network has made it possible for companies to source goods and services throughout the world and to reconfigure production lines quickly and easily, meaning that a country or a supplier can be cut out of the network if the conditions change and they are not able to react rapidly enough.[21]

Much of the empirical evidence that exists on the treatment of workers in EPZs in fact seems to show that the wages in those zones are higher than in comparable alternative employment in the country concerned.[22] Whether this evaluation would still be as positive after controlling for productivity

[19] See generally on export processing zones, the study of the ILO, 'Free Trade Zones' in *Employment Effects of Multinational Enterprises in Developing Countries* (Geneva: ILO,1981); the joint study of the ILO and the United Nations Centre on Transnational Corporations, ILO/UNCTC, *Economic and Social Effects of Multinational Enterprises in Export Processing Zones* (Geneva: ILO, 1988); ILO, *Labor and Social Issues Relating to Export Processing Zones* (Geneva: ILO, 1998). The estimates are that, in December 2002, 116 countries had such special economic zones, of which there are altogether 3,000, providing employment for 43 million workers (of which 30 million in China alone). The phenomenon is expanding rapidly. In 1995, for instance, 73 countries had such zones, of which there were 500 in total. In 1997, the first year for which this data is available, there were still only 22.5 million employees in EPZs. These figures are from ILO calculations based on a diversity of sources, and presented in the report presented to the Governing Body of the ILO in March 2003 (*Employment and social policy in respect of export processing zones (EPZs)*, 286th session of the ILO Governing Body, GB.286/ESP/3, para. 4).

[20] ICFTU, *Export Processing Zones—Symbols of Exploitation and a Development Dead-End*, September 2003, 10. Other interesting reports on the situation of labour rights in export processing zones include two reports from Human Rights Watch, *From the Household to the Factory: Sex Discrimination in the Guatemalan Labour Force*, February 2002; and Human Rights Watch, *A Job or Your Rights: Continued Sex Discrimination in Mexico's Maquiladora Sector*, December 1998. A comparative analysis has been prepared by the International Labour Office, Committee on Employment and Labour Policy, *Employment and Social Policy in Respect of Export Processing Zones*, GB.285/ESP/5, Geneva, ILO, November 2002.

[21] ICFTU, ibid.

[22] This seems to be confirmed by the recent work of the ILO on the employment and social aspects of EPZs (see ILO, Report of the Tripartite meeting of Export Processing Zone-Operating Countries, ILO doc. GB. 273/STM/8/1 (1998)), as well as by other studies, such as the report of the World Bank, *The Philippines: The Case of Economic Zones* (Washington

differentials attributable, in particular, to the efficiency gains due to the
technology of the TNC, and to the economies of scale its organization permits,[23] remains to be seen; and it may also be suggested that such higher
wages are merely to be seen as a compensation for the compliance required
from the workforce in EPZs and the long working hours, with maximum
flexibility and adaptability to new requirements, which the companies
established in such zones generally expect from workers. But these debates
miss the point which is made here. The question whether the presence of
EPZs truly benefit the countries which create such incentives to attract foreign
investors, beyond the immediate gains of employment creation and relatively
higher wages for those who manage to be recruited, is distinct from the
question whether the workers' rights are respected in such special zones, and
whether the wages they receive are fair. In particular, the absence or quasi-
absence of fiscal revenues for the host country from companies investing in
such zones, or the uncertainty about the long-term presence of the investor
which could easily relocate production elsewhere, seem to be in clear tension
with the right to development of that country. These concerns have been
clearly expressed by the Worker Vice-Chairperson of the ILO Governing
Body, in the course of a discussion of export processing zones held in March
2003 on the basis of a paper prepared within that organization.[24] He noted:

Economic analysis was needed to evaluate the true impact of EPZs as there were
open and hidden costs to EPZs. Companies were attracted by benefits and incentives
leading to growth, but this came at a cost to government in terms of forgone tax
revenues and payments for other services. The key issue was whether the costs
exceeded the benefits. This was not a matter which could be asserted by intuition; it
was a matter for research and measurement based on downstream inputs and links to
the local economy. Inputs sourced from a foreign country represented a loss for the
host country. If companies imported technology and know-how which did not filter
down through the rest of the supply chain, they would not have a sustainable
economic impact.[25]

It is a rather similar diagnosis the UNCTAD arrives at in its recent *Work
Investment Report 2002: Transnational Corporations and Export Competitiveness*, where it notes the difficulty of undertaking such a cost-benefit analysis as
the one advocated by the ILO Governing Body Worker Vice-Chairman.

D.C.: World Bank, 1999), and D. Madani, *A Review of the Role and Impact of Export
Processing Zones*, Policy Research Paper, Series No. 2238 (Washington D.C.: World Bank,
1999) 45.

[23] On this feature of transnational corporations, see James R. Markusen, 'Multinationals,
Multiplant Economies, and the Gains from Trade' 16 *Journal of International Economics* 205
(1984).

[24] ILO, *Employment and social policy in respect of export processing zones (EPZs)*, above n. 19.

[25] ILO, Governing Body, 286th session—fifteenth item on the Agenda: 'Report of the
Committee on Employment and Social Policy', GB.286/15, March 2003, para. 61.

Cautioning against a 'race to the top' in terms of incentives to attract foreign capital, the UNCTAD report notes that 'successful EPZs should not be judged solely on their capacity to attract FDI or increase exports and foreign-exchange earnings. They should also be assessed by the extent to which they help meet broader economic and social objectives.'[26] However, the kind of analysis this would require—what we may call 'macro-analysis', in the distinction proposed at the beginning of this chapter—the report notes, is

difficult to undertake. In particular, some potential long-term and structural contributions to the local economy are more difficult to appraise as they derive from dynamic gains that can only be realized over time and through deliberate effort, such as learning and absorbing foreign technologies and transforming the pattern of economic growth from an inward-looking to an outward-looking one ... Furthermore, costs such as environmental degradation and foregone revenues are difficult to quantify and may reveal their extent only over time. An additional cost and danger is the risk of 'leakage' of duty-free goods into the domestic market. This has the potential to undermine the development of backward linkages by preventing local enterprises from emerging or it can even destroy local enterprises.[27]

Rémi Bachand and Stéphanie Rousseau add an even more fundamental critique, which replaces the consequences of FDI on the global relationship between industrialized countries and developing countries and, again, questions the contribution of FDI to sustainable development. They note that

FDI from industrialized countries typically comes in the form of loans taken out with host country banks; when the debt is repaid and the profits are repatriated to the investors' countries of origin, what was originally classified as an export becomes an import of capital and wealth into Northern countries. FDI, then, does not always have the effect of capitalizing the host country; it may, on the contrary, cause a flight of the wealth and capital so necessary to the effective protection of human rights such as the right to health and education.[28]

16.2.2 The Crowding Out of Local Producers and Investors

Or consider the argument, put forward in its most recent annual report on Trade and Development by the United Nations Conference on Trade and Development, that the arrival of FDI can have very negative effects on local producers or investors, if no accompanying measures are adopted and if the sequencing and rhythm of the opening up of the country to foreign investments are not carefully considered. According to the UNCTAD, 'transnational corporations (TNCs) operate in highly imperfect markets, where their financial and technological strengths enable them to crowd out

---

[26] UNCTAD, *Work Investment Report 2002: Transnational Corporations and Export Competitiveness* (Geneva: UNCTAD, 2003) 244. [27] Ibid. 215.
[28] Bachand and Rousseau, above n. 15, 9.

domestic producers or pre-empt their investment opportunities'.[29] In the
course of a discussion held at Rights & Democracy, it was mentioned for
instance that the opening in 1996 of the gold mine of Bulyanhulu in
Tanzania, owned by a Canadian undertaking, led to the eviction of local
artisan miners without any compensation for the loss they incurred or to
faciliate their resettlement—moreover all the benefits from this mine are
repatriated to Canada, therefore hardly serve to promote the economic
development of Tanzania.[30] Such examples could be multiplied: whether or
not they respect human rights in their sphere of influence, the impact of the
presence of transnational corporations on sustainable development in the
host country, far from being automatic, depends on the conditions in which
investment takes place and the regulatory framework in place.

16.2.3 The Contribution of TNCs to Technology Transfers

The question of technology flows offers another example. In many cases,
TNCs possess technologies which companies in host countries do not have.
One of the advantages the host country may expect from the presence of
TNCs therefore is that these technologies be transferred, and that local
producers will be able to improve their efficiency by acquiring them. Not
infrequently, however, the TNC will seek to protect its technological
advance. It may preserve technological secrets with the parent company and
transfer only limited parts of the technology to local affiliates or subsidiaries.
It may reserve technological secrets to the personnel from the home country.
It may equip the activities which are outsourced to local subsidiaries or
affiliates with outdated machinery, in order to limit the risk of technology
being diffused within local producers, who may be perceived as potential
competitors. The technological superiority of the TNC therefore does not
automatically result in the transfer of technology to the country hosting its
investment, even if the conditions for FDI are liberalized and the presence of
TNCs, thus, encouraged.

16.2.4 The Limitations Imposed on the Exercise by the Host Government of its Regulatory Powers

Still a further question is raised by the so-called 'stability' clauses in agreements between the foreign investor and the host state which provide that the

[29] UNCTAD, *Trade and Development Report*, above n. 11, 76.

[30] Rights & Democracy (International Centre for Human Rights and Democratic
Development), *Concilier investissement direct à l'étranger et droits humains*, Rapport du groupe
de réflexion de Droits et démocratie, Ottawa, 11 June 2003, 14. This example has been put
forward in the discussion by Joan Kuyek, the national co-ordinator of Mines Alert Canada.

latter will not impose further regulations on the investor which would diminish the profitability of the investment.[31] This constituted one of the most disputed aspects of the Baku-Tbilisi-Ceyhan pipeline project, which may serve here as an illustration. This 3.6 billion US dollars-worth project[32] is for a consortium (BTC) led by British Petroleum (BP) to build two 1,760 km-long pipelines (oil and gas) from the Caspian sea through Azerbaijan, Georgia, and Turkey. The pipeline is expected to function for at a minimum 40 years, and possibly up to 60 years. The legal framework is constituted by one Inter-Governmental Agreement (IGA) concluded between the three countries and three Host Government Agreements (HGAs),[33] with disputes being subjected to the International Centre for the Settlement of Investment Disputes (ICSID). The HGA concluded between the consortium and Turkey in October 2000, which will be in force for 40 years and may be extended for a further period of 20 years, contains the following provisions:

Art. 21.2. The Parties hereby acknowledge that it is their mutual intention that no Turkish Law now or hereafter existing (including the interpretation and application procedures thereof) that is contrary to the terms of this Agreement or any other Project Agreement shall limit, abridge or affect adversely the rights granted to the MEP Participants or any other Project Participants in this or any other Project Agreement or otherwise amend, repeal or take precedence over the whole or any part of this or any other Project Agreement.

Art. 7.2 (vi) . . . . if any domestic or international agreement or treaty; any legislation, promulgation, enactment, decree, accession or allowance; any other form of commitment, policy or pronouncement or permission, has the effect of impairing, conflicting or interfering with the implementation of the Project, or limiting, abridging or adversely affecting the value of the Project or any of the rights, privileges, exemptions, waivers, indemnifications or protections granted or arising under the Agreement or any other Project Agreement it shall be deemed a Change in Law under Article 7.2(xi) [which, if it affects the 'economic equilibrium'[34] of the project, will require Turkey to pay compensation].

These clauses create the impression that Turkey has committed itself not to impose further regulations on the Project participants, for instance in the

---

[31] See in particular F. V. Garcia Amador, 'State Responsibility in case of "Stabilization" Clauses' 2 *Journal of Transnational Law and Policy* 23 (1993).

[32] See www.caspiandevelopmentandexport.com.

[33] These agreements were made public due to the insistence of the International Finance Corporation, the private sector lending institution which is part of the World Bank group, after it was requested to contribute to financing the project.

[34] The 'economic equilibrium' of the project refers according to an Appendix to the HGA to 'the economic value to the Project Participants of the relative balance established under the Project Agreements at the applicable date between the rights, interests, exemptions, privileges, protections and other similar benefits provided or granted to such Person and the concomitant burdens, costs, obligations, restrictions, conditions and limitations agreed to be borne by such Person'.

areas of labour or environmental rights or human rights generally, which could lead to economic losses for the consortium—unless that loss is compensated for. This would of course imply a considerable restriction to the regulatory powers of Turkey, agreed to in the name of the protection of the rights of the investors.[35] However, these clauses of the Turkish HGA should be read in combination with Article IV of the IGA which stipulates that the 'standards and practices generally prevailing in the international petroleum industry for comparable projects' which the project shall comply with must be at least as stringent as those applied within the European Union (EU). The IGA has precedence above the HGAs in cases of conflict, so that any challenge to the exercise by Turkey of its regulatory powers when this would lead to disruption of the 'economic equilibrium' of the project could be contested by Turkey, if it does no more than seek to impose standards equivalent to those in force in the EU. Moreover, confronted by a large number of reports from civil society organizations hostile to the project—a project which these organizations accused of creating social and environmental damage and of creating disincentives for the host states to develop their commitments under human rights treaties—the three states concerned, with the consortium BTC, signed a joint statement on 16 May 2003 containing a number of commitments, including compliance of the project participants with the OECD Guidelines on Multinational Enterprises, confirming that the references in the project to EU standards are references to those standards as they evolve over time, and that all parties are committed to specified labour standards and to any other international labour standards which may be in force in a project state from time to time. On 22 September 2003, a 'BTC Human Rights Undertaking' was published, under which BTC stated, *inter alia*, that it would not contest any regulation by the relevant host government of the human rights or health, safety, and environmental aspects of the project

in a manner (1) reasonably required by international labour and human rights treaties to which the relevant Host Government is a party from time to time, and (2) otherwise as required in the public interest in accordance with domestic law in the relevant Project State from time to time, provided that such domestic law is no more stringent than the highest of European Union standards as referred to in the Project Agreements, including relevant EU directives . . . , those World Bank standards referred to in the Project Agreements, and standards under applicable international labour and human rights treaties.

In that same undertaking, BTC confirmed that it would not seek compensation under the 'economic equilibrium' clause of the HGAs 'in connection with . . . any action or inaction by the relevant Host Government that

---

[35] See, in particular, the report by Amnesty International, *Human rights on the Line: The Baku-Tbilisi-Ceyhan Pipeline Project*, May 2003.

is reasonably required to fulfill the obligations of the Host Government under any international treaty on human rights (including the European Convention on Human Rights), labour or HSE in force in the relevant Project State from time to time to which such Project State is then a party'.

These clarifications seem to constitute adequate answers to the concerns expressed about the legal regime created for the BTC pipeline.[36] In fact, the 'BTC Human Rights Undertaking' is not dissimilar to the 'overriding clause' proposed by Amnesty International just a few months earlier for the HGA between Turkey and BTC, which would have read 'Nothing in this [Agreement] shall be interpreted or applied by the parties in a way that would make it more difficult for Turkey to satisfy its international human rights obligations, at present or in future, as they arise under customary international law or under specific treaties or other instruments to which Turkey is a party.' But, however we evaluate the final outcome of the wide-ranging public debate on the BTC pipeline, the episode illustrates the risk that investors, under agreements concluded directly with host states, or *mutatis mutandis* under bilateral investment treaties or regional free trade agreements, will seek to protect their investments by challenging, as a form of expropriation, any use by the host government of its regulatory powers which may lead to certain economic losses for the investor, in comparison to which gains could be anticipated at the moment the investment was made. Been and Beauvais have documented this risk in detail in their study of Chapter 11 of the North American Free Trade Agreement, which relates to the rights of investors.[37] No doubt similar studies could be produced about the consequences of other legal frameworks protecting the right of foreign investors to be immune from expropriation, as this notion is understood to go beyond nationalization—the transfer of property by unilateral decision of the host state—and may extend to economic losses subsequent to the exercise by the host state of its regulatory powers.[38]

16.2.5 The Contours of an Economic Responsibility

The implication of these examples for the understanding of the responsibilities of transnational corporations is clear. We cannot satisfy ourselves with the fact that, in the particular project concerned, the corporation will not

---

[36] See International Finance Corporation, *BTC Pipeline and ACG Phase 1 Projects, Environmental and Social Documentation—IFC Response to submissions received during the 120-day Public Comment Period,* 27 October 2003, 22–23.

[37] V. L. Been and J. C. Beauvais, 'The Global Fifth Amendment: NAFTA's Investment Protections and the Misguided Quest for an International "Regulatory Takings" Doctrine' 78 *New York University Law Review* 1 (2003).

[38] Bachand and Rousseau, above n. 15, 16–22.

violate human rights. We also have to ask whether, in seeking to invest in the most favourable conditions from the point of view of its profitability—in order to satisfy its shareholders—the TNC is not contributing to a situation which is detrimental to the host country, for instance by immiserizing its population in making it more difficult for the state authorities to finance certain public programmes by taxing foreign investment, or by raising unemployment due to the privatization of certain public sectors taken over by private economic actors. It is perfectly plausible for a TNC to respect all the social, environmental, and human rights standards we believe it is bound by under international law, and nevertheless for its presence to be, on balance, detrimental to the population of the country where it extends its activities, at least in the short run. We therefore have to identify the contours of a form of economic responsibility, understood as a responsibility towards the eradication of poverty and towards development, beyond the banal and outdated conception of development as economic growth. The precise extent of this economic responsibility and the mechanisms through which it could be imposed on private corporations are questions still awaiting answers. But it will already be an important step forward if we acknowledge that such a responsibility weighs on TNCs, as one of the primary agents of globalization: to ensure that globalization works to the benefit of the populations whose needs are greatest, and that they contribute to reducing inequalities between countries rather than accentuate such disparities.

16.3 THE INCAPACITY OF MICRO-ANALYSIS TO IMPOSE AN OBLIGATION TO PROMOTE HUMAN RIGHTS IN THE HOST COUNTRY

There is a second reason why we should try to move beyond an understanding of the human rights responsibilities of transnational corporations which limits itself to imposing negative obligations on these actors, *not to violate human rights directly or indirectly* in the course of a particular investment. Transnational corporations not only are powerful actors when measured by how much they 'weigh' as vis-à-vis states;[39] they exercise—more importantly—an important pressure on the states where they consider

---

[39] The comparison between the economic power of states and that of multinational corporations has led to some debate, revolving around the validity of such comparisons and, specifically, on whether the GNP of countries should be compared with the sales volumes of TNCs or with their added values (or profits). See Bhagwati, above n. 5, 166. Such comparisons, however, fail not only for the lack of adequate, generally agreed, methodological criteria to perform them. The 'power' of states—their ability to exercise control on other actors—has to do, rather than with their economic weight, with the exercise of their regulatory functions, i.e., with their sovereignty, which TNCs are deprived of.

investing in order to obtain the most favourable conditions. The coercion, naturally, is mutual: not only the corporation, but also the host state seeks to conclude the agreement which, in each partner's view, will be the most advantageous possible. But although the situations which will present themselves are as a matter of course extremely diverse, there will be situations where the corporation will seek to squeeze out as many advantages as possible from its negotiation with the host state, and will obtain most of what it has sought, simply because of the need in which the state is of foreign investment and because of the expectations the state has as to the consequences of the arrival of the investor: such an investment, the host state authorities may be hoping, will lead to the creation of quality and well-paid employment; it may lead to the transfer of new technologies or, at least, know-how, to local producers; it may be beneficial to local producers also in that the hosted TNC may subcontract more or less important parts of the production process to local firms. What matters, however, is not that such an agreement between the host state and the TNC deciding to invest in that state will be in the mutual interest of both parties (that it is in their mutual interest may be said to be a pure tautology, for how otherwise could the agreement be concluded?), it is that the framework under which the negotiation takes place, defining the respective bargaining powers of both parties, may dramatically affect the outcome of the negotiation process, and thus, in the final instance, the impact on human rights of the private investment.

The imposition on TNCs of direct obligations under international law may be seen as an attempt to modify precisely this framework, as the effect of affirming such obligations is that certain elements relating to labour rights, the environment, or human rights will simply not be treated as items open for negotiation. Again however, these obligations can be conceived of in two different ways. We may insist that TNCs are bound to respect certain social, environmental, and ethical standards, and that remedies must be created for the benefit of those whose corresponding rights have been violated as a consequence of their activities. Alternatively, we may require that TNCs use their influence to promote human rights in the countries where they operate and with the authorities of which, therefore, they interact: we may seek to ensure that TNCs, as agents of globalization, contribute to globalization being benign, and working in favour of reducing the inequalities between countries and within countries, rather than being negative and accentuating inequalities, even where the TNC contributes to economic growth. The imposition of positive obligations on TNCs to promote human rights implies that, where their bargaining power allows them to do so, TNCs will be under an obligation to use the leverage they have to seek improvements in the situation of human rights in the country where they invest. In this context, the influence TNCs may exercise on the developing states in which they invest is not simply a means for these corporations to obtain the best conditions possible for their investment; it also should be made to work for the benefit of human rights.

This, I would submit, is the direction which we have been taking recently. The *Declaration on the Right and Responsibility of Individuals, Groups and Organs of Society to Promote and Protect Universally Recognized Human Rights and Fundamental Freedoms*, adopted by the UN General Assembly in March 1999,[40] essentially seeks to affirm the importance of the role of human rights defenders, and the protection they must be guaranteed in the states where they operate. However, the language unmistakably refers to a positive obligation of all actors to protect and to promote human rights, which goes beyond an obligation to respect—i.e., not to violate—those rights. It states that 'Individuals, groups, institutions and non-governmental organizations have an important role to play and a responsibility in safeguarding democracy, promoting human rights and fundamental freedoms and contributing to the promotion and advancement of democratic societies, institutions and processes.'[41] Building on Article 28 of the Universal Declaration of Human Rights, it refers to the 'important role and responsibility' of private actors 'in contributing, as appropriate, to the promotion of the right of everyone to a social and international order in which the rights and freedoms set forth in the Universal Declaration of Human Rights and other human rights instruments can be fully realized'.[42] Quite apart from the question of the legally binding *vel non* character of this Declaration—which, formally speaking, is not as such the source of legal obligations—the formulations are interesting in that they demonstrate that positive obligations (obligations to act in order to protect and fulfil human rights) may be imposed not only on states, despite the primary duties they have in this respect due to the sovereign powers they are attributed, but also on private actors, to the extent that they may contribute to human rights in their sphere of influence.

The *Norms on the Responsibilities of transnational corporations and other business enterprises with regard to human rights* adopted on 13 August 2003 by the Sub-Commission on the Promotion and Protection of Human Rights,[43] and presently pending for adoption by the UN Commission on Human Rights, move further in this direction. According to their Preamble, these Norms are based on the understanding that TNCs[44] 'have the capacity to foster economic

[40] G.A. res. 53/144, annex, 53 U.N. GAOR Supp., U.N. Doc. A/RES/53/144 (1999).

[41] Universal Declaration of Human Rights, above n. 7, Art. 18(2).

[42] Ibid. Art. 18(3).

[43] Commentary on the Norms on the responsibilities of transnational corporations and other business enterprises with regard to human rights (UN Sub-Commission on the Promotion and Protection of Human Rights, fifty-fifth session, E/CN.4/Sub.2/2003/38/Rev.2, 26 August 2003).

[44] The expression is used here as a shorthand for the larger set of adressees of these Norms proposed by the UN Sub-Commission on the Promotion and Protection of Human Rights.

well-being, development, technological improvement and wealth, as well as
the capacity to cause harmful impacts on the human rights and lives of individuals through their core business practices and operations, including…
relationships with suppliers and consumers, interactions with Governments
and other activities'. The capacity of the TNCs to contribute positively to
human rights is seen as a source of obligations no less than their capacity to
produce harm. Although the Norms reaffirm that the states have the 'primary
responsibility' to 'promote, secure the fulfilment of, respect, ensure respect of
and protect human rights', they clearly index the obligations of TNCs on the
influence they may exercise. Paragraph 1 of the Norms stipulates:

Within their respective spheres of activity and influence, transnational corporations
and other business enterprises have the obligation to promote, secure the fulfilment
of, respect, ensure respect of and protect human rights recognized in international as
well as national law, including the rights and interests of indigenous peoples and
other vulnerable groups.

The Commentary to the Norms indicates that TNCs shall 'use their
influence in order to help promote and ensure respect for human rights'.
This, I would submit, goes beyond a simple obligation—also stated in the
Commentary—imposed on TNCs to 'inform themselves of the human
rights impact of their principal activities and major proposed activities so that
they can further avoid complicity in human rights abuses'. Where TNCs are
required to 'use their influence', they are required to interfere with the course
of policies pursued in the countries where they operate, and thus to contribute to ensuring that their presence in those countries will facilitate a
human rights-driven form of development. The reference in title E of the
Norms to 'respect for national sovereignty and human rights' should not
discourage us from identifying such an obligation imposed on TNCs to
promote human rights wherever they operate. In paragraph 10 of the Norms,
where this title is explicitated, the concern for 'national sovereignty' appears
clearly subordinated to the requirement that TNCs contribute to the right to
development. It states:

Transnational corporations and other business enterprises shall recognize and respect
applicable norms of international law, national laws and regulations, as well as
administrative practices, the rule of law, the public interest, development objectives,
social, economic and cultural policies including transparency, accountability and
prohibition of corruption, and authority of the countries in which the enterprises
operate.

Strictly speaking, these Norms are intended to apply not only to transnational corporations,
but also to 'other business enterprises' having any relation with the transnational corporation,
the impact of the activities of which is not purely local, or—even where neither of these
conditions is fulfilled—where their activities involve violations of the right to security. See
para. 21 of the Norms for a fuller description of their scope of application *ratione personae*.

The commentary to this provision of the Norms mentions that TNCs are under a duty to 'encourage social progress and development by expanding economic opportunities—particularly in developing countries and, most importantly, in the least developed countries'. The right to development which TNCs must respect is undertstood broadly as comprising 'the right to enjoy economic, social, cultural and political development in which all human rights and fundamental freedoms can be fully realized and in which sustainable development can be achieved so as to protect the rights of future generations'. Thus, although the enterprises to which the Norms are addressed must respect the authority of the countries in which they are present, they are encouraged to act so as to influence the direction these countries are taking. Wherever they can to an extent commensurate to their influence, they are invited to favour the right to development rather than to remain passive in the face of governmental policies, including the policies the government pursues vis-à-vis foreign investors, which fly in the face of that right—a right which we should conceive of as a right of the local populations rather than as a right of governments to determine without any outside influence the course of their evolution.

That corporations operating in foreign jurisdictions may be under a positive obligation to contribute to the improvement of human rights in those jurisdictions, and therefore to leave the position of the silent observer complying with the local norms, may sound like a bold proposition. The difficulty is not only that one hardly sees how, practically, such an open-ended obligation could be satisfactorily translated in legal terms, and by which mechanisms it could be implemented. This is a difficulty which shall be returned to. But the main problem is, if the term fits, of an ideological nature.

First, since the early 1970s, the emphasis has been put on the requirement that corporations do not interfere with internal policies of the states in which they have operations. This has been, in fact, one of the aspects of the call for a 'new international economic order' by newly decolonized states,[45] who feared that the end of colonialism would be followed by a form of 'neo-colonialism' from the northern states, a less visible but not necessarily less damaging form of domination of which private economic actors were seen as among the most important instruments. Well-known historical episodes, such as the influence of the U.S.-based corporations ITT, Pepsi-Cola, and the Chase Manhattan Bank in the coup d'état which put Pinochet into power in Chile or the role of the Union Minière in the secession of Katanga from Congo in the months following the declaration of independence from Belgium, contributed widely to this perception.[46] The Draft UN Code of

[45] See the Resolution adopted by the UN General Assembly on 1 May 1974, UN Doc. A/Res/3201 (S-VI).

[46] See Bhagwati, above n. 5, 168 (and the reference to research by Christopher Hitchens, 'The Case Against Henry Kissinger', at http://archive. 8m.net/hitchens.htm); and Nicola

Conduct on Transnational Corporations for instance, the latest version of which dates from 12 June 1990 but the work on which was launched in 1974 following a call from the UN Economic and Social Council,[47] stipulates that corporations must abstain from involving themselves in domestic policies and respect the priorities of the host government in the countries in which they operate in the fields of employment, the environment, and socio-economic policy.[48] Therefore a first difficulty with imposing on TNCs an obligation to promote improvements in the democratic regime, in the human rights record of the host state, and in its good governance is that this seems to modify the balance between the corporation and the state, whose sovereignty it must respect and whose laws it must comply with. A second difficulty is that the imposition of such an obligation seems, to some extent, to affect the very nature of the TNC as an organization instituted to make profit—to ensure a return on their investments to the shareholders—and whose business, to use the famous formula attributed to Milton Friedman, is not to promote good, but to do business.

The view that foreign investors should abstain from any kind of inter-ference with internal policies, however, appears both outdated and verging on hypocrisy. The emergence of the notion of corporate social responsibility, if it means anything at all, means that the goal of profit making cannot be the sole objective of the corporation, exclusive of any other. The notion that respect for the internal affairs of the state constitutes an obstacle to the imposition of internationally recognized human rights has lost the currency it once had. It may be symptomatic, for instance, that the Organisation for Economic Co-operation and Development (OECD) Guidelines for Multi-national Enterprises, after their revision in 2000, state in paragraph 2 of the chapter on General Policies that:

enterprises should take fully into account established policies in the countries in which they operate, *and consider the views of other stakeholders.* In this regard enterprises should: . . . respect the human rights of those affected by their activities *consistent with the host government's international obligations and commitments.*[49]

The formulations which have been emphasized indicate not only that the drafters of the guidelines considered—rightly—that the interests of the communities affected by the activities of TNCs should not be defined exclusively by the government, but also that the obligation of these

---

Jägers, *Corporate Human Rights Obligations: In Search of Accountability* (Antwerpen and New York: Intersentia, 2002) 100–101 and 120.

[47] UN Doc. E/5500/Rev.1/Add. 1 (Part 1), 24 May 1974.

[48] Articles 7–11, 13, and 16 of the Draft Code (UN Doc. E/1990/94).

[49] OECD, *The OECD Guidelines for Multinational Enterprises: Text, Commentary and Clarifications*, DAFFE/IME/WPG/(2000)15/FINAL, 31 October 2001, 12 (emphasis added).

corporations to respect the sovereignty of the host states—in particular, by complying with the local regulations and by abstaining from interfering with public policies—is subordinated to the obligation of the host state to comply with its international human rights obligations. This is in contrast with the original version of the OECD Guidelines, which emphasized the non-interference by corporations in the policies of the countries in which they operate, without mentioning an obligation to comply with international human rights or, *a fortiori*, to promote them.[50]

Why is it important to insist that the presence of the TNC in a country should serve to improve its human rights record? Empirical studies performed separately by Dani Rodrik and David Kucera have demonstrated that FDI flows are encouraged where the country of destination respects civil and political rights, and therefore preserves social and political stability.[51] This conforms with surveys of managers of transnational corporations which indicate the importance of such stability for the choice of where to invest in foreign jurisdictions.[52] Therefore governments whose human rights records are good are rewarded by higher foreign investment flows. This constitutes an incentive for governments to ensure an investment-friendly environment by offering the adequate legal framework for the benefit of their populations: the attractiveness of jurisdictions whose human rights record is good confers on them a competitive advantage, which is only partially offset by the fact that, in such jurisdictions, the wages will generally be higher.[53] In fact, the positive correlation between TNC investment and human rights has led William H. Meyer to postulate that, on the average, the presence of TNCs has a positive

[50] See also, alluding to this evolution, Jägers, above n. 46, 104. Jägers comments further: '... the emphasis has shifted from non-interference by corporations in the countries in which they operate to requiring corporations to take a more active stance regarding labour rights and human rights' (106).

[51] See Dani Rodrik, 'Democracies pay Higher Wages' 114 *Quarterly Journal of Economics* 707 (1999); Kucera, above n. 17. These studies and the study mentioned in the following note are cited by the helpful review of the literature made by D. K. Brown, A. V. Deardorff, and R. M. Stern, 'The Effects of Multinational Production on Wages and Working Conditions in Developing Countries', Research Seminar in International Economics, School of Public Policy of the University of Michigan, Discussion Paper No. 483, August 2002, available at http://www.spp.umich.edu/rsie/workingpapers/wp.html.

[52] Fabrice Hatem, *International Investment: Towards the Year 2001* (New York: United Nations, 1997).

[53] As pointed out by Brown, Deardorff, and Stern, above n. 51, this constitutes one of the most interesting results from the research by David Kucera for the International Labour Organization: 'FDI is attracted to countries with a higher civil liberties index of one point (on a 10-point scale), controlling for wages, is associated with a 18.5 per cent increase in FDI flows. When the negative impact of increased wages in democracies is factored in, a one-unit increase in the civil-liberties index raises FDI inflows by 14.3 per cent. So even though democracies pay higher wages for a given level of worker productivity, they still provide an attractive location for foreign investors.'

effect on the level of respect for human rights in the host country.[54] However, the results of this research have been questioned[55] and, today, Meyer sees 'no reason to challenge the validity or reliability' of the study of his contradictors,[56] and has turned his thoughts instead to the methodological difficulties in testing the validity of theories in international relations.[57] In fact, although better governance may attract higher levels of foreign direct investment, the sensitivity to this dimension may be relativized in certain industries, particularly in extractive industries, where the foreign investor may not have the same choice as to the location of the investment or may have difficulties relocating—it may not be surprising, in that respect, that certain of the most striking examples of investments made in countries with a bad human rights record, leading to accusations of complicity with the regime in place of the foreign investor, have occurred in the oil or the mining sectors. More importantly, Daniel Kaufmann has shown, in an accompanying essay in this volume,[58] that any positive correlation we might identify between the level of FDI in a particular country and the indicators of good governance do not demonstrate that the presence of FDI is the causal factor leading to improvements in governance. On the contrary, the direction of causality may be exactly opposite: though good governance attracts FDI, FDI may not contribute to good governance where it has not taken hold otherwise. The absence of such an automaticity between the presence of FDI in the country and the improvement of the human rights record of that country encourages us to identify the need to impose on TNCs an affirmative duty to contribute to such an improvement, by taking the initiatives required to bring about such an evolution.

Another reason why we need to think further about this dimension of the responsibility of TNCs is that the conditions under which they may be found liable for doing business in a repressive regime remain undefined, which creates a situation of legal uncertainty. International criminal tribunals have considered that the 'moral support' given by the accomplice to the principal perpetrator of the crime could suffice to constitute the *actus reus* of aiding

---

[54] William H. Meyer, 'Human Rights and MNCs : Theory v. Quantitative Analysis' 18 *Human Rights Quarterly* 368 (1996); and William H. Meyer, *Human Rights and International Political Economy in Third World Nations : MNCs, Foreign Aid and Repression* (Westport, Connecticut: Praeger, 1998) Ch 3.

[55] Jackie Smith, Melissa Bolyard, and Anna Ippolito, 'Human Rights and the Global Economy: A Response to Meyer' 21 *Human Rights Quarterly* 207 (1999).

[56] William H. Meyer, 'Activism and Research on TNCs and Human Rights: Building a New International Normative Regime' in J. G. Frynas and S. Pegg, eds., *Transnational Corporations and Human Rights* (London: Palgrave Macmillan, 2003) 33–52, 35.

[57] William H. Meyer, 'Confirming, Infirming and "Falsifying" Theories of Human Rights: Reflections on Smith, Bolyard and Ippolito through the Lens of Lakatos' 21 *Human Rights Quarterly* 220 (1999).   [58] See Chapter 15 in this volume.

and abetting in international criminal law,[59] and that the *mens rea* of aiding and abetting could consist simply in the accomplice accused being 'aware that one of a number of crimes will probably be committed'. Indeed, if one of those crimes is then indeed committed, the accomplice 'has intended to facilitate the commission of that crime'.[60] As a result, under these standards, a company may be found to be complicit in the commission of an international crime where its presence in the state where such a crime is committed may be interpreted as offering a form of 'moral support' to the perpetrator of that crime, at least in so far as the company could have anticipated the commission of the crime in question. Even before it could be tested in international criminal law with respect to corporate actors, this understanding of the notion of complicity has influenced the regime of civil liability of those actors under national law, in particular in the context of the United States Alien Tort Claims Act 1789.[61] It results in a situation where any corporation doing business in a repressive state, and not speaking out to denounce the human rights violations committed by the organs of that state or left unpunished, may potentially be held liable for being complicit in those violations, if it was in a position to exercise influence on the organs directly responsible for those violations and did not do so.

A notion of 'silent complicity' has emerged.[62] It does not amount to a total prohibition for TNCs from being present in certain states because of

---

[59] See *Prosecutor v. Furundzija*, IT-95–17/1-T (10 December 1998) (38 I.L.M. 317 (1999), para. 235 (International Criminal Tribunal for Yugoslavia); *Prosecutor v. Musema*, ICTR-96–13-T (27 January 2000), http://www.ictr.org/, at para. 126 (International Criminal Tribunal for Rwanda).

[60] *Furundzija*, ibid. at para. 245. These standards pre-date the cited cases. Indeed, the *Furundzija* Tribunal bases its understanding of complicity on decisions by the American and British military courts and tribunals dealing with Nazi war crimes, and on the cases decided by the German courts created at the end of the Second World War in the British and French occupied zones of Germany.

[61] Now codified as 28 U.S.C. § 1350. In its judgment of 18 September 2002 in the case of *John Doe I and others v. Unocal Corp. and others*, the United States Court of Appeals for the Ninth Circuit considered in the face of allegations from the plaintiffs that the defendants had aided the Burmese military in subjecting them to forced labour in the course of the construction of the Yadana pipeline, that 'given that there is . . . sufficient evidence in the present case that Unocal [the California-based corporation which participated in the pipeline consortium] gave assistance and encouragement to the Myanmar Military', it did not need to decide 'whether it would have been enough if Unocal had only given moral support to the Myanmar Military'. The discussion of the Court of Appeals leaves, however, little doubt that the answer to this question would have been affirmative. *John Doe I and Others v. Unocal and Others*, available at http://caselaw.lp.findlaw.com/data2/circs/9th/0056603p.pdf.

[62] See on the degrees of proximity which may exist between a corporation and a repressive regime the typology proposed by Margaret Jungk, 'A Practical Guide to Addressing Human Rights Concerns for Companies Operating Abroad' in M. K. Addo, ed., *Human Rights Standards and the Responsibility of Transnational Corporations* (The Hague: Kluwer Law International, 1999) 171–186. On the notion of complicity in evaluating the liability of

their repressive regime. But it does seem to require that, if TNCs do choose to be present, they use their influence to promote changes. Although it offered a clear distinction in its Final Report between 'first order involvement' of business under the apartheid regime in South Africa (where it played 'a central role in helping to design and implement apartheid policies'), 'second order involvement' (where companies 'made their money by engaging directly in activities that promoted state repression'), and 'third order involvement' (which refers to 'ordinary business activities that benefited indirectly by virtue of operating within the racially structured context of an apartheid society'),[63] the South African Truth and Reconciliation Commission (TRC) considered that all businesses active under apartheid South Africa should be responsible for restitution, to the extent that they did not use their power to promote change. The TRC noted that 'overwhelming economic power resided in a few major business groupings with huge bargaining power vis-à-vis the State. This power could have been used to promote reform.'[64] It answered to a submission from South African businesses according to which

Any notion that business could have acted as a watchdog of the government as far as human rights violations are concerned is totally unrealistic and should be dispelled. Business [under the apartheid regime] was unable to act in that way in the past and will not be able to do so in the future (. . .) government is so powerful and dominant that a business organisation will seriously jeopardise its prospect of success by crossing swords with politicians

that

While there are clear constraints imposed by political power, to say that business was incapable of crossing swords with politicians is to deny the power (and responsibility) that accompanies financial muscle and personal contacts.[65]

Although the final destination remains unknown, the general direction which we are taking emerges clearly from these developments. At a minimum, an obligation not to co-operate with repressive regimes is imposed on TNCs. Such an obligation has been defined by Nicola Jägers as an obligation that 'requires from the corporation operating in States where widespread and systematic human rights violations occur, to either abstain from operations or to take measures to ensure that its operations do not amount to complicity in these human rights violations'.[66] But even outside situations of widespread

corporations for human rights violations, see Andrew Clapham and Scott Jerbi, 'Towards a Common Understanding of Business Complicity in Human Rights Abuses', background paper for the Global Compact Dialogue on the role of the private sector in zones of conflict, New York, 21–22 March 2001, http://www.globaldimensions.net/articles/cr/complicity. html.

[63] See the Truth and Reconciliation Commission of South Africa, *Final Report*, Vol. 4, Ch. 2, 'Business and Labour' at paras. 23–36.   [64] Ibid., para. 39.
[65] Ibid., paras. 142–143.   [66] Jägers, above n. 46, 94.

and systematic human rights violations, corporations, especially TNCs, are increasingly expected to contribute to bringing about positive evolutions by using their influence on the governments in the states where they invest. The fact that it is in their business interest to work in a politically and socially stable climate will contribute to accelerating this development. However, before an obligation of the TNC to exercise influence on the authorities of the host state can be concretized, many questions remain to be answered. How is the influence of the TNC on the host state's government to be measured? Which requirements of transparency in the financial and contractual relationships between the TNC and that government should be imposed to ensure that this influence can be evaluated with precision? Which forms should the exercise of that influence take, and for instance, should the pressure put by the TNC on the host government be public, or may it remain confidential? Should we expect from the TNC that it make its continued presence in the country conditional upon certain changes in the attitudes of the local authorities towards human rights? Should we impose conditionalities on the use of the revenues accruing for the government from the presence of the TNC—for instance, that it be spent on education, health, or other social services? The incapacity of the existing tools to impose human rights obligations on TNCs operating in developing countries, here, also is a consequence of the lack of generally agreed criteria, and of the absence of the methodology we would require to apply such criteria once they are agreed upon.

16.4 THE INCAPACITY OF MICRO-ANALYSIS TO EVALUATE THE CONSEQUENCES ON RELATIVE WAGES OF THE INTERNATIONAL DIVISION OF LABOUR

Where they invest in foreign jurisdictions, the motivation of TNCs may be to penetrate the local market, in which case the choice to proceed to that investment is considered to be a better alternative than to export the same goods from the home country (or any other country where the TNC produces the same goods) or to franchise its production to a local firm in the host country. Such strategy will be preferred, for instance, where tariffs are imposed which would render the exported goods less competitive on the local market, or where the franchising of a local firm would require controlling the quality of its performance or giving away protected technology. However, in most cases, the investment by TNCs in foreign jurisdictions is motivated by the aim to produce goods for the global markets at the most competitive prices, by dividing the production process into different segments, located in different countries, in the most efficient way possible.[67]

---

[67] On this distinction, see Brown, Deardorff, and Stern, above n. 51, 25–26.

In that case, the TNC will be moved in its decision to invest by the comparison of the endowments in production factors of different possible locations for the investment. Where the benefits of outsourcing outweigh the costs in communication, transport, and co-ordination of the production process, and any reputational costs involved in choosing a location whose human rights record is contesed, it will be the preferred option.

That the international division of labour depends on the respective endowments of the different countries reminds us, of course, of the Ricardian analysis of the benefits of international trade. But we have long ceased to inhabit the world where England produces cloth and Portugal wine, and where both countries exchange for their mutual benefit. With the exception of extractive industries, most of the inflows of FDI into developing countries today are in the sectors of manufactured goods or of services,[68] for which the attractiveness of particular locations to foreign investment typically depend—rather than on natural endowments of the countries concerned—on the level of economic development and, especially, on the regulatory context. This is one of the explanations put forward by Jagdish Bhagwati for the exacerbation of competition under the current form of globalization, and the growing worries of producers in all jurisdictions that their competitors situated abroad are receiving an 'unfair' advantage because of the standards under which they operate. He writes:

... today, in most commodities and activities, technology matters and has diffused greatly, both because many have access to similar pools of knowledge and because multinationals can take scarce knowledge almost everywhere if they choose, as they often do, and they do produce globally. The buffer [between competitors situated in different countries, due to the differences in natural conditions and therefore in the relative costs of production] has therefore shrunk dramatically in most activities, and international competition is fierce and feared. The inevitable effect has been to prompt firms everywhere to worry about 'fair trade'. Each looks over his foreign rival's shoulder to see if any difference in domestic policy or institutions gives this competitor an 'unfair' advantage. The result has been a growing demand for ironing out any such differences, including in labour and environmental standards, as firms seek 'level playing fields', ignoring the fact that it is differences, whether of climate or skills or of domestic institutions and policies reflecting local conditions, that lead to beneficial trade among nations.[69]

Fears have been regularly expressed about 'regulatory competition' and, therefore, about the risk that we will be facing a 'race to the bottom' in the areas of labour rights and environmental standards, as each country will seek, by deregulating in these areas, to attract foreign investors, induced by the

---

[68] David Kucera notes that in 1997, '50.1 percent of FDI flows into LDCs went to manufacturing (down from 66.8 percent in 1988), compared to 41.3 percent to services ... and 4.6. percent to the primary sector': Kucera, above n. 17, 17).

[69] Bhagwati, above n. 5, 12.

prospect to be able to produce at economically more favourable conditions. The available empirical studies seem to demonstrate that these fears have not yet translated into reality, at least concerning the basic labour rights.[70] Whether this is attributable to the more demanding scrutiny from civil society or international unions federations under which transnational corporations operate or whether it is due, as appears more likely, to the understanding by businesses that an investment in jurisdictions where legislation does not adequately protect labour rights is more risky, these studies indicate that, in general, a legal environment which secures these rights is preferred by investors. This conclusion has been spectacularly confirmed in a much-publicized OECD study from 2000.[71] From their useful review of this literature, Drusilla K. Brown, Alan V. Deardorff, and Robert M. Stern conclude: 'Labour rights that promote political stability and enhance labour quality may in fact make a particular location attractive to foreign investors.'[72] More recently, a report commissioned by the International Finance Corporation—a member of the World Bank Group to which this chapter returns in section 16.6—arrives at the conclusion that, in order to appear attractive to foreign investors, developing countries should invest in the development and effective enforcement of laws on corporate social responsibility.[73]

Labour costs, and in particular the level of wages, constitute however an entirely different matter. The difference in wages, and therefore of labour costs, constitutes a major determinant of the location of foreign investment. TNCs typically pay their workers wages situated comfortably above both the legally required minimum and the wages which the same workers would receive for equivalent alternative employment in local firms—a bonus which is only partially explained by the improved productivity of the workers hired by the TNC and thus benefiting its superior technology and the economies

---

[70] See, in particular, Linda Y. C. Lim, *The Globalization Debate: Issues and Challenges* (Geneva: ILO, 2001) ; William Cooke and Deborah Noble, 'Industrial Relations Systems and U.S. Foreign Direct Investment Abroad' 34 *British Journal of Industrial Relations* 581 (1998).

[71] OECD, *International Trade and Core Labour Standards* (Paris: OECD, 2000).

[72] Brown, Deardorff, and Stern, above n. 51, 50.

[73] Political and Economic Link Consulting for the IFC-World Bank Group, 'Race to the Top: Attracting and Enabling Global Sustainable Business', October 2003. However, the report has serious methodological flaws. For instance, although the surveys made for the report tend to show that businesses may prefer locales with high and especially reliable regulatory standards, they express this preference only all other things being equal: the relative weight of corporate social responsibility (CSR) considerations and other more classical determinants of the investment choices are not examined. In fact, certain data from the report itself seem to demonstrate that, when they choose in favour of better CSR regulatory standards, they may be moved by the risk of legal sanctions, for example because of the requirements set by the legislation of their home state—this being the case, especially, for U.S. corporations. Therefore preference for CSR would not be spontaneous, but the result of strong legal mechanisms. The market will not take care of itself in respect of CSR.

of scale the multinational character of the production authorizes. Nevertheless, at least for labour-intensive fragments of the production, FDI accrues, all other things being equal, to the countries where the wages are the lowest.[74] This constitutes an incentive for the developing countries to keep the costs of labour down, and thus to preserve their attractiveness to foreign capital. Moreover, the easiness with which capital can be moved from one location to another—and thus the FDI be redirected in the relatively short term—diminishes the bargaining power of workers' unions, thus pressuring wages to fall or, more precisely, not to rise in the proportions they would were the threat of relocation not available to the employing company.[75] In other terms, although FDI will generally raise the average level of the wages in the host country, this rise remains limited by structural conditions linked to the multinational character of the investor. Even more important, FDI may accentuate the wage gaps between the high skilled labour and the low skilled labour, both in the home country (the 'North') and the host country (the 'South'). Indeed, in the countries from where capital is moved—the home countries—the less skilled labour is most often victim of such a relocation, as the production segments which are labour-intensive and require relatively low skills are most easily outsourced in developing countries. In the host country, FDI will benefit instead the most skilled segment of the workforce, which will be in the highest demand from the TNC.[76]

Therefore there is a real possibility that FDI will actually accentuate inequalities in both the country of origin and in the host country, even where

[74] In fact, this is precisely why a number of international free trade economists have opposed the mandatory imposition of labour standards or the imposition of wages at certain levels deemed reasonable: this would lead a number of least developed countries to lose the comparative advantage they have in this respect, and could induce firms to seek out lower cost production locations, to the detriment of precisely those workers which such mandatory requirements sought to help. See, for example, the position of the Academic Consortium on International Trade (ACIT) against the 'anti-sweatshop' campaign in the United States, which the ACIT considers to be motivated by protectionist purposes and, in the final instance, to constitute a danger for precisely those workers in developing countires the conditions of which such campaigns seek to improve.   [75] Brown, Deardorff, and Stern, above n. 51, 37.

[76] Ibid. 29. These authors also cite some empirical evidence for this phenomenon. See for instance Robert C. Feenstra and Gordon H. Hanson, 'Foreign Direct Investment and Relative Wages: Evidence from Mexico's Maquiladoras' 42 *Journal of International Economics* 371 (1997). In fact, Brown, Deardorff, and Stern are careful to indicate that this is just one of possible consequences on the relative wages of skilled and unskilled labour in the countries concerned by the flow of capital: on the basis of their theoretical discussion, they conclude that no unambiguous conclusions can be derived from the examination of the consequences of FDI on wages (at the end of section III of their paper), and therefore they examine the empirical evidence in detail in section IV. They do assert, however, that the increasing disparity between the wages of relatively unskilled labour and the wages of relatively skilled labour is, according to empirical evidence, 'exactly what a great deal of FDI into developing countries actually does' (29).

the TNC pays wages in the latter country which are above the wages which
would accrue to alternative employment in a local firm. Accompanying
measures should be devised to limit such consequences. For instance, workers
in industrialized countries who suffer the consequences of delocalization
could be granted forms of vocational training which would facilitate their
re-employment in higher skilled, better-paid positions. The consequences of
the FDI on relative wages in the host country could be mitigated by the
training to non-skilled workers, which the TNC making the investment
should be made to provide, so that the arrival of the TNC will not lead to
a sudden increase in the demand for relatively skilled labour without any
compensation. The loss of the bargaining power of workers' unions, in
a context of economic globalization, could be compensated for at least to
some extent by the development of framework agreements between TNCs
and global union federations;[77] the wage policies of the TNC should not be
excluded, as a matter of principle, from the ongoing dialogue such framework agreements seek to encourage between the parties.

The preceding arguments have sought to highlight that an analysis of the
human rights obligations of transnational corporations, as long as it remains
confined to an analysis of the obligations of TNCs not to violate those rights
in the course of the operations they undertake, fails to address the wider
impact of the activities of TNCs as a channel of economic globalization. It
fails, especially, to realize the potential TNCs present to ensure that globalization contributes to a human rights-driven form of development. Such a
'micro-analysis', conducted at the level of each individual project, cannot
guarantee that—by their way of acting, by the form under which they decide
to invest, by the conditions under which they negotiate with the host
country—the TNCs will contribute to guaranteeing the right to development. Questions such as under which form the TNC has made its investment
(for instance, in the context of a privatization programme of the host
country, by acquiring one or more local firms, or by bringing in fresh capital), which technologies have been transferred to the host country and
therefore been made available to local producers, or which prohibitions are
imposed on the government of the host country to impose certain regulatory
obligations on the TNC, are generally not asked when we remain at such a
level of analysis. Neither do we ask how the TNC could contribute, by the
influence it may exercise on the host government, to improving its record in
the field of human rights, or, more generally, its governance. Finally,
the question of relative wages is usually not addressed, except for the general
obligations not to pay wages under the legal minimum prescribed under
the laws of the host country and not to substract wages for disciplinary
reasons. Instead, what we require is to identify the building blocks of a legal

---

[77] See for a list of such agreements www.global-unions.org.

framework for foreign direct investment which would ensure that FDI will truly benefit the populations of the host countries—that, in other terms, economic globalization will serve development, and not only contribute to economic growth. What we require is for human rights lawyers to turn their efforts to another level of analysis: beyond that of individual investment projects, which of course have to comply with human rights, they should ask where the rules of the game of economic globalization are unfavourable to human development, and, where this is the case, how they can be modified.

In the course of the preceding discussion, we have identified a list of obligations which could be imposed on TNCs to ensure that they will be responsible actors in the process of economic globalization—that, apart from not violating human rights in the course of their activities, TNCs will contribute to the promotion of human rights by the activities they perform, and thus favour a form of globalization more conducive of human development. This is the common denominator of obligations such as to accept a form of economic responsibility for the consequences of the impact foreign direct investment has on the populations of the host country, to avoid crowding out local producers or investors, to transfer technology when operating in developing countries whose local firms lack knowledge about certain production processes, to abstain from challenging the right of the host state to exercise its regulatory functions in the public interest, to promote human rights in the host country by exercising its influence, or to limit the impact of outsourcing on the relative levels of wages in both the country of origin and the host country—other examples, of course, could further enrich this preliminary listing.

Thus, it would be tempting to simply expand the list of obligations imposed on TNCs, perhaps by identifying which obligations could correspond to a 'right to development' of the populations of the countries in which they conduct their activities. The *Norms on the Responsibilities of transnational corporations and other business enterprises with regard to human rights* adopted by the Sub-Commission on the Promotion and Protection of Human Rights go some way in that direction. For instance, the Commentary to the Norms indicates that TNCs 'shall respect, protect and apply intellectual property rights in a manner that contributes to the promotion of technical innovation and to the transfer and dissemination of technology, to the mutual advantage of producers and users of technological knowledge, in a manner conducive to social and economic welfare, such as the protection of public health, and to a balance of rights and obligations'.[78] But the facile, albeit implicit, reliance on the notion of abuse of rights, and the resulting vagueness with which the Norms define the obligation of TNCs vis-à-vis the exercise of intellectual property rights, illustrate the obstacles we face once we seek to impose on

---

[78] Commentary to Norm 10, (d), above n. 43.

corporate actors legal obligations which require from them that they abstain from doing precisely what they are set up for: to benefit from the opportunities offered by economic globalization. More generally, the obligations of TNCs which have been identified above all remain relatively open and undefined, either because—like the obligation formulated in the *Norms on the Responsibilities of transnational corporations and other business enterprises with regard to human rights* on intellectual property rights and the need to balance their exercise against the right to health—they require from TNCs that they renounce using those opportunities to their full extent, or because they do not correspond to clearly identified internationally recognized human rights, as they seek, rather, to promote a kind of social and international order in which the rights and freedoms of the Universal Declaration of Human Rights can be realized.[79] In such a context, simply to affirm the existence of such obligations and attempt to list them will not suffice; it is necessary to identify mechanisms through which compliance with such obligations may be encouraged.

Rather than expanding the list of obligations which should be imposed on TNCs on the basis of the existing international law of human rights—many of the obligations mentioned above could only be related to those rights with some artificiality, and in a rather indirect fashion—we should turn to the other major actors of the globalization process: states and international organizations. Of course, the state receiving the foreign direct investment has the primary responsibility to ensure that the FDI, as it directed, is conducive of the well-being of its population. But this is a point too obvious to be elaborated upon, and moreover this again does not appear to be the most promising route. Our preceding discussion has identified two typical situations: either the developing state is in need of foreign investment, and will seek to appear as attractive as possible to potential investors by identifying their expectations and trying, as far as possible, to satisfy them[80]—its negotiating capacity, therefore, will be weak; or the state is prone to commit human rights violations and to repress its own populations, and, although it may need the presence of foreign investors, it will not be its priority to ensure that the arrival of FDI will truly benefit its population, in which case it will be illusory to count on the state to ensure that FDI is channelled towards the satisfaction of the needs of the population. More generally, the current context of economic globalization and, especially, the international legal regime of investment, would in many cases make it impossible for the

[79] Universal Declaration of Human Rights, above n. 7, Art. 28.

[80] This is not tantamount to saying that the state seeking to attract foreign capital will necessarily be tempted to deregulate in the social and environmental areas: as we have seen, a strong and—especially—reliable legal framework in these fields may in fact prove an advantage, rather than a liability, for the state offering such a framework, in the race to attract foreign investors.

developing state to impose on the foreign investor the kinds of obligations mentioned above, even where this would be its intention. It is not the developing states seeking the arrival of foreign investors, but the industrialized countries from which those investors originate, and intergovernmental organizations, which have set the rules of globalization. It is they which have the power to modify them.

16.5 PROMOTING A FRAMEWORK FOR FOREIGN DIRECT INVESTMENT CONDUCIVE OF HUMAN DEVELOPMENT: THE ROLE OF THE DEVELOPED STATES

Consider, first, the responsibility of industrialized countries, from which the overwhelming majority of TNCs originate, in organizing the legal framework of foreign direct investment in the way most favourable to the interests of the foreign investors. Bilateral investment treaties (BITs) represent the main tool in this regard. Such treaties have proliferated throughout a number of years.[81] They form today a vast array of agreements creating a legal framework favourable to investment.[82] This network of agreements now appears de facto as a substitute for the failed multilateral agreement on investment (MAI), negotiated within the OECD until it failed in 1999 under the pressure of a large coalition of civil society organizations; it is complemented by regional free trade agreements such as the North American Free Trade Agreement (NAFTA), which often have served as models for the preparation of such treaties; and it anticipates further liberalization of investment negotiated under the auspices of the World Trade Organization (WTO), beyond the existing agreement on Trade-Related Investment Measures (TRIMs). The bilateral investment treaties typically contain national treatment and most-favoured-nation clauses in favour of investors from the other party; they prevent states hosting the investment from imposing performance requirements on foreign investors, for example to require that the production contains a certain percentage of domestic content, that it uses a certain amount of goods or services purchased on the territory of the host state, or that the investor transfers technology or knowledge about production processes to a person on that territory. However, as noted in the report prepared for *Rights & Democracy*: 'When States

---

[81] 2099 BITs were inventoried as being in force at the end of 2001. See UNCTAD, *World Investment Report 2002*, above n. 26, 8.

[82] Important studies on these treaties include G. Sacerdori, 'Bilateral Treaties and Multilateral Instruments on Investment Protection' 269 *Recueil des cours de l'Académie de droit international* (1997) and Kenneth Vandevelde, 'Investment Liberalization and Economic Development: The Role of Bilateral Investment Treaties' 36 *Columbia Journal of Transnational Law* 501 (1998).

are prevented from requiring investors to attain certain levels of domestic content or purchase domestic products and services, they are deprived of an important means of ensuring that private economic activity has an impact of social development and, a fortiori, on the progressive realization of human rights.'[83] Obviously, this is even more the case where, under the pretext of protecting the foreign investors from forms of expropriation which amount to 'regulatory takings', the host states agree to renounce the exercise of their regulatory powers in certain areas such as labour rights or the protection of the environment, to avoid inflicting unexpected economic losses on the investors. As we have seen from the example of the Baku-Tbilisi-Ceyhan pipeline project, this risk is not present only in intergovernmental agreements: it is also a risk entailed in the negotiation and conclusion of agreements between the foreign investors and the host governments.

The *Draft Guidelines on a Human Rights Approach to Poverty Reduction Strategies* insist, on the contrary, that

[w]hen a developing State is engaging in bilateral, multilateral or corporate negotiations, the State should give the most careful attention to its international human rights obligations to the poor in its jurisdiction. The State may wish to argue that these obligations constitute an international minimum threshold below which individuals and groups within its jurisdiction may not fall and that, therefore, it is impermissible for the State to conclude any agreement that is inconsistent with the international human rights it owes to the poor in its jurisdiction.[84]

It is of course the responsibility of the state hosting the foreign investment to ensure that the conditions attached do not constitute an obstacle to its full compliance with its international human rights commitments. But it is also the responsibility of all states not to pressure developing countries, in need of foreign direct investment for their economic growth, to accept agreements which lead to creating such an obstacle. A first step towards ensuring that foreign direct investment truly promotes human development in the countries towards which it is directed would be to review the full range of existing bilateral investment treaties and to examine which clauses of those instruments conflict with the ability of the receiving states to comply with their human rights obligations and to realize the right to development. Similarly, the other instruments which industrialized states resort to in order to facilitate investment in other countries by TNCs incorporated in their jurisdiction and to protect the rights of these investors should undergo such a scrutiny. A concern for human rights should be proactively included in such instruments, for example in the conditions imposed by state export credit agencies.

---

[83] Bachand and Rousseau, above n. 15, 18.

[84] OHCHR, *Draft Guidelines on a Human Rights Approach to Poverty Reduction Strategies*, above n. 14, para. 222.

The reason for imposing such obligations on the industrialized countries is not that the acts of transnational companies incorporated under their laws would necessarily be imputable to those states, under the rules of international responsibility—indeed, such acts of private actors in principle are not attributable to the state, under those rules in their current state of development. Rather, the justification for requiring from industrialized countries that they take steps to ensure that the liberalization of foreign direct investment will truly serve as an instrument for human development—as it will not automatically have that effect—is that, under Article 28 of the Universal Declaration of Human Rights, all states must contribute to a social and international order in which the rights and freedoms of the Declaration can be realized.[85] As noted by the International Council on Human Rights Policy, the question of whether there exists an

obligation to act should be considered separately from the question of *responsibility for the abuse*. Where a party is responsible for violations, it has a duty to change its policies and behaviour so that the violations cease. However, in many circumstances outsiders have an obligation to help end violations of economic, social and cultural and other rights abroad even when they have no responsibility for causing them. Indeed, in many cases of unfulfilled ESC [economic, social, and cultural] rights, there is no clear perpetrator.[86]

Although any particular developed country may not be responsible either for the constraints facing a developing country in need of FDI and prepared therefore, in order to attract foreign investors, to sacrifice certain social objectives which it would be in the interest of its population to fulfil, or for the behaviour of the foreign investors themselves, even when they are TNCs incorporated under its jurisdiction, each developed state nevertheless arguably is under a duty to facilitate the achievement by developing states of their human development objectives, in particular the eradication of poverty and more specific objectives in the areas of health, education, housing, or nutrition. This obligation cannot be simply ignored, or put between brackets, when developed states negotiate bilateral investment treaties, when they sponsor their transnational corporations by granting loans or by insuring their investments against risk, or when they act in multilateral negotiations: in such contexts, developed States are obliged to put their international human rights obligations and those of the developing countries concerned at the centre of their preoccupations.

---

[85] See the commentary by Asbjørn Eide on this provision, in G. Alfredsson and A. Eide, eds., *The Universal Declaration of Human Rights* (The Hague: Kluwer Law International, 1999) 597.

[86] International Council on Human Rights Policy, *Duties sans Frontières. Human Rights and Global Social Justice* (Geneva: International Council on Human Rights Policy, 2003) 41 (emphasis added).

This shared responsibility for human development, in particular the elimination of poverty, is clearly affirmed in the United Nations Millennium Declaration of 2000, in which some 150 heads of state and government confirmed that states parties to international human rights treaties have obligations that go beyond their own territory, and asserted their common resolution 'to create an environment—at the national and global levels alike—which is conducive to development and to the elimination of poverty'. Moving towards that same end, the *Draft Guidelines on a Human Rights Approach to Poverty Reduction Strategies* explicate, under the Guideline relating to the right to international assistance and co-operation, that this right 'should not be understood as encompassing only financial and technical assistance: it also includes an obligation to work actively towards equitable multilateral trading, investment and financial systems that are conducive to the reduction and elimination of poverty'.[87] And, as elements of a strategy for realizing the right to international assistance and co-operation, the Draft Guidelines refer to the formulation by developed states of an *international* poverty-reduction strategy, defined as 'a strategy for poverty reduction beyond [national] borders'. Under such an international poverty reduction strategy, developed states are expected to take measures to ensure that their international human rights obligations are coherently and consistently applied in their international policy-making processes; this should be understood especially by 'those in finance and trade who represent the State in international negotiations on those issues'. Under this strategy, developed states moreover are to 'take reasonable measures to ensure that the overseas operations of companies headquartered in their jurisdiction are respectful of the international human rights obligations of both the home and the host State'.[88]

16.6 PROMOTING A FRAMEWORK FOR FOREIGN DIRECT, INVESTMENT CONDUCIVE TO HUMAN DEVELOPMENT: THE ROLE OF THE MULTILATERAL LENDING INSTITUTIONS

We should equally pay careful attention to the obligation of multilateral lending organizations (MLIs) to create a framework for foreign direct investment which will ensure that it effectively contributes to the objective of human development. In its statement on globalization and its impact on the enjoyment of economic, social, and cultural rights, the UN Committee on Economic, Social and Cultural Rights urged international organizations 'to take whatever measures they can to assist Governments to act in ways which

---

[87] OHCHR, *Draft Guidelines on a Human Rights Approach to Poverty Reduction Strategies*, above n. 14, para. 216.   [88] Ibid. 218.

are compatible with their human rights obligations and to seek to devise policies and programmes which promote respect for those rights'.[89] To the extent that MLIs contribute to shape the framework under which FDI is channelled towards developing states, they are under an obligation to take into account the human rights obligations of those countries. They should not only abstain from creating conditions which will make it more difficult or even impossible for them to comply with those obligations, but also actively promote such compliance within their sphere of influence. In their final report to the UN Sub-Commission on the Promotion and Protection of Human Rights on 'Globalization and its impact on the full enjoyment of human rights', J. Oloka-Onyango and Deepioka Udagama consider that international organizations 'must, at a minimum, *recognize, respect, and protect* human rights'.[90] An obligation to protect is a positive obligation to ensure that any actor, whose behaviour the MLI effectively influences, will not violate his own human rights obligations. MLIs must use their influence, in other terms, to encourage compliance with human rights, within the sphere in which that influence may be exercised.

With respect to the private sector, the most relevant MLI is the International Finance Corporation (IFC), a member of the World Bank Group alongside the International Bank for Reconstruction and Development (IBRD), the International Development Association (IDA), and the Multilateral Investment Guarantee Agency (MIGA). The IFC invests in projects led by the private sector, in particular by granting loans. In the selection of the prospective projects, the IFC not only verifies whether the projects comply with the local requirements, but also whether they comply with the environmental, health, and safety guidelines imposed on all the projects of the World Bank Group or, in sectors for which no such guidelines exist, with the internationally recognized standards applicable. Each project is evaluated according to a complex, potentially time-consuming procedure, to ensure that it is environmentally and socially sound.[91] The departure point for this

---

[89] Statement on Globalization and its Impact on the Enjoyment of Economic, Social and Cultural Rights, adopted by the UN Committee on Economic, Social and Cultural Rights at its eighteenth session, E/1999/12-E/C.12/1998/26, para. 515.

[90] E/CN.4/Sub.2/20903/14, 25 June 2003 (at para. 39, emphasis added). As the authors recognize themselves, 'left out of this formulation are the obligations to promote and fulfil, which we believe are obligations that properly belong to the State'. This restriction is apparently linked to the need to respect the principle of specialty of international organizations, whose powers do not go beyond those attributed to them by the States which have created them by international agreement, and whose goals are limitatively defined by that instrument—whether a charter, articles of agreement, a statute, or any other form. This of course does not mean that the mandate of the organization cannot include such goals, nor that human rights considerations may not be relevant to the policies pursued by the international organization within the limits of its mandate.

[91] See for a description www.ifc.org/enviro.

process is, for all projects except those which are likely to have minimal or no adverse environmental impacts (category C projects), the preparation of an environmental assessment, addressing a wide range of issues (including for instance occupational health and safety, socio-economic impacts, land use and involuntary resettlements, all dimensions of the project for which the notion of an 'environmental' assessment may be too restrictive in its wording) and on the basis of which a consultation of the stakeholders is organized. The example set by this framework (the IFC Sustainability Framework) has contributed to the adoption on 4 June 2003 of the 'Equator Principles', a set of principles which a number of leading banks have agreed to follow in their investment decisions, to ensure that the projects they finance will be socially and environmentally responsible. Apart from the scope of the initiative measured in terms of the financial weight of the participating financial institutions or the range of sectors concerned, the importance of these Principles is that they constitute a clear recognition from these institutions, including the IFC, that, as they exercise in fact an influence on the borrowers, they must use this influence to promote socially and environmentally responsible development.

Again, however, it is perfectly possible that a private sector project will be environmentally and socially sound when considered in isolation, and still not contribute to human development in the country where it is conducted. To ensure that it will be conducive of human development, the financiers have to use their considerable leverage to impose forms of conditionalities which go beyond not only the economic viability of the project, but also beyond compliance with the social and environmental standards mentioned above. Such conditionalities could translate, for instance, into guarantees that accompanying measures will contribute towards the development of the affected communities. Or they could ensure that the revenues accruing to the governments concerned will be wisely spent.

The example of the Baku-Tbilisi-Ceyhan pipeline project again may serve to illustrate this. When the promoters of the BTC project addressed themselves to possible lenders, including the European Bank for Reconstruction and Development (EBRD), a number of export credit agencies from Europe, the United States, and Japan, and others (in total, the financing sought amounted to 2.6 billion U.S. dollars), they also turned to the IFC. As one of the major aspects of the BTC pipeline concerns the expropriation of approximately 17,700 parcels of land and the resettlement of the landowners, the IFC required from the consortium that they develop three comprehensive Resettlement Action Plans (RAPs), one for each country, although these RAPs are linked together by one overaching document ensuring parity across the project. These RAPs provide that compensation will be offered to the households affected by the pipeline, at a rate significantly higher than the prevailing local market rates. The IFC document released in October 2003 in response to submissions received on the project comments that

[i]n communities with limited opportunities to acquire cash income this has enabled many households to acquire additional agricultural equipment/machinery, livestock and to afford increased agricultural inputs (such as fertilizer), which will hopefully result in increased production and returns and improved livelihoods. Compensation payments are also being used for a number of other purposes, which will ultimately result in developmental benefits (e.g., education, setting up of small household enterprises, improving homes, acquiring vehicles for transportation of agricultural produce and other goods, etc.).[92]

The land acquisition and compensation procedures, moreover, have led to clarify the existing land rights and to improve the capacity of local organizations, instituted for the purpose of dialoguing with the project promoters. The IFC believes that 'the project's standards of compensation, consultation and contribution to development impact associated with involuntary resettlement will "raise the bar" considerably in [all three affected countries: Azerbaijan, Georgia, and Turkey]. These standards will become the benchmarks for similar projects involving land acquisition in the future.'[93]

Still other precautions taken by the project promoters upon the insistance of the IFC deserve highlighting. Confronted in the course of the public consultation it organized with allegations of corruption of the SOCAR (the Azerbaijan State Oil Company), IFC responded that BTC has agreed to 'publish what they pay' and that

Azerbaijan has agreed to 'publish what they receive'. This fiscal transparency together with the commitments made to the entire donor community under the Poverty Reduction Strategy Programs is in IFC's view one of the most effective ways to ensure that revenues will be wisely spent. In addition, IFC has worked closely with the World Bank with respect to the State Oil Fund of Azerbaijan's operations including the use of outside auditors. Furthermore, IFC continues to work with the World Bank and the IMF, advocating the need for ongoing transparent management and utilization of Azerbaijan's oil revenues.[94]

We may identify why these conditions imposed by the IFC and other lenders to the project are worth highlighting without it being necessary to take a position on the adequacy of these responses to the many concerns raised by non-governmental organizations in the context of the BTC pipeline project. By imposing conditions such as the inclusion of development aspects in the resettlement action plans in the context of land acquisitions or the adoption of a poverty reduction strategy programme ensuring that the revenues going to the public authorities will be 'wisely' spent, i.e., invested in

[92] International Finance Corporation, *BTC Pipeline and ACG Phase 1 Projects, Environmental and Social Documentation—IFC Response to submissions received during the 120-day Public Comment Period*, 27 October 2003, 10.   [93] Ibid.
[94] Ibid. 23.

development-related benefits to the population, the IFC in fact recognizes that it may use the leverage power it exercises on the borrowers to ensure that they will impose, in turn, certain conditions on the countries concerned which will contribute to fulfilling the development potential of the project.

What emerges is a chain of conditionalities, in which each actor is acknowledged to have an obligation to promote a form of human rights-oriented development in its sphere of influence. If the BTC project is indeed, as asserted by the IFC, exemplary in the standards it sets for the future, it may be so in precisely this respect. For instance, just in the same way that the countries receiving loans from the International Bank for Reconstruction and Development are required to produce poverty reduction strategy papers describing by which economic, social, and structural programmes they intend to reduce poverty[95]—a requirement also imposed on recipients of debt relief under the 'Heavily indebted poor countries' (HIPC) initiative—the IFC could condition funding of private sector projects for which its support is requested to the adoption of such a programme by the country concerned, and to its approval of the PRSP by the Board of the World Bank. This is especially important as most PRSPs adopted to date insist on the importance of the private sector in contributing to growth and thus to development, on the necessary inclusion into the world economy of the country concerned, and on the need to encourage foreign direct investments. Whether the macroeconomic components of the actual PRSPs actually contribute to a form of development directed towards the full realization of the internationally recognized human rights may of course be contested. But what deserves attention is that support from the international community of donors or lenders to private sector projects, no less than support to governmental projects, may be conditional upon certain undertakings of the receiving state. The question therefore naturally arises as to what responsibility should be imposed on the institutions which are in a position to influence indirectly the behaviour of those states, via the influence they exercise directly on the project partners they finance, to encourage these states to use the resources accruing from the investment in a way conducive to the realization of the human rights which they are internationally bound to respect. Where we accept that such a responsibility may exist in principle, we are led to ask not only whether the individual project is socially and environmentally responsible, but also how it may be used as an instrument to promote change in the receiving state. It is in precisely this sense that, in the kind of international governance we are presently inventing, TNCs may be

---

[95] For preliminary appraisals, see J. Klugman, *Poverty Reduction Strategy Papers: Objectives, Process and Experience to Date* (Washington D.C.: World Bank, 2003) and IMF and World Bank, 'Poverty Reduction Strategy Papers—Detailed Analysis of Progress in Inplementation', http://www.worldbank.org/poverty/strategies/progrep.htm.

made to become agents for the transformation of economic globalization into a process genuinely oriented towards human development.

16.7 CONCLUSION

The power of transnational corporations fascinates. Our reaction to this power has been fed by much-publicized situations in which, effectively controlled neither by their state of incorporation nor by the state where they operate, these global actors seemed to be able to commit human rights violations in complete impunity: our reaction has been to restrain that power, by imposing on transnational corporations obligations to comply with internationally recognized human rights. But, as we have discovered when we undertook to impose positive obligations on the state to protect and to fulfil human rights, power is not unidimensionally evil. It may also be exercised in the name of the good. TNCs could be seen also as a potential tool, and a powerful one, for the realization of the right to development.

However, this will not result from the initiatives of some enlightened corporations: apart from the still very exceptional circumstance where it may be accused of 'silent complicity' with a regime where widespread and systematic human rights violations occur, a corporate actor generally will accept a responsibility only for the human rights impact of its particular operations, but it will deny that it has a role in contributing to the development of the countries where it operates, and that, in particular, it should accept an 'economic responsibility' for the consequences of its economic decisions whether and when to invest or to disinvest, under which form, and with which accompanying measures, if any. Indeed, these are not issues TNCs need to worry much about: the tools which exist today to ensure the accountability of TNCs focus on the impact of their activities on the enjoyment of human rights, but no equivalent tools address the structural, often macroeconomic, questions raised by the presence of FDI in developing countries and by the legal framework under which such investment is made.

Change, if it is to occur at all, must probably come from elsewhere. A first step towards channelling TNCs in the direction of becoming agents of human development is for the developed states to recognize the paradox of the situation they have created. Although they insist that developing states should fully comply with their international human rights obligations, the developed states, in both their bilateral and their multilateral international policy making, have consistently sought to protect the rights of investors. They have thus made it impossible or very costly—even illegal in many cases—for developing states to effectively seek to impose on TNCs obligations in order to ensure that their presence will benefit human development in the countries where they operate. Multilateral lending institutions, too, have a responsibility to effectuate this change. They already see private investment as an opportunity not only for economic growth, but for improvements in the modes of governance of the countries in which such investment is made. They should go further in including such conditionalities in their lending policies. The more such measures will be taken, the more incentives will be devised to encourage TNCs to contribute to realizing the development aims of the countries where they operate, the more they will appear as the driving belts of this other economic globalization we anticipate—one which works for the poor.

Part F

Building Human Rights into Development
Planning Processes: The PRSP Exercise

17

Poverty Reduction Strategy Papers within the Human Rights Perspective

FRANCES STEWART AND MICHAEL WANG

17.1 INTRODUCTION

This chapter reviews how far the Poverty Reduction Strategy Papers (PRSP) exercise, which covers most very poor countries and involves considerable resources, contributes to the realization of human rights, and whether changes in the process might enhance this contribution.[1] PRSPs incorporate a set of policies intended to reduce poverty in particular countries. Countries are required to produce such papers in order to qualify for debt relief under the Heavily Indebted Poor Country debt reduction process (HIPC). PRSPs were first introduced in 1999, and 39 had been completed by April 2004. An essential aspect of PRSPs is the *process* by which they are produced, which is through participatory mechanisms, involving a variety of national and international actors, co-ordinated by the government: 'Poverty Reduction Strategies should be country-driven, promoting national ownership of strategies *by involving broad-based participation by civil society*.'[2]

The intention of the World Bank and International Monetary Fund (IMF), which initiated PRSPs, was to increase national ownership of poverty strategies,[3] for three reasons: first, because the ineffectiveness of many of the conditions of the international financial institutions (IFIs) was widely attributed to lack of national ownership, and it was intended that the PRSP

---

[1] A good deal of the analysis of PRSPs is derived from an earlier paper on which we received very helpful comments from Jeni Klugman. See F. Stewart and M. Wang, *Do PRSPs Empower Poor Countries and Disempower the World Bank, or is it the Other Way Round?* Queen Elizabeth House Working Paper 108 (Oxford, 2003).

[2] International Monetary Fund (IMF), *Poverty Reduction Strategy Papers: A Factsheet*, available from http://www.imf.org/external/np/exr/facts/prsp.htm, emphasis added.

[3] 'Country ownership is the guiding principle ... the process and content [of PRSPs] must be designed nationally to suit local circumstances and capacities, and should be useful to the country, *not only* external donors': J. Klugman, *Poverty Reduction Strategy Papers: Objectives, Process and Experience to Date* (Washington D.C.: World Bank, 2003), emphasis added.

process would improve implementation by increasing ownership of the programmes; second, that a participatory process might bring about a better set of policies, more in tune with local conditions and needs; and third, there was a belief in participation as a virtue in itself, because it empowered the poor.

The human rights agenda has a much longer history, going back to Thomas Paine, and earlier, for general advocacy of 'the rights of man', and to 1948 for internationally agreed human rights. Since 1948, recognition of human rights has extended to so-called 'positive' as well as 'negative' rights, notably in the International Covenant on Economic, Social and Cultural Rights (ICESCR),[4] the Declaration of the Right to Development,[5] and several other conventions.[6] However, while human rights have come to the front of much international debate, and have become prominent in United Nations (UN) and non-governmental organization (NGO) advocacy, implementation has been much slower.

In principle, the UN Commission on Human Rights (the Commission), supported by the Sub-Commission on the Promotion and Protection of Human Rights (the Sub-Commission), promotes the implementation of these internationally agreed covenants and conventions. In practice, much of the attention of the Commission has been on civil and political rights, where it has investigated and condemned the human rights situation in a large number of countries.[7] Only a fifth of the resolutions adopted in the spring 2003 session of the Commission, for instance, were explicitly concerned with economic, social, and cultural issues. Of the eleven Special Rapporteurs (or Experts) appointed since 1984 with respect to specific countries, only one has been concerned with development issues (an Independent Expert on technical co-operation for Liberia, appointed in 2003). However, over the last five years, four Special Rapporteurs and three independent experts have been appointed dedicated to positive rights,[8] accounting for one fifth of the total

[4] G.A. res. 2200A (XXI), 21 U.N. GAOR Supp. (No. 16) at 49, U.N. Doc. A/6316 (1966), 993 U.N.T.S. 3, *entered into force* 3 January 1976.

[5] G.A. res. 41/128, annex, 41 U.N. GAOR Supp. (No. 53) at 186, U.N. Doc. A/41/53 (1986).

[6] For example, Convention on the Elimination of All Forms of Discrimination against Women, G.A. res. 34/180, 34 U.N. GAOR Supp. (No. 46) at 193, U.N. Doc. A/34/46, *entered into force* 3 September 1981 and the Convention on the Rights of the Child, G.A. res. 44/25, annex, 44 U.N. GAOR Supp. (No. 49) at 167, U.N. Doc. A/44/49 (1989), *entered into force* 2 September 1990.

[7] For example, in 1992, Alston wrote: 'The Commission's lengthy debates have done very little to promote the core normative content of economic rights let alone the human rights dimensions of debt, world trade and development cooperation': P. Alston, ed., *The United Nations and Human Rights: A Critical Appraisal* (Oxford: Clarendon, 1992) 191.

[8] These are: the Independent Expert of the Commission on Human Rights on the right to development; the Special Rapporteur on the right of everyone to the enjoyment of the highest attainable physical and mental health; the Special Rapporteur on the right to education; the Special Rapporteur on the right to food; the Special Rapporteur on the right to adequate housing; the Independent Expert on human rights and extreme poverty; and the Independent Expert on structural adjustment and foreign debt.

appointed under thematic mandates, indicating greater attention being paid by the Commission to positive rights. The Committee on Economic, Social and Cultural Rights (the Committee) was established by the Economic and Social Council as a body of independent experts to monitor the achievement of positive rights. The Committee has clarified the norms contained in the ICESCR, expanded the information base about economic, social, and cultural rights, and set in place a system of monitoring country performance. However, the Committee has no effective power of enforcement if states are not fulfilling their obligations under the ICESCR.

Thus while the Commission and the Committee report on countries' achievements (or failures), as yet they have not been able to do much about them beyond advocacy. Progress in realizing positive rights has been made in a few countries which have incorporated various human rights in their own laws (for example India and South Africa), which has helped, though not ensured, realization of some human rights. But most of the progress in realizing human rights (both positive and negative) has stemmed from independent developments not directly related to human rights discourse— i.e., from democratization and the gradual extension of negative rights, from activist pressure, and from rising per capita incomes and improved social services that have improved the realization of positive rights, including the right to development. However, progress has been imperfect, and there remain many gaps in achievements.[9]

The question that this chapter considers is whether the realization of human rights could be improved by the PRSP process. It is plausible to suppose it might. First, the process of participation and empowerment could improve the realization of negative rights, extending people's control over decisions that affect them. Secondly, to the extent that PRSPs do realize their objective and lead to effective poverty reduction along the many dimensions of poverty, they would contribute to the realization of positive rights even though this is not the main intention. Hence in order to assess the potential contribution of the PRSP process to human rights we need to assess, first, their contribution to participation and empowerment and, second, to effective poverty reduction. The PRSPs do not use the language of rights. A third question, therefore, is whether this matters if de facto they improve the realization of rights. It is arguable that, unless achievements are firmly grounded in rights, they may prove ephemeral. Moreover, the PRSP process is itself likely to have a short lifespan, judging by the many changes in process that the IFIs have initiated over the years. For long-term success in the realization of rights, therefore, these rights need to be embedded both in legal and constitutional processes and in the norms of society. It is this sort of embeddedness that has broadly preserved negative rights in developed

---

[9] United Nations Development Program, *Human Development Report, 2000* and *Human Development Report, 2002* (New York: Oxford University Press, 2000, 2002).

countries (in the United Kingdom, for example, through habeas corpus, and in the U.S., through the Constitution). Hence, even if we get a positive answer to the first two questions, we shall need to consider whether PRSPs could be changed to produce embedded rights, or whether this must depend on other mechanisms and processes.

The next section will provide an overview of PRSPs. Section 17.3 will then consider how far the process of the PRSPs contributes to empowerment. This will explore who is involved, in what manner, and on what, all of which help indicate the extent of empowerment. Whether the process has actually changed poverty reduction programmes, compared with what happened before, is another indication of empowerment to be assessed. This issue will be considered in section 17.4. This is also relevant to the question of the PRSP contribution to poverty reduction. Section 17.5 will present conclusions and discuss changes to the PRSP process which might enhance the contribution to empowerment and poverty reduction. Since PRSPs are relatively new, the analysis has to rely on exploring the process and content of PRSPs, and not the actual impact, especially given data lags.

17.2 OVERVIEW OF PRSPS

PRSPs now form the basis for all multilateral lending to the poorest developing countries. They are policy documents produced by borrower countries outlining the economic and social programmes to reduce poverty, to be implemented over a three-year period.

Since 1999, recipients of debt relief under the enhanced HIPC initiative, as well as of concessional international development agency lending and the IMF's Poverty Reduction Growth Facility (PRGF), have been required to produce a PRSP. Finished documents must receive endorsement from the Boards of both the World Bank and the IMF, part of which, in principle, is based upon an acceptable participatory process. Following one year's implementation, countries which qualify for HIPC relief receive the full cancellation of their agreed-upon debt, the so-called 'completion point'. Countries can access temporary ('decision point') debt relief before completing a full PRSP by producing an interim document (I-PRSP) outlining strategies to be employed in the final document.

Nearly all low-income and highly indebted countries have either produced, or are in the process of producing, a PRSP. As of April 2004, 55 countries had undertaken a full or an interim PRSP, of which 39 had completed a full PRSP. In terms of geographic distribution, the majority of countries involved are in sub-Saharan Africa (SSA) (30), with the remaining distributed across East and South Asia and Pacific (8), Europe and Central Asia (11), Latin America & Caribbean (5), and the Middle East (1).

Table 17.1. *Countries in the PRSP process (April 2004)*

FULL	FULL (cont)
Albania	Serbia and Montenegro
Armenia	Sri Lanka
Azerbaijan	Tajikistan
Benin	Tanzania
Bolivia	Uganda
Bosnia and Herzegovina	Vietnam
Burkina Faso	Yemen
Cambodia	Zambia
Cameroon	**INTERIM**
Chad	Bangladesh
Djibouti	Burundi
Ethiopia	
Gambia	Cape Verde
Georgia	
Ghana	Central African Republic
Guinea	Côte d'Ivoire
Guyana	
Honduras	D.R. Congo
Kyrgz Republic	
Madagasgar	Dominica
Malawi	Guinea Bissau
Mali	Indonesia
Mauritania	
Mongolia	Kenya
Mozambique	Laos
Nepal	Lesotho
Nicaragua	Macedonia
Niger	Moldova
Pakistan	Sao Tome and Principe
Rwanda	
Senegal	Sierra Leone

Source: World Bank website.

17.3 DO PRSPS' PARTICIPATORY PROCESSES ENHANCE EMPOWERMENT?

PRSPs cover most low-income countries and might potentially be an important instrument to advance negative human rights by enhancing empowerment. Achieving this objective depends on how participation is interpreted in the PRSP process. One important distinction is whether the participation involves significant control over decision making, which could be understood to entail 'empowerment', or whether it simply means rudimentary levels of consultation.[10] A related issue is between whether participation is viewed as a means or an end.[11] An instrumental approach regards participation as a means to improving implementation, efficiency, and equity, while an empowerment approach values the process of increasing participation as an important end in itself.

At a minimum, participation clearly requires that individuals and groups are in some way involved in the decision making process. This engagement runs along a spectrum, which has been defined as ranging from (1) information sharing, (2) consultation, (3) joint decision making, to (4) initiation and control by stakeholders.[12] At one end, 'information sharing' involves very limited decision making powers but potentially important knowledge transfers. At the other lies 'initiation and control', which implies a high degree of citizen control over decision making. In between, 'consultation' exists when participants are able to express opinions but their perspectives are not necessarily incorporated into the final product; 'joint decision making', on the other hand, gives participants the shared right to negotiate the content of strategy. The boundaries of this classification are of course not clear-cut, and the type of participation involved varies with different stages of the policy-making process (e.g., early stages might involve more information sharing, while later stages more consultation and joint decision making).

Moreover, it is also important to find out *who* has been involved and thus empowered. This depends partly on who is consulted, and partly on whether their opinions are incorporated into the PRSPs. In this connection, the selection of groups, and how group representatives are chosen, are important elements influencing the extent to which the process contributes to extensive empowerment, especially since the PRSP process clearly cannot consult *everyone*.

In principle, a democratically elected government constitutes a comprehensive and legitimate representative of the people. But governments vary notoriously with respect to which groups they represent, and in the extent to which they are influenced by special (including their own private) interests rather than the people they supposedly represent. Consequently, empowerment of some groups, particularly of poor people, may require special efforts over and above the normal democratic processes. This is one reason that the

---

[10] N. Nelson, and S. Wright 'Participation and Power' in N. Nelson and S. Wright, eds, *Power and Participatory Development* (London: ITDG Publishing) 1–18.

[11] D. Goulet, 'Participation in Development: New Avenues' 17 *World Development* 165 (1989).

[12] World Bank, *The World Bank Participation Sourcebook* (Washington D.C.: World Bank, 1996); R. McGee, J. Levene, A. Hughes, *Assessing participation in poverty reduction strategy papers: a desk-based synthesis of experience in sub-Saharan Africa*, IDS Research Report 52 (Brighton: IDS, 2002); D. Narayan et al., *Voices of the Poor: Can Anyone Hear Us?* (Oxford: Oxford University Press, 2000).

PRSP process was introduced, although the deep suspicion of government shared by the IFIs was probably also an underlying motive. If governments do not provide adequate representation, realizing negative human rights may be assisted by PRSPs if participation is *comprehensive*, since human rights, by their nature, are comprehensive. A special focus on the poor may be needed because they particularly lack ways of affecting government decisions, while other parts of society can influence events in a number of other ways. To support negative human rights, then, participation needs to be at the 'initiation and control' end of the participation spectrum. There needs to be comprehensive participation, and the poor should be well represented. It is also important that participation and empowerment should be objectives in themselves and not merely seen as means to an end—partly because this is in the spirit of the philosophy of human rights, which are not mere means but ends in themselves, and partly because an instrumental approach may make any participation rather insecure, dependent on its (somewhat unproven) instrumental achievements.

An important consideration relevant to the extent and nature of empowerment concerns the manner in which participants are involved. Issues here are (1) whether the mechanisms for participation (for example, conferences, voting procedures, etc.) are conducive to generating broad-based participation (the timing and location of events can significantly impact the character of participants); (2) whether information is widely available; and (3) the policy areas and stages of the decision making process in which participation occurs.

The World Bank's definition of participation provides the basis for the PRSP process. According to the *SourceBook for Poverty Reduction Strategies*,[13] participation is 'the process by which stakeholders influence and share control over priority setting, policymaking, resource allocations, and/or program implementation'. The *Sourcebook* expects the following groups to participate: (1) the general public, particularly the poor and vulnerable groups; (2) the government, including parliament, local government, line and central ministries; (3) Civil Society Organizations (CSOs) such as NGOs, community-based organizations, trade unions and guilds, academic institutions; (4) private sector actors such as professional associations; (5) donors, both bilateral and multilateral.[14]

It would appear, therefore, that the World Bank envisages participation in PRSPs to be towards the initiation and control end of the spectrum. Participants should be able to 'influence' and 'share control' of policy making and agenda setting, as well as budgeting and implementation. The World Bank's vision of participation is an inclusive one, encompassing extremely

---

[13] See World Bank, *The World Bank Participation Sourcebook*, above n. 12, 237.
[14] Ibid. 250.

broad sectors of domestic society and international stakeholders, not only poor marginalized individuals, but also relevant representative institutions and umbrella groups.

Human rights pertain to individuals, and, in the case of the Right to Development, to a whole society or nation. Consequently, in the list above only the first two (the general public and the government, representing people) are directly relevant. Whether involving category (3) (civil society represented by NGOs and community organizations) will empower individuals and the poor depends very much on the nature of those organizations. Community organizations of the poor would seem to have more legitimacy from this perspective than NGOs, which can be quite unrepresentative. Consultation and empowerment of the private sector, (4), is unlikely to empower in a human rights direction, but could be helpful instrumentally in securing efficient solutions. Category (5), external actors, are hardly relevant to empowerment within a society—since they come from outside it—but they too might contribute instrumentally and/or to international issues. However, in order for their involvement not to negate any national empowerment effects, it is important that they do not dominate the process by setting the agenda, by their articulateness in discussions, and by their implicit financial clout.

The next sections examine whether the reality of the PRSP participatory process has indeed empowered citizens and particularly the poor, by operating at the initiation and control end of the spectrum, and through the comprehensiveness of participation, especially the extent of participation of the poor. We limit ourselves to examining participation in the policy-making process only, not in budgeting or implementation. We will assess participation along two lines: first, the 'process' of policy formation, assessing the degree of inclusion, asking *who* has participated, and in *what manner* they have participated, and the *issues* in which they have participated; and secondly in terms of the *content* of PRSPs, asking whether the PRSP process has affected the policy content of the final documents. The process question gives some indication of who has potentially been empowered, and whether the process was such as to make it probable that significant empowerment occurred; the content question is also relevant to the extent of empowerment because it seems likely that if empowerment occurs this would change the content of the policy package.

17.3.1 Who Participates?

It is difficult to generalize about the range of actors consulted in PRSPs given the diversity of country experience. In some cases, there has been broad involvement across all the categories outlined in the World Bank's *Sourcebook*.

Uganda, Rwanda, and Vietnam have been acknowledged by civil society and donors alike as having fostered such comprehensive participation.[15]

In Uganda, participation was widespread with a large scale and high profile media campaign and workshops that made concerted efforts to include stakeholders beyond the capital.[16] The creation of an umbrella organization to channel civil society efforts ensured wide civil society participation. In Rwanda, broad participation was achieved by incorporating existing indigenous participatory practices known as *Ubedehe* into the process. This involved a bottom-up approach, the government targeting 9,000 *cellules* to produce priority rankings and community development plans, and a participatory poverty assessment exercise to collect poor peoples' opinions on the relevance of sectoral policies.[17] There is broad consensus that there was grass-roots participation at most stages, which helped in the post-conflict reconciliation process. Vietnam also had extensive participation according to both donor and civil society observers, largely due to good pre-existing relations between government structures and Vietnamese NGOs, particularly at the local level.[18]

In other countries, some categories of participants were more engaged than others, while some were left out. For example, the private sector was particularly active in Mozambique,[19] while it was absent elsewhere, including Rwanda.[20] Religious organizations were quite important in Bolivia and Nicaragua but missing elsewhere. There was generally substantial government involvement, as the government managed the process of participation, though the breadth of government involvement was variable, with some (e.g., Kenya) extending participation across different levels of government and ministries, while in others the process was led principally by the finance or planning ministry and concentrated at the national level (e.g., Mali and Malawi).[21]

---

[15] For Uganda see Z. Gariyo, *The PRSP Process in Uganda* (2001), available from http://www.eurodad.org; C. Robb and A. Scott, *Reviewing Some Early Poverty Reduction Strategy Papers in Africa*, IMF Policy Discussion Paper PDP/01/5 (Washington D.C.: IMF, 2001), available from http://www.imf.org; and D. Worodofa, *The Role of Civil Society Organisations in Formulation of Poverty Reduction Strategies in Uganda* (Oxford: Oxfam U.K., 2002). For Vietnam see SGTS & Associates, *Civil Society Participation in Poverty Reduction Strategy Papers: Report to the Department for International Development* (2000), available from http://www.dfid.gov.uk. For Rwanda, see references in McGee et al., above n. 12; E. Bugingo, *Missing the Mark? Participation in the PRSP process in Rwanda* (2002), Christian Aid Research Report available from http://www.christian-aid.org.uk/indepth/0212rwanda/rwanda.pdf; F. Mutebi, S. Stone, and N. Thin, 'Rwanda' 2 *Development Policy Review* 253 (2003).

[16] McGee et al., above n. 12, 70.   [17] Bugingo, above n. 15.

[18] SGTS, above n. 15, 23.

[19] R. McGee and N. Taimo, *Civil Society in the PRSP Process*, report for DFID Mozambique, 2001.   [20] Mutebe, Stone, and Thin, above n. 15, 260.

[21] For Kenya, see L. Hanmer, G. Ikiara, W. Eberlei, and C. Abong, 'Kenya' 2 *Development Policy Review* 179 (2003); Mali, see I. Dante, J-F. Gauteir, M. Marouani, and M. Raffinot, 'Mali' 2 *Development Policy Review* 217 (2003); Malawi, see R. Jenkins and M. Tsoka, 'Malawi' 2 *Development Policy Review* 197 (2003).

Donors, including IFI representatives, also displayed differing levels of engagement, ranging from assuming an observer's role to organizing and financing consultations directly. It is reported that most donors have taken a relatively 'hands-off' approach in the design of the process, allowing national government greater space than before in conducting national and regional consultations.[22] At later stages, donor involvement has varied. In some countries such as Ghana, Killick and Abugre report that IFI representatives specifically avoided excessive involvement in drafting the PRSP.[23] But there are reports of heavy IFI involvement in the drafting of Tanzania's I-PRSP.[24]

Several key categories of participants were *excluded* from the participatory process consistently across a number of countries:

- *Parliamentarians:* In a number of countries, the role of national Parliaments in formulating PRSPs was minimal, particularly in Africa,[25] although this has also been a problem in Latin America.[26] In Malawi, for example, 'only 5 MPs were involved in the process'.[27] In Kenya, less than 10 per cent of MPs attended consultations.[28] In Senegal and Mali parliamentarians were only officially included in the final ratification of the PRSP.[29] In general, it appears that in most African countries there is a tendency for PRSPs to be seen as 'technical planning processes that are properly the affair of the government, and not a subject for party-political debate'.[30]

- *Trade Unions:* The International Confederation of Free Trade Unions (ICFTU) reports that trade unions were not systematically consulted in many early PRSP processes. In Tanzania and Uganda national trade unions were told they could participate in the PRSP process only after the PRSP had already been completed and endorsed by the IFIs.[31] In Mali, neither trade unions and nor the important Cotton Producers' Association

---

[22] D. Booth, 'Chapter 1: Overview of PRSP processes and monitoring' in *Report Submitted to the Strategic Partnership with Africa* (2001) 27.

[23] T. Killick and C. Abugre, 'Chapter 3: Institutionalising the PRSP approach in Ghana' in *Report Submitted to the Strategic Partnership with Africa* (2001) 13.

[24] A. Evans, 'Tanzania' 2 *Development Policy Review* 271 (2003).

[25] Booth, above n. 22.

[26] Trocaire, *PRSPs—Policy & Practice in Honduras and Nicaragua* (2002), available from http://www.eurodad.org.

[27] Eurodad, *Many Dollars, Any Change?* available at http://www.eruodad.org, at 9.

[28] Panos Institute, *Reducing Poverty—Is the World Bank's Strategy Working?* available from http://www.eurodad.org at 25.

[29] W. Phillips, 'All for Naught? An Analysis of Senegal's PRSP Process' in A. Whaites, ed., *Masters of their Own Development?* (Monrovia, California: World Vision, 2002) 47–71; Dante et al., above n. 21.   [30] Booth, above n. 22, 41.

[31] International Confederation of Free Trade Unions (ICFTU), *Brief to the IMF/World Bank Review on the PRSP Process* (2002), available from http://www.imf.org/external/np/prspgen/review/2002/comm/v2.pdf.

participated at all.[32] There is some evidence, however, of trade unions enjoying substantive participation in transition countries where there have traditionally been close relations between governments and trade unions.[33]

- *Women:* In a number of countries, participation of women's groups appears to be weak.[34] In Senegal, the United Nations Development Fund for Women (UNIFEM) found 'civil Society organisations were ignored, especially women'.[35] In Tanzania, Bolivia, and Malawi it is reported that consultations with women's groups were very limited.[36] In Azerbaijan only 10 per cent of those consulted were women.[37] But there are reports that some countries made special efforts to include women, such as Lesotho.[38]

- *Marginalized Groups:* The process has been widely criticized for not consulting the poor. Action Aid reports that at least five of its country programmes complained of little direct involvement of associations of the poor in PRSP deliberations.[39] In Bolivia, the poor were represented by local authorities that were only weakly connected to the poor, particularly to indigenous groups.[40]

Participation was often extremely selective, excluding groups out of favour with the government. In Ghana, for example, trade union members reported that 'the Government preferred to consult with more sympathetic institutions, like the Civil Servants Union (which was not a member of the TUC), than with bodies which carry real weight within civil society'.[41] Christian Aid reports that, in Bolivia, civil society participants felt that the government's selection of participants for the 'National Dialogue' was not impartial or

---

[32] Dante et al., above n. 21.

[33] Overseas Development Institute, 'Experience with PRSPs in transition countries' *PRSP Synthesis Note 6*, February 2003, available from http://www.prspsynthesis.org.

[34] World Bank, *Gender in the PRSPs: A Stocktaking* (Washington D.C.: World Bank, 2001) available from http://www.gtz.de/forum_armut/download/bibliothek/GenderPRSP.PDF.

[35] UNIFEM, *Contribution to the World Bank and IMF PRSP Review* (2001), available from http://www.imf.org/external/np/prspgen/review/2002/comm/v1.pdf.

[36] E. Zuckerman, *Engendering Poverty Reduction Strategy Papers, Why it Reduces Poverty and the Rwanda Case* (2001), available from http://www.wider.unu.edu/conference/conference-2001-2/conference2001-2.htm; McGee et al., above n. 12.

[37] IMF and World Bank, *Poverty Reduction Strategy Papers—Detailed Analysis of Progress in Implementation* (2003), available from http://www.worldbank.org/poverty/strategies/progrep.htm.

[38] Overseas Development Institute, 'Assessing Participation in PRSPs in sub-Saharan Africa' *PRSP Synthesis Note 3*, February 2002, available from http://www.prspsynthesis.org; Panos Institute, above n. 28, 43.

[39] Action Aid, *Inclusive Circles Lost in Exclusive Cycles* (2002), available from http://www.imf.org/external/np/prspgen/review/2002/comm/v2.pdf.

[40] R. Uriona, J. Requena, J. Nunez, R. Eyben, and W. Lewis, 'Crafting Bolivia's PRSP: 5 Points of View' 39 *Finance and Development* (2002), available at http://www.imf.org/external/pubs/ft/fandd/2002/06/cavero.htm.   [41] Cited in SGTS, above n. 15, 19.

representative.[42] In Cameroon, the Catholic Relief Services note that the government hand-picked participants in civil society consultations, bypassing important civil society institutions such as the Catholic Church, which were key campaigners for debt relief.[43] In some cases, NGO participation was limited to international NGOs (INGOs), or NGOs in the capital area. Smaller and rural NGOs, generally those with the most contact with the poor, were often excluded. In Bolivia, for example, only one NGO outside La Paz was invited to initial consultations, while one of the most prominent local NGOs in La Paz was not invited,[44] and smaller NGOs were poorly represented in Senegal.[45] NGOs that did participate were not always representative of broader societal concerns. This is particularly a concern in very divided communities, where local elite interests may dominate.[46] Killick and Abugre report that the non-state actors involved in drafting Ghana's PRSP were donor-driven and not representative of pro-poor constituencies.[47]

To summarise: comprehensive empowerment did not occur in many cases, with an under-representation of the poor, of NGOs and community organizations representing the poor, and of women.

17.3.2 How is Participation Organized?

There have been a variety of strategies for consultation and information dissemination, including national and regional conferences to discuss PRSP drafts and proposals, with invited participants from civil society. In several countries (e.g., Nicaragua and Bolivia) they built upon participatory mechanisms that had already been embodied in national legislation.[48] Other methods include local surveys asking villagers for inputs into prioritizing public action and resource allocation, as well as media campaigns including

---

[42] Christian Aid, *Ignoring the experts: Poor People's Exclusion from Poverty Reduction Strategies* (2001), available from http://www.imf.org/external/np/prspgen/review/2002/comm/v2.pdf at 14.

[43] Catholic Relief Services, *Review of the Poverty Reduction Strategy Paper Initiative* (2001), available from http://www.imf.org/external/np/prspgen/review/2002/comm/v2.pdf at 10.

[44] World Development Movement, *Policies to Roll-Back the State and Privatise? Poverty Reduction Strategy Papers Investigated*, available from http://www.eurodad.org.

[45] Phillips, above n. 29, 52.

[46] J. Hoddinott, 'Participation and Poverty Reduction: An Analytical Framework and Overview of the Issues' 11 *Journal of African Economies* 146 (2002).

[47] Killick and Abugre, above n. 23, 32. Nonetheless, there are examples of attempts to ensure that the CSOs are representative. In Uganda, for example, the composition of the task force charged with representing CSOs was determined through an election involving 45 NGOs: Gariyo, above n. 15.

[48] Overseas Development Institute (ODI), 'Experience with Poverty Reduction Strategies in Latin America and the Caribbean', *PRSP Synthesis Note 5*, February 2003, available from http://www.prspsynthesis.org.

TV, radio, and newspaper announcements (e.g., Malawi, Tanzania, Rwanda, and Kenya). Participatory Poverty Assessments (PPAs) occurred in some countries (e.g., Uganda, Vietnam, and Rwanda) to provide the poverty analysis that underpins the PRSP. However, there have been problems with the design and implementation of participatory processes, including the time frame, information sharing, and level of consultations.

17.3.2.1 Time Frame

Because debt relief is conditional on producing PRSPs, there is a strong incentive for HIPC-eligible countries (accounting for more than half the countries producing PRSPs) to complete PRSPs as soon as possible in order to lock in debt relief.[49] Extensive evidence suggests this link has compromised the quality of participation. The Mozambique Debt group reported that 'the consultation process was driven inordinately by a deadline for the completion of the PRSP, which even with good faith on the part of the government, provided inadequate time to carry out a comprehensive consultation process'.[50] In Ethiopia, the government attempted consultations in over 100 districts in just three days.[51] In many cases, CSOs were not given sufficient time to prepare for consultation. From a review of its country programmes, Action Aid reports that there was

a lack of adequate prior notice regarding meetings and consultations. Many were informed only 2 or 3 days in advance, and in the case of Nepal, 24-hour prior notice was given on one occasion... nearly all country programs felt such last minute notification prevented them from preparing adequately for PRS consultations; lengthy reports and documents could not be commented upon and the views of community partners could not be sought.[52]

In Bolivia, Honduras, and Cameroon, the Catholic Relief Service also complained of being given only a day's notice before consultations, with insufficient preparatory information or material.[53] There were reports of local consultation workshops taking place only once over the course of a day without any further possibilities for participation at the local level (e.g., Honduras and Cameroon).[54] Tanzania, for example, had an extremely compressed PRSP timetable (six months from initiation to cabinet approval) and the only local consultations took place over the course of a single day.[55]

---

[49] C. S. Adam, and D. Bevan, *PRGF Stocktaking Exercise on behalf of DFID* (2001), available from http://www.econ.ox.ac.uk/Members/david.bevan/Reports/PRGFStocktake02.pdf.
[50] Cited in Christian Aid, above n. 42, 33.
[51] J. Muwonge, B. Geleta, S. Heliso, 'Working towards an Ethiopian PRSP' in A. Whaites, ed., *Masters of Their Own Development?* (Monrovia, California: World Vision, 2002) 73–87.
[52] Action Aid, above n. 39, 7.   [53] Catholic Relief Services, above n. 43, 22.
[54] Save the Children, *Save the Children UK Submission to the IMF/World Bank Review of PRSPs* (2001), available from http://www.imf.org/external/np/prspgen/review/2002/comm/v2.pdf.   [55] Evans, above n. 24.

17.3.2.2 Information Availability

Mostly, the consensus is that access to drafts and final versions of PRSPs and I-PRSPs was relatively good. But in some cases the availability of information was hampered by:

- *Access:* Many CSOs complained about lack of access to core World Bank and IMF documents. In Nicaragua, the draft interim PRSP was available in English in Washington D.C. before it was available in Managua.[56] In a survey of eight PRSP countries McGee et al. found that the sharing of information with CSOs who take an active part in PRSP processes was patchy.[57] Governments often appeared reluctant to share early drafts of PRSPs. In general, information seems not to have reached rural populations in time to encourage broad and well-informed participation in consultations.[58] In Haiti, civil society groups had trouble obtaining even basic information such as which government ministry was leading the process and the timeline for its formulation.[59] In Bolivia, civil society participants did not realize the promised opportunity to review the final PRSP.[60] Zambian NGOs complained that they did not receive all key documents or necessary information, even basic information such as the amount of interim debt reduction.[61]
- *Language:* In several cases the choice of language limited participation. For example, Cambodia's PRSP was only made available in Khmer in the final version, not in earlier drafts.[62] In Bolivia some PRSP documents were initially only produced in English.[63] A Spanish version followed but documents were never translated into local languages.

17.3.2.3 Level of Consultations

In a number of countries, particularly in Africa, consultations were mainly held in urban areas.[64] In Mozambique, for example, rural communities and northern districts were far less involved in the consultation process than Maputo-based organizations.[65] Tanzanian officials and the PRSP itself states that the poor at the village level were not adequately consulted.[66]

---

[56] ODI, 'Experience with Poverty Reduction Strategies in Latin America and the Caribbean', above n. 48.   [57] McGee et al., above n. 12.
[58] Ibid. 9.   [59] Christian Aid, above n. 42, 14.   [60] Ibid. 33.
[61] CRS, above n. 43, 21.
[62] NGO Forum on Cambodia, *Results of Initial Discussions among NGOs/CSOs on the National Poverty Reduction Strategy of Cambodia* (2001), available from http://www.bigpond.co.kh/users.ngoforum/workshop/att/default.htm.   [63] Christian Aid, above n. 42, 13.
[64] ICFTU, above n. 31.   [65] Christian Aid, above n. 42, 33.
[66] McGee et al., above n. 12.

17.3.2.4 Pre-Prepared Drafts

A recurrent complaint was that governments came to discussions with pre-prepared draft frameworks; participants were rarely involved in the design of frameworks. CRS claims this was the case in Zambia, Honduras, and Bolivia.[67]

In Bolivia, citizen participation in the PRSP drafting process was severely limited. Instead, a small circle of government economists undertook drafting to the PRSP plan for more than four months without including or even informing civil society organizations that had participated in the National Dialogue. Bolivian organizations tried repeatedly to pressure the government to be more inclusive, even appealing to international donors and the World Bank and IMF, but to no avail.

In Bolivia the final PRSP was received by CSOs through the German Ministry of International Development.[68] In Senegal, when the PRSP process was launched, the government appeared with its analysis already prepared.[69] In Zambia, CSOs were denied representation on the Technical Committee for drafting the PRSP, despite a large and active coalition of groups organized to co-ordinate inputs.[70] A UNDP assessment of Lesotho's PRSP found that the procedures were designed to conduct the participatory process *after* the PRSP draft was already prepared.[71]

17.3.2.5 Summary of the Participation Process

Countries implementing PRSPs start from very different positions, and processes should be judged relative to starting conditions. Participation may be less in countries with unstable and fractionalized polities than in more stable and unified societies. Yet, even taking this into account, the fact remains that in many countries key elements of participation were seriously flawed. Important sections of civil society (e.g., women, religious organizations, workers' movements, rural groups) and parts of government (e.g., line ministries and parliament) were missing from the process or inadequately represented, either because they were not included at all, or because of rushed time frames, deficient information, poor dissemination in appropriate languages, and failure to reach many local, especially rural, communities. In almost every case, civil society participants were presented with drafts formulated by small teams of external consultants or central ministry staff. Poor people's priorities were consequently often not embodied in the PRSP.

Within the government, the position of the Ministry of Planning or Finance seems to have been enhanced, since it is these ministries who organize the process and prepare drafts, while the role of the so-called 'line'

---

[67] CRS, above n. 43, 10.

[68] IBIS, *Input for the PRSP Review. Poverty Reduction and Participation* (2001), available from http://www.imf.org/external/np/prspgen/review/2002/comm/v2.pdf, 124.

[69] Phillips, above n. 29, 56.   [70] CRS, above n. 43, 11.

[71] McGee et al., above n. 12, 66.

ministries which are perhaps more likely to represent the interests of the poor (e.g., Ministries of Health or Education) has been weak.

To date defects in process of the PRSPs, including selective participation, mean that they have not played a significant role in realizing human rights through a comprehensive increase in empowerment. We now turn to an assessment of whether the PRSP process changed the *content* of country programmes. If it has, then this does suggest some empowerment, albeit not comprehensive. Also, some change in content would be needed if PRSPs were to be a useful mechanism for promoting the realization of positive human rights.

17.4 THE CONTENT OF PRSPS

This section examines whether countries are empowered from a policy-making perspective. Previous adjustment programmes were criticized for their 'one-size-fits-all' approach to policy design, and the resulting uniformity of reform packages across different countries. If PRSPs are genuinely country-owned, we would expect to see considerable variation across country programmes reflecting different national priorities and inputs from participation, and for policies to diverge from standard orthodox packages. We investigate this issue by analysing a wide range of reviews of PRSPs and by a detailed analysis of actual content of full PRSPs.

17.4.1 Reviews of the Content of PRSPs

ActionAid Vietnam reports that 'PPAs and other consultative exercises . . . have created a lot of opportunities for government participants to learn more about the causes of poverty. This has led to national plans becoming more "people-centred and pro-poor".'[72] In many countries, a multidimensional definition of poverty was adopted as a result of the PPA work associated with PRSPs. However, a move towards a multidimensional approach to poverty has formed an important element in the recent international poverty agenda, independently of PRSPs.[73]

Most PRSPs have involved significantly more ambitious social targets than the country's historic achievements, although countries with PRSPs under implementation have sometimes revised targets downwards.[74] An IMF

---

[72] Cited in M. Zaman, *Are We Getting Lost in Exclusive Anti-poor, Adjustment Lending Policy Cycles?*, Action Aid Policy Brief, 2002, available from http://www.esrftz.org/ppa/documents/aa_1.pdf at 22.

[73] World Bank, *The World Bank Participation Sourcebook*, above n. 12; Narayan et al., above n. 12.

[74] IMF and World Bank, 'Poverty Reduction Strategy Papers—Detailed Analysis of Progress in Implementation', above n. 37, 11–12.

evaluation of selected PRSPs shows an increase of between 2 and 3 per cent of GDP in planned poverty reducing expenditures in PRSP countries, 1999–2002, though no comparison is made with non-PRSP projections.[75] Vietnam's PRSP commits itself to implementation of the 20/20 initiative— 20 per cent of aid and 20 per cent of government expenditure to be spent on basic social services.[76] Nicaragua's PRSP aims to make additional investment in water and sanitation,[77] while Bolivia's PRSP has allocated social spending according to positive discrimination criteria, favouring the poorest municipalities.[78] PRSPs have also emphasized agricultural sector policies and promoted improved gender equality, and protection of ethnic minorities and the vulnerable (children and the disabled). While all these changes are very much in line with the international poverty agenda, the PRSPs have been a helpful mechanism in promoting them.

Specific elements of civil society have been effective in lobbying national government to incorporate affirmative action policies in PRSPs. For example, in Kenya, pastoralist groups successfully lobbied to have their concerns over access to assets included in the PRSP,[79] and women's groups brought gender concerns into Kenya's final PRSP.[80] Action Aid country offices report that HIV/AIDS groups in Malawi and rural peasant producers in Rwanda and Vietnam were influential in shaping sectoral polices.[81] In several countries CSOs have successfully lobbied to have user fees abolished.[82]

These are positive changes, but, by and large, it appears that participation has had a limited impact on the content of PSRPs. Many observers report that the recommendations made during consultations were mostly not incorporated in final documents.[83] In Bolivia, for example, civil society participants felt the initial draft bore little relation to the recommendations from the 'National Dialogue'.[84] Only after mass demonstrations did the policy content shift, but still remained largely void of civil society recommendations for extending the poverty agenda beyond social expenditure to land reform and political issues.[85] Leading NGO groups were so frustrated with their lack of impact that they lobbied Washington D.C. for Bolivia's

---

[75] IMF, 'Draft PGRF-PRSP Evaluation: Main Report' (Washington D.C.: IMF, 2004) 24.
[76] Government of Vietnam, *Comprehensive Poverty Reduction and Growth Strategy* (2002), available at http://www.poverty.worldbank.org/files/Vietnam_PRSP.pdf.
[77] Government of Nicaragua, *A Strengthened Growth and Poverty Reduction Strategy* (2001) available from http://poverty.worldbank.org/files/Nicaragua_PRSP.pdf.
[78] Government of Bolivia, *Poverty Reduction Strategy Paper* (2001), available from http://poverty.worldbank.org/files/boliviaprsp.pdf.   [79] McGee et al., above n. 12, 42.
[80] Ibid. 43.   [81] Zaman, above n. 72.
[82] Klugman, personal communication.
[83] In some cases this was because the recommendations from civil society were vague and unimplementable.   [84] Christian Aid, above n. 42.
[85] A. Bendana, *Poverty Reduction Policy Politics in Bolivia* (2001), available from http://www.aidc.org.za/sapsn/kampala/alejandro_2.htm.

final document not to be approved.[86] The recommendations from parallel PRSP processes initiated and conducted by civil society in Honduras and Nicaragua were also effectively ignored in the final PRSP.[87] Killick and Abugre report that in Ghana 'it appears that the results of the community consultations did not feed into the analyses and recommendations'.[88] A survey of seven countries found that, while in some countries the adoption of inputs appeared to be good (Rwanda, Vietnam), in the majority, most civil society proposals were not incorporated, particularly in areas of tax reform, budget making, and civil service reforms.[89] The weak tangible impact on policies would appear to corroborate the complaint from many civil society participants that their involvement was limited to information dissemination and consultation exercises at an early stage, and that they were excluded from later decision making.

The lack of influence over policy is even more evident when it comes to structural reform issues. Most CSOs report that they were barred from participating in macroeconomic and structural policy discussions.

There is broad consensus among our civil society sources in Ghana, Malawi, Mozambique, Tanzania, Zambia and Bolivia that NGOs and their coalitions have been totally unable to influence macroeconomic policy or even engage governments in dialogue about it.[90]

In Bolivia, the umbrella NGO organization complained that the economic model was 'a given' and they were only permitted to tinker around the edges.[91] Honduran NGOs complain of exclusion from workshops on the macro-economic chapter of the PRSP, which was included in the final document without ever having been circulated to CSOs or parliamentarians.[92] In six African PRSP exercises, it is reported that discussions rarely considered sequencing or alternative policies, and only in one (Uganda) was there discussion of the impact of structural adjustment.[93]

While national governments were the agents of this exclusion, it appears they too were constrained in influencing the macroeconomic framework. The Honduran NGO network, *Interforos*, was told by government officials that 'the Fund's position with regard to macro-economic policies were not negotiable'.[94] In Kenya, the Finance Minister was reportedly sacked after a series of public statements that alleged the IMF and the World Bank were forcing

[86] ODI, 'Experience with Poverty Reduction Strategies in Latin America and the Caribbean', above n. 48.   [87] IBIS, above n. 68.
[88] Killick and Abugre, above n. 23, 31.   [89] Zaman, above n. 72, 8.
[90] McGee et al., above n. 12, 13.   [91] Christian Aid, above n. 42, 11.
[92] ODI, 'Experience with Poverty Reduction Strategies in Latin America and the Caribbean', above n. 48, 12.   [93] Robb and Scott, above n. 15, 30.
[94] I. Knoke and P. Morazan, *PRSP: Beyond the Theory. Practical Experiences and Positions of Involved Civil Society Organisations* (2002), available from http://www. brot-fuer-die-welt.de, 16 note 2.

the Government to undertake unwanted changes in its PRSP.[95] There was a perception among government officials that altering the macroeconomic framework would prevent endorsement from the Boards of the IFIs, leading to self-censorship in some countries. A Finance Minister in a country developing a PRSP is quoted as saying: 'We do not want to second guess the Fund. We prefer to pre-empt them by giving them what they want before they start lecturing us about this and that. By doing so, we send a clear message that we know what we are doing—i.e., we believe in structural adjustment.'[96] In their study of Ghana's PRSP process, Killick and Abugre similarly describe

a strong reported tendency towards self-censorship on the part of the Ghanaian authorities, writing into the GPRS drafts wording designed to meet the anticipated demands of the IFIs ... such second-guessing ... does qualify the claim of Ghanaian ownership, which implies the GoG [Government of Ghana] was free to write what it wanted.[97]

17.4.2 How Far Have Programmes Changed?

The most effective way to assess whether the PRSPs have empowered people in decisions about policy making is to explore how far they have altered the basic thrust of reform programmes: do they differ from one another and from standard structural adjustment programmes, as one would expect if they made a significant contribution to policy content?

A striking feature of nearly all PRSPs is the consistency of their approaches to poverty reduction. All country programmes are based on the premise that private sector led growth is the most effective way to reduce poverty. Although this growth is described variously as 'pro-poor' (e.g., Cambodia), 'equity-based' (Burkina Faso), or 'broad-based' (Nicaragua), none consider alternative approaches to poverty reduction, particularly ones containing an element of resource redistribution or that are rights-based. Indeed, there is a general disregard for distributional issues; projections of the beneficial impact of growth in country papers tend to assume a scenario where growth is accompanied by neutral distribution (e.g., see Tanzania's PRSP). Even in the few PRSPs that explicitly recognize the necessity for redistribution to ensure the poor benefit from growth, policies are either vague about how this should be done in practice (e.g. Azerbaijan, Ethiopia, and Sri Lanka) or take redistribution simply to mean increasing the share of social spending devoted

---

[95] Zaman, above n. 72, 12.

[96] Cited in F. Cheru, *Economic, Social and Cultural Rights—The Highly Indebted Poor Countries (HIPC) Initiative: a human rights assessment of the Poverty Reduction Strategy Papers (PRSPs)*, Report submitted to the 57th session of the Economic and Social Council of the United Nations, Commission on Human Rights, agenda item 10E/CN.4/2001/56 (2001), available from http://www.unhchr.ch.   [97] Killick and Abugre, above n. 23, 14.

to the poor (e.g., Albania, Kyrgyzstan, Malawi, Tajikistan). Where land reforms are mentioned, they usually refer to consolidating property rights and establishing legal titles for the development of property markets rather than reallocating resources to the landless (e.g,. Albania, Benin, Bolivia, Cameroon, Niger, Rwanda, Tajikistan, Tanzania). In only a few countries, such as Mozambique and Uganda, are land reforms specifically targeted at improving the access of marginalized groups.

A closer examination of the macroeconomic and structural reform policy contents of the 30 completed PRSPs reveals that there is no fundamental departure from the kind of policy advice provided under earlier structural adjustment programmes. Current policies contain all the elements of the first generation of policy reforms designed to promote the role of the market and 'get the prices right', and share a similar format and content involving all of the following reforms: financial and trade liberalization; privatization; public sector reform; sectoral policies (e.g., infrastructure, energy, and manufacturing); and social sector reform (see Appendix Table 17A.1 below).

With regards to fiscal and monetary matters, the emphasis is still on maintaining current-account and fiscal balances consistent with low and declining debt levels; inflation in the low single digits; and rising per capita GDP, even though in Participatory Poverty Assessments conducted in many countries (e.g., Ethiopia and Nigeria) the rural poor stress that contractionary macroeonomic policies resulting in lower employment and declining wage bills in the public sector are more of a concern than inflation.[98] Tight monetary and fiscal policies to control inflation and budget deficits are generally proposed, and a flexible exchange rate or movement towards one.

HIPC Ministers themselves appear to question the stance taken with respect to inflation and growth. At the declaration of the 6th HIPC Ministerial meeting, they urged the IFIs to:

> ... think more closely about ways to increase growth and employment rather than further reducing inflation, about the supply-side (as well as demand-side) causes of inflation and about defining sustainability of the budget deficit as including grants and debt relief.[99]

Other familiar first generation reforms which reappear in all PRSPs include measures to deregulate the financial sector: movement towards market-based interest rates, liberalizing the domestic banking sector, and the elimination of exchange controls and opening up of the capital account (see Appendix Table 17A.2 below). Yet the connection between these policies and poverty reduction is remote, particularly in the context of poor countries with shallow capital markets.

---

[98] Narayan et al., above n. 12, 21 and 150.
[99] Cited in UNCTAD, *From Adjustment to Poverty Reduction: What is New?* (Geneva: UNCTAD, 2002) 25.

Trade policy advice in poverty reduction strategy programmes conforms to the view that rapid integration into the world economy is the best way to combat poverty. In every country, there is commitment to maintaining open and liberal trading regimes. A very few cases diverge somewhat from the conventional wisdom. Mozambique's PRSP, for example, advocates the use of 'case-by-case, selective intervention, limited in time' for manufactured goods.

There is also universal emphasis on the continued privatization of state-owned enterprises; reliance on private agents in the provision of public goods; the liberalization of prices for most utilities and key markets; cost-recovery in curative health care and secondary/tertiary education; and a general reduction of state involvement in the economy (see Table 17A.2). The PRSPs also endorse 'second generation' reforms, including anti-corruption measures; more participatory and accountable public administration; greater transparency in budgets; and legal reforms aiming at securing property rights and protecting private sector activity, as well improving the rule of law.

A general lack of explicit linkage between macroeconomic policies and poverty reduction goals also suggests that macro-reforms have not been substantially affected by the PRSP process. In every country document, poverty analysis and macroeconomic strategies are presented as two independent sections of the PRSP, with the macroeconomic sections largely void of any *ex ante* assessments of the impact of structural reforms on poverty apart from considerations of how various growth scenarios will impact poverty levels in the future. Only Cambodia's PRSP, and to a lesser extent that of Rwanda, recognize the potential negative impact of various reforms on poverty and the need to conduct qualitative assessments of their possible effects. Moreover, several country papers (e.g., Albania, Nicaragua, and Senegal) exhibit inconsistency, noting the failure of adjustment programmes in the past, but going on to advocate the very same policies in the macro section. This, together with the separation of the two parts of the documents and the lack of *ex ante* assessments of poverty consequences of macro-measures, lends support to the view that, on the macro side, PRSPs basically endorse the conventional IFI-designed programmes.

The purpose here is not to discuss whether the structural strategies pursued in PRSPs are the most appropriate for combating poverty, but, rather, to highlight the similarity of the policy package contained in PRSPs across countries with earlier structural adjustment programmes. Although the emphasis on various reforms differs in different countries—for example, transition countries (e.g., Azerbaijan, Albania, and Tajikistan) tend to emphasize privatization reforms more than others—the fact remains that all countries' documents pursue the same core set of structural reforms. These trends suggest a low impact of PRSPs in changing the major features of programmes, and from this one can deduce that they have had a low impact both on the extent of realized empowerment and on changing the rate of poverty reduction.

17.5 CAN THE PRSPS BE CHANGED TO BE MORE SUPPORTIVE OF HUMAN RIGHTS?

The limited experience with PRSPs so far would suggest that PRSPs have not achieved very much in improving the realization of human rights. On the one hand, the process has been such that consultations are selective, missing or under-representing important groups, and are carried out too rapidly to allow considered inputs from outside the government. Moreover, the discussions do not seem to include major macro-issues relevant to growth and distribution which are critical to the progressive realization of positive human rights. A review of the content of programmes suggests only marginal changes compared with previous structural adjustment programmes. Consequently, it appears that to date PRSPs have not been a very powerful mechanism for promoting either negative or positive human rights.

An important question is whether reforms in the PRSPs might make them a more useful instrument for promoting human rights. The UN's Office of the High Commissioner for Human Rights (OHCHR) has issued draft guidelines on 'A Human Rights Approach to Poverty Reduction Strategies'.[100] This basically consists of a summary of what the main human rights are and some suggested indicators of achievement. It does not consider the nature of the PRSP process. Yet it is clear from the review in this chapter that, as well as providing documentation to those conducting PRSPs about the nature of human rights, some important changes would need to be made in the PRSP process if they were to be an important source of advancement in human rights.

A major issue to be decided is whether a reformed PRSP should be a conscious vehicle for the achievement of human rights, or whether the aim should be to make PRSPs more effective in promoting the fulfilment of human rights, without an explicit basis in human rights. Since PRSPs have such comprehensive coverage in poor countries, it might be argued that they should become a conscious and important instrument for promoting human rights. The empowerment aspect would then help promote negative human rights, while the policy content of PRSPs would promote positive human rights, including the right to development. In this case, PRSPs would be explicitly tasked with achieving human rights. Each PRSP process would need to be provided with some guidance on the nature of human rights, and perhaps be supported by a human rights expert. A major advantage of such an approach would be that the PRSP apparatus could be used to define the steps needed to achieve improved human rights in particular contexts, moving from the general to the particular—which has rarely been done in human rights work to date, and is needed if human rights are to provide policy guidance in particular contexts.

---

[100] United Nations High Commissioner for Human Rights, *Draft Guidelines: A Human Rights Approach to Poverty Reduction Strategies*, 10 September 2002 (Geneva: United Nations).

PRSPs would then need to adopt the language of human rights. We noted earlier that PRSPs currently do not use the language of rights. The internationally agreed human rights instruments adopt the language of rights deliberately and explicitly to imply that human rights are more than goals; that every person in the world has equal entitlements to them by virtue of being human; and that governments and the international community have an obligation to help realize them. The fact that PRSPs—and more generally IFI discourse—do not use the language of rights is not accidental. It reflects the fact that the international community and governments do not wish to accept the obligations that rights imply. The question which arises is whether, if the donor community were persuaded to use human rights as the basis of PRSPs, this would simply be a matter of a change in language, or would they also accept the obligations that the human rights language implies. The danger is that they might accept the language but not real change in the rich-poor relationship. It's a matter of judgement, but to us it seems likely that if PRSPs accepted human rights explicitly as their basis, the change would mostly be confined to language with little change in reality, which could even weaken the human rights movement by discrediting the language.

A more pragmatic proposal is to reform PRSPs so that de facto they contribute to the greater achievement of human rights, but without becoming an explicit vehicle for them, and without the use of human rights language. Whichever choice is made, there are some important reforms needed in the PRSP process. With respect to negative rights, *comprehensive empowerment* is needed. Consultation, therefore, needs to be much more inclusive, and must include sufficient representation of groups presently under-represented, including marginalized peoples and women. In general, community or popular organizations would be preferable to NGOs to represent these groups, since NGOs have little legitimacy as representatives. This is particularly true of INGOs. Both local and international NGOs are self-selected and quite arbitrary in which people and interests they represent.

In democratic systems, parliamentarians should have an important role, as representing their constituencies. Representation of particular interest groups (including private sector representatives) or external agencies should be curtailed, from this perspective, involving them only to the extent that it is clearly important to get policies implemented efficiently; by including them, local groups and individuals inevitably lose power. Similarly, donors do not have the legitimacy required to be consulted—the more their views prevail, the less the role of local voices.

In general, consultation alone is unlikely to bring about empowerment, as indicated by the small changes achieved by existing PRSPs. Empowerment is a political process that is rarely conferred without struggle. The PRSPs are too apolitical to achieve major redistribution of power against the interests involved in the prevailing system. Where there are real conflicts of interest— e.g., with respect to land reform or progressive taxation—deprived groups need to organize and lobby if the PRSPs are to bring about significant change. Any human rights agenda must recognize this, and work outside the PRSP process as well as within it.

It would not be reasonable to expect PRSPs to carry the full weight of realizing negative human rights. Negative rights, such as protection against arbitrary detention and freedom of speech, go well beyond what PRSPs can deliver. Negative rights require an effective democratic system of government and a fair judicial system. These are not part of the central remit of PRSPs, though a multidimensional approach to poverty suggests that providing such rights arguably should be part of a poverty reduction strategy. While support for negative rights must go beyond the PRSP process, there is a case for widening the PRSP remit to include support for representative government, for an independent judiciary, and for access to law among the poor.

With respect to promoting positive human rights, changes are needed in process and in coverage. Apart from much more extensive coverage of the powerless, it is essential that the process be given considerably more time; that papers are prepared in advance; that they are translated into local languages. As far as content is concerned, the arena of PRSPs needs to be extended to include genuine participation in deciding macroeconomic and structural issues. This must include the possibility of challenging the usual policy package. Redistribution of assets and incomes should be on the agenda, as essential to achieve major improvements in human rights fulfilment in many countries. Budgetary targets may need to be relaxed. Import restrictions may be needed. Intellectual property rights may need to be challenged. Such policies are virtually never considered, let alone adopted in PRSPs. Yet without them, little change in human rights achievements is likely.

Even without PRSPs becoming the major vehicle of human rights, it would be helpful for human rights inputs to be made into the PRSP process. If human rights experts were added to the team, this would enhance consciousness of human rights and provide the human rights community with a valuable opportunity to define the progressive realization of human rights in particular contexts, and identify the specific problems confronting the realization of human rights in such contexts. For some countries, human rights fulfilment will depend on changes outside a country's control, including flows of resources (aid, private capital, debt relief), the terms of trade, and technology transfer. PRSPs do not extend to international issues (e.g., the amount of aid, debt relief, terms of trade, technology transfer, commodity subsidies). If PRSPs became a major vehicle for promoting human rights, other mechanisms would still be needed for the consideration of international issues. But it would seem appropriate that local groups should have some input into their determination (as with other policies that affect them), so that the PRSP process should encompass consideration of international issues, which at present it does not.

A reformed PRSP process could bring about some improvements in the achievement of human rights, but they are likely to be modest. However, there are some problems about relying on PRSPs as the major instrument to promote human rights. PRSPs claim to be aimed at country ownership of programmes. But at the same time the international community is not prepared truly to let go, and allow countries genuine control. The process therefore only works so long as the area of decision making is confined to relatively small arenas—the precise balance of social expenditure, whether water should be provided before secondary schools and so forth—and even here only within limits. The defects in PRSPs are not, we conclude, altogether an accidental feature of a system that has only begun or mere learning difficulties, but rather mechanisms that are essential to ensure a small role for substantive national ownership, participation, and control, and which will allow what the international community regards as 'good policies' to continue while giving them a veneer of ownership that may make them more effective. If this view is correct, it is unlikely that the process could be changed radically enough to make PRSPs a major vehicle of human rights fulfilment.

PRSPs are intended to define local priorities. Yet to some extent the internationally agreed human rights have already decided the priorities favoured. Of course, the human rights are sufficiently vague and all-embracing to leave considerable leeway for local inputs and choices, and the PRSP process would be helpful in this regard. But sometimes insisting that the PRSPs follow the human rights agenda conflicts with local choices. This sort of conflict might not happen, but if it did not—and introducing human rights did not change the PRSP priorities—then what would be the gain from a human rights perspective in incorporating human rights into the process?

Finally, we return to the issue of the need to embed human rights in the norms and legal system of every country. This is essential to ensure that they are sustained over the long term. The PRSPs can do a little in this regard, but not very much—a simple reform would be that each PRSP could be supported by a human rights expert for guidance, as suggested above. But ultimately the education system, the press, and the politicians need to be convinced of the value of human rights and incorporate them in norms and laws.

With their comprehensive country coverage, and the heavy resources invested in them, PRSPs have become a major instrument for policy change in poor developing countries. Moreover, PRSPs seem to be more open to outside influence than the policy conditionality they replaced. It is therefore tempting to incorporate important agendas, such as human rights, into them. However, for this to mean much, there would have to be a radical transformation in the process and content of PRSPs. In the absence of such a transformation, PRSPs are likely to remain a rather insignificant instrument for promoting human rights, but they could become more effective with some more modest changes noted above.

Table 17.A1. *Checklist of reforms contained in PRSPs*

REFORMS	Albania	Azerbaijan	Benin	Bolivia	Burkina FASO	Cambodia	Cameroon	Chad	Ethiopia	Ghana	Guyana	Honduras	Kyrgyzstan	Malawi	Mali	Mauritania	Mozambique	Nicaragua	Niger	Rwanda	Senegal	Sri Lanka	Tajikistan	Tanzania	Uganda	Yemen	Zambia
Economic Management																											
Reliance on macroeconomic stability for poverty reduction	x	x		x	x	x	x	x	x	x	x	x	x	x	x		x	x	x	x	x	x	x	x		x	
Trade Policy (tariff reduction/export promotion)	x	x	x	x	x	x		x	x	x	x	x	x	x	x	x	x	x	x	x	x	x	x	x	x	x	x
Monetary Restraint	x	x	x	x	x	x	x	x	x	x	x	x	x	x	x	x	x	x	x	x	x	x	x	x	x	x	x
Exchange Rate Policy	x	x	x	x	x		x	x	x	x	x	x	x	x	x	x	x	x	x		x	x	x	x	x	x	x
Fiscal Restraint	x	x	x	x	x		x	x	x	x	x	x	x	x	x		x	x	x	x	x	x	x	x	x	x	x
Tax & Customs Reforms	x	x	x	x	x	x	x	x	x	x	x	x	x	x	x		x	x	x	x	x	x	x	x	x	x	x
Price Control/Wage Policies	x	x										x				x								x			
User Fees		x				x				x		x	x			x			x			x	x			x	
Sectoral Policies	x	x	x	x	x	x	x	x	x		x		x	x	x	x	x	x	x	x	x	x	x		x	x	x
Public Sector Governance and Management																											
Budget Management	x	x	x	x	x	x	x	x	x	x	x	x	x	x	x	x	x	x	x	x	x	x	x	x	x	x	x
Medium-Term Expenditure Framework	x	x	x	x	x	x	x	x	x	x	x		x	x	x	x	x	x	x	x	x	x	x	x	x	x	x
Decentralization	x		x	x	x			x	x	x			x	x	x	x	x	x	x	x	x	x	x	x	x	x	x
Public Administration Reform	x		x	x	x	x	x	x	x	x	x		x	x	x	x	x	x	x	x	x	x	x	x	x	x	x
Anti-corruption	x		x	x	x	x	x	x	x	x	x		x	x	x	x	x	x	x	x	x	x	x	x	x	x	x

Financial Sector Reform

	1	2	3	4	5	6	7	8	9	10	11	12	13	14	15	16	17
Financial Institutions	x	x		x	x	x	x		x	x	x		x	x		x	x
Financial Intermediation Policies	x	x		x	x	x	x	x	x	x	x	x	x	x		x	x
Private Sector Development																	
Privatization	x		x	x	x		x	x	x	x	x	x	x	x		x	x
Price Liberalization	x	x			x	x	x		x	x							
Legal and Judicial Reform	x		x	x	x	x		x	x	x	x	x	x		x		x
Land Tenure Laws	x			x	x		x	x	x	x	x	x	x		x	x	x
Social Sector Reforms																	
Education		x		x	x	x	x	x	x	x	x	x	x	x		x	x
Health		x		x	x	x	x	x	x	x	x	x	x	x	x	x	x
Social Protection/			x	x	x	x	x	x	x	x	x	x	x	x		x	x
Employment Promotion	x	x		x	x	x	x	x	x	x	x	x	x	x	x	x	x
Rural Livelihoods	x				x	x	x		x	x	x	x	x	x	x	x	
Food Security		x	x	x	x	x	x		x	x	x	x	x	x	x	x	x
Environmental Protection	x	x						x	x	x	x	x	x	x	x	x	x
Ethnic Minority Protection		x						x	x		x					xx	
Gender Equity	x	x	x	x	x		x	x	x	x	x	x	x	x	x		x
Children/Disabled	x	x		x				x	x	x	x	x	x	x	x	x	
Vulnerable Groups							x	x	x	x	x	x	x	x	x	x	
Macro and Poverty																	
sections separate?	Y	Y	Y	Y	Y	Y	Y	Y	Y	Y	Y	Y	Y	Y	Y	Y	Y
Ex ante assessment of impact?	N	N	N	N	N	N	N	N	N	N	N	N	N	N	N	N	N

Source: F. Stewart and M. Wang, *Do PRSPs Empower Poor Countries and Disempower the World Bank, Or Is It The Other Way Round?* Queen Elizabeth House Working Paper 108 (Oxford, 2003).

Table 17.A2. *Poverty and macro-reform linkages*

	Albania	Azerbaijan	Benin	Bolivia	Burkina Faso	Cambodia	Cameroon	Chad	Ethiopia	Ghana	Guyana	Honduras	Kyrgyzstan	Malawi	Mali	Mauritania	Mozambique	Nicaragua	Niger	Rwanda	Senegal	Sri Lanka	Tajikistan	Tanzania	Uganda	Yemen	Zambia
Links between Growth and Poverty Reduction	x	x	x	x	x	x		x	x		x	x	x				x	x	x	x	x	x	x	x	x	x	x
Links between Poverty and Trade Policy						x																					x
Links between Poverty and Monetary Policy																				x							
Links between Poverty and Tax Policies/Fiscal Reform		x																									
Links between Poverty and Privatization																				x							x
Legal/Judicial Reforms						x							x														
Links between Poverty and Civil Service Reforms						x																					
Links between Poverty and Financial Sector Reforms						x																					
Assessment of Past Policies	x										x	x		x				x			x					x	
Discussion of Policy Trade-Offs																											
Poverty Impact Evaluation						x														x							

Source: F. Stewart and M. Wang, *Do PRSPs Empower Poor Countries and Disempower the World Bank, Or Is It The Other Way Round?* Queen Elizabeth House Working Paper 108 (Oxford, 2003).

18

Human Rights and Poverty Reduction Strategies: Moving Towards Convergence?

GOBIND NANKANI, JOHN PAGE, AND
LINDSAY JUDGE[1]

18.1 INTRODUCTION

Since 1999, the World Bank, the International Monetary Fund (IMF)—and increasingly the development community in general—have undertaken a new way of doing business in low-income countries, using a Poverty Reduction Strategy Paper (PRSP) as the basis for access to concessional lending and other forms of development assistance.[2] A PRSP is a national document that is expected to provide a comprehensive analysis of poverty, exploring macroeconomic and structural impediments to poverty reduction as well as sectoral issues. Drawing on this diagnostic, it should present a costed and prioritized plan of action that the government will implement to reduce poverty. The PRSP approach also embodies a number of 'process conditionalities', most notably that the government develop the PRSP through a participatory process, discussing the strategy with relevant stakeholders and taking their views into account.

The PRSP reflects the convergence of three key trends. First, the concept of poverty expanded in the 1980s and 1990s. The path-breaking work of Sen on capabilities,[3] for example, made it clear that poverty could no longer be regarded as a purely economic phenomenon measured in terms of income alone. Instead, he argued that lack of opportunities, assets, and entitlements all conspired against the well-being of poor people. This thinking found operational expression in the Human Development Indicators introduced by

[1] The views and opinions reflected in this paper are those of the authors and do not represent those of the World Bank, its Executive Directors, nor the countries they represent.

[2] For documentation on the PRSP and critical commentaries on the PRSP process, see http://www.worldbank.org/prsp.

[3] A. Sen, *Commodities and Capability* (Amsterdam: North Holland, 1985).

the UNDP in 1990, and was absorbed into the development mainstream early in that decade. The World Bank's Voices of the Poor exercise[4] extended the concept of poverty further still, providing critical evidence of the impact of skewed power relations on the lives of poor people. This growing understanding of the complexity of poverty underlined the need for comprehensive solutions that addressed all determinants, a belief that found expression in the World Bank through the launch of the Comprehensive Development Framework in 1998.[5]

Second, there was a growing recognition throughout the 1990s that development assistance was not resulting in the outcomes it aimed to achieve. Disappointing results were observed in low-income countries and especially in sub-Saharan Africa, and it was clear that many countries were not on track to meet their international development goals for 2015. Empirical studies highlighted the critical role played by good policies in aid-recipient countries as a key determinant of the growth and poverty reduction impact of development assistance.[6] A positive and significant relationship was identified between democracy and growth,[7] and between good institutions and aid effectiveness.[8] As a consequence, the question of how aid could best support poverty reduction became increasingly pertinent.

Third, the Heavily Indebted Poor Countries (HIPC) initiative was undergoing reform in the late 1990s and many G7 governments saw this as an opportunity to strengthen the links between debt relief, poverty reduction, and governance. The first round of HIPC had been criticized for being too narrowly tied to social sector spending and many stakeholders advocated that further debt relief refocus on poverty reduction more generally. Moreover, countries such as the United Kingdom proposed a shift from policy to process conditionality to provide an incentive to low-income countries to address systemic issues such as weak public expenditure and closed national processes which undermined the effectiveness of development assistance, while United States aid policy maintained that debt relief should be tied to reform commitments on both the political as well as economic front.[9]

---

[4] D. Narayan, R. Chambers, M. K. Shah, and P. Petesch, *Voices of the Poor: Crying Out for Change* (Washington D.C.: World Bank, 2000).

[5] See 'The Other Crisis', speech by James Wolfensohn, Washington D.C., 6 October 1998, in which he stated 'Too often we have focused too much on the economics, without a sufficient understanding of the social, the political, the environmental, and the cultural aspects of society.' Available at http://www.worldbank.org/html/extdr/am98/jdw-sp/am98-en.htm.

[6] C. Burnside and D. Dollar, *Aid, Policies and Growth*, Policy Research Working Paper 1777 (Washington D.C.: World Bank, 1997).

[7] J. Svensson, 'Aid, Growth and Democracy' 11 *Economics and Politics* 275 (1999).

[8] P. Collier and D. Dollar, 'Aid Allocation and Poverty Reduction' 26 *European Economic Review* 1475 (2002).

[9] K. Christiansen and I. Hovland, *The PRSP Initiative: Multilateral Policy Change and the Role of Research*, ODI Working Paper 216 (London: ODI, 2003).

In the light of these factors, the PRSP approach proposes a break with previous practice in several respects. To begin, it places poverty reduction centre stage as the objective for both the country and its donor partners. Second, the country itself is expected to formulate and write the PRSP, as compared with the Policy Framework Papers that previously determined access to concessional finance which were written by the IMF and World Bank and then negotiated with governments. Third, the PRSP is envisaged as the product of a participatory process, with the views of relevant stakeholders being solicited by government and informing the strategy, thereby opening up the 'black box' of policy making to scrutiny and influence. Fourth, the PRSP is expected to usher in a more evidence-based approach to reform in low-income countries, with policy actions subject to review, impacts monitored, and remedial actions taken if the results fall behind expectations. Finally, the PRSP approach is premised on the notion of partnerships, and a commitment from many donors to orient their financing to the poverty reduction priorities set out in the strategy, rather than to use aid policy to further their own domestic agenda.

Thus, the PRSP approach represents a compact between states, their citizens, and the international community to leverage their efforts and resources to achieve poverty reduction. But where do human rights, which also compel these parties to work towards specific ends, fit into this picture? This chapter explores this question. The first section seeks to locate where poverty reduction fits conceptually within the human rights domain. The following three sections analyse key aspects of the PRSP approach, namely country ownership, comprehensiveness, and results orientation. Each section presents the ideal embedded in the PRSP paradigm, assesses the interface between this and human rights, and then provides a brief overview of both progress to date and ongoing challenges in realizing these principles. Finally, the chapter concludes with an assessment of the extent to which the PRSP model is consistent with the principles embedded in the human rights framework.

18.2 HUMAN RIGHTS AND POVERTY REDUCTION

This section suggests a way of viewing the relationship between human rights and poverty reduction, and in doing so seeks to expose the degree of affinity that exists between the two concepts. It requires as its starting point a working definition of a human right which, for the purposes of our discussion, we take to be a claim to a particular outcome which is encoded in international law. This definition thus has two elements which we believe are important to distinguish: first, it points to the *outcomes* sought, which embody a range of norms and values on which there is such extensive consensus that these outcomes have been elevated to the status of human rights; and second, implicit in this definition is the *strategy* through which these outcomes are to be achieved, namely the assertion and fulfilment of various claims.

This section explores both these aspects in turn, aiming, in the process, to expose further some of the complex links between human rights, poverty reduction, and the development process.

18.2.1 Human Rights and Poverty Reduction Outcomes

While there can be little dispute that human rights and poverty reduction are both concerned with the well-being of vulnerable groups in society, the precise relationship between the two has been delineated in many different ways. It is relatively easy to take stock, however, of the outcomes human rights approaches aspire to achieve by virtue of the fact that they have been encoded in positive international law. The two International Covenants, the International Covenant of Civil and Political Rights (ICCPR)[10] and the International Covenant on Economic, Social and Cultural Rights (ICESCR),[11] set out clearly a range of valuable ends. The outcomes these core documents seek to achieve have, of course, also been amplified over many years by further texts seeking to provide additional protection to specific groups (for example, women and children) or against particularly egregious forms of denial (such as genocide, torture, or racism).

There have been several efforts to record poverty reduction outcomes in a similarly definitive manner. In the 1990s, the UN set out a number of International Development Goals, which, in a slightly modified form, were endorsed by 191 nations at the UN General Assembly in 2000 as the Millennium Development Goals (MDGs). Grouped under eight broad headings, the MDGs point to the importance of educational attainment, gender equality, improved health status, and environmental protection as, among others, the critical outcomes that underpin poverty reduction.[12]

These objectives found endorsement in the World Development Report (WDR) 2000/2001 which presents the most comprehensive statement of the World Bank's understanding as to what constitutes poverty, and hence what outcomes we should strive towards in the name of development and poverty reduction. The WDR defines poverty as a lack of opportunity, security, and empowerment, thereby extending the concept of poverty far beyond the orthodox notion of lack of resources. This definition captures Sen's capabilities concept, noting that poverty impedes the freedom to live one's

---

[10] G.A. res. 2200A (XXI), 21 U.N. GAOR Supp. (No. 16) at 52, U.N. Doc. A/6316 (1966), 999 U.N.T.S. 171, *entered into force* 23 March 1976.

[11] G.A. res. 2200A (XXI), 21 U.N. GAOR Supp. (No. 16) at 49, U.N. Doc. A/6316 (1966), 993 U.N.T.S. 3, *entered into force* 3 January 1976.

[12] See http://www.un.org/millenniumgoals/for further information on the MDGs.

life to the full because of the absence of education, good health, and the like. In addition, the WDR observes that poverty is also the product of systems of entrenched discrimination, or what one writer has called 'structural violence'.[13] The *Voices of the Poor* report, which pointedly informed the WDR, exposed this dimension of poverty: in testimony, poor people repeatedly defined their experience as marked by a lack of respect, by social exclusion, and by fear of violence.[14]

So, if we compare the outcomes sought by the human rights world with those of the poverty reduction community, to what extent do they map with each other? As poverty has increasingly come to be regarded as a multi-dimensional concept, it is clear that the alignment between human rights and poverty reduction objectives has become more extensive. This is true not just for many of the outcomes encoded in the ICESCR, such as improvements in health status and educational attainment, but also many of the ends aspired to through the ICCPR. The empowerment pillar of the WDR in particular has effectively extended the poverty reduction concept to include outcomes such as increased voice, participation, and respect, which are intrinsic to the ICCPR. Thus, we contend that poverty reduction outcomes have increasingly converged with the ends that human rights seek to obtain, and that the development and human rights communities are increasingly motivated by a shared set of norms and values.

That said, some have suggested that the overlap between rights and poverty reduction outcomes is not total, and that some human rights outcomes remain outside the purview of poverty reduction. The Office of the High Commissioner for Human Rights (OHCHR), for instance, has recognized that the intersection between poverty reduction and human rights objectives is not complete. For example, their Draft Guidelines on PRSPs state that they 'do not address all aspects of human rights with equal emphasis because they are formulated for the specific context of poverty reduction, which is only part of the broader human rights agenda'.[15]

Broadly speaking, we would agree with the notion that poverty reduction objectives should be viewed as a subset of human rights outcomes. For example, while it is clear that non-discrimination, liberty and security of the person, and good health and education are critical aspects of the poverty reduction equation, the relevance to poverty reduction of rights such as the right to marry and found a family or the right to rest and leisure are perhaps less evident. It is important to note, however, that these are examples only, and the exact scope of the overlap, while perhaps interesting to debate, is not the issue we seek to resolve here. We recognize that the rights outside of the

---

[13] P. Farmer, *Pathologies of Power* (Berkeley: University of California Press, 2003).

[14] Narayan et al., above n. 4.

[15] Office of the High Commissioner for Human Rights, *Draft Guidelines: Human Rights Approach to Poverty Reduction Strategies* (Geneva: United Nations, 2002) para. 27.

intersecting subset are important and valid, and also contend that focusing on only selected outcomes is not inconsistent with the principle of indivisibility, as has sometimes been suggested.[16] Instead, it represents an honest attempt to clarify the relationship between human rights and poverty reduction more clearly, and to mark out where development practitioners have the greatest contributions to make.

18.2.2 Strategies for Human Rights Promotion and Poverty Reduction

Given this, what strategies should policy makers and advocates who are concerned about the achievement of poverty reduction and human rights ends pursue? Implicit in our definition of a human right is the idea that the desired outcome is to be achieved through the exercise of a claim. We can distil from this formulation two key conclusions as to the nature of rights-based approaches. First, the concept of a claim implies that there is an entity which has a duty to deliver on the outcomes embedded in each right. By virtue of the fact that human rights are encoded in international law, this entity is first and foremost identified as the state.[17] Second, the human rights framework highlights the importance of enabling marginalized and vulnerable people to claim their rights for themselves, indicating that the process as well as result is critical.

Let us examine both of these aspects in turn, and consider the extent to which these are also considered important by development practitioners. Rights-based strategies stress the imperative that the state delivers on a range of outcomes. Their success, however, is premised on three assumptions: first, that there is a functioning state with institutions that are capable of delivering the desired outcomes; second, that those in charge of the state have the political will to address the question of disparities that exist within the country; third, that sufficient resources are available to deliver on commitments. This final point is important: as is now broadly accepted, even those rights which are styled as 'negative rights' require public policy interventions and hence expenditures. For example, challenging inhumane behaviour by security services requires investigations, efforts to bring perpetrators to justice, training programmes for new staff, and the like.

---

[16] See, for example, the paper by Jose Miguel Vivanco, Executive Director of Human Rights Watch America, presented at the World Bank/World Vision Democratizing Development Conference, September 2002 available at http://www.worldbank.org/poverty/strategies/events/092502_vivanco.pdf, and World Vision International, *Do the Rights Thing: the World Bank and the Human Rights of People Living in Poverty* (Monrovia, California: World Vision, 2003).

[17] This is not to deny the important work that many scholars have undertaken in recent years to delineate the responsibilities of private actors for human rights. See, for example, A. Clapham, *Human Rights and the Private Sphere* (Oxford: Oxford University Press, 1996).

Rights principles provide less guidance, however, as to the best course of action in low-income countries where these three conditions are often absent. It is here that development thinking has a contribution to make, as it has grappled for many years with the challenge of achieving poverty reduction in institutionally weak, politically deficient, and resource constrained environments. Of these three constraints development practitioners have arguably thought most deeply about the question of resources, both how they can be increased in aggregate as well as best used to achieve poverty reduction ends. The centrality of economic growth to poverty reduction approaches is something that some in the human rights world, however, find inimical. It has been argued, for example, that development economics insists on a utilitarian calculation of welfare which is concerned only with aggregate improvements and is blind to both the existence of and reasons for inequitable distribution of outcomes in societies.[18]

However, this debate between development and human rights thinkers on the subject of growth is, in our opinion, counter-productive. It is important to be honest about the essential role that growth plays in achieving poverty reduction and hence also many human rights outcomes. For any low-income country, which by definition has a GDP/capita of below $750 per year, even a perfectly equal distribution of income would not result in a satisfactory level of well-being. Without additional resources, no low-income country government can afford to deliver better and more widely available services to its population, nor protect its citizens no matter how much it sees this as a desirable end. That is not to say that all forms of growth have widespread benefits. The relationship between growth and inequality has been the subject of much attention by development thinkers for many years, and continues to be widely debated.[19] The World Bank, in collaboration with several other development partners, has, for example, an extensive work programme examining which types of growth most benefit poor people, and how this can best be facilitated through public policy interventions.[20] Consequently, we consider growth to be a necessary, but not sufficient condition for the achievement of poverty reduction outcomes. And we see a pro-poor growth focus as consistent with the attainment of human rights.

In addition to the question of how to increase the means at the disposal of society, development thinkers have also grappled (perhaps more successfully than the human rights world) with the critical question of how best to use

[18] See, for example, R. Eyben, *International Development Organisations and Rights Based Approaches*, paper delivered at Institute for Development Studies, Rights and Power Workshop, November 2003, Brighton, UK.

[19] See M. Ravallion, *Pro-Poor Growth: A Primer* (Washington D.C.: World Bank, 2004) for an overview of the extensive literature on growth and inequality.

[20] See http://www.worldbank.org/poverty/inequality for further information on this programme.

these finite resources. In highly resource constrained environments where there is so little room for manoeuvre, selecting the optimum policies is of vital importance. However, while there is some consensus on certain priorities—for example, most would agree on the vital role of primary education in reducing poverty—many questions remain about which policies can best tackle the multiple determinants of poverty most effectively given a specific set of country conditions. This points to the need for good diagnostics that explore the role of economic, social, and cultural factors that inhibit opportunities, undermine security, and stifle voice, as well as empirical studies that assess which policy interventions have or have not worked in similar conditions. New tools are emerging to help practitioners do just this: for example, the last three years have seen the emergence of Poverty and Social Impact Analysis (PSIA), a tool kit which brings together quantitative and qualitative methods to assess the impacts of both proposed and ongoing public interventions.[21] A good evidence base of this nature allows governments to design policies and leverage resources to tackle the real causes of poverty, rather than the symptoms.

Finally, let us return to the other aspect that human rights approaches highlight as an important component of any strategy, that of enabling people to assert their claims to various outcomes themselves. The human rights world has certainly done an excellent job over many years in stimulating awareness about human rights and building capacity at the grass-roots level. This has motivated many to take action and campaign on both their own and others' behalf. However, social mobilization is not just the preserve of human rights activists: much of the practice of social development considers how marginalized people can be enabled to take control of their lives and to claim their entitlements. The discipline has recognized for many years that lack of voice, participation, justice, and identity are key determinants of poverty, and that strategies are required to tackle these dimensions. More recently, much of this thinking has crystallized around the notion of empowerment, which increasingly is bringing together development and human rights thinkers as they seek to learn from each other's experience.[22]

So, how should we conceive of the relationship between the strategies proposed by the human rights advocates and those suggested by poverty analysts? We hope the foregoing has shown that, in practice, there are significant areas of convergence between both human rights and development approaches, even if the two communities sometimes employ different language. When one considers the supply side—what governments need to do in order to ensure various positive outcomes for their citizens—we see

---

[21] See http://lnweb18.worldbank.org/essd/sdvext.nsf/81ByDocName/PovertySocialImpact Analysis for further information on the tool kit.

[22] See http://lnweb18.worldbank.org/essd/sdvext.nsf/68ByDocName/Empowerment for further information.

some divergence, with development practitioners, for example, highlighting the importance of overall economic good health, but also areas of agreement such as on the importance of primary health and education provision. On the demand side—how people can be empowered to claim these outcomes for themselves—we see both the human rights and development communities making valuable and mutually reinforcing contributions to the debate.

18.2.3 Summary

As the development community's understanding of poverty has grown increasingly sophisticated in recent years, our notion of what needs to be achieved to obtain poverty reduction has also expanded. However one defines poverty reduction—the achievement of the MDGs, increased opportunities, security, and empowerment, or the like—it is our contention that the attainment of poverty reduction outcomes and human rights overlap considerably. Consequently, poverty reduction objectives are, in our opinion, coterminous with the fulfilment of many, although arguably not all, human rights.

However, the means by which these outcomes are best achieved are not so simply set out. The disciplines of development and human rights suggest a multitude of different strategies, although there is a considerable area of convergence on actions proposed by both schools of thought. That said, human right principles point to two elements that perhaps should be central to any approach if it is to be regarded as consistent with the rights framework. First, as the state has primary responsibility for ensuring its citizens' welfare, increasing and supporting the capacity of the state to design and implement appropriate public policy measures is of critical importance. Second, capacities and opportunities for citizens to assert their claims also require attention.

Given these preliminary conclusions, how should we view the relationship between development assistance and human rights? If our initial assertion is accepted, the efforts that have gathered force in recent years to align aid more explicitly with poverty reduction ends also represent greater alignment with human rights outcomes. The question of the extent to which development assistance and human rights strategies are reinforcing requires further examination however, and, as the PRSP is now the dominant aid modality, it is to a more detailed exploration of this that we now turn.

18.3 COUNTRY OWNERSHIP AND THE PRSP

In the 1990s it became increasingly clear that highly aid dependent countries were often more responsive to the concerns of donor agencies than they were to their own populations, and that the national policy process was fragmented as the government sought to appease its multiple funders. The PRSP approach was designed to confront this state of affairs, and to shift the locus of policy making and accountability back to the country and its citizens. By increasing country ownership of the poverty reduction agenda, it was hoped that policies which reflect the concerns of poor people would be identified, and that their sustained implementation would be ensured by the emergence of new alliances and constituencies.

Country ownership demands a set of changes to previous behaviour. First, it requires that low-income country governments develop a broad consensus on a poverty reduction plan across government, convincing key policy makers and implementers as well as seeking high-level buy-in for the reorientation of domestic policies to poverty reduction ends. Second, ownership needs to extend beyond government, and countries are expected to solicit the participation of a wide range of stakeholders such as civil society organizations in the design, implementation, and monitoring of the PRSP. Third, donors are expected to respect the leadership of the government, align their resources with the emerging national strategy, and thus no longer distort national priorities or undermine capacity.

In our view, the precept of country ownership resonates with human rights principles on a number of counts. To begin, there is a clear acknowledgement that the primary responsibility to develop and implement policies that benefit the most marginalized sections of society is held by national governments. Country ownership seeks to promote greater transparency and accountability within government, within countries, and with international development partners. The emphasis on participation in the PRSP is also critical, and effectively promotes key rights such as freedom of expression, of association, and the right to self-determination. Overall, the emphasis on country ownership highlights that process is as important as policies in developing strategies to achieve poverty reduction outcomes, and that aid modalities should support the development of institutions and behaviour that are essential for success on this front.

Four years on from the launch of the PRSP initiative there is a stock of experience which we can draw upon to assess the extent to which country ownership has increased to date.[23] However, any evaluation at this stage needs to recognize that many of the changes demanded by the PRSP exercise are non-trivial, tackling entrenched patterns of behaviour and often requiring significant institutional reform. While it is important to be candid about the

---

[23] As of June 2004, 41 countries have completed their full PRSP. An additional 14 have finalized their Interim PRSP (I-PRSP) which provides an initial poverty diagnostic and sets out a plan of action for developing the full document, thereby allowing countries to access concessional finance prior to the completion of the full strategy. It is important to note that governments are not expected to prepare an I-PRSP in a participatory manner, although they should outline the process they plan to adopt in developing the full PRSP.

shortcomings of the approach to date, it is also necessary to recognize the initial conditions within which PRSPs have been developed, and not impose an impossible 'gold standard' on countries where gains are likely to be small and gradual. In addition, the stock of PRSPs represents a diverse range of experience, spanning from high performers to countries that have struggled to embrace PRSP principles, and, as a result, generic conclusions are often difficult to draw at this early stage. Despite these caveats, it remains useful to examine experience to date and to consider how the ideals embedded in the PRSP approach can be further realized.

18.3.1 Government Ownership

Much of the analysis of the PRSP to date has focused on the participatory process and we will consider this in more depth further below. However, less attention has been given to the vital question of whether intra-governmental relations have changed for the better and whether poverty reduction as a desirable goal has been mainstreamed throughout government as a result of the PRSP process. Buy-in from three key stakeholders is critical for the success of the strategy: sector ministries and decentralized agencies which will implement the programme of action; the Ministry of Finance which will decide whether and how PRSP priorities are funded; and the top political leadership whose support is needed to ensure that the ambitions of the PRSP are reflected across government and that the programme stays on track.

Reviews to date suggest that one of the key gains of the PRSP approach has been the broadened ownership throughout government of the poverty reduction agenda.[24] In particular:

- Poverty reduction is increasingly recognized as a goal for all line agencies, rather than seen as a concern for social sector ministries alone. Ministries such as infrastructure, agriculture, and justice which have traditionally not engaged with debates on poverty reduction have been brought into discussions with counterparts from other agencies, often for the first time.
- While there is a wide range of practice with respect to the role played by Ministries of Finance in the PRSP process, most commentators see their increased engagement with the PRSP as a positive sign, indicating that poverty reduction outcomes are receiving greater political attention. In addition, the involvement of finance ministries increases the

[24] D. Booth, 'Are PRSPs Making a Difference? The African Experience' 21 *Development Policy Review* 131–159 (2003) and IMF/IDA, *Poverty Reduction Strategy Papers: Detailed Analysis of Progress in Implementation* (Washington D.C.: IMF, 2003).

likelihood that PRSP priorities will be reflected in resource allocation decisions.[25]

- Although experience varies, there is evidence to suggest that poverty reduction objectives are receiving high-level as well as cross-governmental endorsement, through, for example, discussion at cabinet level.

However, it would be wrong to be complacent about the extent of government ownership as there are various practices which undermine greater collective responsibility for the PRSP. To begin, there are some parts of the government where further effort needs to be made to bring them into the PRSP discussion. The engagement of local governments with the PRSP, for example, has been limited, an omission which is of particular concern in the increasingly decentralized context of many low-income countries. In addition, some governments continue to manage the PRSP disconnected from other government processes. Special units have been set up in some countries to draft the document, and while these enclaves represent a pragmatic approach to kick-starting the PRSP in often weak institutional environments, they clearly militate against the mainstreaming of the strategy and the upgrading of government processes more generally.

18.3.2 Participation

Participation is probably the best studied aspect of the PRSP approach to date, in part because the requirement that governments solicit the opinions of their citizens and extend opportunities to them to engage throughout the policy cycle constitutes a real innovation. Most studies agree that new space for dialogue has opened up as a result of the PRSP, an achievement that, for many low-income countries with no tradition of consultation or participation, is particularly impressive.[26] There is evidence that an increasingly broad range of stakeholders is engaging with the process, from civil society organizations, private sector bodies, women's groups, church bodies, and trade unions. Participatory poverty assessments have been conducted in some countries to ensure that the voices of poor people themselves find expression in the PRSP.

[25] Analysis of the composition of public expenditures for 14 PRSP countries showed that, on average, poverty reduction priorities were receiving an additional 3.9% of total government expenditures comparing 1999 with 2001. See IMF/IDA, above n. 24, for more details.

[26] Booth, above n. 24; K. Cash and D. Sanchez, *Reducing Poverty or Repeating Mistakes: A Civil Society Critique of Poverty Reduction Strategy Papers* (Sweden: Church of Sweden Aid/Diakonia/Save the Children Sweden/The Swedish Jubilee Network, 2003); Oxfam International, *From 'Donorship' to Ownership? Moving Towards PRSP Round Two*, Oxfam Briefing Paper 51 (Washington D.C.: Oxfam, January 2004); F. Stewart and M. Wang, *Do PRSPs Empower Poor Countries and Disempower the World Bank, Or Is It The Other Way Round?* Queen Elizabeth House Working Paper 108, Oxford, October 2003.

Table 18.1. *Participation in PRSPs (shown as percentage)*

	Explicit outcome	Instrumental in PRSP design	Instrumental in implementation
Participation	71	79	34
Access to information	48	48	32
Organizational capacity	31	71	13

Source: Heinsohn and Sehagiri, forthcoming.

Note: Sample comprises all countries that had full PRSPs at the outset of the study.

Furthermore, a recent review of the experience of 14 PRSP countries showed that participation is perceived as not only of instrumental value for the development of the PRSP in many countries, but also as a worthwhile end in itself. Table 18.1 presents the findings of this study, showing the percentage of PRSPs sampled that rate participation as of high importance. However, this table also highlights some noteworthy weaknesses to date. First, while esteemed as an end in itself as well as for its process value, some key aspects which underpin participation, such as access to information and capacity, received less emphasis in the PRSPs reviewed. Second, the analysis exposes what some commentators have called the 'participation gap' which is observed as PRSPs enter the implementation phase, when finding appropriate roles for non-governmental stakeholders becomes more challenging.[27]

In addition to these two observations, participation in the PRSP has also been subject to a number of other shortcomings to date.[28] Many studies have raised questions as to who has been allowed to participate in the development of the PRSP. Some country cases have suggested, for example, that key stakeholders such as trade union representatives, women's groups, and civil society organizations (CSOs) based outside the capital city or main urban areas were notably absent from discussions. Others have questioned the extent to which those groups that are brought into discussions truly represented the perspectives of poor people. A further criticism levelled at the process is that participation has often been cursory, conducted according to timetables that have not allowed meaningful contributions to be prepared, and undermined by inadequate information dissemination.

Moreover, in most countries, governments' efforts to open up policy debates have been limited to consultation with relevant groups. Consequently, many CSOs have refused to accept that this constitutes participation, which implies at the least shared decision making, and ideally initiation and control by

[27] IMF/IDA, above n. 24.

[28] Cash and Sanchez, above n. 26; Oxfam International, above n. 26; J. Entwistle, *Country Ownership of Poverty Reduction Strategies: The Experience of 5 Countries* (Washington D.C.: World Bank, forthcoming 2005).

stakeholders.[29] This raises interesting questions, however, about the role of participatory processes in societies which either are, or are in transition to, democracies. Country experience suggests that the focus on participation in the earliest PRSPs was achieved at the cost of minimal engagement of elected representatives in the process. While subsequent evidence suggests that parliamentarians have become more actively involved, this points to the need to find an appropriate balance between participatory and representative mechanisms.

To summarize, the requirement that countries actively engage with relevant constituencies in the development and implementation of the PRSP has led to some real gains over the last five years. However, there continue to be a number of shortcomings in the way that governments manage the process: for example, experience to date points to the need for greater clarity as to the nature of the participatory exercise as well as how participants' inputs are to be used. Countries need to manage carefully the development of parallel participatory processes and their effective articulation with government structures which, in the medium term, should strengthen efforts to improve the functioning of the state and its ability to develop and manage policy to achieve poverty reduction goals.

18.3.3 Donor Behaviour

The transformation of the aid relationship envisaged by the PRSP is dependent on donors taking a much-reduced role in the formulation of policy in low-income countries. To date, there is evidence that many have taken a step back at least during the preparation of the PRSP, and certainly much of their early scepticism that countries would be unable to lead the process successfully has been overcome.

That said, some have argued that because the PRSP is required by the World Bank and IMF in order to access funding, the ideal of country ownership is fatally undermined. They assert that the intellectual origins of a programme are a key dimension of ownership, and that no government is able to own an initiative that it did not develop itself.[30] This ignores the fact that some low-income countries such as Uganda and Vietnam had PRSP-type planning processes in place prior to the formal introduction of the concept in 1999. Furthermore, others have disputed whether the prospects of a programme being implemented are automatically compromised by the fact that it emerged from another agency.[31] Instead, it is argued that a

[29] Stewart and Wang, above n. 26.

[30] T. Killick with R. Gunatilaka and A. Marr, *Aid and the Political Economy of Policy Change* (London: Routledge, 1998).

[31] O. Morrissey, 'Pro-poor conditionality and Debt Relief in East Africa', paper prepared for the WIDER Development Conference on Debt Relief, Helsinki, 17–18 August, 2001, quoted in D. Booth, above n. 24.

government's broad commitment is the critical indicator of ownership. Measuring commitment is, of course, a challenge but we would point to the fact that PRSPs have often endured changes in administration, are increasingly integrated into other domestic processes or combined with other planning documents, and progressively have traction over domestic as well as external finances as positive signs on this front. Some have pointed to the similarities between the policies proposed in PRSPs and the previous policy frameworks under which aid was provided and have concluded from this that donor influence has not diminished, and that ownership remains elusive.[32] However, this assumes that PRSPs were developed on a blank sheet, rather than importing a whole range of commitments and ongoing policy reforms from previous years. In addition, it also implies that all policies prior to the PRSP were not effective, and thus should be discarded. Both of these assumptions are clearly questionable, and we conclude that continuity between pre-PRSP and the PRSP programmes is not sufficient evidence to imply a wholesale dominance of the process by donors.

However, there is clearly a delicate balance to be struck between donors providing useful advice, guidance, and analytical inputs and their overwhelming the often fragile government processes through which the PRSP is being developed. There is much to suggest that this balance has not yet been found in some countries, where donor concerns continue to distort national priorities. That said, there is some emerging good practice: as a result of the PRSP, for example, some governments have been able to assert themselves and demand donors co-ordinate their inputs more successfully. Thus, while many challenges remain for governments, citizens, and donors, there have been changes in the way that all engage as a result of the PRSP approach which, in our view, resonates with human rights principles.

18.4 A COMPREHENSIVE APPROACH TO POVERTY REDUCTION

The PRSP approach demands that countries develop a comprehensive diagnostic of poverty and, on the basis of this, propose a plan of action to tackle its various determinants. Drawing on inputs from the participatory process, the poverty analysis is expected to reflect the multidimensional nature of poverty, identifying not just the economic but also the social, political, and cultural constraints that need to be overcome if poverty reduction outcomes are to be achieved. It thus demands good disaggregated quantitative data, indicating not only who is poor, but also key aspects of their identities such as where they live, their gender, ethnicity, and age. In addition, qualitative

---

[32] Oxfam International, above n. 26.

information which explores perceptions, experiences, and preferences is of critical value in providing additional depth to the analysis.

It is argued that this emphasis on developing a comprehensive picture of poverty is consistent with the principle of indivisibility, a key principle of human rights approaches. Clearly, the PRSP recognizes that achievements are needed on many fronts, with an interdependency between those outcomes that the human rights community has encoded as political and civil rights and those recognized as economic, social, and cultural rights. Furthermore, disaggregating poverty data and cross-referencing with qualitative studies exposes systems of discrimination and exclusion and points to the necessity of dismantling these if poverty reduction is to be achieved. Thus, the PRSP is preoccupied with rigorously identifying the most marginalized in society, and is informed by notions of equality and non-discrimination that are central human rights principles.

One need only look at many of the issues that have emerged in countries' poverty diagnostics to see that governments are, through the PRSP, developing a better sense of the concerns and vulnerabilities in society. Figure 18.1

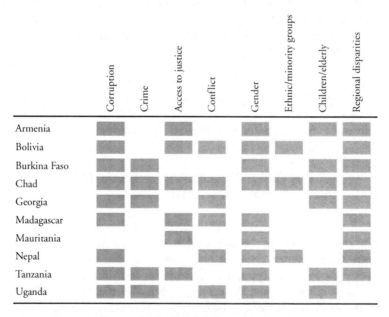

Figure 18.1. Poverty diagnostics in full PRSPs

Source: Own analysis.

Note: Randomly selected sample comprises first 5 full PRSPs produced (Bolivia, Burkina Faso, Mauritania, Tanzania, and Uganda) and most recent 5 as of February 2004 (Armenia, Chad, Georgia, Madagascar, and Nepal).

provides an overview of the issues that have emerged in the poverty analysis of a randomly selected 10 countries. This shows how prevalent issues such as governance and corruption, access to justice, and personal security are in the PRSPs, as well as illustrating the extent to which countries have disaggregated the experience of poverty and identified specific vulnerable groups.

However, while a comprehensive diagnostic implies that a comprehensive action is required to address the various dimensions of poverty, any such plan also needs to make realistic trade-offs. Rather than producing 'wish lists', governments need to recognize the resource constraints within which the PRSP must be implemented, and, given this, develop a costed, prioritized, and sequenced programme of actions. In practice, one of the key short-comings of the PRSPs to date has been their inability to prioritize actions and indicate how policies will be sequenced as resources become available. This failure to prioritize stems in part from technical constraints: it has proven difficult to estimate available resources accurately and costing programmes has been a challenge. However, long and unfocused PRSPs also point to the difficulties inherent in managing the multiple inputs generated by the participatory processes, where many expect their concerns to be reflected.

Nevertheless, the PRSP has led to the development of new tools which help countries assess the likely impacts of policy actions on the most vulnerable groups, and hence make informed choices as to programmes with the highest poverty reduction effects. With much in common with the idea of consequential evaluation advocated by Sen, Poverty and Social Impact Analysis (PSIA) provides a set of tools to help countries assess *ex ante* as well as *ex post* the distributional impacts of proposed reforms. The methodology captures both the income and non-income dimensions of well-being, employing, for example, indicators that measure risk, vulnerability, and social capital, and utilizes both qualitative and quantitative techniques. While some have criticized the slow progress to date in subjecting key reforms in the PRSP to PSIA, the emergence of new techniques such as this points to a way of advancing countries' understanding of how policy actions can translate into the desired results.[33]

In our view, it is critical that choices be made and trade-offs negotiated if the PRSP is to move beyond a list of aspirations to a plan which offers guidance to policy makers and implementing agencies as to which actions should be taken first. This may constitute a genuine difference of perspective between rights-based approaches, which stress the interdependency of all human rights outcomes, and the PRSP which is premised on the notion of prioritization. However, differences on this front may have been overstated: the principle of progressive realization of some rights clearly recognizes that

---

[33] Social Forum of External Debt and Development of Honduras (FOSDEH) and Oxfam International, *The PRSP in Honduras: Perpetuating Poverty?* Draft, 2003.

resource availability does constrain progress. But tensions remain with respect to the achievement of those rights which human rights approaches insist are immediately compelling.

18.5 FOCUSING ON RESULTS

A PRSP is expected to be results-focused and to set out clearly long-term outcomes that will benefit poor people and enable them to move out of poverty. In addition, the approach also puts a great deal of emphasis on the importance of tracking progress towards these outcomes, and on feeding evidence back into policy making. Consequently, the PRSP is expected to set intermediate and annual targets as well as define both monetary and non-monetary long-term goals for poverty reduction. Indicators of progress derived from these goals allow the country to monitor the ongoing impacts of their policy actions. This focus on results requires that robust monitoring and evaluation systems be developed to collect and manage information. In addition to data collection and analysis, effective implementation of the PRSP also demands that results are reported regularly and that findings are broadly shared.

The PRSP model thus seeks to increase accountability and transparency, key precepts of a rights-based approach. As more information is generated and disclosed, there is greater scope for citizens to hold their governments to account as well as new opportunities to engage in debates about what works and what does not. Furthermore, the prominence given to tracing results in the PRSP requires governments to link inputs to outcomes, thereby creating new incentives to track expenditures more effectively than before, and exposing leakage and corruption in the process. To our mind, such achievements are linked to gains on a number of human rights fronts such as greater freedom of information and increased participation in the policy process. In addition, the results focus of the PRSP ensures that poverty reduction outcomes remain centre stage: in particular, governments are encouraged to think about how the PRSP can enable the country to work towards the achievement of the MDGs.

More specifically, while the MDGs present a set of extremely useful targets for low-income countries and their development partners, the PRSP provides a vital accountability mechanism that would otherwise be lacking. The PRSP is increasingly an instrument which allows countries to reconfirm their commitment to the MDGs, set out the actions both they and their development partners need to undertake in order to achieve the goals, and report on progress towards the goals over time. In particular, as the PRSP implementation is monitored, and the results of policy actions reported to both citizens and development partners through PRSP Progress Reports, all have more opportunity to scrutinize government performance as well as identify areas where the anticipated results are not being achieved, thereby allowing for remedial action to be taken.

Some tensions have been observed, however, in setting sufficiently ambitious yet relevant long-term objectives in the PRSP. In particular, the relationship between the objectives a country sets out in its PRSP and the MDGs has been the subject of some discussion.[34] However, while there is clearly not a one to one mapping between PRSP targets and MDGs in all PRSPs, there is emerging good practice of countries using the PRSP to explore alternative scenarios, thereby illuminating how improved policies and governance could interact with more and better aid in helping them accelerate progress towards the MDGs. In addition, some countries have sought to reconcile the aspirations of the MDGs with a realistic assessment of the constraints they face, customizing the targets to their local conditions while spelling out a longer term game plan for their achievement. Overall, the PRSP clearly has a critical role to play in exposing both the capacity and resource constraints which currently impede the country's efforts to reach the goals by 2015.

However, a number of challenges remain to be addressed. In practice, monitoring the inputs, outputs, and outcomes of policies presented in the PRSP has proven technically difficult. The ability of a country to isolate resources which are directed at certain programmes, and thereby be able to trace through the consequences of these expenditures, is dependent on underlying public expenditure systems. In order to provide useful information on inputs any such system needs to contain accurate data and to present this appropriately. However, as recent studies have shown, many low-income countries are slow to collect information on how the budget is actually spent, even slower to audit this, and often use budget classifications that do not allow analysts to establish which programmes were funded.[35] Moreover, appropriate intermediate indicators which enable progress to be tracked and help countries steer implementation on an ongoing basis have been problematic to define. Common pitfalls include selecting too many indicators or loosely defined proxies, neither of which are useful to monitor. That said, more recent experience suggests that countries are choosing indicators more carefully, including those which allow them to track disparities between gender, social groups, rural/urban areas, and the like. In addition, many countries are now including key process indicators in their PRSPs: for example, they seek to track improvements in corruption and public expenditure management as well as use quantitative methods to solicit perceptions on, for example, service delivery and civil service performance.

---

[34] See, for example, J. Sachs, *The Millennium Development Goals: Desirable, But Are They Achievable?* Water and Sanitation Lecture Series, World Bank, May 2003.

[35] R. Alonso, J. Almagro, L. Judge, and J. Klugman, *Budgets and the PRSP: A Synthesis of Five Case Studies* (Washington D.C.: World Bank, 2003).

Overall, the PRSP has clearly provided added impetus for poverty monitoring which will track trends over a longer time horizon and allow countries to report on their overall targets. There is evidence that greater emphasis is being placed on disaggregating by vulnerable groups thereby exposing the differential impacts of specific policies. Moreover, the PRSP has revealed more clearly than ever how the move towards an evidence-based approach to policy making is much more than a technocratic exercise. Establishing monitoring systems that seek to support and improve what already exists is a major exercise, and often demands challenging entrenched institutional practices. Most countries, to date, have sketched out plans for such systems in only the most general terms, and have yet to grapple with clarifying the roles and responsibilities of the multitude of agencies which will need to be engaged if any system is to be a success.

Finally, most countries envisage an active role for non-governmental actors in monitoring the implementation of the PRSP and providing feedback on services. CSOs are being brought into formal mechanisms such as committees or working groups which are set up to track progress. Furthermore, in countries which have not formalized the role of civil society in their monitoring structures, NGOs have often successfully carved out a space for themselves as suppliers of additional poverty data and information, as well as performing a watchdog function and ensuring governments live up to their PRSP commitments. The use of citizens' report cards and public expenditure tracking surveys also point to the emergence of new tools which facilitate greater citizen engagement with monitoring and reporting.

18.6 CONCLUSIONS

This chapter has explored the interface between human rights and the PRSP initiative, aiming to identify both commonalities as well as points of departure between the two approaches. Section 18.2 suggested that there is significant, but not complete, coincidence between the outcomes pursued by human rights approaches and the ends sought by development and poverty reduction practitioners. Thus, we see poverty reduction as a subset of the human rights value system. Furthermore, we have gone on to suggest that while the fields of human rights and development implicitly suggest different approaches to the achievement of these shared ends, in recent years there has been greater convergence in the programmes of action suggested by both disciplines.

Moreover, we believe that the PRSP is an aid modality which is consistent with many human rights principles, and therefore there is greater alignment between development strategies and human rights since its introduction. The PRSP model developed as a result of the literature on growth, poverty, and inequality, from debates about aid effectiveness, and from valuable analysis which extended our understanding of what it meant to be poor such as Sen's work on capabilities and the Voices of the Poor exercise. However, despite a different intellectual starting point from rights-based approaches, a high level of congruence exists between the PRSP model and human-rights-based approaches to development. Most notably:

- The emphasis placed on reconfiguring the aid relationship so that both government and domestic stakeholders assert greater control over policy making and resources is, in our view, consistent with the notion that states have the primary responsibility for the welfare of their citizens and should respond to their concerns.
- By supporting the development of domestic capacity, the PRSP approach aims to ensure that aid no longer undermines the essential condition for its success: a fully functioning government without which few, if any, rights can be guaranteed.
- By requiring that governments open up the policy process to their citizens, the PRSP seeks to create new political space for debate and expression. While few cases of the participatory process have been models of good practice, in most PRSP countries the achievements observed over the last five years have been impressive given their relative starting points, and clearly, if the many lessons can be taken on board, greater gains could be achieved.
- The requirement that PRSPs are based on a comprehensive diagnostic of poverty has resulted in analysis emphasizing not only issues which could be classified as the outcomes sought by economic, social, and cultural rights, but also those pursued by civil and political rights.
- The focus on results and the monitoring of inputs, outputs, and outcomes has the potential to lead to real gains in terms of increased transparency of governments, and empowers citizens to hold the state to account.

At the same time, we also see some areas of non-intersection between the PRSP and rights-based approaches. In particular, it is difficult to square convincingly the principle of indivisibility with two critical aspects of the PRSP. First, as outlined in section 18.2, poverty reduction does not necessarily encompass all rights and hence the PRSP is not a strategy that aims to deliver results on all human rights fronts. Second, the PRSP is a pragmatic approach which, to be successful, has to work within the parameters of both resource and capacity constraints. In practice, hard choices have to be made and policies sequenced over time. This chapter has argued that, on both points, the extent to which the PRSP is consistent with the key human rights principle of indivisibility is indeed significant but nonetheless some differences remain.

Since the introduction of the PRSP many human rights advocates have suggested that the World Bank adapt the model further to bring it into line with human rights approaches. The OHCHR, for example, while acknowledging that many of the norms embedded in human rights are currently reflected in PRSPs, has argued there are six key aspects of the human rights agenda that would strengthen the PRSP process, as follows:

- The process of achieving poverty reduction, and especially the participation of poor people in decisions affecting their lives, should be as important as the end result.
- The principles of non-discrimination and equality in the human rights canon should be emphasized to expose discriminatory practices that underpin poverty.
- The complementarities between civil and political rights and economic, social, and cultural rights should be underscored.
- Accountability of the state to its citizens should be paramount.
- A rights-based approach would prohibit trade-offs and protect against a state regressing on rights that have previously been achieved.
- Because human rights encode international legal obligations, framing poverty reduction policies in human rights terms would give them additional legitimacy.[36]

We hope that this chapter has shown convincingly that the first four lines of reasoning are already central to the PRSP model. The principles of country ownership, comprehensiveness, and results focus on which the PRSP is premised are, to our mind, fully resonant with the approach advanced by the OHCHR in its draft guidelines. The relationship between the other two points and the PRSP is, however, more nuanced. The PRSP is an instrument designed to help governments make choices and assess trade-offs that are a fact of life for all, but are especially pertinent for low-income countries. However, implicit in the PRSP is the belief that policies should, first and foremost, benefit poor people. In addition, governments should be cognizant of the possible detrimental impacts that reforms pursued in the name of development may have on vulnerable sections of the population and that these impacts should be mitigated. Thus, while any realistic strategy cannot avoid facing up to trade-offs, the PRSP does seek to improve the lives of poor people and protect them from possible transitional costs.

The final point made by the OHCHR, that human rights provide added legitimacy to poverty reduction strategies by virtue of their legal status, is one where perhaps more thought is needed. The PRSP is, of course, not disconnected from internationally agreed texts: most importantly, PRSPs are intimately linked to the achievement of the MDGs which arguably have

---

[36] Office of the High Commissioner for Human Rights, above n. 15, paras 16–24.

achieved the status of international customary law. More problematic perhaps is how employing the language of the international treaties and pointing out governments' obligations under such documents is consistent with the principle of country ownership. It would be interesting, however, to explore how the discourse on human rights can further the achievement of poverty reduction outcomes, and, in particular, to spell out more clearly its relation to the empowerment agenda.

There are many challenges implicit in the PRSP model. It is clear that the PRSP demands a reconfiguration of relationships between governments, their citizens, and donors but behavioural change takes time, as vested interests have to be overcome, incentives altered, and new skills learned. In practice, resource and capacity constraints have also limited what the PRSP approach has been able to deliver to date, although the alternative scenarios being developed in the context of the MDGs are usefully exploring the nature and scope of these constraints, and highlighting appropriate remedial actions. As the most recent World Bank/IMF Progress Report on PRSPs noted,

The PRSP is an instrument being charged with multiple objectives, many of which imply tensions—for example, the range of proposals emerging from the participatory process versus prioritization; comprehensiveness in addressing the different dimensions of poverty versus selectivity and focus of the strategy and national implementation capacity; the pace at which public expenditure management can improve against that needed for successful PRSP implementation; and meeting the expectations of the international community versus country ownership.[37]

Despite the significant issues that remain to be resolved, in our opinion the PRSP ideal offers a genuinely different way forward for low-income country governments, their citizens, and development partners. This approach has the potential not only to deliver on poverty reduction, and hence many human rights outcomes, but also to do so in a way that is broadly consistent with key human rights principles. We believe that the dichotomy presented by some between the PRSP and human rights approaches is thus a false one. We also believe that poor people the world over are better served by our recognizing that many synergies exist between the PRSP and human rights approaches, and, that while there are differences, the two reinforce one another. Indeed, their comparative advantages ensure that both human rights advocates and development practitioners have critical and complementary roles to play in the fight against poverty, and the achievement more broadly of human rights.

---

[37] IMF/IDA, above n. 24.

19

Human Rights, Poverty Reduction Strategies, and the Role of the International Monetary Fund[1]

MARK W. PLANT

19.1 INTRODUCTION

The Office of the High Commissioner for Human Rights (OHCHR) recently issued a set of draft guidelines that provide a framework for integrating human rights into poverty reduction strategies (PRSs).[2] These guidelines transform the often abstract discussion of the role of human rights in the development process into practical advice. This is valuable not just for low-income countries developing PRSs but also for their international partners using PRSs to frame their development assistance. In reading the guidelines, one could come easily to the conclusion that there is nothing more to be said at this point, given their thoroughness and depth. They point to how PRSs can be framed by a rights approach to development and how the PRS process, as it has been developing over the last four years, can reinforce the efforts of the international community to ensure governments the world over live up to the obligations incumbent upon them in the Universal Declaration of Human Rights and ensuing international agreements. In sum, these guidelines provide practical means to enter into what has heretofore been mostly rhetorical—the virtuous circle of human rights promotion and poverty reduction.

[1] I would like to thank my IMF colleagues for their assistance on this paper, particularly Mark Allen, Michael Bell, Klaus Enders, Peter Fallon, Elliott Harris, Peter Heller, Amber Mahone, and Simonetta Nardin. They bear no responsibility for any remaining errors or errant ideas. The opinions expressed in the paper are mine and do not necessarily represent the official position of the International Monetary Fund.
[2] United Nations High Commissioner for Human Rights, *Draft Guidelines: A Human Rights Approach to Poverty Reduction Strategies*, 10 September 2002 (Geneva: United Nations).

The temptation is to let the experiment begin—promote the guidelines, provide assistance to those wanting to implement them, and observe how low-income country governments, donors, and the international institutions in fact use them. In a few years, we can hold conferences, laud best practices, point fingers at each other's misunderstanding or misuse of, or disregard for, the approach, revise and resubmit the guidelines and begin again. That is, we can enter into our own virtuous (or is it vicious?) cycle of re-framing the development challenge and creating another mini-industry to succor the international bureaucracy and academic community.

This rhetoric points to a skepticism about succumbing to this temptation, but this skepticism does not come out of any doubt about the human rights approach—in fact, the rights approach should be seen as a foundation for development efforts. The skepticism stems instead from watching the development of the PRS approach over the last four years. As the PRS approach gains increasing breadth and momentum, we owe it to our colleagues in low-income countries to step back a bit and ensure that the PRS approach is aimed at helping them solve the very basic problem they confront—reducing poverty in all its aspects. There are three questions to be answered about the integration of the PRS approach with the effort to address the human rights challenges faced by developing countries:

- Is there a good balance between ambition and realism?
- Is there a good balance between process and content?
- What role can the human rights approach play in the international community's efforts to support poverty reduction?

None of these can be answered definitively in this chapter. Instead, the chapter will offer some observations informed by the ongoing effort to define the international community's role in meeting the Millennium Development Goals (MDGs) in low-income countries.

19.2 BACKGROUND

To begin to answer the question of whether the integration of the human rights approach will make the PRS approach more effective for development, we need to consider briefly the international context for the PRS process. The international community adopted the MDGs and, at the United Nations Financing for Development Conference in Monterrey, Mexico, came to a consensus about how to proceed to reach those goals (known as the two-pillar approach): the international community will assist low-income countries that adopt the right policies and pursue sound strategies for poverty reduction through sustained economic growth. The International Monetary Fund (IMF) fully supports both the MDGs and the Monterrey Consensus, and its

Executive Board has reaffirmed that the PRS approach provides the frame-work for the IMF's support to low-income countries.[3] The World Bank, the regional development banks and bilateral donors, and the agencies of the United Nations System, notably the United Nations Development Program (UNDP), have taken similar stances—the PRS approach will frame the international community's work with low-income countries.

19.3 AMBITION, REALISM, AND HEAVY DEMANDS

After four years of implementing the PRS approach, there is now a substantial body of experience on which to draw. A recent paper, jointly prepared by the IMF and World Bank staffs and considered by the two Executive Boards, underscored that a number of tensions are beginning to emerge in the PRS process as countries confront the reality of crafting comprehensive poverty reduction strategies formulated through a broad-based participatory process and aimed at providing practical blueprints for policy formulation and execution.[4]

There is a marked tension between the ambitious goal of providing a comprehensive strategic vision for poverty reduction and the desire to for-mulate a realistic and operational tactical blueprint for making the myriad of policy choices governments confront every day. The incorporation of the MDGs as the ultimate objectives in the PRS process makes that tension even more acute. For example, some critics of the IMF's involvement in the PRS process have alleged that macroeconomic frameworks in PRS papers (PRSPs) restrict country policy choices through their reliance on realistic projections (or, in their eyes, conservative projections) of donor support and through their emphasis on the fundamental need for fiscal and monetary discipline. This approach is seen as short-sighted, offering no more than incremental progress rather than the kind of step change needed to meet the MDGs. Such critics would instead prefer to see the IMF open up space for policy choices by helping countries construct ambitious macroeconomic frameworks that would light the path to meeting the MDGs, giving the donor community the information required to make decisions about how much support is needed

---

[3] See 'The IMF Executive Board Reviews the Role of the Fund in Low-Income Countries Over the Medium Term', Public Information Notice 3/117, International Monetary Fund, 10 September 2003 (http://ww.imf.org/external/np/sec/pn/2003/pn03117.htm) and 'Role of the Fund in Low-Income Member Countries over the Medium Term—Issues Paper for Discussion', International Monetary Fund, 21 July 2003 (http://www.imf.org/External/np/pdr/sustain/2003/072103.htm).

[4] See 'Poverty Reduction Strategy Papers—Progress in Implementation', International Monetary Fund, 23 September 2003 (http://www.imf.org/external/np/prspgen/2003/091203.pdf).

to meet the MDGs and in which countries. The IMF, while recognizing the global need for such information, views its role in the Monterrey Consensus as helping countries maintain macroeconomic stability as a necessary prerequisite for growth and, in practical terms, helping them ensure that growth can be increased and sustained and poverty reduction accelerated without jeopardizing hard-won gains in stabilization. The IMF can be seen, perhaps, as the realistic macroeconomic and growth tactician, and needs to become an integral part of the overall strategic decision-making process to achieve the ambition of the MDGs. Of course, tactics are only effective in the context of a good strategy. So how, in the PRS process, do we, as an international community, intermediate between strategy and tactics? How can we ensure that strategy informs tactics, yet be informed as the day-to-day implementation efforts succeed or fail?

The guidelines for a human rights approach to poverty reduction strategies also struggle with the tension between ambition and realism. They attempt to provide a broader context for the PRS approach by placing it in the frameworks of international legal obligations and binding international rights, broadening its scope to address structures of discrimination and helping to structure mechanisms for accountability through the human rights paradigm. At the same time they suggest rather specific guidance on strategies for realizing rights, including appropriate targets and indicators of progress. The guidelines recognize that all the human rights and associated objectives will not be attained immediately, and that priorities must be set. But do the guidelines simplify or complicate low-income countries' policy choices and the provision of donor support? Do they limit policy choices or broaden them? There is a risk that, fairly or unfairly, the human rights approach will be seen by low-income countries or their international partners as being grafted onto the PRS process and thus more of a burden than a help. The operational vision for the guidelines is clear—they are to frame and focus the PRS process and thus be integrated into it rather than added on. But how can that be effected, especially in the face of similar guidelines from other multilateral organizations, bilateral donors, and civil society organizations?

One gets a sense, in talking to officials of low-income countries, that they are becoming confused as to what poverty reduction strategies are really supposed to be and to do. A measure of the success of the PRS approach is that many of the international players see it as valuable and that it has become 'the only game in town'. But the risk we take in making it the principal development instrument for addressing the full panoply of development-related issues is that it could collapse under the weight of the demands put on it. Perhaps what is needed is the development of closer links (i.e., links extending beyond rhetoric) between economic growth, achieving the MDGs, advancing the human rights agenda, and reducing poverty. But how can these links be forged?

19.4 PROCESS OR CONTENT?

This leads to a second tension in the PRS process, which is mirrored in the human rights process—that between the process of developing policies and the content of the policies. A key feature of the PRS process, as underscored in the human rights guidelines, is the participatory process that underpins the actual strategy. This process is meant to broaden the policy debate and include those most affected by policy decisions, thereby strengthening societal consensus and on-the-ground implementation of the strategy. Embedding participation in many low-income countries' decision-making frameworks has been heralded as one of the important successes thus far of the PRS process. Equally, those schooled in the human rights approach underscore the salutary effects of giving voice to all in society and empowering the poor.

Although participation in formulating the PRS can be seen as an end in and of itself, it is an empty objective if the content of the policies designed through participation is poor or if participation only amounts to involvement. For example, some PRSs have been criticized as being so general that they fail to provide any effective basis for choice; some are seen as internally contradictory or ignoring key policy areas and thus avoiding difficult choices; and some seem to espouse policies that may sacrifice longer-term gains for short-term political solutions. These aspects are characteristic, perhaps, of any political process, but this does not obviate the objective of getting good policies and not just good process. The IMF's experience in this regard provides some interesting insights, as does the human rights approach as embodied in the PRS guidelines.

The IMF has been criticized for grafting its macroeconomic framework onto some countries' PRSPs rather than subjecting macroeconomic policy making to a participatory process and integrating the result into the development of the PRSP. Although this criticism is, in fact, a caricature of what happens, it does raise the question as to the level at which meaningful input can be made into macroeconomic decision making. Can villagers be informed about and have some meaningful input into decisions that might have to be made regarding trade-offs between delivery of high-quality secondary education and the inflationary effects of a more expansive monetary policy? Here I am not calling into question the intellectual capacity of village elders but only their perspectives and information bases. Are either sufficiently broad to enable these leaders to make meaningful choices? Is it effective to broaden both so they can give opinions? Given the ultimate responsibility of the government to make difficult societal choices in the face of a budget constraint that spans the country's entire economy and whose impact may last for generations, how much participation is needed? How many voices need to be heard and whose are they? Often governments are uneasy about letting non-elected civil society representatives have a voice in making very difficult, complex, and sensitive macroeconomic policy choices.

The IMF is trying to understand how to open the macroeconomic policy debate to a broader range of stakeholders, recognizing the benefits of such a broadening and knowing full well that we may not have all the answers to the country's macroeconomic problems. However, like the proverbial central banker, the IMF's responsibility to the international community is often 'to take the punch bowl away just as the party is getting started'. We aim to help governments understand the constraints they face—and typically these constraints will not be changed through discussion. Governments must decide how to engage in a full and responsible discussion of macroeconomic policy choices with their people. That discussion should be part of their interaction with the IMF—not just for process's sake but to find policies that will work better and to understand the societal trade-offs involved in the making of policy decisions. But these discussions need to lead to cogent choices, often in a very short period of time. Difficult macroeconomic choices cannot be avoided by adopting empty or internally contradictory policies; if this is done, the choices will be made by markets—where, for example, currency depreciation or inflation may occur—or postponed until later generations through indebtedness. Politicians may prefer to avoid such discussions, but the responsibility of the IMF is to discourage this.

How do process and content interact in the human rights approach to poverty reduction? A strong point of the guidelines is that they separate how the human rights approach should influence the process aspects of the PRS from how it should influence the content of policies themselves. As noted before, the very existence of a participatory process reinforces voice and empowerment. Although this is an end in itself, if the participatory process is to be effective, it must be focused on what people care about and have knowledge of. The guidelines state clearly that there are limits to parti-cipation by the poor, with the proper focus being on their inclusion in setting priorities and benchmarks, often in the context of community-level activities rather than in the technical deliberations on policy formulation.

However, some questions arise. What if the participatory process leads to a policy conclusion at variance with one of the key elements for realizing basic human rights? Can a trade-off between participation and voice and other rights be acceptable? Economists would have a similar difficulty determining an appropriate trade-off between participation and, for example, macro-economic stability. How can this be done in the human rights domain?

Another difficulty in sorting through the guidelines is discerning the hard constraints—that is, what is the minimum pace of introduction of human rights into PRSs that will be tolerated? Any notion of hard constraint is made a bit more elusive by the fact that the full set of rights cannot be achieved overnight and thus progress made toward this goal is what needs to be measured. Although governments may recognize the wisdom of adopting such an approach, adopting such a stance risks putting them in a quandary as to what the operational implications of the rights approach are for the PRS. For example, the right to education implies, in the first instance, that primary education should be compulsory and available free to all, but the guidelines put forward some six key features of a strategy for realizing the right to education in a PRS. On the one hand, the principal feature is ensuring access to primary education for the most vulnerable, which would seem to meet the test of being a well-defined policy objective that is not vacuous, inherently contradictory, or time-inconsistent. On the other hand, the last feature states that 'education should be directed to the full development of the human personality and strengthen respect for human dignity, tolerance, human rights and fundamental freedoms', which, while clearly a valuable principle, seems so general as to offer little guidance to governments as how to go about making good education policy decisions.

The point here is not to criticize any particular key feature or interpretation of how the human rights approach should influence PRSs. Instead, it is to underscore that the international community is confronting the low-income countries engaged in the PRS process with a myriad of imperatives, demands, constraints, and guidelines on both process and content. Getting the process right will not guarantee the content of policies, and arriving at the right content by a deficient process may be self-defeating. Can countries get the balance right, especially in the face of severe capacity constraints?

19.5 INTEGRATION OF INTERNATIONAL EFFORTS

This leads back to the Monterrey Consensus, one part of which was not mentioned earlier. The international community's assistance to low-income countries is supposed to leverage the expertise of each partner. Given the imperative of reaching the MDGs by 2015, the various players do not have the luxury of treading on each other's turf but rather must specialize in their respective areas of comparative advantage. At the same time, each institution should be held accountable for the advice and support it promises and provides.

If the donor community transfers its responsibilities on to each country's PRS process, and implicitly to low-income countries, the process will indeed collapse. If each international institution and donor proposes separate guidelines on what it expects from a PRS, low-income countries will either produce PRSPs that wallow in general principles that can be supported but not implemented or produce encyclopedic documents that no one reads or understands and that certainly cannot be used to hold low-income governments or their partners accountable.

The way out is to consider documents such as that produced by the OHCHR not as guidelines for low-income countries to fulfill, but instead as offers by institutions of the developed world to help in their areas of expertise. This cogent and well-crafted document sets out what the OHCHR thinks an ideal PRS looks like from the perspective of its background, expertise, and experience. Following their logic above, it should not be seen by low-income countries as yet another demand on what they must do to live up to some externally or self-imposed standard. Instead it should be seen as an offer by the OHCHR of expertise that it can bring to bear to the benefit of low-income countries. It should be used as a measure of accountability not for Chad or Guinea-Bissau, for example, but instead as a measure of the accountability of the OHCHR. When Chad or Guinea-Bissau decides that it wants to pursue a policy of ensuring that education is directed to the full development of the human personality, it should be able to call on the OHCHR for help in doing so, just as Chad can call on the IMF to help design an efficient tax system or monetary policy. With such an approach, a low-income country's PRSP would truly become its contribution toward fulfilling the Monterrey Consensus—drawing on the expertise and support offered by international partners through such guidelines, with each country deciding what it was going to do.

Further, with such an approach, international partners would begin to understand how their demands fit together or conflict. For example, confronted with the OHCHR guidelines, an IMF mission chief might view them as yet another demand on the government's scarce human and financial resources to be satisfied, or as a framework to guide government policy that competes with macroeconomic prudence, or not. If instead the guidelines were recast as OHCHR's idea of what human rights mean in the PRS process and as an offer of how it can assist low-income countries, then a conversation may be opened up as to how, for example, the IMF's efforts to establish transparent and sound accounting mechanisms in the budgetary process fit in with the human rights imperatives and how it can complement the OHCHR's efforts to ensure accountability. Similarly, the OHCHR could begin to understand how the IMF frames its macroeconomic assistance, and the OHCHR could offer ideas as to how participation can best be used to help the discussion of macroeconomic policy choices.

There are several advantages to such an approach. First, the development of guidelines for ourselves in providing assistance to low-income countries begins to make members of the international community accountable in concrete and measurable ways. Second, it makes the various institutions and governments think about their own constraints. If we commit ourselves to helping willing countries meet the standards we lay out, then we are likely to be more parsimonious in what we choose to be criteria worth meeting. Third, it takes a weight off the PRS process and lets the country's voice be more clearly heard. The country can say what it will do and what expertise it wants to draw on without having to jump through all the hoops set for it by the diverse bodies of the international community.

Each international institution should undertake this kind of reflection. The IMF is in the process of thinking about what its role in low-income countries should be in the coming years. The process that began in August 2003 and continues today is meant to describe to the international community what low-income countries and their partners can expect of the IMF in the two-pillar process. In addition, the World Bank and the IMF have recently received the reports of their independent evaluation offices on the PRSP process. In that context, we will look again at the PRSP and at how each of our institutions uses the PRSP to structure its assistance to low-income countries. That reflection will present us with the opportunity to engage other institutions using the PRS process to see how we can work together to ensure the PRS process does not collapse under the weight of our multiple demands.

The OHCHR guidelines will serve low-income countries and their partners well by ensuring that human rights considerations underpin all their work together. The importance of the human rights approach for our work in low-income countries and the high quality of the work that went into crafting the guidelines make it all the more clear that the international community needs to find a mechanism for making sure that countries can make effective use of the human rights approach. Equally, such an approach needs to support the efforts of those countries judiciously, wisely, and with the minimum amount of wasted effort.

Part G

The World Bank and Human Rights

20

The Legal Aspects of the World Bank's Work on Human Rights: Some Preliminary Thoughts

ROBERTO DAÑINO[*]

20.1 INTRODUCTION

The focus of this volume of essays is on the ways in which efforts to promote development and human rights can reinforce one another.[1] Development is precisely what the World Bank works for and we believe that this work consistently contributes to the progressive realization of human rights in our member countries.[2] I welcome the opportunity to share some of my initial

[*] This chapter is based upon a speech delivered at a conference held at New York University Law School in March 2004. The speech represents the personal views of the General Counsel. It should not be taken as a statement of World Bank policy.

[1] A number of leading resources on human rights were consulted in the process of preparing this chapter. They provided general background to the thinking it contains and informed the normative and principled bases of the arguments and the basic precepts underpinning these views. These include, but are not limited to, the following titles: J. Donnelly, *The Concept of Human Rights* (London, Croom Helm, 1985); L. Henkin, *The Age of Rights* (New York, Columbia University Press, 1990); P. Sieghart, *The Lawful Rights of Mankind* (Oxford, Clarendon Press, 1986); R. Falk, 'The Theoretical Foundations of Human Rights' in R. Newburg (ed.) *The Politics of Human Rights* (New York, New York University Press, 1980) 31; P. Alston (ed.), *Human Rights Law* (Aldershot, Dartmouth, 1996); B. Ramcharan, *The Concept and Present Status of the International Protection of Human Rights Forty Years After the Universal Declaration* (Dordrecht, Martinus Nijhoff, 1989); F. Butler (ed.) *Human Rights Protection: Methods and Effectiveness* British Institute of Human Rights (The Hague, Kluwer, 2002); H. Hannum, *Guide to International Human Rights Practice* (Philadelphia, University of Pennsylvania Press, 3rd edn., 1999); P. Alston, *The United Nations and Human Rights: A Critical Appraisal* (Oxford, Clarendon Press, 1992); S. Horowitz and A. Schnabel (eds.). *Human rights and Societies in Transition: Causes, Consequences, Responses* (New York, United Nations University Press, 2004).

[2] In this chapter, the concept of progressive realization is understood as a principle of human rights law which recognizes that the realization of human rights is often constrained by the scarcity of resources, and that such constraints cannot be remedied instantly. Its special

personal thoughts about the legal considerations regarding the work of the World Bank with respect to human rights.

One of my first acts on assuming my position at the end of 2003 was to establish a Work Group on Human Rights within the Legal Vice-Presidency. The response from our lawyers to my invitation for expressions of interest in serving on this committee was overwhelming. That Group has been analyzing the legal framework applicable to the Bank's work in connection with human rights. It is also developing a matrix of Human Rights and the activities of the Bank—to help us get a better understanding of the interconnections between the work of the Bank and each of the human rights obligations of our members,[3] and more generally, on the connections between development and

relevance to economic, social, and cultural rights and to the context of the ICESCR is also acknowledged, see, for example, P. Alston and G. Quinn, 'The Nature and Scope of States Parties' Obligations under the International Covenant on Economic, Social and Cultural Rights, 9 *Hum. Rts. Q.* (1987) 156–229 at 159.

[3] The following example illustrates the framework employed in the human rights matrix being developed by the Legal Vice-Presidency:

Human Right	International HR Instrument Provisions	IBRD Policy	IBRD Practice
Right to freedom of opinion and expression;	UDHR Article 19	Disclosure; Public Consultation requirements in Operational Policy/ Bank Procedure 4.01	Access to information; Public Information;
Right to hold opinions without interference;	ICCPR Article 19	Environmental Assessment; Operational Policy/ Bank Procedure 4.04 Natural Habitats;	Economic and Sector Work (ESW);
Right to receive and impart information and ideas through any media and regardless of frontiers		Operational Policy 4.09 Pest Management; Operational Policy/ Bank Procedure 4.12 Involuntary Resettlement; Operational Policy 4.20 Indigenous Peoples; Operational Policy/Bank Procedure 4.36 Forests; Operational Policy 11.03 Cultural Property	Document translation framework; public information centers; Education; Education for the knowledge economy; Global distance learning; technology diffusion; telecom projects;
		Public Information Centers and ESW	Dissemination of Environmental Assessments and other reports.

human rights.[4] I did this, not only because of my personal conviction that work in this area is a moral imperative, but also because of my sense that human rights are progressively becoming an explicit and integral part of the Bank's work, just as has happened over the last twenty years with the environment[5] and in the last five years with anti-corruption.[6]

However, it appears that concerns and uncertainties about the 'constitutional' restrictions under the Articles of Agreement of the Bank[7] have somewhat inhibited a more proactive and explicit consideration of human rights as part of our work. I would therefore like to offer my preliminary thoughts on the nature of our legal boundaries.

What I have to say falls into three broad parts.

First, I want to discuss the Bank's legal framework—the Articles of Agreement. Our framework has limitations—as it should—for it is important to bear in mind that the Bank is a financial institution. As a specialized agency of the United Nations it has a specific financial purpose and a clearly designated role within the structure of the UN,[8] as well as within the structure of the two International Human Rights Covenants.[9]

---

[4] Some research has shown that a modern economic approach to service provision (and development more broadly) overlaps substantially with a rights-based approach—both emphasize transparency, accountability, and strengthening the position of clients. See, for example, V. Gauri, 'Social Rights and Economics: Claims to Health Care and Education in Developing Countries', Chapter 5 in this volume.

[5] *World Bank Environment Strategy* (2001). See especially chapter 1, which addresses the connections between development policy and the environment. For a more general narrative of the evolution of environmental considerations in the work of the World Bank, see R. Wade, 'Greening the Bank: The Struggle Over the Environment' in D. Kapur, J. Lewis, R. Webb (eds.) *The World Bank: Its First Half Century* (Brookings Institution Press, Washington D.C., 1997) 611–734; World Bank, *Development and the Environment* (World Development Report 1992, Washington D.C., 1992); D. Freestone, 'Incorporating Sustainable Development into the Development and Investment Process—the World Bank Experience' in M. Fitzmaurice and M. Szuniewicz (eds.) *Exploitation of Natural Resources in the 21st Century* (The Hague, Kluwer Law International, 2003), 91–112.

[6] See I.F.I. Shihata, 'Corruption—A General Review with an Emphasis on the Role of the World Bank' 15 *Dickinson Journal of International Law* (1997) 451. See also *Helping Countries Combat Corruption: The Role of the World Bank Poverty Reduction and Economic Management* (Washington D.C., World Bank, 1997); *Helping Countries Combat Corruption: The Role of the World Bank: Progress at the World Bank Since 1997* (Washington D.C., World Bank, 2000); *Anticorruption in Transition: A Contribution to the Policy Debate* (Washington D.C., World Bank, September 2000); and *Reforming Public Institutions and Strengthening Governance, A World Bank Strategy* (Washington D.C., World Bank, November 2000).

[7] International Bank for Reconstruction and Development, Articles of Agreement. Entered into force on 27 December 1945, 2 UNTS 134 (amended 17 December 1965, 16 UNTS 1942).

[8] Agreement concluded with the United Nations in 1947, 16 UNTS 346. Article 57 of the United Nations Charter makes specific provision for the specialized agencies and for their relationship to the United Nations.

[9] See ICESCR, Articles 16, 17, 18, 19, 20, 21, 22, and 24. See ICCPR, Articles 40, 44, and 46.

Within these limitations, the objectives of the institution have been, and should continue to be, dynamically interpreted and applied. And my view is that this legal framework can also be seen as enabling.

Second, in order to put these discussions in context, I want to discuss the evolution of the Bank's role in development. As the world has changed over the past sixty years, so too has the Bank and its practice. Its emphasis has shifted dramatically from bricks and mortar infrastructure to the large-scale inclusion of human development, institutional reform, and social development.[10] In other words, the focus of our work has clearly evolved from 'hard lending' to 'soft lending'.[11] A significant proportion of the Bank's lending portfolio also is directly aimed at the attainment of the Millennium Development Goals (MDGs).[12] It is clear that, as a result of this progress, the Bank has made major contributions to the substantive furtherance of a broad array of human rights in a range of fields.[13]

Third, bearing in mind that I am a newcomer to the Bank, I will try to articulate my own preliminary thinking about the way forward for the Bank in this area.

---

[10] See World Bank Social Development Strategy, approved by the Board of Executive Directors in 2004. '*Action 2015' Accountability, Cohesion, Transparency, Inclusion, and Opportunity—Now: An agenda of social progress.* http://web.worldbank.org/WBSITE/EXTERNAL/NEWS/0,,content MDK:20263268 ~ menuPK:34480 ~ pagePK:34370 ~ theSitePK:4607,00.html.

[11] *World Bank Annual Report 2004*, 91.

[12] *The World Bank Annual Report 2004*, 87–90.

[13] See generally, *Development and Human Rights: The Role of the World Bank* (Washington D.C., World Bank, 1998) http://www.worldbank.org/html/extdr/rights/hrtext.pdf. In his 1995 Legal Opinion on 'The Prohibition of Political Activities in the Bank's Work' (11 July 1995), the then General Counsel concluded, 'In fact, the Bank's work has promoted a broad array of economic, social and cultural human rights. Its proclaimed overriding objective at present is to enable its borrowing countries to enjoy freedom from poverty, a basic freedom which many find to be required for the full enjoyment of human rights. The Bank increasingly contributes to the borrowing countries' efforts to develop their human resources, through its lending for education, health and nutrition, and to strengthen their systems of governance, through its lending for legal, regulatory, judicial and civil service reform. It encourages the involvement of affected peoples and local NGOs in the design and implementation of the projects it finances. It, and the Global Environment Facility of which it is the trustee and the main implementing agency, currently represent the multilateral organization with the greatest involvement in the protection of the human environment. It has also integrated the promotion of the role of women in development in its operations. It tries to ensure, through its pioneering directives, humane conditions for the resettlement and rehabilitation of the people affected by the projects it finances and protection for the rights and distinctive cultures of indigenous peoples. More broadly, it advocates through its lending operations and policy advice the liberalization of investment and the free flow of services, goods and information. Clearly, these activities have a direct effect on the amelioration of non-political human rights. They may even pave the way for greater awareness and protection of political rights in the borrowing countries.' Reproduced in I.F.I. Shihata, *World Bank Legal Papers* (The Hague, Martinus Nijhoff, 2000) 219 at 233.

20.2 LEGAL FRAMEWORK

The legal framework within which the Bank must operate with respect to human rights as with all its activities is anchored in the Articles of Agreement. They contain important limitations but they have been and must continue to be interpreted dynamically so as to achieve the mission of the Bank.[14]

There are three key issues in the Articles which need to be discussed:

(i) First and foremost, all Bank activities must further the purposes for which it was established.[15] Article I sets out the purposes of the Bank. Drafted as it was in 1944 at the end of World War II, it sets out a variety of activities related to reconstruction and development, such as the facilitation of investment capital for productive purposes, the restoration of economies after wars, and the development of productive facilities and raising of standards of living.

(ii) Second, the Articles provide that only economic considerations shall be relevant to the decisions of the Bank and its officers, and these must be weighed impartially. When Bank lending is involved, funds must be used without regard to political or other non-economic influences or considerations.[16]

(iii) Third, there are two distinct political prohibitions:

(a) the Bank and its officers may not interfere in the political affairs of any Member;[17]

---

[14] The Articles themselves vest the role of interpretation in the Executive Directors. This is provided for in Article IX of the Articles of Agreement. The General Counsel's role is distinct: 'As a general matter, a General Counsel of an international organization does not decide on the questions addressed to him; he only provides advice based on thorough legal analysis.' Ibid., xxxviii and xlii. See also A. Broches, 'Legal Aspects of the World Bank', in Hague Academie de droit international, Receuil des cours 1959 III, 297 at 312–314.

[15] Article I provides, 'The Bank shall be guided in all its decisions by the purposes set forth above.' It is generally accepted also that the process of the Articles' interpretation is itself subject to the requirement that all the decisions of the Bank be guided by Article I, See I.F.I. Shihata, note 13 above, lviii.

[16] Article III, Section 5:

b) The Bank shall make arrangements to ensure that the proceeds of any loan are used only for the purposes for which the loan was granted, with due attention to considerations of economy and efficiency and without regard to political or other non-economic influences or considerations.

[17] Article IV, Section 10 Political Activity Prohibited:

The Bank and its officers shall not interfere in the political affairs of any member; nor shall they be influenced in their decisions by the political character of the member or members concerned. Only economic considerations shall be relevant to their decisions, and these considerations shall be weighed impartially in order to achieve the purposes stated in Article I.

(b) the Bank cannot be influenced in its decisions by the political character of the Member or Members concerned.[18]

Let me consider each of these three norms in a little more detail.

20.2.1 Purposes

Article I sets out the purposes of the institution. Although it was drafted sixty years ago, its provisions have stood the test of time. Nevertheless, as the challenges of development have changed, the Bank's mission has also evolved to serve a broader concept of development.[19] The Bank's mission as currently defined is the alleviation of poverty[20] through economic growth and social equity[21]—this conception of the alleviation of poverty has an especially strong human rights dimension.[22]

This approach to the alleviation of poverty understands poverty as a multidimensional and relational phenomenon. As Nobel Laureate, Amartya Sen has argued, we must view development in terms of freedom and the removal of obstacles to it, including poverty, tyranny, poor economic opportunities, systemic social deprivation, the neglect of public facilities, as well as intolerance.[23]

Social equity, which is at the heart of my conception of poverty alleviation, includes fighting inequality, giving the poor and marginalized a voice

There is one further limitation that applies specifically to Bank lending—the requirement that funds be used for the purposes intended and 'without regard to political or other non-economic influences or considerations' (Article III, Section 5). This limitation, coupled with the need for economy and efficiency, strengthens the economic and technical character of Bank operations. It can be considered a protection against corruption and misuse of funds.

[18] Article IV, Section 10, ibid.

[19] This broadened understanding of development is clear from the Comprehensive Development Framework launched in 1999, http://web.worldbank.org/WBSITE/EXTERNAL/PROJECTS/STRATEGIES/CDF, Part 1, and in the Bank's more recent emphasis on human development, social development, and social protection.

[20] On poverty and the Bank's mission generally, see *World Development Report 2000/2001 Attacking Poverty*.

[21] Of general relevance to this is the *World Development Report 2006* on *Equity* (forthcoming).

[22] Speaking recently at the opening of the 61st Session of the Commission on Human Rights, United Nations High Commissioner for Human Rights, Louise Arbour made the following observation about poverty in relation to human rights: 'When we talk of the need to end poverty, to entrench systems of good governance and the rule of law, of the importance of democratic institutions, of ending racism and intolerance in whatever form, and of the need to protect the dignity and safety of all, we are talking *directly* of the reality of human rights.' (Geneva, 14th March 2005) http://www.unhchr.ch/huricane/huricane.nsf/view01/527ED2F6E7DD06ADC1256FC400406C8D?opendocument.

[23] A. Sen, *Development as Freedom* (New York, Anchor Books, 1999) 3. See also A. Sen, *Commodities and Capabilities* (Oxford, Clarendon Press, 1999).

(i.e., empowerment),[24] freedom from hunger and fear, as well as access to justice.[25] Social equity has, therefore, an obvious human rights content.

It is clear that under President Wolfensohn the Bank is moving towards a conception of development, and of its mandate, that is more grounded in equity and the social face of development.[26] In our interpretation of the Articles of Agreement, we must therefore maintain a focus on the purposes of Article I and the overall mission of the Bank.[27] Let me turn now to the issue of economic considerations.

20.2.2 Economic Considerations

The Articles provide that only economic considerations[28] of economy and efficiency shall be relevant to the decisions of the Bank and its officers, and these must be weighed impartially. What then constitute economic considerations for these purposes?

Let me start by reminding ourselves that the World Bank, although a development institution, is primarily a financial institution. In making decisions about the investment of limited available public resources, the Bank—like its private sector counterparts—needs to evaluate the wisdom of its proposed investments. It must rely upon analysis of *all* the factors that can affect the investment,[29] including the 'investment climate' in the recipient country.[30] The Bank has already accepted the fact that issues of

---

[24] See, for example, D. Narayan (ed.), *Empowerment and Poverty Reduction: A Sourcebook* (Washington D.C., World Bank, 2002); R. Alsop (ed.), *Power, Rights and Poverty: Concepts and Connections* (Washington D.C., World Bank, 2004).

[25] The World Bank's Social Development Strategy paper is strongly supportive of and imbued with the concept of social equity. Its core principles are those of cohesion, inclusion, and accountability. 'Empowering People by Transforming Institutions: A Strategy and Implementation Plan for Social Development in Bank Operations' (2005).

[26] J.D. Wolfensohn, *A Proposal for a Comprehensive Development Framework*, 21 January 1999 http://www.worldbank.org/cdf/cdf-text.htm#part1.

[27] I.F.I. Shihata, note 13 above, lix. Shihata went on to state that 'A teleological, functional approach to interpretation based on the purposes stated in the text has in fact been found by the World Bank and its members to be the most appropriate for the Bank's Articles, as it has been generally for charters of other multilateral institutions', lix–lx.

[28] While the Articles of Agreement speak of 'considerations of economy and efficiency'— the term 'economic considerations' is used throughout this chapter.

[29] A number of the Bank's policy instruments are designed to assess this. See for instance, the CPIA—Country Policy Institutional Assessment—which rates a variety of dimensions of a country's policy and institutional framework.

[30] See I.F.I. Shihata, 'Issues of "Governance" in Borrowing Members: The Extent of their Relevance under the Bank's Articles of Agreement'. Memorandum of the Vice-President and General Counsel (21 December 1990):

i) The degree of political instability of the government of a member requesting a loan and of the security of its territories could be such as to affect the development prospects of the country including its governance[31] are relevant for purposes of such economic analysis but, in my view, it goes further than this—it is now widely recognized that there are a host of political and institutional factors which may affect economic growth.[32] Research has shown that substantial violations of political and civil rights are related to lower economic growth.[33]

Similarly, it has long been recognized in the Bank that political considerations can have direct economic effects. For instance, in judging country creditworthiness, as required by the Articles, the Bank has to consider the degree of political stability of the government.[34] In my opinion, therefore, it is consistent with the Articles that the decision-making processes of the Bank

prospective creditworthiness. Political changes may also affect the borrower's ability to keep its commitments under a loan agreement or the ability of the Bank to supervise project implementation or to evaluate the project after its completion.

As a result, partial or full foreign occupation of the country's territories or civil strife in such territories cannot be deemed irrelevant to the Bank's work simply because they are of a political nature. Bank lending in such circumstances may run counter to the financial prudence required by the Bank's Articles (Article III, Section 4(v)). It may also threaten the standing of the Bank in financial markets or otherwise adversely affect its reputation as a financial institution. Indeed, the Bank has long recognized that it 'cannot ignore conditions of obvious internal political instability or uncertainty which may directly affect the economic prospects of a borrower.' This position has been consistently upheld by the Bank's Legal Department, most recently in the Legal Memorandum of December 23, 1987. It is important to recall, however, that in such situations the Bank would still be taking into account relevant economic considerations; political events would represent only the historical origins or the causes which gave rise to such considerations.

Reproduced in I.F.I. Shihata, note 13 above, 245, at 265–266.

[31] *Governance: The World Bank Experience* 58 (Washington D.C., World Bank, 1990). See also D. Kaufmann, A. Kraay and P. Zoido-Lobaton (1999), 'Aggregating Governance Indicators', World Bank Policy Research Working Paper No. 2195; D. Kaufmann, A. Kraay and P. Zoido-Lobaton (1999). 'Governance Matters', World Bank Policy Research Working Paper No. 2196.

[32] See generally, A. Alessina and R. Perotti, 'The Political Economy of Growth: A Critical Survey of the Recent Literature', 8 *World Bank Economic Review* (1994) 351–371. For an example of research suggesting a link between the quality of institutions and investment and growth, see J. Aron, 'Growth and Institutions: A Review of the Evidence', 15 World Bank Research Observer (2000) 99–135; for other work on related issues, see M. J. Isham, D. Kaufmann and L.H. Pritchett, 'Civil Liberties, Democracy and the Performance of Government Projects', 11(2) *World Bank Economic Review* (1997) 219, 237; see also A. Baerji and H. Ghanem, 'Does the Type of Political Regime Matter for Trade and Labor Market Policies?', 11 *World Bank Economic Review* (1997) 171; R. J. Barro, 'Economic Growth in a Cross Section of Countries', 106 *The Quarterly Journal of Economics* (1991) 407 at 432.

[33] R. Barro, *Determinants of Economic Growth: A Cross-Country Empirical Study* (Cambridge, Mass: MIT Press, 1997).

[34] Article III, Section 4 Conditions on which the Bank may Guarantee or Make Loans provides:

(v) In making or guaranteeing a loan, the Bank shall pay due regard to the prospects that the borrower, and, if the borrower is not a member, that the guarantor, will be in a position to meet its obligations under the loan; and the Bank shall act prudently in the interests both of the particular member in whose territories the project is located and of the members as a whole.

should incorporate social, political, and any other relevant factors which may have an impact on its economic decisions.

This same line of analysis applies to the discussion of which human rights are relevant for the making of economic decisions. Some assert that only economic rights are relevant, not political rights. In my view there is no stark distinction between economic and political considerations: there is an interconnection among economic, social, and cultural rights on the one hand, and civil and political rights on the other.[35] Indeed, it is generally accepted at the political level that 'all human rights are universal, indivisible, interdependent and interrelated'.[36]

Also from a financial point of view I believe the Bank cannot and should not make a distinction between different types of human rights. It needs to take all these considerations into account. In all cases, however, Bank decision making must treat these considerations impartially, treating similarly situated countries equally.

20.2.3 Political Prohibitions

The other limitations in the Articles relate to politics. There are two general political prohibitions in the Articles which must also be respected. First, Bank interference in a country's political affairs is barred—this applies to both domestic and foreign partisan politics.[37] Second, Bank decisions cannot be influenced by the political character of the member country.[38] The ban on political interference requires the Bank to distance itself from partisan politics, from favoring political factions, parties, or candidates in elections,

---

[35] A number of General Assembly resolutions also affirm the principles of indivisibility and interdependence or interrelatedness of human rights, see, for example, General Assembly Res. 32/130 (1977).

[36] Proclamation of Teheran. Proclaimed by the International Conference on Human Rights at Teheran on 13 May 1968, paragraph 14 reads: 'Since human rights and fundamental freedoms are indivisible, the full realization of civil and political rights without the enjoyment of economic, social and cultural rights is impossible. The achievement of lasting progress in the implementation of human rights is dependent upon sound and effective national and international policies of economic and social development': http://www.unhchr.ch/html/menu3/b/b_tehern.htm. United Nations World Conference on Human Rights (Vienna, 14–25 June 1993) issued the Vienna Declaration and Programme of Action (A/CONF.157/23) 12 July 1993, Section 5 of which provides: 'All human rights are universal, indivisible and interdependent and interrelated. The international community must treat human rights globally in a fair and equal manner, on the same footing, and with the same emphasis. While the significance of national and regional particularities and various historical, cultural and religious backgrounds must be borne in mind, it is the duty of States, regardless of their political, economic and cultural systems, to promote and protect all human rights and fundamental freedoms.'

[37] I.F.I. Shihata, note 13 above, 271–272.   [38] Article IV.10, note 18 above.

and from active participation in political life. The prescribed neutrality with respect to political character keeps the Bank from endorsing or mandating a particular form of government, political bloc, or political ideology.[39] But neither of these limitations would prevent the Bank from considering political issues that have economic consequences or implications—so long as this is done in a non-partisan, non-ideological, and neutral manner.[40]

Just as the prevailing understanding of what can constitute economic considerations has evolved over the past sixty years, it is clear that the concept of interference in the sovereign affairs of a country has undergone a similar process.[41] In interpreting the meaning of these political prohibitions, we need to recognize that the concepts of sovereignty and interference have also evolved.[42] In the modern world, sovereignty is no longer an absolute shield against scrutiny of states' respect for international norms.[43] That should not be taken to mean that human rights involve a 'loss' of sovereignty, but rather

[39] I.F.I. Shihata, note 13 above, 270.

[40] Thus, these prohibitions do not bar all political considerations, since not all such considerations amount to interference in the political affairs of a member, and not all such considerations relate to the political character of a member. Y. Yokota, 'Non-Political Character of the World Bank', 20 *Japanese Annual of International Law* (1976) 39.

[41] 'Unlike many components of classical international law, the human rights movement was not meant to work out matters of reciprocal convenience among states... Rather it reached broad areas of everyday life within states that are vital to the internal rather than international distribution of political power. As international law's aspirations grew, as the law became more critical of and hence more distanced from states' behavior, the potential for conflict between human rights advocates within a state and that state's controlling elites escalated.' H. Steiner, 'The Youth of Rights', 104 *Harvard Law Review* (1991) 917 at 929.

[42] 'At its very threshold and to this day, the human rights movement has inevitably confronted antagonistic claims based on conceptions of sovereignty. How could its premises coexist with the then reigning concepts of state sovereignty? Or have the nature of the state, and the concept of that protean concept as well as of allied concepts like domestic jurisdiction and autonomy, themselves undergone substantial change over the half century of this movement?' H.J. Steiner and P. Alston, *International Human Rights: Law, Politics and Morals* (Oxford, Oxford University Press, 2nd edn., 2000) 573. See also, Louis Goodman, 'Democracy, Sovereignty and Intervention', 9(1) *Am. U. J. Int'l Law and Policy* (1993) 27; A. Rosas, 'State Sovereignty and Human Rights: Towards a Global Constitutional Project', 43 *Political Studies* (1995) 61–78; G. Lyons and M. Mastanduno (eds.) *Beyond Westphalia?: State Sovereignty and International Intervention* (Baltimore, Johns Hopkins University Press, 1995) *passim*; L. Henkin, Lecture 'That "S" Word: Sovereignty, and Globalization and Human Rights, Et Cetera', 68 *Fordham L. Rev.* (1999) 4.

[43] The UN Charter, adopted in 1945, balances the principles of sovereignty and non-interference with that of respect for human rights. Moreover, the emergence of what Louis Henkin called 'the new law of human rights' (L. Henkin, 'Introduction', in L. Henkin (ed.), *The International Bill of Rights* (New York, Columbia University Press, 1981) 6) or what Thomas Buergenthal referred to as 'contemporary international human rights law' (T. Buergenthal, 'The Normative and Institutional Evolution of International Human Rights', 19 *Human Rights Quarterly* (1997) 703) is properly traced to the United Nations Charter.

that human rights flow from the inherent dignity of every human being, which lies at the heart of the United Nations Charter.[44]

International law now recognizes that there are issues which traverse national boundaries.[45] The examples abound: corporate or financial crimes, money laundering, corruption,[46] environmental hazards,[47] the work of the International Criminal Court,[48] the work of the International Criminal Tribunal for the former Yugoslavia and the International Criminal Tribunal for Rwanda,[49] and the special jurisdictional rules for crimes against humanity.[50]

The significance of this for the Bank is that, in my opinion, it can and should take into account human rights in the process it uses and the instruments it relies on to make economic decisions. Moreover, because of the way international law has evolved with respect to concepts of sovereignty and interference, and the range of issues that are considered to be of global concern, the Bank would not, in doing so, fall foul of the political

[44] See Separate Opinion of Judge Weeramantry in Application of the Genocide Convention (Judgment of 11 July 1996) at 54. See also O. Schachter, 'Human Dignity as a Normative Concept' 77 *American Journal of International Law* (1983) 848–854.

[45] N. Passas (ed.), *International crimes* (Aldershot, Ashgate, 2003); M. Cherif Bassiouni, *Introduction to international criminal law* (Ardsley, NY: Transnational Publishers, 2003).

[46] E. Savona and L. Mezzanotte, 'Double Standards in Public Life: The Case of International Corruption' in B. Rider (ed.) *Corruption: The Enemy Within* (Kluwer, 1997) 105–111; I.F.I. Shihata, 'Corruption—A General Review with an Emphasis on the Role of the World Bank' in the same volume 255–283. More generally, see Global Corruption Report 2004, http://www.transparency.org/pressreleases_archive/2004/2004.10.20.cpi.en.html.

[47] See, for example, preambular provisions of the United Nations Framework Convention on Climate Change (which entered into force on 21 March 1994) acknowledging the need for the widest possible co-operation by all countries and their participation in an effective and appropriate international response. 1770 UNTS 107, http://unfccc.int/2860.php.

[48] I. Brownlie, *Principles of Public International Law* (Oxford, Oxford University Press, 6th edn, 2003) 571–575; A. Cassese, P. Gaeta, and J. Jones (eds.) *The Rome Statute of the International Criminal Court: A Commentary* (3 vols.) (Oxford, Oxford University Press, 2002).

[49] On the proliferation of international criminal courts and tribunals more generally, P. Sands (ed.) *From Nuremberg to The Hague: the future of international criminal justice* (Cambridge, Cambridge University Press, 2003).

[50] A different, though related issue is that of universal jurisdiction which is recognized by a number of international law experts: D.J. Bowett, 'Jurisdiction: Changing Patterns of Authority Over Activities and Resources', 53 *British Yearbook of International Law* (1982) 11–14; K. Randall, 'Universal Jurisdiction Under International Law', 66(4) *Texas Law Review* (1988) 785; O. Schachter, 'International Law in Theory and Practice, General Course in Public International Law', 178 *Coll. Courses Hague Acad. Int'l Law* 262 (1982-V); I. Brownlie, note 48 above, at 303; E. David, *Principes de droit des conflits armés* (Brussels, Bruylant, 1994) 592. The Third Restatement provides as follows: '[t]hat genocide and war crimes are subject to universal jurisdiction was accepted after the Second World War' (Restatement of the Law (Third), The Foreign Relations Law of the United States, American Law Institute (1987), Reporter's Note on §404, p. 254). Another formulation is 'crimes under international law' for breaches of the laws of war, especially the Hague Convention of 1907 or the Geneva Conventions of 1949: such crimes may be punished by any state having custody of those suspected to be responsible, see I. Brownlie, ibid., 303–304.

prohibitions of the Articles. Globalization has forced us to broaden the range of issues that are of global concern. As President Wolfensohn noted in his address to the Bank's Board of Governors in Dubai, we face an immense challenge in creating a new global balance.[51] Human rights lie at the heart of that global challenge.

These, in sum, are my preliminary thoughts on the legal framework applicable to the Bank on this topic. Let us turn now to the Bank's practice.

20.3 THE BANK'S PRACTICE

Operating within the legal framework that I have described, it is clear that the work of the Bank, as well as the concept of development itself, will continue to reflect trends and changes in the world at large. As early as 1973, then World Bank President Robert McNamara, addressing the Board of Governors on the meaning of development, said: '[We] believe that economic progress remains precarious and sterile without corresponding social improvement. Fully human development demands attention to both. We intend, in the Bank to give attention to both.'[52] Jim Wolfensohn endorsed a similar vision in the Comprehensive Development Framework, in which he emphasized an integral approach and the two dimensions of development: 'The macroeconomic aspects on the one side, and the social, structural and human on the other, must be considered together.'[53]

Overall, there has been a marked shift in emphasis from infrastructure lending to human development. Thirty years ago, the Bank had 58 per cent of its portfolio in infrastructure, today it is reduced to 22 per cent while human development and law and institutional reform represent 52 per cent of our total lending. The evolving practice of the Bank has an important legal dimension for the interpretation of our Articles, since Article 31 of the Vienna Convention on the Law of Treaties regarding the general rule of interpretation makes provision for '. . . any subsequent practice in the application of the treaty which establishes the agreement of the parties regarding its interpretation'.[54]

---

[51] Address by James D. Wolfensohn, President of the World Bank Group, to the Board of Governors of the World Bank Group at the joint Annual Discussion, Dubai, United Arab Emirates, 23 September 2003, http://web.worldbank.org/WBSITE/EXTERNAL/EXTA-BOUTUS/ORGANIZATION/PRESIDENTEXTERNAL/0,,contentMDK:20129148 ~ menu PK:232083 ~ pagePK:159837 ~ piPK:159808 ~ theSitePK:227585,00.html.

[52] R. McNamara, Address to the meeting of the Board of Governors, Copenhagen, Denmark, 21 September 1970 as quoted in E. Mason & R. Asher, *The World Bank Since Bretton Woods* (Washington D.C., Brookings Institution Press, 1973) 475.

[53] See CDF, note 26 above.

[54] Article 31 of Vienna Convention on the Law of Treaties (which entered into force on 27 January 1980). UNTS vol. 1155; at p. 331.

Another dimension of the evolving mandate of the Bank is embodied in the world community's commitment towards realizing the MDGs.[55] The Bank has joined other global partners to pledge the attainment of the major targets which relate to the eradication of extreme hunger, the achievement of universal education, the promotion of gender equality, reduction of child mortality, improving maternal health, combating HIV/AIDS, ensuring environmental stability, and developing a global partnership for development.

The Bank's work contributes to the realization of all eight MDGs, and all eight MDGs involve more than one human right.[56] One concept that the Bank has taken a leading role in developing is governance.[57] Our consideration of this issue followed from our deepened understanding of how to achieve effective development.[58] The importance of effective governance is now well appreciated, as a result of which the Bank now finances a range of activities in support of these concerns.[59] Governance itself has a strong human rights content, indeed, this is an area in which our research has found a rich set of connections in charting the work of the Bank to key international human rights provisions. Governance incorporates transparency, accountability, and a predictable legal framework.[60]

[55] http://www.developmentgoals.org/.

[56] Indeed, each MDG can be traced to the furtherance of one or several core human rights. For instance, MDG #2 embodies a commitment to achieve universal primary education. This is a right provided for in Article 26 of the Universal Declaration on Human Rights (GA res. 217A (III), UN Doc A/810 at 71 (1948)); and Articles 6, 10, 13, and 14 of the ICESCR (993 UNTS 3, which entered into force 3 January 1976). In the ICCPR (999 UNTS 171, which entered into force 23 March 1976), the right to education is provided for in Article 18 and Article 19. Of general relevance to this point is the Sachs Report on the UN Millennium Project (2005) which also highlights the relevance of human rights to the attainment of the MDGs, see, for example, pages 36, 108, 118–120. http://www.unmillenniumproject.org/reports/index.htm.

[57] *Governance: The World Bank Experience* (Washington D.C., World Bank, 1990), note 31, above.

[58] On the link between good governance practices and economic growth, see D. Kaufmann, A Kraay and P Zoida-Lobaton, *Governance Matters* (Washington DC, The World Bank, 1999). See also R.M. Sherwood et al., 'Judicial Systems and Economic Performance', 34 *Q. Rev. Econ. & Fin.* (1994) 101. The authors estimate that countries that attempt economic liberalization under a weak judicial system suffer 'at least a 15 percent penalty in their growth momentum', id. at 113. I.F.I. Shihata, 'Preface: Good Governance and the Rule of Law in Economic Development' in A. Seidman, R.B. Seidman and T. Walde (eds.) *Making Development Work: Legislative Reform for Institutional Transformation and Good Governance* (The Hague; Boston: Kluwer Law International, 1999).

[59] I.F.I. Shihata, *The World Bank in a Changing World* (Dordrecht, Martinus Nijhoff, 1991) (especially Chapter 3, 'The World Bank and Governance in its Borrowing Members'). I.F.I. Shihata, *The World Bank in a Changing World, Volume III* (The Hague; London; Boston: Kluwer International, 2000) especially Chapter 6, 'Relevant Issues in the Establishment of a Sound Legal Framework for a Market Economy'.

[60] I.F.I. Shihata, 'Legal Framework for Development and the Role of the World Bank in Legal Technical Assistance'. *The World Bank in a Changing World, Volume II* (The Hague, Martinus Nijhoff, 1995), Chapter 3.

All of these principles are clearly linked to the 'rule of law' with its inherent notions of fairness and social justice.[61] The 'rule of law' itself includes access to justice, recognition before the law, proper public sector management,[62] and the independence of the judiciary;[63] all of which are protected under international human rights law.[64] However, the rule of law must also be supported by a number of other indispensable factors, such as public participation, a free press, and a voice for civil society. These too relate to important provisions of a number of international human rights instruments, particularly those of the International Covenant on Civil and Political Rights.[65]

So, while governance is a crucial concept, my personal view is that governance does not go far enough: we must go beyond it to look at the issues of social equity alongside economic growth. Here legal and judicial reform programmes have a key role to play if they support the development of such concepts within national legal systems.[66] Social equity programmes should be seen as falling squarely within the mandate of the Bank. Our legal and judicial reform projects already advance social equity.

The Bank supports a wide array of 'Legal and Judicial Reform' initiatives: there are approximately 600 Bank-financed activities related to legal and judicial reform and to date there are sixteen active 'free-standing' projects in

---

[61] S. Schlemmer-Schulte, 'The World Bank's role in the Promotion of the Rule of Law in Developing Countries' in Schlemmer-Schulte & K.Y. Tung (eds.), *Ibrahim Shihata Liber Amoricum* (Boston, Kluwer Law International, 2001) 677.

[62] The Bank has also worked to improve public sector management and reform the civil service, see, for example, I.F.I. Shihata, 'Some Aspects of Civil Service Reform' in I.F.I. Shihata (ed.) *Complementary Reform, Essays on Legal, Judicial and Other Institutional Reforms Supported by the World Bank* (The Hague, Kluwer Law International, 1997) 119–138.

[63] See, for instance, Georgia Judicial Reform Project, which had as its objective the development of an independent and professional judiciary, committed to high standards of judicial ethics, and capable of efficient and effective dispute resolution. Credit No. 3263-GE, approved 29 June 1999, US $13.4 million (equivalent).

[64] The right to be recognized as a person before the law is provided for in Article 6 of the Universal Declaration on Human Rights, and in Articles 2, 9, 14, 16 of the ICCPR. The right to an effective remedy by a competent national tribunal is provided for in Article 8 of the UDHR and in Articles 2, 14 of the ICCPR. The right to a fair and public hearing by an independent and impartial tribunal in the determination of one's rights is provided for in Article 10 of UDHR. The right to be presumed innocent unless proved guilty according to law in a public trial is provided for in Article 11 of the UDHR, and in Articles 14 and 15 of the ICCPR.

[65] For instance, freedom of thought, conscience, and religion are provided for in Article 18 of the UDHR, Article 10 of the ICESCR, and Article 18 of the ICCPR. The right to freedom of opinion and expression, the right to hold opinions without interference, and the right to receive and impart information and ideas through any media and regardless of frontiers are provided for in Article 19 of the UDHR, and Article 19 of the ICCPR.

[66] A. Sen, *What is the Role of Legal and Judicial Reform in the Development Process?* Presentation at the World Bank Legal Conference, Washington D.C., 5 June 2000. http://www1.worldbank.org/publicsector/legal/legalandjudicial.pdf.

four regions. The Bolivia Judicial Reform Project,[67] for example, was designed to support the development of the national judicial system that contributed to economic growth in Bolivia by facilitating private sector activity and promoting social welfare by guaranteeing the basic rights of all citizens. The project comprised two principal components: one related to reforming the judicial system and another related to supporting the work of the Ministry of Justice. Another illustrative example emerged in the Ecuador Judicial Reform Project,[68] the object of which was to improve access to justice, the efficiency of judicial services, and participation of civil society in judicial reform.[69]

20.4 THE WAY FORWARD

Let me conclude with some personal thoughts about the way forward. I strongly believe that an objective assessment of the work of the Bank leads inevitably to the conclusion that it has made a substantial positive contribution to the realization of human rights, and that it will increasingly continue to do so. In particular it has fulfilled and will continue to fulfill an important role in assisting its Members to progressively realize their human rights commitments.

However, there are limits that must be respected.

There are legal limits. We need to interpret them in a way that is consistent with the purposes of the Bank, in a dynamic way and in a contemporary context. But these limits do exist. We must work within the legal framework that I have described in this chapter to tackle the challenges presented by human rights issues as they evolve.

There are also institutional limits. The Bank is a specialized financial agency. We cannot lose sight of the specificity of our function as a financial institution in the development context. We also have finite capacity and limited resources. For now at least, I believe we should embrace the centrality of human rights to our work instead of being divided by the issue of whether or not to adopt a 'rights-based approach' to development.[70]

[67] Bolivia Judicial Reform Project, Credit No. 2705-BO, approved 13 April 1995 for US $11.0 million (equivalent).

[68] Ecuador Judicial Reform Project, Loan No. 4066-EC, approved 13 April 1995 for US $10.7 million (equivalent).

[69] See generally, *World Bank, Legal and Judicial Reform: Observations, Experiences and Approach of the Legal Vice Presidency* (Washington D.C., World Bank, 2002) and *Legal and Judicial Reform: Strategic Directions* (Washington D.C., World Bank 2003).

[70] A well-established definition of a rights-based approach to development is that promulgated by the Office of the United Nations High Commissioner for Human Rights. http://www.unhchr.ch/development/approaches.html. See also the *UN Common Understanding on the Rights Based Approach to Development* (2003).

Within both these constraints there is still a great deal of latitude. In so far as human rights constitute a valid consideration for the investment process, they are properly within the scope of issues which the World Bank must consider when it makes its economic decisions. And this consideration should include all human rights: those classified as economic, social, and cultural, as well as those classified as civil and political. Moreover it stands to reason that we must address the potential economic consequences of human rights situations, and consider the risks *ex ante*, not only *ex post facto*.

However, as a development institution we must also ensure that we work in a manner that does not inflict a 'double punishment' on the people of our client countries by turning our backs on them because of the human rights record of their governments. It is easier for a private company to walk away from a particular investment than for the Bank to walk away from an investment program for a whole country and thus inflict additional hardship on those who may already be suffering governmental abuse as a result of the government's failure to respect or protect human rights. It should also be clear that the Bank's role is not that of enforcer. Enforcement belongs primarily to the mandate of the member countries, and to other non-financial entities. Our role is a collaborative one in the implementation of our member countries' human rights obligations. It is also a complementary one to that of our UN partners entrusted with the job of respecting, protecting, promoting, and fulfilling human rights globally.

We do need to work within countries to exert a positive influence, to deepen the dialogue, and to share our knowledge and expertise. And in this venture we need to accept that we must work with countries that do not respect human rights as well as those that do. So, how does the Bank move forward in this area? The way forward in the area of human rights and development must be consistent with the mission of the Bank, that is to say, poverty alleviation through economic growth and social equity. The human rights content of this direction is beyond question.

As we move in this direction there is a clear and unmet demand from our member countries for legal and judicial reform programs. We certainly need to scale up substantially our interventions in this field with a wide range of partners. Through these programs, as well as through every other aspect of the Bank's work, many of the human rights aspirations can be progressively realized.

During my tenure as Legal Counsel, my office will be fully committed to the Bank's institutional mission of poverty alleviation through economic growth and social equity. And, given that the rule of law is an indispensable component of these goals, we will strongly support legal and judicial reform, and thus contribute to the progressive realization of human rights everywhere in the world.

Index